ANTIQUES
Handbook
& Price Guide

Miller's Antiques Handbook & Price Guide
By Judith Miller

First published in Great Britain in 2017 by Miller's, a division of Mitchell Beazley,
imprints of Octopus Publishing Group Ltd., Carmelite House,
50 Victoria Embankment, London, EC4Y 0DZ.
www.octopusbooks.co.uk

An Hachette UK Company
www.hachette.co.uk

Distributed in the US by Hachette Book Group
1290 Avenue of the Americas, 4th and 5th Floors, New York, NY 10104

Distributed in Canada by Canadian Manda Group
664 Annette St., Toronto, Ontario, Canada, M6S 2C8

Miller's is a registered trademark of Octopus Publishing Group Ltd.
www.millersguides.com

ISBN: 9781784723514

A CIP record for this book is available from the British Library

Set in Frutiger

Printed and bound in China

Publisher Alison Starling
Editorial Co-ordinators Katie Lumsden & Zenia Malmer
Proofreader John Wainwright
Advertising Sales Julie Brooke
Indexer Hilary Bird
Creative Director Jonathan Christie
Designer Ali Scrivens, T J Graphics
Production Controller Meskerem Berhane

Photograph of Judith Miller, page 7, by Chris Terry

Page 1: An early 19thC mahogany library chair. $25,000-32,000 CHEF
Page 3: A Chinese Republic Period Tibetan style temple vase. $400,000-500,000 LC
Page 4 from left to right: Chinese porcelain snuff bottle. $900-1,000 POOK;
A rare brass Sundail, by Thomas Jones. $3,800-5,000 CM;
A George III carved giltwood wall mirror. $3,200-3,800 SWO;
A pair of Brussels faience figural water cisterns, by Philippe Mombaers. $5,000-6,500 WW;
Page 5 from left to right: A George II silver coffee pot, by William Shaw and William Priest. $1,000-1,100 WW;
An Alfa Romeo P2 tinplate clockwork toy model, by C.I.J. Paris. $7,500-10,000 HW;
A late 19thC glazed earthenware garden seat. $550-700 BELL;
A Fine Bronze Ormolu Striking Mantel Clock. $6,500-7,500 TEN

ANTIQUES
Handbook
& Price Guide

Judith Miller

MILLER'S

Contents

LIST OF CONSULTANTS

At Miller's we are extremely lucky to be able to call on a large number of specialists for advice. My colleagues and friends on the BBC Antiques Roadshow have a wealth of knowledge and their advice on the state of the market is invaluable. It is also important to keep in touch with dealers as they are really at the coalface dealing directly with collectors. Certain parts of the market have been extremely volatile over the past year, so up-to-date information is critical.

CERAMICS

John Axford
Woolley & Wallis
51-61 Castle Street
Salisbury SP1 3SU

Fergus Gambon
Bonhams
101 New Bond Street
London W1S 1SR

DECORATIVE ARTS

Michael Jeffrey
Woolley & Wallis
51-61 Castle Street
Salisbury, SP1 3SU

John Mackie
Lyon & Turnbull
33 Broughton Place
Edinburgh EH1 3RR

Will Farmer
Fieldings
Mill Race Lane
Stourbridge DY8 1JN

Mike Moir
www.manddmoir.co.uk

FURNITURE

Lennox Cato
1 The Square, Edenbridge
Kent TN8 5BD

Lee Young
Lyon & Turnbull
33 Broughton Place
Edinburgh EH1 3RR

ORIENTAL

John Axford
Woolley & Wallis
51-61 Castle Street
Salisbury SP1 3SU

Lee Young
Lyon & Turnbull
33 Broughton Place
Edinburgh EH1 3RR

GLASS

Will Farmer
Fieldings
Mill Race Lane
Stourbridge DY8 1JN

SILVER

Alistair Dickenson
90 Jermyn Street
London SW1 6JD

Duncan Campbell
Beau Nash
31 Brock Street
Bath BA1 2LN

JEWELRY

Trevor Kyle
Lyon & Turnbull
33 Broughton Place
Edinburgh EH1 3RR

Gemma Redmond
5 Roby Mill, Wigan,
Skelmersdale WN8 0QF

CLOCKS & BAROMETERS

Paul Archard
Derek Roberts
25 Shipbourne Road
Tonbridge TN10 3DN

MODERN DESIGN

John Mackie
Lyon & Turnbull
33 Broughton Place
Edinburgh EH1 3RR

HOW TO USE THIS BOOK

Running head Indicates the sub-category of the main heading.

Page tab This appears on every page and identifies the main category heading as identified in the Contents List on pages 4-5.

Essential Reference Gives key facts about the factory, maker or style, along with stylistic identification points, value tips and advice on fakes.

Closer Look Does exactly that. We show identifying aspects of a factory or maker, point out rare colors or shapes, and explain why a particular piece is so desirable.

The object The antiques are shown in full color. This is a vital aid to identification and valuation. With many objects, a slight color variation can signify a large price differential.

Caption The description of the item illustrated, including when relevant, the period, the maker or factory, medium, the year it was made, dimensions and condition. Many captions have **footnotes** which explain terminology or give identification or valuation information.

The price guide These price ranges give a ball park figure of what you should pay for a similar item. The great joy of antiques is that there is not a recommended retail price. The price ranges in this book are based on actual prices, either what a dealer will take or the full auction price.

Judith Picks Items chosen specially by Judith, either because they are important or interesting, or because they're good investments.

Source code Every item has been specially photographed at an auction house, a dealer, an antiques market or a private collection. These are credited by code at the end of the caption, and can be checked against the Key to Illustrations on pages 588-589.

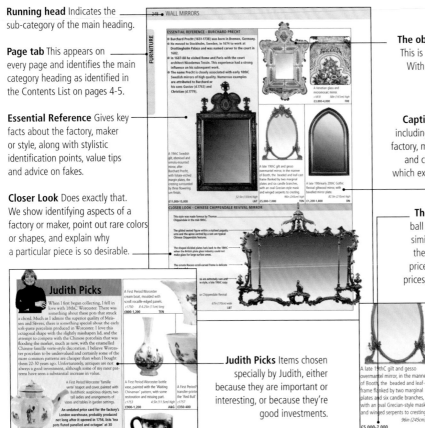

INTRODUCTION

Welcome to the 2018-2019 edition of 'Miller's Antiques Handbook & Price Guide'. The Guide is, as always, packed with over 8,000 images of antiques and fine decorative objects that are completely new to this edition. I am often asked if we update the prices in each edition. We don't. When we publish an edition we start again - trying to reflect changes and developments in the antiques market.

It seems unbelievable to think the first Guide was published in 1979. How the antiques world has changed! When I was collecting in the early 1970s, there were many more antiques shops in every High Street. There were more general auction sales where potential 'sleepers' (unidentified treasures) could be found. There was no internet. Collectors scoured the country and abroad to find that hidden gem. The recession and changing tastes have hit the antiques market. Many shops have closed and many traditional areas of the market are struggling to survive. However, there are indications of an up-turn. Many dealers have joined together in antiques centers, many display their antiques at fairs and many deal primarily online. Across the board there is a certain cautious optimism. Some areas are very strong, such as the Oriental, Russian and Indian markets. Any good quality top end antique in original condition that is fresh to the market will excite collectors' interest. Look at the highly important blue and white 'dragon' stem cup Lyon and Turnbull sold in Hong Kong for over £3,500,000 ($4,500,000). I am often asked 'Do Antiques have a Future?' It's an interesting question. Some people quote the fact that young people seem less interested in collecting

A miniature Bow model of a hare, seated on his haunches and scratching his left ear with one paw, his fur finely incised, raised on a low pad base, highlighted with puce scrolls, a little good restoration to the ears. c1760 2.75in (7cm) $7,500-9,000 WW

and are keener on a minimal look. But there is always demand for antiques. There is a shortage of good antiques - the dealers' lament is that, when they have made a sale, the hardest part of the business today is finding good quality antiques to replace it.

There is also the 'green' argument. Buying solid mahogany furniture is more ethically sound than buying disposable MDF pieces. In many cases it is cheaper than the alternative and no one is going to convince me that MDF will prove to be a good investment. That solid, plain mahogany mid-19thC chest of drawers will still be a practical storage piece in another 200 or 300 years.

The internet has meant that antiques are more accessible than ever. We can browse large numbers of pieces of different styles and periods. Due to the power of the internet, auction houses outside the big cities are getting record prices for rare pieces. Just look at the wonderful Emile Gallé 'Passion Flower' vase sold by Charles Hanson in Derbyshire.

An Emile Gallé 'Passion Flower' vase, acid-etched and engraved with a naturalistic passion flower, with a verse by Marceline Desbordes Valmore 'O vie, O fleur d'orage, O menace, O mystere, O songe aveugle et beau', incised to the socle 'Galle, Expo 1900'. 20in (51cm) high $50,000-60,000 HAN

It really is an exciting time in the world of antiques. I am constantly asked what is my advice about buying antiques. What is the next 'big' thing? My answer is always the same. Buy what you like. Buy something that will bring you pleasure - if it increases in value that's a bonus. But one thing is certain: however high or low antiques rank as good investments, no other investment brings with it the daily pleasure that an antique does. People love their antiques; they buy them in order to live with them, not to sell them in the near future.

We live in an uncertain time. With all the changes in the US and Brexit in Europe - who knows what the future will hold? However, in times of economic uncertainty top quality antiques are often seen as a good investment - and you have the added benefit of enjoying them.

It's a great time to buy. Use the Guide to increase your knowledge and enjoyment. Those hidden treasures are out there just waiting to be discovered.

A blue and white 'dragon' stem cup, finely painted with two five-clawed dragons chasing the eternal flaming pearl amongst clouds, above a sea, the interior painted with the six-character Xuande reign mark 3.75in (10cm) diam $4,500,000+ L&T

Judith Miller.

THE PORCELAIN MARKET

Although there is a certain feeling that the market is improving, there has been continued nervousness fueled by porcelain collectors' very real concern that the ceramic market is 'soft'. Private collectors are, however, prepared to buy when items that are rare and of excellent quality are on offer. You only have to look at the exceptionally rare porcelain group manufactured by Charles Gouyn. Much research has been done into these rare figures, which has increased the interest and their value.

In many respects there has been very little change to the market over the last few years. The market leaders Sèvres and Meissen have remained in demand, particularly early 18thC examples. The 'golden age' of Meissen, from the early years of the factory to the end of the Seven Years War (1710-1759) is still very strong and, in this area, collectors are even prepared to accept some damage. Later 18thC pieces, however, have tended to struggle, unless the piece has some rare features. Dresden, Vienna and Limoges pieces have to be particularly impressive to sell well. The Paris factories have also struggled and buyers are suspicious of many so-called 'Samson' pieces that do not have the quality of the true Samson copies. However good quality 'genuine' Samson continues to attract collectors.

Another area that is still struggling is British blue-and-white from both the 18th and 19thC. What buyers will pay for is pieces in exceptional condition and with a rare early pattern. Large platters are also in demand but not if they have a common transfer-printed pattern. Worcester has been in demand, but only the First Period Dr. Wall pieces with rare hand-painted patterns. Later transfer-printed pieces have struggled to find pre-recession prices, with many auctioneers combining pieces in job lots. If someone is considering starting a collection of 18thC English porcelain, this is a good time to start. Many pieces fail to find the price levels that I was paying 30 years ago.

However, rarity is again a key fact. Woolley and Wallis sold a miniature Bow model of a hare, seated on his haunches and scratching his left ear with one paw, his fur finely incised, c1760, for around £5,500 ($7,000). The rarity and 'cuteness' of this figure assured a good price.

Another factory that has really bucked the trend is Lowestoft - again this is particularly true when rare shapes and patterns are on offer. Nantgarw and Swansea are also still in demand due in part to rarity and superb quality. Unrecorded early Derby figures always excite the market. Royal Worcester ewers and vases painted by such artists as Charles Baldwin, Harry Davis and the Stintons still have their collectors and prices have remained steady, but the pieces have to be of a good size and preferably fresh to the market.

Top Left: A rare Worcester teapot and cover, decorated in the famille rose palette, spoiled red anchor mark, restoration to spout and cover.

c1753-54 *8in (20.5cm) wide*

$3,800-5,000 WW

Above: A St James's Factory pastoral figure group, by Charles Gouyn, the lady cradling a lamb on her lap, seated beside a tree stump, the man sitting beside her with his hand raised to the lamb's chin.

c1750-54 *5.25in (13.5cm) high*

$19,000-25,000 DUK

ESSENTIAL REFERENCE - BERLIN

Wilhelm Kaspar Wegely founded the first porcelain factory in Berlin in 1752.

● Molded flowers and foliage and basketwork rims were specialities.

● In 1757 Wegely sold his stock to Johan Ernst Gotzkowsky. In 1761 Gotzkowky founded his porcelain factory.

● In 1762 Prussian king Frederick II acquired it. From then on it was called the 'Königliche Porzellan-Manufaktur Berlin'.

● From c1850 Rococo Revival wares were influenced by Meissen.

● Vases with fine landscape cartouches are noteworthy.

● Porcelain produced between 1752-57 was marked with a 'W' in underglaze blue. After Frederick II acquired the Berlin factory in 1763, the scepter mark was used to mark wares. From 1832 onward the 'KPM' mark was used. Between 1849 and 1870 a mark featuring a Prussian eagle holding an orb and scepter was used.

● The Berlin Porcelain Factory is still active.

A Berlin Wegely porcelain lady with a snuffbox, painted in pastel colors, incised 'W' mark to the base, stamped '29/2'.

1751-57　　　5.5in (14.5cm) high

$1,500-2,000　　　MTZ

A Berlin Wegely porcelain cup and saucer, glazed in white, decorated with blooming branches in relief, stamped 'W' mark.

1751-57

$450-500　　　MTZ

A Berlin porcelain plate, from the Earl of Rothenburg's service, 'Antikzierrat' pattern, painted in colors with birds and branches bearing fruit and butterflies, underglaze blue scepter mark.

1772　　　10in (25cm) diam

$1,300-1,900　　　MTZ

A Berlin porcelain vase, commemorating the soprano Henriette Sontag, decorated with a view of the Berlin State Opera and theatre images, underglaze blue scepter mark, brown 'KPM' mark, and imperial eagle.

Henriette, Countess Rossi (3 January 1806-17 June 1854), was a German operatic soprano of great international renown. She possessed a sweet-toned, lyrical voice and was a brilliant exponent of florid singing.

1827　　　19.75in (50cm) high

$4,500-5,000　　　MTZ

A pair of Berlin porcelain vases, on pedestals, decorated with panels and views of Berlin castle, underglaze blue scepter mark with red-brown 'KPM' mark and orb, painter's mark, dated.

1838　　　15in (38cm) high

$5,000-5,700　　　MTZ

A Berlin porcelain amphora vase, egg-shaped body painted with a pair of cherubs, gilt borders, J-shaped handles, square pedestal, underglaze blue scepter mark.

1795-1800   *11in (28cm) high*

$5,500-6,500   **MTZ**

A Berlin porcelain plate, possibly 'Antikglatt' pattern, painted with an oriental warrior riding a horse, underglaze blue scepter mark.

1810-20   *9.75in (24.5cm) diam*

$1,900-2,500   **MTZ**

A KPM porcelain plaque, depicting a woman wearing a blue dress, signed 'R. Wagner' in the lower left corner, marked to the reverse with impressed scepter mark 'KPM' and '145 203', in a period frame.

14.5in (37cm) high

$2,500-3,200   **JDJ**

A KPM porcelain plaque, painted with a young woman standing by a well, plaque is marked to the reverse with impressed scepter mark 'KPM' and 'H', in a gilt frame with red velvet liner (not shown).

17.75in (45cm) high

$1,900-2,500   **JDJ**

A KPM porcelain plaque, depicting two young maidens and an elderly woman, artist signed in lower right corner 'Thumann', marked on back with impressed scepter mark 'KPM' and 'H', the plaque is housed in elaborate gilt frame (not shown).

15.75in (40cm) high

$3,800-4,400   **JDJ**

A 19thC German porcelain plaque, possibly Berlin, painted with the 'Grecian Bride' after Friedrich August von Kaulbach, in velvet mount and ebony easel backed frame (not shown).

10in (25cm) high

$1,300-1,900   **CHEF**

A 20thC Berlin porcelain tureen, cover, and stand, painted with scenes of figures drinking, with insects and a turquoise paneled border, underglaze blue mark, one handle restored.

tureen 11.5in (29.5cm) diam

$650-900   **SWO**

A Bow model of a sphinx, modeled reclining on a tall scrolling base, wearing a mob cap, beaded necklace and buttoned lace-edged cuffs, the head broken off and restuck.

This model is traditionally believed to represent the actress Margaret 'Peg' Woffington (1717-60), who lived for many years with David Garrick but repeatedly refused his offers of marriage.

See Raymond C. Yarbrough, 'Bow Porcelain and the London Theatre', pages 49-52 and plate 3, for an enameled pair.

c1752-53 　　　　　　　　　5in (12.5cm) high
$2,300-2,800　　　　　　　　　　　　　**WW**

CLOSER LOOK - BOW TOY WARE COFFEE CUP

Size and value often have an inverse relationship in the antiques world where small can be beautiful.

Tableware known as 'toys' or miniatures are thought to have been children's playthings or small-scale functional pieces.

This is an unusual piece from the London factory.

The early c1750 cup was in good condition with no obvious defects save some pitting.

A rare early Bow toy ware coffee cup, painted in underglaze blue.
c1750-55 　　　　　　　　　1.75in (4.5cm) high
$10,000-11,000　　　　　　　　　　　　**PBE**

A rare pair of English porcelain models of recumbent sphinxes, possibly Bow, with female heads wearing mob caps, somewhat restored.

Again the identity of the female on both Bow and Chelsea models has been given to Margaret 'Peg' Woffington, the well known 18thC actress. This attribution has been questioned in recent years.

c1755 　　　　　　　　　each 5.25in (13.5cm) long
$7,000-7,500　　　　　　　　　　　　　**CAN**

A pair of Bow 'New Dancers', modeled as a boy and girl standing in dancing pose before a colorful bocage, raised on a scroll-molded base, red anchor and dagger marks.
c1765　　　　　　　9.5in (24cm) high
$900-1,000　　　　　　　　　**BELL**

A Bow figure of 'Autumn', from a set of Seasons, modeled as a young man seated on a basket of grapes and holding a bowl and a bunch of grapes, a flask at his feet on the mound base, some damage.
c1760　　　　　　　5in (13cm) high
$500-650　　　　　　　　　**MAB**

A set of four Bow porcelain figures of the elements, water as Neptune with a dolphin, air as Juno with an eagle, fire as Vulcan with a pot of fire, and Ceres as earth holding a cornucopia, a lion at her feet.

See Bradshaw (Peter) 'Bow Porcelain Figures, c1748-74', plates 94 and 95 for similar examples.

c1760　　　　　　　tallest 8.5in (22cm) high
$3,200-4,400　　　　　　　　　**TEN**

A Bow teapot and matched cover, printed with a figure on a bridge before pagodas, the reverse with bamboo and fence, the cover painted with Oriental landscapes.

Transfer-printing in Bow underglaze blue never reached the output of contemporary factories such as Worcester, Caughley, and Lowestoft.

c1760-65　　　　　　　7in (18cm) across
$750-900　　　　　　　　　**WW**

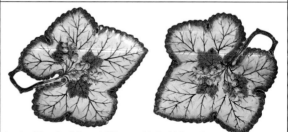

A pair of Bow leaf-shaped dishes, molded with branches of yellow berries, with turquoise leaves, the veins picked out in puce inside a green and yellow rim, some restoration.
c1760　　　　　　　9in (23cm) long
$700-800　　　　　　　　　**MAB**

ESSENTIAL REFERENCE - 'GIRL ON A HORSE' FACTORY

This candlestick comes from a factory about which almost nothing is known. These wares are referred to as the 'Girl on a Horse' factory, 'Transitional Derby' or the Compass factory, although the surviving body of work is tiny. There are fewer than 21 pieces known. The British Museum and the V&A have two each, and the wares rarely appear at auction. The mark is missing from most reference books, and is similar to that of Chelsea, but not exactly. The first piece to define this enigmatic factory was a figure of a girl riding a horse which surfaced some 40 years ago. The collector who bought it decided to refer to similar works as being from the 'Girl on a Horse' factory, in the way that Charles Gouyn's St James' factory was for many years known as 'Girl in a Swing' after the white-glazed figure in the V&A. Books on 18thC ceramics have sometimes included these wares alongside early Derby figures - hence the alternative reference, 'Transitional Derby'.

An 18thC Chelsea candlestick, in the form of a pheasant-like bird within foliage on a naturalistic base, incised triangle mark within circle, lacking its sconce, some chips.

4.25in (10.5cm) high

$11,000-12,000   PFR

A Chelsea tea bowl, studio of Jefferyes Hamett O'Neale, painted with the Aesop fable the 'Lion and the Mouse', the mouse released the lion from a trap, the lion with mouse in his paw, with other mice, red anchor mark, stilt marks to base, glaze chip at front, wear to top rim.

c1750-52   2.5in (6.5cm) high

$4,500-5,000   CHOR

A rare bell-shaped Chelsea mug, of unusually large size, finely painted with birds, the reverse with apple blossom, perhaps after George Edwards, a well-restored crack.

This unusual form is believed to have been copied from the Vincennes/Sèvres factory which produced a small amount of such mugs or cups (known as a bardaque) for the Turkish market.

c1754-55   5in (12.5cm) high

$1,900-2,500   WW

A Chelsea lemon box and cover, the fruit forming part of a posy with stems of flowers, tied with an orange ribbon, the cover with a rosebud finial, some restoration.

c1754   7.5in (18.5cm) wide

$1,200-1,400   WW

A pair of Chelsea soup plates, painted with flowers and insects, within molded garlands and bouquets, with fluted brown rims.

c1755   9.25in (23.5cm) diam

$650-750   BELL

A Chelsea botanical plate, painted with flowers and scattered nuts, the feathered rim in brown and green, brown anchor mark, some wear, a chip to the rim.

c1758-60   8.5in (21.5cm) diam

$180-250   WW

A Chelsea 'The Cat and the Fox' fable candlestick group, with a dog attacking the fox, the cat in the bocage, gold anchor mark, restoration to dog's tail, light chipping to flowers.

c1765-70   12in (30cm) high

$750-1,000   CHOR

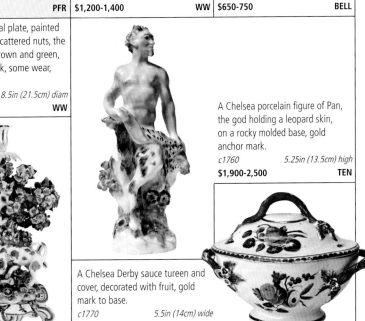

A Chelsea porcelain figure of Pan, the god holding a leopard skin, on a rocky molded base, gold anchor mark.

c1760   5.25in (13.5cm) high

$1,900-2,500   TEN

A Chelsea Derby sauce tureen and cover, decorated with fruit, gold mark to base.

c1770   5.5in (14cm) wide

$550-700   BELL

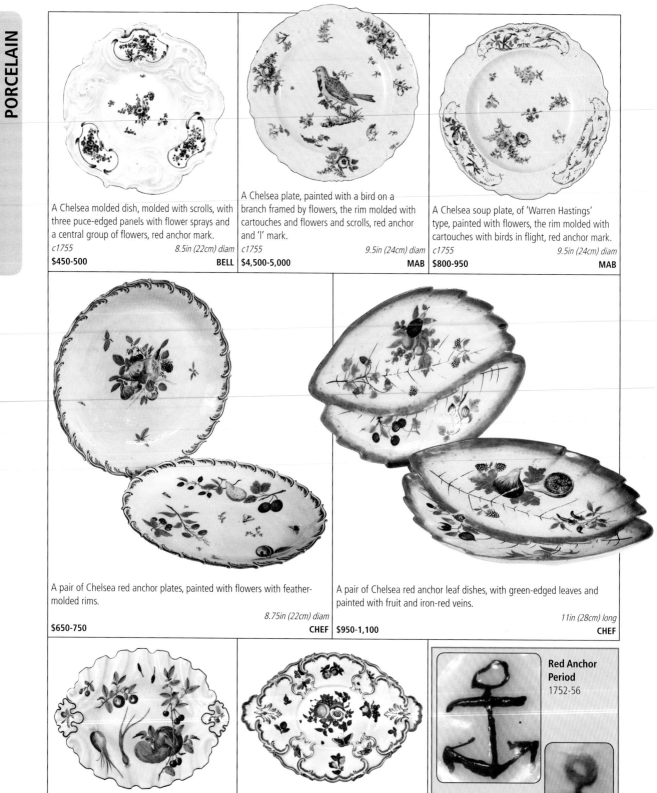

A Chelsea molded dish, molded with scrolls, with three puce-edged panels with flower sprays and a central group of flowers, red anchor mark.
c1755   *8.5in (22cm) diam*
$450-500   **BELL**

A Chelsea plate, painted with a bird on a branch framed by flowers, the rim molded with cartouches and flowers and scrolls, red anchor and 'I' mark.
c1755   *9.5in (24cm) diam*
$4,500-5,000   **MAB**

A Chelsea soup plate, of 'Warren Hastings' type, painted with flowers, the rim molded with cartouches with birds in flight, red anchor mark.
c1755   *9.5in (24cm) diam*
$800-950   **MAB**

A pair of Chelsea red anchor plates, painted with flowers with feather-molded rims.
    8.75in (22cm) diam
$650-750   **CHEF**

A pair of Chelsea red anchor leaf dishes, with green-edged leaves and painted with fruit and iron-red veins.
    11in (28cm) long
$950-1,100   **CHEF**

A Chelsea silver-shaped dish, the molded form painted with branches of plum and cherry, with strawberry sprigs, and two onion bulbs, brown anchor mark.
c1758   *8.5in (21.5cm) wide*
$950-1,100   **WW**

A Chelsea porcelain silver-shaped dish, with shell-molded handles, painted, possibly in the workshop of James Giles, with fruit and insects, gold anchor mark.
c1760   *11.5in (29cm) wide*
$1,300-1,800   **BELL**

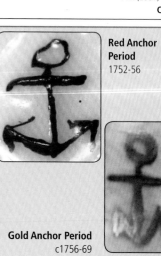

Red Anchor Period
1752-56

Gold Anchor Period
c1756-69

A pair of Derby busts of classical figures, from the 'Four Seasons', after Meissen, emblematic of Summer and Winter, some restoration.
c1765-70   *4.25in (10.5cm) high*
$400-450   **WW**

A small matched pair of Derby figures of children, dressed as Harlequin and Columbine, raised on low bases applied with flowers, some restoration.
c1765   *4.5in (11.5cm) high*
$900-1,000   **WW**

A pair of Derby figures of a shepherd and shepherdess.
c1770   *9.75in (24.5cm) high*
$500-550   **BELL**

A Derby porcelain group, modeled as a nun kneeling before an abbot making her confession.
c1775   *5in (12.5cm) high*
$500-650   **BELL**

A Derby figure of a shepherd, playing a pipe before bocage, some damage.
c1775   *9in (23cm) high*
$80-110   **CHOR**

A Derby figure of Diana, a hunting dog at her side, on flower-applied mound, some chips and losses.
                                       11in (28cm) high
$300-400   **MAB**

A pair of Derby porcelain bocage groups with white rabbits, verso with thumb piece with flower terminal, some small chips to the bocage.

This model is more usually seen with a candle sconce. This pair has no evidence that they have lost sconces so must have been intended as purely ornamental pieces even though the thumb-piece for carrying purposes was still provided.
c1765   *7in (18cm) high*
$1,000-1,200   **DN**

A Derby group of a cow and calf, some damage.
c1800   *6.25in (16cm) high*
$80-150   **MAB**

A Derby figure of a pug dog, the scroll-molded base in green, turquoise, and gilt, incised '2' to base.
c1800   *2.75in (7cm) high*
$300-400   **BELL**

A Derby pierced rose basket, formed as two wreaths of leaves, wrapped around a central flowerhead colored in puce.

c1758   *8in (20.5cm) diam*
$2,500-3,200   **MAB**

ESSENTIAL REFERENCE - 'QUAKER' PEGG

William 'Quaker' Pegg (1775-1851) worked as an apprentice studying porcelain painting from the age of 10. In 1796 he started working for the Derby factory, where he initially spent five years, before leaving and returning. His second time with the company saw new developments in his work, and this botanical dish is an example of his level of skill as a decorator and observer of botanical specimens. This 'Large Double China Aster', is thought to have originated from a hand-colored etching included in John Edward's 'A Collection of Flowers...', which was originally published with 79 similar plates in January 1795. It is believed that Derby acquired a copy of this book in the mid-1790s, and it provided much inspiration for the factory's painters. A similar painted dish, also made and decorated at Derby, is held within the collection at the Victoria & Albert Museum in London.

A Derby porcelain botanical dish, decoration attributed to William Pegg, painted with a China Aster within gilt borders, back inscribed 'LARGE DOUBLE CHINA ASTER', maker's marks '392'.

c1800   *8.75in (22cm) wide*
$3,200-3,800   **L&T**

A Derby porcelain dish, painted with cherries with insects, rim chip.

c1758   *10.75in (27.5cm) long*
$250-320   **MAB**

A Derby porcelain dessert plate, painted with 'Gentiana Acaulis - large-flowered gentian' within a gilt lily border, printed mark and title in blue.

c1795   *9.25in (23.5cm) diam*
$550-650   **TEN**

A pair of Derby dessert dishes, painted with titled views, 'In Cumberland' and 'In Holland', red painted crowned crossed batons and 'D', painted number '24'.

c1810   *11in (28cm) wide*
$500-650   **BELL**

A Derby porcelain dessert dish, painted in the manner of William 'Quaker' Pegg with 'Square Stemmed Passion Flower or Granadella Vine', painted mark and title in red.

c1815   *10in (25.5cm) wide*
$750-900   **TEN**

One of a pair of Derby biscuit porcelain plaques, modeled perhaps by James Goadsby, mounted in giltwood frames behind domed glass.

c1820-30   *15in (38cm) high*
$4,500-5,000 pair   **WW**

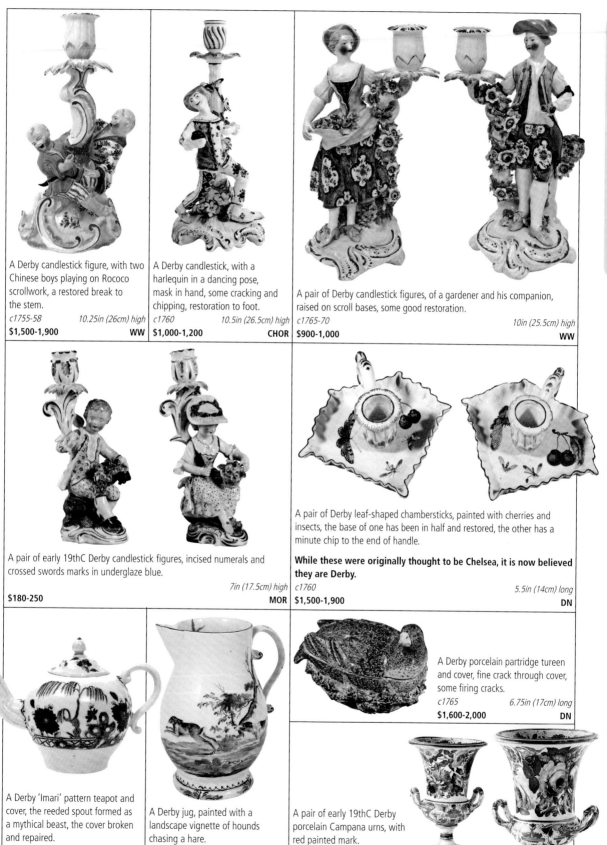

A Derby candlestick figure, with two Chinese boys playing on Rococo scrollwork, a restored break to the stem.
c1755-58   *10.25in (26cm) high*
$1,500-1,900   **WW**

A Derby candlestick, with a harlequin in a dancing pose, mask in hand, some cracking and chipping, restoration to foot.
c1760   *10.5in (26.5cm) high*
$1,000-1,200   **CHOR**

A pair of Derby candlestick figures, of a gardener and his companion, raised on scroll bases, some good restoration.
c1765-70   *10in (25.5cm) high*
$900-1,000   **WW**

A pair of early 19thC Derby candlestick figures, incised numerals and crossed swords marks in underglaze blue.
7in (17.5cm) high
$180-250   **MOR**

A pair of Derby leaf-shaped chambersticks, painted with cherries and insects, the base of one has been in half and restored, the other has a minute chip to the end of handle.

While these were originally thought to be Chelsea, it is now believed they are Derby.
c1760   *5.5in (14cm) long*
$1,500-1,900   **DN**

A Derby porcelain partridge tureen and cover, fine crack through cover, some firing cracks.
c1765   *6.75in (17cm) long*
$1,600-2,000   **DN**

A Derby 'Imari' pattern teapot and cover, the reeded spout formed as a mythical beast, the cover broken and repaired.
c1756   *7.5in (19.5cm) long*
$1,300-1,800   **WW**

A Derby jug, painted with a landscape vignette of hounds chasing a hare.
c1758   *6.25in (16cm) high*
$2,500-3,200   **MAB**

A pair of early 19thC Derby porcelain Campana urns, with red painted mark.
12.75in (32.5cm) high
$1,000-1,200   **L&T**

PORCELAIN

A 19thC Bloor Derby pedestal ewer, decorated with birds on an acanthus leaf support.

13.5in (34cm) high
$300-400   **LOC**

A Royal Crown Derby vase and cover, painted with Conway Castle, printed marks, including 'Tiffany & Co. New York', titled and no '680', dated.

1894   *14in (36cm) high*
$500-650   **SWO**

CLOSER LOOK - ROYAL CROWN DERBY PLATE

The birds are signed 'C Harris' who specialized in game birds.

Albert Gregory was regarded as the best flower painter at the factory.

A Royal Crown Derby 'pâte-sur-pâte' cabinet plate, painted by Desire Leroy, signed, printed mark and Royal Warrant mark in puce.

Leroy developed the use of raised white enamel decoration in imitation of Limoges enamels and pâte-sur-pâte whilst at the Minton factory.

c1900   *9in (23cm) diam*
$5,000-6,500   **TEN**

The gilding is signed 'G W Darlington' who succeeded his tutor, Desire Leroy, as principal flower painter and gilder.

So this service involved the best decorators at Derby at this period. Hence the high value.

A Royal Crown Derby plate, from 'The Judge E.H. Gary' service, painted with partridges, three baskets to the rim, with gilding, printed marks, with 'Tiffany & Co. New York'. dated.

1909   *9in (23cm) diam*
$5,000-6,500   **SWO**

A pair of Royal Crown Derby campana shape vases and covers, painted by Cuthbert Gresley, signed, printed mark.

c1905   *9in (22.5cm) high*
$900-1,300   **TEN**

A Royal Crown Derby miniature teapot, decorated in the Imari 'Witches' 6299 pattern, printed mark with date cipher, spout restored.

1911   *3.5in (9cm) long*
$180-250   **FLD**

A Royal Crown Derby 'Cheshire Cat' paperweight, limited edition 45/500, with a gold stopper and initialed to the base, boxed, with certificate.

$1,000-1,200   **HAN**

A Royal Crown Derby 'Lady Amherst Pheasant' paperweight, 'The 250 Collection', with gold stopper, boxed.

$1,000-1,300   **HAN**

ESSENTIAL REFERENCE - LIVERPOOL

A number of porcelain factories were established in Liverpool in the 18thC.

- Richard Chaffers and Philip Christian were the most successful Liverpool porcelain makers.
- Samuel Gilbody made porcelain in Liverpool from 1754-60 without much success.
- Three branches of the Pennington family operated their own works from 1769 to c1800.
- William Reid's Brownlow Hill factory operated from 1756-1761.
- Precise dating plays a vital part in identifying Liverpool blue and white porcelain.

A Chaffers Liverpool coffee pot and cover, painted with the chinoiserie 'Trellis Fence' pattern.

c1760   9.5in (24cm) high
$400-650   BELL

A small Chaffers mug or coffee can, painted with two figures standing on a rocky outcrop, a small pagoda on an adjacent island, two small rim chips.

c1758-60   2.5in (6cm) high
$500-650   WW

A Richard Chaffers coffee pot and cover, painted with a Chinese hut beneath willow issuing from rockwork, a chip to the cover.

c1758-60   9in (23cm) high
$1,300-1,800   WW

A Chaffer's figure of a nun, probably decorated in London, wearing a puce veil, white surplice with scattered flowers over a turquoise habit.

c1756   4.75in (12cm) high
$750-900   BELL

A William Reid teapot and cover, painted in polychrome enamels with a standing Chinaman holding a long spear beside a pine tree and a potted plant, some chipping.

c1755   6.5in (16.5cm) wide
$2,800-3,500   WW

A Philip Christian teapot and cover, enameled with panels of flowers, the spout and handle with gilt foliate motifs.

c1770   8.5in (21.5cm) wide
$3,500-4,000   WW

A John Pennington teapot and cover, painted in the atelier of James Giles, with panels of fruit and flowers, the spout as a mythical beast, the cover's finial attached to the handle with a chain.

c1775   8.25in (21cm) wide
$1,900-2,500   WW

A Lowestoft miniature or toy teabowl and saucer, painted with peony and willow, a few small rim chips.

c1760   *3.25in (8cm) high*

$450-500   **WW**

A Lowestoft miniature or toy teapot and cover, painted with boats and pagodas in a Chinese island landscape.

c1762   *4in (10.5cm) wide*

$1,600-2,000   **WW**

A Lowestoft molded Hughes type sparrowbeak jug, decorator's mark.

1762-65

$1,500-1,900   **LOW**

A Lowestoft teapot and cover, painted with a building beneath trees and a fence, a small island in the distance, workman's mark to the base.

c1765   *8.25in (21cm) high*

$750-900   **WW**

A small Lowestoft sparrowbeak jug, painted with peony beside rockwork.

c1765   *3in (8cm) high*

$450-500   **WW**

A Lowestoft miniature teabowl and saucer, decorated with a river island scene, decorator's marks.

c1765

$450-500   **LOW**

A Lowestoft plate, painted with a Chinese lady holding a parasol, with a zigzag fence, the pattern echoed to the large vase, the rim with vignettes of prunus.

c1770   *8.5in (22cm) diam*

$1,200-1,500   **WW**

A 1770s Lowestoft plate, decorated with a fence, tree, and floral pattern.

8in (20.5cm) diam

$1,300-1,900   **LOW**

An 18thC Lowestoft mug, painted with flowers and a named cartouche 'John Elden Carpenter at Colthorp', minute chips.

John Elden is recorded at Calthorpe, Norfolk (1714-88).

4.25in (11cm) high

$13,000-18,000   **CHOR**

A Lowestoft fluted cress dish stand, printed with a pine cone pattern.

1775-85   *9.75in (25cm) diam*

$1,000-1,200   **LOW**

A Lowestoft 'Tulip Painter' teapot and cover, with unusual green leaf painting to handle, tiny chip to edge of cover.

$3,200-3,800 LOW

A Lowestoft 'Curtis' teapot and cover, painted with flowers and sprigs, some staining.
1770s *6in (15cm) high*
$400-500 MAB

A Lowestoft sparrowbeak jug, painted in the Chinese manner with the 'Blackbird' pattern, a bird on a branch on rockwork, its head pointing down toward two large pink fruits.
c1770 *3.5in (8.5cm) high*
$550-700 WW

A 1780s Lowestoft sparrowbeak jug, decorated with the 'Thomas Rose' pattern.
$650-750 LOW

A 1780s Lowestoft sparrowbeak jug, decorated with a cornucopia pattern.
$700-800 LOW

A Lowestoft tea bowl and saucer, decorated with a Mandarin pattern.
c1775
$550-650 LOW

A 1780s Lowestoft coffee cup, decorated with a rose pattern.
$400-450 LOW

A Lowestoft coffee cup, decorated with pink flower sprays, gilt chain internal border.
c1770
$1,000-1,200 LOW

A rare Lowestoft vase, painted with vase and flowers.
7in (18cm) high
$3,800-5,000 LOW

A rare Lowestoft ram, molded with twisted horns, restored stump behind ram.
$5,000-6,500 LOW

ESSENTIAL REFERENCE - MEISSEN

The Meissen factory was established in 1710. It became Europe's first porcelain factory after German chemist Johann Friedrich Böttger discovered hard-paste porcelain. This discovery was also due to Augustus the Strong, Elector of Saxony and King of Poland, who had a passion for Oriental porcelain.

- The Meissen factory prospered under J.G. Höroldt, who was appointed as chief painter in 1720.
- The crossed sword mark was added in 1720.
- Early decoration showed Oriental influence.
- From the 1730s onward, Meissen's shapes, decoration and crossed swords mark was widely copied by other European porcelain makers.
- Johann Joachim Kändler became chief modeller in 1733. He helped produce some of Meissen's most striking figures.
- Decorative motifs such as the naturalistic flowers known as 'Deutsche Blumen' (German flowers) were popular from c1740.
- From the early 19thC, pieces in popular styles, such as Empire, Gothic Revival and Rococo, were produced in large quantities.
- New and original designs were produced by Paul Scheurich and Max Esser during the Art Nouveau and Art Deco periods.
- The factory is still active today.

A Meissen teapot, by Johann Gregorius Horoldt, decorated with figures, flowers, and panels, highlighted with a gold scroll border, underglaze blue sword mark and 'KPM', inscribed '72' on the cover and base.

1723-24   4.75in (12cm) high
$13,000-18,000   MTZ

A Meissen 'silber Chinesen' brown-glazed teabowl and saucer, with chinoiserie figures beneath palm trees, the interior of the teabowl with exotic birds, later silvered and tooled by Joseph Hackl in the Seuter workshop, brown 'JHC' monogram and '37' mark with three dots, some oxidisation to the decoration.

c1725   5in (13cm) diam
$2,500-3,200   WW

A Meissen beaker, painted to each side with a quatrefoil panel, one with a Chinaman with a colorful bird, the reverse with a figure holding a tray of incense, reserved in borders of Böttger luster, gilt 'r' mark to the base.

c1723   3in (8cm) high
$2,500-3,200   WW

A Meissen Hausmaler beaker and similar saucer, probably decorated in Augsburg, perhaps by Elizabeth Wald, with chinoiserie scenes, blue crossed swords mark to the saucer, the two associated, the beaker restored.

Hausmalerei (German: home painting) is a tradition originating with the freelance enamelers on glass in Bohemia. It was developed in Germany on white tin-glazed earthenware in the 17thC, in which glazed and fired but unpainted wares 'in the white' were purchased on speculation by unsupervized freelance ateliers of china painters, who decorated them in overglaze enamel colors and gilding, which were fixed by further firing in their own kilns. A few such freelance decorators of faience operated in Nuremberg in the late 17thC, but hausmalerei developed in Augsburg into a notable feature of tin-glazed earthenware production during the early 18thC, before the workshops turned entirely to porcelain. Hausmalerei reached an artistic pinnacle with paintings on Meissen porcelain and Vienna porcelain in the second quarter of the 18thC; sometimes Meissen porcelains remained blank for decades before they were painted.

c1730   5.75in (14.5cm)
$1,300-1,800   WW

A Meissen beaker, painted in the 'Kakiemon' palette with a gnarled spray of prunus, the reverse with a bird in flight, caduceus mark in underglaze blue.

c1730   3in (7.5cm) high
$2,500-3,200   WW

A Meissen plate, painted in the 'Kakiemon' palette, with two cranes, flowering plants, a bird and insect, inside a 'Sulkowski-Ozier' molded border, crossed swords mark in underglaze blue.

c1735   *9.25in (23.5cm) diam*

$800-950   **BELL**

A Meissen plate, painted in the 'Kakiemon' palette, with a bird, fruiting plants issuing from rockwork, inside a 'Sulkowski-Ozier' molded border, crossed swords mark in underglaze blue.

c1735-40   *9.25in (23.5cm) diam*

$800-950   **BELL**

A Meissen teapot and cover, painted with figures, the spout issuing from a molded mask, the handle with a spray of 'Indianische Blumen', blue crossed swords mark.

c1735   *6in (15cm) across*

$3,800-5,000   **WW**

A Meissen coffee cup and saucer, painted with chinoiserie figures and flying insects, blue crossed swords mark, Dreher's mark to the saucer's footrim.

It is worth noting that the early Meissen porcelain sometimes had a dreher's mark impressed in the foot rim of cups and saucers and a gilder's mark in addition to the eponymous cross swords. These were introduced in the 1720s.

c1735   *saucer 5in (13cm) diam*

$3,200-3,800   **WW**

A Meissen teabowl and saucer, the teabowl painted with two quatrefoil panels of figures in harbour scenes, the interior with a puce monochrome landscape, the saucer with a similar scene to the well, blue crossed swords marks.

c1735-40   *5in (13cm) long*

$800-950   **WW**

A Meissen model of a bustard, naturalistically modeled on a reed-molded base, the decoration perhaps later, damage, loss, and marks.

c1735   *17.25in (44cm) high*

$11,000-12,000   **DN**

A Meissen roller, model by J.J. Kändler, underglaze sword mark.

A roller is a type of European bird with very distinct plumage.

1735   *14in (35.5cm) high*

$13,000-15,000   **MTZ**

A Meissen bowl, from the service of Clemens August of Bayern, Elector of Cologne, with gold border, chinoiserie pattern with figures and flowers, raised gold monogram 'CA', underglaze blue sword mark, potter's mark for Paul Wildenstein.

1735   *5in (13cm) diam*

$9,000-10,000   **MTZ**

A Meissen 'Angry Harlequin' figure of Hanswurst, modeled by J.J. Kändler.

1735-40   *7.5in (19cm) high*

$38,000-45,000   **MTZ**

PORCELAIN

The most famous Rococo porcelain dinner service of the 18thC was commissioned in 1736 by Count Heinrich Graf von Brühl, Prime Minister to Augustus II of Saxony, and director of the Meissen factory. The 'swan' service, the name of which derives from its relief molded swans, took four years to produce and is estimated to have numbered over 2,200 pieces. Kändler was insistent that the enamel decoration be kept to a minimum, allowing the molded detail to be the focal point of the service, with only a scattering of Indianische Blumen around the borders. The service remained intact in the possession of the Brühl family at their castle Schloss Pförten until the end of the 19thC. From the 1880s onward, pieces were given to museums, so by the turn of the century it is estimated only about 1,400 pieces of the service remained. At the end of World War II, the Russian army occupied the Schloss and when the family returned, they found the castle and its collections in ruins. The famous Swan Service, the apogee of 18thC porcelain production, had been smashed, reputedly used as target practice by Red Army marksmen.

A Meissen plate, from the 'Christie-Miller' service, painted with a scene of figures standing at the quayside before an Italian palace, blue crossed swords mark.

The scenes depicted on this service are derived from etchings by Melchior Küsel after Johann Wilhelm Baur. The decoration on this plate is largely copied from 'View of the Palace at Muran of the Count Widman of Ständig', although the statues on top of the building are more akin to those in another print of Venetian palaces; both prints dating from 1681.

c1740   *9.5in (24cm) long*
$13,000-19,000   **WW**

A Meissen 'Imari' plate, painted with a bird perched on rockwork beneath a pine tree, blue crossed swords mark.

The pattern was directly copied from a Japanese original.

c1740   *8.75in (22cm) diam*
$2,500-3,800   **WW**

A Meissen 'swan' service plate, with shell-like molded rim border, gilt rim and 'Indianische Blumen' flanking a coat of arms for Count Brühl and his wife, Maria Anna Franziska von Kolowrat-Krakowsky, central molded scene of two swans and a heron, blue crossed swords marks.

c1736   *9in (23cm) diam*
$13,000-18,000   **L&T**

A Meissen model of the lace maker Barbara Uttman, modeled by J.F. Eberlein, with a lacemaking pillow on her knee, holding bobbins, small restoration to her left hand.

Barbara Uttman (1514-1575) established the lacemaking industry in her home town of Annaberg, Germany. Her tombstone credits her with the invention of bobbin lacemaking in 1561.

c1745   *5in (12cm) high*
$1,500-1,900   **WW**

A pair of Meissen pugs, modeled by J.J. Kändler and P. Reinicke, the bases decorated with flowers, minor restoration, chipped, no marks.

1744   *6in (15.5cm) high*
$25,000-32,000   **MTZ**

A Meissen sauce jug and cover, the ribbed body painted with 'Deutsche Blumen', blue crossed swords mark, a little chipping to the finial.

c1750   *7in (18cm) high*
$1,000-1,500   **WW**

A Meissen flower encrusted candlestick, modeled with a cockerel and hen atop a C-scroll base, blue crossed swords mark.

c1755   *5.75in (14.5cm) high*
$450-500   **BELL**

A Meissen Marcolini teacup and saucer, painted with birds below a 'puce mosaik' border.

c1770
$200-250   **CHOR**

A mid-18thC Meissen butter cooler, pierced to the sides and base, painted with 'Deutsche Blumen', blue crossed swords mark.

Butter coolers were designed to allow condensation to drain from the butter, which formed owing to the change in temperature when it was brought into the dining room from the scullery.

6in (15cm) wide

$300-400　　　　　　　　　　　**WW**

A mid-18thC Meissen coffee cup and saucer, the rims molded with osier panels, painted with birds, insects and moths, blue crossed swords marks.

saucer 5.5in (14cm) diam

$300-400　　　　　　　　　　　**WW**

A near pair of mid-18thC Meissen figures, of a shepherd and his companion, a dog and sheep at their feet, blue crossed swords marks, she marked '3' underneath, minor faults.

5.5in (13.5cm) high

$1,000-1,500　　　　　　　　　　**WW**

A pair of mid-18thC Meissen cutlery handles, attached to a steel fork and knife.

the handles 3.5in (9cm) long

$250-400　　　　　　　　**BELL**

A pair of 18thC Meissen Harlequin and Columbine figures, modeled by J.J. Kändler, some damages and restoration.

5.75in (14.5cm) high

$1,300-1,900　　　　　　　　**WW**

A Meissen figure, of the town crier dancing with five people, blue crossed swords and dot, impressed 'H'.

c1770　　　　　　*8.75in (22cm) high*

$700-1,000　　　　　　　　**BELL**

A mid-18thC Meissen tea caddy and cover, indistinct blue crossed swords mark to base.

4.75in (12cm) high

$300-400　　　　　　　　**BELL**

A Meissen chocolate pot and cover, painted with a dog seated on its haunches gazing at a colorful bird, the reverse with a rabbit boxing a parrot's tale, blue crossed swords mark.

c1775　　　　　　*6in (15cm) high*

$700-750　　　　　　　　**WW**

ESSENTIAL REFERENCE - MARCOLINI OR DOT PERIOD

The Marcolini or Dot Period of Meissen manufacture takes its name from Count Camillo Marcolini, Prime Minister of the German kingdom of Saxony, where the Meissen factory was located, who was named director of the Meissen works in 1774, a position he held until 1814. Marcolini perfected the Neo-classical style of Meissen forms and decoration introduced by his predecessor and these products are highly valued and sought-after. Meissen products from the Marcolini period were marked with the traditional crossed swords plus a star (sometimes looking like an asterisk) located near the short ends of the swords, all in underglaze blue.

A pair of Meissen flower encrusted pot pourri vases and covers, painted with courting couples, incised '2745/50', some chips and losses to the flowers and petals, minor rubbing to gilt.

23.25in (59cm) high

$7,500-9,000 CHOR

A Dot Period Meissen écuelle, cover, and stand, painted with two reserves of pairs of figures in landscapes within burnished gilt frames, crossed swords and dot marks.

saucer 8.5in (21.5cm) diam

$1,900-2,500 CHEF

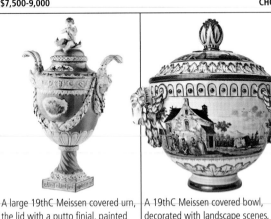

A large 19thC Meissen covered urn, the lid with a putto finial, painted with classical figures, blue crossed sword marks.

19in (48cm) high

$1,900-2,500 L&T

A 19thC Meissen covered bowl, decorated with landscape scenes, ram's head handles, blue crossed swords mark.

6in (15.5cm) high

$800-950 BELL

A late 19thC Meissen flower-encrusted clock case and movement, the clock case set with brass dial and indistinctly inscribed 'Gustav Bulaud (?) Dresden', the two-train movement with outside count-wheel strike on a bell, blue crossed swords mark and incised '1047', lacks pendulum, finial has been restored.

27in (69cm) high

$2,300-2,800 DN

A pair of 19thC Meissen tureens and covers, modeled as partridges, blue crossed swords mark, incised '480/60'.

5.5in (14cm) long

$950-1,100 HT

A late 19thC Meissen figure, emblematic of 'smell' from the 'senses', underglaze blue crossed swords marks and remnants of a blue paper label, some damage.

5.25in (13.5cm) high

$500-650 BELL

A late 19thC pair of Meissen busts, of Prince Louis Charles de Bourbon and Princess Marie-Zephirine de Bourbon.

6in (15cm) high

$650-750 BELL

A 19thC Meissen 'The Broken Egg' figure, blue crossed swords mark, incised and impressed numerals to base, slight damage.

9.5in (24cm) high

$1,000-1,100 TRI

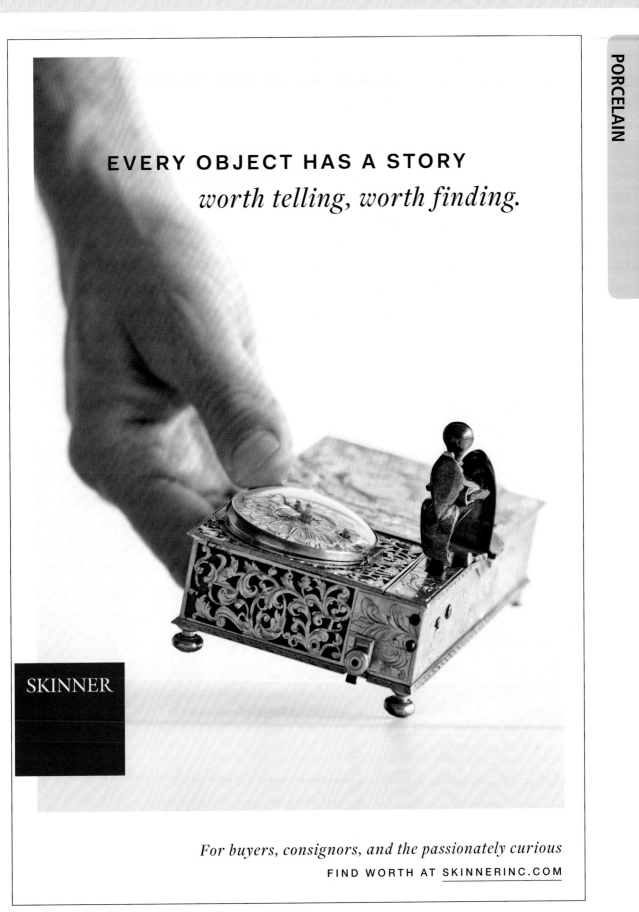

EVERY OBJECT HAS A STORY
worth telling, worth finding.

SKINNER

For buyers, consignors, and the passionately curious
FIND WORTH AT SKINNERINC.COM

PORCELAIN

A late 19thC Meissen 'Poetry' figure group, after Michel-Victor Acier, blue crossed swords mark, some chips and restoration.

12.25in (31cm) high

$1,300-1,500   **DN**

A late 19thC set of five Meissen figures, of classical maidens allegorical to the senses, 'Smell' holding a flower and sensor, 'Hearing' with a lute, 'Taste' with an apple and basket, 'Sight' with a telescope and a mirror, 'and 'Touch' with a parrot, on scroll molded bases applied with their attributes.

11.25in (28.5cm) high

$9,500-10,500   **TEN**

A Meissen crested cockatoo, on a tree stump, underglaze crossed sword mark, inscribed 'No. 57a', impressed '50'.

8.5in (22cm) high

$1,500-1,900   **SWO**

An early 20thC Meissen waxwing figure, blue crossed swords and incised marks.

9in (23cm) high

$130-180   **BELL**

CLOSER LOOK - MEISSEN FIGURE

The original 18thC figure is considered Kändler's masterpiece.

These figures give a more evocative sense of this form of theatre than most illustrations.

The bearded figure in a contrapposto stance in gilt-lozenged costume.

All details are crisply executed and detailed. The flagon is inscribed 'ZM1738' and with crossed swords.

A Meissen 'Drunken Harlequin', after J.J. Kändler, on a gilt scroll base, underglaze blue crossed swords, impressed '64 551'.

9.75in (24.5cm)

$650-750   **SWO**

A 20thC Meissen twenty-two piece monkey band, after the original by J.J. Kändler and wearing 18thC dress, comprising a conductor, a music stand, four singers, and sixteen musicians, blue crossed swords marks, some damage and restoration to several figures.

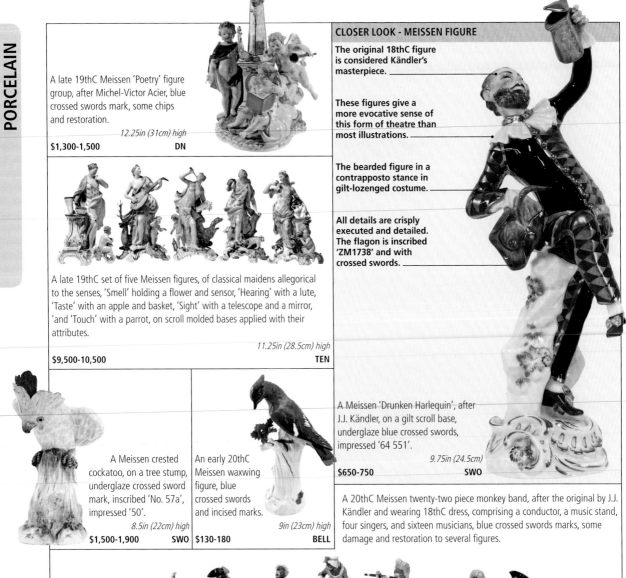

The Monkey Band was created in the mid-18thC by Johann Joachim Kändler, the most celebrated and famous of all Meissen sculptors. They were based on the satirical illustrations of the French artist Christophe Huet, working in the 'singerie' style of elegant monkeys that was hugely popular with the French aristocracy during the 18thC. The figures were first produced in 1746, and have been reproduced ever since. They are one of the most famous lines of all Meissen animal figurines, and the designs were widely copied by other porcelain manufacturers across Europe.

7.5in (19cm) high

$9,500-10,500   **DN**

A Nantgarw Welsh porcelain dish, part of the 'Duke of Cambridge' service.

This Nantgarw dish was produced by the most desirable of Welsh porcelain factories. It was recognized as part of the so-called 'Duke of Cambridge' service which was a wedding present to the duke from his brother the Prince Regent in 1818. The decoration of fruit, landscapes and birds is by Thomas Martin Randall of Clerkenwell and Islington. More than one such service to this design may have been made at Nantgarw.

$5,000-5,700   BRI

A Nantgarw plate, of 'Brace Service' type, painted in London in the Bradley workshop, impressed 'NANTGARW CW' mark.

c1817-20   *10in (25cm) high*

$2,300-2,800   WW

Two Nantgarw oval dessert dishes, painted with a botanical study 'Princes Feather' and 'Red flowerd Chelone' (sic) with scroll molded borders.

c1820   *10.5in (26.5cm) long*

$1,900-2,500   CHOR

A pair of early 19thC Nantgarw dessert plates, painted with scattered flower sprays, enriched in gilding, with impressed marks.

9.75in (24.5cm) diam

$450-500   BELL

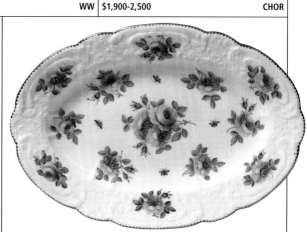

A Nantgarw porcelain dish, probably painted in the Sims Workshop, London, with scattered pink rose sprigs and insects, impressed 'NANT-GARW C.W.'.

c1818-20   *10.5in (26.5cm) wide*

$1,300-1,800   TEN

A Nantgarw porcelain plate, painted in London with a flower spray and insects, the rim with flower sprays, impressed 'NANT-GARW C.W.'.

9.25in (23.5cm) diam

$2,500-3,200   TEN

A Nantgarw coffee cup and saucer, by Thomas Pardoe, painted with flowers and an insect.

c1820   *saucer 5.25in (13.5cm) diam*

$750-1,000   BELL

A Nantgarw sauce tureen and cover, painted with summer flowers, impressed 'Nantgarw CW', one handle restored, restoration to chips on shoulder.

7in (18cm) diam

$450-500   CHOR

ESSENTIAL REFERENCE - SÈVRES

The Sèvres porcelain factory was founded in Vincennes in 1740. It was first known as the Vincennes factory. It became one of the most important porcelain manufacturers in Europe during the second half of the 18thC. It moved to Sèvres in 1756.

● Jean-Jacques Bachelier was appointed as art director in 1751. The factory flourished under his direction.

● Its early wares were inspired by Meissen. Typical features were small flower sprays in soft color palettes.

● Rococo shapes and patterns were introduced around 1750.

● The crossed 'L's of the Royal cipher were adopted as the Vincennes (and later the Sèvres) mark in 1753.

● Louis XV bought the factory in 1759.

● The factory lost its royal patronage as a result of the French Revolution. It was near bankruptcy at the beginning of the 19thC.

● The factory's output in the 19thC was extensive. It included porcelain services decorated with portrait cameos, landscape views and colorful enamels.

● The decoration of 19thC porcelain was inspired by historical styles.

A Vincennes cup and saucer, the cup with a putto, the saucer with a further putto seated beside a goat, gilt dentil rims, blue interlaced 'LL' marks and painter's mark for Viellard.

A covered cup and saucer with near identical decoration is in the collection at Upton House, Warwickshire.

c1754   saucer 5.5in (14cm) diam

$2,800-3,500   WW

A Sèvres cup and saucer, painted with birds in flight, on a blue lapis ground, interlaced 'LL' mark, date code 'E' to the cup.

1757   saucer 5.25in (13.5cm) diam

$650-750   WW

A Sèvres porcelain stand, painted by Louise Papette, painted marks in blue.

c1766   9in (22.5cm) diam

$750-900   TEN

An 18thC Vincennes soft-paste yellow ground ware lidded sucrier, 'double Louis' factory mark to the base in underglaze blue for 1753 and a painter's mark for the artist A-V Vielliard.

This item is decorated with two vignettes of cherubs, after an engraving by François Boucher in monochrome blue (camaïeu bleu).

$70,000-80,000   PW

A Sèvres porcelain custard cup and cover, painted with flower sprigs, painted mark in manganese.

c1770   3in (8cm) high

$650-900   TEN

A Sèvres porcelain triple salt, from the 'Dubarry Service', painted by Jean-Nicholas Le Bel, painted marks in blue.

c1771   4in (10cm) wide

$2,500-3,200   TEN

A pair of Sèvres porcelain plates, painted and molded with the 'Feuille de Choux' pattern, painted marks in manganese.

1772   9.75in (24.5cm) diam

$650-900   TEN

A Sèvres porcelain dish, painted and molded with the 'Feuille de Choux' pattern, painted mark in manganese.

1772   8.75in (22cm) wide

$650-900   TEN

A Sèvres coffee cup and saucer, painted with panels of fruit and flowers, interlaced 'LL' mark and 'B' painter's mark, perhaps for Barré.

c1773   saucer 5.25in (13.5cm) diam

$1,300-1,800   WW

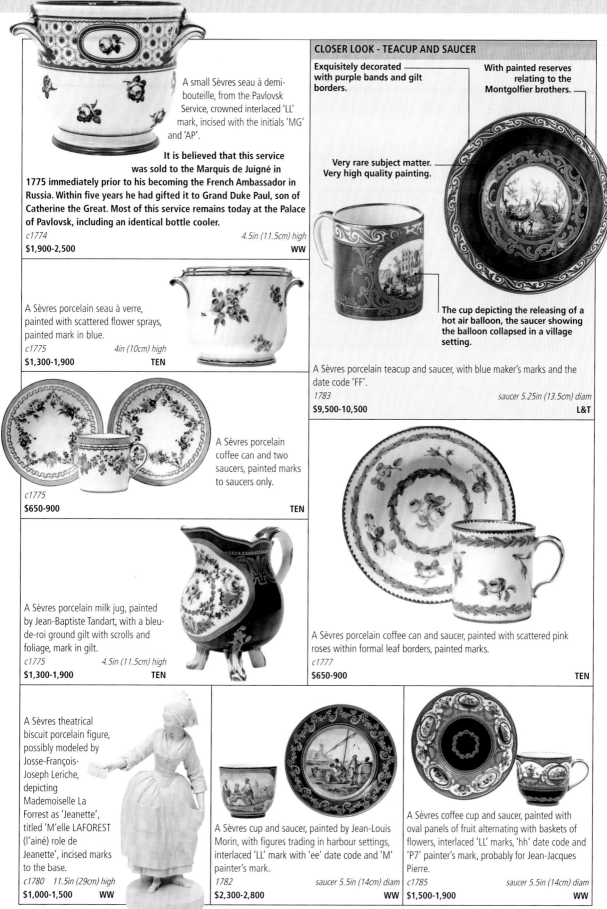

A small Sèvres seau à demi-bouteille, from the Pavlovsk Service, crowned interlaced 'LL' mark, incised with the initials 'MG' and 'AP'.

It is believed that this service was sold to the Marquis de Juigné in 1775 immediately prior to his becoming the French Ambassador in Russia. Within five years he had gifted it to Grand Duke Paul, son of Catherine the Great. Most of this service remains today at the Palace of Pavlovsk, including an identical bottle cooler.

c1774   *4.5in (11.5cm) high*
$1,900-2,500   **WW**

A Sèvres porcelain seau à verre, painted with scattered flower sprays, painted mark in blue.
c1775   *4in (10cm) high*
$1,300-1,900   **TEN**

A Sèvres porcelain coffee can and two saucers, painted marks to saucers only.
c1775
$650-900   **TEN**

A Sèvres porcelain milk jug, painted by Jean-Baptiste Tandart, with a bleu-de-roi ground gilt with scrolls and foliage, mark in gilt.
c1775   *4.5in (11.5cm) high*
$1,300-1,900   **TEN**

CLOSER LOOK - TEACUP AND SAUCER

Exquisitely decorated with purple bands and gilt borders.

With painted reserves relating to the Montgolfier brothers.

Very rare subject matter. Very high quality painting.

The cup depicting the releasing of a hot air balloon, the saucer showing the balloon collapsed in a village setting.

A Sèvres porcelain teacup and saucer, with blue maker's marks and the date code 'FF'.
1783   *saucer 5.25in (13.5cm) diam*
$9,500-10,500   **L&T**

A Sèvres porcelain coffee can and saucer, painted with scattered pink roses within formal leaf borders, painted marks.
c1777
$650-900   **TEN**

A Sèvres theatrical biscuit porcelain figure, possibly modeled by Josse-François-Joseph Leriche, depicting Mademoiselle La Forrest as 'Jeanette', titled 'M'elle LAFOREST (l'ainé) role de Jeanette', incised marks to the base.
c1780   11.5in (29cm) high
$1,000-1,500   WW

A Sèvres cup and saucer, painted by Jean-Louis Morin, with figures trading in harbour settings, interlaced 'LL' mark with 'ee' date code and 'M' painter's mark.
1782   *saucer 5.5in (14cm) diam*
$2,300-2,800   **WW**

A Sèvres coffee cup and saucer, painted with oval panels of fruit alternating with baskets of flowers, interlaced 'LL' marks, 'hh' date code and 'P7' painter's mark, probably for Jean-Jacques Pierre.
c1785   *saucer 5.5in (14cm) diam*
$1,500-1,900   **WW**

A Sèvres coffee can (gobelet litron) and saucer, interlaced 'LL' mark, 'ii' date code, marks for Jean-Joseph-Philippe Boucot fils and Jacques-Francois-Louis de Laroche, with date code, chip to the underside of the saucer's rim.

1786

saucer 5.5in (14cm) diam

$3,800-4,400

WW

A Sèvres porcelain ice cup, painted by Vincent with 'Moineau Jeune de France Male', painted mark and title in blue and painter's mark in white.

c1788

2.5in (6cm) high

$1,500-1,900

TEN

A pair of Sèvres plates, painted with an entwined floral monogram within bleu nouveau borders.

c1790

9.75in (24.5cm) diam

$500-650

BELL

A Sèvres porcelain cup and saucer, with 'Merle du Siniges Appellè Podobe' and 'Gorge Rouge', painted marks and titles in blue.

c1790

$1,300-1,900

TEN

A mid-19thC pair of Sèvres-style turquoise ground gilt bronze bowls, painted with birds and flowers, blue painted 'No IH' marks, the mounts late 19thC.

6.75in (17.5cm) high

$950-1,100

BELL

A rare Sèvres candle snuffer stand, the two snuffers formed as bee skeps with a butterfly forming the handle of each, printed marks to the base.

c1855

6.25in (16cm) long

$1,300-1,900

WW

A late 19thC Sèvres-style trembleuse cup, cover and saucer, decorated with a panel of lovers in a garden and river landscapes, interlaced 'Ls' and script 'D' mark in blue.

5.5in (14cm) high

$500-650

MOR

A late 19thC Sèvres-style porcelain inkstand, fitted with double inkstands and a central reservoir, painted with puce figures of cherubs, with blue maker's marks from later date.

9in (23cm) wide

$450-550

L&T

A pair of early 20thC gilt metal mounted Sèvres-style porcelain vases and covers, decorated with 18thC lovers in landscape, signed 'Verjot', painted 'FRANCE' marks.

18in (46cm) high

$1,900-2,500

TEN

ESSENTIAL REFERENCE - VAUXHALL

Around 1752 Nicholas Crisp set up a small porcelain factory in Vauxhall.

- **The factory's main output was blue and white porcelain. Forms and decoration were influenced by Chinese export wares and Meissen.**
- **The factory experimented with polyglaze printing.**
- **Vauxhall products were recently identified following the discovery of broken porcelain shards.**
- **The underglaze blue may be inky, wet-looking, and rather smudged.**
- **Glazes may be 'peppered'.**
- **The Vauxhall factory closed in 1764.**

A Vauxhall blue and white coffee cup, painted with a Chinese landscape scene, the interior rim with a hatched border.
c1755-8   2.25in (6cm) high
$550-700   WW

A rare Vauxhall cider jug, painted in the Imari palette with a single Chinese figure, a small chip to the spout and the footrim.
c1756-60   5.25in (13.5cm) high
$950-1,100   WW

A Vauxhall blue and white saucer, painted with two Chinese figures, within a cell diaper border.
c1755-60   4.5in (12cm) long
$500-650   WW

A Vauxhall teapot and cover, painted with sprays of English flowers, including chrysanthemum and tulip, some faults.
c1758   7in (18cm) high
$1,300-1,800   WW

A rare Vauxhall teapot and cover, printed and hand-colored, one side with a couple standing on a small island with a third figure, the reverse with a couple standing before buildings in a harbour setting, the cover with a shepherdess and musician, some chipping to the spout.
c1785   7in (18cm) wide
$5,000-6,500   WW

PORCELAIN

ESSENTIAL REFERENCE - VIENNA

In 1718, Claudius Innocentius du Paquier founded the first porcelain factory in Vienna, Austria, with the help of runaway workmen from Meissen. Vienna porcelain was popular amongst members of the Viennese aristocracy.

- The Vienna factory was one of the first to make hard-paste porcelain.
- Early Vienna pieces were strongly influenced by Meissen. They can be distinguished by a denser style of decoration.
- Du Paquier sold the factory to Maria Theresa in 1744, before she became empress of Austria.
- F. Joseph Dangel, a highly regarded porcelain modeller, worked at the factory from 1762 to 1804. His work is characterized by Rococo styling.
- The Vienna factory also became known for their Baroque-style porcelain wares.
- The Neo-classical influence was introduced after Konrad Sörgel Von Sorgenthal became director in 1784.
- The factory declined in the 1820s. It shut down in 1864.

A mid-18thC pair of Vienna porcelain figural salts, impressed beehive mark.

7in (17.5cm) high

$300-400   **BELL**

A Vienna group of two Masqueraders, with blue shield mark, painter's numerals '30' to the footrim.

These figures are possibly Pantalone and Columbine from the Comedia dell'Arte.

c1755   *5.75in (14.5cm) high*

$700-800   **BELL**

A pair of Vienna monteiths, blue shield marks, puce 19 for Jakob Reibler.

c1770   *11in (28cm) wide*

$1,800-2,300   **WW**

A late 18thC Vienna eyebath, painted with sprays of flowers, blue shield mark, restoration to the bowl.

2.5in (6cm) high

$300-400   **WW**

A late 19thC Vienna-style mythological ewer, painted with scenes titled 'Jupiter et Claisto' and 'Konnigin Eleonore', each against a gilt, burgundy, turquoise, and cream foliate ground, underglaze blue shield mark.

18.5in (47cm) high

$750-900   **BELL**

A late 19thC Vienna-style jar and cover, painted with two panels of mythological scenes, titled 'Venus' to the base.

13in (33cm) high

$1,500-1,900   **BELL**

A late 19thC 'Vienna' cabinet plate, painted with a titled scene 'Amor und Aglaia' after Angelica Kauffmann, blue shield, painted title.

9.75in (24.5cm) diam

$450-500   **BELL**

A Vienna portrait plaque, painted with an Eastern lady, signed 'M. Stadler', within a giltwood frame, with incised shield mark and pressnummern.
1862   *12.75in (32cm) high*
$650-750
                                                    BELL

A late 19thC Vienna oval dish, decorated later, painted with a mythological scene, indistinct title to reverse, impressed and painted marks, underglaze blue shield mark.
                                          14.25in (36cm) wide
$650-900
                                                    BELL

A late 19thC Vienna-style charger, decorated with classical figures and signed 'Ed Barschneieler', with blue shield mark.
                                    14.25in (36cm) diam
$950-1,100
                                                    BELL

A late 19thC Vienna-style cabinet plate, titled 'Fisher und Nixe', painted with a man pulling a mermaid from a stream, underglaze blue shield mark.
                              9.75in (24.5cm) diam
$800-950
                                                    BELL

A late 19thC Vienna-style cabinet plate, titled 'Die Underweisung de Achillies', underglaze blue shield marks.
                              9.25in (23.5cm) diam
$750-900
                                                    BELL

A late 19thC Vienna porcelain cabinet plate, painted with Bacchus and Venus, signed 'L. KNOELLER', with blue beehive mark and painted title 'BACCHUS & VENUS'.
                              9.75in (24.5cm) diam
$550-700
                                                    L&T

A Royal Vienna Franz Josef Diamond Jubilee commemorative porcelain plate, with red printed Vienna and underglaze blue marks, dated.
Franz Josef was born in 1830. He became Emperor of Austria in 1848 and died in 1916.
1848-1908   *7.75in (20cm) long*
$400-500
                                                    H&C

An early 20thC Vienna porcelain cabinet plate, painted with a woman holding an amphora, signed 'WAGNER', with blue beehive mark and inscribed 'APFELBLÜTHEN'.
                              9.75in (24.5cm) diam
$750-900
                                                    L&T

PORCELAIN

A rare Worcester beaker or tea bowl, decorated in the Chinese manner, a little restoration to the rim.
c1753-55 *2in (5.5cm) high*
$1,500-1,900 **WW**

A pair of early first period Worcester porcelain sauce boats, painted with figures in chinoiserie landscapes, painted workman's marks in red.
c1754 *6.75in (17cm) long*
$1,300-1,900 **TEN**

A Worcester sauce boat, painted with two boats beside small pagodas on rock strata, the handles modeled with grotesque animal heads, workman's mark, a small rim chip.
c1755-60 *9in (22.5cm) across*
$650-900 **WW**

A Worcester sauce boat, molded with foliate scroll panels, painted 'Plantation' pattern on one side, the reverse with a pavilion, blue workman's mark.
c1755 *7.5in (19cm) long*
$250-400 **BELL**

A Worcester tea bowl and saucer, penciled in puce with a chinoiserie scene of two gentlemen in a fenced garden, one or two minute chips to rim of bowl.
c1756-8
$1,000-1,200 **CHOR**

A Worcester teapot and cover, penciled 'Boy on a Buffalo' pattern, incised mark to the base, a small chip to the cover.
c1755 *7.5in (19cm) wide*
$1,200-1,400 **WW**

A Worcester coffee cup, penciled in black with two figures bowing before buildings in a mountainous Oriental landscape, incised cross mark.

This design is based on an original Chinese pattern in 'encre de Chine'.
c1756 *2.5in (6cm) high*
$1,800-2,300 **WW**

A Worcester mug, printed with a titled portrait of Frederick II of Prussia, signed 'R H Worcester' for Robert Hancock, with an anchor rebus for Richard Holdship.
1757 *3.5in (8.5cm) high*
$650-750 **WW**

A Worcester chocolate cup and saucer, painted 'Departing Chinaman' pattern, workman's marks, some damages.

Illustrated: Branyan, French and Sandon, 'Worcester Blue and White Porcelain', page 132 (the saucer) where it is stated to be one of only two known to exist at the time of writing.
c1757 *saucer 6.5in (16cm) diam*
$2,300-2,800 **WW**

A Worcester vase and matched cover, painted 'Fancybird in a Tree' pattern, a long-tailed bird perched in flowering branches, workman's mark, the cover with a blue crossed swords mark.
c1758 *15in (38.5cm) high*
$7,000-7,500 **WW**

A Worcester tea bowl, coffee cup, and saucer, painted 'Heron on a Floral Spray' pattern, workmen's marks.

c1758-60   *saucer 4.75in (12cm) diam*

$2,800-3,200   **WW**

A Worcester water bottle or guglet, painted 'Willow Bridge Fisherman' pattern, the reverse with a figure beside a pagoda, open crescent mark, short rim crack.

The term 'guglet' is believed to derive from the sound made by liquid pouring out of the wide neck of such shaped bottles, though in fact the flared neck of this bottle is less common at Worcester than the narrow truncated opening on similar bottles.

c1760-65   *11in (28cm) high*

$950-1,100   **WW**

A Worcester tea bowl and saucer, painted 'Feather Molded Floral' pattern, blue workman's mark.

c1760   *saucer 4.75in (12cm) diam*

$180-230   **BELL**

A Worcester mug, printed 'La Terre' pattern depicts three Chinese figures, cracked.

c1760   *3.5in (9cm) high*

$450-550   **WW**

A Worcester mug, rare printed 'The Harvesters' pattern by Robert Hancock, depicts three workers, the reverse with 'The Minuet' pattern after a design by Francis Hayman, some faults.

c1760   *3.5in (8.5cm) high*

$550-700   **WW**

A Royal commemorative Worcester porcelain mug, with a profile of George II, with a vignette of trophies of war and inscribed 'Liberty'.

c1760   *3.5in (8.5cm) high*

$800-950   **H&C**

A Worcester chestnut basket, cover, and stand, the stand painted with a red anchor mark, the cover incised '10', the basket incised '2', firing crack to cover, restoration to rim, with hairline crack, some chips to flowers.

The red anchor mark was sometimes added to wares of this date which were decorated by independent workshops. It could also be used to emulate the Chelsea mark.

c1760

$1,600-2,300   **CHOR**

A Worcester pierced dish, with basket weave and lattice panels, heightened in puce, some cracks, some kiln specks, a little wear to the enamels.

c1760   *10.75in (27cm) wide*

$750-1,000   **CHOR**

Two Worcester plates, attributed to James Giles, painted with an exotic bird upon rocks.

c1765-70   *8.25in (21cm) diam*

$1,900-2,500   **L&T**

A Worcester cabbage leaf-molded dish, painted in the atelier of James Giles.

c1765-70   *10.25in (26cm) long*

$800-950   **MAB**

PORCELAIN

A Worcester basket, the interior with a pavilion in the 'Imari' palette, slight chipping to petals.
c1765   *7.75in (19.5cm) wide*
$750-1,000   **CHOR**

A Worcester chocolate cup and saucer, 'Jabberwocky' pattern, cup with one spot of staining in base, saucer rim with glaze speckling.
c1765
$1,000-1,100   **CHOR**

A Worcester mug, painted with an exotic bird, hatched square mark, some chips to footrim.
c1765   *3.75in (9.5cm) high*
$1,800-2,300   **CHOR**

A Worcester tea bowl and saucer, painted 'Candle Fence Pavilion' pattern, open crescent marks.
c1765   *saucer 5in (13cm) diam*
$500-650   **WW**

A Worcester dessert plate, painted 'Old Japan Fan' pattern, pseudo Oriental marks.
c1765   *7.5in (19cm) diam*
$180-250   **BELL**

A Worcester jug and cover, painted 'Eloping Bride' pattern, depicts a couple on horseback being chased by three figures, pseudo Chinese mark, chip to the cover.
c1765-70   *5in (13cm) high*
$1,800-2,300   **WW**

A Worcester tea bowl, coffee cup, and saucer, 'Arcade' pattern, character marks.
c1765-70   *saucer 4.25in (10.5cm) diam*
$2,300-2,800   **WW**

A Worcester coffee cup and saucer, painted 'Bird in a Ring' pattern, open crescent marks.
c1765-70   *saucer 4.75in (12cm) diam*
$500-650   **WW**

A Worcester sparrow beak jug and cover, painted 'Eloping Bride' pattern, depicts an archer with a female companion on horseback taking aim at figures holding banners, blue painter's mark.
c1765-68   *5in (12.5cm) high*
$1,900-2,500   **MAB**

A Worcester tea bowl and saucer, painted 'Gardener' pattern depicting a Chinese figure kneeling, watched by a further figure.
c1768   *saucer 4.75in (12cm) diam*
$1,500-1,900   **WW**

A Worcester 'gu' beaker vase, painted with two panels of birds beneath trees, within gilt cartouches, blue square seal mark.

A 'gu' is a type of ancient Chinese ritual bronze vessel from the Shang and Zhou dynasties. It was used to drink wine or to offer ritual libations. A 'gu' is tall and slender, with a slightly flared base that tapers to a slim center section before widening again into a trumpet-like mouth, wider than the base.

c1770   *6in (15.5cm) high*
$2,300-2,800   **WW**

A Worcester mug, painted with exotic birds, within gilt cartouches, crescent marks.

c1770   *5.5in (14cm) high*
$2,500-3,200   **CHOR**

A Worcester chocolate cup and matching cover, painted with exotic birds within gilt scroll cartouche and gilt stripe ground, some rubbing.

c1770
$1,900-2,500   **CHOR**

A Worcester garniture of pot pourri vases, mazarine-blue ground, painted with exotic birds, the shoulders pierced with diamond-shaped apertures, crescent marks, a smaller vase with restoration to neck.

c1770   *largest 9in (23cm) high*
$7,000-8,000   **CHOR**

A Worcester tea canister and cover, painted with exotic birds, flat chip under cover rim, hatched square mark.

c1770   *6in (15.5cm) high*
$6,500-7,000   **CHOR**

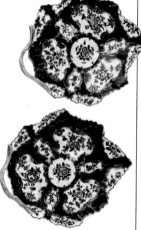

Two Worcester vine dishes, painted with flowers within gilt cartouches, one dish with chip to foot rim.

c1775   *9in (23cm) long*
$1,300-1,800   **CHOR**

A Worcester coffee cup and saucer, painted with exotic birds, landscape and buildings, crescent marks.

c1775
$1,900-2,500   **CHOR**

A Worcester cabbage leaf jug, with mask spout, painted with exotic birds in landscape, small restoration to spout.

c1775   *7in (18cm) high*
$3,200-3,800   **CHOR**

An 18thC Worcester tankard, decorated with exotic birds and insects, underglaze blue square mark.

5in (12.5cm) high
$800-950   **L&T**

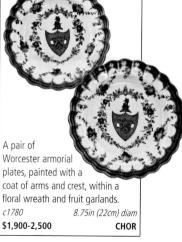

A pair of Worcester armorial plates, painted with a coat of arms and crest, within a floral wreath and fruit garlands.

c1780   *8.75in (22cm) diam*
$1,900-2,500   **CHOR**

PORCELAIN

ESSENTIAL REFERENCE - WORCESTER

The term 'Worcester' includes several factories that operated in the city.

- The best-known Worcester factory was managed by the Flight family in the 18thC.
- Important names and periods in Flight's history include: Flight (1783-92), Flight & Barr (1792-1804), Barr, Flight & Barr (1804-13) and Flight, Barr & Barr (1813-40).
- Humphrey Chamberlain and his son opened their own factory around 1786. They were active until 1840.
- From 1840 to 1851, Flight's and Chamberlain's merged to form Chamberlain & Co.
- Former Chamberlain employee Thomas Grainger established a factory in c1806. It operated under various guises until 1902.
- Kerr & Binns took over the management of the Chamberlain & Co. works from 1852 to 1862.

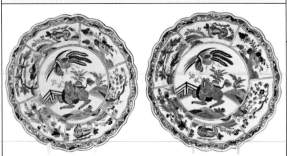

A pair of Worcester dessert plates, from the Bishop Sumner service.

The pattern is a direct copy of a Chinese original from the Kangxi period (1662-1722) although the palette is not true to the Chinese porcelain. There are several Bishop Sumners after whom the service could be named - perhaps the most likely the brothers John Sumner, Archbishop of Canterbury (1780-1862) and Charles Sumner, Bishop of Winchester (1790-1874) - but as both lived in the 19thC, the service cannot have been originally made for them. It is possible that a link was made when the service was sold as part of one of the bishops' estates.

c1775   *9in (22.5cm) long*
$1,900-2,500   **WW**

A Worcester sugar bowl and cover, of 'Lord Henry Thynne' type, crescent mark, tiny chips to flower finial, rubbing to gilding on bowl.
c1775
$700-800   **CHOR**

A Worcester teacup and saucer, painted 'Royal Wedding' pattern, the saucer with a slight trembleuse to the well, open crescent marks.

The pattern was so named when a service of this type was presented by the Borough of Cheltenham to HRH Queen Elizabeth and the Duke of Edinburgh on their wedding in 1948.
c1780-85   *5.5in (13.5cm)*
$250-320   **WW**

A Worcester ribbed teapot, cover, and stand, with turquoise shagreen borders, the pot with small sliver chips to finial, tiny chip to flange.
c1780   *the teapot 5.5in (13.5cm) high*
$1,300-1,900   **CHOR**

A Worcester 'Flight' oval dish, from the 'Hope' service ordered by the Duke of Clarence, decorated by John Pennington, blue 'Flight' mark, a few small flakes and areas of wear to the gilding.
c1790   *13.5in (34cm) long*
$3,200-4,400   **DN**

A Flight & Barr Worcester 'Japan' pattern coffee can, saucer and plate, incised 'B' marks to coffee can and saucer.
c1800   *plate 8.25in (21cm) diam*
$250-320   **BELL**

A Flight, Barr & Barr plate, painted with an Oriental figure in a landscape inside an elaborate 'Japan' pattern border, printed and impressed marks.
c1815   *8in (20.5cm) diam*
$250-320   **BELL**

An early 19thC Grainger & Company, Worcester blush ivory candle snuffer, modeled as a monkey's head, marked '1812'.
3.75in (9.5cm) high
$300-400   **LOC**

A Kerr & Binns Worcester pot pourri vase and cover, modeled with three classical maidens, iron-red printed shield mark, restoration.
1852-62   *9in (23cm) high*
$250-400   **MAB**

A pair of Chamberlain's Worcester ice pails with liners and covers, printed marks to the inside of the covers.
c1810-20 *8.75in (22cm) high*
$1,900-2,500 WW

A pair of Chamberlain's Worcester ice pails and covers, of 'Warwick vase' form, with simulated marble interiors.
c1820 *13in (33cm) high*
$1,300-1,900 BELL

A Chamberlain's Worcester topographical basket, painted with a view of Great Malvern Priory, titled 'Malvern' to the underside, puce factory mark.
c1840 *8.75in (22cm) wide*
$550-650 CHOR

A Chamberlain's Worcester jardinière, with blue painted script mark.
c1820 *15in (38.5cm) wide*
$450-500 BELL

A Royal Worcester vase, by Charles Henry Clifford Baldwyn, shape no.1553, painted with flying swans, there is minor factory polishing to a blemish on the underside, with factory gilding over the top.
c1903 *10.75in (27cm) high*
$4,500-5,000 CHOR

A Royal Worcester vase, painted with swans in flight, signed 'C Baldwyn', shape no.1539.
1903 *6in (15.5cm) high*
$2,300-2,800 SWO

A Royal Worcester vase, painted with sheep on a hillside, signed 'H Davis', shape no.2701.
1894 *6.25in (16cm) high*
$1,300-1,900 SWO

A Royal Worcester porcelain vase, painted by Harry Davis with sheep in a highland landscape, signed, printed mark in puce, dated.
1908 *8.5in (21.5cm) high*
$950-1,100 TEN

A Royal Worcester vase, painted with a crane in a desert rock pool, signed 'W Powell', shape no.2260, with date code.
1909 *6in (15cm) high*
$1,000-1,200 SWO

A Royal Worcester pot pourri vase, painted with highland cattle, signed 'J Stinton', with an internal lid and pierced cover, no.'2048', with date code.
1919 *13in (33cm) high*
$2,500-3,800 SWO

PORCELAIN

A Royal Worcester pedestal vase and cover, signed 'F Parker', factory marks to base, registration no.329876, date code.
1905   *10.75in (27.5cm) high*
$550-700   **TRI**

A Royal Worcester 'Hadley Ware' vase, painted with a brace of pheasants in landscape, unsigned, green mark, shape no.F114/6940.
1905   *7in (18cm) high*
$400-450   **HT**

A Royal Worcester vase, commemorating the 1911 Coronation, the cover modeled as the crown.
6in (15.5cm) high
$1,000-1,100   **H&C**

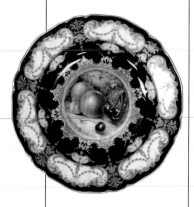

A Royal Worcester comport, decorated by Richard Seabright, manufactured for H.G Stephenson Ltd., Manchester, puce mark with date code.
1911   *9.5in (24cm) diam*
$400-500   **FLD**

A Royal Worcester vase, painted by W. Ricketts with a still life of apples, grapes and other fruits on a mossy bank, signed, puce mark, shape no.1572.
1913   *8.75in (22.5cm) high*
$650-700   **HT**

A matched pair of Royal Worcester vases, painted in by W. Ricketts with a still life of apples, grapes and peaches on a mossy bank, signed, puce mark, shape no.1410.
1912 and 1913   *11in (28cm) high*
$2,300-2,800   **HT**

A Royal Worcester vase, painted with fruit, signed 'Ricketts', numbered '287', with date code.
1921   *7.75in (20cm) high*
$650-700   **SWO**

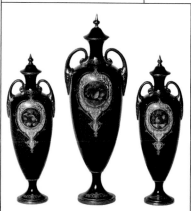

A Royal Worcester mantel garniture, largest painted by E. Townsend with peaches and cherries on a mossy bank, the smaller vases painted by W. Bee, puce mark, shape no.2710.
1928-30   *largest 12.5in (32cm) high*
$750-900   **HT**

A small Royal Worcester 'Fallen Fruits' cabinet plate, decorated by Leaman, signed, black printed mark.
6in (15cm) diam
$230-280   **FLD**

A Royal Worcester gilt decorated figural table piece.
10in (25cm) high
$50-60   **LOC**

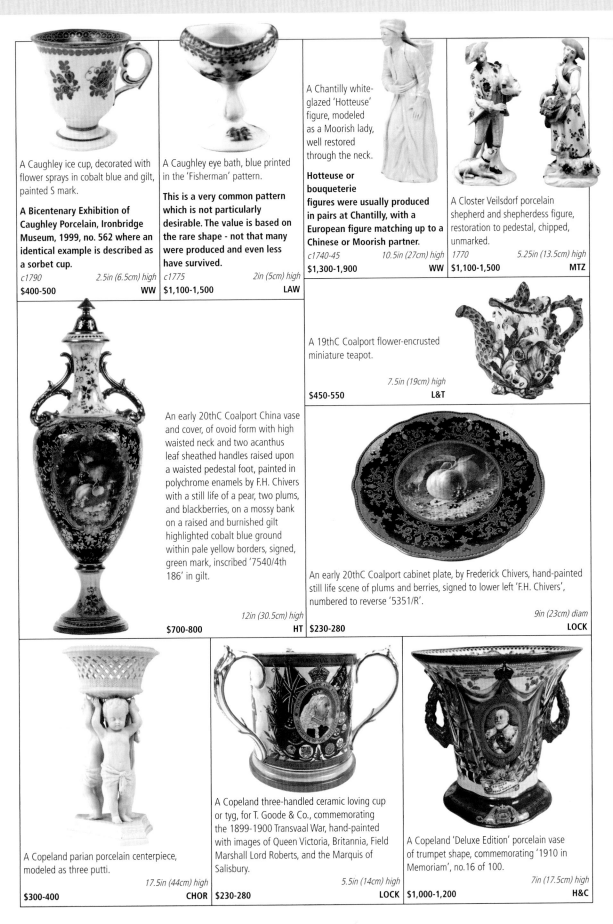

A Caughley ice cup, decorated with flower sprays in cobalt blue and gilt, painted S mark.

A Bicentenary Exhibition of Caughley Porcelain, Ironbridge Museum, 1999, no. 562 where an identical example is described as a sorbet cup.

c1790   *2.5in (6.5cm) high*
$400-500   **WW**

A Caughley eye bath, blue printed in the 'Fisherman' pattern.

This is a very common pattern which is not particularly desirable. The value is based on the rare shape - not that many were produced and even less have survived.

c1775   *2in (5cm) high*
$1,100-1,500   **LAW**

A Chantilly white-glazed 'Hotteuse' figure, modeled as a Moorish lady, well restored through the neck.

Hotteuse or bouqueterie figures were usually produced in pairs at Chantilly, with a European figure matching up to a Chinese or Moorish partner.

c1740-45   *10.5in (27cm) high*
$1,300-1,900   **WW**

A Closter Veilsdorf porcelain shepherd and shepherdess figure, restoration to pedestal, chipped, unmarked.

1770   *5.25in (13.5cm) high*
$1,100-1,500   **MTZ**

A 19thC Coalport flower-encrusted miniature teapot.

7.5in (19cm) high
$450-550   **L&T**

An early 20thC Coalport China vase and cover, of ovoid form with high waisted neck and two acanthus leaf sheathed handles raised upon a waisted pedestal foot, painted in polychrome enamels by F.H. Chivers with a still life of a pear, two plums, and blackberries, on a mossy bank on a raised and burnished gilt highlighted cobalt blue ground within pale yellow borders, signed, green mark, inscribed '7540/4th 186' in gilt.

12in (30.5cm) high
$700-800   **HT**

An early 20thC Coalport cabinet plate, by Frederick Chivers, hand-painted still life scene of plums and berries, signed to lower left 'F.H. Chivers', numbered to reverse '5351/R'.

9in (23cm) diam
$230-280   **LOCK**

A Copeland parian porcelain centerpiece, modeled as three putti.

17.5in (44cm) high
$300-400   **CHOR**

A Copeland three-handled ceramic loving cup or tyg, for T. Goode & Co., commemorating the 1899-1900 Transvaal War, hand-painted with images of Queen Victoria, Britannia, Field Marshall Lord Roberts, and the Marquis of Salisbury.

5.5in (14cm) high
$230-280   **LOCK**

A Copeland 'Deluxe Edition' porcelain vase of trumpet shape, commemorating '1910 in Memoriam', no.16 of 100.

7in (17.5cm) high
$1,000-1,200   **H&C**

A pair of Copeland jardinières, possibly made for the 1862 Exhibition, painted by Charles Ferdinand Hürten, signed 'Hürten' to both sides, printed marks.

Charles Ferdinand Hürten (1820-1901) was an active porcelain painter in Paris where he came to the attention of William Taylor Copeland, who took two years to persuade him to come and work at Copeland. Many of his first works were for the factory's exhibits at the London International Exhibition of 1862. Hürten received many special commissions, including a set of panels for the Grand Drawing Room at Chatsworth created for the Duchess of Devonshire. However, he stayed loyal to the Copeland factory where he remained until the 1890s. In 1874 the Art Journal reported, 'Hürten has no superior in flower painting, especially on pieces sufficiently large to give full scope to his vigorous yet delicate pencil; and his perfect feeling for all the beauties of texture and color in his favorite subjects is sufficiently obvious.'

1850-1900   *13.75in (35cm) across*
$9,500-10,500   **WW**

A rare Copeland porcelain vase and cover, the vase in two sections united by a silver metal bolt and butterfly nut, decorated with portraits of Qyeen Victoria.

11in (28cm) high
$2,000-2,500   **H&C**

A Frankenthal porcelain horse, modeled by Karl Gottlieb Lück, underglaze blue and crowned 'CT' mark, restored.

1777   *8in (20cm) high*
$1,000-1,100   **MTZ**

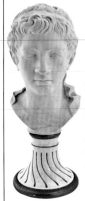

A 1770s Furstenberg biscuit bust of Ptolemaeus, probably modeled by Desoches, incised 'PTOLOMEUS' above 'No.5', with impressed running horse over 'W', the base with blue script 'F' mark.

10.75in (27cm) high
$750-900   **BELL**

A Herend porcelain serving dish, yellow Imari decorated, centered with two carp over four shell-shaped dishes, with blue printed marks.

19.5in (50cm) long
$800-950   **BELL**

A Höchst porcelain 'The Broken Egg' figure of a boy, modeled by Johann Peter Melchior, painted in colors, underglaze blue 'Radmarke', incised 'N25'.

1771   *5in (12.5cm) high*
$450-550   **MTZ**

A Höchst porcelain 'The Disturbed Slumber' figure, modeled by Johann Peter Melchior, underglaze blue wheel mark.

1770   *5.5in (14cm) high*
$1,900-2,500   **MTZ**

A Höchst porcelain sultan and sultaness, modeled by Johann Peter Melchior, underglaze blue crowned wheel mark.

1770   *7.5in (19cm) high*
$3,800-4,400   **MTZ**

A Longton Hall bell-shaped mug, printed with the arms of the Ancient and Honourable Society of Bucks, signed 'sadler Liverpool', between smaller prints of Justice and Fame, some damages.

The print is after an engraving by H Copeland, dated 1748 and is attributed to Jeremiah Evans. The same print can be found on Worcester porcelain and also on Liverpool porcelains and creamwares. It is likely that Sadler bought Longton Hall blanks in the last years of the factory.

c1758-60   *5in (12.5cm) high*
$650-750   **WW**

A Longton Hall leaf dish, molded and painted in the 'Trembly Rose' manner with English flowers.

c1755   *9in (23cm) long*
$1,300-1,800   **WW**

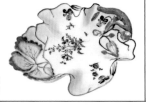

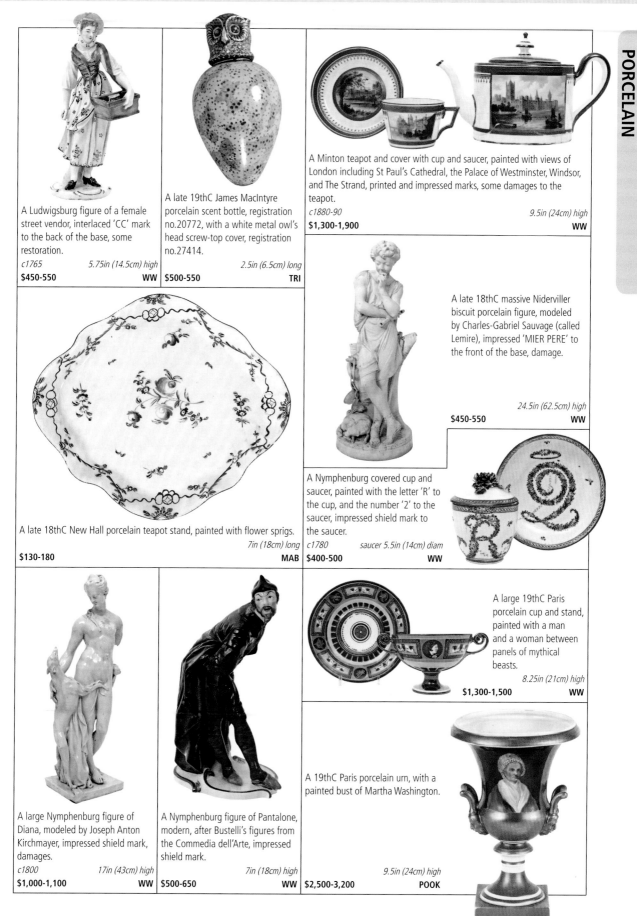

A Ludwigsburg figure of a female street vendor, interlaced 'CC' mark to the back of the base, some restoration.
c1765   5.75in (14.5cm) high
$450-550   WW

A late 19thC James MacIntyre porcelain scent bottle, registration no.20772, with a white metal owl's head screw-top cover, registration no.27414.
                    2.5in (6.5cm) long
$500-550   TRI

A Minton teapot and cover with cup and saucer, painted with views of London including St Paul's Cathedral, the Palace of Westminster, Windsor, and The Strand, printed and impressed marks, some damages to the teapot.
c1880-90   9.5in (24cm) high
$1,300-1,900   WW

A late 18thC massive Niderviller biscuit porcelain figure, modeled by Charles-Gabriel Sauvage (called Lemire), impressed 'MIER PERE' to the front of the base, damage.

                    24.5in (62.5cm) high
$450-550   WW

A late 18thC New Hall porcelain teapot stand, painted with flower sprigs.
                    7in (18cm) long
$130-180   MAB

A Nymphenburg covered cup and saucer, painted with the letter 'R' to the cup, and the number '2' to the saucer, impressed shield mark to the saucer.
c1780   saucer 5.5in (14cm) diam
$400-500   WW

A large 19thC Paris porcelain cup and stand, painted with a man and a woman between panels of mythical beasts.
                    8.25in (21cm) high
$1,300-1,500   WW

A large Nymphenburg figure of Diana, modeled by Joseph Anton Kirchmayer, impressed shield mark, damages.
c1800   17in (43cm) high
$1,000-1,100   WW

A Nymphenburg figure of Pantalone, modern, after Bustelli's figures from the Commedia dell'Arte, impressed shield mark.
                    7in (18cm) high
$500-650   WW

A 19thC Paris porcelain urn, with a painted bust of Martha Washington.
                    9.5in (24cm) high
$2,500-3,200   POOK

PORCELAIN

A Paris porcelain mug, or pot à boire, by Christopher Potter, Rue de Crussol, with gilt mark 'Potter a Paris', faint crack to base.

Christopher Potter (c1751-1817) was originally a Cambridgeshire landowner and army victualler. By 1789 he seems to have been in Paris, probably as a result of the scandal surrounding his unseating from the parliamentary constituency of Colchester for corrupt practices. In June 1789 he petitioned the National Assembly for an exclusive right to open a workshop to decorate and print on glass and ceramics but was turned down. He nevertheless took premises on the Rue de Crussol under the name Manufacture du prince de Galles and completed his first order in 1790 before selling the company to its director, Louis Blancheron in 1794. Around this time he re-opened the Chantilly Factory, closed because of the Revolution and had further potteries at Montereau and Forges-les-Eaux.

1790-94   *5in (13cm) high*
$500-550   **DN**

A Victorian parian bust of the Duke of Wellington, by Joseph Pitts, London.

9.5in (24cm) high
$200-250   **DW**

A Plymouth porcelain figure of Minerva, on a brown rocky mound base, with damage.

c1770   *7.25in (18.5cm) high*
$550-650   **BELL**

A pair of 19thC Carl Thieme (Potschappel) figures of badminton players, after Meissen, some restoration.

6.5in (16.5cm) high
$180-250   **WW**

A Ridgway porcelain dessert service, comprising a comport, two oval stands, two rectangular stands, four circular stands and twelve plates, painted pattern '6/4694'.

c1850
$1,300-1,900   **BELL**

A Rockingham shallow basket, painted with the north-west side of Salisbury Cathedral, puce mark, titled in red to the base.

c1835   *12in (30cm) wide*
$650-700   **WW**

A late 19thC Samson figure group of 'The Betrothal', after the Meissen model by J.J. Kändler, imitation crossed swords mark, some damages and restoration.

8in (20cm) high
$60-100   **WW**

A Soviet state porcelain figurine of Tamara Karsavina, after a design by Ivanov, depicting the ballerina for a performance of Stravinsky's 'Firebird', underglazed factory stamp, artist's monogram and date.

c1921   *9in (23cm) high*
$2,800-3,500   **TRI**

A Spode pot pourri vase and cover, with pierced cover and set on a triple dolphin support and triform base, restoration to cover and dolphin.

6.5in (16.5cm) high
$650-750   **CHOR**

A Spode Copeland 'édition de luxe' Trafalgar centenary porcelain tyg, no.78 of a limited edition of 100.

This is the rare larger sized version of this decorative celebration tyg.

1905   *6in (15cm) high*
$700-800   **CM**

A pair of Samson figural pot pourri vases, pseudo gold anchor mark, some damage.

13.5in (34cm) high
$500-650   **CHOR**

A St. Petersburg porcelain dinner plate, from the Raphael Service, from the Imperial Porcelain Factory, the cavetto painted 'en grisaille' with Venus and Cupid.
1897   *9.5in (24cm) diam*
$10,000-11,000   **DN**

A St. Petersburg Imperial porcelain factory Rococo Revival coffee cup and saucer, by repute from the service at the Imperial Dacha, with central Imperial monogramme beneath crown, under-glazed blue printed cipher for Nicholas I, with two small chips.
c1840
$2,300-2,800   **DN**

A Swansea plate, printed and painted in the 'Mandarin' pattern with a group of men in a garden.
c1815   *8.25in (21cm) diam*
$400-500   **CHOR**

A pair of Swansea plates, painted probably by Henry Morris.
c1815-17   *9in (23cm) diam*
$650-750   **WW**

A Volkstedt figure of Diana, her dog at her feet, the dog's collar inscribed 'JCW 1786'.
1786   *7.75in (19.5cm) high*
$550-700   **WW**

A late 19thC Volkstedt porcelain basket and cover, modeled as a hen with four yellow chicks, crossed pitchforks mark in blue, two cracks across footrim.
                          7.75in (19.5cm) wide
$650-750   **CHEF**

A West Pans blue and white bottle or guglet, painted with bamboo issuing from rockwork beside a fence, a small chip to the rim.
c1770   *8in (20.5cm) high*
$1,000-1,100   **WW**

A late 19thC Zsolnay Pecs charger, impressed and printed factory marks on reverse.
                          18in (46cm) diam
$700-750   **TRI**

A rare Suffragette porcelain model of a cat, molded, to the base 'I Want My Vote', covered in straw colored glaze.
$250-320   **MOR**

An English porcelain plate, commemorating the wedding of the Duke of Clarence (later William IV), with coats of arms surmounted by the crown of a younger son of the Monarch.

On 11 July 1818 William married Princess Adelaide of Saxe-Meiningen (whose arms appear on the right of the plate) at Kew. It is probable that this plate is from the service used at the banquet in celebration of that union.
$950-1,100   **H&C**

THE POTTERY MARKET

As with most areas, pottery collectors have been affected by the economic climate. There is some evidence that things are looking up. As always when good, rare, early pieces, and especially dated, come fresh to the market, top prices are paid. Mid-priced and low-end pieces have struggled, particularly if they were produced in large quantities, like some of the more common transfer-printed Staffordshire patterns. Some Staffordshire is doing considerably better with US collectors.

The American market for pottery is generally stronger than the UK market. Business is mainly through the internet as we are still not seeing the number of American buyers travelling around the country as in the past, although there are indications that the collectors are returning. Good quality pre-1830 pottery is still in demand. Even with some restoration, the rarity of the Yorkshire Toby jug featured was enough to ensure a good price at a time when prices of Toby jugs are at best sluggish.

Victorian pottery and Staffordshire figures have to be exceptionally rare to attract any interest. As I always say, it is an excellent time financially to start a collection. There is still the problem of fake 'Staffordshire' coming from the Far East. They are really quite easy to spot, and don't have the quality of period examples. If in any doubt, you should always buy from a reputable dealer or auction house, and remember, it is worth looking at good, original 'right' pieces to 'get your eye in'.

Delftware again has to be early and a rare shape to achieve strong prices. Dates also help - as with the rare delft dish on this page, sold by Cheffins for in excess of £25,000 ($35,000). The significance of the 1682 date on a number of delft pieces is uncertain. It could relate to the death of Prince Rupert of the Rhine, cousin of King Charles II, who was Royalist commander during the English Civil War. This intrigue increases interest.

For the more modest collector interested in delft and slipware, it is an excellent time to buy. At many sales there is strong competition for top-end pieces, but the market is generally sluggish for more common pieces.

Again there have been some dramatic prices paid for some early pottery, particularly the Italian maiolica 'istoriato' ware plates, dishes and apothecary jars created in the 16thC. Interest in good and early (16thC) Hispano Moresque pottery remains strong, but little comes to the market. Mason's ironstone has to be an interesting shape with strong colors to make any money. Good quality early Wedgwood, particularly pieces with unusual color combinations, seems to be selling better in the US rooms. American stoneware continues to have a strong collectors market, particularly for rare shapes and makers and unusual designs. Redware has seen a sluggish period where only the most unusual pieces fetch high prices. Early spatterware continues to fetch substantial prices when it comes onto the market.

Top Left: A rare delft dated dish, probably from London, the center painted with a large crown and dated '1682', decorated in blue and yellow.

13in (33cm) diam

$32,000-38,000   **CHEF**

Above: A rare Yorkshire Toby jug, holding a large churchwarden's pipe in his left hand and a bottle in his right, his breeches, coat and hat washed in manganese, the handle formed as a caryatid with folded arms, a very small amount of good restoration.

c1780   *10in (25.5cm) high*

$4,400-5,700   **WW**

POTTERY

A Bristol delftware bowl, painted with two ladies with trees and a building.
c1750-70   *7in (17.5cm) high*
$900-1,000   **WW**

A Bristol delft chinoiserie dish, with a crane in a stylized Chinese water garden, typical wear to rim.
c1760   *13in (33.5cm) diam*
$950-1,100   **DN**

ESSENTIAL REFERENCE - BRISTOL DELFT

So many pieces of English tin-glazed earthenware remain anonymous - most cataloged according to region or city rather than by potter or factory. An exception is a series of delft blue dash chargers associated with Josiah Bundy of the Limekiln Lane pottery in Bristol. The son of a local confectioner, he joined the pottery at a young age, ultimately running the Lower Pot-House for a couple of years from 1739 until his death in 1741. This 14in (35cm) dish, c1727 (presumably a coronation piece), was decorated with a portrait of George II. The sponged bushed to either side of the stylized figure are close to the decoration on Bristol farmyard plates with the bold palette and glaze color of the type normally associated with either Brislington or Bristol. It had been completely broken in half and reglued but was otherwise in good condition with little in the way of chips or damage to the glaze.

An 18thC Bristol delft charger, in the manner of Josiah Bundy.

$12,000-13,000   **DUK**

A delftware tulip charger, probably Brislington, damages and restoration.
c1730-40   *13in (32.5cm) diam*
$900-1,000   **WW**

A Dublin delftware blue and white guglet, probably Delamain's 'World's End Pottery', painted with jardinières of flowers.
c1760   *10in (25cm) high*
$300-400   **BELL**

A delftware flowerbrick, probably Dublin, minor restorations.
c1750   *5.5in (14cm) long*
$550-700   **WW**

A Liverpool delftware tile, painted with an Oriental, inside a 'Michaelmas daisy corner'.
c1750-55   *5in (12.5cm) wide*
$900-1,000   **BELL**

A pair of Liverpool delftware wall pockets.
c1750-60   *8.5in (21.5cm) high*
$1,300-1,900   **WW**

A pair of mid-18thC delftware wall pockets, probably Liverpool, one with painted numeral '4' to reverse.
8.5in (21.5cm) high
$1,500-1,900   **MAB**

A Liverpool delft puzzle jug, decorated with a verse, 'Here Gentlemen Come try your skill; I'le [sic] hold a wager if you will: That you don't Drink this Liquor all; without you spill or lett [sic] some fall', two small restored chips.

c1760   *7in (18cm) high*

$1,300-1,800   **DN**

A London delftware Royal charger, with William and Mary beneath the initials 'WMR', a long crack.

c1690   *13.5in (34cm) diam*

$6,500-7,500   **WW**

A Royal commemorative delft dish, probably London, with a crowned portrait of Queen Anne, restored.

c1702   *13.75in (35cm) diam*

$6,500-7,500   **H&C**

A mid-18thC London delft chinoiserie plate, some surface scratching and wear to rim.

12in (30.5cm) diam

$450-500   **DN**

A London delft plate, commemorating the balloon ascent of Vincenzo Lunardi, cracked in half and restored.

Vincenzo Lunardi (1759-1806), pioneering ballonist born in Lucca, Tuscany, was famous for his balloon flights in England and Scotland which did much to engage the public. After initial favorable acclaim he left Britain in 1786 when one of his balloon flights caused a fatality. Monuments to his various landing spots can be seen in both England and Scotland.

c1785   *13.75in (35cm) diam*

$3,200-3,800   **DN**

A mid-18thC London delft water bottle or guglet, painted with stylized Chinese lotus reserved on a scroll pattern ground, some small chips.

9.5in (24cm) high

$750-900   **DN**

A mid-18thC delftware syrup jar, detailed 's. Althae' within a cherub and foliate border.

6.5in (16cm) high

$500-550   **BELL**

A mid-18thC English delftware plate, painted with a chinoiserie cockerel, hen and chick, rim chipping.

9.25in (23.5cm) high

$800-900   **WW**

A small English delftware vase, decorated with flowers, a bird and insects, a little glaze chipping.

c1730   *4.75in (12cm) high*

$180-250   **WW**

A late 18thC English delftware clock dial, painted with Roman numeral hours and Arabic minutes.

9.5in (24cm) diam

$950-1,100   **WW**

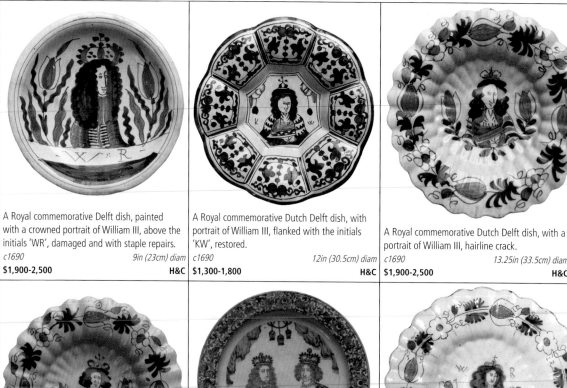

A Royal commemorative Delft dish, painted with a crowned portrait of William III, above the initials 'WR', damaged and with staple repairs.
c1690   *9in (23cm) diam*
$1,900-2,500   **H&C**

A Royal commemorative Dutch Delft dish, with portrait of William III, flanked with the initials 'KW', restored.
c1690   *12in (30.5cm) diam*
$1,300-1,800   **H&C**

A Royal commemorative Dutch Delft dish, with a portrait of William III, hairline crack.
c1690   *13.25in (33.5cm) diam*
$1,900-2,500   **H&C**

A Royal commemorative Dutch Delft dish, a half-length crowned portrait of Queen Mary, repaired.
c1690   *13.5in (34cm) diam*
$1,900-2,500   **H&C**

A Royal commemorative Dutch Delft dish, painted with crowned portraits of William and Mary, inscribed 'W.H.K.V.G.B' and 'M.K.IN', restored.
c1690   *15.75in (40cm) diam*
$2,500-3,200   **H&C**

A late 17thC Delft dish, commemorative of William III.
13.5in (34.5cm) diam
$1,500-1,900   **CHEF**

An 18thC Delft blue and white dish, painted with a lion, with a 'Kraak' type rim-decoration.
13.75in (35cm) diam
$950-1,100   **CHEF**

A Dutch Delft doré buttertub with cover and stand, painted with ships at sea, iron red 'VH' marks, two small reglued chips to the cover.
c1750   *7in (18cm) long*
$1,900-2,500   **WW**

A possibly 18thC Delft tulip vase or flower pyramid, the sections resting on lions and painted with figures in a tiled interior, blue 'AP' mark perhaps for Anthony Pennis, some damage.

Anthony Pennis is recorded as working at The Two Little Ships (De twee Scheepjes) between 1759 and 1770.
18.25in (46.5cm) high
$2,300-2,800   **WW**

A 18th/19thC large Dutch Delft tile, with fisherfolk harvesting against a seascape.
10in (25cm) square
$700-750   **BELL**

A late 17thC Rouen faience wine cistern and cover, modeled as a young Bacchus on a barrel, the barrel set with a metal tap, the top of his head lifting as a cover, the cover a replacement.

23.25in (59cm) high

$6,500-7,000   WW

An early 18thC French faience pilgrim flask, in the Nevers style, painted after the Chinese, applied with four simple handles with blue dash decoration, '4.P' mark to the base perhaps for the Desvres factory.

16.75in (42.5cm) high

$1,300-1,900   WW

CLOSER LOOK - FAIENCE TRAY

A large rectangular shaped tray is an unusual form of faience.

It is well decorated in the Rococo manner.

The subject matter, an amorous Watteauesque couple set in a stylized garden setting and titled 'LE BAIN' and 'Il Faut ceder a la force', is also unusual.

Although this has been in several pieces and restored, its rarity accounted for the value.

A mid-18thC Rouen faience tray.

25in (63cm) long

$13,000-15,000   DN

A French faience ewer, probably 18thC, Rouen, of helmet shape, decorated with a lambrequin design above a flared foot, the spout molded with a mythical mask, a little glaze chipping.

11.75in (30cm) high

$400-650   WW

A 19thC French faience model of a pigeon.

The shaped base fitted with a narrow hole to two sides suggesting that this might have been intended to cap a newel post or similar.

10.5in (26.5cm) high

$130-180   WW

A 19thC faience model of a cat.

Cats are highly collectable. This example, modeled lying on its side with head turned in a playful pose, is particularly endearing.

8.5in (21.5cm) long

$450-550   WW

A German faience barber's bowl, Arnstadt, painted in blue with a rabbit and floral decoration.

c1650   *11.5in (29cm) diam*

$1,900-3,200   WKA

A German faience pewter-mounted tankard, decorated with an image of St Simon.

c1700   *11.25in (28.5cm) high*

$1,500-2,300   WKA

An early 18thC Frankfurt faience pewter-mounted jug or ewer, molded with horizontal bands, painted with Chinese figures, minor faults.

8in (20.5cm) high

$300-650   WW

A late 18thC German faience pewter-mounted tankard, with Fayencekrug hinged cover, inscribed blue 'K' mark to base, crack through handle.

This is of mining or masonic interest, decorated with arms supported by two bearers and surmounted with a crown and eye, above the motto 'GLICKH.AVF'.

9in (23cm) high

$1,200-1,500   DN

A large 18thC Italian faience dish, Savona, decorated with a knight on horseback, surrounded by buildings and foliage.

18in (45.5cm) diam

$2,500-3,800   CSB

POTTERY

ESSENTIAL REFERENCE - TIN-GLAZED EARTHENWARE

Maiolica, delftware, and faience are common tin-glazed wares from different parts of Europe such as France, Britain, Holland, Ireland, Germany, Portugal, Italy, and Spain.

- The manufacture of British tin-glazed earthenware began in the 16thC. It was originally known as 'galleyware'.
- Important centers of production in Britain were Southwark, Brislington, Bristol, Liverpool, Glasgow, and Wincanton.
- Maiolica is the term for Italian tin-glazed earthenwares. Production started in the 13thC.
- German wares were first produced in the early 16thC by the stove-makers of the south in Bavaria and Tyrol.
- The majority of German faience dates from the late 17th until the early 19thC.
- Tin glazes were used to make earthenware less porous.
- Most tin glazes are prone to chipping because the glaze does not fuse well with the earthenware body.

Two 17thC Caltagirone maiolica albarelli.

9in (23cm) high

$950-1,100 BELL

A Sicilian Caltagirone maiolica albarello, painted to one side with the profile portrait of a soldier, the reverse inscribed '1784', the base drilled and repaired, dated.

1784 *9in (23cm) high*

$300-400 WW

A late 17thC unusual Sicilian Caltagirone maiolica albarello, painted with a lady wearing a pair of leather-rimmed nose spectacles, some glaze chipping.

7in (18cm) high

$1,600-2,000 WW

A Sicilian maiolica albarello, painted with a double portrait panel of two people facing each other, a few small rim chips.

c1790 *8.75in (22.5cm) high*

$200-250 WW

A mid-18thC Castelli maiolica teabowl and saucer, the saucer painted with a lady seated with a basket of fruit, the teabowl with Cupid holding a circular mirror.

saucer 5in (13cm) diam

$650-900 WW

A pair of 18thC Italian maiolica urns and covers, Castelli, one decorated with a buccholic scene, the other with Cupid and a water god.

15in (38cm) high

$3,200-4,400 WW

A maiolica dish, from Deruta or Savona, painted with Demeter in a chariot leaving a classical building in a landscape, extensively repaired.
c1700   *13.5in (34.5cm) diam*
$500-650   **SWO**

A 16thC Hispano-Moresque copper luster charger.
13.5in (34.5cm) diam
$650-750   **L&T**

An Italian maiolica drug jar or albarello, probably Naples, painted with a winged figure holding a sword and scales, standing on the back of the recumbent devil, inscribed 'Ung. Di Piombo'.

Ointment of lead also included antimony, rose oil, turpentine and yellow wax, and was used in the treatment of ulcers.
1720-40   *7.5in (19cm) high*
$180-320   **WW**

A 16thC Venetian maiolica albarello, painted to each side with a portrait of a man, perhaps in the workshop of Domenego da Venezia.

See 'Italian Maiolica in the Fitzwilliam Museum', pages 418-9 for other examples of work by Domenego da Venezia.
6.5in (16.5cm) high
$900-1,000   **WW**

A 16thC Italian maiolica albarello, Venice, probably from the workshop of Domenego Da Venezia.
c1560-80   *6in (15.5cm) high*
$5,500-7,000   **L&T**

A possibly 16thC Italian maiolica dish, painted with a Renaissance mendicant holding a branch of herbs, one half of this dish has been broken off in four pieces and museum-restored back.
15in (38cm) diam
$1,900-2,500   **CHEF**

A large 18thC Italian maiolica urn, decorated with a soldier on horseback and a beggar, the reverse with cipher and dated.
1702   *17.25in (44cm) high*
$3,200-4,400   **FRE**

POTTERY

A mid-18thC Staffordshire redware coffee pot, with engine-turned decoration and a foliate molded spout.

9in (23cm) high

$300-450   L&T

An English redware teapot, with molded chinoiserie decoration, cover with knop, metal band to tip of spout, character mark impressed to base.

c1760   4.5in (11cm) high

$230-280   HW

A 19thC Pennsylvania redware centerpiece bowl, the applied handles with stamped pinwheels at the terminals.

12in (30.5cm) wide

$1,900-2,300   POOK

ESSENTIAL REFERENCE - PRESTONPANS PUNCH BOWL

This large punch bowl is believed to have come to Dollerie House in 1829, when Anthony Murray of Dollerie married Georgina Murray of Ochtertyre. She was the great-granddaughter of George Mackenzie, 3rd Earl of Cromartie, whose family crest is depicted in the well of this punch bowl. Mackenzie was known for joining the Jacobite rebellion in 1745. In April 1746 he was arrested and taken prisoner following his prominent role in the Battle of Littleferry. Although he received a pardon and was not sentenced to death, he forfeited his peerage, estates and wealth, which reduced him to extreme poverty before his death in 1766. Mackenzie's youngest daughter, Lady Augusta, married into the Murray family of Ochtertyre in 1770, and it is believed that

this bowl passed to the Murray family through this connection. At the period this bowl was made, there were three potteries in Prestonpans. Given its size and quality, we can be fairly sure that this bowl was thrown either at the 'Old Kirk Pottery' owned by William Cadell or the 'Bankfoot Pottery' owned by his nephew, also a William Cadell.

A rare Prestonpans ceremonial lead-glazed redware punch bowl, with a heraldic crest to the interior with motto 'CAPER FEY', the base inscribed and dated 'M.C., P. PANS, 1776' in part below a glaze patch (broken and repaired), with late19thC ebonized table stand.

1776   bowl 30.75in (78cm) diam

$5,000-6,500   L&T

An early 19thC Connecticut redware oval loaf dish.

10.75in (27.5cm) wide

$5,500-6,500   POOK

A mid-19thC Southeastern Pennsylvania redware advertising charger, with an inscription 'G.W. Rhoads Dealer in Dry Goods Groceries & Co. also Schwitzer Kase (Swiss Cheese)'.

13.5in (34.5cm) diam

$6,500-7,500   POOK

An early 19thC Southeastern Pennsylvania redware plate.

11.75in (28.5cm) diam

$14,000-18,000   POOK

An early 19thC Bristol, Massachusetts redware pitcher and cover, with speckled green glaze.

10.5in (26.5cm) high

$14,000-18,000   POOK

An early 19thC New England redware bulbous jar, attributed to Hartford, Connecticut.

8in (20.5cm) high

$700-800   POOK

A 19thC Virginia redware crock, by Solomon Bell, impressed 's. Bell & Sons Strasburg'.

9in (23cm) high

$1,900-2,500   POOK

A 19thC Pennsylvania redware bowl and cover.

5.5in (14cm) diam

$1,000-1,100   POOK

A 19thC New England redware crock, with manganese and yellow splotches on an orange and green ground.

9in (23cm) high

$1,900-2,500   POOK

A 19thC New England redware jar, possibly Gonic, New Hampshire, having a bold green, orange, and manganese oxide glaze.

10in (25.5cm) high

$5,500-7,000   POOK

A 19thC Pennsylvania redware monkey man and jug match holder.

6.5in (16.5cm) high

$7,000-8,000   POOK

A late 18thC creamware satirical jug, printed and hand-colored with a bawdy scene of figures, titled 'The Devil of a Job - Satan at the bottom of all Mischief', restored.

6.75in (17.5cm) high

$1,800-2,300   WW

A creamware tankard, commemorating the 1782 Battle of the Saintes, with named portraits of Lord Rodney and Lord Hood, molded with a ship named 'Ville de Paris', restored.

The Battle of the Saintes, fought in the West Indies, saw the British fleet under Rodney and his second in command Hood vanquish the French, capturing their flag ship the 'Ville de Paris'.

4.5in (11.5cm) high

$700-800   H&C

A documentary creamware mug, the front inscribed 'Je crains Dieu, et je n'ai point d'autre crainte; Capt. Samuel Parker' and 'When this you see, Remember me, Tho' many miles We distant be, Dec. 20th 1788' beside an anchor, fitted with a glass bottom.

Samuel Parker is a common name in 18thC America, particularly in the six states of New England. Rather than a memorial, the French inscription appears to indicate that the mug was made by a sea captain for his beloved when he set off on a voyage.

6in (15cm) high

$650-750   WW

A creamware tankard, commemorating George III's recovery in 1789, inscribed with loyal verse, dated 'March 17 1789'.

The significance of 17 March is unclear. However, there was held at St. Paul's Cathedral on 15 March 1789 a service of thanksgiving for the King's recovery from ill health.

3.5in (9cm) high

$1,900-2,500   H&C

A creamware tankard, with interlaced handles, with the inscription 'Liberty to Subject And Loyalty to King', chips to foot rim.

Whilst in the midst of the Revolution in 1793 the French executed their King, while the British rallied behind their Monarch.

c1793   *6in (15.5cm) high*

$950-1,100   H&C

A creamware Liverpool Amnesty jug, commemorating the 1801 Golden Jubilee, two chips to foot.

8.25in (21cm) high

$800-950   H&C

A creamware jug, printed and hand-colored to one side with a French soldier standing beneath the American flag, titled 'success to America whose Militia is better than Standing Armies, May Its Citizens Emulate Soldiers and its Soldier Heroes', to the reverse a ship, beneath the spout the American Eagle surrounded by a quote from Thomas Jefferson's inaugural speech of 1801, some restoration.

c1804   *9in (23cm) high*

$450-550   WW

A creamware jug, printed to one side with two racehorses with jockeys, the reverse with a sad-looking old nag, each above an eight-line poem, inscribed 'Peter Unsworth Sadler-Newton, 1815', some restoration, dated.

The surname of Unsworth is common in the Newton area of Lancashire. However, it has not been possible to find definite record of the gentleman in question.

1815   *10in (25cm) high*

$300-450   WW

A rare political commemorative creamware mug, with a named portrait of Henry Brougham, with eulogy, chipped.

Brougham was MP for Camelford between 1810 and 1812, Winchelsea from 1816 and Westmorland from 1818 (for which event this mug is most likely made). He represented Queen Caroline in 1820 and subsequently championed reform in the great bill of 1832.

c1818   *3.5in (9cm) high*

$800-900   H&C

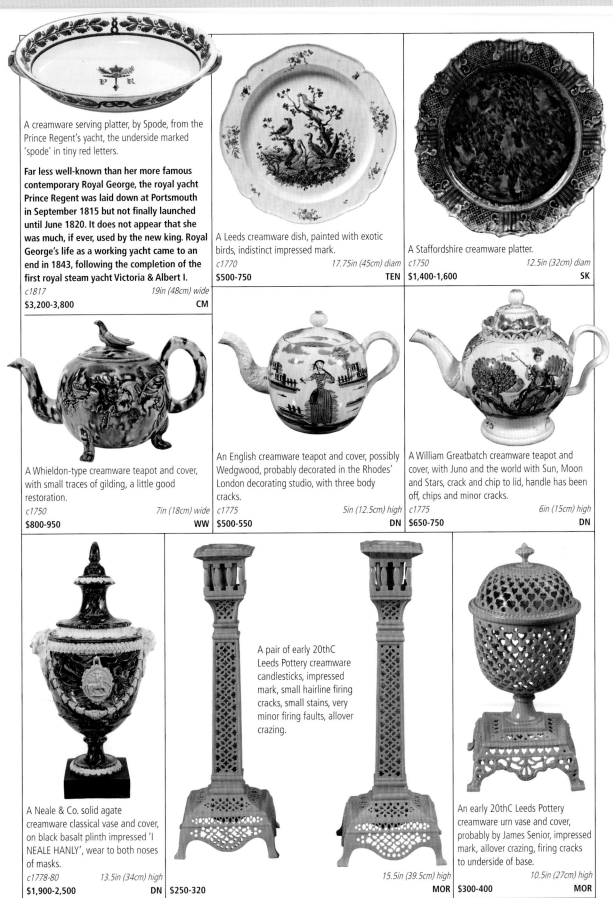

A creamware serving platter, by Spode, from the Prince Regent's yacht, the underside marked 'spode' in tiny red letters.

Far less well-known than her more famous contemporary Royal George, the royal yacht Prince Regent was laid down at Portsmouth in September 1815 but not finally launched until June 1820. It does not appear that she was much, if ever, used by the new king. Royal George's life as a working yacht came to an end in 1843, following the completion of the first royal steam yacht Victoria & Albert I.

c1817   *19in (48cm) wide*

$3,200-3,800   **CM**

A Leeds creamware dish, painted with exotic birds, indistinct impressed mark.

c1770   *17.75in (45cm) diam*

$500-750   **TEN**

A Staffordshire creamware platter.

c1750   *12.5in (32cm) diam*

$1,400-1,600   **SK**

A Whieldon-type creamware teapot and cover, with small traces of gilding, a little good restoration.

c1750   *7in (18cm) wide*

$800-950   **WW**

An English creamware teapot and cover, possibly Wedgwood, probably decorated in the Rhodes' London decorating studio, with three body cracks.

c1775   *5in (12.5cm) high*

$500-550   **DN**

A William Greatbatch creamware teapot and cover, with Juno and the world with Sun, Moon and Stars, crack and chip to lid, handle has been off, chips and minor cracks.

c1775   *6in (15cm) high*

$650-750   **DN**

A Neale & Co. solid agate creamware classical vase and cover, on black basalt plinth impressed 'I NEALE HANLY', wear to both noses of masks.

c1778-80   *13.5in (34cm) high*

$1,900-2,500   **DN**

A pair of early 20thC Leeds Pottery creamware candlesticks, impressed mark, small hairline firing cracks, small stains, very minor firing faults, allover crazing.

15.5in (39.5cm) high

$250-320   **MOR**

An early 20thC Leeds Pottery creamware urn vase and cover, probably by James Senior, impressed mark, allover crazing, firing cracks to underside of base.

10.5in (27cm) high

$300-400   **MOR**

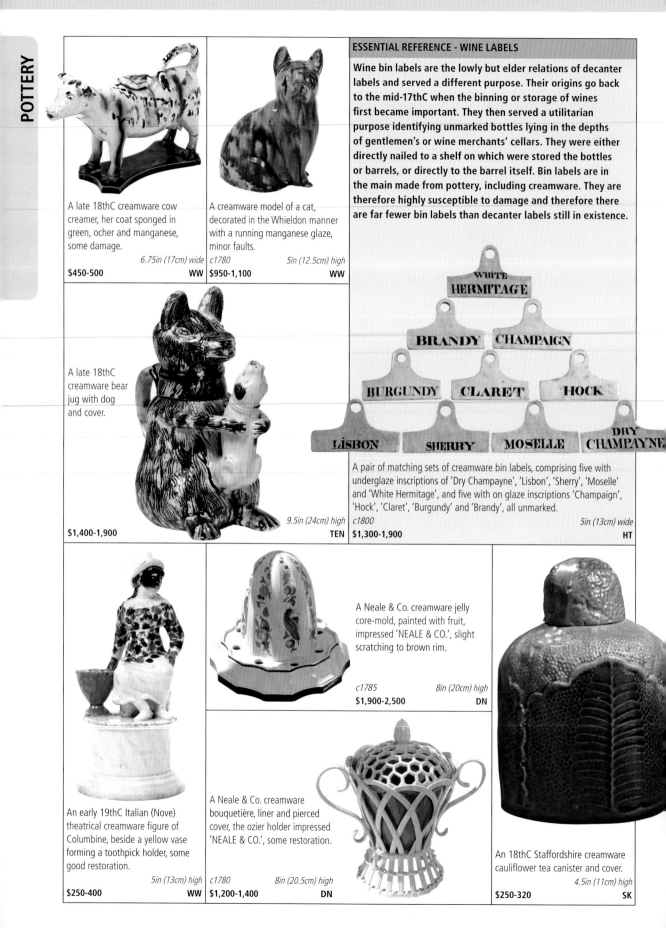

A late 18thC creamware cow creamer, her coat sponged in green, ocher and manganese, some damage.

6.75in (17cm) wide

$450-500 WW

A creamware model of a cat, decorated in the Whieldon manner with a running manganese glaze, minor faults.

c1780 *5in (12.5cm) high*

$950-1,100 WW

ESSENTIAL REFERENCE - WINE LABELS

Wine bin labels are the lowly but elder relations of decanter labels and served a different purpose. Their origins go back to the mid-17thC when the binning or storage of wines first became important. They then served a utilitarian purpose identifying unmarked bottles lying in the depths of gentlemen's or wine merchants' cellars. They were either directly nailed to a shelf on which were stored the bottles or barrels, or directly to the barrel itself. Bin labels are in the main made from pottery, including creamware. They are therefore highly susceptible to damage and therefore there are far fewer bin labels than decanter labels still in existence.

A late 18thC creamware bear jug with dog and cover.

9.5in (24cm) high

$1,400-1,900 TEN

A pair of matching sets of creamware bin labels, comprising five with underglaze inscriptions of 'Dry Champayne', 'Lisbon', 'Sherry', 'Moselle' and 'White Hermitage', and five with on glaze inscriptions 'Champaign', 'Hock', 'Claret', 'Burgundy' and 'Brandy', all unmarked.

c1800 *5in (13cm) wide*

$1,300-1,900 HT

An early 19thC Italian (Nove) theatrical creamware figure of Columbine, beside a yellow vase forming a toothpick holder, some good restoration.

5in (13cm) high

$250-400 WW

A Neale & Co. creamware jelly core-mold, painted with fruit, impressed 'NEALE & CO.', slight scratching to brown rim.

c1785 *8in (20cm) high*

$1,900-2,500 DN

A Neale & Co. creamware bouquetière, liner and pierced cover, the ozier holder impressed 'NEALE & CO.', some restoration.

c1780 *8in (20.5cm) high*

$1,200-1,400 DN

An 18thC Staffordshire creamware cauliflower tea canister and cover.

4.5in (11cm) high

$250-320 SK

A late 18th/early 19thC yellow ground pearlware mug, decorated with a large ship at sail, minor faults.

5.75in (14.5cm) high

$400-500   **WW**

A pearlware loving cup, painted with the instruments of a tailor beneath the inscription 'Robert Kirby 1805', within floral sprays, some restoration.

7in (18.5cm) high

$650-900   **WW**

A rare pearlware Napoleonic jug, printed and hand-colored to one side with a Russian soldier holding a rifle over his shoulder from which are suspended the corpses of five Frenchmen, titled 'A Russian Boor returning from his Field sports', the reverse with Napoleon surrendering to a further Russian who holds an axe aloft, a short rim crack.

The French defeat in Russia at the end of 1812 demonstrated that Napoleon was not invincible nor the military genius that many supposed him to be. Both prints are taken from cartoons etched by George Cruikshank after Russian originals by Terebenev, and were published in January 1813. The second print is sometimes titled 'specimen of Russian chopping blocks'.

c1813   *5.75in (14.5cm) high*

$500-650   **WW**

A late18thC pearlware coffee pot, transfer-printed in blue with a Willow-type pattern, minute chip to finial of cover.

10in (25cm) high

$130-180   **TRI**

A T. Lakin & Sons pearlware blue printed eggcup stand, with six egg cups, with lion's head finial carrying handle.

c1810

$250-400   **DN**

A Ralph Wood-type pearlware lion.

c1780   *11in (28cm) long*

$1,300-1,800   **TEN**

An early 19thC pearlware stirrup cup, possibly Ralph Wood, modeled as a fox mask, crack on the underside, chips, light crazing, restored.

5in (13cm) long

$650-750   **MOR**

Five Staffordshire pearlware garden labels, impressed marks, retailer's name of G.A. Stubbs, Warwick, registration lozenge, minor rim chips and staining.

c1878   *12.25in (31cm) high*

$230-280   **DN**

A pearlware maskhead mug, molded 'success to Lord Rodney' around the rim, rim restored.

Although Rodney held various Parliamentary seats it was for his naval career he is best remembered culminating in his success at the Battle of the Saintes for which he was raised to the Peerage in June 1782.

c1782   *5in (12.5cm) high*
$550-700   H&C

A Royal Commemoratives George III pearlware mug, with an inscribed superimposed portraits medallion.

c1809   *5in (12.5cm) high*
$400-450   H&C

A Royal Commemoratives pearlware nursery plate, for Queen Caroline.

1821   *6.5in (16.5cm) diam*
$180-230   H&C

A pearlware bust of Handel, by Ralph Wood.

c1780   *8.5in (21.5cm) high*
$800-900   SWO

A pearlware jar, probably Yorkshire, possibly Ferrybridge, with pink luster, inscribed, 'John and Elizabeth Withy, Octr. 21st 1826', small chip and crack, pitting, discoloration, some flaking and scratches.

1826   *5.75in (14.5cm) high*
$180-230   MOR

A pearlware pottery plaque, painted in the palette of Obadiah Sherratt, with a Regency couple, some hairline cracks, restoration, allover crazing.

c1820   *9.25in (24cm) high*
$300-350   MOR

A pair of pearlware plaques, with portraits of Louis XVI and Marie Antoinette, hairline cracks, some restoration, light crazing.

c1790   *7.25in (18.5cm) high*
$950-1,100   MOR

A pearlware plaque, painted with Judith and Holofernes, firing faults to glaze, crack on reverse, allover light crazing.

c1800   *8.75in (22cm) high*
$250-400   MOR

An English pearlware cow creamer, Staffordshire or Yorkshire, repairs.

c1820   *6in (16cm) long*
$500-750   DN

A Staffordshire salt-glazed stoneware teapot and cover, with a putto reaching through the clouds to a bird perched on flowers, minor faults.
c1750 *8in (20cm) wide*
$2,500-3,200 **WW**

A Staffordshire salt-glazed stoneware teapot and cover, painted with English flowers, cracked, the cover broken and restuck.
c1750 *6.25in (16cm)*
$180-250 **WW**

A rare Liverpool tin-glazed stoneware teapot and cover, with a building, trees in a landscape, the cover with a hatched border, cracked.
1760 *7in (18cm) wide*
$3,800-5,000 **WW**

A Staffordshire salt-glazed stoneware teapot and cover, of Jacobite significance, enameled in the 'famille rose' palette, some restoration.
c1760 *8in (20cm) wide*
$900-1,000 **WW**

A Staffordshire salt-glazed stoneware commemorative teapot and cover, for Frederick The Great of Prussia, inscribed 'Fred.III.Prussiae Rex' and verso with eagle and inscription 'semper Sublimis', replacement cover, impact cracks in the body.

Frederick II of Prussia, 'The Great', was popular in Britain at the time this teapot was made as he was Britain's ally in the Seven Years' War.
c1760 *4.5in (11cm) high*
$400-450 **DN**

An English salt-glazed stoneware chinoiserie coffee pot and cover, of 'Lighthouse' shape, three sizeable cracks to the body.
c1760 *6.25in (16cm) high*
$1,300-1,800 **DN**

An early 19thC Staffordshire smear-glaze stoneware bough pot and cover, of 'D' shape.
6.25in (16cm) high
$550-700 **TEN**

A 'George III in Memoriam' nursery plate, the reverse with impressed mark 'R W & Co Stone Ware'.
1820 *7.5in (19cm) diam*
$500-550 **H&C**

A Duke of York salt-glazed stoneware Reform flask.
c1820 *9.5in (24cm) high*
$350-400 **MART**

A 19thC salt-glazed stoneware stirrup cup, possibly Brampton, modeled with a metamorphic grinning face.

5in (12.5cm) high

$1,400-1,800   MOR

A 19thC salt-glazed stoneware figure of a lion, roaring showing tongue and teeth.

5.25in (13cm) high

$90-110   TRI

A German Raeren salt-glaze stoneware beer jug, with dancing couples above an inscribed banner and incised date, dated.

1597   *10in (25.5cm) high*

$750-900   HT

A Rhenish stoneware Bellarmine jug, with applied bearded mask, chips.

c1680   *5in (13.5cm) high*

$650-750   SWO

A William III Westerwald jug, with a relief portrait of the monarch flanked by his coat of arms, with a 1.5in crack to the neck, and typical wear to the raised points of the incised decoration.

As a general rule, prices for Westerwald blue and gray stonewares are lackluster. The subject is unusual (more difficult to find than similar vessels with the cipher of German royalty) and this crossover into the sphere of British royal commemoratives prompted a bidding war. The jug was in relatively good condition for its 300-plus years.

11in (28cm) high

$9,500-10,500   CHEF

A German Westerwald pewter-mounted stoneware tankard, with the coat of arms for the Kingdom of Great Britain.

c1707-14   *7in (17.5cm) high*

$1,000-1,250   WW

An 18thC German stoneware jug, of Westerwald type, decorated with 'GR' rosette, small foot rim chip.

9.75in (25cm) high

$180-230   DN

A Pennsylvania four-gallon stoneware lidded crock, impressed 'Cowden & Wilcox Harrisburg, PA', with a rare cobalt decoration of a dog holding a basket in its mouth.

14.25in (36cm) high

$20,000-25,000   POOK

A 19thC blue spongeware jug, inscribed J.E. Merser.

11.5in (29cm) high

$1,200-1,500   POOK

A late17thC Dutch East Indian Company stoneware flagon, possibly Japanese, with a leather rope-twist twin handle to the neck, with 'VOC' monogram.

10.75in (27cm) high

$200-250   BELL

A 19thC Staffordshire 'states' pitcher and basin, the basin impressed 'Clews'.

basin 12in (30.5cm) diam

$2,500-3,200   POOK

A 19thC Staffordshire 'Arms of Massachusetts' serving dish, impressed 'T. Mayer'.

7.75in (19.5cm) long

$1,900-2,500   POOK

A 19thC Staffordshire 'Alms House, Boston' tureen and ladle, stamped 'Ridgway'.

12.5in (32cm) long

$2,300-2,800   POOK

A 19thC Staffordshire 'General Lafayette' cup plate, impressed 'A. Stevenson'.

3.75in (9.5cm) diam

$2,500-3,200   POOK

A 19thC blue Staffordshire 'Boston Hospital' platter, stamped 'J & W Ridgway'.

12.5in (31.5cm) wide

$2,500-3,200   POOK

A 19thC Staffordshire 'New York from Weehawk' platter, impressed 'A. Stevenson'.

18.5in (47cm) wide

$1,900-2,500   POOK

A 19thC Staffordshire 'New York Heights from near Brooklyn' platter, impressed 'stevenson'.

16.5in (42cm) wide

$1,000-1,200   POOK

A 19thC 'Battle of Bunker Hill' platter, impressed 'stevenson'.

12.5in (32cm) long

$1,300-1,900   POOK

A 19thC Staffordshire 'Castle Garden Battery, New York' platter, impressed 'Wood & Sons'.

18.5in (47cm) long

$2,000-2,500   POOK

POTTERY

A 19thC Staffordshire 'Constitution and Guerrière' plate, impressed 'Wood'.

10in (25.5cm) diam

$1,900-2,500   POOK

A 19thC Staffordshire 'Highlands Hudson River' platter, impressed 'Wood & Sons'.

12.75in (32.5cm) long

$1,500-2,000   POOK

A 19thC Staffordshire 'Capitol Washington' platter.

20.25in (51.5cm) long

$1,300-1,800   POOK

A 19thC Staffordshire 'Fairmount near Philadelphia' undertray.

14in (35.5cm) long

$1,800-2,300   POOK

A 19thC Staffordshire 'Bellville on the Passaic River' soup tureen, with a 'Hope Mill Catskill, New York' tureen undertray.

tureen 15in (38cm) long

$3,800-5,000   POOK

A 19thC Staffordshire 'American Eagle and Shield' cup plate.

3.75in (9.5cm) diam

$1,800-2,300   POOK

A 19thC Staffordshire 'Exchange of Baltimore' cup plate.

4.25in (11cm) diam

$2,500-3,200   POOK

A 19thC Staffordshire 'Exchange Charleston/ Bank Savannah/New York City Hall' fruit compote.

11in (28cm) long

$1,300-1,800   POOK

A transferware soup tureen and cover, by Elkins & Co., printed with Blenheim Palace, Oxford, with swan handles, printed marks.

The print was engraved by William Radclyffe after John Preston Neale.

c1830-40   *15.5in (39cm) wide*

$180-250   WW

A late 18thC Ralph Wood figure of Jupiter, titled 'Jupiter' in black to the underside, the front of the black base titled 'Hercules' beneath the paint, some restoration.

The decorator has incorrectly titled this figure as Hercules on the front of the base. When this error was pointed out after the model had been fired, it was given back to the painter to correct the mistake. The normally white base was then overpainted in marbled black to hide the error, while the correct name of Jupiter was painted on the underside.

11.25in (28.5cm)

$300-400   WW

A Ralph Wood model of the Vicar and Moses, typically modeled with the sleeping cleric above his industrious clerk, titled to the front, a small amount of good restoration.

c1785-90   9.5in (24cm) high

$900-1,000   WW

A late 18th/early 19thC Ralph Wood-type figure, of the 'Lost Sheep Found', number '60' to the base, a little restoration.

8.25in (21cm) high

$650-750   WW

A Staffordshire group of a Savoyard and dancing bear, a small monkey between them, some restoration.

c1820-30   7.5in (19.5cm) long

$1,300-1,600   WW

A 19thC pair of Staffordshire models, of smoking dogs, each with a pipe held in its mouth, their textured coats decorated with red wheels of fire.

With Staffordshire dogs it is important to look for the more unusual. Very common examples are difficult to sell whereas these relatively rare dogs with pipes are more desirable.

8.5in (21.5cm) high

A pair of Staffordshire pottery mastiff dogs, with ocher-tinged body, on bright maroon base, the muzzle details in black.

c1880   7in (18cm) high

$300-400   SWO

$900-1,000   WW

A 19thC Staffordshire pottery bear jug and cover, the bear clutching a struggling, outstretched dog.

12.5in (32cm) high

$1,500-1,900   TEN

An early 19thC Staffordshire pottery bear jug and cover, the bear holding a caricature of Napoleon in his forepaws, the hat inscribed 'BONEY'.

11in (28cm) high

$1,500-1,900   TEN

An early 19thC pair of Staffordshire pottery figures of eagles, with sockets to top of heads.

8in (20cm) high

$650-750   TEN

An early 19thC Price & Gosnell bears grease pot lid, marked 'FOR THE GROWTH of HAIR FROM THE ANIMAL in its NATIVE CLIMATE'.
$300-400   **MART**

A 'JAMES ANDERSON BEARS GREASE' advertising lid, 2/6 size.
$70-80   **H&C**

A 'GENUINE RUSSIAN BEARS GREASE For increasing THE GROWTH OF HAIR' advertising lid, framed.
$150-190   **H&C**

A 'WHITAKER & Co's GENUINE BEAR's GREASE' Staffordshire pot lid, decorated with a bear in a ravine, well restored.
$1,100-1,400   **H&C**

A blue printed lid depicting soldiers attacking a bear, framed.
$160-200   **H&C**

A mid-19thC Prattware pot lid Windsor Park, 'Return from Stag Hunting', with decorative raised and gold band border.
$100-130   **MART**

A Staffordshire 'The Listener' pot lid, the exhibition lid with wide gold banded border, framed.
$900-1,000   **H&C**

A Staffordshire pot lid, commemorating The Great Exhibition of 1851 opening ceremony.
$500-650   **H&C**

A Staffordshire pot lid, depicting Admiral Sir Charles Napier.
$450-500   **H&C**

Judith Picks

The transfer-printed image depicts Princess Charlotte and her husband, Prince Leopold of Saxe-Coburg and Gotha, visiting Dame Bewley, a grace-and-favor occupant of one of the cottages on the Claremont estate, their royal residence near Esher, in Surrey. Dame Bewley (also known as 'Goody') is depicted with an old small-print Bible that she had difficulty reading - a state of affairs that prompted a subsequent visit by the Princess and Prince bearing the gift of a large, beautifully bound, and much easier to read Quarto Bible. This act of largesse was typical of Princess Charlotte: the only daughter of the Prince Regent (later George IV) and Princess Caroline of Brunswick she was, unlike her father, hugely popular with the British public.

Her tragic death in 1817, aged just 21 and after giving birth to a stillborn son, caused a national outpouring of grief and mourning, to the extent that most draper's shops ran out of black fabric! Not surprisingly, it also prompted the production of numerous commemorative souvenirs, of which this is an example.

A nursery plate, by Stevenson, of Princess Charlotte and Dame Bewley, printed in black and decorated in colors with an inscribed scene, impressed mark.
1816   *6.75in (17cm) diam*
$130-200   **H&C**

A brown salt-glazed quart mug, attributed to Vauxhall, decorated with a profile of Queen Anne guarded by men with guns, the lower half with spotted hounds chasing a stag, inscribed 'Ambrose Thomson 1722', chips to rim, glaze losses.
8.25in (21cm) high
$7,500-9,000   **CHEF**

A rare pottery plaque of George IV's visit to Scotland, with inscription 'Welcome King George IV', in colored enamels and pink luster, some flaking to enamel and chipped.
1822   *5.5in (14cm) wide*
$1,500-1,900   **H&C**

A stoneware commemorative jug depicting Queen Caroline, with a hatted profile and on the reverse a bird flanked by laurel branches centered by flowers of the Union.
c1820   *7in (17.5cm) high*
$300-400   **H&C**

A pink luster and colored enamel decorated jug, molded with a named Queen Caroline.
1821   *4.75in (12cm) high*
$250-320   **H&C**

A pottery jug, printed in pink with a scene from the 1831 Coronation, small chip to foot.
1831   *5.5in (14cm) high*
$200-250   **H&C**

A Victoria Coronation jug, by Read & Clementson, printed with portraits including the Duchess of Kent, printed mark.
1837   *7.75in (19.5cm) high*
$350-400   **H&C**

A pottery mug, printed with an early locomotive pulling three carriages and a wagon inscribed 'Victoria, Coronation, London Royal Mail Liverpool'.
c1838   *4in (10cm) high*
$950-1,100   **H&C**

A large commemorative 'Election' jug, with gilt inscriptions celebrating the election of 'Twelve Conservative Members to the County of Salop' in the General Election of 1841, with the coat of arms for Shrewsbury.
1841   *9.5in (24cm) high*
$750-900   **WW**

POTTERY

A mid-19thC chocolate cup, probably by Samson after the Imperial Sèvres original, of Josephine Bonaparte, the portrait signed 'O. Brun', the underside with stencilled 'M. Imple de Sevres' mark in red.

4in (10cm) high

$150-190   **H&C**

An enameled metal 'Cup of Sorrow', commemorating the 1896 Tsar Nicolas II Coronation.

1896

$300-400   **H&C**

A pottery beaker, commemorating the Tsar Nicolas II Coronation, molded with monograms, inscription and coat of arms of Moscow.

1896

$300-400   **H&C**

A Copeland 'subscribers copy' pottery tyg, commemorating the Boer War Transvaal, very faint star crack to underside.

1900   *5.5in (14cm) high*

$400-500   **H&C**

A Bristol Pottery plate, by Kepple, detailing the English League, 1st division, 1907 Football Association.

$300-400   **H&C**

A Paragon teapot and cover, commemorating the birth of Princess Elizabeth.

1926   *5in (12.5cm) high*

$400-450   **H&C**

A Copeland pottery tyg, commemorating the 'silver Jubilee', for Goode 'subscribers Copy', numbered 50.

1935   *5.75in (14.5cm) high*

$250-320   **H&C**

A Copeland pottery tyg, for Goode, commemorating the Coronation of George VI and Queen Elizabeth, numbered 10.

1937   *6in (15cm) high*

$400-500   **H&C**

A composition plaque, by W.H. Bossons, commemorating the Conquest of Everest, molded with figures of Hillary and Norgay in oxygen masks at the summit and impressed with an inscription, paintwork flaking.

This plaque is a visually impressive commemorative of the conquest of Everest. These plaques were made from an inferior composition with the result that few survive in good order.

1953   *14.25in (36cm) diam*

$180-250   **H&C**

A Ralph Wood type pottery Toby jug.

c1780 10in (25cm) high

$4,500-5,000 TEN

A rare Yorkshire creamware Toby jug, seated with a massive clay pipe, holding an empty jug molded with Cupid to two sides and with a face beneath the spout, with caryatid handle, all picked out in a deep manganese and raised on a rare flat base, the top of his pipe stem restored.

c1780 9.5in (24.5cm) high

$5,500-6,500 WW

A Toby jug, of Ralph Wood type, with a gadrooned foaming jug of ale resting on one knee.

c1790 10in (25cm) high

$1,500-1,900 WW

A late 18thC pearlware Toby jug, holding a foaming jug of beer and a pipe, unmarked.

7in (18cm) high

$2,300-2,800 FLD

A late 18thC Wood family Toby jug and cover, unmarked.

10.25in (26cm) high

$1,800-2,300 FLD

A late 18thC Ralph Wood Toby jug, ordinary model with a roman nose, impressed '51'.

9.75in (25cm) high

$1,900-2,500 FLD

A creamware Toby jug, seated with a large clay pipe between his knees, a foaming jug of ale on his left knee, decorated in running splashes of green, blue and manganese, some good restoration to his hat.

c1790 10in (25cm) high

$1,500-1,900 WW

A Prattware 'sailor' Toby jug, of Rodney type, seated on a rectangular sea chest, a jug of ale in his left hand, a cup of the same clutched in his right, wearing a blue coat with yellow trim over trousers striped in blue and ocher, some good restoration.

c1790 11in (28cm) high

$2,500-3,200 WW

An 'Ordinary' Toby jug, by Enoch Wood, seated with a large round jug of ale and holding his long-stemmed pipe in his right hand, wearing a pale lilac coat over a yellow and green striped waistcoat, some good restoration to his hat.

c1800 9.75in (25cm) high

$250-400 WW

A 'Drunken Parson' Toby jug, by Enoch Wood, seated with a jug of ale and a cup, raised on a low colored marbled base, some restoration.

c1815-20 7.75in (20cm) high

$500-650 WW

A Mexborough Yorkshire Toby jug, typically modeled with an empty jug of ale and a hexagonal goblet, restoration to his hat.

c1820-30 10in (25cm) high

$500-650 WW

POTTERY

A Wedgwood Queen's Ware dish, painted by Emile Lessore, with three putti fishing, titled 'The Young Anglers', signed, impressed and painted marks.

c1860-70 12.5in (32cm) wide

$250-320 BELL

A Wedgwood Queen's Ware commemorative mug, for the Friendly Society of Cordwainers of England, with a coat of arms and supporters, with inscriptions 'We unite to maintain our Rights inviolate.', 'Prosperity attend the justness of our Cause.' and 'THE FRIENDLY SOCIETY OF CORDWAINERS OF ENGLAND', impressed mark, slight rubbing to gilding.

c1770 5in (13cm) high

$2,300-2,800 DN

A Wedgwood jasper tripod urn and cover, modeled as a classical censor supported on legs with rams' masks and cloven feet, impressed 'WEDGWOOD', some firing cracks, legs warped in firing, small chips.

c1790 8.5in (21.5cm) high

$1,900-2,500 DN

A 19thC Wedgwood pottery footbath, decorated with vine leaves and grapes, with a pair of handles, impressed mark 'WEDGWOOD'.

19in (48cm) wide

$300-450 WW

A large Wedgwood and Bentley black basalt vase, the Classical form highlighted in red enamel with a continuous leaf border to the shoulder, the square base with a Greek key design, the shoulders applied with two handles, applied roundel mark for Etruria, Wedgwood & Bentley, the cover lacking, some damage to the base.

c1775 16.25in (41.5cm) high

$900-1,000 WW

A late 19thC Wedgwood bronzed black basalt vase, the Classical form applied in bronze with a continuing grapevine border above leafy swags issuing from centaur masks, impressed mark, gilded pattern no.Z3920, the cover lacking.

Basalt vases decorated with bronze and gilt were produced in small quantities at Wedgwood from 1875, probably to feed the contemporary hunger for Japanese bronze vases.

6.5in (16.5cm) high

$700-800 WW

A pair of 19thC Wedgwood tricolor jasperware vases, the slender ovoid bodies decorated with applied Classical equestrian figures in white on a sage-green ground, between formal acanthus leaf bands on pale blue, with later silver mounts to the rims, impressed 'WEDGWOOD' marks, hallmarked for Chester.

1911 7.75in (19.5cm) high

$400-500 WW

A Wedgwood black basalt pot pourri vase and two covers, of Krater form, with wide two-handled body painted with Oriental flowers in polychrome enamels, edged in terracotta bands and raised on a square base, impressed 'WEDGWOOD' mark, some chipping.

c1820 9.5in (24.5cm) high

$400-500 WW

A 19thC Wedgwood tricolor jasperware preserve pot and metal cover, the squat waisted form applied with a continuous scene of Classical figures flanked by trees and vases of flowers, in white on a green ground between lilac bands, with silver-plated mount and cover, impressed Wedgwood mark.

6in (15cm) high

$300-400 WW

ESSENTIAL REFERENCE - THE SOUTH WALES POTTERY

William Chambers Jnr. built The South Wales Pottery in 1839. Because of the closure of the Glamorgan Pottery in Swansea, he was able to acquire plant, expertise and a large number of their designs. William Bryant, previously employed by the Glamorgan pottery, was taken on as manager and very soon not only was the pottery being sold locally but it was also exported all over the world. In 1855, the pottery was sublet to the partnership of Charles Coombs and William Holland. William Holland took over the lease himself in 1858. This period is considered the high spot of pottery manufacture at Llanelli, with the best quality 'body' being used alongside transfer-printing of the highest standard. Llanelli pottery was displayed at the International Exhibition in London in May 1862. David Guest joined William Holland in 1868. The pottery closed in 1875. It was then reopened by David Guest in 1877. Due to the popularity of The Arts and Crafts Movement, Llanelli pottery began to use, along with their transfer patterns, brightly-colored, hand-painted designs, including the cockerel plates which are now so symbolic of it. An artist called Samuel Shufflebotham arrived from Bristol in 1908 and his work has become highly desired. He left in 1915. The factory closed in 1921.

A Llanelly pottery meat platter, hand-painted with two figures in folk costume, no marks to base.

One or possibly both of the figures painted on this meat platter could be Mari Jones. The daughter of a weaver from Llanfihangel-y-Pennant in Gwynedd, it is said that in 1800, Mari Jones famously walked 25 miles in barefoot across the mountains to buy a Welsh language Bible from the Reverend Thomas Charles of Bala.

13.5in (34cm) long

$10,000-11,000   **JON**

An undocumented and exceptionally rare Llanelly pottery oval meat platter, painted by Shufflebotham, painted title to border 'Welsh Cattle', inscribed 'Llanelly' to base.

16in (41cm) long

$10,000-11,000   **JON**

A Staffordshire agateware teapot and cover, marbled with striations of blue, cream and manganese, some restoration to the spout.

Agateware was sometimes called solid agate to distinguish it from ware with surface marbling. Agateware was probably introduced about 1730 by Dr Thomas Wedgwood of Rowley's Pottery, Burslem, Staffordshire. The random mingling of colored clays, such as red and buff, gave a broad veining to domestic and ornamental pieces. The English potter Thomas Whieldon greatly improved agateware in the 1740s by using white clays stained with metallic oxides. Repeated mixing of different layers of brown, white, and green or blue clay yielded a striated marbling throughout the substance; the clay 'cake' difficult to manipulate without blurring, was shaped in two-part molds, polished after firing, and glazed. A typical golden-yellow glaze is on early ware, but after about 1750 it is transparent or blue-gray, being tinted by the by the cobalt in the blue-stained clay. Whieldon's agateware commenced with snuffboxes and knife shafts, and Josiah Wedgwood used the process at Etruria for classical onyx or pebbled vases closely imitating natural agate. Other makers of agateware were Thomas Astbury and Josiah Spode. It was an unsuitable medium for human figures but was used in models of cats or rabbits and for tableware. Its manufacture ceased c1780.

c1755

$1,800-2,300   **WW**

6.75in (17cm) long

A Pratt type pottery bear jug and cover, with a dog in its forepaws.

c1800   *8in (20.5cm) high*

$950-1,100   **TEN**

A slipware model of a cradle, incised and decorated in cream slip, the cradle's head inscribed with the initials 'sB', a chip to one rocker, dated.

1800   *7.5in (19cm) wide*

$700-800   **WW**

A pottery plaque, possibly Scottish, small glaze chip, allover light crazing.

c1830   *4.5in (11.5cm) high*

$350-400   **MOR**

THE ORIENTAL MARKET

In the past few years, in a depressed economic climate, oriental works of art have bucked the trend. It seems that not a week passes without some record being broken: whether jade or ceramic. However the market is getting a lot more discerning, with top prices being reserved for rare early pieces with Imperial provenance. Also prices fluctuate - a lot may fetch a record price in Hong Kong and a similar piece fail to meet its much lower reserve in London, or the reverse.

In May of 2016, Lyon and Turnbull hosted their first auction of Chinese Works of Art in Hong Kong, where a highly important Xuande blue-and-white 'dragon' stem cup went under the hammer to fetch over £3,500,000 ($4,500,000) after a long bidding battle. The stem cup was the highlight of a specially curated sale of Chinese Works of Art produced in conjunction with Freeman's of Philadelphia, America's oldest auction house. The stem cup's journey to Hong Kong began at Asian Art in London in November 2015 - with its first public exhibition in 20 years - followed by a trip to both Philadelphia and New York, before travelling to Hong Kong in perfect time for the prestigious Asian Week Hong Kong festival this May. Its extensive travels emphasise the increasingly global nature of the collecting market. In late 2016 Woolley and Wallis in Salisbury sold a Chinese doucai vase, probably Republic Period, for in excess of £400,000 ($500,000), while at the same sale a Chinese Yongzheng Imperial doucai jar and cover 1723-35 sold for well over £1,000,000 ($1,250,000).

There is a strong demand for rare and unusual Chinese snuff bottles, but they must be top quality.

Jade continues to excite buyers. In March 2017 Bonhams in San Francisco sold an 18th/19thC carved jade group of three rams and Taiji symbol for $43,750 (£34,715).

As to the market for Japanese antiques, Lee Young, head of Asian Art at Lyon & Turnbull in Edinburgh said. 'We have, over the last few years, seen a noticeable increase in the number of buyers for Japanese items, resulting in higher prices in key areas such as cloisonné and mixed metal wares… However, the regained vigour of the Japanese market is still considerably overshadowed by the incredible strength of the Chinese market. With European and American collectors now often unable to compete with newly and extremely affluent Chinese purchasers intent on buying back their heritage.'

The Chinese collectors are also much more discerning and are looking for excellent quality, rare Imperial pieces. As in many areas it helps if they are 'fresh to market'.

CHINESE REIGN PERIODS AND MARKS

Imperial reign marks were adopted during the Ming dynasty, and some of the most common are illustrated here. Certain emperors forbade the use of their own reign mark, lest they should suffer the disrespect of a broken vessel bearing their name being thrown away. This is where the convention of using earlier reign marks comes from - a custom that was enthusiastically adopted by potters as a way of showing their respect for their predecessors.

It is worth remembering that a great deal of Imperial porcelain is marked misleadingly, and pieces bearing the reign mark for the period in which they were made are, therefore, especially sought after.

EARLY PERIODS AND DATES

Xia Dynasty	c2000-1500 BC	Three Kingdoms	221-280	The Five Dynasties	907-960
Shang Dynasty	1500-1028 BC	Jin Dynasty	265-420	Song Dynasty	960-1279
Zhou Dynasty	1028-221 BC	Northern & Southern Dynasties	420-581	Jin Dynasty	1115-1234
Qin Dynasty	221-206 BC	Sui Dynasty	581-618	Yuan Dynasty	1260-1368
Han Dynasty	206 BC-220 AD	Tang Dynasty	618-906		

EARLY MING DYNASTY REIGNS

Hongwu	1368-1398	Zhengtong	1436-1449
Jianwen	1399-1402	Jingtai	1450-1457
Yongle	1403-1424	Tianshun	1457-1464
Hongxi	1425-1425	Chenghua	1465-1487
Xuande	1426-1435		

MING DYNASTY MARKS

Hongzhi
1488-1505

Zhengde
1506-21

Jiajing
1522-66

Wanli
1573-1619

Chongzhen
1628-44

QING DYNASTY MARKS

Kangxi
1662-1722

Yongzheng
1723-35

Qianlong
1736-95

Jiaqing
1796-1820

Xianfeng
1851-61

Tongzhi
1862-74

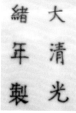
Guangxu
1875-1908

Xuantong
1909-11

Hongxian
1915-16

A Han dynasty red pottery figure of a seated dignitary, two cracks at the back.

This figure is covered in encrustations from having been buried.

18in (46cm) high

$250-400　　　　　　　CHEF

A Qin or Western Han dynasty cocoon vase, the gray pottery with pink tinges, with some chips.

13in (33cm) high

$400-500　　　　　　　CHEF

A large Chinese Han dynasty green glazed pottery 'Hu' wine jar.

18in (45.5cm) high

$550-650　　　　　　　BELL

A Chinese Tang dynasty painted pottery figure, of an equestrian figure of a female polo player, later black perspex stand, some restoration.

With an Oxford Authentication Certificate, confirming that the figure was last fired between 900 and 1500 years ago, Sample No. C115j10.

12.25in (31cm) long

$3,200-3,800　　　　　　MAB

A Southern Song Ding-type 'Phoenix head' teapot, with a phoenix head neck, covered in persimmon-brown glaze with striations of metallic black.

6in (15cm) high

$38,000-50,000　　　　　L&T

A 12thC Chinese Song or Jin dynasty Cizhou 'Partridge Feather' glazed vase, the glaze stopping short of the foot.

8.5in (21.5cm) high

$1,900-2,500　　　　　　WW

A Chinese Yuan Dynasty Junyao ware tripod purple splash censer, on tripod legs.

Provenance: This piece was given to the Rt. Honourable Malcolm McDonald Commisioner General for South-East Asia 1948-1954 by Leonard Bluett. This piece comes with additional handwritten note from Mr Bluett.

2.25in (5.5cm) high

$13,000-15,000　　　　　ROS

A Chinese Ming dynasty Cizhou-type vase, painted in brown with panels, depicting scenes from the tale of Deng Bodao.

This comes with a copy of Thermoluminescence Analysis Report, sample no.P115e31, dated 24 June 2015. This vase tells the Jin (265-420 AD) story of Deng Bodao, who was taken prisoner while serving as the governor of Hedong by the rebel leader Shi Le. Following his eventual escape, Bodao, along with his wife, son and nephew, were pursued by the rebel mounted troop. The couple realised they would be unable to remain uncaptured carrying both young boys. Thus, in the knowledge that they could have another child, they agreed to abandon their own son, tying him to a tree, in order to continue the bloodline of his late brother.

11in (28.5cm) high

$6,500-7,500　　　　　　WW

A Ming pottery shrine, slab-built in the form of a pavilion, the opening at the front topped by ocher trefoil band of cresting and flanked by ocher trellis squares above green panels.

19in (48cm) high

$650-750　　　　　　　CHEF

A mid-17thC Ming dynasty ge-type glazed tripod censer, with a brown-crackled, cream glaze, with original black-painted lotus stand.

10in (25cm) wide

$750-1,000　　　　　　SWO

ORIENTAL

ESSENTIAL REFERENCE - CELADON

Celadon is a type of high-fired, iron-derived glaze, and although employed both earlier and later, it is best-associated with the Song Dynasty. Mostly applied to stoneware, its semi-translucent greenish color varies in tone, depending on ingredient proportions, firing temperature, the underlying body, and thickness of application.

● Northern celadon thinly applied over gray stoneware bodies has an olive-green hue.

● Southern celadon more thickly applied over whiter bodies is more opaque and a cooler green or blue in color.

● Important centers of production include Yaozhou, in the north, and Longquan in the south.

● The most distinctive Yaozhou celadon wares feature incised or molded floral scroll decoration. The most desirable Longquan celadon wares include bowls and vases.

A Chinese Song Dynasty Yaozhou conical bowl, delicately carved to the interior with peony, the exterior with incised bands radiating from a short ring foot.

Yaozhou is typically a Northern Song 'greenware'. Established in the Tang Dynasty and prospering in the Northern Song Dynasty, the Yaozhou Kiln was one of the most well-known 'celadon' kilns in China. The clay sources in Yaozhou were rocks that were turned into workable clay for ceramics through grinding and washing. The decoration was mostly molded or incised with a knife with a curved blade with which the decoration was incised in the pieces before the clay was completely dry. The pieces were then bisque-fired before they were glazed, making the decoration come out as different shades of the thick green glaze.

8in (20cm) diam

$11,000-13,000 **WW**

A Yue celadon ram water dropper, possibly Western Jin dynasty, on later zitan stand, the poll of the head pierced to form a chamber between the horns, feet have been ground down.

5in (14cm) wide

$1,500-1,900 **CHEF**

A Chinese Ming dynasty Longquan celadon glazed stand, with a central flowerhead within foliate scrolls, the rim with a scalloped edge.

8.25in (21cm) diam

$9,500-10,500 **WW**

A Chinese Ming dynasty Longquan celadon-glazed 'yen yen' vase, molded with flowering peony blooms amongst leafy foliage, on a fitted three-legged hardwood stand.

20in (50.5cm) high

$1,900-3,200 **WW**

A Chinese Yongzheng period pale celadon vase, the neck ribbed in bamboo style and with trumpet mouth rim, decorated around the neck and shoulder with chrysanthemum petals, the base with a Zhuanshu script, with six-character Yongzheng mark.

During Yongzheng's 13-year reign, the emperor personally supervised the production of a profusion of new shapes and colors at the ceramic kilns in Jingdezhen, many inspired by ancient ceramics preserved in the Imperial collection.

1723-35 *9.25in (23.5cm) high*

$1,100,000-1,400,000 **MLL**

A Chinese Qianlong Guan-type celadon glazed 'Hu' vase, covered with greenish-gray glaze suffused with dark gray craquelures, the unglazed foot ring painted in dark brown.

11.5in (29cm) high

$7,500-10,000 **L&T**

A 19thC Chinese 'Ge-type' vase, in the form of a bronze vessel, with crazing to the glaze on a dark celadon ground.

11.5in (29cm) high

$5,000-6,500 **CHOR**

A 19thC blue and white decorated celadon vase, applied with elephant head handles and painted with the Daoist Immortals and attendants, the reverse with two bats.

19.25in (49cm) high

$1,500-1,900 **CHEF**

A Chinese blanc-de-Chine model of Guanyin, standing on an over-turned vase, the base with lotus flowers and swirling waves, an impressed mark to the reverse for 'He Chaozong'.

Blanc-de-Chine is the traditional European term for a type of white Chinese porcelain, made at Dehua in the Fujian province, otherwise known as Dehua porcelain. It has been produced from the Ming dynasty (1368-1644) to the present day. Large quantities arrived in Europe as Chinese Export Porcelain in the early 18thC and it was copied at Meissen and elsewhere. It was also exported to Japan in large quantities.

c1620

15in (38cm) high

$9,000-10,000 WW

A Chinese blanc-de-Chine wine pot, decorated in relief with a tied double ribbon, the spout and handle formed as chilongs, with a hardwood cover.

c1640   *5.75in (14.5cm)*

$3,500-4,000 WW

A 17thC Chinese blanc-de-Chine model of Guanyin, a bundle of books and a vase placed at her side, with two acolytes standing before her.

10in (25cm) high

$750-1,000 WW

A blanc-de-Chine tripod censer, the body encircled by key fret beneath sprigged motifs, sides with chilong handles and on three mask and paw feet.

c1680   *5.75in (14.5cm) high*

$2,500-3,200 SWO

A late 17thC blanc-de-Chine ewer, molded with sprigs of prunus.

4.75in (12cm) high

$950-1,100 SWO

A pair of Chinese Kangxi blanc-de-Chine Buddhistic lion joss stick holders, on plinth molded with dragons.

9in (23cm) high

$1,000-1,100 CHOR

An early 18thC blanc-de-Chine libation cup, of rhinoceros form, molded with a tiger and a deer beneath pine, crane, prunus and dragon.

6in (15cm) high

$1,200-1,400 SWO

An 18thC Chinese blanc-de-Chine model of two Europeans, with a small dog at their feet.

6.75in (17cm) high

$1,300-1,500 WW

An 18thC Chinese Qianlong lavender-blue glazed moon flask or 'bianhu', one side with cranes beneath lotus, the reverse with two magpies on a prunus branch.

9.25in (23.5cm) high

$15,000-18,000 WW

An 18thC Chinese turquoise glazed moon flask, with two cloud-shaped handles to the neck.

10in (25.5cm) high

$7,500-10,000 WW

A Chinese violet-blue glazed anhua-decorated bottle vase, with two five-clawed scaly dragons amongst clouds and flame wisps, all above crashing waves, with six-character Jiaqing seal mark.

1796-1820 *12.75in (32.5cm) high*

$5,000-6,500 WW

A 19thC Clair de Lune 'Dragon' bottle vase, with light blue glaze and a Qilong dragon on the shoulder, the base with six-character seal mark, with Yongzheng mark.

13.5in (34.5cm) high

$2,500-3,200 L&T

A 19thC Chinese blue glazed flower vase, with Yongzheng marks.

15.75in (40cm) high

$4,500-5,000 CHOR

A 19thC turquoise glazed group, possibly taken from the 'Journey to the West', the central horseman depicting Xuanzang accompanied by Sun Wukong, Zhu Wuneng and Lidiehguei.

20in (51cm) wide

$1,300-1,900 CHEF

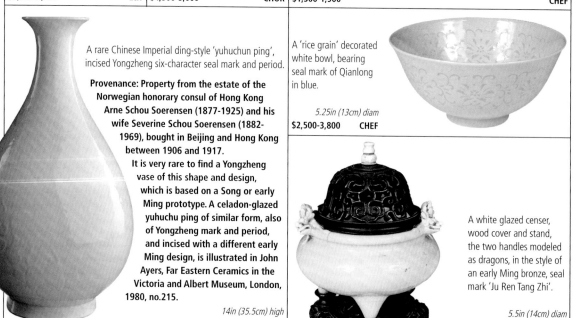

A rare Chinese Imperial ding-style 'yuhuchun ping', incised Yongzheng six-character seal mark and period.

Provenance: Property from the estate of the Norwegian honorary consul of Hong Kong Arne Schou Soerensen (1877-1925) and his wife Severine Schou Soerensen (1882-1969), bought in Beijing and Hong Kong between 1906 and 1917.

It is very rare to find a Yongzheng vase of this shape and design, which is based on a Song or early Ming prototype. A celadon-glazed yuhuchu ping of similar form, also of Yongzheng mark and period, and incised with a different early Ming design, is illustrated in John Ayers, Far Eastern Ceramics in the Victoria and Albert Museum, London, 1980, no.215.

14in (35.5cm) high

$550,000-700,000 NAG

A 'rice grain' decorated white bowl, bearing seal mark of Qianlong in blue.

5.25in (13cm) diam

$2,500-3,800 CHEF

A white glazed censer, wood cover and stand, the two handles modeled as dragons, in the style of an early Ming bronze, seal mark 'Ju Ren Tang Zhi'.

5.5in (14cm) diam

$2,500-3,800 CHEF

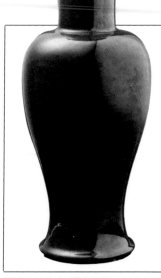

A Chinese Kangxi langyao copper-red glazed baluster vase, 'guan yin ping', suffused with a network of fine crackle, the interior and the base covered with a crackled ivory colored glaze.

13.5in (34.5cm) high

$25,000-32,000 **L&T**

A purple flambé spherical bowl, with masks on the shoulders, with four-character mark of Yongzheng.

12.25in (31cm) high

$3,800-5,000 **CHEF**

A Chinese Qianlong bottle vase, the exterior covered overall with an even liver-red glaze, the interior and the base covered with a transparent glaze, the base inscribed in underglaze blue with a Qianlong six-character seal mark.

9.25in (23.5cm) high

$25,000-38,000 **L&T**

An 18thC Chinese copper-red glazed stem bowl, the interior glazed white, with a six-character Xuande mark within concentric bands.

3.75in (9.5cm) high

$11,000-14,000 **WW**

An 18thC Qing dynasty flambé-glazed 'Hu' vase, with a glaze of red tone streaked with darker shades of red and burgundy, thinning to a clear pale-blue and cream at the rim, the base unglazed.

11in (28cm) high

$3,200-4,400 **L&T**

An 18thC Chinese Meiping vase, decorated with the Three Abundances, Sandou, with fruiting sprays of finger citron, peach and pomegranate, in a rich purple glaze.

11.75in (29.5cm) high

$2,500-3,800 **WW**

An 18th/19thC Chinese 'langyao' bottle vase, decorated with an unctuous deep red glaze, the interior glazed white.

12.5in (32cm) high

$6,500-7,500 **WW**

A pair of Chinese coral ground bowls, painted to the interior with birds, peaches, flowers and a bat, the exteriors with flowers, foliage and rockwork, with six-character Daoguang marks.

1821-50 *7.25in (18.5cm) diam*

$2,500-3,800 **WW**

ORIENTAL

A Chinese flambé glazed vase, of the Qing dynasty or later, the body with chamfered corners, the neck with two zoomorphic handles, the base with a four-character Yongzheng mark.

20in (50.5cm) high

$1,600-2,000   **WW**

An early 20thC flambé 'Hu' vase, with 'arrow handles', four-character seal mark of Yongzheng.

Hu is a type of wine vessel with a pear-shaped cross-section and handles to each side. The shape probably derives from its ceramic prototype prior to the Shang dynasty (1600-1045 BC). As wine played an important part in the Shang ritual, the Hu vessel might be placed in an ancestor's grave to ensure a good relationship with the ancestor's spirit.

11in (27.5cm) high

$700-800   **SWO**

A Chinese Yongzheng tea dust glazed bottle vase, the pear-shaped body with a metal-mounted flaring neck, decorated with a deep mottled brown glaze, with six-character Yongzheng mark.

13.5in (34cm) high

$14,000-18,000   **WW**

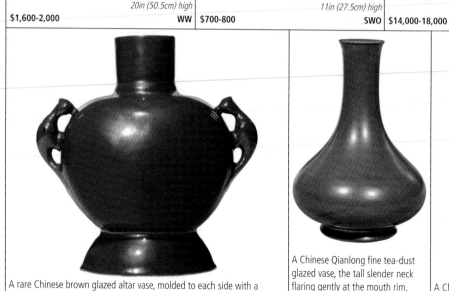

A rare Chinese brown glazed altar vase, molded to each side with a peach-shaped panel, raised on a domed elliptical foot, with two handles formed as birds to the shoulder, decorated with a rich brown glaze, with six-character Yongzheng mark.

1723-35   *9in (22.5cm) high*

$100,000-130,000   **WW**

A Chinese Qianlong fine tea-dust glazed vase, the tall slender neck flaring gently at the mouth rim, covered in an olive-green glaze with thin dark speckles throughout, Qianlong mark.

9in (23cm) high

$14,000-18,000   **L&T**

A Chinese Qianlong tea-dust glazed vase, evenly glazed tea-green, seal mark of Qianlong impressed within the footrim.

11.75in (30cm) high

$1,500-2,300   **CHEF**

A Chinese Kangxi bowl, decorated with a bright yellow glaze, the base with a six-character Jiajing mark.

1662-1772   *8in (20.5cm)*

$2,500-3,800   **WW**

A small Chinese bowl, the U-shaped body decorated with a vibrant yellow glaze, six-character Yongzheng mark.

1723-35   *4in (10cm) diam*

$11,000-12,000   **WW**

A Chinese bowl, the exterior covered with a bright lemon-yellow glaze, the interior famille rose with lingzhi and orchid, six-character Yongzheng mark within a double circle.

4.75in (12cm) diam

$9,500-10,500   **SWO**

A Kangxi period pierced Yixing teapot, the flattened sides with central reserve with pierced floral decoration, the body of typical color.

These teapots date back to the 15thC and are made from clay produced near Yixing (pronounced yeeshing) in the Eastern province of Jiangsu. From the early 16thC these teapots were popular with the scholarly class and their fame spread. It is said that if you use a Yixing teapot for many years, you can brew tea by just pouring boiling water into the empty pot. The very simplicity and early date of this teapot add to its desirability.

5.5in (14cm) high

$2,500-3,200   **L&T**

An 18thC Chinese Yixing teapot and cover, decorated in relief to one side with Shoulao riding a deer, to the other with a phoenix, the cover with flowerheads, the base inscribed with a poem and a signature.

4.25in (10.5cm) high

$5,000-6,500   **WW**

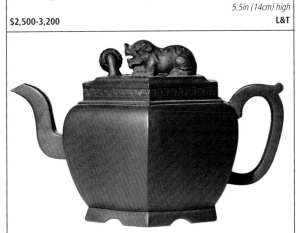

An 18thC Chinese Yixing teapot and cover, the cover surmounted by a Buddhist lion dog facing a large brocade ball.

8.25in (21cm) high

$3,800-5,000   **WW**

A Qing dynasty Chinese Yixing Duanni teapot and cover, with a bail handle, inscribed to one side with a poem, the base marked 'Chen Ming Yuan', the cover marked 'Ming Yuan'.

7.25in (18.5cm) high

$1,300-1,900   **WW**

A 20thC Yixing teapot, with short spout, loop handle and mammiform cover, the body mottled orange with oatmeal inclusions, impressed mark.

7in (18cm) high

$650-750   **SWO**

A 20thC Chinese Yixing teapot and cover, incised with calligraphy around the shoulder, the base and cover with seal marks attributed to Wang Ying Chun.

8in (20.5cm) high

$5,000-6,500   **WW**

ORIENTAL

A Chinese Yuan dynasty charger, painted with rocks issuing plantain, bamboo leaves, and lotus flowers borne on leafy tendrils, the cavetto decorated with scrolling lotus with six flowerheads, the base unglazed.

15.5in (39cm) diam

$140,000-180,000   **L&T**

A 15th/16thC rare Chinese blue and white kendi, made for the Islamic market, unusually formed after a leather water bag, with a tall garlic-mouthed neck to the center, a pointed finial to each end, decorated with a diamond-shaped cartouche containing dense geometric designs and cloud scrolls.

9in (22.5cm) long

$38,000-45,000   **WW**

A rare Chinese Jiajing period boys jar, Guan, painted with sixteen boys at play, one riding a hobby horse, a group simulating school lessons, a boy pulling a toy on a string, another group playing with a cart, one holding a fan, three boys playing a game, with lotus leaf lappets to the base, on a cell ground divided by auspicious symbols, with six-character Jiajing mark.

This auspicious subject of boys at play represents a wish for an abundance of male descendants and the continuing performance of filial duties. It can also be linked to the 'hundred boys' decoration, which refers to Zhou Wenwang, the founder of the Zhou dynasty who was blessed with ninety-nine sons by his twenty-four wives, as well as an adopted son.

1522-66   *15.5in (39cm) high*

$110,000-150,000   **WW**

A Chinese Tianqi period ko-sometsuke dish, painted with three ladies and a gentleman in a fenced garden.

Ko-sometsuke ('old blue and white') porcelain was produced specifically for the Japanese market during the final decades of the Ming dynasty (1368-1644). The lack of Chinese Imperial patronage during this period prompted the potters at the Jingdezhen kilns to seek out new markets for their porcelain. This coincided with the rising popularity of the tea ceremony in Japan. Fulfilling the orders from Japanese tea masters resulted in the flourishing of Chinese porcelain trade to Japan at this time. Ko-sometsuke wares were made to Japanese taste, in contrast to the traditional wares produced at Jingdezhen, ko-sometsuke porcelain was deliberately potted in a rough manner from poorly levigated clay. The 'moth-eaten' edges, were particularly prized in Japan.

1621-27   *11.25in (28.5cm) diam*

$2,500-3,200   **WW**

CLOSER LOOK - DRAGON DISH

This is a fine example of a 'Dragon' dish from the Chenghua Dynasty (1465-87).

It is elaborately painted in soft blue tones with a medallion enclosing a single five-clawed dragon amongst crested waves, its sinuous body with powerful legs and finely detailed scales.

The dragon is surrounded on the cavetto by three striding five-clawed dragons chasing each other amongst ruyi clouds.

This dish has Imperial significance and auspicious symbols.

A Chinese 'dragon' dish, with Chenghua six-character reign mark, the base unglazed.

12in (30cm) diam

$50,000-60,000   **L&T**

A pair of Chinese Wanli bottle vases, with Kraak-type decoration.

This segmented form of decoration was called 'Kraaksporselein' after the caraaks - the Portuguese ships - that transported the porcelains to the west from the Wanli dynasty to the end of the Ming. Normally thinly potted, often molded, its designs are divided into decorative panels, with reserves that might include flowers and animals, taotie masks and stylized tulips.

11.75in (30cm) high

$3,800-5,000   **CHOR**

A Chinese vase, painted with 'the Three Friends of Winter' emerging from rockwork, with a hardwood reticulated cover carved with scrolling foliage.

The Three Friends of Winter, symbolize the pine, bamboo, and plum. The Chinese observed that the pine, bamboo and plum do not wither in winter season. They symbolize steadfastness, perseverance, and resilience.

c1640   *10.75in (27cm) high*

$3,200-3,800   **WW**

Judith Picks

This bitong, or brush pot, is a good example from one of my favorite periods in Chinese porcelain.

During the reign of the Emperor Wanli (1573-1619) the quantity of porcelain made for export increased dramatically. The main center was still the ancient kilns at Jingdezhen in Jiangxi province. During the Transitional Period potters, who had lost the imperial patronage, had more creative freedom and new shapes and decoration combined with an improved body and glaze resulted.

For the sake of providing a working date, the Transitional Period in Chinese ceramics is considered to have started with the death of the Wanli emperor in 1620. It spanned the changeover from the Ming to Qing dynasty in 1644 and extended to the arrival of Zang Yingxuan as director of the imperial factories at Jingdezhen in 1683.

A Chinese bitong, of the Transitional period, painted with four boys and two ladies, in a garden with rocks, clouds and a banana tree, one boy flying a kite, on a hardwood stand.
c1640   *8in (20cm) diam*
$7,000-8,000   **WW**

A mid-17thC Chinese vase, painted with a single kylin beneath flame wisps, in a fenced garden with plantain, with a later wood cover.
10.75in (27.5cm) high
$3,200-3,800   **WW**

A Chinese Kangxi period bitong, painted with a crane and a Buddhist lion dog, with tables displaying vases, a qin, incense burners and auspicious things, the reverse with chrysanthemum and other flowers.
1622-1722   *7.25in (18.5cm) diam*
$13,000-15,000   **WW**

A 17thC Chinese Wanli Kraak porcelain kendi, with panels of flowers and scroll work.

A kendi was a ritual water sprinkler.
7.5in (19cm) high
$1,400-1,600   **CHOR**

A Chinese Kangxi rouleau vase, painted with mountain landscapes, flowers, animals, birds and auspicious things, on a ground of lotus and peony flowers and foliage, the neck with ruyi and key fret.
18in (46cm) high
$8,000-9,500   **WW**

A large Chinese vase, with two incised bands of scrolls and painted with vases and jardinières with peony, chrysanthemum, plantain, a fan-shaped panel with a figure beside a dwelling, the shoulder with a single kingfisher beside lotus.
c1640   *17.5in (44.5cm) high*
$19,000-25,000   **WW**

A late Chinese Ming dish, the central qilin enclosed by a band of lotus, nick to the rim, hair crack to the qilin.

The crack to the central qilin severely reduces the value of this dish.
12.5in (32cm) diam
$500-650   **CHEF**

A Chinese ewer, painted with huts and a pagoda in a mountainous landscape amongst trees, the neck and S-shaped spout with lotus designs.
c1640   *5in (13cm) high*
$1,500-1,900   **WW**

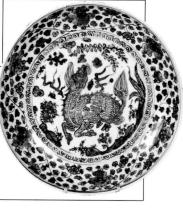

Judith Picks

This rare, early, exquisitely decorated vase also has a great story of survival. Originally it was acquired by the owner's great-aunt in Cornwall, who was a dealer and collector, probably in the 20s or 30s. When the owners inherited it, it was used as a doorstop in the family's modest bungalow because it is so large and heavy. Their children even played football around it when they were growing up and it almost ended up at a car boot sale. It was then revealed as a rare Chinese antique with a price tag to match.

A mid-17thC Chongzhen porcelain vase, the decoration exhibits the Ming 'heaping and piling' effect and also has a Baroque influence.
26in (66cm) high
$1,000,000-1,200,000   **HAN**

A Chinese Kangxi jar, decorated with ladies discussing with scholars, with a later wooden lid.

9.5in (24cm) high

$5,000-6,500   **TRI**

A Chinese Kangxi period jar and cover, painted with fan-shaped panels depicting a figure beside lanterns, and with vases, scrolls and other auspicious objects, the cover with a vase of peacock feathers

12.5in (32cm) high

$6,500-7,500   **WW**

A Chinese Kangxi bowl, painted with figures in a landscape.

Provenance: The Collection of Ethel Bedford Fenwick née Manson (1857-1947). In 1881, aged twenty-four, she became the matron of St. Bartholomew's Hospital, UK. After years of lobbying at the highest level she became the General Nursing Council's first Registered Nurse.

8.5in (21.5cm) diam

$4,500-5,000   **CHOR**

A Chinese Kangxi period box and cover, each painted with vases and buddhist emblems.

4.75in (12cm) diam

$5,000-6,500   **BELL**

A Chinese Kangxi period brushpot, painted with two confronting dragons chasing a flaming pearl amongst cloud scrolls.

7.25in (18.5cm) diam

$1,600-2,000   **BELL**

A Chinese Kangxi period triple gourd vase, painted with precious objects between banana leaves, the uppermost trumpet section with a rare lustrous pale ocher glaze.

The beige luster café-au-lait glaze is uncommon, but see 'Chinese Ceramics in the Topkapi Sarayi Museum Catalogue', 1986, III Nos. 2659-2678, for similarly decorated examples.

1662-1722

9.75in (24.5cm) high

$2,300-2,800   **SWO**

A Chinese Kangxi 'gu' beaker-vase, painted with mountainous landscapes, figures in boats and peony emerging from rocks.

17in (43cm) high

$2,500-3,800   **WW**

A Chinese Kangxi vase and cover, decorated with rocky mountainous scenes with willow, pine and dwellings, the cover painted with six triangular landscape cartouches.

24in (60.5cm) high

$5,500-7,000   **WW**

A Chinese Kangxi blue and copper-red 'yen yen' vase, decorated with a ferocious Buddhist lion dog, landscapes, the neck with birds above peony, with stylized dragons to the shoulder, on a shagreen-like ground.

17.75in (45cm) high

$5,500-7,000   **WW**

A Chinese Kangxi kendi, molded with peony, prunus, chrysanthemum and lotus, the spout modeled as a phoenix's head.

9.25in (23.5cm) high

$3,200-4,400   **WW**

A Chinese Kangxi period 'bitong', painted with Kui Xing, standing on a giant turtle amidst waves, holding a calligraphy brush in his hand.

Kui Xing is a character in Chinese mythology, the god of examinations, and an associate or servant of the god of literature, Wen Chang.

5in (13cm) high
$1,800-2,300   WW

A Chinese Kangxi period dish, the well with a gnarled prunus tree, incense burner, a scroll, with lotus, chrysanthemum, poeny and pomegranate, the rim with pagoda scenes, with fishermen and other figures.

14in (35.5cm) diam
$1,100-1,500   WW

A Chinese Kangxi porcelain double-gourd jar, painted with sprays of lotus, peony and orchid.

4in (10.5cm) high
$300-400   BELL

A Chinese Kangxi porcelain rouleau vase, painted with a dignitary and attendants within lattice borders, artemisia leaf mark.

18in (45.5cm) high
$11,000-14,000   TEN

A Chinese Kangxi period bowl, cover and wood stand, painted with precious objects, the cover with seated lion finial.

10in (25.5cm) high
$2,300-2,800   CHEF

A pair of Chinese Kangxi period chargers, each with a medallion surrounded by flowers, the rims with stylized foliage, one repaired.

15in (38cm) diam
$3,800-4,400   DN

A Chinese Kangxi period vase, painted with a peony scroll with leafy tendrils, the neck with a band of stylized leaf lappets.

1662-1722   16.25in (41.5cm) high
$1,800-2,300   WW

A Chinese Kangxi period jardinière, Gang, painted with a dragon amongst auspicious things, the reverse with a bird, a butterfly, rocks and flowers.

1662-1722   9in (23cm) high
$5,000-6,500   WW

A Chinese 'yen yen' vase, painted with two deer in a mountain landscape crossing a rocky bridge, with a single crane, the neck with a deer beneath a pine tree.

1662-1722   18.5in (47cm) high
$6,500-7,500   WW

A pair of Chinese Kangxi 'gu' beaker-vases, painted with attendants carrying banners and swords and greeting a general, the lower section with a scholar in a fenced rocky garden and a boy with geese, all divided by floral sprays to the center, each with a six-character Chenghua mark to the base.

1662-1722

17in (43cm) high
$25,000-38,000   WW

ORIENTAL

A Ming-style blue and white dish, the center of the interior painted with peaches, the exterior with a band of scrolling foliage, with six-character mark of Yongzheng.

10.75in (27cm) diam

$3,800-5,000   **CHEF**

CLOSER LOOK - QIANLONG PERIOD VASE

The vase is extremely large - hence difficult to pot.

It's decoration is of the archaistic style.

It is painted to the exterior with stylized dragons and taotie panels reserved on dense geometric grounds.

The vase has a reticulated zitan and hardwood stand, carved with bands of the Three Friends of Winter.

A Chinese Qianlong brush washer, painted with two five-clawed dragons amongst cloud scrolls, with breaking waves beneath, with six-character Qianlong seal mark.

1736-95   *8.25in (21cm) diam*

$11,000-14,000   **WW**

A Chinese Qianlong period vase, the shoulder with ring handles surmounted by mythical creatures masks.

1736-95   *20in (51cm) high*

$25,000-38,000   **WW**

A mid-18thC rouleau vase, painted with two figures on donkeys on a mountain track amongst rocks and trees, the neck with ruyi and key fret borders.

18.5in (47cm) high

$38,000-45,000   **SWO**

A Chinese Qianlong bottle vase, decorated with ten elongated panels with flower heads on leafy stems, bordered by two bands of scrolling foliage, Qianlong seal mark.

12.25in (31cm) high

$18,000-23,000   **L&T**

A Chinese Qianlong bottle vase, Shangping, with a continuous flowerhead design, with six-character Qianlong mark.

1736-95   *14.75in (37.5cm) high*

$25,000-32,000   **WW**

A late 18thC Chinese Meiping vase, in Ming style, painted with sprays of fruit above a border of stiff leaves.

14.25in (36cm) high

$350-400   **BELL**

An 18thC Chinese brush pot, painted with pavilions amongst mountains in an archipelago scene.

7.75in (19.5cm) diam

$9,000-10,000   **CHEF**

An 18thC Chinese bowl, made for the Ottoman market, molded with bands of lappets with cornflower stems, the interior with a rim band of flower heads, minor nicks, scratching to glaze.

8in (20cm) diam

$650-750   **CHEF**

A Chinese saucer dish, painted with a five-clawed dragon amongst clouds in pursuit of a flaming pearl, the exterior painted with two dragons chasing pearls, blue Jiaqing seal mark.

6.75in (17cm) diam

$1,500-1,900   BELL

A Chinese quatrefoil dish, a double band of scrolling lotus enclosing the central inscription and seals, seal mark of Jiaqing.

6.5in (16.5cm) long

$2,500-3,200   CHEF

An early 19thC vase, painted on one side with a lakeside village, flanked by mountains between elephant head handles, the reverse with magpies in prunus.

23.75in (60cm) high

$2,500-3,200   SWO

A Chinese bowl, the rosette enclosed by Buddhist objects, the exterior with flowers above ruyi lappet band on the foot, bearing seal mark of Daoguang.

8.25in (21cm) diam

$1,300-1,900   CHEF

A 19thC Peony charger, with five large peonies amongst scrolling leaves and further blossoms, apocryphal Qianlong mark to the base.

21in (53cm) diam

$1,300-1,900   L&T

A pair of mid-19thC temple vases and covers, with scrolling lotus after Kangxi originals and between bands of false gadroons and cloud collars.

25.5in (64.5cm) high

$1,300-1,800   SWO

A 19thC Chinese underglaze blue and copper-red vase, painted with five five-clawed dragons amongst clouds and flame wisps, the base with a six-character Qianlong mark.

3.25in (8cm) high

$900-1,000   WW

A Chinese charger, Chinese fisherman pattern with mountains in the distance.

21.75in (55cm) diam

$3,200-3,800   CHOR

A late 19thC Chinese Kangxi-style jar, painted with prunus blossom against a 'cracked ice' ground.

8.25in (21cm) high

$1,300-1,800   BELL

A 19thC Chinese Kangxi-style dish, painted with geometric designs within a border of auspicious gifts and flowers.

8in (20.5cm) diam

$500-650   **CHOR**

A 19thC Kangxi bottle vase.

8.5in (21.5cm) high

$700-750   **TRI**

A late 19thC Chinese vase, painted with bands depicting crashing waves, scrolling lotus designs and stylized acanthus leaves, with elephant head handles, with a Qianlong seal mark, raised on a stand carved with lotus.

24in (60.5cm) high

$13,000-15,000   **WW**

A late 19thC Chinese beaker, painted with maidens and pots of flowers, tiny rim chips, with associated hairline crack, with Chenghua reign mark.

3.5in (8.5cm) high

$500-650   **TEN**

A 19thC Chinese bottle vase, painted with two five-clawed dragons above a flaming pearl, waves above the foot and ruyi cloud band on the rim.

17.25in (44cm) high

$1,000-1,100   **CHEF**

A 20thC Republic period plaque, painted by Wang Bu, a bird calls from a branch with blossoms, with two peaches below, inscribed and with two seal marks, with wooden frame carved with flowers.

Wang Bu's father Wang Xiuqing, was a porcelain painter during the reigns of Tongzhi and Guangxu. It was common for children to follow in their father's footsteps, and at the age of nine, Wang Bu was apprenticed to Xu Yousheng, a porcelain painter at Jingdezhen. He completed his apprenticeship in 1912. After the closure of the imperial workshops at Jingdezhen, Wang Bu made a living painting bird feeders, before he was hired by the ceramic artist Wu Aisheng to make reproductions of Ming and Qing porcelains. This laid the foundation for his later innovation. From the time Wang Bu arrived at Jingdezhen in 1907, till his death in 1968, he created numerous ceramic art works. His work in underglaze blue and white decoration earned him the title of 'qinghua dawang' (the king of blue and white).

21in (53cm) high

$1,500-1,900   **CHEF**

A Xuantong blue and white bowl, decorated with the eight trigrams and flying cranes interspersed with ruyi-head clouds, with Xuantong mark.

5.25in (13.5cm) diam

$3,200-3,800   **L&T**

A Chinese Kangxi famille verte teapot and cover, molded with eight panels, painted with peony, prunus and chrysanthemum, the neck with key fret.
1662-1722 *7in (17.5cm) high*
$1,500-1,900 **WW**

A pair of Chinese Kangxi famille verte Buddhist lion dogs, one with a puppy, the other a brocade ball, each with articulated eyes and a ribbon in its mouth.
1662-1722 *7.75in (19.5cm) high*
$1,300-1,900 **WW**

A Chinese Kangxi famille verte dish, painted with two long-tailed birds amongst peony, the rim with two bands of flowers, birds and insects.
1662-1722 *14in (35.5cm) diam*
$1,300-1,900 **WW**

A 17thC Chinese Kangxi famille verte dish, decorated with exotic birds and flowering bushes, the border with four floral panels, leaf marked in underglaze blue.
11.25in (28.5cm) diam
$1,300-1,900 **CHOR**

One of a pair of Chinese Kangxi famille verte chargers, painted with a mythical creature running in a landscape, with four panels enclosing further animals, the diaper and cell pattern border with panels of shrubs.
15in (38cm) diam
$3,200-3,800 pair **BELL**

A Chinese Kangxi famille verte dish, painted with a vase with flowers and foliage, the handle tied with a ribbon, the rim with panels with lotus, prunus, peony and other flowers, the base with a shop mark.
1662-1722 *14.5in (36.5cm) diam*
$1,000-1,200 **WW**

A pair of Chinese Kangxi famille verte bottle vases, painted with two birds amongst cherry blossom, the trees growing from overglaze blue and green rocks to one side.
8in (20cm) high
$6,500-7,500 **CHEF**

A Chinese Kangxi famille verte vase, painted with flowers in overglaze blue, red, aubergine, and yellow, between lappets on the rims.
8.25in (21cm) high
$750-900 **CHEF**

A pair of Chinese Kangxi famille verte bottle vases, painted with Buddhist lions and ribbons.
10.5in (27cm) high
$5,000-6,500 **BELL**

ORIENTAL

A pair of Yongzheng vases, enameled and gilt with ladies admiring two feng under a tree with peony, prunus and chrysanthemum flowers and fruit, between Kangxi famille verte borders of fish and crustacea.

1723-25   *13in (33cm) high*

$19,000-25,000   **SWO**

A 19thC Chinese famille verte vase, painted with figures engaged in various activities, blue six-character Kangxi mark.

14in (36cm) high

$550-700   **BELL**

ESSENTIAL REFERENCE - FAMILLE ROSE

The famille rose palette was first created in the early 18thC at the end of the Kangxi period.

- It includes dominant shades of opaque pink and carmine, which were sometimes achieved using gold.
- Opaque white and yellow enabled painters to blend and shade colors.
- This gave rise to the refined decoration seen on Yongzheng porcelain.
- Famille rose colors were often referred to as 'foreign' in China because they originated from Europe.
- The style was widely copied in European countries such as the Netherlands.

A pair of Chinese famille verte vases, with warrior scenes.

21.75in (55cm) high

$1,300-1,900   **POOK**

A 19thC Chinese famille verte ginger jar with lid, decorated with figures crossing a bridge.

8.25in (21cm) high

$1,000-1,200   **TRI**

A 19thC Chinese famille verte vase, decorated with four panels of baskets on a floral ground, on an ormolu stand with festoons of laurel.

14.75in (37.5cm) high

$400-500   **WW**

A Yongzheng famille rose vase and cover, enameled with precious objects amongst flowers and butterflies, a pair of cockerels, and lingzhi fungus.

1722-35   *15.5in (39cm) high*

$2,500-3,800   **SWO**

A Chinese Yongzheng famille rose bowl and saucer, the saucer enameled with flowering sprays and two butterflies, the bowl with a peony spray to the well, each decorated to the exterior with a pink glaze.

saucer 6in (15.5cm) diam

$5,000-6,500   **WW**

A Chinese famille rose bowl, enameled with a single figure, pointing toward a vase of lotus, with six-character Yongzheng mark in underglaze blue.

4.5in (11.5cm) high

$7,500-9,000   **WW**

A rare Chinese Imperial famille rose bowl, delicately painted in mogu (boneless) enamels with chrysanthemum and peony, two butterflies in flight, the interior with a single flower, with Yongzheng mark in underglaze blue.

7in (17.5cm) long

$50,000-60,000   **WW**

A Chinese Yongzheng famille rose 'immortal' bowl, the exterior painted with Shoulao on a deer, with an attendant, with Yongzheng six-character mark.

3.75in (9.5cm) diam

$38,000-50,000   **L&T**

A Chinese Yongzheng famille rose charger, painted with a man holding a chime and standing with two ladies in a garden.

14in (35.5cm) diam

$3,500-4,300   **BELL**

A Chinese Qianlong famille rose teapot and cover, decorated with panels of bulls fighting.

9.5in (24cm) high

$1,000-1,200   **CHOR**

A Chinese famille rose bottle vase, with bats amongst scrolling foliage, with six-character Qianlong seal mark in red.

11in (27.5cm) high

$2,800-3,800   **TEN**

A Chinese Qianlong famille rose, enameled with two ladies with six playing boys and two cranes, a shallow chip which has been filled to the right of the cranes, with Qianlong seal mark.

11in (28cm) high

$3,800-5,000   **CHOR**

A 19thC massive Qianlong period Chinese famille rose bottle vase, brightly enameled with peony, poppy, lotus and hibiscus entwined together with other flowers and foliage, all reserved on a yellow ground, the rim with a band of ruyi-heads, the foot with formal stiff lappets, the base and interior glazed turquoise, with a six-character Qianlong seal mark in iron-red.

23.75in (60cm) high

$8,000-9,500   **WW**

An 18thC Chinese famille rose jardinière, painted with birds amongst flowering lotus, peony and chrysanthemum with insects, the rim with key fret and foliate bands.

14.25in (36cm) high

$5,000-6,500   **WW**

CLOSER LOOK - A FAMILLE ROSE PUNCH BOWL

This punch bowl is of a good early date and is massive in size.

The enamelling is of exceptional quality with scenes of figures and attendants in domestic settings and rocky fenced gardens, bordered by stylized gilt scrolls and bats.

The interior with peony, chrysanthemum, prunus, and rose hips with butterflies and insects, the well painted with a shepherdess and her flock, with a band of Moor fish amongst ferns.

All reserved on a gilt cell diaper ground above a band of key fret.

An 18thC massive Chinese famille rose punch bowl.

21.75in (55cm) diam

$32,000-38,000   **WW**

ORIENTAL

A late 18thC Chinese famille rose fluted sugar bowl, applied with lotus flowers and leaves and painted with a cockerel, a hen and chicks.

4.5in (11.5cm) wide

$1,000-1,100   PC

An 18thC Chinese famille rose barber's bowl, painted with an incense burner, a bowl of fruit and two vases.

12in (30.5cm) wide

$1,800-2,300   WW

An 18thC Chinese famille rose incense burner, with two colorful dragons with a flaming pearl of wisdom and clouds.

7in (17.5cm) high

$950-1,100   WW

A late 18thC Chinese famille rose vase, decorated with pink scales, the body with European flower sprays, with small foot chips.

8.75in (22cm) high

$550-700   PC

Judith Picks

According to legend, the name of this portable potty comes from Louis Bourdaloue (1632-1704), one of King Louis XIV of France's Jesuit priests. Bourdaloue's oratorical skills were reputedly so accomplished that huge numbers of people queued at great length to hear his equally lengthy and interval-free sermons. Unfortunately, however, most churches, like theatres of the period, had no toilet facilities - a state of affairs that presented something of a problem to anyone, and especially a lady, 'taken short'. The solution was the 'bourdaloue': a portable urinal that could be discretely placed under skirts or dresses, enabling the lady to relieve herself in it from either a semi-squatting or standing position without too much risk of mishap. As you might imagine - given the history and intended function - I have on more than one occasion been much amused when attending a dinner party to discover a bourdaloue being used as a gravy boat!

An early 19thC Cantonese famille rose bourdaloue, with ladies in a fenced garden, possibly originally with cover, some minor surface wear.

10in (25cm) long

$750-900   TEN

A pair of Chinese Imperial famille rose medallion bowls, enameled to the exterior with trees, divided by stylized lotus sprays and on a pink sgraffito ground, the interior painted in underglaze blue with a rabbit, with six-character Daoguang seal marks.

6in (15cm) wide

$38,000-50,000   WW

A Chinese Daoguang famille rose vase, turquoise bands of ruyi lappets on the shoulders and foot enclosing chrysanthemums, seal mark of Daoguang.

10.25in (26cm) high

$1,000-1,100   CHEF

A mid-19thC Cantonese famille rose vase, decorated with figures, dignitaries and attendants and warriors on horseback, on a typical ground of birds, flowers, insects and Buddhistic emblems, applied at the shoulders with gilt chilong, double Buddhist lion handles.

35in (89cm) high

$2,500-3,200   MOR

A pair of mid-19thC gilt bronze mounted Cantonese famille rose vases, painted with figures on a ground of precious objects, bases have been drilled for electricity, some minor wear.

18.5in (47cm) high

$2,500-3,800   TEN

A mid-19thC pair of Cantonese famillle rose jars and covers, with four dog knops and mask handles, painted with figures in interiors and birds and butterflies, the knops on the covers are different and so covers possibly matched.

17.5in (44cm) high

$750-900   **TEN**

A mid-19thC large Canton celadon ground famille rose two-handled vase, painted with three figurative panels, the reverse painted with two equestrian figures.

23.75in (60cm) high

$400-500   **BELL**

A Guangxu blue ground famille rose bowl, the exterior with three roundels each containing a dragon and a phoenix chasing the flaming ball, the interior painted with a coiled dragon, six-character iron-red mark to the base.

10.25in (26cm) diam

$1,500-1,900   **L&T**

A 19thC Chinese famille rose tulip vases, in the Dowager Empress style, decorated with dragons on a yellow ground.

10in (25cm) high

$1,000-1,100   **WW**

A 19thC Chinese famille rose model of Shoulao, holding a peach in his detachable hand.

Shoulao, the God of longevity, is usually recognizable by his over-sized forehead, representing wisdom and long beard representing long life. Attributes include peach and a staff, both symbols of longevity themselves, and said to come from Xi Wangmu's magical garden in Heaven.

19in (48.5cm) high

$1,300-1,800   **WW**

A 19thC pair of Canton famille rose vases, painted with a procession of officials and warriors, the shoulders applied with chilong and set with buddhist lion and cub handles, some restoration to one rim.

25in (63.5cm) high

$2,500-3,200   **BELL**

A 19thC pair of Chinese Canton famille rose vases, enameled with figures engaged in courtly duties, the foot with formal lappets, molded to the shoulders with gilt dragons, the handles formed from pairs of iron-red dragons.

30.5in (77.5cm) high

$13,000-15,000   **WW**

A 19thC Chinese famille rose dish, painted with nine boys, each standing and with various attributes including vases, ruyi scepters and flower stems, the reverse with a further seven boys, the base with a six-character Jiaqing mark.

9in (23cm) diam

$1,000-1,100   **WW**

ORIENTAL

A late Qing or Republic period Chinese famille rose vase, painted with a single colorful bird perched on a blossoming branch, a butterfly in flight, the reverse with a peony bloom, the base with a six-character Qianlong mark.

8.5in (21.5cm) high

$4,500-5,000 **WW**

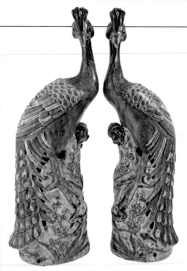

A late 19thC pair of Chinese famille-rose figures of peacocks.

12.5in (32cm) high

$1,100-1,500 **BELL**

A late 19th/early 20thC pair of Chinese yellow ground famille-rose reticulated lanterns and stands, molded four character mark to base.

15.75in (40cm) high

$2,500-3,200 **BELL**

A pair of Republic period famille rose figures, of Guanyin and a Maiden Immortal, Guanyin with gilt vase and fly whisk, her companion with a basket of peach and peony, and on a red dragon swimming through waves, the latter with relief mark Fujian huiguan.

Guanyin illustrates well the Dehua style of using a gaping dragon as the base, common at this period, while the workers later moved to Jingdezhen setting up a kiln there and from which the Maiden heralds.

1912-49 *male 17.5in (44.5cm) high*

$2,300-2,800 **SWO**

A Republic period Chinese famille rose nine peach bottle vase, the base with a six-character Qianlong mark.

21.5in (54.5cm) high

$2,500-3,200 **WW**

An unusual Republic period famille rose figure, of Liu Hai, the corpulent god holding the bottle of the Elixir of Life and a string of square-holed coins, on the back of a toad, molded mark 'Huang Yuanshun zao'.

1912-49 *13.5in (34.5cm) high*

$1,900-2,500 **SWO**

A Chinese Republic period famille rose vase, enameled with five boys playing in a fenced garden amongst rocks and bamboo, the base with a Qianlong seal mark.

9.75in (24.5cm) high

$1,300-1,900 **WW**

A pair of Chinese Republic period famille rose 'wu zi deng ke' jardinières and stands, enameled with scenes of boys accompanied by their attendants holding auspicious symbols, bearing an iron-red four-character mark to the underside, with pierced wood stands, with Linzhi Chengxiang four-character mark.

7.75in (20cm) high

$20,000-25,000 **L&T**

A 20thC Chinese famille rose vase, painted with Immortals in a boat beneath a pine tree, and with symbols of longevity, a four-character hallmark to the base.

12in (30.5cm) high

$2,800-3,500 **WW**

A pair of Kangxi famille verte and Chinese Imari armorial saucer dishes, the rims decorated with a phoenix crest.

The arms are of Fenwick of Northumberland, prosperous merchants in Newcastle-upon-Tyne, family seat Brenkley and Morpeth. These dishes were probably made for Mr Fenwick, Chief Supercargo on East Indiaman 'Marlborough' at Canton 1716.

1731 8.75in (22cm) wide

$3,800-4,400 CHOR

A pair of early 18thC Chinese Yongzheng export armorial porcelain chargers, painted with King coat of arms, the borders painted with auspicious items and flowering urns.

The arms are of King impaling Seys for Peter King, 1st Baron King of Ockham, and his wife Anne, daughter of Richard Seys of Boverton, Glamorgan. They married in 1704. These plates were produced c1726 and are the remaining pair from a once larger and now dispersed service.

14in (35cm) diam

$15,000-18,000 L&T

A Chinese Qianlong porcelain armorial custard cup and cover, decorated similarly with the arms of Francis, Earl Annesley, a chip to the inside footrim.

c1795 3.5in (8.5cm) high

$800-950 WW

A Chinese Qianlong porcelain armorial dish, decorated with the arms of Francis, Earl Annesley, the rim with a gilt and blue vine garland, the crest supported by a Roman Knight and a Moorish Prince above the motto Virtutis Amore, some damages to the rim.

Francis, the 1st Earl of Annesley and 2nd Viscount Glenawly was born in 1740 and created an earl in 1789. He died in 1802.

c1795 10in (25cm) diam

$180-250 WW

A Chinese Qianlong export armorial famille rose guglet, each side painted with a monogram within a shield and surmounted by an eagle.

10.5in (27cm) high

$400-500 BELL

One of a set of nine Chinese Qianlong export armorial plates, made for the Portuguese market, painted with a group of tied flowers beneath the enameled coat of arms of Joaquim Inacio da Cruz Sobral.

c1775 9in (22.5cm) diam

$3,200-3,800 set BELL

A Chinese porcelain armorial dish, of small size, painted with the quartered arms of Chadwick, the reverse inscribed 'Canton in China 24th Jan. 1791'.

The arms are those of the old Staffordshire family of Chadwick quartering the ancient family coats of Malvesym, Carden and Bagot.

1791 6.5in (16cm) diam

$650-750 WW

An 18thC Chinese famille rose armorial tureen and lid, with iron red pomegranate finial and hare handles, with the arms of Lovett on the lid and two pheasants on rocks to the sides.

14in (35.5cm) wide

$1,600-2,300 TRI

A pair of late 18thC armorial bourdalou and covers, for the Dalling family with Pinnock in pretence, the rims of the slipper shapes with roses and gilt foliage, some damage.

10in (25.5cm) wide

$2,300-2,800 CHEF

ORIENTAL

A Chinese Kangxi doucai rouleau vase, painted with four Immortals riding on mythical creatures amongst crashing waves and rockwork, the shoulder with lotus panels beneath ruyi and key fret bands.

Doucai can be translated as 'colors which fit together' but also 'contrasting colors'. Decoration in a combination of underglaze cobalt blue outlines and enamels added on top of the fired glaze. Invented during the Xuande period, they are mostly associated to the Chenghua reign (1465-87). The production of imperial porcelain declined after the Chenghua emperor died. The technique was revived in the 18thC, during the Qing dynasty.

1662-1722   *17.75in (45cm) high*
$1,900-2,500   **WW**

A Chinese doucai wine cup, with two gilt shou characters beneath swastikas, with flowers and ruyi-heads in ribbons, above a band of lappets, with six-character Daoguang mark.

1821-50   *2.75in (7cm) diam*
$2,300-2,800   **WW**

A rare Chinese Kangxi doucai dragon bowl, with four scaly five-clawed dragons amongst clouds, with waves crashing upon rocks, the interior with a fifth dragon within a roundel with flames, with six-character Kangxi mark.

1662-1722   *7.25in (18.5cm) diam*
$32,000-38,000   **WW**

A Chinese Daoguang doucai bowl, painted with three groups of lotus sprays with leafy scrolls, the interior with a single lotus sprig, with seal mark.

5in (12.5cm) diam
$10,000-11,000   **BELL**

An early 17thC late Ming wucai jar, with a band of Buddhist lions in yellow and turquoise amongst peony and green scrolls and underglaze blue leaves.

Wucai meaning five enamels or 'five color ware' is mostly three enamels (red, green and yellow) within outlines in blackish cobalt, underglaze blue, plus the white of the porcelain body, making up five colors.

The name wucai refers to Chinese porcelain decorated in this palette dating from the Ming period, especially during the reign of Jiajing (AD 1522-66), Longqing (AD 1567-72) and Wanli (1573-1619) emperors. The name wu-cai, or five-color ware, may well have developed as the number five has an important symbolic significance in Chinese art. As shown by the examples on this page, the techniques were revived in the Qing Dynasty.

9in (23cm) high
$1,100-1,500   **SWO**

A Chinese doucai dish, probably late Qing dynasty, painted with bands of foliate designs, within a ruyi border, the base with a six-character Qianlong mark.

9.5in (24cm) diam
$1,500-1,900   **WW**

A pair of late Ming wucai vases, each with a central band of dragons and lotus within bracket and zig-zag borders, fixed ormolu stands.

13.5in (34cm) high
$6,500-7,500   **SWO**

A fine and rare Chinese Ming wucai 'dragon' zun-shaped porcelain vase, with Wanli six-character mark within double circles.

The vase is decorated in vibrant enamels with pairs of sinuous dragons in turquoise and iron-red, around the foot and on the tall trumpet neck, each pair divided by sets of vertical flanges, and the sections separated by bands of scrolls and petal lappets. The form of this rare, archaistic zun-shaped porcelain vase was one that found considerable favor with the Wanli court, as evidenced by the pair of smaller vases of this form, with aubergine decoration on a yellow ground, which were excavated in 1958 from the Dingling tomb of the Wanli emperor. Although there were several versions of the ancient bronze zun form made in porcelain over the centuries, the form seen on the vases from the Wanli emperor's tomb and on the current vase is one of the closest to the bronze original, bearing appropriate flanges.

1573-1639   *12.5in (32cm) high*
$320,000-380,000   **NAG**

A Chinese Transition period wucai porcelain jar, painted with fish amongst weeds, on a lattice ground, with matched hardwood cover and stand.

1620-23   *7.75in (19.5cm) high*

$1,600-2,000   TEN

A mid-17thC wucai vase, painted with feng (pheonix) and peony below stylized flowers.

5.75in (14.5cm) high

$450-500   SWO

A 17thC Chinese wucai gourd-shaped vase, with peony blooms and scrolling foliage, the neck with two scaly dragons divided by flaming pearls of wisdom.

17.75in (45cm) high

$5,000-6,500   WW

A 17thC Chinese wucai vase and cover, painted with fruiting vines, with squirrels playing, a band of peony to the neck.

The vine and squirrel, songshu putao, when seen together represent the wish for ceaseless generations of male descendants.

c1680   *15.75in (40cm) high*

$19,000-25,000   WW

A 17thC Chinese wucai vase, painted with figures in a garden amongst clouds, with rockwork and plantain.

13in (32.5cm) high

$4,400-5,700   WW

A 17thC Chinese wucai tiered box and cover, the top painted with five roundels containing cranes divided by clouds, the sides with chrysanthemum flowers, the middle sections each with a six-character Chenghua mark.

3.75in (9.5cm) high

$3,200-3,800   WW

A pair of 17thC Chinese wucai vases, painted with horses leaping amongst rockwork and precious emblems, later wood covers and stands.

13in (33cm) high

$3,300-3,800   BELL

An 18thC Chinese wucai plate, the lotus flowers in an overglaze yellow roundel within blue scrolling lotus band overglazed with a turquoise ground.

8in (20.5cm) diam

$1,500-1,900   CHEF

An 18thC Chinese wucai bowl, the cavetto with colored flowers outside a fish scale band in blue enclosing a central flower stem, chipping and hair crack to the rim.

10.5in (26.5cm) diam

$300-450   CHEF

ORIENTAL

An early 17thC miniature stem cup, enameled with fish amongst weeds, the flared stem with a rudimentary oxo stand, with wood stand.

This was probably made for the Japanese market.

cup 1.5in (4cm) high

$1,900-2,500   SWO

Two Chinese Kangxi Brinjal porcelain bowls, incised with flower sprays, glazed in aubergine, white, green, or yellow against an olive-green ground, blue seal marks.

Bowls of this type are made of thinly glazed biscuit porcelain, with incised decoration and colored in a limited palette. This group of wares are generically described as Brinjal bowls. The earliest known bowls of this type, are dated to the 1620s, but production continued well into the Kangxi period. The name Brinjal derives from an old Anglo-Indian word for aubergine, and was adopted due to the aubergine-brown color employed in the decoration.

7.5in (19cm) diam

$650-750   BELL

An 18thC pair of Chinese Imari guglets, each ribbed body painted with sprays of flowers.

10in (25cm) high

$1,600-2,000   BELL

A Chinese Imari barber's bowl, painted with a fenced garden with peony, bamboo, and rocks beneath a border of foliage and scrolls.

Imari is a style of porcelain named after the Japanese port from which it was shipped to the West, beginning in the late 17thC. Chinese Imari is a decoration style with predominantly a dry iron-red enamel highlighted with gilt applied on underglaze blue and white porcelain. By the early 18thC, China was flooding the export market with inexpensive Chinese Imari of its own, making Japanese Imari prohibitively costly in the West.

c1720-50   *12in (30.5cm) wide*

$700-800   BELL

A mid-18thC Chinese Qianlong chamber pot and cover.

10.5in (27cm) wide

$500-650   CHOR

A Mandarin palette punch bowl, painted with two panels of European hunting scenes and two panels of finches, the interior with a hunting panel within a floral and scrolled border, well restored.

c1760   *14.25in (36cm) diam*

$1,900-2,500   SWO

An underglaze red meiping, with flowers and a stiff leaf band on the foot, bearing a seal mark of Qianlong in blue.

9in (23cm) high

$1,300-1,900   CHEF

A Chinese Qianlong wall vase, the body on a gilt iron-red stand and flanked by a finger citron, the inscription in black, with four-character Qianlong mark and inscription.

8.25in (21cm) high

$1,300-1,900   CHEF

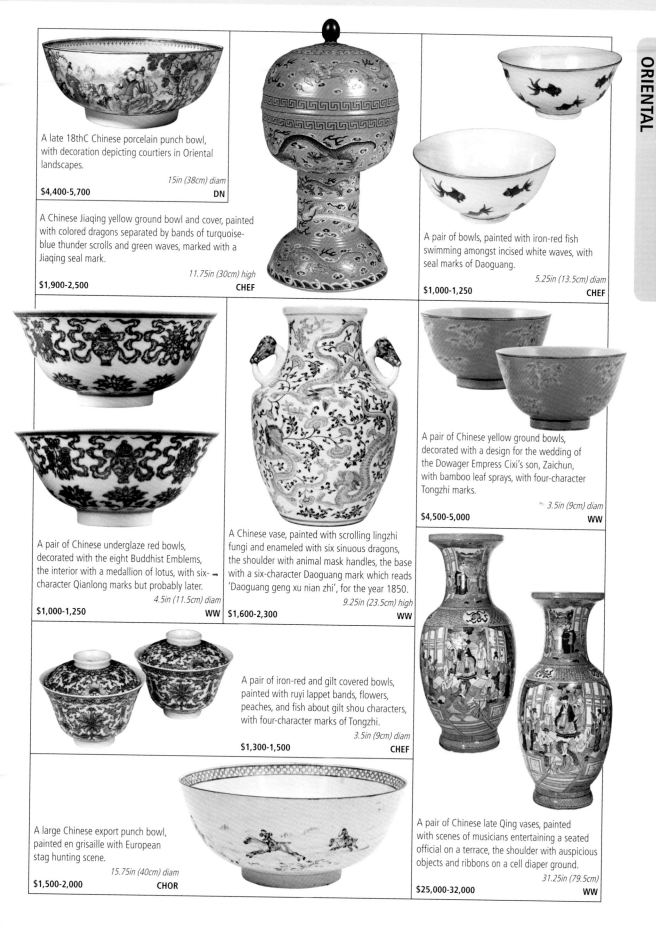

A late 18thC Chinese porcelain punch bowl, with decoration depicting courtiers in Oriental landscapes.

15in (38cm) diam

$4,400-5,700   DN

A Chinese Jiaqing yellow ground bowl and cover, painted with colored dragons separated by bands of turquoise-blue thunder scrolls and green waves, marked with a Jiaqing seal mark.

11.75in (30cm) high

$1,900-2,500   CHEF

A pair of bowls, painted with iron-red fish swimming amongst incised white waves, with seal marks of Daoguang.

5.25in (13.5cm) diam

$1,000-1,250   CHEF

A pair of Chinese underglaze red bowls, decorated with the eight Buddhist Emblems, the interior with a medallion of lotus, with six-character Qianlong marks but probably later.

4.5in (11.5cm) diam

$1,000-1,250   WW

A Chinese vase, painted with scrolling lingzhi fungi and enameled with six sinuous dragons, the shoulder with animal mask handles, the base with a six-character Daoguang mark which reads 'Daoguang geng xu nian zhi', for the year 1850.

9.25in (23.5cm) high

$1,600-2,300   WW

A pair of Chinese yellow ground bowls, decorated with a design for the wedding of the Dowager Empress Cixi's son, Zaichun, with bamboo leaf sprays, with four-character Tongzhi marks.

3.5in (9cm) diam

$4,500-5,000   WW

A pair of iron-red and gilt covered bowls, painted with ruyi lappet bands, flowers, peaches, and fish about gilt shou characters, with four-character marks of Tongzhi.

3.5in (9cm) diam

$1,300-1,500   CHEF

A large Chinese export punch bowl, painted en grisaille with European stag hunting scene.

15.75in (40cm) diam

$1,500-2,000   CHOR

A pair of Chinese late Qing vases, painted with scenes of musicians entertaining a seated official on a terrace, the shoulder with auspicious objects and ribbons on a cell diaper ground.

31.25in (79.5cm)

$25,000-32,000   WW

CLOSER LOOK - CHINESE ICE PAILS

It is rare to find a pair of ice pails in such excellent condition, with all the associated parts still together.

The decoration is of particularly high quality, finely painted with figures gathered in gardens about pavilions.

The metal handles suspended from gilt masks and gilt lion finials add to their decorative appeal.

These would have been expensive at the time and would have been made in small quantities, which accounts for their rarity.

A large 19thC Canton vase, painted with figural court scenes and birds and insects amongst flowers.

24in (61cm) high

$750-1,000 **BELL**

A pair of 19thC Chinese ice pails, liners, and covers, with seal marks of Doaguang in red.

7.75in (19.5cm) diam

$9,500-10,500 **CHEF**

A pair of Chinese Qing coral ground vases, painted to one side with Magu and a deer, to the other with a landscape, a four-character Qianlong mark to the base, raised on a rectangular hardwood stand.

Magu is a legendary Taoist immortal associated with the elixir of life, and a symbolic protector of females in Chinese mythology.

11.5in (29cm) high

$3,800-4,400 **WW**

A Chinese Qing dynasty millefleurs vase, with gilt coral handles, the base with a four-character mark which reads 'qing mu de tang'.

15in (38cm) high

$1,000-1,250 **WW**

A 19thC Chinese Canton enamel floor vase, decorated with figures against an enameled and gilded ground with fruit, flowers, foliage, and exotic birds.

33.5in (85cm) high

$550-700 **FLD**

A 19thC Chinese Canton enamel floor vase, decorated with exotic birds and butterflies over an enameled and gilded ground.

34.75in (88cm) high

$300-400 **FLD**

A pair of 19thC Chinese porcelain vases, painted with warriors, dignities, attendants, and mythical beasts above a formal border, bear six-character reign marks in blue.

36.75in (93cm) high

$7,500-9,000 **TEN**

A late 19thC Chinese porcelain vase, decorated with figures, dragons and clouds.

16.5in (42cm) high

$180-250 **LOC**

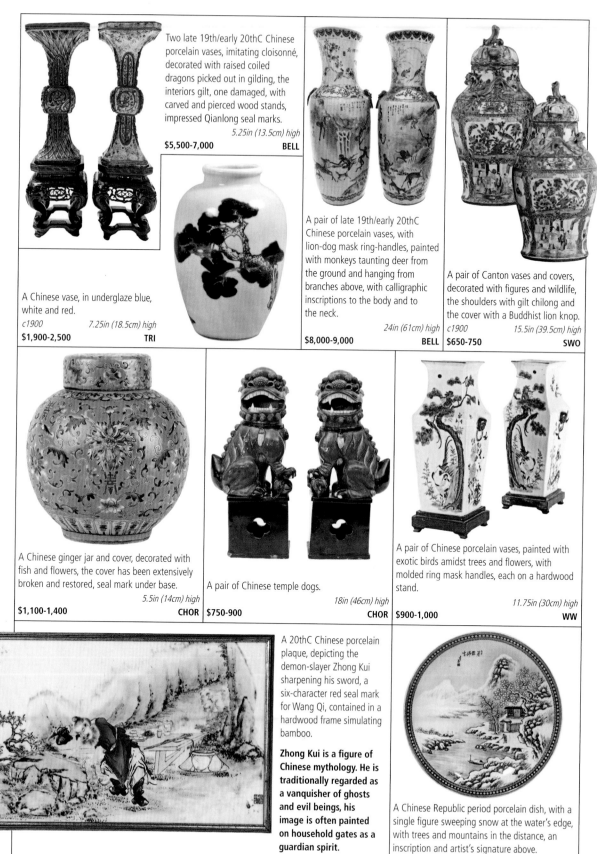

Two late 19th/early 20thC Chinese porcelain vases, imitating cloisonné, decorated with raised coiled dragons picked out in gilding, the interiors gilt, one damaged, with carved and pierced wood stands, impressed Qianlong seal marks.

5.25in (13.5cm) high

$5,500-7,000   **BELL**

A Chinese vase, in underglaze blue, white and red.

c1900   *7.25in (18.5cm) high*

$1,900-2,500   **TRI**

A pair of late 19th/early 20thC Chinese porcelain vases, with lion-dog mask ring-handles, painted with monkeys taunting deer from the ground and hanging from branches above, with calligraphic inscriptions to the body and to the neck.

24in (61cm) high

$8,000-9,000   **BELL**

A pair of Canton vases and covers, decorated with figures and wildlife, the shoulders with gilt chilong and the cover with a Buddhist lion knop.

c1900   *15.5in (39.5cm) high*

$650-750   **SWO**

A Chinese ginger jar and cover, decorated with fish and flowers, the cover has been extensively broken and restored, seal mark under base.

5.5in (14cm) high

$1,100-1,400   **CHOR**

A pair of Chinese temple dogs.

18in (46cm) high

$750-900   **CHOR**

A pair of Chinese porcelain vases, painted with exotic birds amidst trees and flowers, with molded ring mask handles, each on a hardwood stand.

11.75in (30cm) high

$900-1,000   **WW**

A 20thC Chinese porcelain plaque, depicting the demon-slayer Zhong Kui sharpening his sword, a six-character red seal mark for Wang Qi, contained in a hardwood frame simulating bamboo.

Zhong Kui is a figure of Chinese mythology. He is traditionally regarded as a vanquisher of ghosts and evil beings, his image is often painted on household gates as a guardian spirit.

11.25in (28.5cm) high

$3,200-3,800   **WW**

A Chinese Republic period porcelain dish, with a single figure sweeping snow at the water's edge, with trees and mountains in the distance, an inscription and artist's signature above.

12.5in (31.5cm) diam

$900-1,000   **WW**

ORIENTAL

A Japanese Meiji Satsuma kogo and cover, painted with figures in boats and at a lakeside, with trees, dwellings and mountains, with a seal mark for Yabu Meizan, with a label 'from Yamanaka & Co. 68 New Bond Street, 1906'.

3.5in (8.5cm) high

$1,600-2,000 WW

A Japanese Meiji Satsuma vase, decorated to one side with women and children playing musical instruments, the other with warriors, the neck with tennin floating amongst auspicious objects, unsigned.

1868-1912 *8in (20cm) high*

$500-650 WW

A Japanese Meiji Satsuma figure of a young woman, by Kinkozan, wearing a kimono painted with insects and chrysanthemum, her obi painted with coiled dragons, impressed seal mark 'Kinkozan zo'.

17in (43cm) high

$7,000-7,500 BELL

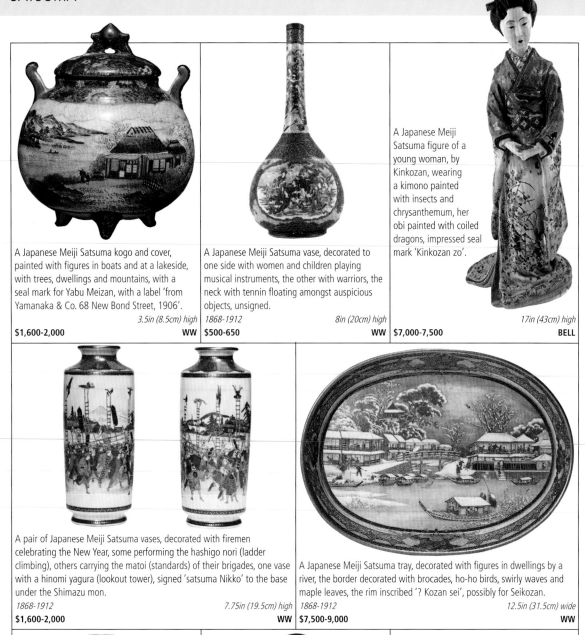

A pair of Japanese Meiji Satsuma vases, decorated with firemen celebrating the New Year, some performing the hashigo nori (ladder climbing), others carrying the matoi (standards) of their brigades, one vase with a hinomi yagura (lookout tower), signed 'satsuma Nikko' to the base under the Shimazu mon.

1868-1912 *7.75in (19.5cm) high*

$1,600-2,000 WW

A Japanese Meiji Satsuma tray, decorated with figures in dwellings by a river, the border decorated with brocades, ho-ho birds, swirly waves and maple leaves, the rim inscribed '? Kozan sei', possibly for Seikozan.

1868-1912 *12.5in (31.5cm) wide*

$7,500-9,000 WW

A Japanese Meiji Satsuma vase, painted with four skeletons, one playing the drum, two doing handstands and the fourth, a child, running away, seal mark for Baikei, possibly Nakamura Baikei.

1868-1912 *5in (12.5cm) high*

$5,000-5,700 WW

A Japanese Meiji Satsuma vase, by Kinkozan, painted with three figurative panels, with silvered ho-ho birds, impressed mark, with wood stand.

13in (33cm) high

$2,300-2,800 BELL

A Satsuma vase, by Kinkozan, one side painted with pigeons feeding below wisteria, the other with two mallard, the butterfly topped ginko leaf frames gilt on a deep blue ground, with wood stand.

14.25in (36.5cm) high

$2,800-3,500 CHEF

A 17thC Japanese Arita kendi (ritual water sprinkler), painted with landscape panels.

8.75in (22cm) high

$750-900 CHOR

A 17thC Japanese Kakiemon ewer, decorated in relief with crashing waves, the spout and handle forming a dragon emerging from water.

Kakiemon is a style of Japanese ceramic, usually porcelain, with overglaze enameled decoration. It was originally produced at the factories around Arita, in Japan's Hizen province from the mid-17thC onward. Kakiemon wares had asymmetrical designs allowing the fine white body to be admired. The palette of cerulean blue, coral red, green, yellow and black enamels was applied onto the glazed surface and fired again at a lower temperature. One studio in Arita was owned by the Kakiemon family from whom the whole category of ware takes its name. The superb quality of its decoration was widely imitated by the major European porcelain manufacturers.

5.5in (14cm) high

$5,000-5,700 WW

A 17thC Japanese dish, molded and painted with three cranes.

5.5in (14cm) diam

$1,300-1,900 WW

A Japanese Kakiemon porcelain dish, decorated with a plant pot with rocks and flowering plants, the border with flowering prunus branches.

c1690-1710 *5in (12.5cm) wide*

$1,500-1,900 PC

A Japanese Kakiemon porcelain dish, decorated with a plant pot with rocks and flowering plants, the border with flowering prunus branches.

c1690-1710 *5in (12.5cm) wide*

$1,500-1,900 PC

A late 17th/early 18thC Arita VOC dish, the central roundel with a bird amongst flowers, the rim with alternating garden panels in the Kraak style.

The VOC mark is that of the Dutch East India Company (Verenigde Oostindische Compagnie) that was originally established as a chartered company in 1602, when the Dutch government granted it a 21-year monopoly on Dutch spice trade. Statistically, the VOC eclipsed all of its rivals in the Asia trade. Between 1602 and 1796 the VOC sent almost a million Europeans to work in the Asia trade on 4,785 ships.

13in (33cm) diam

$2,300-2,800 CHEF

A pair of Nabeshima porcelain dishes, painted in red, green, yellow, and underglaze blue with stylized plants, the foot with stiff leaves.

The Japanese porcelain industry was actually pioneered by Korean potters living in Japan. Many of them came to Japan during two invasions of Korea in the 1590s. An appreciation of Korean ceramics had recently developed in Japan, and many of the feudal lords brought back Korean potters to build up the ceramic industry. The Nabeshima lord took Korean potters back to his province of Hizen on Kyushu, the southernmost of Japan's main islands. These potters would eventually become the first producers of porcelain in Japan. In the early 17thC the Korean potters living in the Arita district of Hizen found suitable clay for the manufacture of porcelain. The Hizen region thus became the major center of porcelain production in Japan.

4.5in (11.5cm) diam

$5,500-6,500 TEN

A Japanese Nabeshima dish, painted with two minogame, beneath leaves, the reverse with three flower sprays and a comb foot.

c1700 *8in (20cm) diam*

$4,500-5,000 WW

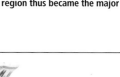

A 18thC Japanese Kakiemon-style decagonal bowl, with kiln mark, minor frits to the rim.

8.25in (21cm) diam

$750-900 PC

An 18thC Imari jar and cover, painted with flowers alternating on a blue ground gilt with flowerhead-centered diamond diaper, the cover with lion finial, finial restored, crack across the foot, chip repaired with glue.

22in (56cm) high

$180-250　　　　　　　　　　　　　　　CHEF

A late Meiji Japanese Imari porcelain vase, decorated with boats, prunus, birds and flowers.

30.5in (77.5cm) high

$1,000-1,100　　　　　　　　　　　　　L&T

A 19thC Japanese Imari charger, decorated in iron-red gilt and cobalt blue to show chrysanthemums, peony and a central medallion.

21.25in (54cm) diam

$1,900-2,500　　　　　　　　　　　　　PC

A Koransha Fukagawa vase and cover, painted with flowers on a ground of diaper and stylized flowers, the cover with shi-shi knop, red orchid and Fukagawa sei, paper label of 'Blairman & Sons' and selling price '3/5/-'.

c1885 *18in (46cm) high*

$450-550　　　　　　　　　　　　　　　SWO

A late 19thC Japanese Imari charger, depicting horses on a white ground, red scroll and grassy hill to the foreground.

16in (40.5cm) diam

$1,000-1,250　　　　　　　　　　　　　PC

A 19thC Japanese Imari charger, decorated with lobsters, shells and tortoises.

24in (61cm) diam

$1,100-1,500　　　　　　　　　　　　　CHOR

A late 19thC pair of Kyoto vases, with panels of a girl with a sunshade and a retainer, another with warriors, six-character mark for Dai Nihon Ogawa Zo.

12in (30cm) high

$250-320　　　　　　　　　　　　　　　SWO

A Japanese Meiji Fukagawa porcelain vase, painted with floral motifs and blossoming branches, mark to base 'Used c1900-1920'.

12.5in (32cm) high

$80-90　　　　　　　　　　　　　　　　APAR

A Japanese Ko-Imari beaker vase, decorated with shaped panels of birds and foliage, on a French ormolu foot rim.

15.75in (40cm) high

$150-190　　　　　　　　　　　　　　　PW

ESSENTIAL REFERENCE - CLOISONNÉ

Cloisonné is a decorative technique that involves firing enamel into compartments (cloisons) formed by metal wires.

- **The technique was introduced into China from Western Asia.**
- **It was first practiced during the 14thC.**
- **Soft glass pastes colored by minerals and metallic oxides are applied within fields formed by wire. Firing melts the enamel, after which it is ground flush with the surface.**
- **The earliest palette included basic colors like dark green, cobalt blue, red, yellow, and white, which were used on a turquoise background.**
- **Cloisonné pieces tend to be heavy as the enamel decoration is applied to a cast bronze base.**
- **Animal and bird figures became popular during the Qing dynasty.**
- **Rose pink was added to the range of colors in the 18thC.**
- **Chinese cloisonné appears to have first reached Europe during the 19thC.**

A late Ming Chinese cloisonné box and cover, decorated with a kylin and flowers, ground decorated with cranes, bats and cloud scrolls.

7in (18cm) diam

$3,800-5,000   **WW**

A late Ming Chinese cloisonné bowl, decorated to the interior with two winged dragons chasing a flaming pearl of wisdom amongst clouds, the exterior with a continuous lotus flowerhead design.

8in (20.5cm) wide

$6,500-7,500   **WW**

A pair of Chinese Qianlong cloisonné gu beaker vases, decorated with taotie masks within stylized stiff leaves containing lotus, the rims with key fret.

13in (33cm) high

$19,000-25,000   **WW**

A Chinese Qianlong cloisonné stem bowl, decorated to the exterior with four dragon roundels, with bands of ruyi-heads and lappets, the interior gilt.

See H Brinker & A Lutz, 'Chinese Cloisonné: The Pierre Uldry Collection', page 263, no.262, for a related example with a Qianlong mark.

4in (10cm) high

$18,000-23,000   **WW**

An 18thC Chinese cloisonné lozenge-shaped vase and cover, decorated with six lotus flowerheads, each encircled by scrolling leaves, the neck and shoulder with key fret borders, all reserved on a bright turquoise ground, the gilt metal handles and finial formed as ribbons.

8.5in (21.5cm) high

$13,000-15,000   **WW**

An unusual rare 18thC Chinese cloisonné stand or arm rest, decorated with auspicious objects.

16.5in (42cm) long

$32,000-38,000   **BE**

An 18th/early 19thC Chinese cloisonné gourd-shaped vase, decorated with flowers, gourds and swastikas.

14in (35cm) high

$10,000-13,000   **WW**

A Chinese cloisonné enamel cockerel, decorated with plumage, scrollwork, precious objects, rockwork and waves, the crest and base with some damage and repair to enamel.

38.25in (97cm) high

$3,200-3,800   **TEN**

An early 19thC Chinese cloisonné panel, decorated with flowers, a jardinière with narcissus, a ruyi scepter, a jue vessel and other auspicious things, a four-character mark which reads 'bai shi ru yi'.

23.5in (67cm) diam

$19,000-25,000   **WW**

A 19thC Chinese cloisonné bitong, decorated with flowerheads and scrolling foliate tendrils, the rim with a band of ruyi-heads.

4.5in (11.5cm) high

$950-1,100   **WW**

A Chinese Qianlong cloisonné censer, enameled with scrolling lotus, the cloisons also gilt, four-character Qianlong mark.

5in (12.5cm) diam

$900-1,000   **CHEF**

A pair of Chinese cloisonné vases, probably late Qing dynasty, decorated with two birds with peony blooms and other flowers, the necks with bats and shou characters.

12.5in (32cm) high

$2,800-3,500   **WW**

A pair of late Qing Chinese cloisonné elephants, the saddle cloths to the backs decorated with bats, surmounted by a vase, on an ormolu base with elephant head feet.

10.75in (27.5cm) high

$13,000-15,000   **WW**

A pair of late Qing Chinese cloisonné chickens.

7.5in (19cm) high

$1,900-2,500   **WW**

A pair of 19thC Chinese cloisonné hounds, the naturalistically modeled beasts with blue and turquoise markings highlighted in gilt, some typical minor surface wear.

7in (17.5cm) high

$5,000-5,700   **TEN**

A pair of Chinese late Qing cloisonné caparisoned elephants, with saddle cloths decorated with bats, lotus and shou designs and adorned with beaded bridles.

7.25in (18.5cm) high

$2,500-3,800   **WW**

A Chinese cloisonné quatrefoil jardinière, decorated with lotus scrolls, the body raised on four short feet, a metal liner to the interior.

c1900   *15.5in (39cm) wide*

$2,800-3,500   **WW**

A Yongzheng Canton enameled potiche, with scrolling foliage and blue chrysanthemum, the mouth with peony, with wood stand.

1723-35 *potiche 2.5in (6.5cm) high*

$3,400-3,800 SWO

A rare Chinese black ground and green enameled dish, painted with flowers, lingzhi fungus and fruiting berry sprays emerging from rockwork, decorated to the rim's reverse with a continuous scroll of lotus flowers and foliage, with six-character Qianlong seal mark.

1736-95 *12in (30cm) diam*

$70,000-75,000 WW

An 18thC Chinese Canton enamel famille rose teapot and cover, with peony, prunus, chrysanthemum and camellia, the neck with roundels with a dog, a rabbit and a mythical creature.

7in (18cm) high

$3,800-5,000 WW

An 18thC Chinese Canton enamel famille rose vase and cover, painted with European figures, mountain landscapes, birds, a deer and a tiger, the neck with prunus on a cracked-ice ground, the cover associated.

12in (30.5cm) high

$1,900-2,500 WW

An 18th/19thC enamel and gilt-metal stand, with stylized flowers and scrolling below lotus gadroons, below a gilt bracketed neck and on six ruyi feet.

8.75in (22cm) wide

$2,800-3,500 SWO

A 19thC Chinese enamel and ivory-mounted mirror, the frame painted with gilt flowers, the reverse with the eight Buddhist Emblems, encircling a 'xi' character, above a carved stained ivory bat inverted above a 'shou' character.

11in (28cm) high

$5,000-5,700 WW

A 19thC Chinese gilt metal enameled presentation snuff box and hinged cover, Guangzhou workshops, the cover painted with a Chinese immortal holding a peach, flanked by engraved floral sprigs, the base compartment opening withan abacus with blue glass beads.

3.75in (9.5cm) long

$4,500-5,000 L&T

A mid-19thC Chinese silver mug, marked for Sunshing, decorated with figures playing go, reading scrolls and playing qin, with buildings, with cartouche with crest and legend of the Scottish Wemyss clan, 'Je Pense' beneath a swan, with dragon handle, struck 'sS' and 'Hui'.

4.5in (11cm) high

$1,900-2,500 SWO

A 19thC Chinese export silver mug, by Leeching, Canton, with figures in landscapes, dragon scroll handle, the front with a vacant shield cartouche.

c1860 *4in (10cm) high 5.5oz*

$1,100-1,400 WW

ORIENTAL

A late 19thC Oriental silver cigarette box, embossed with village and battle scenes.

4.5in (11.5cm) long

$2,300-2,800 TRI

A Chinese Export silver box, by Wang Hing, pierced and chased with two duelling dragons and a flaming pearl, raised on bracket feet.

c1900 7.5in (19cm) wide 10oz

$1,900-2,500 TEN

CLOSER LOOK - BRONZE HU VASES

These vases are from the Warring States period 475-221 BC.

Hu is a type of wine vessel that has a pear-shaped cross-section. Its body swells and flares into a narrow neck, creating S-shaped profile. The shape of hu probably derives from its ceramic prototype prior to the Shang dynasty (1600-1045 BC).

They are sophisticated - decorated in relief with four concentric relief bands simulating twisted rope, the shoulder with two mythical beast masks.

The surface with evidence of malachite encrustations - meaning they were burial finds.

A pair of Chinese bronze hu vases, with removable crowns, with eight ogee-shaped radiating petals decorated with stylized geometric scrolls.

15.75in (40cm) high

$32,000-38,000 WW

A Chinese Sui/Tang parcel-gilt bronze 'Lion and Grapevine' mirror, cast in high relief with five lion-like animals, light malachite encrustation sides and reverse.

3.75in (9.5cm) diam

$7,000-8,000 L&T

A rare Chinese Ming Imperial gilt-bronze bianzhong ritual bell, with a handle of swirling clouds above pairs of cranes and phoenix, the sides with five bands of alternating bosses and stylized flames between a frieze of dragon-tortoise and phoenix, the narrower sides decorated with a five-clawed dragon amongst swirling clouds.

10.75 (27cm) high

$200,000-250,000 L&T

A Chinese Yongle gilt bronze figure of Vajrapani, the bodhisattva finely cast seated in dhyanasana on a double-lotus base, the base plate incised with a double vajra with remains of red lacquer, Yongle incised mark.

The front of the base incised with a six-character mark reading 'Da Ming Yong Le Nian Shi' - bestowed in the Great Ming Yongle period. Vajrapani is one of the earliest-appearing bodhisattvas in Mahayana Buddhism. He is the protector and guide of Gautama Buddha and rose to symbolize the Buddha's power. The Golden Light Sutra titles him 'great general of the yakshas'.

9.75in (25cm) high

$550,000-650,000 L&T

A Chinese Ming bronze 'Champion' vase, vases cast with daodieh and joined by the wings of an eagle standing on the head of a bear, crack to the shoulders of one vase, eagle's feet are loose.

18in (45.5cm) high

$45,000-50,000 CHEF

A 17thC Chinese bronze censer, with Arabic calligraphy in three reserves, with Zhengde four-character seal mark.

5.5in (14cm) diam

$150,000-250,000 NAG

A 17thC Chinese bronze and parcel-gilt archaistic vase, with bands of taotie designs above eight taotie mask lappets, with handles with mythical beasts' heads, the inscription reads 'SOUVENIR A L.MEGNEN MON GENDRE ET MEILLEUR AMI J.SEBILLE'.

19in (48cm) high

$3,200-3,800 WW

A Chinese Ming bronze 'you' vase and cover, after an early Western Zhou original, with gold and silver inlay with taotie masks, the cover and interior with archaic inscriptions.

16.5in (42cm) high to top of handle
$50,000-55,000   **JN**

A Chinese bronze incense burner, a mark to the base which reads 'da Qing Kang Xi nian zhi yan tai shi shi jing zao', with twelve-character Kangxi seal mark.
1662-1722
$8,000-9,000
7in (17.5cm) wide
WW

CLOSER LOOK - QING 'DRAGON' STAND

These fine Kangzi stands are amazingly detailed.

They are heavily cast as a pair of striding five-clawed dragons whose sinuous bodies entwine.

The faces have bulging eyes showing a ferocious expression, the mouth agape at a ball held in its left forepaw.

Each creature is finely detailed with powerful legs, scaly bodies and spiky dorsal fins.

A rare 17th/18thC Chinese Qing gilt bronze 'dragon' stand.
9.5in (24cm) long
$19,000-25,000   **L&T**

An 18thC Chinese bronze tripod censer and stand, the stand as a mallow flower with overlapping petals, the base bearing an apocryphal six-character Xuande mark.

8.25in (21cm) long
$5,000-5,700   **L&T**

A Chinese Qing bronze censer, in the form of a fingered citron issuing from a gnarled leafy stem, with wood stand.

7.75in (20cm) long
$8,000-9,000   **L&T**

A Chinese Qing bronze incense burner, raised on three legs, surmounted by an animal mask and tapering to a hoof.
16.25in (41cm) wide
$1,300-1,900   **WW**

A Chinese gilt bronze temple bell or bianzhong, the top cast with pairs of phoenix, with dragon cast sides.
10.5in (27cm) high
$1,000-1,200   **CHEF**

A bronzed copper potiche and cover, possibly Wanli, with hammered relief and incised horses racing through waves against clouds, dark brown patination.
8.25in (21cm) high
$900-1,000   **SWO**

A Japanese Meiji bronze samurai, clothing with large 'mon' designs in gilt, holding a hammer over his head, signed 'Yoshimitsu', on a wooden base.
1868-1912 *15.25in (38.5cm) high*
$5,500-6,500 **WW**

A Japanese Meiji bronze table group, a man holding a rice bowl to a child, a table of food beside them.
26in (66.5cm) long
$4,500-5,000 **TEN**

A large Japanese Miyao bronze figure of a samurai, the samurai's leggings with a seal mark, mounted on wood stand.
bronze 15.5in (39.5cm) high
$1,900-2,500 **JN**

A pair of Meiji Japanese bronze vases, carved in low relief and inlaid in high relief with birds amongst chrysanthemums in copper, silver and gilt, signed.
9.75in (24.5cm) high
$1,900-2,500 **BELL**

A Japanese Meiji bronze striding elephant, by Genryusai Seiya, signed.
10in (25cm) high
$950-1,100 **BELL**

A Japanese Meiji bronze vase, cast in relief with elephants.
15.5in (40cm) high
$3,200-3,800 **JN**

A Japanese Meiji bronze jardinière, cast in high relief with elephants, the base with a seal mark.
9.5in (24cm) high
$2,500-3,200 **JN**

A Japanese Meiji mixed-metal okimono, with a pair of oshidori (Mandarin ducks) on a rocks.
1868-1912 *8.25in (21cm) wide*
$2,500-3,200 **WW**

A pair of Japanese Meiji mixed metal vases and stands, decorated with warriors beneath pine, onlaid and inlaid in gold, silver and copper metals, bases with maker's marks.
30in (76cm) high
$8,000-9,000 **JN**

A pair of Japanese Meiji cloisonné vases, with birds amongst branches of flowering blossom, the necks with dragons and cloud scrolls.
48in (122cm) high
$3,800-4,400 **BELL**

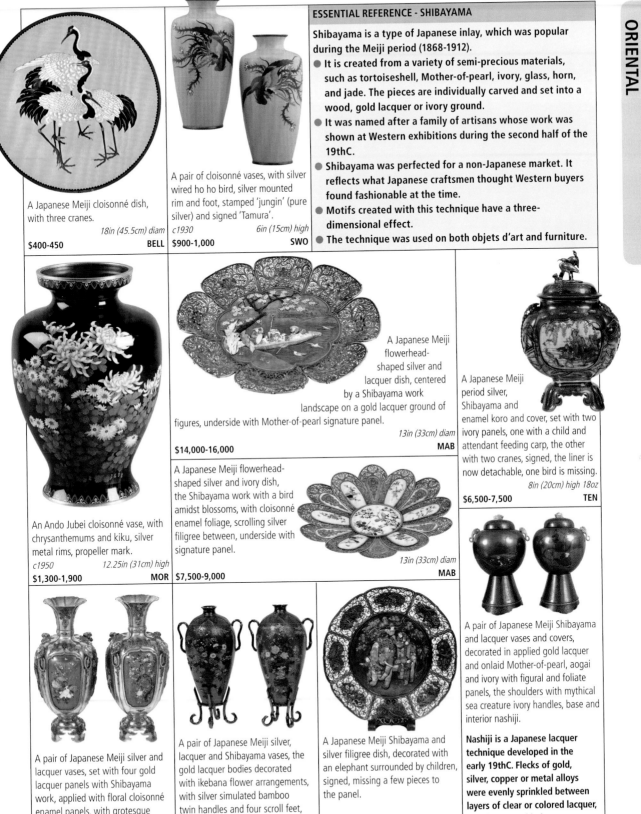

A Japanese Meiji cloisonné dish, with three cranes.

18in (45.5cm) diam

$400-450   BELL

A pair of cloisonné vases, with silver wired ho ho bird, silver mounted rim and foot, stamped 'jungin' (pure silver) and signed 'Tamura'.

c1930   6in (15cm) high

$900-1,000   SWO

ESSENTIAL REFERENCE - SHIBAYAMA

Shibayama is a type of Japanese inlay, which was popular during the Meiji period (1868-1912).

- It is created from a variety of semi-precious materials, such as tortoiseshell, Mother-of-pearl, ivory, glass, horn, and jade. The pieces are individually carved and set into a wood, gold lacquer or ivory ground.
- It was named after a family of artisans whose work was shown at Western exhibitions during the second half of the 19thC.
- Shibayama was perfected for a non-Japanese market. It reflects what Japanese craftsmen thought Western buyers found fashionable at the time.
- Motifs created with this technique have a three-dimensional effect.
- The technique was used on both objets d'art and furniture.

A Japanese Meiji flowerhead-shaped silver and lacquer dish, centered by a Shibayama work landscape on a gold lacquer ground of figures, underside with Mother-of-pearl signature panel.

13in (33cm) diam

$14,000-16,000   MAB

An Ando Jubei cloisonné vase, with chrysanthemums and kiku, silver metal rims, propeller mark.

c1950   12.25in (31cm) high

$1,300-1,900   MOR

A Japanese Meiji flowerhead-shaped silver and ivory dish, the Shibayama work with a bird amidst blossoms, with cloisonné enamel foliage, scrolling silver filigree between, underside with signature panel.

13in (33cm) diam

$7,500-9,000   MAB

A Japanese Meiji period silver, Shibayama and enamel koro and cover, set with two ivory panels, one with a child and attendant feeding carp, the other with two cranes, signed, the liner is now detachable, one bird is missing.

8in (20cm) high 18oz

$6,500-7,500   TEN

A pair of Japanese Meiji silver and lacquer vases, set with four gold lacquer panels with Shibayama work, applied with floral cloisonné enamel panels, with grotesque mask drop-rings, underside with signature panel.

9.25in (23.5cm) high

$5,500-6,500   MAB

A pair of Japanese Meiji silver, lacquer and Shibayama vases, the gold lacquer bodies decorated with ikebana flower arrangements, with silver simulated bamboo twin handles and four scroll feet, unsigned, one has been reattached to the base.

7.75in (19.5cm) high

$4,000-4,800   TEN

A Japanese Meiji Shibayama and silver filigree dish, decorated with an elephant surrounded by children, signed, missing a few pieces to the panel.

9.5in (24cm) wide 13oz

$2,800-3,500   TEN

A pair of Japanese Meiji Shibayama and lacquer vases and covers, decorated in applied gold lacquer and onlaid Mother-of-pearl, aogai and ivory with figural and foliate panels, the shoulders with mythical sea creature ivory handles, base and interior nashiji.

Nashiji is a Japanese lacquer technique developed in the early 19thC. Flecks of gold, silver, copper or metal alloys were evenly sprinkled between layers of clear or colored lacquer, creating a speckled appearance similar to that of aventurine glass.

7.5in (19cm) high

$10,000-11,000   JN

A mid-19thC Chinese ivory card case, carved with figures in gardens with buildings, with tablet with initials.

4.25in (10.5cm) high

$1,000-1,200 LAW

An early 19thC Canton ivory card case, carved with Laozi and figures in a garden, a boy in the clouds, the reverse with a boy on a buffalo.

Laozi (also Lao-Tzu, literally 'Old Master') was an ancient Chinese philosopher and writer. He is known as the reputed author of the 'Tao Te Ching' and the founder of philosophical Taoism, and as a deity in religious Taoism and traditional Chinese religions.

4.5in (11.5cm) high

$750-900 SWO

A 19thC Canton ivory workbox, densely carved with figures in leisurely pursuits, the interior with lift-out tray fitted with compartments and two carved covers, with turned and carved accessories including six thread barrels, two cylindrical containers and covers and a sewing clamp.

11in (27.5cm) wide

$15,000-18,000 BELL

An early 20thC pair of Chinese ivory figures, of an Emperor and Empress, signed.

13.75in (35cm) high

$1,000-1,200 BELL

An early 19thC Chinese ivory carving of a lady and a phoenix.

9.25in (23.5cm) high

$1,900-2,500 WW

A 19thC Chinese ivory figure of a maiden, holding a lily, section of lily stem lacking, some typical staining, surface splitting and minor losses.

13.75in (35cm) high

$500-650 TEN

A pair of ivory cranes, on bronze legs with finely detailed feathers, the eyes inlaid in Mother-of-pearl, on fixed wooden stands.

c1890 *8in (20cm) high*

$2,500-3,200 SWO

A 19thC carved ivory tusk on wooden stand, pierced and carved as a riverside village scene, some details are raised outside the natural curve of the tusk and have been glued on.

ivory 44.5in (113cm) long

$5,000-6,500 CHEF

A Republic period ivory vase, carved in relief and tinted in green and red with a literatus under a pine, books and a teapot on a rock, the neck with cranes, red heraldic lion mark.

1912-49 *11in (27.5cm) high*

$1,900-2,500 SWO

A 19thC Chinese ivory libation bowl, carved in high relief with twisting pine on a tree bark ground.

3in (7.5cm) high

$650-750 JN

A Meiji Japanese ivory okimono, carved as figures smoking over a bundle of sticks, signed.

Okimono is a Japanese term meaning ornament for display, objet d'art, decorative object, typically displayed in a tokonoma (alcove) or on a butsudan (Buddhist altar).

3.25in (8cm) high

$180-250   BELL

A Meiji Japanese ivory okimono of a fisherman, holding a spear and a basket of fish, signed on red lacquer tablet.

7.5in (19cm) high

$130-180   BELL

A Japanese Meiji carved ivory okimono of a tiger, by Okada Tsunekichi, the tiger reaching to wash its heel, with inset Mother-of-pearl eyes, with artist's signature.

Okada Tsunekichi went by the artist's name of Tomokazu. He was a member of the Tokyo School of Artists and Tokyo Chokokai (Tokyo Carvers Association) from 1906-10.

4.75in (12cm) long

$10,000-11,000   HW

An early 20thC Japanese wood and ivory okimono of a street vendor, some pipes lacking, typical minor splitting and wear throughout, figure and hat loose, some staining.

13.75in (35cm) high

$1,300-1,800   TEN

A Japanese Meiji ivory okimono, depicting a tanuki carrying a mokugyo on its back, the bell with a lotus flower mon, the base with a two-character signature, possibly for Shigeyasu.

A tanuki is a Japanese raccoon. A wooden fish, Mokugyo, is a wooden percussion instrument. The wooden fish is used by monks and laity in the Mahayana Buddhist tradition. It is often used during rituals usually involving the recitation of sutras, mantras, or other Buddhist texts.

1868-1912   3.5in (8.5cm) high

$2,300-2,800   WW

A Japanese Meiji ivory okimono of a man gathering coral, by Ju/Toshi, he has coral in his hands, a basket containing rope, and a tobacco pouch with pipe case and netsuke slung at his waist, signed.

10in (25cm) high

$500-650   BELL

A Japanese Meiji ivory okimono of a tradesman, carrying flowers upon which sits a hare, a basket, a fox, and a bird at his feet, signed.

8.25in (21cm) high

$700-800   BELL

A signed Japanese Meiji ivory okimono of a puppeteer, three costumed mice at his feet, the details stained and engraved, the base with a finely engraved signature.

6.5in (16.5cm) high

$4,500-5,000   JN

A Japanese Meiji ivory okimono of a group of rats, clambering over a fallen stand, their eyes inlaid.

5.5in (14cm) wide

$1,300-1,900   JN

A Japanese Meiji ivory okimono of a corn cob, naturalistically carved and partially stained in green, with a wood stand.

ivory 6in (15cm) long

$2,500-3,200   JN

A signed Japanese Meiji ivory okimono of a female lion, with a rabbit in its mouth, a group of cubs playing, the base with an engraved signature.

4.75in (12cm) high

$1,300-1,900   JN

A signed Japanese Meiji ivory okimono of a fisherman, on rockwork above waves and carrying a boy on his back, another boy at his feet.

12in (30.5cm) high

$3,200-3,800   JN

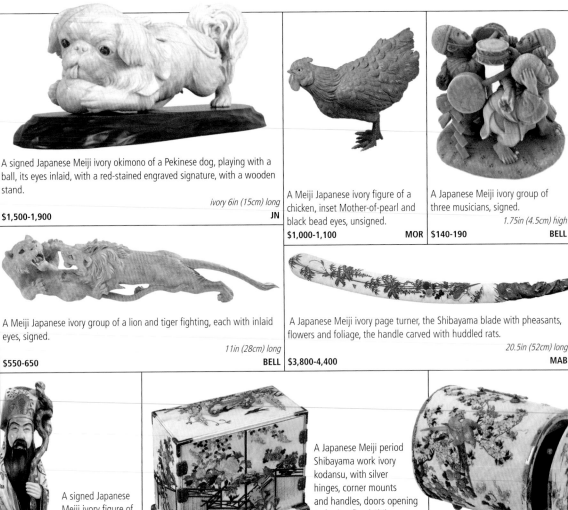

A signed Japanese Meiji ivory okimono of a Pekinese dog, playing with a ball, its eyes inlaid, with a red-stained engraved signature, with a wooden stand.

ivory 6in (15cm) long

$1,500-1,900   JN

A Meiji Japanese ivory figure of a chicken, inset Mother-of-pearl and black bead eyes, unsigned.

$1,000-1,100   MOR

A Japanese Meiji ivory group of three musicians, signed.

1.75in (4.5cm) high

$140-190   BELL

A Meiji Japanese ivory group of a lion and tiger fighting, each with inlaid eyes, signed.

11in (28cm) long

$550-650   BELL

A Japanese Meiji ivory page turner, the Shibayama blade with pheasants, flowers and foliage, the handle carved with huddled rats.

20.5in (52cm) long

$3,800-4,400   MAB

A signed Japanese Meiji ivory figure of Jurojin, the bearded deity holding a long knarled staff, his robes with gilded and stained decoration, the base with a red stained seal mark.

22.5in (57cm) high

$4,500-5,000   JN

A Japanese Meiji period Shibayama work ivory kodansu, with silver hinges, corner mounts and handles, doors opening to further floral Shibayama inlays to reverse of doors and an arrangement of four short and one long drawer.

Kodansu is the Japanese for 'small box-chest', describing a small lacquer cabinet containing a nest of drawers enclosed by a door for holding personal accessories. It often has, as here, engraved silver mounts.

6in (15.5cm) long

$7,000-8,000   MAB

A Japanese Meiji Shibayama casket, with decoration of exotic birds, with a hinged door set with two lacquered drawers, signed to a plaque to one side.

6in (15cm) high

$6,500-7,500   APAR

A Japanese Meiji Shibayama ivory figure of an elephant, caparisoned with beaded mesh and fringing, with flower, butterfly and bird inlaid howdah blanket, with signature panel.

7.25in (18.5cm) long

$5,000-5,700   MAB

A Japanese Meiji Shibayama ivory figure of an elephant, caparisoned with beaded mesh and horn harnessing, the howdah blanket with flower filled panels, signed under one foot.

13.5in (34cm) long

$11,000-12,000   MAB

A Japanese Meiji Shibayama ivory figure of an elephant, caparisoned with beaded mesh, the howdah blankets with panels of birds amidst foliage and a flower-filled cart, with signature panel, with wood stand.

14in (36cm) long

$7,000-8,000   MAB

A Japanese Meiji ivory and lacquer table screen, with a gold lacquer Shibayama panel, one with a gardener, the other of a lady and a boy amidst blossoming foliage, with silver hinges and corner mounts.

9in (23cm) high

$11,000-14,000   MAB

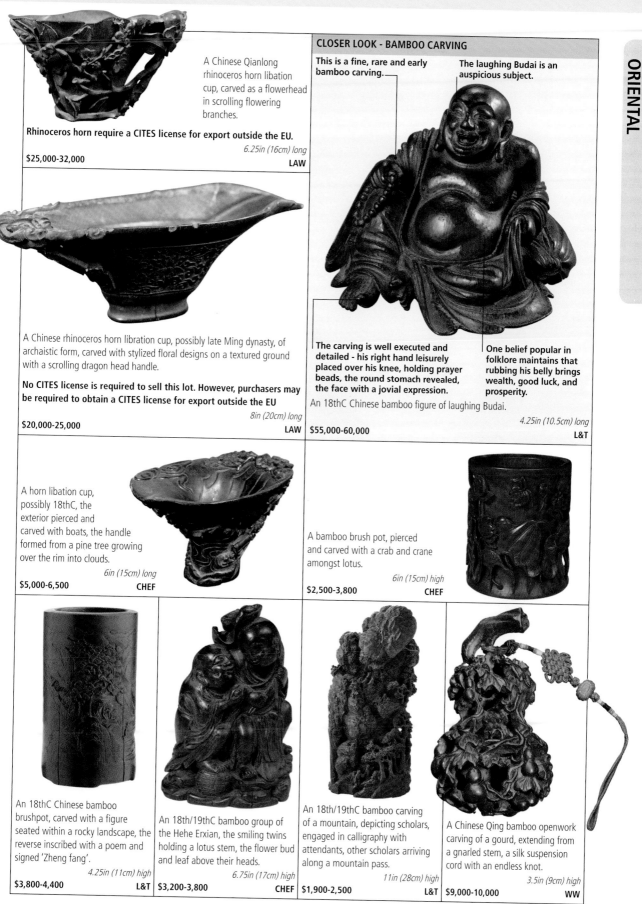

A Chinese Qianlong rhinoceros horn libation cup, carved as a flowerhead in scrolling flowering branches.

Rhinoceros horn require a CITES license for export outside the EU.

6.25in (16cm) long

$25,000-32,000   **LAW**

A Chinese rhinoceros horn libation cup, possibly late Ming dynasty, of archaistic form, carved with stylized floral designs on a textured ground with a scrolling dragon head handle.

No CITES license is required to sell this lot. However, purchasers may be required to obtain a CITES license for export outside the EU

8in (20cm) long

$20,000-25,000   **LAW**

CLOSER LOOK - BAMBOO CARVING

This is a fine, rare and early bamboo carving.

The laughing Budai is an auspicious subject.

The carving is well executed and detailed - his right hand leisurely placed over his knee, holding prayer beads, the round stomach revealed, the face with a jovial expression.

One belief popular in folklore maintains that rubbing his belly brings wealth, good luck, and prosperity.

An 18thC Chinese bamboo figure of laughing Budai.

4.25in (10.5cm) long

$55,000-60,000   **L&T**

A horn libation cup, possibly 18thC, the exterior pierced and carved with boats, the handle formed from a pine tree growing over the rim into clouds.

6in (15cm) long

$5,000-6,500   **CHEF**

A bamboo brush pot, pierced and carved with a crab and crane amongst lotus.

6in (15cm) high

$2,500-3,800   **CHEF**

An 18thC Chinese bamboo brushpot, carved with a figure seated within a rocky landscape, the reverse inscribed with a poem and signed 'Zheng fang'.

4.25in (11cm) high

$3,800-4,400   **L&T**

An 18th/19thC bamboo group of the Hehe Erxian, the smiling twins holding a lotus stem, the flower bud and leaf above their heads.

6.75in (17cm) high

$3,200-3,800   **CHEF**

An 18th/19thC bamboo carving of a mountain, depicting scholars, engaged in calligraphy with attendants, other scholars arriving along a mountain pass.

11in (28cm) high

$1,900-2,500   **L&T**

A Chinese Qing bamboo openwork carving of a gourd, extending from a gnarled stem, a silk suspension cord with an endless knot.

3.5in (9cm) high

$9,000-10,000   **WW**

An early Chinese Qing bamboo bitong, by Zhou Zhiyan (1685-1773), carved with mountains, with pine trees and figures, the reverse inscribed with a poem and signed 'Zhiyan'.

6in (15cm) high

$1,900-2,500   **WW**

A Chinese Qing hardwood bitong, carved to simulate natural knots in the wood.

7.5in (19cm) high

$3,500-4,300   **WW**

A Chinese late Qing zitan bitong, carved with scholars with a scroll, others playing a board game, all amongst craggy rocks, bamboo, pine and maple trees, with an inscription 'kui chou zhong dong yue, Jiang Chun Bo zhi'.

5.25in (13.5cm) high

$700-800   **WW**

A 19thC Chinese bamboo model of Liu Hai, riding on his three-legged toad, holding cash in his right hand, a bowl raised in his left.

10in (25cm) high

$1,600-2,300   **WW**

A 19thC Japanese hardwood group, of two nude warriors wrestling, elbow missing from standing figure.

37in (94cm) high

$2,500-3,200   **TEN**

An 18th/19thC boxwood Guanyin, carved from a single section of trunk, one hand in meditation, the other holding the Elixir of Life, her face with a serene expression.

28.75in (73cm) high

$12,000-14,000   **SWO**

An unusual pair of 19thC rootwood Immortals, depicting Fu and Lu, each holding an attribute or child, other figures below on the mountainous base, dark stained.

35in (89cm) high

$6,500-7,500   **SWO**

A 19thC Chinese soapstone bitong, modeled as bamboo, the exterior carved with mountains, pagodas, trees and dwellings, with three stems of bamboo.

4.75in (12cm) high

$650-750   **WW**

A signed Japanese Meiji/Taisho lacquered wood and ivory fisherman, with small areas of Mother-of-pearl inlay.

14.25in (36cm) high

$3,200-3,800   **JN**

A signed Japanese Meiji/Taisho lacquered wood and ivory woman and child, with small areas of Mother-of-pearl inlay.

11in (28cm) high

$1,900-2,500   **JN**

A signed Japanese Meiji/Taisho lacquered wood and ivory street vendor, with areas of Mother-of-pearl inlay.

6.5in (16.5cm) high

$2,300-2,500   **JN**

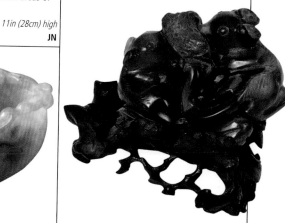

A 19thC Chinese agate brush washer, carved on the rim with a bat.

4in (10cm) high

$150-190   **MOR**

A Chinese 19thC carved agate group of squirrels, nibbling peanuts, with carved wood stand.

2in (5cm) long

$2,500-3,800   **MAB**

A Japanese Meiji/Taisho lacquered wood and ivory young woman, with small areas of Mother-of-pearl inlay, inlaid with an engraved signature on a red lacquer reserve.

14.5in (37cm) high

$2,500-3,200   **JN**

A Chinese mid-19thC lapis lazuli brush washer, the sage resting against a jar.

According to the note affixed to the underside, this object was on the table next to Governor Yeh Ming-ch'en (1807-1859) when he was taken prisoner.

4in (10cm) long

$2,100-2,500   **MAB**

A Chinese two-tone agate vase, possibly of the Republican period, carved with a leaping dragon fish and chilong climbing the rocks.

$15,000-19,000   **TOV**

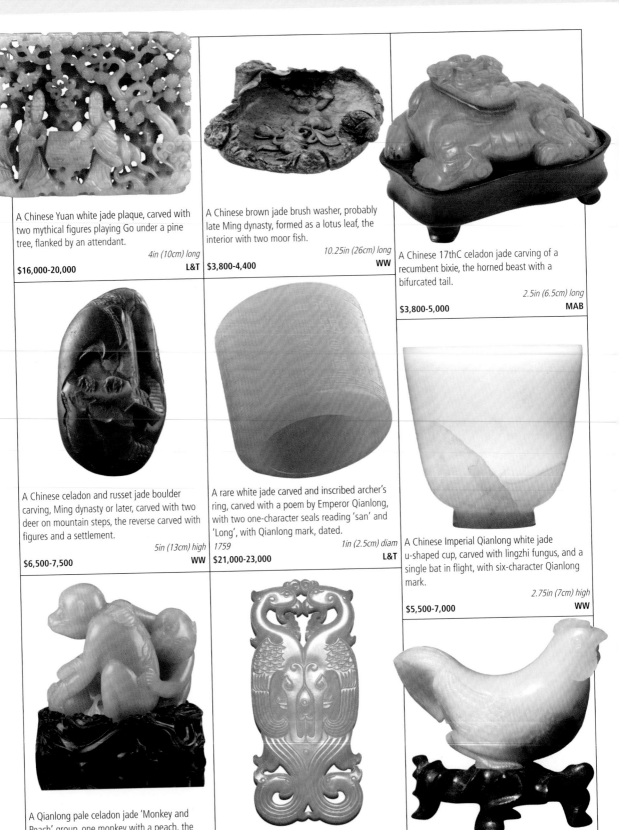

A Chinese Yuan white jade plaque, carved with two mythical figures playing Go under a pine tree, flanked by an attendant.

4in (10cm) long

$16,000-20,000 **L&T**

A Chinese brown jade brush washer, probably late Ming dynasty, formed as a lotus leaf, the interior with two moor fish.

10.25in (26cm) long

$3,800-4,400 **WW**

A Chinese 17thC celadon jade carving of a recumbent bixie, the horned beast with a bifurcated tail.

2.5in (6.5cm) long

$3,800-5,000 **MAB**

A Chinese celadon and russet jade boulder carving, Ming dynasty or later, carved with two deer on mountain steps, the reverse carved with figures and a settlement.

5in (13cm) high

$6,500-7,500 **WW**

A rare white jade carved and inscribed archer's ring, carved with a poem by Emperor Qianlong, with two one-character seals reading 'san' and 'Long', with Qianlong mark, dated.

1759 *1in (2.5cm) diam*

$21,000-23,000 **L&T**

A Chinese Imperial Qianlong white jade u-shaped cup, carved with lingzhi fungus, and a single bat in flight, with six-character Qianlong mark.

2.75in (7cm) high

$5,500-7,000 **WW**

A Qianlong pale celadon jade 'Monkey and Peach' group, one monkey with a peach, the other with its arms around the other, grasping a branch of a peach tree, with later dark spinach jade stand.

3.5in (9cm) high

$55,000-60,000 **L&T**

A Chinese Imperial Qianlong white jade plaque, carved with a pair of phoenix, their wings and tail plumage in mirror image.

1736-95 *3.5in (8.5cm) high*

$55,000-60,000 **WW**

An 18thC Chinese pale celadon jade cockerel, with a fitted hardwood stand.

2.75in (7cm) high

$8,000-9,500 **WW**

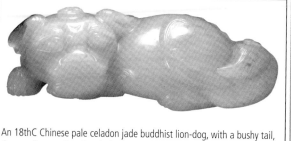

An 18thC Chinese pale celadon jade buddhist lion-dog, with a bushy tail, the ears flattened against its body.

4in (10cm) long

$14,000-18,000 **WW**

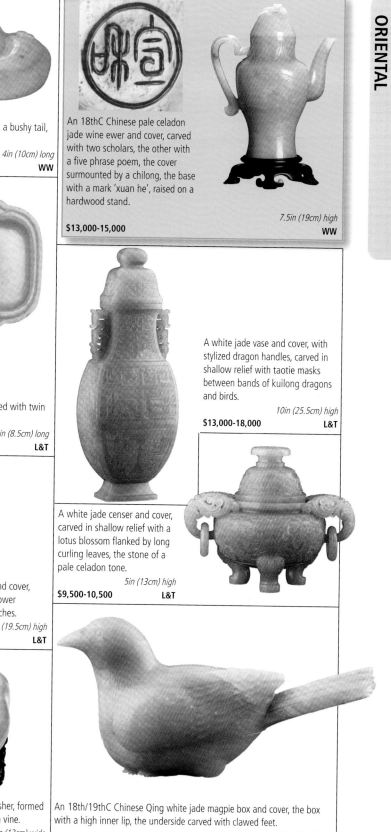

An 18thC Chinese pale celadon jade wine ewer and cover, carved with two scholars, the other with a five phrase poem, the cover surmounted by a chilong, the base with a mark 'xuan he', raised on a hardwood stand.

7.5in (19cm) high

$13,000-15,000 **WW**

An 18thC Chinese Qing white jade 'Fenghuang' box, decorated with twin phoenix to cover top and edge.

3.25in (8.5cm) long

$4,400-5,700 **L&T**

A white jade vase and cover, with stylized dragon handles, carved in shallow relief with taotie masks between bands of kuilong dragons and birds.

10in (25.5cm) high

$13,000-18,000 **L&T**

A white jade censer and cover, carved in shallow relief with a lotus blossom flanked by long curling leaves, the stone of a pale celadon tone.

5in (13cm) high

$9,500-10,500 **L&T**

A celadon jade ewer and cover, decorated with lotus flower amongst scrolling branches.

7.75in (19.5cm) high

$7,000-8,000 **L&T**

A large Chinese 18th/early 19thC pale celadon jade brush washer, formed as a gourd, with two bats, on a hardwood stand carved with a vine.

5in (13cm) wide

$11,000-15,000 **WW**

An 18th/19thC Chinese Qing white jade magpie box and cover, the box with a high inner lip, the underside carved with clawed feet.

7in (18cm) long

$25,000-32,000 **L&T**

ORIENTAL

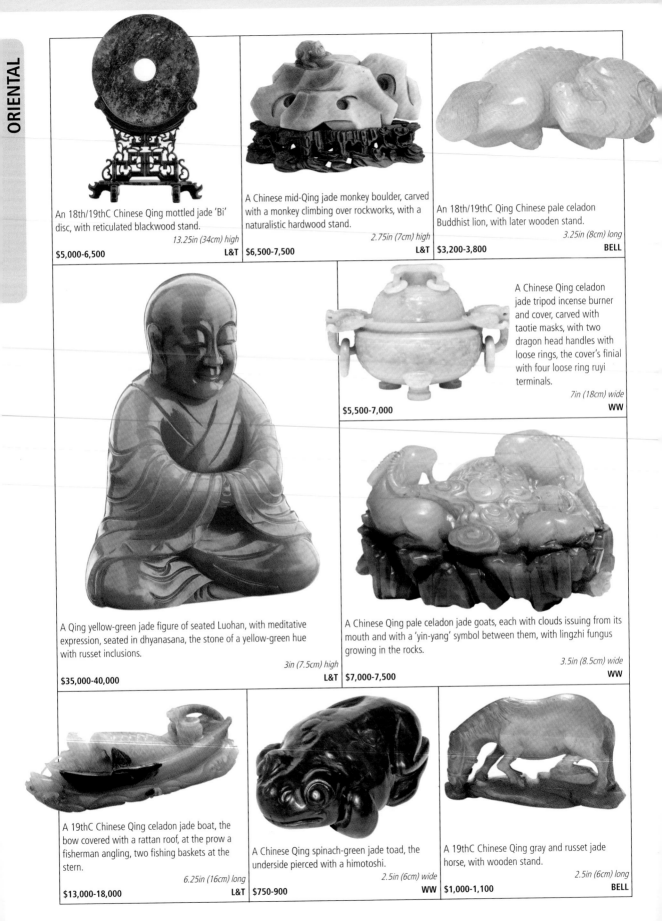

An 18th/19thC Chinese Qing mottled jade 'Bi' disc, with reticulated blackwood stand.

13.25in (34cm) high

$5,000-6,500 **L&T**

A Chinese mid-Qing jade monkey boulder, carved with a monkey climbing over rockworks, with a naturalistic hardwood stand.

2.75in (7cm) high

$6,500-7,500 **L&T**

An 18th/19thC Qing Chinese pale celadon Buddhist lion, with later wooden stand.

3.25in (8cm) long

$3,200-3,800 **BELL**

A Chinese Qing celadon jade tripod incense burner and cover, carved with taotie masks, with two dragon head handles with loose rings, the cover's finial with four loose ring ruyi terminals.

7in (18cm) wide

$5,500-7,000 **WW**

A Qing yellow-green jade figure of seated Luohan, with meditative expression, seated in dhyanasana, the stone of a yellow-green hue with russet inclusions.

3in (7.5cm) high

$35,000-40,000 **L&T**

A Chinese Qing pale celadon jade goats, each with clouds issuing from its mouth and with a 'yin-yang' symbol between them, with lingzhi fungus growing in the rocks.

3.5in (8.5cm) wide

$7,000-7,500 **WW**

A 19thC Chinese Qing celadon jade boat, the bow covered with a rattan roof, at the prow a fisherman angling, two fishing baskets at the stern.

6.25in (16cm) long

$13,000-18,000 **L&T**

A Chinese Qing spinach-green jade toad, the underside pierced with a himotoshi.

2.5in (6cm) wide

$750-900 **WW**

A 19thC Chinese Qing gray and russet jade horse, with wooden stand.

2.5in (6cm) long

$1,000-1,100 **BELL**

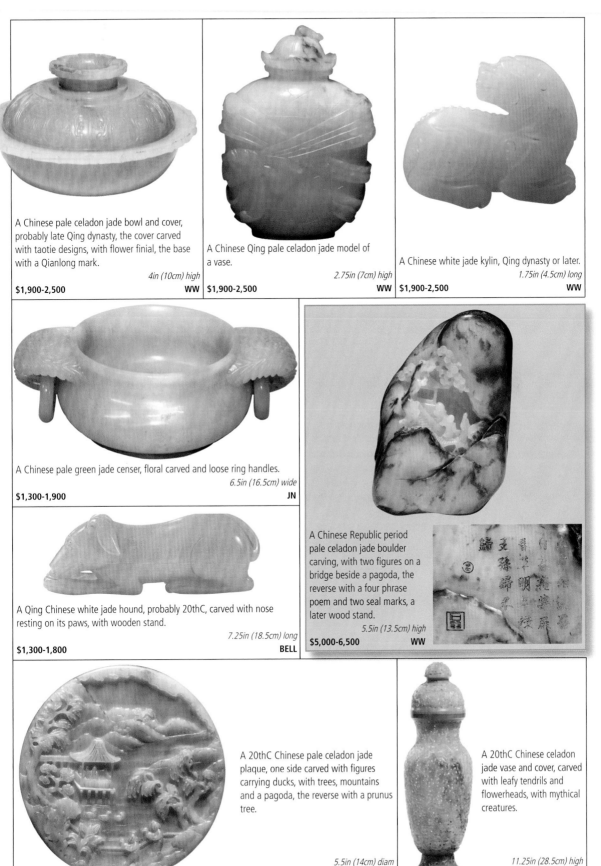

A Chinese pale celadon jade bowl and cover, probably late Qing dynasty, the cover carved with taotie designs, with flower finial, the base with a Qianlong mark.

4in (10cm) high

$1,900-2,500 **WW**

A Chinese Qing pale celadon jade model of a vase.

2.75in (7cm) high

$1,900-2,500 **WW**

A Chinese white jade kylin, Qing dynasty or later.

1.75in (4.5cm) long

$1,900-2,500 **WW**

A Chinese pale green jade censer, floral carved and loose ring handles.

6.5in (16.5cm) wide

$1,300-1,900 **JN**

A Qing Chinese white jade hound, probably 20thC, carved with nose resting on its paws, with wooden stand.

7.25in (18.5cm) long

$1,300-1,800 **BELL**

A Chinese Republic period pale celadon jade boulder carving, with two figures on a bridge beside a pagoda, the reverse with a four phrase poem and two seal marks, a later wood stand.

5.5in (13.5cm) high

$5,000-6,500 **WW**

A 20thC Chinese pale celadon jade plaque, one side carved with figures carrying ducks, with trees, mountains and a pagoda, the reverse with a prunus tree.

5.5in (14cm) diam

$4,500-5,000 **WW**

A 20thC Chinese celadon jade vase and cover, carved with leafy tendrils and flowerheads, with mythical creatures.

11.25in (28.5cm) high

$2,500-3,800 **WW**

CLOSER LOOK - TIXI LACQUER BOWLS

The design elements of this object are similar to abstract designs found on carved lacquer pieces dating to the Song (1127-1279) and Yuan (1279-1368) dynasties.

The motif carved out on the bowls is known as 'pommel scroll', since it resembles the shape of the ring-pommel on early Chinese swords.

In Chinese texts, this type of decoration is generally referred to as tixi, meaning 'marbled lacquer.'

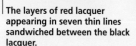

The layers of red lacquer appearing in seven thin lines sandwiched between the black lacquer.

The interiors are applied with a silver lining.

A pair of Chinese Yuan tixi lacquer bowls.

4.5in (11.5cm) diam

$18,000-23,000　　L&T

ESSENTIAL REFERENCE - RUYI

Ruyi is a curved decorative object that serves as a ceremonial scepter in Chinese Buddhism or a talisman symbolizing power and good fortune in Chinese folklore. A traditional ruyi has a long S-shaped handle and a head fashioned like a fist, cloud, or lingzhi mushroom. Ruyi are constructed from diverse materials. For example, the Palace Museum in Beijing has nearly 3000 ruyi that are variously made from valuable materials like gold, silver, iron, bamboo, wood, ivory, coral, rhinoceros horn, lacquer, crystal, jade, and precious gems. Qing Dynasty lacquer ruyi scepter. During the Qing Dynasty (1644-1912 AD), ruyi scepters became luxuriant symbols of political power that were regularly used in imperial ceremonies, and were highly valued as gifts to and from the Emperor of China.

A mid to late Qing cinnabar deeply carved lacquer ruyi scepter, the head, plaque and terminal with the Eight Buddhist Emblems, the reverse with wan diaper.

14in (35.5cm) long

$8,000-9,500　　SWO

A Chinese Qianlong carved cinnabar lacquer ingot-shaped vessel, the long exterior sides each carved with a sword, tied with a ribbon, the ends with lotus, the interior carved with prunus and lotus.

8.25in (21cm) long

$10,000-11,000　　L&T

A pair of 18thC Chinese Qing carved cinnabar lacquer 'Chrysanthemum' boxes and covers, with thirty-two lobed sides, the center of each top carved with a blossom surrounded by five registers of decoration, the feet decorated with leiwen.

7in (18cm) diam

$38,000-45,000　　L&T

A cinnabar lacquer box and cover, possibly 18thC, carved with Shou Lao and two boys under a lomquat tree.

Lacquer has been used in China since Neolithic times, and it is perhaps its durability coupled with its aesthetic properties that make it appealing to this day.

2.75in (7cm) diam

$1,200-1,400　　SWO

A Chinese Qing cinnabar lacquer vase, with mask handles, carved with figures in landscape, some minor surface splitting and losses, some staining.

12.25in (31cm) high

$3,800-5,000　　TEN

A late Qing Chinese red cinnabar lacquer vase, carved with figures in a rocky landscape with pine, maple and willow trees, the flaring neck with lotus flowers beneath a band of ruyi-heads, raised on a hardwood stand.

17.75in (45cm) high

$1,000-1,100　　WW

A Chinese lacquer scribe's box and cover, bears Kangxi reign mark, decorated with phoenix amongst peony, some surface wear and chips to angles.

13.75in (35cm) wide

$1,500-1,900　　TEN

A pair of 19thC Chinese Qing dynasty carved ocher-yellow lacquer jardinières, the rim decorated with shou characters, the exterior carved with elderly scholars and attendants, with wood stands.

8.5in (21.5cm) long

$15,000-19,000　　L&T

A 20thC Japanese Komai-style inlaid brass miniature cabinet, the doors open to five drawers, applied in gilt, the doors with a river scene with Mount Fuji, the top with cranes, the reverse with a pagoda, with gilt Mount Fuji mark, with wooden stand.

5.5in (13.5cm) high

$3,200-3,800 **BELL**

A Japanese Meiji period lacquer and mixed metal tea caddy, the exterior with river landscapes, applied in shakudo, gilt-bronze and silver, with workers in fields, the interior fitted with two canisters with sliding lids.

9.5in (24cm) wide

$450-550 **BELL**

A Japanese Meiji tortoiseshell and lacquer stationary box, ryoshibako, decorated in gold and red takamakie and silver hirame with two phoenixes, the underside of the lid with a landscape, the interior with autumn grasses, all in hiramakie, signed 'Hogetsusai Fujiwara (no) Masaaki', with kakihan.

13in (32cm) high

$1,900-2,500 **BELL**

A lacquered metal natsume, with colored carp, one, gold, leaping the waterfall, signed 'Nobuhito'.

A natsume is a type of chaki (tea caddy) used in a Japanese tea ceremony.

1930s *8.25in (21cm) high*

$1,300-1,900 **SWO**

A Japanese Edo document box and cover, bunko, decorated with gold lacquer with a kago (sedan chair), the interior with mountains, a water wheel containing a mercury waterfall, which tilts to provide the illusion of water and which turns the wheel, the background in gold nashiji.

1615-1868 *9in (22.5cm) high*

$2,500-3,800 **WW**

A Japanese Edo incense box and cover, the side wrapped in coarse red cloth covered in red lacquer, decorated in gold lacquer and gold leaf, fitted with two metal loose ring handles.

14.5in (35.5cm) wide

$1,300-1,900 **JN**

A Japanese Meiji lacquer kettle and cover, decorated in thin gold lacquer with flowerheads.

9.5in (24cm) high

$250-400 **JN**

A Japanese Meiji Shibayama box, the cover decorated in raised gilding and inlaid in Mother-of-pearl and coral with birds in shrubs, the sides decorated with birds and insects.

4.25in (10.5cm) wide

$800-950 **BELL**

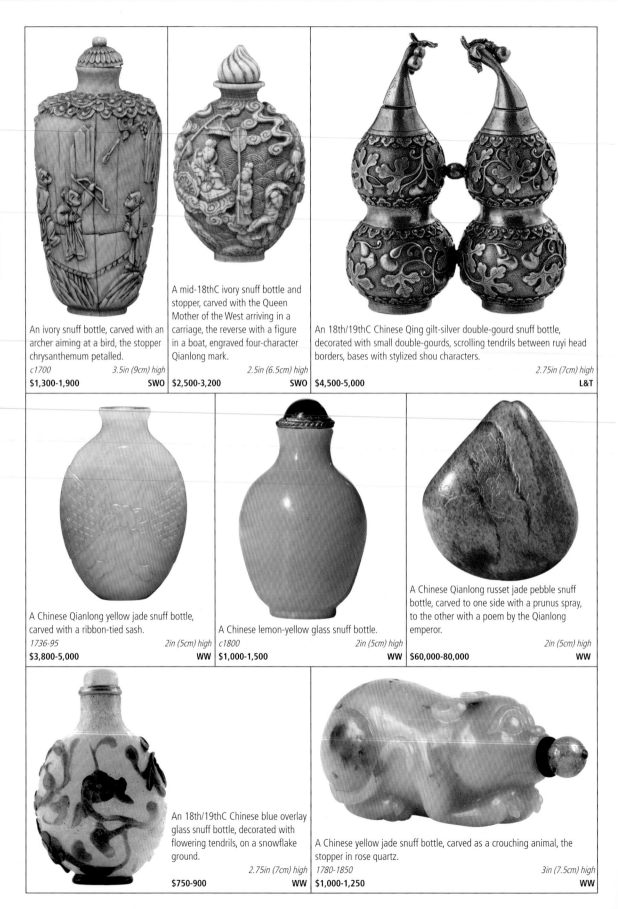

An ivory snuff bottle, carved with an archer aiming at a bird, the stopper chrysanthemum petalled.

c1700   3.5in (9cm) high
$1,300-1,900   **SWO**

A mid-18thC ivory snuff bottle and stopper, carved with the Queen Mother of the West arriving in a carriage, the reverse with a figure in a boat, engraved four-character Qianlong mark.

2.5in (6.5cm) high
$2,500-3,200   **SWO**

An 18th/19thC Chinese Qing gilt-silver double-gourd snuff bottle, decorated with small double-gourds, scrolling tendrils between ruyi head borders, bases with stylized shou characters.

2.75in (7cm) high
$4,500-5,000   **L&T**

A Chinese Qianlong yellow jade snuff bottle, carved with a ribbon-tied sash.

1736-95   2in (5cm) high
$3,800-5,000   **WW**

A Chinese lemon-yellow glass snuff bottle.

c1800   2in (5cm) high
$1,000-1,500   **WW**

A Chinese Qianlong russet jade pebble snuff bottle, carved to one side with a prunus spray, to the other with a poem by the Qianlong emperor.

2in (5cm) high
$60,000-80,000   **WW**

An 18th/19thC Chinese blue overlay glass snuff bottle, decorated with flowering tendrils, on a snowflake ground.

2.75in (7cm) high
$750-900   **WW**

A Chinese yellow jade snuff bottle, carved as a crouching animal, the stopper in rose quartz.

1780-1850   3in (7.5cm) high
$1,000-1,250   **WW**

Attributed to Youqua (Chinese, active mid 19th c.), pair of monumental China Trade oil on canvas panoramic landscapes, ca. 1840.

Sold for $768,000

Pook & Pook, Inc. provides expert appraisal services for estates, individual and corporate collections, and museums. At auction, we sell a large variety of period furniture, fine art, and decorative accessories.

463 EAST LANCASTER AVENUE, DOWNINGTOWN, PA 19335
P: (610) 269-4040 | F: (610) 269-9274
INFO@POOKANDPOOK.COM | WWW.POOKANDPOOK.COM
ONLINE BIDDING: WWW.BIDSQUARE.COM

A Chinese Qing pale celadon jade pebble snuff bottle, carved to one side with a phoenix, to the other with a four-character mark which reads 'ming feng lai yi', the stopper of red coral.

2in (5cm) high

$2,300-2,800   **WW**

A mid-19thC biscuit ginger-glazed porcelain snuff bottle, molded with a writhing dragon amongst clouds, with a coral, stained ivory and pearl stopper, engraved four character Qianlong seal mark.

2.75in (7cm) high

$3,200-3,800   **SWO**

A 19thC Chinese aragonite snuff bottle, carved with ring handles to the sides.

3in (7.5cm) high

$1,000-1,500   **WW**

A 19thC Chinese coral snuff bottle, carved to simulate bamboo, the stopper jadeite.

2.5in (6cm) high

$2,500-3,200   **WW**

A Chinese Qing tortoiseshell snuff bottle, decorated in gilt with inscriptions, one a hallmark which reads 'shi zhen xuan cang', another the collector's name Wu Rang zhi Qing Wan.

3.25in (8cm) high

$5,000-6,500   **WW**

A Chinese late Qing agate snuff bottle, carved to one side with Shoulao and an attendant.

2.75in (7cm) high

$750-1,000   **WW**

A Chinese late Qing agate snuff bottle, carved to one side with Shoulao and an attendant.

2.75in (7cm) high

$750-1,000   **WW**

A late Qing Chinese cloisonné snuff bottle, decorated with flowerheads.

3in (8cm) high

$300-400   **WW**

A rare Chinese Qianlong Beijing yellow glass water pot (zhadou), carved to the exterior with four Manchu characters, and an inscription which reads 'Qian Long yu zhi wan shou tian zi guan', the base with a tian (heaven) mark in relief, and a smaller incised bing mark, contained in a fitted silk box.

The character bing is one of the Heavenly Stems used in counting cyclical years, and is also used in inventory systems.

3in (7.5cm) diam

$25,000-32,000   WW

ESSENTIAL REFERENCE - CHINESE GLASS

Chinese glassmaking can be traced back to the Eastern Zhou period (770-256 BC). However, it was not until the Qing dynasty (1662-1722) and under the rule of the Kangxi Emperor that glass production thrived.

- The Kangxi Emperor established workshops within the palace.
- Experimentation took place, which resulted in new ways to create colored glass.
- Qing dynasty glass is often carved to reveal colored layers of glass underneath.
- Other decorating techniques involved fluting, faceting, carving with inscriptions, wheel engraving, stippling, and etching.
- Colored glass was often used to imitate jade and other hardstones, as well as other materials such as gold, amber, and coral.
- Jade craftsmen often worked in the Imperial glass workshops. This had an impact on glass designs.
- Chinese glass appears regularly at auction in small numbers.
- Prices still don't reflect those of other collecting areas, such as porcelain.

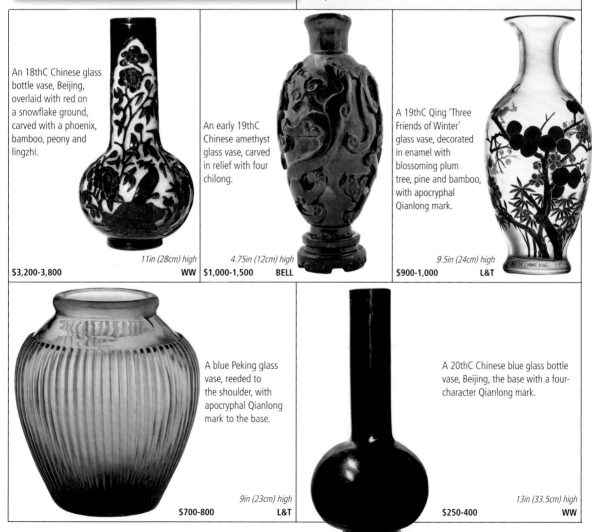

An 18thC Chinese glass bottle vase, Beijing, overlaid with red on a snowflake ground, carved with a phoenix, bamboo, peony and lingzhi.

11in (28cm) high

$3,200-3,800   WW

An early 19thC Chinese amethyst glass vase, carved in relief with four chilong.

4.75in (12cm) high

$1,000-1,500   BELL

A 19thC Qing 'Three Friends of Winter' glass vase, decorated in enamel with blossoming plum tree, pine and bamboo, with apocryphal Qianlong mark.

9.5in (24cm) high

$900-1,000   L&T

A blue Peking glass vase, reeded to the shoulder, with apocryphal Qianlong mark to the base.

9in (23cm) high

$700-800   L&T

A 20thC Chinese blue glass bottle vase, Beijing, the base with a four-character Qianlong mark.

13in (33.5cm) high

$250-400   WW

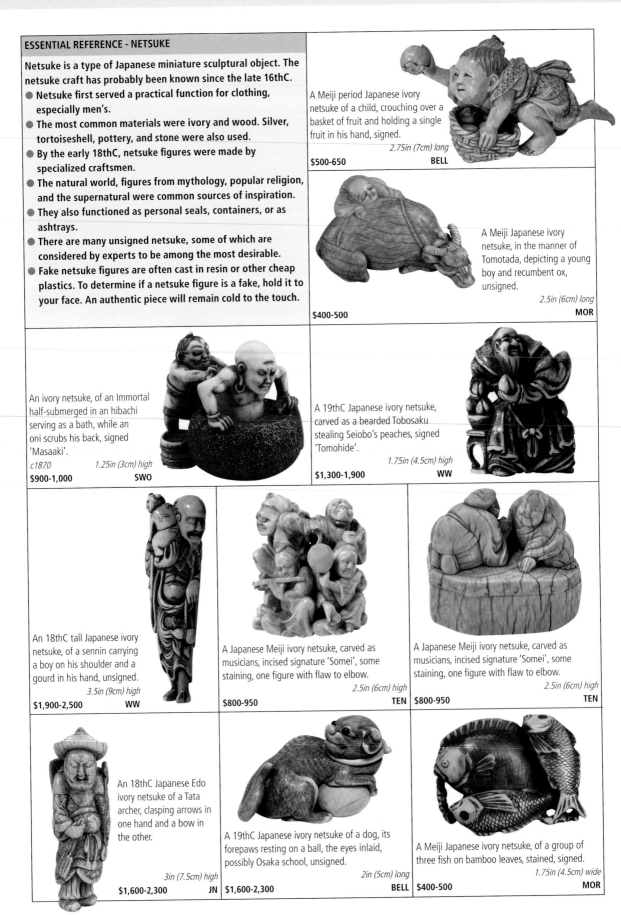

ESSENTIAL REFERENCE - NETSUKE

Netsuke is a type of Japanese miniature sculptural object. The netsuke craft has probably been known since the late 16thC.

- Netsuke first served a practical function for clothing, especially men's.
- The most common materials were ivory and wood. Silver, tortoiseshell, pottery, and stone were also used.
- By the early 18thC, netsuke figures were made by specialized craftsmen.
- The natural world, figures from mythology, popular religion, and the supernatural were common sources of inspiration.
- They also functioned as personal seals, containers, or as ashtrays.
- There are many unsigned netsuke, some of which are considered by experts to be among the most desirable.
- Fake netsuke figures are often cast in resin or other cheap plastics. To determine if a netsuke figure is a fake, hold it to your face. An authentic piece will remain cold to the touch.

A Meiji period Japanese ivory netsuke of a child, crouching over a basket of fruit and holding a single fruit in his hand, signed.

2.75in (7cm) long

$500-650   BELL

A Meiji Japanese ivory netsuke, in the manner of Tomotada, depicting a young boy and recumbent ox, unsigned.

2.5in (6cm) long

$400-500   MOR

An ivory netsuke, of an Immortal half-submerged in an hibachi serving as a bath, while an oni scrubs his back, signed 'Masaaki'.

c1870   1.25in (3cm) high

$900-1,000   SWO

A 19thC Japanese ivory netsuke, carved as a bearded Tobosaku stealing Seiobo's peaches, signed 'Tomohide'.

1.75in (4.5cm) high

$1,300-1,900   WW

An 18thC tall Japanese ivory netsuke, of a sennin carrying a boy on his shoulder and a gourd in his hand, unsigned.

3.5in (9cm) high

$1,900-2,500   WW

A Japanese Meiji ivory netsuke, carved as musicians, incised signature 'Somei', some staining, one figure with flaw to elbow.

2.5in (6cm) high

$800-950   TEN

A Japanese Meiji ivory netsuke, carved as musicians, incised signature 'Somei', some staining, one figure with flaw to elbow.

2.5in (6cm) high

$800-950   TEN

An 18thC Japanese Edo ivory netsuke of a Tata archer, clasping arrows in one hand and a bow in the other.

3in (7.5cm) high

$1,600-2,300   JN

A 19thC Japanese ivory netsuke of a dog, its forepaws resting on a ball, the eyes inlaid, possibly Osaka school, unsigned.

2in (5cm) long

$1,600-2,300   BELL

A Meiji Japanese ivory netsuke, of a group of three fish on bamboo leaves, stained, signed.

1.75in (4.5cm) wide

$400-500   MOR

A 19thC Japanese ivory netsuke, carved as two quail seated on millet, with inlaid eyes, signed 'Okatomo'.

1.5in (4cm) wide

$2,500-3,200　　　BELL

A 19thC Japanese ivory netsuke, carved as a puppy playing with an awabi shell, unsigned.

1.5in (3.5cm) high

$650-750　　　WW

CLOSER LOOK - IVORY NETSUKE

Much of the attraction of a netsuke lies in its being of its period and well-carved, this being an excellent example.

The subject is delightful - it is carved as a monkey examining a flea between his fingers.

His other hand scratching his leg where the insect has bitten him.

The hair is finely depicted and the eyes inlaid in dark and yellow horn.

It is signed 'Masatsugu' the most famous Osaka based carver renowned for his flawless technique.

A Japanese Meiji ivory netsuke.

1868-1912

2in (5cm) high

$19,000-25,000　　　WW

A 19thC Japanese ivory netsuke, carved as a sika deer, the eyes inlaid, signed 'Ranmei'.

1.5in (4cm) high

$2,500-3,200　　　WW

An early 19thC Japanese ivory netsuke, of a kirin, baring its teeth, the body covered in scales and with a long curly tail, the eyes inlaid, signed 'Gyokuzan' to the reverse.

The kirin is a mythical hooved chimerical creature known in Chinese and other East Asian cultures, said to appear with the imminent arrival or passing of a sage or illustrious ruler. It is often depicted with what looks like fire all over its body.

1.5in (4cm) high

$3,200-3,800　　　WW

An 18th/19thC Japanese ivory netsuke, carved as a fierce-looking shishi climbing on a large tama, baring its teeth.

Shishi is translated as lion but it can also refer to a deer or dog with magical properties and the power to repel evil spirits. A pair of shishi traditionally stand guard outside the gates of Japanese Shinto shrines and Buddhist temples.

The Shishi are traditionally depicted in pairs, one with mouth open and one with mouth shut. The opened/closed mouth relates to 'Ah' (open mouth) and 'N' (closed mouth). 'Ah' is the first sound in the Japanese alphabet, while 'N' (pronounced 'un') is the last. These two sounds symbolize beginning and end, birth and death.

1.75in (4.5cm) high

$1,300-1,900　　　WW

A 19thC Japanese ivory netsuke, of a hare, carved licking its right foreleg, the eyes inlaid, signed 'Ranichi'.

1in (2.5cm) high

$650-900　　　BELL

A Japanese Meiji ivory netsuke, carved as a fierce-looking shishi, its right paw resting on a reticulated brocade ball with a loose ball inside, the eyes inlaid, signed 'Kô/Mitsu Tô'.

1868-1912　　1.75in (4.5cm) high

$1,900-2,500　　　WW

A 19thC Japanese ivory netsuke, carved as a persimmon, signed 'Unsho Hakuryu' with kakihan.

1.25in (3cm) high

$2,500-3,200　　　WW

A 19thC Japanese marine ivory rysua netsuke, carved with a cock on a war drum, a hen by its side, unsigned.

1.75in (4.5cm) high

$1,300-1,900　　　WW

A Japanese Meiji period wood netsuke, signed 'Minko', carved as a child holding a mask to his face, signed to the figure's back.

1.25in (3cm) high

$1,300-1,900　　　L&T

A Japanese Meiji wood netsuke, carved as an emaciated temple servant, his straw hat misshapen by the wind, his face contorted in dismay as he holds his broken sandal, unsigned.

3.25in (8cm) high

$750-1,000   WW

A 19thC Japanese wood netsuke, of a court gardener, the himotoshi lined with green stained ivory and signed 'shumin', for Hara Shumin II.

See F Meinertzhagen, 'The Meinertzhagen Card Index on Netsuke in the Archives of the British Museum', Part B, page 775, where a netsuke of a gardener by Shumin is illustrated, possibly this very piece.

1.5in (4cm) high

$1,100-1,400   WW

A 19thC Japanese wood netsuke, carved as a tiger with a goofy expression, the eyes inlaid with brass studs, unsigned.

1.75in (4.5cm) high

$1,900-2,500   WW

A 19thC Japanese wood netsuke, carved as four rats climbing on Daikoku's mallet, the eyes inlaid, signed 'Kiyomitsu'.

1.75in (4.5cm) high

$1,000-1,500   WW

A 19thC Japanese wood netsuke, carved as a blind masseur, a tumour on the back of his head, his lifeless eye and teeth inlaid with ivory, signed 'Gyokkei'.

See F Meinertzhagen, 'The Meinertzhagen Card Index on Netsuke in the Archives of the British Museum', Part A, pages 84-85 for a biography of Gyokkei and two other examples of blind masseurs by the same carver.

1.5in (3.5cm) high

$1,300-1,900   WW

A 19thC Japanese wood netsuke, carved as a squirrel on leaves and gnawing on berries, the eyes inlaid in horn, unsigned.

2in (5cm) high

$1,800-2,300   WW

A 19thC Japanese wood netsuke, carved as a coiled rat gnawing on its tail, the eyes inlaid, unsigned.

1.75in (4.5cm) high

$1,900-2,500   WW

An 18th/19thC Japanese wood netsuke, carved as a pot-bellied tanuki seated in the pose of a maneki-neko, the eyes inlaid, signed 'Minko'.

The maneki-neko, meaning beckoning cat, is a common Japanese lucky charm, which is believed to bring good luck to the owner.

1.5in (4cm) high

$1,800-2,300   WW

A 19thC Japanese wood netsuke, carved as a shishi mask, the articulated jaw opening to a tongue and pointy teeth, the eyes inlaid, signed 'Tomokazu' with kakihan.

1.25in (3cm) high

$1,900-2,500   WW

A 19thC Japanese wood netsuke, carved as a monkey biting biwa fruit, its eyes inlaid in amber, its teeth in bone or ivory, back leg signed 'Tomokazu'.

1.25in (3cm) high

$8,000-9,500   WW

A 19thC Japanese wood netsuke, carved as a cock and hen, the eyes inlaid in horn, signed 'Okatomo'.

2.25in (5.5cm) high

$2,500-3,800   WW

A 19thC Japanese wood and metal netsuke, depicting a matchlock pistol, the iron barrel decorated with vines and flower mon in gold nunome zogan and set into a wood stock, unsigned.

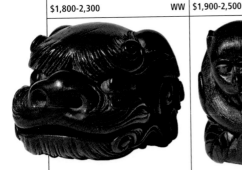

2.5in (6.5cm) high

$3,200-4,400   WW

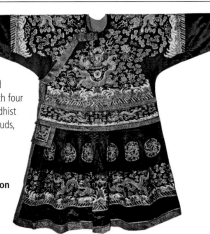

A rare mid-19thC Chinese Imperial Chaopao silk formal robe, embroidered in satin stitch and Peking knot, the upper half with four five-clawed dragons, with Buddhist emblems, bats, flowers and clouds, the skirt with thirteen dragon roundels.

Dr Wolfendale traveled to China in 1896 with the London Missionary Society, having qualified in Edinburgh as a Medical Missionary. He was appointed to the hospital in Chongqing (Chungking), where he was known as Dr Fan I Sen. He spoke fluent Chinese, and was a respected physician. In 1910 he transferred to the Canadian Missionary Society to continue his work, including rebuilding hospital buildings in Luzhou (Luchow) in 1915, and treating wounded soldiers from both sides during fighting between Yunnan and Sichuan (Szechuan) forces. Dr Wolfendale was presented with this robe as a gift in 1914 when he left Chongqing.

82in (208cm) wide

$10,000-13,000   WW

A mid-19thC Chinese silk gauze summer skirt for a robe, worked in counted stitch (petit point), with thirteen five-clawed dragons, above pairs of dragons with bats, peaches and clouds.

41in (104cm) long

$3,200-3,800   WW

A gold embroidered dragon robe, jifu, with nine five-clawed dragons in pursuit of flaming pearls, with a separate hood with couched gold dragon.

c1800s   *55in (140cm) long*

$2,300-2,800   LAW

A Qing silk kesi weave Chinese robe, jifu, woven with romance of butterflies and flora motifs, worn in places.

$9,500-10,500   LAW

A 19thC Chinese Qing embroidered dragon ladies' tabard, with a crane, three crouched gold dragons with five claws, birds, clouds, and auspicious creatures.

48in (123cm) long

$6,500-7,500   LAW

A late Qing Chinese red-brown silk dragon robe, Jifu, embroidered with nine dragons amongst cloud scrolls, flaming pearls and other auspicious things.

85.5in (209cm) wide

$3,800-5,000   WW

An early 20thC blue silk dragon robe, stitched in gilt metal threads with four claws, several loose threads, worn to shoulders, neck and back.

51in (130cm) long

$1,300-1,800   TEN

A 20thC Chinese silk robe, decorated with cranes, phoenix, peacocks with flower sprays, with a cream silk skirt, embroidered with deer, lingzhi, flower sprays and birds.

77.5in (197cm) wide

$800-950   WW

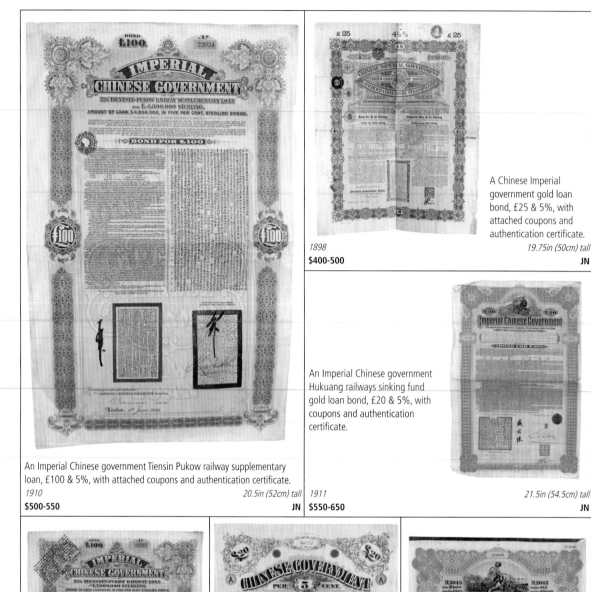

A Chinese Imperial government gold loan bond, £25 & 5%, with attached coupons and authentication certificate.

1898   *19.75in (50cm) tall*
$400-500   **JN**

An Imperial Chinese government Tiensin Pukow railway supplementary loan, £100 & 5%, with attached coupons and authentication certificate.
1910   *20.5in (52cm) tall*
$500-550   **JN**

An Imperial Chinese government Hukuang railways sinking fund gold loan bond, £20 & 5%, with coupons and authentication certificate.

1911   *21.5in (54.5cm) tall*
$550-650   **JN**

An Imperial Chinese government Tientsin Pukow railway loan bond, £100 & 5%, with attached coupons and authentication certificate.
                              20in (51cm) tall
$550-650   **JN**

A Chinese Republic government gold loan bond, £20 & 5%, with attached coupons and authentication certificate.
1912   *18in (45.5cm) tall*
$550-650   **JN**

A Chinese Republic government reorganisation gold loan bond, £100 & 5%, various currencies, with coupons and authentication certificate.
1913   *18in (45.5cm) tall*
$550-650   **JN**

A 19thC Chinese carved hardwood dragon armchair, with carved dragon arms on pierced supports carved with bats.

40in (101.5cm) high

$1,500-1,900   **MART**

A Chinese hardwood throne chair, painted in red and gilded lacquer, with carved dragons with central flaming pearl.

63in (160cm) high

$750-1,000   **CHOR**

ESSENTIAL REFERENCE - HUNTING CHAIR

Originally used only by the Emperors and princes, hunting chairs eventually became equally popular among high ranking officials. The chairs originally accompanied their owners, who often rode ahead on horse-back during hunts while male servants carried them upon their back and followed behind on foot. One of the key features of these chairs is the surface carving. Imbued with traditional Chinese symbols of positive meanings, they also indicate the owner's wealth and status. Running along the façade of the seat are auspicious Chi-dragons, and on the splat are carved fortuitous symbols of good fortune, long life and prosperity which run the gamut from lively Qilin (Chinese unicorn), via lotus blooms, to Buddhist lions and other motifs of fortune. The hunting chair can be folded with ease, and comes with a handsome attached foot-stool with brass inlay. The brass fittings on the chair lends it a sense of strength whilst providing highlights to the piece. The fine figuring and grain of the Huanghuali adds greatly to the chair's good appeal.

A Chinese late Qing dynasty huanghuali horseshoe back folding armchair, the splat with two qilin amongst clouds.

44in (112cm) high

$9,000-11,500   **L&T**

A pair of late 19th/early 20thC Chinese metal banded horseshoe back folding chairs.

51.5in (131cm) high

$1,000-1,500   **BELL**

A pair of Chinese padouk and brass-mounted folding chairs, the splats with dragon motifs.

41.75in (106cm) high

$300-350   **LOC**

A pair of early 20thC Chinese carved hardwood armchairs, each with a hardwood marble back panel.

39.5in (100.5cm) high

$1,900-2,500   **JN**

A pair of 20thC hardwood folding horseshoe back chairs, with engraved bronze fittings, the back splats carved with dragons.

37in (94cm) high

$1,500-2,000   **JN**

An early 20thC Chinese red lacquer bench, carved with dragons chasing pearls.

53in (135cm) wide

$750-1,000   **BELL**

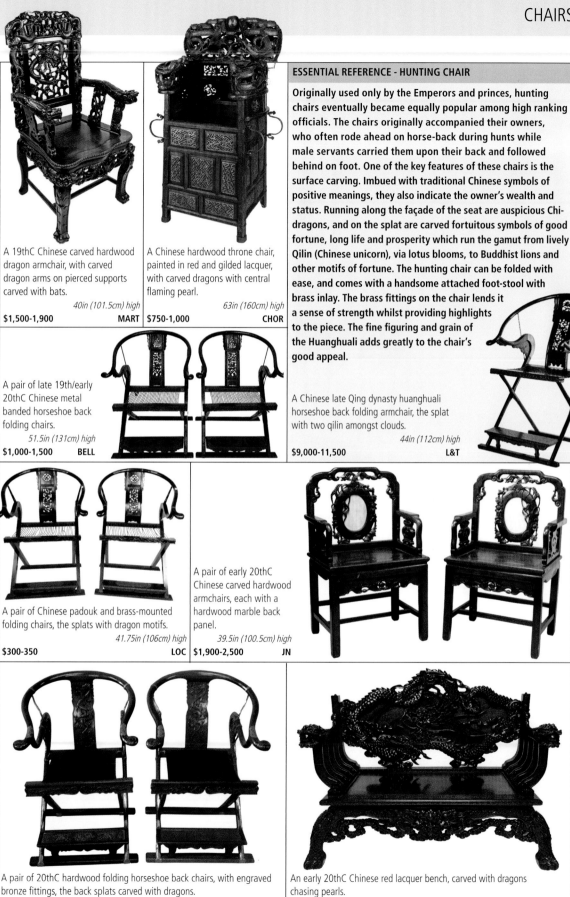

ORIENTAL

A Chinese Ming Huanghuali painting table, Pingtouan.

58in (147.5cm) long

$150,000-230,000   **L&T**

An early 19thC Chinese elm and hardwood writing table.

40in (101.5cm) long

$1,000-1,300   **MART**

A late 19thC Chinese table, with variegated marble revolving top, the base with brass collar, some cracking and damage.

35in (88.5cm) high

$28,000-35,000   **CHOR**

A late Qing Chinese hardwood side table, the frieze with lingzhi-shaped apertures.

56in (142cm) long

$800-1,000   **WW**

A 19thC Chinese Mother-of-pearl inlaid hardwood table, decorated with butterflies, birds, foliage, precious objects and a Shou medallion.

34in (86.5cm) high

$1,900-2,500   **JN**

A Chinese Qing zitan miniature altar table.

6.75in (17cm) long

$3,800-5,000   **WW**

A Chinese Ming black lacquer low table, Kang, inlaid with Mother-of-pearl, the top depicting scholars in a fenced garden, another with a deer, a crane, the apron with kylins, phoenix and Mandarin ducks.

16.5in (42cm) wide

$2,300-2,800   **WW**

A late Qing Chinese hardwood stand, inset with a marbled stone panel.

33in (84cm) high

$1,000-1,250   **WW**

A pair of 19thC Chinese marble top stands.

18in (46cm) wide

$1,000-1,300   **JN**

A late 19thC Chinese hardwood display stand, carved with two dragons to the cresting rail, and with prunus and bands of berries.

80in (204cm) high

$9,000-10,000   **WW**

ESSENTIAL REFERENCE - ZUO ZHUAN CABINET

The Chinese script to the reverse of this cabinet originates from 'Zuo Zhuan' which comprises thirty densely written chapters covering the period 722-468 BC, and focuses primarily on diplomatic and political affairs of that period. The text is from one of the chapters named 'Year Five of King Xi', and narrates the following piece of history: In 655 BC Kingdom Jin planned to attack Kingdom Guo, and Kingdom Yu was in the middle between the two kingdoms geographically. Hence Jin's ambition was to take Guo first and then attack Yu by overrunning Jin's troops within Yu's territory. Yu's minister Gong Zhiqi figured out the plan and advised the king of Yu not to allowing Jin to do so by saying 'if the lips were gone, the teeth would be cold'. Yet the King refused to take his advice and was captured by Jin's troops.

A 19thC Chinese rosewood cabinet on stand, carved with figures in stylized landscapes.

44.5in (113cm) wide

$1,900-2,500   **MOR**

A 19thC Chinese red and black lacquer cabinet, decorated with figures in lanscapes, gardens, and flowers.

71.75in (182cm) high

$1,100-1,400   **L&T**

A late 18th/early 19thC Chinese black coromandel lacquer and gilt-decorated cabinet on stand, with carved decoration depicting figures and traditional buildings, doors opening to incised decoration throughout depicting vases of flowers, trees, birds and dragons, on a later stand.

58.75in (149cm) high

$5,000-6,500   **DN**

A late 19thC Oriental rosewood open cabinet, with applied carved key pattern and foliate borders.

35in (89cm) wide

$10,000-11,000   **TRI**

An early 20thC Chinese hardwood display cabinet, carved with flowers and scrolls.

72.5in (184cm) high

$7,500-9,000   **WW**

A 19thC Chinese export lacquer cabinet, with a fitted interior, the base with a writing slide and single drawer, profusely decorated in gilt.

27.5in (70cm) wide

$1,500-2,300   **CHOR**

A Chinese hardwood alter table, with bronze fittings.

54.5in (138.5cm) wide

$3,800-5,000   JN

A 17th/18thC Chinese black lacquer table cabinet, the front panel removable to reveal two drawers divided by two smaller drawers the interior lacquered red with gilt splashes, the fittings paktong, depicting a garden scene of boys and scholars amongst trees, with pagodas beneath clouds in the distance.

13.75in (35cm) high

$10,000-13,000   WW

A 19thC Chinese Qing dynasty huanghuali box, with original metal clasps and corners.

7.75in (20cm) long

$3,800-5,000   L&T

A 19thC Chinese camphor wood chest, with a frieze carved with two dragons amongst scrolls, mounted on rollers.

65.75in (167cm) wide

$3,200-3,800   WW

An 18th/19thC Chinese Qing huanghuali seal chest, with original metal hardware and hasp.

14.25in (36cm) high

$13,000-18,000   L&T

An early 20thC Chinese hardwood writing desk, carved with a vine and flowers.

53.5in (136cm) high

$2,500-3,200   WW

An early 18thC Japanese black and gilt-lacquer cabinet, on English giltwood stand, the cabinet decorated with landscape scenes, enclosing drawers.

64in (162.5cm) high

$50,000-55,000   L&T

An early 18thC Japanese black lacquer cabinet on stand, decorated with a landscape, the inner faces with exotic birds, on a japanned stand of George II period with cabriole legs carved with 'Green Man' masks to the knees, some damage.

53in (135cm) high

$5,000-6,500   TEN

A late Qing and earlier Chinese hardwood, lacquer and jade six-panel screen, carved with scholar's objects and Buddhist emblems.

85in (216cm) wide

$28,000-35,000 **WW**

A 19thC Chinese eight panel black and gold lacquer screen, painted with mountainous pagoda landscapes, with figures in boats, pine and willow trees.

170in (432cm) wide

$3,800-4,400 **WW**

A six-fold screen, each leaf with two porcelain plaques enameled with insects, foliage, landscapes, each signed, mounted in carved wood flowers between relief He-He Erxian.

c1930 *57.75in (146.5cm) high*

$3,800-4,400 **SWO**

A 20thC large mixed media panel, with a cloisonné vase issuing jade and soapstone lotus and flowers with Mother-of-pearl calligraphy, above a cloisonné elephant.

46in (117cm) high

$5,000-6,500 **SWO**

A 17thC Chinese ivory panel, decorated to one side with a mountain landscape, with figures, the reverse with an inscription and three seal marks, in a hardwood frame.

14.5in (36.5cm) wide

$1,900-2,500 **WW**

A Chinese Qing dreamstone table-screen, simulating a rocky ravine beneath a stormy sky, in a carved hardwood stand.

19in (48.5cm) high

$1,300-1,900 **WW**

A lapis lazuli matrix table screen, on carved hardwood stand, carved with pavilions amongst pine trees in cloud shrouded mountains.

the stone of the screen 8.5in (22cm) high

$1,300-1,900 **CHEF**

A Japanese Meiji carved jade tablet, set in a carved wood frame.

8.25in (21cm) high

$650-750 **TRI**

THE FURNITURE MARKET

The furniture market has continued to be very polarised. The 'brown furniture' market has continued to fall. Most auctioneers are reporting that the plain utilitarian 18thC and 19thC mahogany is proving difficult, if not impossible, to sell. Some dealers are quoting a substantial drop in prices and a general lack of interest. I recently answered a letter to a lady whose parents were moving from a large house with very large Victorian furniture of 'average quality'. It is extremely difficult to advise as the demand is just not there. At the other end, quality furniture that is really top quality, fresh to the market and 'honest', continues to rise in value. It is not just age that determines the value of a piece of furniture, quality and condition and 'eye appeal' are all important factors. At the BADA 2017 fair the London furniture dealer Godson & Coles sold an exceptional early 18thC japanned bureau cabinet for a six-figure sum.

The reasons for the decline in value of 'average', mid-range furniture is complex, most of it is down to fashion. Younger buyers believe that old mahogany furniture is just not 'cool' and does not fit into today's interiors. There is also a lack of really good quality examples on the market. Another problem is that vendors are reluctant to enter good antique furniture to auction while prices are depressed.

Pieces that are too bulky for modern interiors need to be of exceptional quality to attract buyers. There is no doubt that Georgian and especially Regency pieces sell better than their heavy Victorian counterparts. Also pieces like the Davenport, Canterbury and bureau do not have any real function in today's interiors. 'Georgian brown' or just brown furniture has nose-dived in value whereas 20thC, especially Mid-century Modern, furniture has continued its renaissance. Many dealers record that American buyers are still not coming in their previous numbers and this has had a dramatic effect on export sales.

However, good quality American furniture is doing very well.

So has the low- to mid-range furniture market reached its nadir? Some of the prices achieved at auction are ridiculously low. These pieces are made of solid wood, by craftsmen and not merely fashioned out of MDF (medium-density fibreboard which is quite simply wood fibres, combined with wax and a resin binder). There are some indicators that prices may be beginning to climb slightly. People are being persuaded that 'antiques are green' and that recycling old furniture is more responsible than cutting down more of the Amazon jungle. Also with some prices so low, younger buyers are looking at auctions when furnishing their first flat or house. Sturdy, good-quality, highly functional pieces are excellent value for money. These pieces could well provide good investment potential, as prices should increase when (and if!) the economy improves.

Above: A George I walnut and featherbanded kneehole desk, the fitted frieze drawer opening to a baize inset sliding writing surface, the space beneath with divisions and a concealed small drawer to one side, with key, marks, scratches and abrasions commensurate with age and use.

c1720   *34.25in (87cm) high*

$20,000-25,000   **DN**

Top Left: A Gustav Stickley leather-top lamp table, original leather and tacks to top, extensive ring stains, several gouges, deep scratches to top.

c1908   *40.5in (103cm) wide*

$3,800-5,000   **DRA**

FURNITURE

UK PERIOD	USA PERIOD	FRENCH PERIOD	GERMAN PERIOD
Elizabethan *Elizabeth I (1558-1603)*		**Renaissance** *(to c1610)*	**Renaissance** *(to c1650)*
Jacobean *James I (1603-1625)*			
Carolean *Charles I (1625-1649)*	**Early Colonial** *(1620s-1700)*	**Louis XIII** *(1610-1643)*	
Cromwellian *Commonwealth (1649-1660)*			
Restoration *Charles II (1660-1685)* *James II (1685-1688)*		**Louis XIV** *(1643-1715)*	**Renaissance/ Baroque** *(c1650-1700)*
William and Mary *(1689-1694)*	**William and Mary** *(1690-1720)*		
William III *(1694-1702)*			
Queen Anne *(1702-1714)*	**Queen Anne** *(1720-50)*		**Baroque** *(c1700-1730)*
Early Georgian *George I (1714-1727)* *George II (1727-1760)*		**Régence** *(1715-1723)*	
	Chippendale *(1750-1790)*	**Louis XV** *(1723-1774)*	**Rococo** *(c1730-1760)*
Late Georgian *George III (1760-1811)*	**EARLY FEDERAL** *(1790-1810)* **American Directoire** *(1798-1804)* **American Empire** *(1804-1815)*	**Louis XVI** *(1774-1792)*	**Neo-classicism** *(c1760-1800)*
		Directoire *(1792-1799)*	**Empire** *(c1800-1815)*
		Empire *(1799-1815)*	
Regency *George III (1812-1820)*	**Later Federal** *(1810-1830)*	**Restauration** *(1815-1830)*	**Biedermeier** *(c1815-1848)*
George IV *(1820-1830)*		*Louis XVIII (1814-1824)* *Charles X (1824-1830)*	
William IV *(1830-1837)*		**Louis Phillipe** *(1830-1848)*	**Revivale** *(c1830-1880)*
Victorian *Victoria (1837-1901)*	**Victorian** *(1840-1900)*	**2nd Empire** *(1848-1870)*	
Edwardian *Edward VII (1901-1910)*		**3rd Republic** *(1871-1940)*	**Jugendstil** *(c1880-1920)*

A 17thC carved and inlaid wainscot oak chair, with old repairs and restoration.

42.5in (108cm) high

$450-550   **CHEF**

An 18thC yew wood and elm corner armchair, later elm panel seat.

It is considered that there would have originally been a rush seat.

31.5in (80cm) high

$450-500   **CHEF**

A William and Mary walnut elbow dining chair, with carved and pierced crest rail, later upholstered seat, some old worm.

52in (132cm) high

$250-400   **CHEF**

A 17thC oak chair, the carved arched horizontal splats to a solid seat on turned front legs united by stretchers.

$250-400   **CHOR**

A 17thC and later carved oak open armchair, the top rail centered by a crown, with later bun feet.

$250-320   **BE**

A George I oak wainscot armchair.
c1720

$1,800-2,300   **POOK**

Two similar 18thC Italian carved walnut side chairs, with gouged and arcaded spindle backs.

$150-190   **BE**

A pair of South Yorkshire oak chairs, with crescent and acorn backs.

39.75in (101cm) high

$400-500   **CHEF**

FURNITURE

ESSENTIAL REFERENCE - COUNTRY CHAIRS

The Windsor is a type of country chair. It is one of the best-known in Britain and North America.

● Examples date back to the 17thC.
● They are characterized by solid saddle seats into which are dowelled the bow and the turned or rounded spindles and legs.
● Common materials used in Britain are: elm, ash, yew, or beech.
● In North America, pine, poplar, ash, hickory, or oak were used.
● There are two basic types: the comb-back (horizontal toprail) and the hoop-back (also called bow-back).
● High Wycombe, Buckinghamshire, was a major British center of production.
● Their appeal partly lies in a restrained but elegant use of ornamentation.

A late 18thC fan-backed Windsor armchair, branded 'D._aker' on underside.

$550-700   POOK

One of a pair of 18thC elm and ash stick-back Windsor chairs.

$250-320 pair   WHP

A George III ash and elm hoop-back Windsor chair.

$1,000-1,500   BELL

A George III ash and elm stick-back Windsor chair, with unusual arm support.

$1,500-1,900   BELL

An early 19thC yew child's Windsor rocking chair, with an elm seat, with a crinoline stretcher on sleigh rockers.

$3,200-3,800   WW

An early/mid-18thC Thames Valley elm and fruitwood armchair, with vase-shaped splat and turned spindle rails.

$4,500-5,000   SWO

An early 19thC yew highback Windsor armchair, with a pierced splat back, above an elm seat.

$650-750   WW

An early 19thC yew and elm lowback Windsor armchair.

22.5in (57cm) high

$700-800   L&T

A 19thC yew lowback Windsor armchair, with an elm seat.

$300-350   WW

A pair of Gothic Windsor yew wood and elm armchairs.
$1,500-1,900   TRI

A mid-18thC cherry and elm comb-back Windsor armchair, attributed to John Pitt.
$2,500-3,800   WW

A set of four mid-19thC yew Windsor armchairs, attributed to the family of Robert Prior, Uxbridge, Middlesex.
21.75in (55cm) high
$2,800-3,300   HT

A matched set of four Windsor splat-back armchairs, one in yew wood, all with Christmas tree motifs to the splats, dished elm seats and crinoline stretchers.
$750-900   CHOR

A pair of yew and elm Windsor armchairs, with crinoline stretcher, with pierced fret-cut splats.
$450-500   MOR

A 20thC yew and inlaid Windsor chair, with kangaroo motif to top rail and burr seat.

The kangaroo motif relates to the 'Aussie Earl' 6th Earl of Stradbroke. The wood sourced from their English seat Henham Park, Southwold.
50in (127cm) high
$650-750   DN

A 19thC yew wood and burr wood child's high chair, with added oak foot rest, replaced foot rest in oak.
37.5in (95cm) high
$400-500   CHEF

An early 20thC mahogany spindle high-backed armchair with a horn-type back rail.
$80-90   WHP

Three of a harlequin set of eight late 18th/early 19thC ash and fruitwood spindleback dining chairs.
$650-750 set   BE

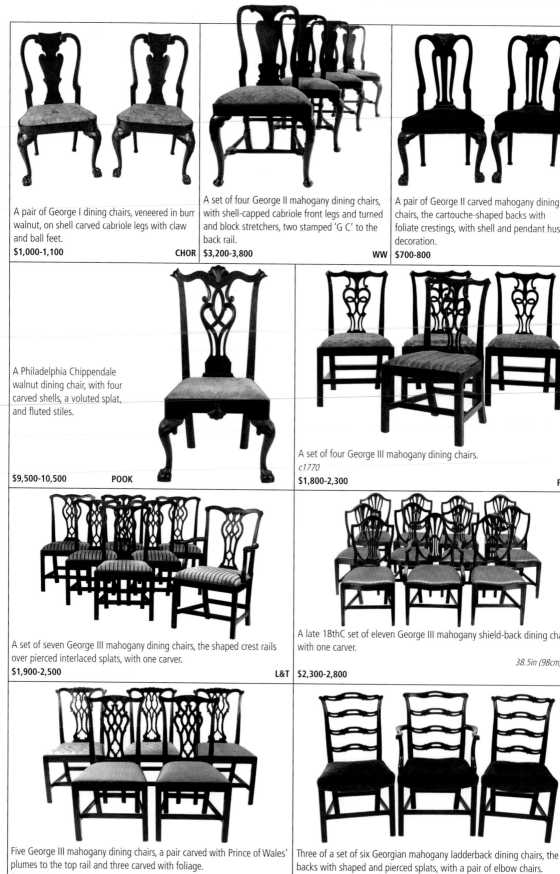

A pair of George I dining chairs, veneered in burr walnut, on shell carved cabriole legs with claw and ball feet.
$1,000-1,100   CHOR

A set of four George II mahogany dining chairs, with shell-capped cabriole front legs and turned and block stretchers, two stamped 'G C' to the back rail.
$3,200-3,800   WW

A pair of George II carved mahogany dining chairs, the cartouche-shaped backs with foliate crestings, with shell and pendant husk decoration.
$700-800   BE

A Philadelphia Chippendale walnut dining chair, with four carved shells, a voluted splat, and fluted stiles.
$9,500-10,500   POOK

A set of four George III mahogany dining chairs.
c1770
$1,800-2,300   POOK

A set of seven George III mahogany dining chairs, the shaped crest rails over pierced interlaced splats, with one carver.
$1,900-2,500   L&T

A late 18thC set of eleven George III mahogany shield-back dining chairs, with one carver.
38.5in (98cm) high
$2,300-2,800   TEN

Five George III mahogany dining chairs, a pair carved with Prince of Wales' plumes to the top rail and three carved with foliage.
$500-650   WW

Three of a set of six Georgian mahogany ladderback dining chairs, the backs with shaped and pierced splats, with a pair of elbow chairs.
$650-750 set   BE

A set of eight late 18thC George III stained ash dining chairs, in the Sheraton style, the square backs with a shell vasiform pieced splat carved with Prince of Wales plumes, with two carvers.

$950-1,100 L&T

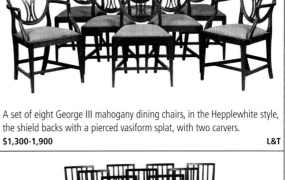

A set of eight George III mahogany dining chairs, in the Hepplewhite style, the shield backs with a pierced vasiform splat, with two carvers.

$1,300-1,900 L&T

A set of twelve George III mahogany dining chairs, with molded frames and pierced splats, on square tapering legs with spade feet, with two carvers.

c1800 *36.75in (93cm) high*

$5,500-7,000 TEN

A set of eleven George III mahogany dining chairs, with molded backs with four vertical splats, with two carvers.

$1,900-3,200 WW

Three of a set of six Regency mahogany dining chairs, the backs with ebony inlaid molded curved bar top rails on reeded square tapered legs, terminating in spade feet.

$1,100-1,500 set BE

Three of a set of six Regency mahogany dining chairs, the backs with reeded and boxwood and ebony strung curved bar top rails.

$650-750 set BE

A set of twelve Regency rosewood dining chairs, the spiral carved top rails above scrolling open work horizontal splats centered by a foliate brass inlaid panel, with two carvers.

c1815

$5,000-6,500 L&T

An early 19thC set of fourteen mahogany and ebony strung dining chairs, with part wrythen-turned back supports, raised on reeded sabre forelegs, some loose joints, with two carvers.

33.5in (85cm) high

$5,000-6,500 TEN

Two of a set of twelve George IV mahogany frame dining chairs, the carved waist rail centered by a Tudor rose, on sabre supports, with drop-in seats mostly stamped 'TV' or 'TB'.

$1,000-1,500 set BELL

FURNITURE

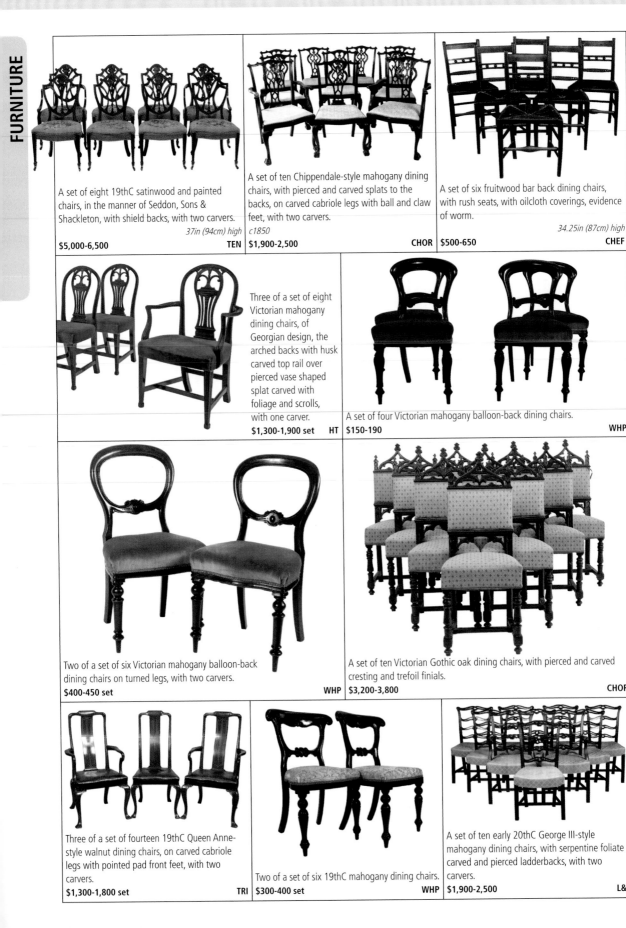

A set of eight 19thC satinwood and painted chairs, in the manner of Seddon, Sons & Shackleton, with shield backs, with two carvers.

37in (94cm) high

$5,000-6,500   **TEN**

A set of ten Chippendale-style mahogany dining chairs, with pierced and carved splats to the backs, on carved cabriole legs with ball and claw feet, with two carvers.

c1850

$1,900-2,500   **CHOR**

A set of six fruitwood bar back dining chairs, with rush seats, with oilcloth coverings, evidence of worm.

34.25in (87cm) high

$500-650   **CHEF**

Three of a set of eight Victorian mahogany dining chairs, of Georgian design, the arched backs with husk carved top rail over pierced vase shaped splat carved with foliage and scrolls, with one carver.

$1,300-1,900 set   **HT**

A set of four Victorian mahogany balloon-back dining chairs.

$150-190   **WHP**

Two of a set of six Victorian mahogany balloon-back dining chairs on turned legs, with two carvers.

$400-450 set   **WHP**

A set of ten Victorian Gothic oak dining chairs, with pierced and carved cresting and trefoil finials.

$3,200-3,800   **CHOR**

Three of a set of fourteen 19thC Queen Anne-style walnut dining chairs, on carved cabriole legs with pointed pad front feet, with two carvers.

$1,300-1,800 set   **TRI**

Two of a set of six 19thC mahogany dining chairs.

$300-400 set   **WHP**

A set of ten early 20thC George III-style mahogany dining chairs, with serpentine foliate carved and pierced ladderbacks, with two carvers.

$1,900-2,500   **L&T**

FURNITURE

ESSENTIAL REFERENCE - GILES GRENDEY

Giles Grendey became an apprentice in 1709, and by 1716 was taking on his own apprentices. He had a workshop in St John's Square, Clerkenwell from where he ran a successful, largely export business. He made a large selection of furniture including tables, chairs, mirrors and case furniture. However, although it is known that he had a thriving workshop, firm attributions are rare, with little evidence of bills in country house records and few pieces still in existence bearing one of his two trade labels. The distinct shell-back design of these chairs relates to a number of sets of chairs that have been attributed to Grendey. Most notably, records show he supplied one such group to Henry Hoare of Stourhead between 1746 and 1756. These include twelve parcel-gilt and fourteen mahogany chairs.

Comparative Literature: Anthony Coleridge, Chippendale Furniture, Faber and Faber, 1968, fig 140 Ralph Edwards, The Shorter Dictionary of English Furniture, Country Life, 1964, fig 107.

A pair of George II walnut chairs, attributed to Giles Grendey, each cartouche-shaped back carved with acanthus terminals throughout and with elaborate molded and pierced splat, on tapering cabriole legs headed by scrolling foliate carved terminals and on carved claw and ball feet, old visible repair to upper corner of each back.

c1735   38.5in (98cm) high
$15,000-19,000   **DN**

A George II Irish mahogany side chair.
$3,200-3,800   **WW**

Judith Picks

These chairs have great provenance and this certainly makes them very desirable. These 'cabriolet' chairs form part of a suite of at least seventeen supplied to George John, 2nd Earl Spencer (1758-1834) either for Spencer House, London or Althorp, Northamptonshire. They relate to chairs by François Hervé supplied for Chatsworth in 1782, which were conceived in a more 'transitional' style. While Hervé restricted himself to chair-making and sometimes caning, the 'japanned'

ornament and gilding was outsourced. A bill presented to Spencer's brother-in-law the 5th Duke of Devonshire by Bickley in 1782 included 'japanned seven dozen backstools cane color' (see I. Hall, 'A neoclassical episode at Chatsworth', The Burlington Magazine, volume 122, June 1980, pages 400-414, fig 39). The 'Curator' 7th Earl recorded that 'many of these chairs had been put away in the stables and were gilded and covered in silk in 1877/78.'

A set of eight George III parcel gilt side chairs, attributed to François Hérve, almost certainly supplied by Henry Holland, each with a husk and guilloche-carved oval caned back above a serpentine seat, on turned tapering fluted legs with stiff-leaf toupie feet, decorations refreshed.

c1791   38.25in (97cm) high
$19,000-25,000   **DN**

A set of six early 19thC Regency rosewood and cane seated music room chairs, the top rails inlaid with brass musical trophies, some damage.
32.25in (82cm) high
$650-750   **TEN**

A set of four George IV simulated rosewood side chairs.
$230-280   **WW**

Six William IV yew wood Gothic side chairs, in the manner of George Smith, with arcaded pierced backs, pierced seat rails.

Closely related designs for 'Parlour Chairs' and 'Drawing Room Chairs' were published in George Smith's 'Collection of Designs for Household Furniture and Interior Decoration', 1808, plates 37 and 54.
$4,400-5,700   **DN**

A pair of 19thC walnut child's chairs, in George II-style, the shell crestings flanked by inward scrolling toprails, on cabriole legs with shell motifs to the knees and claw and ball feet.
$4,400-5,700   **DN**

FURNITURE

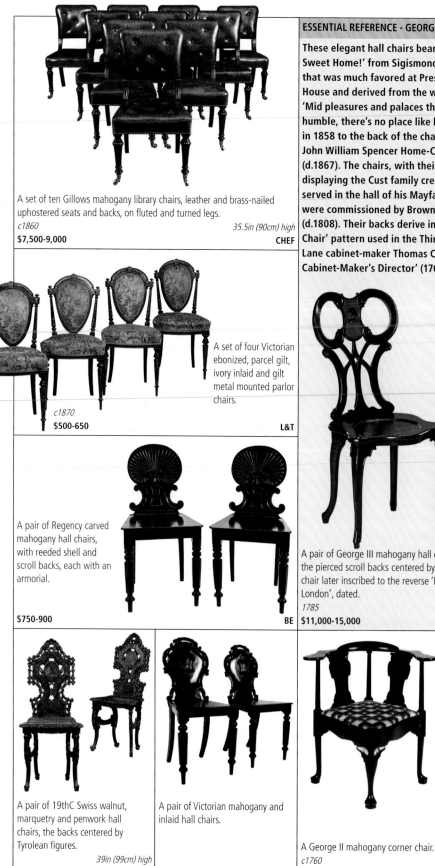

A set of ten Gillows mahogany library chairs, leather and brass-nailed upholstered seats and backs, on fluted and turned legs.
c1860   *35.5in (90cm) high*
$7,500-9,000   **CHEF**

A set of four Victorian ebonized, parcel gilt, ivory inlaid and gilt metal mounted parlor chairs.
c1870
$500-650   **L&T**

A pair of Regency carved mahogany hall chairs, with reeded shell and scroll backs, each with an armorial.

$750-900   **BE**

A pair of 19thC Swiss walnut, marquetry and penwork hall chairs, the backs centered by Tyrolean figures.
39in (99cm) high
$900-1,000   **L&T**

A pair of Victorian mahogany and inlaid hall chairs.

$230-280   **WHP**

ESSENTIAL REFERENCE - GEORGE III CHAIRS

These elegant hall chairs bear the patriotic inscription 'Home! Sweet Home!' from Sigismond Thalberg's 1857 composition that was much favored at President Abraham Lincoln's White House and derived from the words of John Payne's 1823 opera, 'Mid pleasures and palaces though we may roam, be it ever so humble, there's no place like home'. The inscription was added in 1858 to the back of the chairs which belonged to the Hon. John William Spencer Home-Cust, later 2nd Earl Brownlow (d.1867). The chairs, with their rich ribbon-fretted backs displaying the Cust family crest on an azure blue shield, had served in the hall of his Mayfair home since 1785, when they were commissioned by Brownlow Cust, 1st Baron Brownlow (d.1808). Their backs derive in particular from a 1759 'Hall Chair' pattern used in the Third Edition of the St. Martin's Lane cabinet-maker Thomas Chippendale's, 'Gentleman and Cabinet-Maker's Director' (1762).

A pair of George III mahogany hall chairs, in the manner of Chippendale, the pierced scroll backs centered by painted armorial cartouches, one chair later inscribed to the reverse 'Home, Sweet Home, 30 Hill Street London', dated.
1785   *19in (48cm) wide*
$11,000-15,000   **DN**

A George II mahogany corner chair.
c1760
$700-800   **POOK**

An Edwardian mahogany and inlaid corner chair.
$130-180   **WHP**

A Charles I oak long stool or bench, the seat with molded edge above a frieze with decorative shaped apron and turned supports joined by an 'H'-shaped stretcher, marks, scratches and abrasions consistent with age and use patch to the top.

c1630

71.75in (182cm) long

$16,000-23,000

DN

A George II carved walnut stool, the square cabriole legs carved at the knees with acanthus leaves.

This stool belongs to a small group of carved George II walnut stools which feature similar cabriole legs of almost square section, headed by crisply carved flowing acanthus leaves and ending in heavy claw and ball feet. A comparable pair of stools were discovered in the 1990s, one of these is stamped with the initials 'IDS' which are possibly those of the cabinet-maker.

22.75in (58cm) wide

$15,000-18,000

DN

A rare American Windsor kettle stand, Pennsylvania or Southern, with a slate top and splayed walnut legs.

c1790

24.75in (63cm) high

$3,800-5,000

POOK

A Regency mahogany and upholstered stool, on scrolled and acanthus leaf supports.

32.75in (83cm) wide

$300-350

WHP

ESSENTIAL REFERENCE - A PAIR OF GEORGE IV STOOLS

The underlying rail of one stool is incised with numerals 'I & II' ,and the other 'V & VI'. This would imply that they were part of a longer set of stools. The design of these stools relates to the Wentworth Woodhouse giltwood suite supplied by Gillows in 1832 to the 4th Earl Fitzwilliam (also stamped 'H H'). See Susan E. Stuart, 'Gillows of Lancaster and London 1730-1840', Antique Collectors Club, 2008 (page 243, volume II). In further support of these stools having been made in Gillows workshop, the stretcher rails of both lots are stamped 'H H' twice. According to Susan Stuart's book (page 244, vol.II) 'H H' is one of the most common initial stamps on Gillow's chairs made during the first half of the 19thC. One set of twenty four chairs from Mere Hall, Cheshire were inscribed with the firm's name and in particular one chair inscribed 'H Howard W Yates Brook/ Mere' in addition to the 'H H' stamp suggests that 'H H' could be Henry Howard. However it could also stand for Henry Holmes. It is possible that these stools were made for the remodelling of Burlington House in the early 19thC by the 1st Earl of Burlington.

One of a pair of George IV carved mahogany stools, attributed to Gillows of Lancaster, each needlework-covered seat depicting three roses above the plain freeze on profusely acanthus-carved scroll legs, the underside of each central stretcher stamped 'H H' to each end on concealed brass casters, some damage.

c1825

50in (128cm) wide

$13,000-18,000 pair

DN

A 19thC carved giltwood stool, in the manner of Henry Williams, of curule form, decorated with carved Venus shells on acanthus-adorned trusses, terminating in bacchic lion paw feet.

28.5in (72.5cm) wide

$3,800-5,000

DN

A 19thC Louis XV-style Kingwood and gilt bronze mounted stool.

19.5in (50cm) high

$550-700

L&T

A Victorian carved walnut curved X-frame stool.

$180-250

BE

A pair of late 19th/early 20thC Italian walnut and parcel-gilt grotto stools, with revolving seats carved in the round as an open shell, with lions paw feet.

26.5in (67cm) high

$3,800-5,000

HW

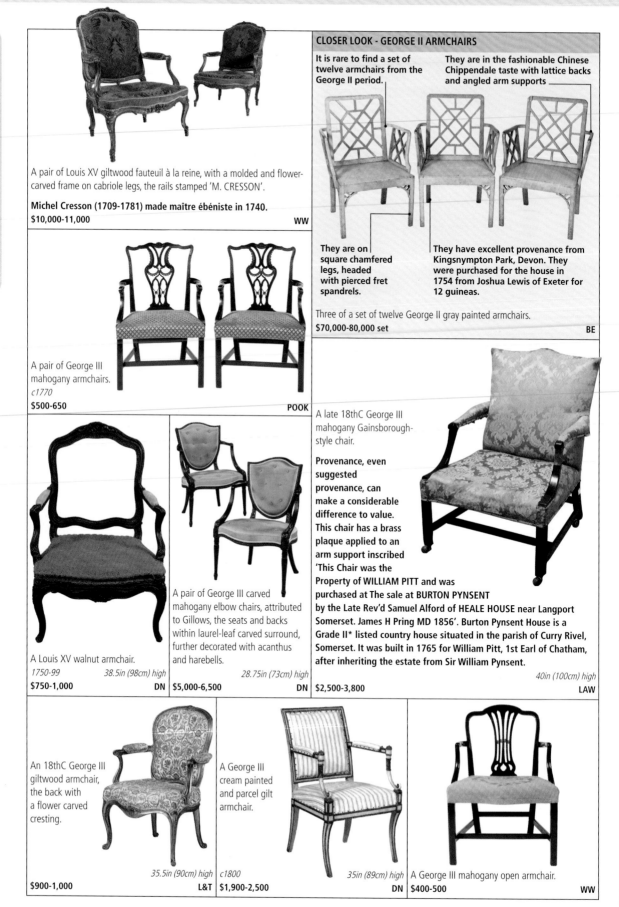

A pair of Louis XV giltwood fauteuil à la reine, with a molded and flower-carved frame on cabriole legs, the rails stamped 'M. CRESSON'.

Michel Cresson (1709-1781) made maître ébéniste in 1740.
$10,000-11,000   WW

CLOSER LOOK - GEORGE II ARMCHAIRS

It is rare to find a set of twelve armchairs from the George II period.

They are in the fashionable Chinese Chippendale taste with lattice backs and angled arm supports

They are on square chamfered legs, headed with pierced fret spandrels.

They have excellent provenance from Kingsnympton Park, Devon. They were purchased for the house in 1754 from Joshua Lewis of Exeter for 12 guineas.

Three of a set of twelve George II gray painted armchairs.
$70,000-80,000 set   BE

A pair of George III mahogany armchairs.
c1770
$500-650   POOK

A Louis XV walnut armchair.
1750-99   *38.5in (98cm) high*
$750-1,000   DN

A pair of George III carved mahogany elbow chairs, attributed to Gillows, the seats and backs within laurel-leaf carved surround, further decorated with acanthus and harebells.
28.75in (73cm) high
$5,000-6,500   DN

A late 18thC George III mahogany Gainsborough-style chair.

Provenance, even suggested provenance, can make a considerable difference to value. This chair has a brass plaque applied to an arm support inscribed 'This Chair was the Property of WILLIAM PITT and was purchased at The sale at BURTON PYNSENT by the Late Rev'd Samuel Alford of HEALE HOUSE near Langport Somerset. James H Pring MD 1856'. Burton Pynsent House is a Grade II* listed country house situated in the parish of Curry Rivel, Somerset. It was built in 1765 for William Pitt, 1st Earl of Chatham, after inheriting the estate from Sir William Pynsent.
40in (100cm) high
$2,500-3,800   LAW

An 18thC George III giltwood armchair, the back with a flower carved cresting.
35.5in (90cm) high
$900-1,000   L&T

A George III cream painted and parcel gilt armchair.
c1800   *35in (89cm) high*
$1,900-2,500   DN

A George III mahogany open armchair.
$400-500   WW

A pair of Empire parcel-gilt armchairs, possibly Russian, with top rail carved with floral motif, above open arms with carved swan terminals.
c1810   *40.25in (102cm) high*
$3,800-5,000   **DN**

A pair of Regency mahogany library chairs, the rectangular caned backs, seats and arm supports with paneled moldings, splayed square rear legs terminating in brass cappings and castors, with loose back and seat cushions.
23.75in (60cm) wide
$9,000-10,000   **DN**

One of a pair of Regency simulated rosewood library armchairs, the backs with scroll-over top rails and scrolling uprights, with gilt metal mounts throughout, elements replaced.
37in (94cm) high
$13,000-18,000 pair   **DN**

One of a pair of early 19thC Italian mahogany armchairs, the floral inlaid back rests with unusual protruding carved lion's heads, the arms with boxwood stringing and carved acanthus decoration, terminating in fantastical masks, with outswept back sabre legs, on brass castors.
24.5in (62cm) wide
$6,500-7,500 pair   **DN**

A set of early 19thC Georgian mahogany and needlework open armchairs.
36.5in (93cm) high
$2,500-3,800   **L&T**

A pair of 19thC mahogany framed open-arm carver chairs, stamped 'Gillows No 648'.
$700-800   **BELL**

A pair of 19thC mahogany frame Gainsborough-style armchairs.
40.5in (103cm) high
$3,800-5,000   **TEN**

ESSENTIAL REFERENCE - LIBRARY CHAIR

Percier and Fontaine was a noted partnership between French architects Charles Percier and Pierre François Léonard Fontaine.

● Together, Percier and Fontaine were inventors and major proponents of the rich and grand, consciously archaeological versions of early 19thC Neo-classical architecture known as Directoire style and Empire style.

● Napoleon Bonaparte liked their work. The calculated theatre of the Empire style, its aggressive opulence restrained by a slightly dry and correct sense of the antique taste, and its neo-Roman values, imperial yet separate from the ancien régime, appealed to the future emperor. He appointed them his personal architects and they were at work on Imperial projects almost until the end of Napoleon's time in power.

● They worked for ten years (1802-1812) on the Louvre. The old palace had not been a royal residence for generations, so it was free of any taint associated with the detested Bourbons. Unlike Versailles, it stood in the heart of Paris, so that the vain Emperor could be seen coming and going.

● They also worked at Josephine's Château de Malmaison, at the Château de Montgobert for Pauline Bonaparte, and did alterations and decorations for former Bourbon palaces or castles at Compiègne, Saint-Cloud, and Fontainebleau.

An early 19thC mahogany library chair, after a design by Percier and Fontaine for Georges Jacob, in the French consulate manner, with a curved ebony line-inlaid back with anthemion motif, on later brass gilded casters, replacing the original carved wood lion paw feet.
$25,000-32,000   **CHEF**

A pair of large mid-19thC Victorian oak and painted Glastonbury chairs, in the manner of A.W.N. Pugin, of Gothic style, each with carved toprail above quatrefoil carved back and Lovelace coat of arms.

An original medieval Glastonbury chair survived in the Bishop's Palace at Wells where Pugin almost certainly saw it, and another example was known at Strawberry Hill. Pugin copied the form exactly, although he did not add the original carved decoration to his versions (see V&A collection, British Galleries, Room 122e). The present examples are elaborately carved to the backs with coats of arms. The full coat of arms dates from the 30 June 1838, when William King, 8th Baron King of Ockham was elevated to the titles 1st Earl of Lovelace and Viscount Ockham. The chairs were likely to have been made after 1846, when the 1st Earl started living at Horsley Towers, and before 1860; as on the 29 September 1860 William King adopted the name and arms King-Noel by royal license.
46in (117cm) high
$5,000-6,500   **L&T**

A French Empire mahogany lowback armchair, with ormolu lion's head handholds.

$1,000-1,200   **POOK**

A Victorian mahogany and buttoned leather upholstered adjustable armchair, the padded arms slide to adjust the angle of the back, the concealed footrest sliding forward with ratchet adjustable section.

c1860   *49in (114cm) high*

$3,800-5,000   **DN**

A Victorian mahogany framed open-arm library chair.

$550-700   **BELL**

One of a pair of Victorian mahogany framed green leather upholstered open armchairs.

$1,000-1,200   **BELL**

A Victorian Gothic grained oak armchair, the pierced and carved back with triangular pediment and poppy finials above a crest with scrolling surround of primitive lions.

$1,000-1,100   **CHOR**

A Victorian Gothic oak chair, with four pierced arches to the back above four Tudor roses.

$1,000-1,100   **CHOR**

A late 19thC Swiss inlaid burr walnut musical chair, playing a choice of sixteen airs via two 11in (28cm) pinned brass cylinders and steel combs, the chair with pierced foliate back and central inlaid oval with Chamois motifs, unsigned.

49.5in (126cm) high

$1,800-2,300   **DN**

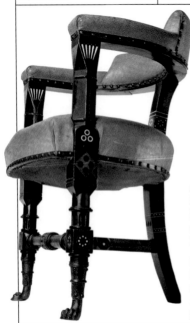

An Aesthetic Movement ivory inlaid ebonized horseshoe-backed chair, with front bronze paw feet, leather dry and cracked.

Provenance: Walter Morrison MP (1836-1921) of Malham Tarn Estate.

c1880   *31in (79cm)*

$23,000-28,000   **TEN**

A late 19thC Moorish-style library armchair, attributed to Liberty, with a spindle and bobbin-turned back support, the molded seat above a conforming seat rail, the legs carved with star symbols, the base stamped 'L25156', brass plaque numbered '2826'.

31in (79cm) high

$1,800-2,300   **TEN**

A 19thC faux rosewood framed library chair, on turned legs and brass wheel casters, stamped no.1766.

38.5in (98cm) high

$700-800   **CHEF**

A 19thC French walnut and needlework upholstered armchair, in the Louis XIV style, on scrolled legs united by a wavy X-form stretcher.
45.25in (115cm) high
$1,000-1,100   **L&T**

A 19thC French beech and tapestry upholstered armchair, in the Louis XIV style.
53.5in (136cm) high
$1,000-1,200   **L&T**

A pair of late 19thC French needlework upholstered beech armchairs.
44in (112cm) high
$800-950   **L&T**

A 19thC Continental walnut open armchair, in the 17thC style.
51.5in (131cm) high
$550-700   **L&T**

A pair of late 19thC William and Mary-style mahogany armchairs, of small size.
37.75in (96cm) high
$400-500   **L&T**

A Victorian mahogany and button upholstered armchair.
$70-80   **WHP**

A pair of Biedermeier-style maple and ebonized bar-back elbow chairs, with over stuff seats and sabre legs.
c1900
$750-900   **SWO**

One of a pair of giltwood and gesso fauteuils, in French Transitional style.
c1900   *41.75in (106cm) high*
$800-950 pair   **TEN**

A late 19thC mahogany armchair, the backrest and arms with spindle panels.
$130-180   **WHP**

A pair of early 20thC William and Mary-style walnut armchairs, by Marsh, Jones & Cribb, each bears makers label 'MARSH, JONES & CRIBB/11457'.
44in (112cm) high
$950-1,100   **L&T**

FURNITURE

An early 18thC wing armchair, the japanned base with a scroll-carved crest and on Braganza-style front feet, previously on castors.
$1,500-1,900 WW

An early 18thC George III barrel shape wingback armchair, raised on square mahogany tapering forelegs with brass toes and castors, legs recently restored.
45.25in (115cm) high
$3,200-3,800 TEN

Judith Picks

I mean if you are going to have a library armchair it's an idea to buy one of the best! This exudes all the best qualities of early Georgian craftsmanship. From the leather upholstery with brass stud border, to the square back S-scroll arms, to the acanthus leaf carved cabriole legs with carved hairy paw feet - all the features you want from this period. Even though the leather is dry and worn, it resonates its period. The leather is probably good enough to renovate and in my opinion it would be criminal to replace it.

A George II mahogany desk armchair.
38.5in (98cm) high
$14,000-18,000 CHEF

A George III mahogany wing armchair.
c1780 *40in (102cm) high*
$1,000-1,200 DN

An early 19thC Scottish Regency green leather armchair, raised on square tapered legs joined by stretchers, bearing an old paper label inscribed 'Walter Biggar, Esq./ 15 Claremont Crescent / Edinburgh'.

Walter Biggar was born in Edinburgh in 1787 and moved to Banff in 1821 where he married Anne Duff, daughter of an old Banffshire family. He is credited with founding the herring trade in the Baltic where his business knowledge and experience helped establish an industry that became the most significant source of wealth in north Scotland in the 19thC. An ornate Gothic style fountain was erected in Low Street, Banff in 1878 in recognition of his and his wife's accomplishments. Walter Biggar is listed as a resident of 15 Claremont Crescent in Edinburgh in the 1850s.
38.5in (98cm) high
$1,500-2,000 L&T

A matched pair of Regency mahogany library bergère armchairs, with rattan seat and sabre legs, brass caps and castors, one seat rail stamped several times 'C', the other 'W', marks, some damage.
c1815 *38.5in (98cm) high*
$8,000-9,500 DN

A Regency mahogany library chair, with cane seat on square legs and large brass wheel castors, old repairs to one leg.
35.5in (90cm) high
$700-800 CHEF

A Regency mahogany bergère armchair, with curved cane panel back, sides and seat, on ring turned tapered legs with brass cappings and castors.
$700-800 BE

A George IV rosewood framed easy chair, the scrolled back and horseshoe-shaped seat between rolled arms with anthemion and acanthus carved end panels.

40in (100cm) high

$2,500-3,200   **TEN**

A 19thC wing back armchair, stamped 'Howard & Sons Ltd, Berners Street', numbered '3793', the curved seat rail raised on short cabriole forelegs joined by a later cross stretcher.

45.25in (115cm) high

$1,900-2,500   **TEN**

A late 19thC pair of carved mahogany armchairs, raised on four gadrooned brackets with carved legs and paw feet, recently restored.

43in (110cm) high

$900-1,000   **TEN**

A 19thC French giltwood upholstered bergère, the foliate- and strap-carved square back and scrolled arms on turned fluted legs.

39in (99cm) high

$800-950   **L&T**

A George II-style mahogany wing armchair, the seat rail carved with foliage, on shell-carved cabriole legs with claw and ball feet.

$2,300-2,800   **CHOR**

An early 20thC Louis XIV-style giltwood chaise d'oreille, with carved rest rail above a padded back and ears.

43in (109cm) high

$900-1,000   **L&T**

A brown goatskin leather button upholstered armchair, in Victorian style, of recent manufacture, minor wear and fading.

45.25in (115cm) long

$1,600-2,300   **DN**

A French carved beech tub-shaped armchair, the panel back with ribbon-tied flowerhead and foliate top rail, with husk-decorated seat rail, on fluted tapered legs, headed with paterae.

$500-650   **BE**

FURNITURE

A Louis XV carved walnut settee, with a serpentine frame carved with acanthus, shells and cabochons, on cabriole legs.

41.25in (105cm) high

$6,500-7,500   **DN**

An 18thC Louis XV walnut framed settee, the carved scrolled top rail and enclosed downswept arms with part pads.

78in (198cm) wide

$6,500-7,500   **L&T**

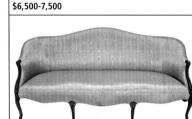

An 18thC gilt framed sofa, with serpentine back and seat, on four shell-capped shallow cabriole front supports.

78in (198cm) wide

$650-750   **BELL**

A late 18thC George III mahogany sofa.

71in (180.5cm) wide

$550-700   **POOK**

A George III mahogany frame campaign sofa, on tapering legs, water marks to linen fabric covering, knocks to the legs.

84.25in (214cm) wide

$4,500-5,000   **CHEF**

ESSENTIAL REFERENCE - IRISH REGENCY GILT SUITE

From 1800-10, Regency gilt Neo-classical-style furniture became very fashionable. Thomas Sheraton (1751-1806) in his influential book 'The Cabinet Dictionary' of 1803 introduced designs subsequently copied and adapted by clients and their designers. A close example in design to Sheraton's drawings in the 'Cabinet Dictionary' is the couch now on display at the Victoria and Albert Museum, London, designed by Gillow & Co. in 1805 for the Reverend Edward Hughes and the Marquess of Sligo. At the same time well-known Regency designers such as Thomas Hope and Henry Holland published their own designs. Thomas Hope's authorative publication of 1807 'Household Furniture and Interior Decoration', included examples of monopedia legs with animal heads. The monopodium, a decorative support consisting of the head and one leg of an animal, often a lion or a leopard, was first seen in Roman furniture but revivied during the late 18thC. As with Sheraton, Hope's designs were taken and adapted by cabinet makers throughout England and Ireland. During his Grand Tour from 1794-1796, the English architect and designer Charles Heathcote Tatham (who studied under the cabinet maker John Linnell) drew similar monopodia to those on this suite and which were later published by Henry Holland.

An Irish Regency gilt suite, in the manner of Thomas Hope, comprising a sofa and a pair of armchairs of Grecian style, carved with fluted cornucopia arms and on monopodia legs, each carved with lion masks and paw feet.

c1805   *sofa 67in (170cm) long*

$32,000-38,000 suite   **CHEF**

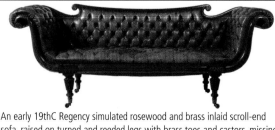

An early 19thC Regency simulated rosewood and brass inlaid scroll-end sofa, raised on turned and reeded legs with brass toes and castors, missing brass inlay section and bracket to roundel.

86.5in (220cm) long

$3,200-3,800   **TEN**

An Irish Regency mahogany double-scroll-back settee, of small proportions, with swept cabriole legs to paw feet.

$1,900-2,500   **APAR**

ESSENTIAL REFERENCE - PENNSYLVANIA PAINTED SETTEE

This decorated settee has one of the boldest and most recognisable forms in rural Pennsylvania chair-making. It was made in the Mifflintown Chair Works, the shop of William F. Snyder, in Mifflintown, Pennsylvania, Juniata County. The huge, scrolled, wooden plank seat is accompanied by an equally oversized crest rail and lyre back slats. The influence of Baltimore furniture makers was not lost on Snyder, who seems to have preferred the much more voluptuous, ogee-profile lines found in his turnings, seats, slats, and crests, but also liked background colors that were more formal. The decoration he used was also gaudier, following Baltimore style, as opposed to Philadelphia or New England.

A Pennsylvania painted settee, the crest with a dramatic landscape decoration, with ten building spires, with bannerette weathervanes.
c1840   78in (198cm) wide
$25,000-32,000   **POOK**

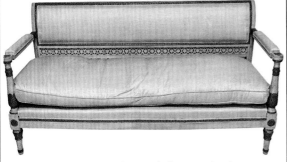

One of a pair of early 19thC Italian parcel gilt cream-painted open-arm sofas, on acanthus carved turned supports.
                                          68.75in (175cm) long
$2,300-2,800 pair   **BELL**

An early Victorian rosewood framed sofa, the arms with scroll-carved rosewood facings, above a molded seat rail raised on short turned tapered legs ending in brass caps and castors.
c1840   75in (190cm) wide
$1,800-2,300   **L&T**

An early Victorian mahogany framed sofa, the arms with rosette-carved mahogany facings, raised on short carved and turned tapered legs with porcelain castors.
c1860   77.5in (197cm) wide
$650-750   **L&T**

A Victorian walnut frame sofa.
                    71in (180.5cm) wide
$500-550   **WW**

A late 19thC French Empire-style sofa, the mahogany frame with twin swan-neck capitals above turned feet with applied brass castors.
                    77.5in (197cm) long
$450-500   **FLD**

A 19thC rosewood frame settee, with acanthus detail to the frame.

56.75in (144cm) long

$300-400   FLD

A George II-style sofa, on carved and gilded cabriole legs with claw and ball feet.

86.25in (219cm) wide

$2,000-2,500   CHOR

A late 19thC George III-style mahogany frame sofa, in the Hepplewhite-style, raised on square tapered legs headed by satinwood fan medallions and carved with husk trails and ending on waisted block feet.

70in (178cm) wide

$3,200-4,400   L&T

A late 19thC mahogany and floral pattern upholstered settee, with brass motifs on turned feet.

$300-350   WHP

A George II-style mahogany sofa, the arms with carved griffin mask terminals, on carved cabriole legs, decorated with acanthus leaf, branch and C-scrolls and claw feet.

c1900   *45.25in (115cm) wide*

$3,800-4,400   CHEF

A Louis XV-style gilt framed salon settee.

$500-650   CHOR

A late Victorian conversation seat, now in three separate sections with ebonized frame.

$450-550   APAR

A Victorian walnut framed chaperone sofa, surmounted by a turned finial, scrolled arms pierced with foliate carving.

46in (117cm) wide

$700-800   HT

A George III mahogany and satinwood chaise longue, the scroll arm inlaid with a patera, on square tapering legs and brass castors.

74.5in (189.5cm) wide

$700-800

WW

A pair of Regency parcel-gilt chaises longues, with sabre legs, some damage.

68in (173cm) long

$1,300-1,900

CHOR

A late 19th/early 20thC ebonized bentwood reclining chaise longue, with paper label 'Thonet'.

75in (190cm) wide

$1,200-1,250

BELL

A 17thC oak settee, the back with molded and carved frieze panels with initials 'Aodnl, date 1667' and c-scroll and rosette ornament having inlaid geometric lozenge panels below.

71in (180cm) wide

$750-900

BE

ESSENTIAL REFERENCE - CHARLES HEATHCOTE TATHAM

Charles Heathcote Tatham, architect, was born in Westminster on 8 February 1772. He was educated at Louth Grammar School, Lincolnshire until 1788 when, aged 19, he began working for Henry Holland. For the next six years Tatham worked in Holland's office working on commissions such as the rebuilding of the Theatre Royal, Drury Lane, for Richard Brinsley Sheridan.

In 1794 Tatham became Holland's agent in Rome as he sent back designs, casts of antiquities as well as original pieces. Tatham visited several archaeological sites including villas, museums, baths and gardens of which he made many drawings. Tatham returned to England in 1796 and soon after exhibited for the first time at the Royal Academy. His first independent commission was for an interior at Stoke Edith, Herefordshire for Edward Foley MP. More importantly, he was employed by the Earl of Carlisle at Castle Howard, Yorkshire, in 1800-01 to fit up Sir Thomas Robinson's Palladian wing. By the end of his career, much of Tatham's work was made up of alterations and additions to both internal and external rooms and houses. Charles Tatham died at Trinity Hospital, Greenwich on 10 April 1842.

A Victorian Gothic oak bench, the pierced and carved back and solid seat on square chamfered legs united by square stretchers, the end finials are both damaged.

71.5in (182cm) long

$1,100-1,500

CHOR

A Regency mahogany hall bench, in the manner of Charles Heathcote Tatham, the seat with an inner molding with scroll bolster ends, with applied rondels on tapering fluted legs and spade feet.

53.75in (136.5cm) wide

$5,000-5,700

WW

A Victorian mahogany bench, the back rest with scrolled and florally carved ends.

108.25in (275cm) long

$450-500

WHP

An oak refectory table, the triple-plank top above a frieze with an S-scroll, on canted square section legs and stretchers, generally fair condition, marks, scratches and abrasions consistent with age and use, old chips and splits and marks, no obvious significant damage, the top faded to each end, and to two legs also faded, evidence of worm, visible to feet and top and elsewhere, the top is likely associated to the base, there are additional holes to the underside where it would have been fixed to an alternate base, several dowel/pegs to joints have been replaced at a later date and colored to match, some division/warping between joins of three planks, one joint in particular will need re-securing.

c1650

$25,000-32,000

108.25in (275cm) long

DN

A late 17thC Charles II oak refectory table, the top with cleated ends, the plain frieze with shaped brackets.

135.75in (345cm) long

$7,000-8,000

TEN

A Jacobean oak and yew wood refectory table.

c1680   89.5in (227.5cm) wide

$1,500-2,300   POOK

A 17thC oak refectory table, with cleated ends, old patch repairs, ring marks.

87in (221cm) wide

$3,200-3,800   CHEF

A 17thC oak refectory table, table top with three pine planks with layers of dark wax.

105in (267cm) wide

$1,900-2,500   CHEF

An 18thC oak dining table, with a triple plank top.

80.25in (204cm) long

$900-1,000   BE

An antique oak and inlaid refectory table, the frieze with diagonal oak and maple banding.

119in (302cm) long

$1,800-2,300   BE

A Flemish oak draw-leaf refectory table, in 17thC-style, the boarded top with cleated ends on gadrooned cup and cover supports.

90in (228.5cm) long

$1,500-2,000   WW

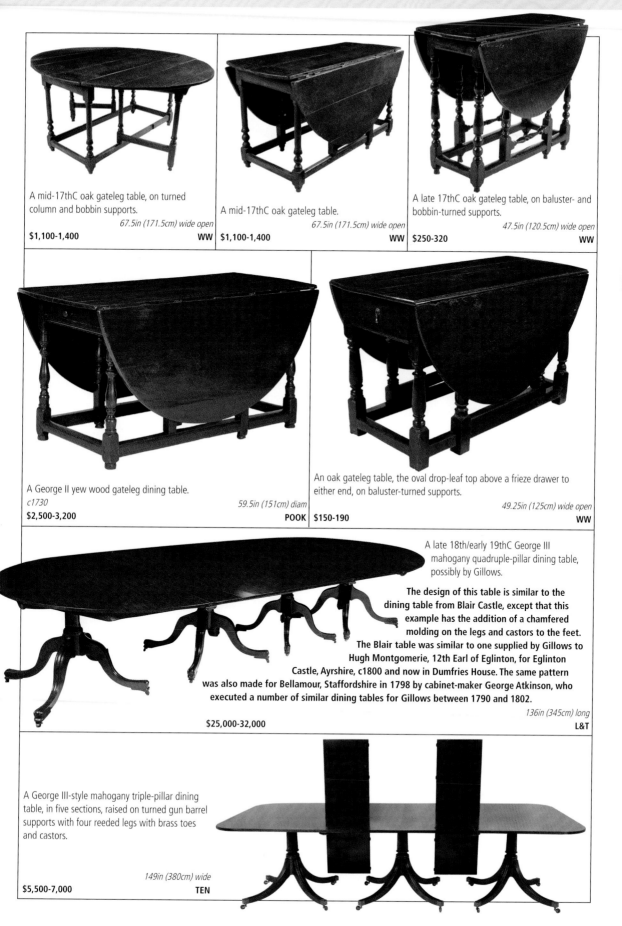

A mid-17thC oak gateleg table, on turned column and bobbin supports.

67.5in (171.5cm) wide open

$1,100-1,400   **WW**

A mid-17thC oak gateleg table.

67.5in (171.5cm) wide open

$1,100-1,400   **WW**

A late 17thC oak gateleg table, on baluster- and bobbin-turned supports.

47.5in (120.5cm) wide open

$250-320   **WW**

A George II yew wood gateleg dining table.

c1730   *59.5in (151cm) diam*

$2,500-3,200   **POOK**

An oak gateleg table, the oval drop-leaf top above a frieze drawer to either end, on baluster-turned supports.

49.25in (125cm) wide open

$150-190   **WW**

A late 18th/early 19thC George III mahogany quadruple-pillar dining table, possibly by Gillows.

The design of this table is similar to the dining table from Blair Castle, except that this example has the addition of a chamfered molding on the legs and castors to the feet. The Blair table was similar to one supplied by Gillows to Hugh Montgomerie, 12th Earl of Eglinton, for Eglinton Castle, Ayrshire, c1800 and now in Dumfries House. The same pattern was also made for Bellamour, Staffordshire in 1798 by cabinet-maker George Atkinson, who executed a number of similar dining tables for Gillows between 1790 and 1802.

136in (345cm) long

$25,000-32,000   **L&T**

A George III-style mahogany triple-pillar dining table, in five sections, raised on turned gun barrel supports with four reeded legs with brass toes and castors.

149in (380cm) wide

$5,500-7,000   **TEN**

FURNITURE

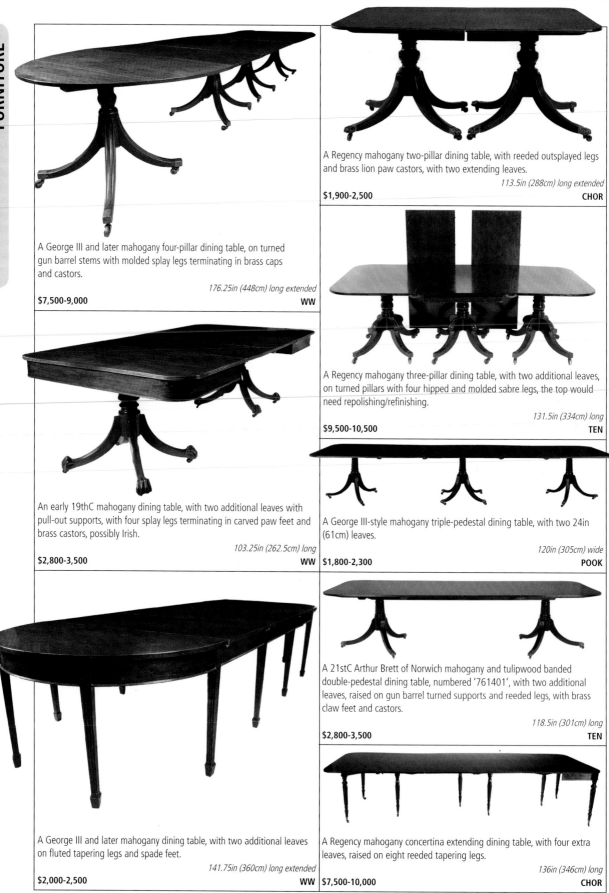

A George III and later mahogany four-pillar dining table, on turned gun barrel stems with molded splay legs terminating in brass caps and castors.

176.25in (448cm) long extended

$7,500-9,000   WW

An early 19thC mahogany dining table, with two additional leaves with pull-out supports, with four splay legs terminating in carved paw feet and brass castors, possibly Irish.

103.25in (262.5cm) long

$2,800-3,500   WW

A George III and later mahogany dining table, with two additional leaves on fluted tapering legs and spade feet.

141.75in (360cm) long extended

$2,000-2,500   WW

A Regency mahogany two-pillar dining table, with reeded outsplayed legs and brass lion paw castors, with two extending leaves.

113.5in (288cm) long extended

$1,900-2,500   CHOR

A Regency mahogany three-pillar dining table, with two additional leaves, on turned pillars with four hipped and molded sabre legs, the top would need repolishing/refinishing.

131.5in (334cm) long

$9,500-10,500   TEN

A George III-style mahogany triple-pedestal dining table, with two 24in (61cm) leaves.

120in (305cm) wide

$1,800-2,300   POOK

A 21stC Arthur Brett of Norwich mahogany and tulipwood banded double-pedestal dining table, numbered '761401', with two additional leaves, raised on gun barrel turned supports and reeded legs, with brass claw feet and castors.

118.5in (301cm) long

$2,800-3,500   TEN

A Regency mahogany concertina extending dining table, with four extra leaves, raised on eight reeded tapering legs.

136in (346cm) long

$7,500-10,000   CHOR

A Regency mahogany concertina-action extending dining table, with five additional leaves, with turned tapering and spiral turned legs, on brass caps and casters.

c1815
117.5in (398cm) long extended
$6,500-7,500
DN

A Regency mahogany extending dining table, in the manner of Gillows of Lancaster, with three leaves, with turned and reeded legs terminating in brass caps and castors.

c1815
125.25in (318cm) long extended
$5,000-6,500
DN

An early 19thC mahogany and inlaid dining table, banded in satinwood bordered with boxwood and ebony lines, with three additional leaves, turned and reeded tapered legs, with brass cappings and castors.

111.75in (284cm) long extended
$950-1,100
BE

An early 19thC mahogany and inlaid D-end dining table, the frieze decorated with ebonized and boxwood lines, with two additional leaves.

87in (221cm) long extended
$1,600-2,300
BE

A Regency patent telescopic extending dining table, by Thomas Butler, London, with four leaf extensions, bearing an engraved brass maker's plaque 'BUTLER's PATENT NO 13 & 14 / CATHERINE ST. STRAND / LONDON', the table extending to two further leaf inserts, not present.

c1820
217in (551cm) long extended
$15,000-19,000
L&T

A George IV mahogany extending dining table, with a pair of 'D' ends, extending on a telescopic frame to accommodate four additional leaves with a molded edge, with ten clips.

134.5in (341.5cm) long extended
$9,500-10,500
WW

An early Victorian mahogany extending dining table, with three additional leaves, with carved and gadrooned bulbous tapering legs with brass castors, no handle.

c1850
118in (300cm) wide extended
$1,500-2,300
TEN

An early Victorian mahogany extending dining table, with three additional leaves, on turned tapering legs and ceramic castors.

123.5in (314cm) long extended
$1,600-2,300
WW

FURNITURE

An early Victorian mahogany extending Imperial dining table, attributed to Gillows, with an oak telescopic mechanism, with three leaves, with brass sprung clips stamped 'PATENT'.

See Susan E. Stuart, 'Gillows of Lancaster and London 1730-1840', page 247, plate 244, for a drawing of an almost identical Imperial telescopic dining table with four legs drawn in 1849 which is housed in the Westminster City Archive.

147.5in (375cm) long extended

$5,000-6,500 WW

A Victorian mahogany wind-out dining table, on plain rails and stout turned lappet-carved legs, with castors, with four additional leaves.

146.5in (372cm) long

$3,500-4,000 TEN

A late Victorian mahogany wind-out dining table, with stout turned and reeded legs, with castors, with three additional leaves.

157.5in (400cm) long extended

$2,800-3,500 TEN

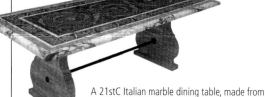

A 21stC Italian marble dining table, made from colored marble fragments, on shaped end supports joined by a turned metal support.

The table is similar to marble wall panelling discovered at Ostia, Italy which has been painstakingly reconstructed from thousands of fragments now at Museo Alto Medioevo, Rome.

87in (221cm) long

$9,500-10,500 TEN

A mid-19thC mahogany dining table, on turned tapering legs with castors.

71.75in (182cm) diam

$2,000-2,500 WHP

A Victorian mahogany extending dining table, with five additional leaves, with turned and fluted legs terminating in 'Copes' patent castors, the winding mechanism with applied plaque for 'JOSEPH FITTER/ PATENT/ BRITANNIA WORKS/ CHEAPSIDE BIRMINGHAM', some damage.

Joseph Fitter was a Birmingham machinist, and applied for a patent for an extending dining table in 1861. Business directories in 1870 list him at this address.

c1870 *153.25in (389cm) long*

$2,500-3,800 DN

A 19thC mahogany extending dining table.

104in (264cm) wide extended

$750-900 CHOR

A Regency mahogany 'Cumberland action' dining table, with two additional leaves, on ring-turned gateleg supports, reeded splay legs and brass castors.

129.5in (329cm) wide extended

$2,500-3,200 WW

A large Regency mahogany extending dining table, in the manner of George Bullock, the finely figured top with four semi-elliptical additional leaves decorated with foliate ebony marquetry, with numbered pull out supports.

91.5in (232cm) diam

$50,000-60,000 **DN**

A Regency rosewood extending dining table, with four additional rosewood effect leaves.

71in (180cm) diam extended

$1,900-2,500 **LAW**

An early 19thC Regency mahogany extending dining table, on a baluster column and tripod base with lion paw feet, with four extra leaves.

110.25in (280cm) long extended

$1,000-1,500 **LAW**

A Regency rosewood breakfast table, the top inlaid with brass, on an acanthus pedestal base with splayed supports and brass castors.

49.25in (125cm) high

$400-500 **DW**

A 19thC mahogany tilt-top dining table on a turned base.

59.5in (151cm) wide

$180-250 **WHP**

A 19thC mahogany extending dining table on turned legs.

47.25in (120cm) diam

$80-150 **WHP**

A Regency rosewood breakfast table, on a reeded and lotus-carved baluster column support, on a tripartite base on acanthus-carved scroll feet.

52in (132cm) diam

$650-750 **L&T**

An early Victorian rosewood breakfast table, with a facetted baluster column support, on a circular base raised on scroll feet with brass castors.

53.5in (136cm) diam

$650-750 **L&T**

FURNITURE

An 18thC Irish mahogany center table, on a shell- and fret-carved frieze and supported on carved slight cabriole legs with pad feet.

31in (79cm) wide

$2,800-3,800   TRI

A Regency mahogany drum table, the rotating top with a later leather inset, over four real and four faux drawers, on a square-paneled base, with a single door and paw feet.

69.5in (176.5cm) diam

$6,500-7,500   SWO

CLOSER LOOK - JOHANNES KLINKERFUSS CENTER TABLE

Everything about this table exudes quality and craftsmanship - from the 'Vert Maurin' marble top.

The sophisticated baluster-shaped stem mounted with a band of palmettes and flowerheads.

The lower-half is elaborately applied with stylized leaves and flowerheads, resting on a stepped-quadripartite base with bun feet.

The paper label with the inventory number 'A.1031' under a Count's crown securing it's royal connection.

An early 19thC German mahogany and ormolu mounted guéridon, attributed to Johannes Klinkerfuss.

Johannes Klinkerfuss (1770-1831) trained under his father Philip Klinckerfuss and Hartman Gürtler (1753-1812). He then trained with the Roentgen firm of cabinet-makers, which he joined in 1789. In 1799 Klinckerfuss was appointed Kabinettebenist to the court shortly after Friederich Eugen's accession the throne and remained in this position until 1812 when he started his own furniture business. However he continued to supply furniture for the Royal court until his death in 1831.

37.5in (95.5cm) diam

$15,000-19,000   DN

ESSENTIAL REFERENCE - JEAN-JOSEPH CHAPUIS

Jean-Joseph Chapuis was born in Brussels in 1765. He was trained in Paris, where he became a master craftsman, entitling him to use a personal mark (estampille) on his work. He had set up his workshop in his home town by 1795 and kept it active to 1830. When the first reference guides on the history of French furniture in the 18thC appeared in Paris, this mark was attributed to Claude Chapuis, who was in fact only a simple trader, of whom little if anything is known. This deprived Jean-Joseph Chapuis of his fame and explains why pieces of furniture by Jean-Joseph Chapuis are rarely found in public collections outside France. The museum of Vleeshuis in Antwerp is an exception. Only single pieces made by Chapuis, not collections, have ever been found, so it is impossible to give a precise account of everything he produced during his lifetime. The museum of Saint-Josse-ten-Noode, Brussels, Belgium, is the only one to possess several marked pieces of Chapuis's furniture. They were collected by Joseph Adolph Van Cutsem, a collector of Empire furniture, who in 1865 supplemented his collection with two significant purchases made during Chapuis's funeral sale.

An early 19thC French Empire mahogany and parcel-gilt marble topped center table, in the manner of Jean-Joseph Chapuis, the marble a later addition.

38in (97cm) diam

$2,300-2,800   L&T

An early 19thC Regency center table, specimen marble top with central chequers board on a red-painted rosewood tripod base.

28.5in (72cm) high

$4,500-5,000   LAW

A Regency fossilized marble-topped painted hardwood center table, possibly Anglo-Indian, the top on three lion's head monopodia and central serpent entwined column.

33in (84cm) wide

$4,400-5,700   L&T

A pair of Italian mahogany center tables, with mosaic tops, the first with a Classical figure above the carved inscription 'Karthago', the second table with a central parrot.

c1830   *28in (71cm) wide*

$15,000-19,000   POOK

A William IV mahogany and specimen marble center table, in the manner of Gillows, the later top inset with various marbles and semi-precious stones, including: malachite, red griotte, porphyry, verde antico, violet jura brocatelle and cipollin.

37in (94cm) wide

$10,000-11,000   WW

ESSENTIAL REFERENCE - BLUE JOHN

'Blue John' is a type of semi-precious mineral.
- A unique fluorspar gives it its characteristic blue and yellow colors and streaky pattern.
- It is said that the Romans discovered it in Castleton nearly 2000 years ago.
- In Western Europe, the best quality stone is found at Blue John Cavern and Treak Cliff Cavern in Derbyshire.
- It is usually mined by hand.
- During the second half of the 18thC, its decorative quality was highly prized. Mining increased as a result.
- Matthew Boulton, an industrialist, championed the use of Blue John in his Neo-classical-style ormolu wares.
- It was also fashionable during the Regency period.
- Blue John can be found on a broad range of items such as furniture, vases, urns, candelabra and clocks.

A 19thC mahogany center table, the top with four segmental additional leaves raised on four turned, fluted, reeded and carved columns, and on X-shaped floor stretcher with carved lion's head terminals.

90.25in (229cm) diam extended

$8,000-9,500   SWO

A rare 19thC Blue John table, the top with a malachite spider inlaid into the center, the veined fluorite appears like a spider's web, on a later gilt brass base with a blue john globe finial and on leaf cast hoof feet.

25.75in (65.5cm) diam

$4,400-5,700   WW

A French Empire guéridon, the dished marble top on a flared mahogany concave sided triangular base and three paw feet.

32in (81cm) wide

$1,500-2,500   BELL

A Victorian figured, burr walnut and floral marquetry inlaid table.

c1860   50.75in (129cm) wide

$1,800-2,300   TEN

An Indo-Portuguese padoukwood center table, the six-plank top with a carved rope-twist edge, the frieze with two deep drawers.

77in (196cm) wide

$2,000-2,500   SWO

An Edwardian inlaid satinwood center table, on square tapering legs, with brass caps and castors.

44.75in (114cm) wide

$1,000-1,500   SWO

A Biedermeier-style maple and ebonized center table, the top rising and falling on a screw thread and extending to accept a single leaf.

60in (152.5cm) diam

$650-750   SWO

A George III mahogany drum library table, the crossbanded top with radiating plum pudding veneers divided by stringing, above four drawers and four false drawers with cast conch shell handles, marks, scratches and abrasions consistent with age and use, no obvious significant damage, cleaned/repolished, cedar lined drawer bases, no physical evidence of handles being replaced or moved, some warping to the top, good original color and patina overall.
c1790 *47.75in (121cm) diam*
$5,500-6,500 **DN**

A Regency mahogany drum library table, with revolving top, fitted alternate drawers with gilt-brass handles.
53.25in (135cm) wide
$2,500-3,200 **CHEF**

A rosewood library table, attributed to William Trotter, Edinburgh, carved to the edge with egg-and-dart moldings, with a tooled leather writing surface, with hinged lidded compartments to each end, on a quadriform base with sabre legs and leaf-cast brass caps and castors.
c1820 *44in (112cm) wide*
$19,000-25,000 **L&T**

A mid-19thC Victorian oak library table, in the manner of A.W.N. Pugin, of Gothic style.
66.5in (169cm) wide
$2,500-3,200 **L&T**

A pair of Regency mahogany and ebony-strung library tables, in the manner of Gillows of Lancaster, overall marks commensurate with age, the first table top with water marks, two ebony moldings detached from the underside corners of the frieze, the font left corner molding possibly a later replacement, rectangular cuts to the veneers to the front and back of the end supports to both tables, but this is presumably constructional, cracks to the high stretcher, the second table with some marks to top, a molding and section of veneer loose to left side of frieze, one long section of molding detached to base of right-hand end support, lacking the short section of molding to the same area.
c1815 *36.25in (92cm) wide*
$6,500-7,500 **DN**

ESSENTIAL REFERENCE - JAMES WINTER

James Winter was an important furniture dealer, broker and licensed appraiser based in Soho, London between 1823 and 1840. However the company that he founded is recorded as having traded in second hand furniture until its demise in 1870, probably long after Winter's death. In the course of its history, the business was renamed 'James Winter & Sons' and even re-located a couple of times, albeit always remaining on Wardour Street, Dictionary of English Furniture Makers, 1660-1840, edited by G. Beard and C. Gilbert, pages 992-3.

A William IV mahogany library table, with leather inset top with rounded corners, above three short and two long drawers to opposing longest sides, each drawer stamped 'JAMES WINTER & SON 101 WARDOUR ST SOHO LONDON'.
c1835 *89.75in (228cm) wide*
$3,200-3,800 **DN**

A mid-19thC Victorian oak library table, in the manner of A.W.N. Pugin, of Gothic style, lacking writing surface.
59in (150cm) wide
$1,800-2,300 **L&T**

A Victorian Gothic oak library table, the top with broad pollard oak border, fitted a surround of four drawers and four false drawers, the top support renewed.
56in (142cm) wide
$3,200-3,800 **CHOR**

A 19thC mahogany library table, leather lined top, fitted two frieze drawers and dummy verso, with damage.
56in (142cm) wide
$1,500-2,000 **CHEF**

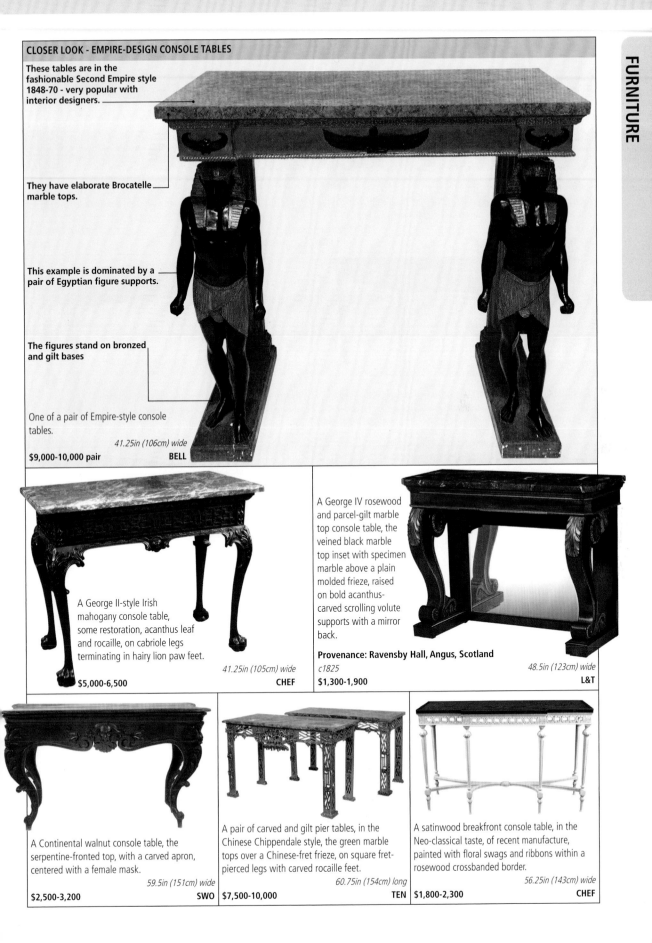

CLOSER LOOK - EMPIRE-DESIGN CONSOLE TABLES

These tables are in the fashionable Second Empire style 1848-70 - very popular with interior designers.

They have elaborate Brocatelle marble tops.

This example is dominated by a pair of Egyptian figure supports.

The figures stand on bronzed and gilt bases

One of a pair of Empire-style console tables.

41.25in (106cm) wide

$9,000-10,000 pair   **BELL**

A George II-style Irish mahogany console table, some restoration, acanthus leaf and rocaille, on cabriole legs terminating in hairy lion paw feet.

41.25in (105cm) wide

$5,000-6,500   **CHEF**

A George IV rosewood and parcel-gilt marble top console table, the veined black marble top inset with specimen marble above a plain molded frieze, raised on bold acanthus-carved scrolling volute supports with a mirror back.

Provenance: Ravensby Hall, Angus, Scotland

c1825   *48.5in (123cm) wide*

$1,300-1,900   **L&T**

A Continental walnut console table, the serpentine-fronted top, with a carved apron, centered with a female mask.

59.5in (151cm) wide

$2,500-3,200   **SWO**

A pair of carved and gilt pier tables, in the Chinese Chippendale style, the green marble tops over a Chinese-fret frieze, on square fret-pierced legs with carved rocaille feet.

60.75in (154cm) long

$7,500-10,000   **TEN**

A satinwood breakfront console table, in the Neo-classical taste, of recent manufacture, painted with floral swags and ribbons within a rosewood crossbanded border.

56.25in (143cm) wide

$1,800-2,300   **CHEF**

FURNITURE

A George III mahogany serving table, with a later marble top, with a frieze with a carved shell center, on turned and stop-fluted supports.

71in (180cm) wide

$25,000-32,000   SWO

A George III mahogany serpentine serving table, on square-molded and chamfered legs, back right hand leg split, molded return missing from back left hand leg.

62in (157cm) wide

$5,000-6,500   CHOR

A late 18thC mahogany serving table, fitted four drawers with upright canted sides, raised on four square-molded legs and set with roundels.

84.25in (214cm) wide

$2,500-3,200   CHOR

A George III mahogany serving table, the top on square-chamfered legs with scroll brackets and block feet.

60.25in (153cm) wide

$1,500-1,900   CHOR

A George III mahogany serving table, with blind fret-carved frieze and pull-out leaf, some damage and repair work.

65.25in (166cm) long

$1,500-2,300   TEN

A William IV mahogany serving table, the inverted breakfront top with egg-and-dart molding above the figured mahogany frieze, each turned pedestal support with a carved acanthus capital and lappet vase terminals. *c1835*

134in (340cm) wide

$5,000-6,500   DN

A Charles II oak side table, with plank top, over a drawer, on bobbin-turned legs and all-round stretcher.

35.5in (90cm) wide

$900-1,100   SWO

A Charles II oak side table. *c1680*

35.5in (90cm) wide

$650-750   DN

A William and Mary walnut and oak side table.

32.35in (82cm) wide

$500-650   WW

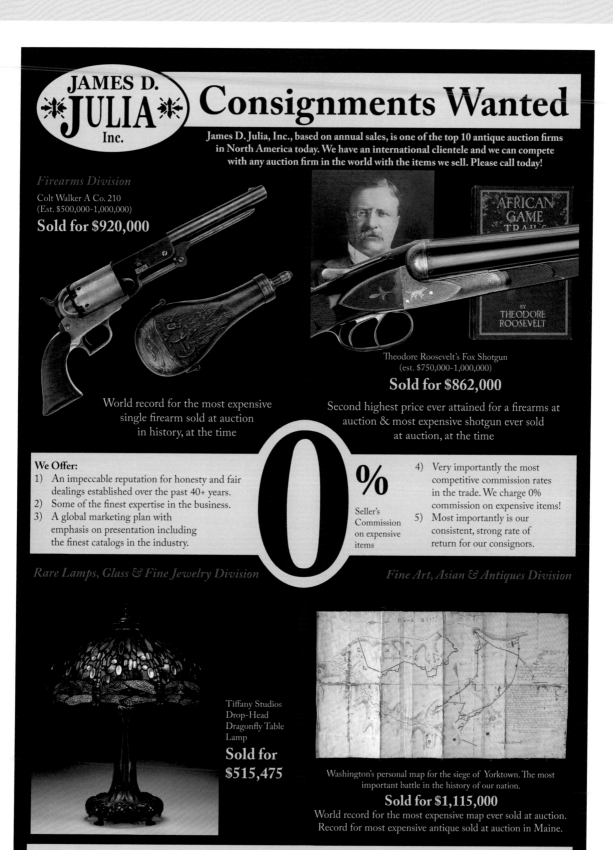

FURNITURE

A George II Irish mahogany side table, the later molded edged top above a frieze centered with a shell.

45.5in (116cm) wide

$4,500-5,000　　WW

A 19thC Irish George III mahogany side table, the frieze centered on the long sides by carved acanthus, on cabriole legs carved with acanthus and flowerheads, with carved hairy paw feet.

45in (114cm) wide

$5,000-6,500　　L&T

An 18thC Piedmontese painted and parcel-gilt side table, in the manner of G.M. Bonzanigo, the brèche violette marble top above a frieze decorated with enclosed anthemia centring on a suspended carved profile portrait of a young lady, decoration refreshed.

Giuseppe Maria Bonzanigo was born in Asti in 1740, and died in Turin in 1820. During his long and distinguished career he established himself as the finest exponent of Neo-classical carved furniture in Piedmont. His commissions included many carried out for Vittorio Amedeo III and, in 1787, Bonzanigo received the accolade of being named a Royal Sculptor, with a salary of 20 lire. Examples of his work can be seen in the Palazzo Reale in Turin, and also in the hunting lodge at Stupinigi, where he supplied many of the furnishings for the royal apartments.

46.5in (118cm) wide

$11,000-14,000　　DN

ESSENTIAL REFERENCE - EDWARDS AND ROBERTS

The firm Edwards and Roberts were among the best English antique furniture cabinet makers of the second half of the 19thC. The company was founded in 1845 and by 1854 was trading as 'Edwards and Roberts', 21 Wardour Street, Antique and Modern Cabinet Makers and Importers of Ancient Furniture'. They became one of the leading London cabinet makers and retailers and the firm produced high quality furniture, as well as good copies of the 18thC and 19thC English, French and Dutch pieces. They were known for restoring and adapting older pieces of antique furniture to suit more modern needs. The quality of timber used was always the best quality and included fine burr walnuts, finely figured mahogany and lighter toned satinwood.

An 18thC Sicilian parcel-gilt side table, the marble top above a central oval cartouche of figures within a band of ribbon-tied laurel leaves, flanked by carved giltwood scrolling acanthus and classical urns against a white painted ground.

54in (137cm) wide

$9,000-10,000　　DN

A 19thC Edwards and Roberts 'Dutch' floral marquetry, ebonized and ivory inlaid side table, on ebonized spirally turned legs united by curved and flattened x-frame stretcher, with ebonized bun feet, the drawer stamped 'Edwards and Roberts, Wardour Street, London'.

44.5in (113cm) wide

$3,200-3,800　　BE

An 18thC Dutch floral marquetry inlaid walnut serpentine side table, with three frieze drawers on cabriole supports.

31.5in (80cm) wide

$1,300-1,500　　BELL

A 19thC George II-style mahogany side table, with a verde antico marble top, with a scrolling leaf-carved apron, on shell-capped and -carved cabriole legs and claw and ball feet.

61in (155cm) wide

$5,000-6,500　　WW

A 19thC Victorian Kingwood, marquetry and gilt-bronze mounted table, in the manner of Holland & Sons, raised on square cabriole legs with bronze mounts.

33.5in (85cm) wide

$2,500-3,200　　L&T

A pair of early 20thC Irish George III-style mahogany side tables, by Hicks, Dublin, raised on acanthus-carved cabriole legs ending in bold hairy paw feet, each bearing 'Hicks Dublin' brass label to reverse.

42.5in (108cm) wide

$3,200-4,400　　L&T

A Regency occasional table, possibly by George Oakley with design by Thomas Hope, the sabicu top inset with brass lines, the frieze with metal rim.

34in (86cm) wide

$4,500-5,000   CHOR

A Louis XV-style Kingwood, tulipwood and ormolu mounted table ambulante, the top with inset Sèvres-style porcelain tray, four panels to the corners, on tapering legs with hoof feet, on a platform base.

c1860   *9.25in (74cm) high*

$7,000-8,000   TEN

A William IV mahogany occasional table, with inset septarian nodule marble top.

The inset top of this table is a section from a large septarian nodule. Formed during the Cretaceous period some 50 to 70 million years ago, the nodules were originally balls of mud which included decomposing sea life and sediment. As the ocean receded, the balls were left to dry and crack. As they did so their Bentonite content shrunk and the space was filled with Calcite crystals formed from decaying sea shells.

$750-1,000   BELL

A pair of mid to late 19thC Indian rosewood occasional tables, the tripartite base with three lions, on bun feet.

30in (74.5cm) high

$3,800-5,000   L&T

ESSENTIAL REFERENCE - E.W. GODWIN

E.W. Godwin (1833-1886), British architect and designer, was described by Max Beerbohm as 'the greatest aesthete of them all'. His work embodied the Aesthetic Movement of 1865-85. He trained as an architect and his work included the original designs for Bedford Park and James Whistler's house in Tite Street Chelsea. However, the scope of his talent was not limited to buildings: he designed wallpaper, textiles, stained glass, lighting and costume and stage designs - particularly during the years he lived with the actress Ellen Terry. His furniture designs were Anglo-Japanese in style, often using ebonized wood. They achieved the perfect balance between the Aesthetic concept of 'art for art's sake' and Godwin's insistence that excess in design (and indeed life) ought to be avoided. He was engaged by many of the leading manufacturers including William Watt, Collinson and Lock, and Gillow and Co. and remains one of the most important designers of his era, with work held in public collections throughout Britain.

A coromandel wood occasional table, attributed to E.W. Godwin, for Collinson & Lock, the square top with parquetry banding above second tier below, repolished, the top is slightly warped.

28.5in (72cm) high

$4,400-5,700   CHEF

A 19thC walnut and micromosaic occasional table, in the manner of Gillows, the rectangular ebony top inset with an Italian micromosaic panel of convolvulus (bindweed), with a red marble border and oval malachite panels, the molded gilt brass edge on a leaf-carved stem, scroll legs and oval pad feet.

In the Turkish secret language of flowers, blue convolvulus means 'repose' or 'night' and pink convolvulus symbolizes 'worth sustained by judicious affection'.

29.5in (75cm) high

$9,500-10,500   WW

A Dutch floral marquetry occasional table.

34in (86cm) diam

$1,000-1,500   CHOR

A Florentine pietra dura table top, a central cartouche framing the Bavarian coat of arms flanked by the monogram ME (the initials of Maximillian and his wife Elizabeth of Lorraine), other stones including jasper, agate, sienna, with four large oval panels of dark blue lapis lazuli and eight smaller panels, minor damage.

70.5in (179cm) wide

$50,000-60,000   TEN

A 19thC Florentine 'pietra dura' octagonal table top, inlaid with various marbles and hardstones, including ruby, cornelian, lapis lazuli, jasper, malachite, sienna, brocatelle stone, and various agates.

98.5in (250cm) wide

$25,000-32,000   TEN

FURNITURE

A George III inlaid partridge
wood Pembroke table.
$25,000-32,000   **SWO**

ESSENTIAL REFERENCE - PEMBROKE TABLE

The term 'Pembroke' table originated with the Countess of
Pembroke, who reputedly ordered the first example of its type.
The Hepplewhite period in late 18thC England is epitomized
by the Neo-classical designs of the cabinetmaker George
Hepplewhite. His furniture patterns are characterized by a
classic simplicity and delicacy, light, curved forms, painted
or inlaid decoration, and distinctive details such as slender
tapering legs terminating in spade feet. The three oval panels
of Neo-classical marquetry, the use of inlaid dentil molding
framing the central drawer and the collars on the legs above
relate to furniture produced by Christoph Furlohg, a Swedish
cabinetmaker who was trained in Europe by the French ebeniste
Jean-François Oeben. He became an employee of John Linnell
at Berkeley Square and was much in demand for his marquetry
work of 'curiously inlaid mahogany and satinwood articles'.
He combined his French techniques with the new Neo-classical
taste in England, which attracted many distinguished patrons
including the Prince of Wales and the Duke of Portland.

A George III satinwood and marquetry Pembroke table, the serpentine
crossbanded top with a central oval
rosewood marquetry medallion inlaid
with a Neo-classical urn, the leaves
each with a fan medallion, the square
tapering legs decorated with water
leaf marquetry feet, with original
brass castors, inlaid throughout with
tulipwood bandings and stringing.
38.5in (98cm) wide
$19,000-25,000   **DN**

A George III mahogany and
inlaid Pembroke table, the
hinged top decorated with
a wide band of ribbon-tied
oak leaves and acorns within
boxwood lines, with later brass
castors, the top with damage.
39.75in (101cm) wide
$650-750   **BE**

A George III satinwood
and inlaid Pembroke table,
crossbanded in tulipwood,
bordered with boxwood and
ebony lines, on tapered legs,
headed with paterae, with brass
cappings and castors.
40in (101.5cm) wide
$2,500-3,200   **BE**

ESSENTIAL REFERENCE - SOFA TABLES

Sofa tables evolved from the Pembroke table during the last
quarter of the 18thC, the Pembroke being a lightweight, easily
movable, drop-leaf table, with one or two drawers, which
could be used at the bedside or for dining, writing and serving
tea. Almost invariably on castors for ease of movement, sofa
tables tend to be narrower and longer than Pembrokes, and
primarily designed to stand behind sofas, their tops used for
candlesticks, table-lamps or decorative artefacts. According
to Sheraton in 'The Cabinet Dictionary' (1803) the sofa table
was specifically for use 'before a sofa' where 'the Ladies chiefly
occupy them to draw, write or read upon'. They usually have
real drawers on one side, and dummy drawers on the other (the
side to face the back of the sofa). Their end supports are usually
united by a stretcher and are mounted on castors. Favored
woods include rosewood, mahogany and satinwood. The best
examples have end supports terminating in ornate metal
mounts. Examples from the Sheraton period are generally the
most sought-after and most Victorian and Edwardian examples
are copies of the tables from that style and period.

A George III fustic,
mahogany and satinwood
crossbanded Pembroke
table, in the manner of Thomas
Chippendale, the top crossbanded
and line inlaid, above a drawer
and an opposing false drawer, each
with a waived apron, above turned
tapering stop-fluted legs with
fluted terminals and surmounted by
carved patera terminals, on brass
caps and leather castors.

A Pembroke table with a similar exotic wood
twin-flap top and of similar proportions, was supplied to William,
5th Earl of Dumfries for Dumfries House, Ayrshire, c1759, possibly
by Thomas Chippendale. Chippendale is known to have employed
exotic woods in the manufacture of everyday furniture, such as
'pidgeon' wood, 'Guadalupe' wood, 'nutmeg' wood and 'Allegozant'.
Maclura tinctoria, commonly known as old fustic or dyer's mulberry
is a medium to large tree of the Neotropics, from Mexico to
Argentina.
c1790   *36.25in (92cm) wide*
$7,500-9,000   **DN**

A Regency rosewood sofa table,
the top inlaid with calamander
wood cross-banding and
boxwood stringing, the pair of
frieze drawers with ebony and
boxwood stringing.
59in (150cm) wide
$7,500-9,000   **DN**

A Regency rosewood and
cut brass inlaid sofa table,
crossbanded in coromandel
wood, fitted a blind drawer, on
a twist carved column, shaped
base and lion paw.
57.5in (146cm) wide
$3,800-5,000   **CHEF**

A Regency mahogany sofa table, with rosewood crossbanded hinged top.

54in (137cm) wide extended

$650-750   BE

A William IV mahogany and crossbanded sofa table, on wrythen reeded twin refectory supports joined by a conforming stretcher.

59in (150cm) long

$1,000-1,500   MOR

A Biedermeier-style maple and ebonized sofa table, with lyre-shaped ends.

c1900   *36.25in (92cm) wide*

$900-1,000   SWO

ESSENTIAL REFERENCE - JOSEPH-EMMANUEL ZWIENER

Joseph-Emmanuel Zwiener (1848-95) was one of the leading Parisian furniture makers of the end of the 19thC. He produced the very finest furniture, often inspired by the public collections in France. In order to differentiate between Messagé's commissions, the gilt bronze mounts were often marked to the reverse with the maker's initials. Several of Zwiener's mounts have been found to have a 'Zw', a 'IZ' or, as in this example, 'Z' on the reverse. This was primarily for the purpose of differentiation, rather than an artist's signature. Some of Zwiener's work was stamped, but not exclusively and only a few pieces have been found with a full signature and/or a date. There is a sketch by Message, dated 1871, of espagnolettes with plumed headdress and bound bodice very similar to those on this bureau plat on page 79 of Christopher Payne's book on Linke. The asymmetric profile of this table reflects the fact that it was originally offered for sale by Zwiener with the option of having a cartonnier standing at the larger end. Literature: Payne, Christopher (2003), 'François Linke, 1855-1946, The Belle Époque of French Furniture', Antique Collectors' Club, Woodbridge.

A Louis XV-style bureau, gilt-bronze mounted, of tulipwood and marquetry, plated with bronze mounts, designed by Léon Messagé and marked 'Z', probably for Joseph Emmanuel Zwiener.

57in (146cm) wide

$45,000-50,000   BELL

A Louis XV ormolu-mounted tulipwood amaranth and marquetry 'table à écrire', in the manner of Jaques Phillipe Carel, the underside with a label inscribed in ink '34731' and another label inscribed 'Mr Gordon', the underside of the slide inscribed ink 'Gailiau F1770/4pt(?) not...at...hait (?), remounted.

31in (79cm) wide

$4,500-5,000   MOR

ESSENTIAL REFERENCE - STOBO CASTLE

Stobo Castle, in the Scottish Borders, was built in 1805 from designs by the Scottish architect James Elliot. It replaced the earlier Manor of Stobo which itself had replaced an even earlier Tower House. In 1767 the estate was sold to the Graham-Montgomery family who owned the property until 1905 when it was sold to the cricketer Hylton Philipson who extensively changed the gardens. This unusual writing table is impressive not only for its scale, but also for the use of the single large slate slab that covers the top surface. While slate surfaces are not uncommon on furniture of the period, it is the sheer size of the piece which makes this table so remarkable. It is believed that the table was commissioned and installed soon after the new house was completed in 1811. It remained there through subsequent owners in the 20thC until the two-day sale of the contents of the Castle in 1972, when it was acquired by Sir James Stirling. The table was on loan for many years to the National Trust for Scotland and was on display in the Trust's previous premises on Charlotte Square, Edinburgh.

A George III satinwood lady's writing table, with Kingwood and harewood crossbanding, with a detachable rest above a cedarwood lined frieze drawer.

28in (57cm) wide

$1,100-1,500   WW

A Regency mahogany and ebonized slate top writing table, raised on fluted square tapered legs ending in bold carved lion paw feet.

c1815   *86.5in (220cm) long*

$9,500-10,500   L&T

ESSENTIAL REFERENCE - BERNARD MOLITOR

Bernard Molitor was born in Betzdorf, Luxembourg in 1755 and trained as a sculptor before moving to Paris, probably before 1778. He survived the French Revolution, the Terror, the Empire and even the Restoration without serious loss. At his death in 1833, he left a substantial fortune. In 1782, he advertised an ingenious patent hand warmer, fashioned as a small pile of books; the box in mahogany or walnut, had a metal liner which could be filled with hot coals. However, his output was not limited to innovative gadgets and he had a furniture workshop which enjoyed considerable success. In 1788, Molitor made the usual 'political' marriage. He married Elizabeth Fessard, daughter of the charpentier du roi. After this, he began to receive regular commissions from the Queen's circle. The Revolution brought ruin to many and death at the guillotine. The ace Molitor held was that his cousin, Michel, had been actively involved in the storming of the Bastille; with his help, Molitor managed to avoid arousing Revolutionary suspicions. Over the following decades, he had commissions from the Emperor Napoleon, King Jerome of Westphalia and many private noble collectors. Above all other factors, Molitor achieved success over this extended period because his work was consistently of outstanding quality.

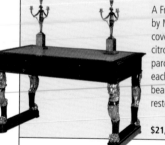

A French Empire rosewood bureau plat, by Molitor, the top with a pair of leather covered slides and a double tier of citronnier-lined drawers in the frieze, on parcel-gilt leopards-head monopodia, each stretcher, signed 'Molitor' and bearing the 'JME' stamp, gilding restored and leather replaced.

49.25in (125cm) wide

$21,000-25,000   DN

A 19thC figured walnut, inlaid and gilt metal mounted writing table.

49.25in (125cm) high

$300-450   WHP

An early 20thC gilt metal mounted Kingwood bureau plat.

58.25in (148cm) wide

$1,900-2,500   BELL

A mid-19thC French Kingwood, tulipwood and marquetry detailed bureau plat, with ormolu mounts in the Louis XV style, the underside of the table bearing a paper label for Princess Margaret, the serpentine shaped top above frieze drawer stamped to the underside 'B932'.

Provenance: This item was in the drawing room of the private apartment of HRH The Princess Margaret, Countess of Snowdon at Kensington Palace.

47in (119.5cm) wide

$4,400-5,700   APAR

A Victorian mahogany writing table.

45in (114cm) wide

$300-400   WHP

ESSENTIAL REFERENCE - TOWN & EMANUEL

Town and Emanuel (1830-1840) traded from 103 New Bond Street, and their trade card from a table formerly in the Duke of Buccleuch's collection is recorded in the Victoria and Albert Museum archives. It bears the trade label dated 183- stating '...Town & Emanuel. Manufacturers of Buhl Marquetrie, Resner & Carved Furniture, Tripods, Screens & c. Of the finest & most superb designs of the times of Louis 14th. Splendid Cabinets & tables inlaid with fine Sevres & Dresden China & c. Old paintings & Curiosities Brought & Exchanged; Buhl & Antique Furniture Repaired. By Appointment to Her Majesty'. Another label recorded on a Kingwood and tulipwood 'bureau plat' of Louis XV style bears the Arms of Queen Adelaide. In 1830, the firm supplied 3rd Lord Braybrooke with a looking-glass costing £8 5s for Audley End, Essex or his London house. In 1838 Town and Emanuel delivered 'new furniture' for Strafford House, London, at a cost of £12 12s. By 1840 they were listed in directories as Town & Co., 'dealers in & Manufacturers of antique furniture, curiosities & pictures'.

A 19thC première partie boulle writing table, by Town & Emanuel, inlaid with brass marquetry on an ebony and rosewood veneered ground, incorporating an early 18thC Regency boulle top, decorated in the manner of Jean Bérain, bearing the trade label of Town & Emanuel.

46in (117cm) wide

$10,000-13,000   DN

A Queen Anne concertina-acton card table, the shaped top is crossbanded and has herringbone inlay borders, the surface lifts to reveal a baize-lined interior with candle stands and guinea wells.

35in (89cm) wide

$15,000-19,000   **DN**

A George II walnut card table, in the manner of Benjamin Crook, the burr veneered fold-over top inlaid with feather banding, the baize lined interior with counter-wells and burr veneered candlestands.

33.5in (85cm) wide

$18,000-23,000   **WW**

A George II Irish mahogany card table, with a baize-lined surface with candlestands and counter-wells, the frieze with an applied carved shell.

36in (93cm) wide

$2,500-3,800   **WW**

A George II Irish mahogany games table, with candle-stands and counter wells, above inlaid chequer and backgammon boards, with a hinged compartment on a ratchet revealing a hinged backgammon frame.

34in (86.5cm) wide

$4,500-5,000   **WW**

An 18thC and later George II-style mahogany card table, with a concertina-action to reveal a baize-lined interior with candle stands and guinea wells, the hinges stamped 'H. Tibats'.

35in (89cm) wide

$9,000-10,000   **DN**

A pair of George III satinwood and marquetry card tables, supported on square tapering legs inlaid with classical marquetry, terminating in spade feet.

34.25in (87cm) wide

$15,000-19,000   **DN**

An 18thC walnut card table, the top with cross and feather banding revealing a baize-lined surface, counter-wells and candlestands, with later adaptations.

35in (89cm) wide

$1,600-2,300   **WW**

FURNITURE

ESSENTIAL REFERENCE - TRIC-TRAC

Tric-trac is a French variant of Backgammon. There are two main forms of the game, 'le Grand Tric-trac' and 'le Petit Tric-trac'. In Tric-trac, the starting point is called a talon; the points, or flèches, are numbered to 12 on both sides of the board, with the 12th point on either side called the 'coin de repos', or, simply, 'coin'. The 11th point (on either side) is often called 'le case d'écolier', or 'schoolboy's point' (case meaning 'square', literally) after the tendency of inexperienced players to rush to this point too soon in the game. Statistically, the most difficult points in the game to reach aside from the coins are the 8th points, and they are named 'les fleches de diable', or 'the Devil's points', for this reason. The home boards are referred to as the 'jan de retour' by either player. Doubles are treated as two identical numbers, unlike Backgammon proper.

A pair of Regency brass inlaid rosewood card tables, each fold-over top with a border of scrolling foliate inlay, with platform base, outswept legs and brass paw castors.

36in (91cm) wide

$6,500-7,500　　　　　　　**SWO**

A pair of Regency rosewood and brass-mounted card tables, each with a crossbanded hinged and swivel top revealing a baize-lined surface, with a bellflower and floret molding and a lyre base.

39.75in (101cm) wide

$8,000-9,500　　　　　　　**WW**

A French Empire mahogany Tric-trac table, the removable top with leather writing surface and green baize to the reverse, the interior with stained and polished ivory set within an ebony frame.

45.25in (115cm) wide

$6,500-7,500　　　　　　　**DN**

A mid-19thC French burr walnut and amboyna crossbanded serpentine card table.

37in (94cm) wide

$1,500-1,900　　　　　　　**APAR**

One of a pair of Anglo-Indian hardwood card tables (probably padouk), the frieze carved with flowerheads and scrollwork on acanthus carved cabriole legs with lion paw feet joined by leaf carved X-stretchers with central urn finial.

37.75in (96cm) wide

$9,000-10,000 pair　　**CHOR**

A George III ormolu-mounted sabicu fustic, mahogany and marquetry dressing table, the top with satinwood panel with a musical trophy and Mercury's Caduceus, with a mahogany lidded padouk interior of hinged lidded wells and one zinc lined well and lid, the underside with labels, one 'Mrs Simon Green', another printed 'Art Treasures Exhibition 1928/No.151', another 'Dept of Woodwork/On Loan from /... Green/~No.9', re-mounted, lacking mirror.

26.5in (67.5cm) wide

$3,200-3,800　　　　　　　**MOR**

An Edwardian late Regency-style mahogany fold-over card table, the table top with oval figured mahogany panel within satinwood framing.

30in (76cm) high

$900-1,000　　　　　　　**TRI**

An early 18thC walnut lowboy, on molded cabriole legs and Braganza feet.

29.5in (74.5cm) wide

$900-1,000　　　　　　　**WW**

A George III oak lowboy, on tapering legs with pad feet.

29in (74cm) wide

$700-800　　　　　　　**CHOR**

A George III mahogany tripod table, the piecrust and shell-carved top on fluted and spiral-fluted stem with acanthus cabriole legs and claw and ball feet, some damage.

28.5in (72cm) high

$450-550   CHOR

A 19thC rosewood tripod table, the top segmented with boxwood lines and centered with a Gothic tracery strung panel, some damage.

27.5in (70cm) high

$1,300-1,800   CHOR

ESSENTIAL REFERENCE - TRIPOD TABLES

Tripod tables were primarily made for holding tea and coffee equipage. Tea had been introduced to England from Holland in the early 17thC and in spite of the high prices and heavy duty imposed, it gradually became a fashionable drink around which great ceremony revolved. Toward the middle of the 18thC there was a shift from the former fashion of drinking in tea gardens to drinking at home. Consequently cabinet-makers turned their attention to the making of suitable ornamental tables, often for a special tea-room. In the 'Spectator' of 1745, a contributor wrote: 'The tea-table costs more to support than would maintain two children at nurse'. William Ince and John Mayhew illustrated designs for 'Tea Kettle Stands' in their 'The Universal System of Household Furniture' (1762), as did Thomas Chippendale in his 'The Gentleman and Cabinet Makers Director', London, third edition, 1762, page LV.

An 18thC-style carved mahogany supper table, after John Channon.

29.25in (74cm) wide

$400-500   BELL

An 18thC George III mahogany tray top tea table, raised on square straight legs with pierced corner brackets and ending in spade feet.

33.5in (85cm) high

$300-400   L&T

A George III mahogany tripod table, with piecrust top.

22.5in (57cm) diam

$3,800-5,000   DN

Judith Picks

I had to choose this table as it hails from the Scottish Borders and I spent many happy childhood weekends in Kelso and particularly Floors Castle. We collectors collect for many reasons and nostalgia is high on the list! The Mein family furniture-making firm operated in Kelso from 1784 until 1851. The principle maker and patriarch James Mein died in 1830 and the business passed to his nephew, also called James, who ran the company until its bankruptcy in 1851. Known for producing furniture of high quality, they counted among their clients the 5th and 6th Dukes of Roxburghe for Floors Castle, and the Earl of Haddington for Mellerstain.

An early 19thC Scottish Regency mahogany, rosewood and amboyne foldover tea-table, attributed to James Mein of Kelso, the pivoting foldover 'D'-shape crossbanded top with a beaded edge above a deep frieze with bird's eye maple panels.

38in (97cm) wide

$1,900-2,500   L&T

A pair of Victorian rosewood tea tables, with hinged swivel tops with molded edges each enclosing a well, the molded friezes having a scroll cartouche, one missing.

36in (91.5cm) wide

$1,500-1,800   BE

A George II mahogany silver table.

30.75in (78cm) wide

$900-1,000   CHOR

A Georgian mahogany and brass-bound cellarette or work table, on later polygonal column, quatrefoil platform and bun feet.

23.5in (60cm) wide

$180-250   BE

A Regency rosewood work table, with wool basket beneath, bearing the label of R. Loader, Cheapside.

21in (53cm) wide

$400-500   CHOR

A Regency rosewood and crossbanded drop-flap combined writing and work table, the frieze drawer fitted with inkwell and pen nib recesses, pen tray and hinged plush inset writing surface.

36.25in (90cm) wide

$450-500   BE

A William IV rosewood, coromandel, and specimen marquetry work table, with a pierced gallery, the drawer opening to a fitted drawer incorporating lidded divisions and Mother-of-pearl mounted accessories, the hexagonal stem with carved acanthus terminal, on carved scroll feet and concealed casters.

c1835   *31in (79cm) high*

$5,000-5,700   DN

A mid-19thC Regency-style rosewood work table, in the style of Gillows of Lancaster, the writing surface with pen drawers, one fitted with two glass inkpots, above a pair of long drawers over a silk-lined sliding work bag.

29in (74cm) high

$1,300-1,800   L&T

A Louis XV-style Kingwood, tulipwood, rosewood and gilt-metal mounted table à ouvrage, with Sèvres-style porcelain mount enclosing a velvet-lined interior and mirror.

c1860   *28in (71cm) high*

$1,900-2,500   TEN

CLOSER LOOK - PAPIER MÂCHÉ CABINET-ON-STAND

This table is by the noted Victorian cabinet maker John Joseph Mechi.

The catalog for the Great Exhibition 1851 illustrates a comparable work table by MECHI, page 739.

It has many desirable features - the hinged cover with silk-lined interior above a pair of paneled doors enclosing two fitted drawers. It has a further drawer with a rosewood writing slope, the ink and vesta boxes gilt stamped 'MECHI, 4 LEADENHALL ST'.

It has a fine quality barleytwist column and quadripartite base with scrolling legs and ceramic castors.

The decoration is excellent with gilt scrolling-framed painted scenes of peacocks and other birds in Neo-classical gardens, the cupboard doors painted with parrots with flowers and fruit.

A Victorian papier-maché work cabinet-on-stand.

38.5in (98cm) high

$11,000-14,000   LAW

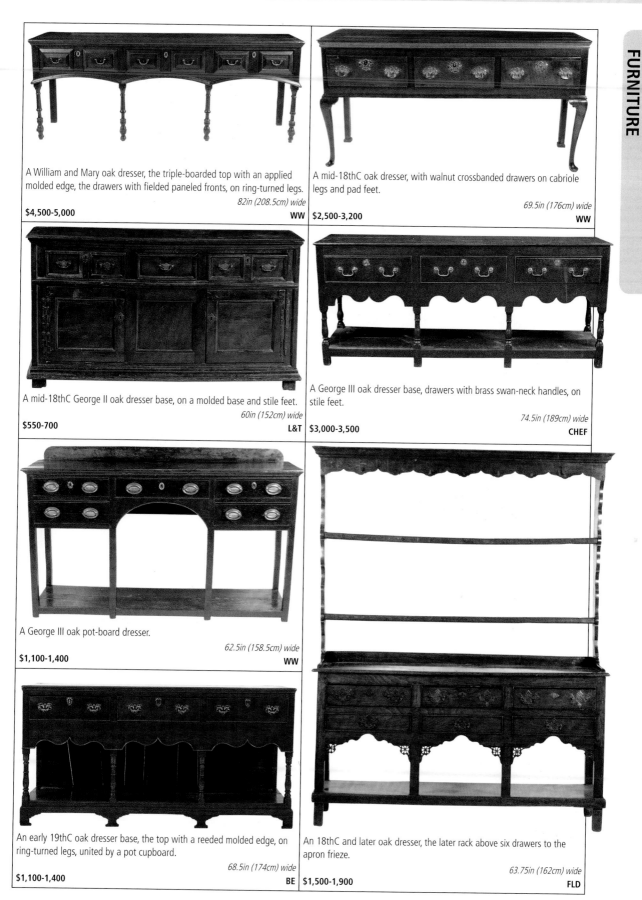

A William and Mary oak dresser, the triple-boarded top with an applied molded edge, the drawers with fielded paneled fronts, on ring-turned legs.

82in (208.5cm) wide

$4,500-5,000 WW

A mid-18thC oak dresser, with walnut crossbanded drawers on cabriole legs and pad feet.

69.5in (176cm) wide

$2,500-3,200 WW

A mid-18thC George II oak dresser base, on a molded base and stile feet.

60in (152cm) wide

$550-700 L&T

A George III oak dresser base, drawers with brass swan-neck handles, on stile feet.

74.5in (189cm) wide

$3,000-3,500 CHEF

A George III oak pot-board dresser.

62.5in (158.5cm) wide

$1,100-1,400 WW

An early 19thC oak dresser base, the top with a reeded molded edge, on ring-turned legs, united by a pot cupboard.

68.5in (174cm) wide

$1,100-1,400 BE

An 18thC and later oak dresser, the later rack above six drawers to the apron frieze.

63.75in (162cm) wide

$1,500-1,900 FLD

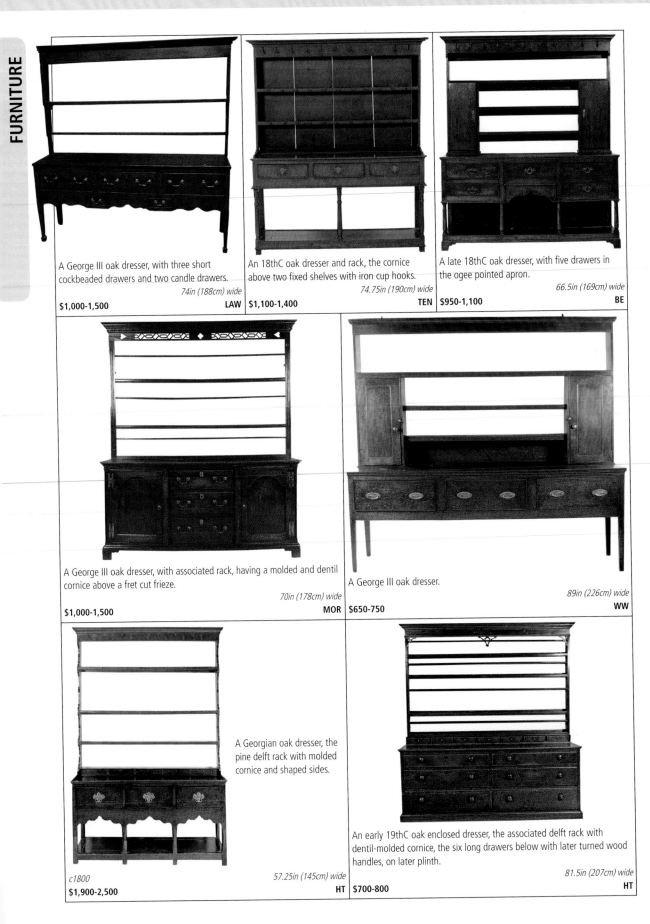

A George III oak dresser, with three short cockbeaded drawers and two candle drawers.

74in (188cm) wide

$1,000-1,500   LAW

An 18thC oak dresser and rack, the cornice above two fixed shelves with iron cup hooks.

74.75in (190cm) wide

$1,100-1,400   TEN

A late 18thC oak dresser, with five drawers in the ogee pointed apron.

66.5in (169cm) wide

$950-1,100   BE

A George III oak dresser, with associated rack, having a molded and dentil cornice above a fret cut frieze.

70in (178cm) wide

$1,000-1,500   MOR

A George III oak dresser.

89in (226cm) wide

$650-750   WW

A Georgian oak dresser, the pine delft rack with molded cornice and shaped sides.

c1800   *57.25in (145cm) wide*

$1,900-2,500   HT

An early 19thC oak enclosed dresser, the associated delft rack with dentil-molded cornice, the six long drawers below with later turned wood handles, on later plinth.

81.5in (207cm) wide

$700-800   HT

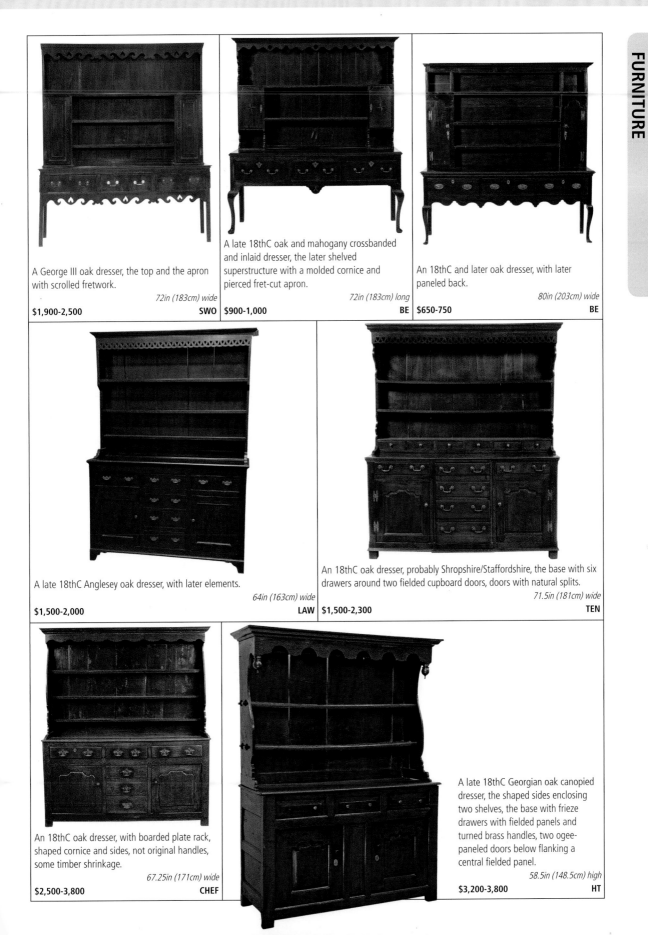

A George III oak dresser, the top and the apron with scrolled fretwork.

72in (183cm) wide

$1,900-2,500   SWO

A late 18thC oak and mahogany crossbanded and inlaid dresser, the later shelved superstructure with a molded cornice and pierced fret-cut apron.

72in (183cm) long

$900-1,000   BE

An 18thC and later oak dresser, with later paneled back.

80in (203cm) wide

$650-750   BE

A late 18thC Anglesey oak dresser, with later elements.

64in (163cm) wide

$1,500-2,000   LAW

An 18thC oak dresser, probably Shropshire/Staffordshire, the base with six drawers around two fielded cupboard doors, doors with natural splits.

71.5in (181cm) wide

$1,500-2,300   TEN

An 18thC oak dresser, with boarded plate rack, shaped cornice and sides, not original handles, some timber shrinkage.

67.25in (171cm) wide

$2,500-3,800   CHEF

A late 18thC Georgian oak canopied dresser, the shaped sides enclosing two shelves, the base with frieze drawers with fielded panels and turned brass handles, two ogee-paneled doors below flanking a central fielded panel.

58.5in (148.5cm) high

$3,200-3,800   HT

A George III oak dresser, on bracket feet.

63.75in (162cm) wide

$1,000-1,500   SWO

A George III oak dresser, with three shelves flanked by a small cupboard to each side, the inverted breakfront base with three frieze drawers over a central bank of three sham drawers.

78.75in (200cm) high

$2,800-3,500   TEN

A George III oak North Wales dresser, fitted six short drawers with diamond-shaped escutcheons, steel locks, replacement brass handles.

60.5in (154cm) wide

$1,000-1,500   PW

An 18thC ash dresser, the base with three paneled frieze drawers above a pair of cupboard doors.

66.75in (169.5cm) wide

$3,200-3,800   WW

An 18thC Welsh oak pewter cupboard.

62.5in (159cm) wide

$2,500-3,200   POOK

A Victorian oak dresser, the pot board base with molded top edging.

73in (185.5cm) wide

$1,300-1,800   HT

A 19thC oak dresser, base with three frieze drawers and two cupboards flanking a central recessed kennel.

67in (170cm) wide

$750-900   PW

An oak paneled and molded chest, with two doors which enclose three further drawers, the front with applied geometric molding and turnings within paneled sides.

c1660   *45in (114cm) wide*

$2,500-3,200   **SWO**

A Charles II cedar and walnut enclosed chest, in two halves, with hinged doors enclosing three oak drawers, with geometric paneled fronts with some ebony veneers on flattened bun feet, some wood off but present.

49in (124cm) high

$3,200-3,800   **WW**

A Charles II and later oak and walnut enclosed chest, in two halves, with ebonized decoration and inlaid with Mother-of-pearl and bone with flowers, portrait busts and rondels, with paneled architectural fronts, with key.

52.75in (134cm) high

$2,800-3,500   **WW**

A 17thC German walnut shrank, the breakfront molded cornice over ogee frieze centered by a carved cherub's head.

89in (226cm) high

$2,500-3,200   **HT**

A late 17th/early 18thC Dutch oak and inlaid 'schrank', with rosette-inlaid frieze, over two rosette inlaid paneled doors.

99.75in (253cm) wide

$2,300-2,800   **L&T**

An oak press cupboard.

c1700   *24in (61cm) wide*

$1,100-1,400   **HT**

A Queen Anne oak press cupboard, probably North Country, the frieze carved with vine leaves and grapes and with triad initials 'TCM' and the date '1704'.

70.5in (179cm) high

$900-1,000   **WW**

A mid-18thC oak press cupboard and base.

92.25in (234cm) high

$450-500   **MOR**

FURNITURE

A Pennsylvania sycamore schrank, with panel doors flanked by linenfold carved pilasters, resting on a three-drawer base.

c1780   *66in (168cm) wide*
$3,800-4,400   **POOK**

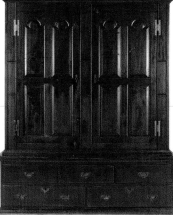

A Pennsylvania tiger maple two-part schrank, probably Chester County, with raised tombstone panel doors.

c1780   *83.5in (212cm) high*
$18,000-23,000   **POOK**

An oak court cupboard, the upper part with a central fall revealing drawers, on a base of three drawers and two doors.

61.5in (156cm) wide
$1,000-1,100   **PW**

A Louis XVI tulipwood, satinwood and specimen wood inlaid secrétaire abbatant, the mottled marble top above a frieze drawer and hinged fall opening to a fitted interior, the parquetry decorated fall centered by an oval medallion centered by initials 'D B'.

The marquetry initials to the fall of the secrétaire possibly relates to Madame du Barry. Jeanne Bécu, Countess du Barry was born on August 19, 1743, in Vaucouleurs, France. From 1743 to 1793, she was the King of France Louis XV's mistress. She was married to Louis XV's brother, Guillaume, for a short time before being installed at court in 1769. Bécu continued to assert her influence on Louis XV until he died and she left the court. In 1793, she was executed for treason in Paris.

c1780   *57.5in (146cm) high*
$3,200-3,800   **DN**

A late 18thC Pennsylvania walnut schrank, with a boldly molded cornice over raised panel doors flanked by fluted quarter columns.

63in (160cm) wide
$4,500-5,000   **POOK**

An early 19thC Pennsylvania Federal cherry corner cupboard, with overall barberpole inlay.

46in (117cm) wide
$2,500-3,200   **POOK**

A George III mahogany estate cabinet, with fitted interior with twenty three short drawers surrounding one open compartment.

39in (99cm) wide
$1,300-1,800   **TRI**

An 18thC English joined oak housekeeper's cupboard.

96in (244cm) high
$1,500-1,900   **TEN**

FURNITURE

A Welsh oak duodarn, the molded cornice above three recessed fielded panel doors above three short drawers and two three-paneled doors, with later shelves and supports.

c1800   59in (150cm) wide

$1,500-1,900   **CHOR**

A 19thC Goanese padoukwood cabinet, the upper section with shelves and two drawers with a secret drawer behind the left drawer.

48.75in (124cm) wide

$1,000-1,500   **SWO**

A pair of late 19thC Jacobean-style carved oak court cupboards.

44.75in (114cm) wide

$1,600-2,300   **POOK**

A Regency mahogany linen press, in the manner of Gillows, with ebonized moldings and stringing, the paneled doors enclosing six cedarwood and oak slides, above two short and two long drawers, with key.

54.25in (138cm) wide

$1,300-1,800   **WW**

A mid-19thC maple wood linen press, interior with fitted sliding trays with three long drawers beneath.

48in (122cm) wide

$1,100-1,500   **CHOR**

ESSENTIAL REFERENCE - A BOMBÉ LINEN PRESS

This unusual cabinet conforms almost exactly to an ambitious Rococo design in Thomas Chippendale's celebrated publication, 'The Gentleman and Cabinet-Maker's Director' of 1754. The Director is composed of a large collection of, as Chippendale said, 'the most elegant and useful designs of household furniture in the Gothic, Chinese and Modern taste.' The modern taste refers to the anglicized version of the forms and styles of France which strongly influenced Chippendale's work at this date and has been called 'for the most part an Anglicisation of the rocaille'. This taste is revealed in the design of this linen press, with the swelling bombé form of the base and the exceptional fine quality of the intricately designed carving to the feet, an interpretation in wood of the fine chased gilt bronze work of French metal-workers. The Director represented an unparalleled undertaking in the publication of furniture designs, with the first and second editions constituting 160 plates of superb engravings. The work exerted a powerful influence on contemporary style that was felt as far afield as the Prussian Court and Lisbon, and it established Chippendale as an inspired and innovative designer. A third edition, somewhat expanded, was to follow in a series of weekly publications in 1762. In the year of publication of the first edition, in which the design related to the present cabinet appears, Chippendale moved to spacious premises in St. Martin's Lane and began to provide furniture for a range of fashionable clients and nobility.

A William IV mahogany wardrobe, the panel cupboard doors opening to hanging space and two sliding trays, on a conforming plinth base.

c1835   74in (190cm) high

$950-1,100   **L&T**

A mid-19thC Victorian mahogany compendium wardrobe, with six drawers, flanked by cupboard doors opening to hanging space.

105in (266cm) wide

$500-650   **L&T**

A carved mahogany bombé linen press, to a design by Thomas Chippendale, slides to the interior, set to the top with two short and one long drawer with cast brass swan neck handles, the base centered below with stylized foliate motif, evidence of repairs around the hinges.

c1900   68in (172.5cm)

$3,200-3,800   **CHEF**

FURNITURE

This type of chest is characterized by its construction using dovetailed boards and decoration of geometrical and architectural designs in marquetry and inlay. In many respects they resemble chests made in Germany, and are now thought to have been made in London, particularly Southwark, by immigrants from northern Germany and the Netherlands from about 1560. Their decoration of picturesque towered buildings probably derive from 16thC printed designs, such as those published by Hans Vredeman de Vries (1527-1604). During the 20thC they came to be known as 'Nonsuch' chests, after Henry VIII's palace of Nonsuch in Surrey, because their decoration of fanciful buildings was thought, wrongly, to represent that building.

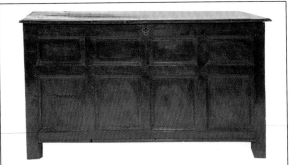

An oak coffer, probably Charles I, with four small and four large panels, enclosing a candle box.

57.5in (146cm) wide

$1,000-1,500　　SWO

A 'Nonsuch' chest, possibly late 16thC, with parquetry inlay in oak, holly and other woods, the front with two pedimented doorways with architectural panels between towers within parquetry borders.

41in (104cm) long

$8,000-9,500　　SWO

A mid-17thC oak coffer, the plank top over a lunette-carved frieze and four panels.

62.75in (159.5cm) wide

$1,500-2,000　　SWO

An oak coffer, probably Sussex, the front profusely carved, the central panel with a Romaine head flanked by panels with stylized flowers.

c1660　　*67.75in (172cm) wide*

$1,900-2,500　　SWO

A 17thC oak paneled coffer, hinged top has been reversed, front panels have been carved later.

53in (135cm) wide

$450-500　　CHEF

An early 18thC oak chest with carved later arches and geometric designs to the three front panels.

48.5in (123cm) wide

$550-650　　CHOR

An early 18thC oak coffer.

52in (132cm) long

$230-280　　BE

ESSENTIAL REFERENCE - PENNSYLVANIA CHEST

German immigrants came to Pennsylvania to build a new life in a new country. Talented immigrant craftsmen expressed their creativity by producing beautiful household furnishings for daily use. One of the most important items was the 'Aus schteier Kischt' (dower chest) also known as the hope chest or blanket chest. Young Pennsylvania immigrant girls between the ages of eight and ten began to sew household items in preparation for marriage. To store their growing accumulation of goods, their fathers or brothers would make them a 'kischt.' These chests were usually painted or stained in a dark color. The girl's name or initials, the date when made and the traditional Pennsylvania Dutch hearts and flowers were often painted on the front panel. Folkloric symbols, including those to ward off evil, were occasionally used. The amount of

decorations varied according to the wealth of the owner and the county in which the chest was made. On her wedding day, the bride proudly displayed her bed linens, quilts, needlework, other personal items and family heirlooms stored in her kischt. Following the ceremony, the kischt was loaded into the 'hochzich watte' (wedding wagon) for the trip to her new husband's home.

A painted poplar dower chest, Berks County, Pennsylvania, inscribed 'Christinna Linnen', retaining its original tulips and pinwheel flowers, with heart corners on a sponge decorated ocher ground.

1786   *47.5in (120.5cm) wide*

$3,800-5,000   **POOK**

A painted poplar dower chest, Lancaster, Pennsylvania, inscribed 'Barbara Waldin', on a blue ground with sponge panels and drawer fronts.

1793   *47.5in (120.5cm) wide*

$3,800-4,400   **POOK**

A child's painted pine dower chest, Lebanon County, Pennsylvania, decorated with two arched panels with star flower and tulips, flanked by heart corners.

c1800   *33in (84cm) wide*

$5,000-5,700   **POOK**

A Pennsylvania painted pine dower chest, the front decorated with stars and tulips on a blue ground.

c1800   *48in (122cm) wide*

$5,000-6,500   **POOK**

Judith Picks

I am quite fascinated by the traditional painted Scandinavian and the similarities with Pennsylvanian Dutch (or more correctly Deutch). Rosemåling is the name of a traditional form of decorative folk art that originated in the rural valleys of Norway, and comprises decorative painting on wood that uses stylized flower ornamentation, scrollwork, lining and geometric elements, often in flowing patterns. Landscape and architectural elements are also common. Many other decorative painting techniques were used such as glazing, spattering, marbelizing and manipulating the paint with the fingers or other objects. Rosemåling is also common in rural Sweden (Swedish: rosmålning). As with its Norwegian counterpart, it was most popular from the latter half of the 18thC until the 1860s. There is evidence to suggest that in the early years of the 19thC some itinerant Scandinavian painters emigrated to the Eastern seaboard of the United States and influenced paint techniques there.

An early 19thC Scandinavian painted pine marriage chest, painted with panels of flowers, the interior with a candle compartment and a drawer, painted with crowns and inscribed 'Christi Ols Pattir Orsund 1819 Fod Din 1ste October Mar 1802', with key.

48in (122.5cm) wide

$500-650   **WW**

An early 17thC and later walnut and oak and inlaid chest, on bun feet.

36.5in (93cm) long

$400-500   **WHP**

A 17thC paneled and molded oak chest, the hinged top over a dummy drawer and three long drawers.

36.25in (92cm) high

$1,000-1,500   **SWO**

A late 17thC William and Mary walnut oyster veneered chest-of-drawers, the molded rectangular top with concentric circle line inlay, raised on turned bun feet.

37.75in (96cm) wide

$3,800-4,400   **L&T**

A late 17thC William and Mary walnut chest-of-drawers, the crossbanded quarter-veneered top, above crossbanded drawers.

38in (97cm) wide

$3,800-4,400   **L&T**

A late 17thC William and Mary olivewood oyster veneered chest-of-drawers, the molded top with tracery stringing, on later feet, restored and polished, later brass.

36.75in (93cm) wide

$4,500-5,000   **TEN**

CLOSER LOOK - A WILLIAM AND MARY KINGWOOD CHEST

This is an excellent example of a late 17thC chest with good color and figuration.

The geometric top has finely figured oyster veneer and cross banded borders.

The brass ring handles and keyhole escutcheons are original.

Although the top has some small splits and signs of some small replacements to the veneers and the feet are later, the quality and early date of the piece commands a high price.

A William and Mary Kingwood chest, fitted with three long and two short drawers with oyster veneer, on bracket feet, the bases of the upper two short drawers look replaced, the right side (as you face it) has some fading and signs of repair near top left corner.

40.5in (103cm) wide

$15,000-19,000   **CHOR**

A William and Mary burr yew and walnut chest-of-drawers, later inlay of diamond and two hearts to top, oak lined and with stains to drawer interior, bun feet from later period.

40in (96.5cm) wide

$2,500-3,200 CHOR

An early 18thC and later walnut and marquetry chest-on-stand.

43in (110cm) high

$1,200-1,400 DN

A George II walnut chest, inlaid with boxwood and ebonized stringing, the quarter-veneered and crossbanded top with a molded edge, above a brushing slide with a later baize lining.

31in (79cm) high

$4,400-5,700 WW

A mid-18thC mahogany bachelor's chest, with fold-over top.

31.5in (80cm) high

$1,600-2,000 SWO

A George III mahogany serpentine chest-of-drawers, with cockbeaded drawers flanked by blind fret-carved angles, the top drawer fitted with a sliding leather lined writing surface with compartments and covered wells.

c1760 *41.75in (106cm) wide*

$5,500-7,000 L&T

A small early George III mahogany bachelor's chest, by George Speer, the pull-out brushing slide with a printed paper trade label, with later castors.

George Speer (1736-1802), was based at 'The Seven Stars' 2 Great Tower Street, London, by 1761 and was a cabinet-maker and undertaker. His first mention in the London directories isn't until 1777. A small number of items have been recorded with his Rococo trade label which he shared with his cousin John.

30.75in (78cm) wide

$1,800-2,300 WW

FURNITURE

An early George III mahogany chest, fitted with a brushing slide, the drawers between ebonized and maple inlaid simulated fluted canted angles, on bracket feet.

37.5in (95cm) wide

$2,500-3,200   BE

A George III figured mahogany serpentine chest-of-drawers, the top with a brushing slide with velvet lining, above cockbeaded drawers with entwined vine brass loop handles with ribbon-tied flowerhead backplates.

c1760   *36in (91cm) wide*

$8,000-9,500   L&T

A Philadelphia Chippendale mahogany chest-of-drawers, with four drawers and fluted quarter columns.

c1770   *35.75in (91cm) wide*

$8,000-9,500   POOK

A rare Pennsylvania Chippendale child's walnut tall chest.

c1770   *25.25in (64cm) wide*

$11,000-12,000   POOK

A late 18thC George III mahogany serpentine chest-of-drawers, with brushing slide above four graduated drawers, reeded canted pilasters and serpentine side.

41in (104cm) wide

$2,500-3,200   LAW

Judith Picks

I do love a good story and it all starts so innocently! The 18thC Scottish father-and-son cabinet-makers Francis and William Brodie specialized in domestic furniture including cabinets, chests-of-drawers and mirrors. Francis was regarded in his time as Edinburgh's leading cabinet-maker. Accounts show that he may have been in partnership with his son from 1764, and they are recorded working together as Brodie & Son in the Edinburgh Street Directory, 1773-74. Both father and son held the title of Deacon of the Incorporation of Wrights, and William acted as a member of the town council. William Brodie is now remembered mainly for having led a double-life. Despite inheriting the business from his father in 1782, in addition to a sum of £10,000, Brodie ran up great debts through two mistresses, numerous children and a gambling habit. Taking advantage of his respected position as craftsman and locksmith, he would make impressions of clients' keys and return to burgle them. In 1788, along with three other men, Brodie attempted his most audacious robbery: to steal the revenues of Scotland from the Excise Office in Edinburgh. Two of his associates who were caught and tempted with a reward for information, named Brodie as the mastermind. He was eventually caught in Holland where he had fled. 25 lock picks were used in evidence against him, some of which were found hidden on Salisbury Crags on Arthur's Seat.
As a result, Brodie was hanged at the Old Tolbooth on Edinburgh's High Street before a crowd of 40,000 people. William Brodie's scandalous life and death is said to be the inspiration for Robert Louis Stevenson's 'Dr Jekyll and Mr Hyde'.

An 18thC George III mahogany bowfront chest-of-drawers, the bowfront top with a molded edge, raised on shaped bracket feet.

49.25in (125cm) wide

$3,200-3,800   L&T

An 18thC Scottish George III mahogany serpentine chest-of-drawers, attributed to the workshop of Francis and William Brodie, raised on scroll carved bracket feet.

40.5in (103cm) wide

$9,500-10,500   L&T

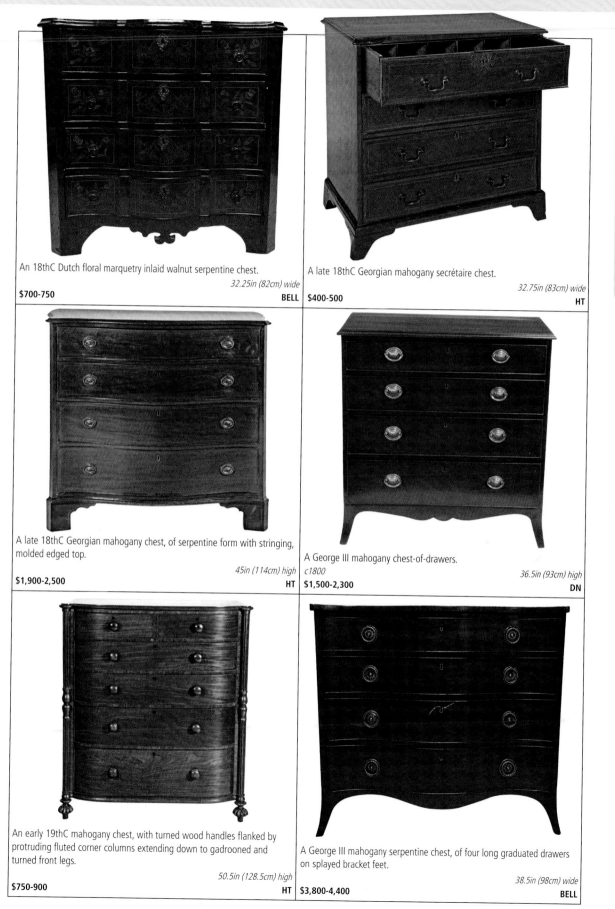

An 18thC Dutch floral marquetry inlaid walnut serpentine chest.

32.25in (82cm) wide

$700-750　　　　　　　　　　　　　　**BELL**

A late 18thC Georgian mahogany secrétaire chest.

32.75in (83cm) wide

$400-500　　　　　　　　　　　　　　**HT**

A late 18thC Georgian mahogany chest, of serpentine form with stringing, molded edged top.

45in (114cm) high

$1,900-2,500　　　　　　　　　　　　**HT**

A George III mahogany chest-of-drawers.

c1800　　　　　　　　　　　*36.5in (93cm) high*

$1,500-2,300　　　　　　　　　　　　**DN**

An early 19thC mahogany chest, with turned wood handles flanked by protruding fluted corner columns extending down to gadrooned and turned front legs.

50.5in (128.5cm) high

$750-900　　　　　　　　　　　　　　**HT**

A George III mahogany serpentine chest, of four long graduated drawers on splayed bracket feet.

38.5in (98cm) wide

$3,800-4,400　　　　　　　　　　　　**BELL**

CHESTS-OF-DRAWERS

FURNITURE

A George III mahogany concave chest-of-three-drawers, with turned reeded columns on tapering bun feet.

46in (117cm) wide

$5,500-6,500

CHOR

A Regency mahogany chest-of-drawers.
c1815
36in (91cm) high
$400-500

DN

A 19thC oak and brass bound military chest/writing desk, in two parts, the upper part with drawers with a writing drawer below, with satinwood veneered and leather writing surface and stationery compartment below, with compartments, the lower part with drawers.

45in (114.5cm) wide

$1,400-1,800

BE

ESSENTIAL REFERENCE - COLLECTORS' CHEST

This type of chest was first seen in the 1820s and is tall and narrow, and usually has a locking flap on one side which, when closed, prevents any of the drawers from opening. They were named after the Duke of Wellington, whose successful campaigns against Napoleon had made him a national hero. They continued to be made in the Victorian period in mahogany, walnut and rosewood. Some had a fitted secrétaire occupying two drawer heights, but these are not considered as desirable as the all-drawer model. Due to their compact size, Wellington chests can be keenly sought and can command high prices, as with these examples here which are a pair, early and made of rosewood. Because of the price differential, be aware that some secrétaire versions may have been converted back to full-drawer models, the give-away being the new drawer linings.

A Victorian mahogany Wellington chest-of-drawers, with seven graduated drawers enclosed by locking bar.

61in (155cm) high

$1,500-1,900

BELL

A pair of Victorian rosewood collectors' chests, each with a glazed lift top display case above a bank of thirteen drawers each containing an antique collection of insects including butterflies, moths, dragonflies, the drawers locked by flanking Wellington action pillasters, the locks hidden behind removable capitals.
c1840
39.75in (101cm) high
$15,000-19,000

DN

A 19thC rosewood Wellington chest, the six drawers enclosed by scroll-mounted locking bar.

24in (61cm) wide

$2,800-3,500

BELL

An early 18thC French ormolu-mounted Kingwood and rosewood parquetry inlaid bowfront commode, minor losses of veneer notable to right side of the bottom two drawers.

53.5in (136cm) wide

$1,900-2,500   **BELL**

A mid-18thC Louis XV-style fruitwood and ebony inlaid Kingwood, tulipwood and marquetry commode, in the manner of Latz, of bombé serpentine form with a molded bréche d'Alep marble top.

47.5in (121cm) wide

$16,000-20,000   **GORL**

A Louis XV walnut commode, with variegated red marble top, drawers with molded fronts and flanking carved foliate decoration, with cabriole legs and stylized hoof feet.

c1750   50in (127cm) wide

$4,400-5,700   **DN**

ESSENTIAL REFERENCE - GEORGE III COMMODE

William Gomm established a cabinet-making and upholstery workshop at Peterborough Court, in the parish of St. Bartholomew, Smithfield c1725. By 1756 Richard William's son was working for the business and in 1763 the company was titled William Gomm & Son & Co. William Gomm is chiefly remembered for his association with Abraham Roentgen having given the famous German cabinet-maker a work experience placement during his time in London in the 1730s. His major commission was to furnish Stoneleigh Park, Warwickshire for the 5th Lord Leigh in 1763, where he worked with the decorators Bromwich & Leigh and produced at least six serpentine dressing commode tables similar to this commode. See Geoffrey Beard and Christopher Gilbert, 'Dictionary of English Furniture Makers 1660-1840', pages 115 and 349-350 for a discussion of William Gomm.

A mid-18thC Italian commode, the serpentine veined marble top over parquetry inlaid rosewood and Kingwood bombé base.

58.5in (149cm) wide

$3,800-5,000   **BELL**

An early George III mahogany serpentine dressing commode, attributed to William Gomm, with crossbanded top, the drawers with original brass swan-neck handles, the top drawer with a slide which part hinges above compartments and divisions, the bracket feet and aprons carved with scrolling leaves and rocaille on brass castors.

46.25in (117.5cm) wide

$45,000-50,000   **WW**

A George III mahogany serpentine commode, with Kingwood banding, the top drawer with a baize-lined slide and with divisions.

39in (99cm) wide

$2,300-2,800   **WW**

One of a pair of 18thC Genoese painted commodes, with Portassanta molded serpentine tops, each with two drawers decorated 'sans traverse' with foliate scrolls and swags on a pale green background, the scroll legs terminating in gilt sabots, the handles are period replacements, decoration restored.

48.75in (123.5cm) wide

$80,000-90,000 pair   **DN**

A George III mahogany commode, in the manner of Thomas Chippendale, with an unusual arrangement of ten drawers surrounding two dummy drawers in the center revealing one deep compartment, the dummy drawers later adapted.

The highly unusual bracket feet on this commode are almost identical to those seen on a pair of serpentine commodes supplied by Thomas Chippendale to Ninian Home for Paxton House, Scotland in 1774. This rare bracket foot is also found on another serpentine commode, almost certainly by Chippendale, supplied to the 10th Earl of Pembroke for Wilton House Wiltshire, c1770. The link to Chippendale is strengthened by the fact that the handles on the present commode are of a pattern frequently used by Chippendale. As well as being of a grand size and of superb color the commode is also distinguished by its highly unusual serpentine outline and drawer arrangement - quite possibly a unique combination.

49in (125cm) wide

$20,000-25,000   **DN**

A late 18thC French marble-topped commode, with an ormolu-mounted marquetry inlaid Kingwood and tulipwood base.

43in (110cm) wide

$1,000-1,500   **BELL**

A late 18thC French secrétaire commode, the marble top over a later adapted secrétaire drawer and two further drawers, with corners stamped 'J.F Leleu' and 'JME'.

51in (130cm) wide

$900-1,000   **BELL**

A George III and later mahogany serpentine commode, the top above a baize-lined brushing slide and four drawers.

35.5in (90cm) wide

$3,200-3,800   **WW**

An early 19thC gilt-metal mounted Kingwood and padauk commode.

52in (132cm) wide

$1,500-2,300   **BELL**

ESSENTIAL REFERENCE - BIEDERMEIER

Biedermeier was an influential German style of furniture design that evolved during the years 1815-1848. The style was also popular in Scandinavia. It is characterized by restraint, conventionality, and utilitarianism. It is often portrayed as boring and conventional, in fact, bourgeois. It derived from the name of Gottlieb Biedermaier, a fictitious German provincial schoolmaster and poet created by L. Eichrodt (1854). It generally was characterized as a simplification of the French Directoire and Empire styles, usually executed in fruitwood with much use of matched veneers, and often displaying architectural motifs. Throughout the period, emphasis was kept upon clean lines and minimal ornamentation consistent with Biedermeier's basis in utilitarian principles. It was a rebellion against Romantic-era fussiness. Middle class growth originated in the English industrial revolution and many Biedermeier

designs owe their simplicity to Georgian lines of the 19thC, as the proliferation of design publications reached the Germanic states and the Austro-Hungarian empire. Biedermeier furniture used locally available materials such as cherry, ash and oak woods rather than the expensive timbers such as imported mahogany. Much local fruitwood was stained to imitate the more expensive timbers. Stylistically, the furniture was simple and elegant. Its construction utilized the ideal of truth through material, something that later influenced the Bauhaus and Art Deco periods.

A matched pair of Biedermeier walnut commodes, each with a beveled caddy top over drawers with ebony shield escutcheons, within fluted pilasters.

c1830   50.5in (128cm) wide

$10,000-11,000   SWO

A Louis XIV-style boulle marquetry, ebony, and ebonized commode, with brass mounts throughout, inlaid with anthemion, arabesques foliate scrollwork, cornucopia and central figures of acrobats, musicians, exotic birds, and animals, raised on short leafy gilt metal feet.

c1860   53in (135cm) wide

$18,000-23,000   L&T

A late 19thC French Louis XV-style rosewood, Kingwood, floral marquetry and gilt metal mounted petit commode, of serpentine form, on slender cabriole legs with gilt mounts and sabots.

32.5in (83cm) high

$1,500-2,300   TEN

A late 19thC gilt-metal mounted rosewood and Kingwood commode in 18thC style.

44in (112cm) wide

$650-750   BELL

A late 19thC Victorian mahogany serpentine commode, painted with flowering urns and flower garlands, opening to two sliding trays, the sides painted with exotic figures in gardens.

50in (128cm) wide

$4,400-5,700   L&T

A William and Mary pollard oak chest-on-stand, with holly stringing throughout.

c1690   *51in (129cm) high*

$6,500-7,500   DN

A William and Mary holly-strung pollard oak chest-on-stand, on barley twist supports, united by concave perimeter stretcher.

51in (130cm) high

$5,000-6,500   BELL

A Queen Anne walnut chest, on a later stand, with feather-banded border decoration, some timber shrinkage cracks, later brass handles and escutcheon.

64.5in (163.5cm) high

$2,500-3,200   CHEF

An early 18thC Queen Anne walnut feather-banded chest-on-stand, in two parts.

63in (160cm) high

$2,500-3,200   L&T

A George II walnut chest-on-stand, handles replaced, evidence of old worm, chips and splits, warping to the pine drawer fonts.

c1740   *63in (160cm) high*

$2,300-2,800   DN

A William and Mary walnut and cherry two-part high chest, Massachusetts, with trumpet-turned legs joined by flat serpentine stretchers.

c1740   *62.5in (159cm) high*

$13,000-15,000   POOK

A Queen Anne walnut two-part high chest, Pennsylvania, retaining its original brass hardware and an old mellow surface.

c1765   *75in (190.5cm) high*

$13,000-18,000   POOK

A late 17thC William and Mary walnut cabinet-on-chest, the doors covered in floral marquetry and opening to drawers, secret compartments and pigeon holes.

66.5in (169cm) high

$5,000-6,500 **L&T**

A 17thC Kingwood oyster-veneered and rosewood cabinet, on 19thC chest, the doors opening to the central cupboard door with three concealed drawers and a secret compartment.

cabinet c1690   58.75in (149cm) high

$3,800-5,000 **DN**

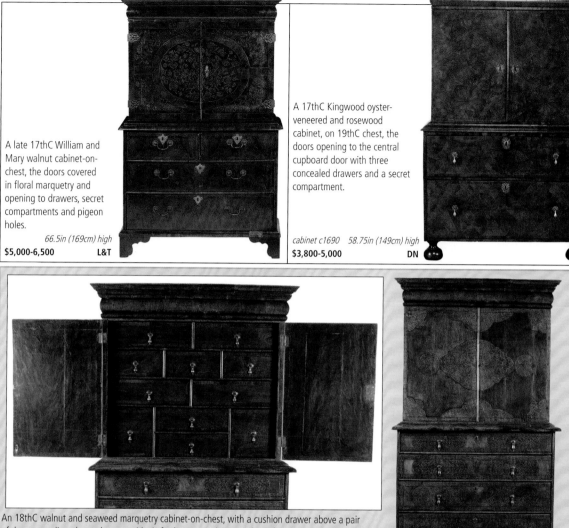

An 18thC walnut and seaweed marquetry cabinet-on-chest, with a cushion drawer above a pair of doors revealing eleven drawers with six further secret drawers, above four long drawers, on bun feet, with key.

72.5in (184cm) high

$3,800-5,000 **WW**

A George II walnut and crossbanded chest-on-chest, the lower part with a brushing slide over three further long drawers, raised on shaped bracket feet.

c1730   77in (195cm) high

$2,500-3,800 **L&T**

A George II walnut chest-on-chest, with three short and six long cross and feather-banded drawers, flanked by fluted angles, on bracket feet.

70.5in (178.5cm) high

$1,300-1,800 **WW**

An important Queen Anne walnut 'Octorara' chest-on-chest, Chester County, Pennsylvania, the upper section with a wall of troy molding, over a linen drawer and three arched drawers, resting on a two-drawer base, supported by ogee bracket feet with closed spurs.

Illustrated in Beckerdite, 'American Furniture 2011', figure 47.

c1760   88in (223.5cm) high
$45,000-50,000   **POOK**

A George III mahogany chest-on-chest, with brass swan-neck handles, on shaped bracket feet.

72in (183cm) high
$650-750   MOR

A George III figured mahogany chest-on-chest, with bracket feet.

74in (188cm) high
$950-1,100   TRI

A George III mahogany chest-on-chest, with an arcaded cornice and blind-fretted frieze, good original condition, section of molding missing to back right middle, minor faults on blind fret carving.

43.25in (110cm) high
$6,500-7,500   **TEN**

A late 18thC Georgian mahogany chest-on-chest, the dentil-molded cornice over plain frieze, on ogee bracket feet.

76.5in (194.5cm) high
$2,500-3,200   HT

A late 18thC George III mahogany chest-on-chest, the molded cornice above a strung frieze.

74in (188cm) high
$1,000-1,500   TEN

A late 18thC Lombardy escritoire, with gilded moldings to the rosewood frieze drawer set with marble specimens and with landscape enamel handle, the fall with central green marble oval panel surrounded by marble specimens on a rosewood and purpleheart ground, interior with two rows of four drawers, flanking pigeon holes, two specimens missing and one replace with wax, the central porcelain drawer roundel cracked.

63in (160cm) high

$32,000-38,000 **CHOR**

A Georgian mahogany secrétaire cabinet, the interior with central division and adjustable shelving, with secrétaire drawer.

c1800 *89.75in (228cm) high*

$450-550 **HT**

A 19thC Dutch mahogany secrétaire abbatant, floral marquetry inlaid decoration, with a blind frieze drawer, fitted interior enclosed by a fall front writing slope and cupboards below.

60.25in (153cm) high

$1,300-1,800 **CHEF**

A Connecticut Chippendale cherry secretary desk, probably Colchester, with philphlot rosettes and fan-carved prospect doors.

c1770 *83.5in (212cm) high*

$6,500-7,500 **POOK**

A George III mahogany 'Estate' secrétaire bookcase, in the manner of Gillows of Lancaster, the broken swan-neck pediment with carved bosses, with an unusual two-tier secrétaire drawer, with three secret drawers over compartments, two slides with letters, some losses.

95.75in (243cm) high

$2,300-2,800 **SWO**

A George III mahogany and Kingwood-banded secrétaire bookcase, the lower part with a fitted, satinwood veneered secrétaire drawer, with key.

91in (231cm) high

$1,300-1,800 **TEN**

A George III mahogany secrétaire bookcase, the base with fitted secrétaire drawer over two paneled doors enclosing four long drawers.

This bookcase is in unrestored condition. The timber is of lovely quality and will be a spectacular piece when fully restored.

90.25in (229cm) high

$8,000-9,500   TEN

A George III satinwood secrétaire bookcase, in the manner of Mayhew & Ince, with amaranth and rosewood banding and stringing, with later swan-neck carved cornice, with a later leather-lined writing surface and pigeon holes and drawers with ivory handles, with two keys and screws.

103.25in (262cm) high

$34,000-38,000   WW

A George III mahogany secrétaire bookcase, the base with secrétaire drawer above three drawers, on bracket feet.

86.25in (219cm) high

$550-700   CHOR

A Georgian mahogany secrétaire bookcase, secrétaire drawer with ebony stringing, with fitted interior with drawers and pigeon holes.

c1800   *95in (241.5cm) high*

$700-800   HT

A William IV colonial teak campaign secrétaire bookcase, possibly camphor, base with fitted secrétaire drawer above three graduated drawers, ivory line inlay and brass swing carry handles.

35in (88.5cm) wide

$2,800-3,800   LAW

An early 20thC Edwardian satinwood, rosewood, inlay and penwork secrétaire bookcase, the lower part with a drawer with a fall front and pigeon holes and drawers.

80.75in (205cm) high

$2,500-3,800   L&T

A Queen Anne walnut bureau bookcase, mirrored arched doors above a cross and feather-banded fall, with a well-and-step interior, mirror plates are later and re-backed, handles and locks replaced, extensive restoration.

40.5in (103cm) wide

$5,000-6,500 CHOR

An early 18thC George I walnut bureau bookcase, the lower part with a slant front, opening to pigeon holes, drawers and a baize line writing surface.

By family repute this came from Glamis Castle. Previously belonged to the late Sir Robert Stodart Lorimer (1864-1929), prominent Scottish architect and furniture designer. Amongst his notable commissions were the renovations for Lennoxlove House as well as his designs for the Scottish baronial houses Rowallan, Ayrshire; Ardkinglas, Argyllshire; and Formakin, Renfrewshire. This piece was in Lormier's drawing room at Gibliston, his house near Kellie, in Fife.

87.75in (223cm) high

$2,800-3,800 L&T

A Queen Anne walnut bureau bookcase, the double-dome top with molded cornice and a pair of mirrored doors enclosing three shelves, the bureau base, the hinged fall with inset writing surface and lidded well, shaped interior with pigeon holes and drawers, the handles, the locks and escutcheons and the feet are later but in keeping with the style of the piece.

c1710   *88.25in (224cm) high*

$10,000-11,000 DN

An early 18thC Queen Anne oak bureau bookcase, the associated lower part with a slant front opening to drawers and pigeon holes.

84in (213cm) high

$900-1,000 L&T

A George I walnut bureau bookcase, the bureau base with fall enclosing an arrangement of pigeonholes, drawers, and concealed well, above two short and two long drawers, on bracket feet.

c1720

$3,800-5,000 DN

A George II walnut bureau bookcase, the bureau base with feather-banded fall opening to a fitted interior with drawers and pigeon holes and a concealed well.

c1735   *79in (200cm) high*

$11,000-13,000 DN

FURNITURE

A George III mahogany bureau bookcase, with breakarch pediment, dentil cornice with blind-fret decorated frieze, the bureau base fitted with drawers, cupboard and pigeon holes.

c1770   *89in (226cm) high*

$1,900-2,500   **CHEF**

An 18thC German figured walnut bureau bookcase, with a fitted interior, the fall also enclosing a fitted welled interior.

      43in (109cm) wide

$2,800-3,800   **BELL**

A Dutch walnut and marquetry bureau bookcase, the fall opening to drawers and central cupboard above a concealed well, the serpentine base with three drawers, on stylized hairy lion paw feet, some damage.

c1800   *97.25in (247cm) high*

$13,000-15,000   **DN**

A late 18thC walnut bureau bookcase, the fall front revealing a stepped interior with a well.

      38.5in (98cm) wide

$2,300-2,800   **PW**

A 20thC Chippendale-style walnut secretary desk and bookcase, by Frank Auspitz, York, Pennsylvania.

Frank Auspitz was a self-educated expert in 18thC furniture and architecture. He specialized in designing and creating reproductions of period furniture and homes and shared his skills with clients around the US. He owned and operated Auspitz Cabinet Shop in York for over 50 years.

      102.25in (260cm) high

$5,500-7,000   **POOK**

A George III mahogany breakfront bookcase, the dentil cornice over four astragal-glazed doors and four paneled doors, enclosing drawers and shelves.

88.5in (225cm) high

$1,300-1,900   **SWO**

A George III mahogany breakfront library bookcase, the internal shelves are possibly later associated.

c1790   *91in (231cm) high*

$8,000-9,500   **DN**

A late George III mahogany, crossbanded and boxwood strung six-door library bookcase, of breakfront form, with keys, in sleepy, unrestored condition.

130in (329cm) wide

$9,000-10,000   **TEN**

A George IV and later mahogany breakfront library bookcase.

81in (206cm) wide

$2,800-3,500   **CHEF**

A William IV mahogany breakfront library bookcase.

94.5in (271cm) wide

$9,000-10,000   **CHEF**

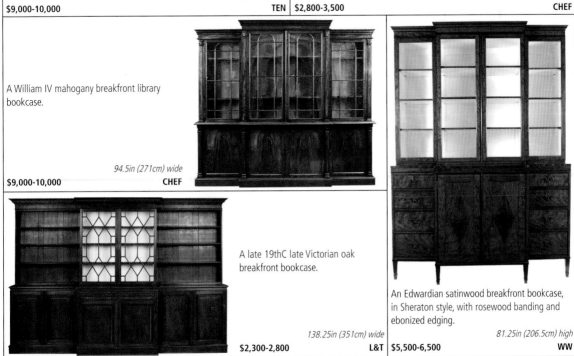

A late 19thC late Victorian oak breakfront bookcase.

138.25in (351cm) wide

$2,300-2,800   **L&T**

An Edwardian satinwood breakfront bookcase, in Sheraton style, with rosewood banding and ebonized edging.

81.25in (206.5cm) high

$5,500-6,500   **WW**

An early 19thC Regency pollard oak bookcase cabinet, in the manner of George Bullock, the base with a pair of paneled cupboard doors enclosing five drawers with turned pulls, the whole with ebony line inlay.

George Bullock made a pair of bookcase cabinets for Napoleon Bonaparte's house on St Helena with a similar arrangement of bookcase and cabinet enclosing drawers.

A late 18thC George III mahogany and ebony library bookcase, the molded cornice with dentil and ebonized egg-and-bead molding above four doors with astragal-glazed panels.

91.25in (232cm) long

$7,500-9,000   **L&T**

75in (191cm) high

$14,000-18,000   **LAW**

A 19thC Italian carved walnut bookcase, in Baroque-style, of breakfront form surmounted by griffins and centered by dragons around a carved cartouche.

107in (272cm) high

$6,500-7,500   **TEN**

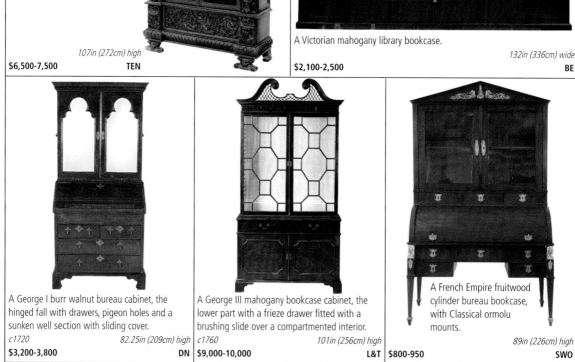

A Victorian mahogany library bookcase.

132in (336cm) wide

$2,100-2,500   **BE**

A George I burr walnut bureau cabinet, the hinged fall with drawers, pigeon holes and a sunken well section with sliding cover.

c1720   *82.25in (209cm) high*

$3,200-3,800   **DN**

A George III mahogany bookcase cabinet, the lower part with a frieze drawer fitted with a brushing slide over a compartmented interior.

c1760   *101in (256cm) high*

$9,000-10,000   **L&T**

A French Empire fruitwood cylinder bureau bookcase, with Classical ormolu mounts.

89in (226cm) high

$800-950   **SWO**

A Victorian walnut, giltwood and ormolu mounted bookcase, the arched mirror back superstructure with an open shelf above the base with tulipwood banding and molded edge, some damage.

This bookcase can be compared to pieces supplied by leading early 19thC dealer Edward Holmes Baldock and his contemporary, the furniture designer Richard Bridgens. Pieces such as this were doubtless influenced by Bridgens' designs for furniture as hybrids of Louis XIV/XV/ English Regency form. To fulfill commissions Baldock worked with London furniture makers like Trollope & Sons, George Blake and Bros., Gillow & Co., G J Morant and Williamson & Sons, all of whose stamps have been found on related furniture.

A Victorian Gothic walnut bookcase, with castellated corners to the cornice and with trefoil finials to the frieze.

100.75in (256cm) high

$3,200-3,800   **CHOR**

c1870   *108.75in (276cm) high*

$5,000-6,500   **DN**

A George IV mahogany open waterfall bookcase, with ebonized edging and turned brass column supports, on spiral twist fluted legs.

51.75in (131.5cm) high

$2,300-2,800   **WW**

A matched pair of Regency rosewood and brass inlaid bookcases, in the manner of George Oakley, each with specimen marble tops with Wellington action pilasters, and brass lion-paw feet, some damage.

c1815   *37.75in (96cm) high*

$15,000-19,000   **DN**

A Regency mahogany freestanding bookcase, attributed to Gillows of Lancaster, each tier supported by pillars fronted by false book bindings, above a reeded stem and base with gadrooned collar, above hipped and downswept reeded legs terminating in lapper cast gilt metal caps and casters.

A design for a 'circular movable bookcase' under the patent of the Catherine Street makers Morgan and Saunders was published in Rudolph Ackermann's 'The Repository of Arts' in 1810 (reproduced in P. Agius, 'Ackermann's Regency Furniture and Interiors', Wiltshire, 1984, page 48, plate 13). According to Ackermann, this 'ingenious and elegant contrivance', derived from the form of dumbwaiters, affords some 'valuable conveniences'.

c1815   *48in (122cm) high*

$7,000-8,000   **DN**

A 19thC satinwood and marquetry-inlaid bookcase, the top inlaid with a classical urn within coconut cross-banding above a single drawer inlaid with paterae and leaves, on square tapering feet.

20in (51cm) wide

$1,900-2,500   **CHOR**

An Edwardian mahogany revolving bookcase, with three drawers and one door, with an ivorine label for Maple & Co.

34.5in (88cm) high

$650-750   **WHP**

FURNITURE

A late 17thC William and Mary oyster-veneered cabinet-on-stand, opening to a shelved and compartmented interior, with later stand.

47in (119cm) wide

$2,500-3,800 **L&T**

A late 17thC North Italian ivory-inlaid ebonized cabinet-on-stand, the doors with panels depicting cavaliers, opening to an interior with drawers around a central drawer.

48.5in (123cm) high

$1,300-1,500 **L&T**

A 17thC Flemish tortoiseshell, ebony, rosewood and ebonized cabinet on a 19thC stand, opening to a green baize-lined interior with further drawers.

60.75in (154cm) high

$2,500-3,800 **L&T**

A William and Mary oyster veneered cabinet-on-stand, with crossbanded doors, enclosing ten drawers around a locked central cupboard, with later stand.

58.5in (148cm) high

$8,000-9,500 **WW**

A William and Mary olivewood oyster-veneered cabinet-on-stand, the doors enclosing ten drawers around a cupboard door and four further drawers, with later stand.

64in (163cm) high

$7,500-9,000 **WW**

A George III mahogany breakfront display cabinet, of 'Chinese Chippendale' style, with a fret-carved gallery with turned finials, with key.

75.5in (192cm) high

$2,800-3,500 **WW**

An 18thC Indo-Portuguese rosewood, ivory and marquetry cabinet on stand, with later stand with slender tapered square legs joined by a stretcher.

This item contains material which may be subject to import/export restrictions, especially outside the EU, due to CITES regulations.

24in (60.5cm) wide

$9,000-10,000 **L&T**

An 18thC Dutch walnut and floral marquetry vitrine, with a bombé-shaped base, on a stretchered base with scroll-molded legs and bun feet, hair crack to the veneers on one canted side.

81.5in (207cm) high

$5,500-6,500 CHEF

An early 19thC Regency mahogany bow-fronted cabinet, in the manner of Gillows, the molded cornice with a central cast-bronze flowerhead the whole with scrolling ebony line inlay.

81in (206cm) high

$5,000-6,500 LAW

An Etruscan Revival ebonized wood and amboyna-inlaid cabinet, by H.Ogden, Manchester, with ivory and parcel gilt embellishments, stamped 'H.OGDEN/MANCHESTER'.

c1870 *70.5in (179cm) wide*

$3,200-4,400 L&T

A late Victorian Irish satinwood and marquetry display cabinet, attributed to James Hicks, Dublin, with gilt brass mounts and inlaid with swags, scrolling foliage, paterae and husks in the Sheraton style, with two keys.

6.75in (195cm) high

$3,200-3,800 WW

A late 19thC South German walnut and marquetry-inlaid cabinet-on-stand, inset with mid-17thC panels carved in low-relief, the panels depicting figures in a garden and another of a warrior on horseback.

53in (135cm) wide

$5,000-6,500 CHEF

A late 19thC Victorian rosewood and mahogany marquetry secrétaire display cabinet, in the Sheraton style, inlaid throughout with foliate swag and garland marquetry.

46in (117cm) wide

$1,300-1,900　L&T

A 19thC amboyna and ebony cabinet, set with Paris porcelain portrait panels, upon an open stand with gilt metal mounts and a porcelain paneled frieze.

24.5in (62cm) wide

$5,000-6,500　CHOR

A 19thC early Victorian mahogany campaign cabinet.

29.5in (75cm) high

$1,300-1,500　L&T

A 19thC Victorian amboyna, ebonized and porcelain-mounted cabinet, the superstructure with pierced gilt-metal galleries.

59in (150cm) high

$4,400-5,700　L&T

A Dutch Kingwood cabinet-on-stand.

c1900　41.75in (106cm) wide

$1,300-1,900　CHOR

A late 19th/early 20thC French Kingwood decorated vitrine, gilt metal-mounted and serpentine-fronted, decorated in the Vernis Martin taste, with figures in wooded arbors and landscapes.

79in (200cm) high

$3,800-4,400　BE

A Louis XV-style satiné and metal-mounted serpentine vitrine, with Vernis Martin-style panels to the base.

79.5in (202cm) high

$3,200-3,800　TEN

An early 20thC Louis XV-style Kingwood, amaranth and marquetry display cabinet, with gilt metal mounts throughout.

72in (183cm) high

$4,500-5,000　L&T

A Regency mahogany chiffonier, the base enclosed by satin and brass grill doors, with lion paw feet.

57in (145cm) high

$1,500-2,000 CHEF

A mid-19thC Napoleon III ebonized, brass-inlaid and mounted breakfront credenza, with porcelain panels in Sèvres style, above a cupboard door centered by an 18thC-style porcelain plaque.

97.75in (248cm) high

$2,500-3,200 TEN

A Regency rosewood and brass inlaid chiffonier, with Gothic arch panel doors opening to a shelved interior.

c1815 *46in (117cm) high*

$5,000-5,700 L&T

ESSENTIAL REFERENCE - CREDENZA

A Credenza is a long side cabinet, with shelves at either end.
- It was originally intended for the display of food.
- The form may have been influenced by the French chiffonier - a small shallow cabinet topped by an open shelf or shelves and sometimes a drawer.
- The Credenza became popular in the later 19thC.
- The most desirable pieces have a serpentine front and glazed side panels.
- The end shelves are often lined with velvet.
- British examples were influenced by Continental models.
- The center door panels are often decorated with pietre dure, marquetry, boullework, panels of ivory, or porcelain.
- French makers generally led the field of furniture making. Italian maker Giovanni Battista Gatti (active 1850-80) was a notable exception.
- In the 19thC, British furniture makers experimented with materials such as papier mâché.

A Victorian burr walnut-inlaid credenza.

66in (168cm) long

$1,500-2,300 SWO

A Victorian gilt metal mounted marquetry-inlaid walnut credenza.

62in (157cm) long

$950-1,100 BELL

A Victorian tulipwood, purplewood, and brass-mounted credenza, with a gilt metal edge over a porcelain-mounted frieze and central door inset with a porcelain plaque.

60.75in (154cm) long

$4,400-5,700 TEN

A large 19thC Victorian burr walnut and mahogany mirrored credenza, with gilt-metal mounts.

99.75in (253cm) long

$3,800-4,400 L&T

A Victorian walnut, tulipwood crossbanded, marquetry and gilt metal mounted breakfront credenza.

73.5in (186.5cm) long

$750-1,000 BE

A mid-18thC French Louis XV marble-topped Kingwood and marquetry gilt-metal-mounted cabinet, the marble top is split.

36in (91cm) high

$1,900-2,500   **L&T**

A George III japanned side cabinet, the original finish decorated in gilt with a chinoiserie landscape to the top.

35in (89cm) wide

$4,000-4,800   **SWO**

An early 19thC Regency mahogany and ebony side cabinet, with cupboard doors lined with silk, flanked by reeded columns ending in carved paw feet.

68in (173cm) wide

$5,500-7,000   **L&T**

A Regency japanned and tôle side cabinet, the drawer with ivory handles and painted Greek key motif decoration, fitted with fifteen small compartments, the cupboard door inset with a tôle panel decorated with a chinoiserie figure.

34.25in (87cm) high

$5,000-6,500   **DN**

An early 19thC mahogany breakfront low side cupboard.

62in (157cm) long

$1,500-2,300   **BE**

A Regency bronze-mounted mahogany and ebonized cabinet, in the manner of George Oakley, inlaid with ebony stringing, with monopodiae with lion paw feet to an inverted breakfront plinth base.

This cabinet bears the distinctive lion mask pilasters that relate to the work of the Regency cabinet-maker George Oakley (1773-1840). With an extensive premises in Bond Street and the City, Oakley undertook commissions for a wide and distinguished circle of patrons, including the Prince Regent, for whom he worked at Carlton House. A pioneer of 'Buhl' inlay, Oakley established himself as one of the most original and innovative designers of the period, and his showrooms in Bond Street became a Mecca for fashionable society. Oakley was commissioned by Charles Madryll Cheere to furnish Papworth Hall, Cambridgeshire, where much of the furniture bears similar Classical Revival elements.

c1810   *31.5in (79.5cm) wide*

$3,200-3,800   **CHEF**

CLOSER LOOK - REGENCY SIDE CABINET

This is a highly sophisticated side cabinet, attributed to George Oakley.

The use of classical anthemion leaf, scroll volutes and carved paw feet show the influence of the designer and connoisseur Thomas Hope.

The base is inlaid with an oak leaf and acorn band, with inlaid ebony bands of stars, lattice work and a stylized Vitruvian scroll.

The use of inlaid brass also shows the popularity of the 18thC French style and the revival of 'buhl' work after Andre-Charles Boulle.

A Regency rosewood, ebony and brass inlaid side cabinet.

52.5in (133.5cm) high

$19,000-25,000   **WW**

A pair of George IV rosewood, Kingwood, yew and ebony detailed marquetry side cabinets, in the manner of George Bullock, each with gray marble top.

48in (122cm) wide

$10,000-15,000   APAR

A late 19thC Victorian boulle marquetry and ebonized serpentine cabinet, with gilt-metal mounts throughout.

82.75in (210cm) long

$5,500-7,000   L&T

A late 19thC burr walnut, amboyna tulipwood and thuya pier cabinet, by Gillow & Co., with gilt foliate mounts, the door stamped 'GILLOW & CO 18'.

44.5in (113cm) high

$3,800-5,000   TEN

A pair of late 19thC Louis XV-style tulipwood and ormolu-mounted cabinets, with porcelain mounts of Sèvres style.

54.75in (139cm) high

$5,500-6,500   TEN

A 19thC mahogany and rosewood-banded breakfront side cabinet.

72in (183cm) long

$1,000-1,100   MOR

A 19thC ebonized gilt metal mounted boullework side cabinet.

54in (137cm) wide

$750-900   BELL

A 19thC ebonized and ormolu-mounted cabinet, in the French style, with boullework cut brass and red tortoiseshell inlaid doors, flanked by figurative column sides.

52.5in (133cm) long

$3,200-3,800   CHEF

A pair of George III figured mahogany bedside tables, the doors with inlaid panels, on tapering legs, the legs slightly reduced.

32in (81cm) high

$8,000-9,000   DN

A George III mahogany tray-top bedside commode, with a hinged retractable door and a pull-out base with a lidded ceramic pot.

32in (81.5cm) high

$1,000-1,100   WW

A Federal mahogany sideboard, with large griffin inlaid cartouches on the center doors and overall line and fan inlays.

c1800   *66.5in (169cm) wide*

$2,800-3,500   **POOK**

A Sheraton period mahogany serpentine sideboard, the drawers inlaid with quarter-fan decoration in satinwood and hardwood.

71.25in (181cm) wide

$3,800-4,400   **CHEF**

An early 19thC Scottish Regency mahogany, ebonized and brass-inlaid stageback sideboard, with two deep drawers, one fitted as a cellaret, raised on tapering faux bamboo legs.

90in (229cm) wide

$2,500-3,200   **L&T**

A Regency mahogany and ebony-lined pedestal sideboard, with two drawers, each with a hinged fall with cellaret to one side and with an enclosed cupboard and zinc lined cupboard below.

91in (231cm) wide

$1,300-1,900   **BE**

A George IV Irish mahogany sideboard, with the label of 'R. STRAHAN & Co, Ltd., Cabinet Makers and Upholsterers 135 St Stephen's Green DUBLIN', larger drawer lining with large hole.

72in (183cm) wide

$2,500-3,200   **TEN**

A George III mahogany breakfront sideboard, in the manner of Thomas Hope, with crossbanded top, the frieze divided by carved lion mask terminals.

c1800   *97.25in (247cm) wide*

$3,800-4,400   **DN**

A George III mahogany crossbanded and inlaid bow-fronted sideboard, bordered with boxwood and ebony lines.

61in (155cm) wide

$1,500-2,000   **BE**

ESSENTIAL REFERENCE - VICTORIAN SIDEBOARD

This sideboard was commissioned for Horsley Towers, Surrey, probably between 1846 and 1860. It shows similarities to examples by J.C. Crace, prominent London interior decorator of the mid-19thC, and collaborator of A.W.N. Pugin. Crace displayed an elaborate sideboard at both the Paris Exhibition in 1855 and the second London Exhibition of 1862 and there are also examples of sideboards by Crace, which rely heavily on Pugin's designs, at Lismore Castle, Co. Waterford, Abney Hall in Cheshire and at Tyntesfield in Somerset. The panelling on this example is reminiscent of designs used in the Palace of Westminster and illustrated in 'True Principles' (1841). The sideboard is embellished with painted coats of arms, all of which pertain to the Lovelace lineage. This style of embellishment relates to furniture designed by Pugin and most particularly to his large bookcase, designed for the Great Exhibition of 1851, and his own dining room cabinet of 1845, both of which incorporate similar shields relating to the owner. The shields here date from after 8 July 1835, when William King, then 8th Baron King of Ockham, married the Hon. Augusta Ada Byron. This sideboard was likely to have been made after 1846 when the 1st Earl of Lovelace started living at Horsley and before 1860 when he adopted the name and arms King-Noel by royal license.

A mid-19thC Victorian oak and painted sideboard, in the manner of A.W.N. Pugin, of Gothic style, the carved paneled back with five painted shields.

113in (287cm) wide

$32,000-38,000   **L&T**

A George II walnut kneehole desk, top later veneered, replaced handles, poor veneer restoration to drawer fronts.

30.25in (77cm) high
$2,300-2,800   **CHOR**

A George I walnut and featherbanded kneehole desk, the fitted frieze drawer opening to a baize inset sliding writing surface, the space beneath with divisions and a concealed small drawer to one side, with key, marks, scratches and abrasions commensurate with age and use.

c1720   *34.25in (87cm) high*
$20,000-25,000   **DN**

A George II walnut kneehole desk, the quarter veneered and crossbanded top above a frieze drawer and central recessed cupboard flanked by two banks of three short drawers, on bracket feet, marks, scratches and abrasions consistent with age, with keys.

c1735   *35.5in (90cm) wide*
$2,300-2,800   **DN**

ESSENTIAL REFERENCE - ANTIQUARIAN DESK

Promoted by the writer Horace Walpole (d.1797) for its 'Elizabethan' character, such ebony furniture became an important element of the Romantic 18th and early 19thC antiquarian interior. An ebony settee, reputed to have been presented by Queen Elizabeth I to the Earl of Leicester, formed part of William Beckford's ebony furnishings in his 'Lancaster State Bedroom', that served for Admiral Nelson's celebrated visit to Fonthill Abbey, Wiltshire in 1803, before being acquired for the Elizabethan mansion at Charlecote, Warwickshire in 1832. Ebony bedrooms were also created at Warwick Castle, Warwickshire, and at Montague House, London, while an ebony dining-room was introduced at Longleat, Wiltshire in the early 19thC. At this period such furniture was particularly associated with antiquarian dealers in Wardour Street, who created new forms of furniture using ancient elements. This desk was constructed re-using the doors, side panels and drawers of a Louis XIV ebony cabinet-on-stand. This type of finely relief carved ebony panel is typical of the oeuvre of Jean Maci, from Blois. Maci has been credited with many similarly decorated cabinets, including the Endymion Cabinet in the Victoria & Albert Museum, London, as well as those cabinets introduced as part of the ebony dining room at Longleat.

A George III mahogany, rosewood and gonçalo alves serpentine desk, the tooled leather inset above an arrangement of nine drawers around the recessed kneehole cupboard, marks, scratches and abrasions consistent with age, veneer splitting, lacking sections of beading, lacking keys.

c1770   *48in (122cm) wide*
$4,500-5,000   **DN**

A George III mahogany tambour desk, on cupboard base flanked by reeded columns and on turned tapering legs, fine marks, scratches and abrasions consistent with age, handles replaced to the large drawer, has original key to the long drawer.

c1790   *47.25in (120cm) high*
$3,200-3,800   **DN**

A George IV 'Antiquarian' desk, constructed during the second quarter of the 19thC using panels from a 17thC French cabinet, the drawers decorated with cherubs in landscapes, the cylinder fall with incised floral decorated panels and border, marks, scratches and abrasions consistent with age and use, one castor to rear leg missing, three Bramah keys but some locks are not operating.

c1825   *61in (155cm) wide*
$9,000-11,500   **DN**

A William IV or early Victorian mahogany partners desk, in the style of Gillows, with three short frieze drawers to each side, on turned leaf form and reeded legs on brass castors, the drawers with Bramah locks.

72.5in (184cm) wide
$5,500-7,000   **ROS**

FURNITURE

A Louis Philippe rosewood and ormolu-mounted desk, with a cartonnier having four drawers above a paneled top with pull-out drawer on a brass cogged wheel mechanism, stencilled 'Lesage & Grandvoinnet Rue de la Chaussee-d'Antin No:11 Paris'.

Antoine-Nicholas Lesage (1784-1841) was one of the most important merchants in Paris of the period, with important clients including the Duchesse de Barry. In 1837 he formed a partnership with Victor-Hyacinthe Granvoinnet (b.1808) who had been working for him for some fourteen years. The partnership at 11 rue de la Chaussee-d'Antin lasted until the death of Lesage in 1841. Many ebenistes worked for them including Remond, Jeanselme, Hervieux and Clavel. See Denise Ledoux-Lebard, 'Le Mobilier Francais Du XIX Siecle', 2000 pages 424-426.

65.75in (167cm) wide

$2,500-3,800   BELL

A mid-19thC early Victorian rosewood pedestal desk and bookcase, the arched kneehole recess flanked by banks of four graduated drawers with ivorine numbers, the reverse fitted as an open bookcase.

28.75in (73cm) wide

$1,300-1,900   L&T

A Victorian satinwood and marquetry kidney-shaped desk, crossbanded with zebrawood, small veneer losses.

48.5in (123cm) wide

$2,500-3,800   TEN

A Victorian figured walnut, tulipwood banded, floral marquetry and gilt-metal-mounted serpentine desk, recent leather top, split to the writing surface.

c1870   *47.5in (121cm) wide*

$2,500-3,200   TEN

A late 19thC Victorian walnut leather inset partners desk.

63in (160cm) wide

$1,900-2,500   L&T

A late Victorian mahogany, satinwood banded and marquetry inlaid cylinder desk, the fall front enclosing a pull-out writing surface, with drawers and pigeon holes, some splits.

c1890   *56in (142cm) wide*

$1,900-2,500   TEN

A solid yew wood single piece kneehole desk.

49.25in (125cm) wide

$2,800-3,300   SWO

A mahogany and satinwood-banded Carlton House desk.

c1900   *54in (137cm) wide*

$1,500-2,000   **TEN**

ESSENTIAL REFERENCE - CARLTON HOUSE DESKS

The Carlton House desk was developed during the Regency period (c1790-1830).

● It was named after the London home of the Prince of Wales (later George IV).

● At the end of the Napoleonic Wars in 1815, the technology required to combine wood and metal was developed. This led to furniture designers experimenting with a wide range of new forms.

● Mahogany and satinwood are typically used.

● New features included: galleries on the tops of tables, small drawers, hinged flaps, curved pull-out ramps, and extending screens that shielded a writer's face from the heat of an open fire.

● Most Carlton House desks are relatively rare because of the craftsmanship and use of expensive materials.

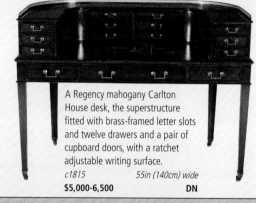

A Regency mahogany Carlton House desk, the superstructure fitted with brass-framed letter slots and twelve drawers and a pair of cupboard doors, with a ratchet adjustable writing surface.

c1815   *55in (140cm) wide*

$5,000-6,500   **DN**

A Sheraton period maplewood bonheur-du-jour, with applied Neo-classical engraved panels, the base with fitted writing drawer and leather lined slope, repair to the gallery, some losses.

50.5in (129cm) high

$1,300-1,900   **CHEF**

A pair of walnut and inlaid bonheur-du-jours, each with a raised superstructure of two cupboards flanking a small mirror, over a slope enclosing a fitted interior with well.

56in (142cm) high

$3,800-4,400   **TEN**

ESSENTIAL REFERENCE - BUREAU MAZARIN

The bureau Mazarin is a 17thC desk form named more or less in memory of Cardinal Mazarin, Regent of France from 1642 to 1661. It is the earliest predecessor of the pedestal desk and differs from it by having only two tiers of drawers or three tiers of rather small drawers under the desktop surface, followed by eight legs supporting the whole. Also, the bureau Mazarin has cross braces between the legs, forming two Xs or two Hs on each side.

An Edwardian bonheur-du-jour, mahogany and marquetry inlaid, with a writing table with folding top above an inlaid drawer.

30.25in (77cm) wide

$1,300-1,900   **CHOR**

A Louis XIV boulle bureau Mazarin, with finely engraved ebony and brass, in geometric and foliate patterns, the eight tapering turned supports with domed brass caps to the knops and feet, the elaborately shaped stretchers uniformly inlaid, with restoration.

47.25in (120cm) wide

$38,000-45,000   **DN**

A late 17thC French Louis XIV ebonized and marquetry bureau Mazarin, with floral urn inlay, above a frieze drawer and kneehole cupboard.

46.5in (118cm) wide

$28,000-35,000   **L&T**

A Chester County, Pennsylvania Chippendale walnut slant-front desk, the interior initialed 'IT', likely for Jacob Taggart.
c1770   *42.5in (108cm) high*
$2,500-3,200   **POOK**

An early 18thC Queen Anne laburnum oyster-veneered bureau.
41.5in (105cm) high
$1,900-2,500   **L&T**

A George III bureau,
with bombé front and lacquered chinoiserie decoration,
fitted interior with well above two candle drawers.
38in (96cm) wide
$1,300-1,800   **LAW**

A George III bureau, the veneers laid in a zigzag pattern, having a fitted interior.
37in (94cm) wide
$1,900-2,500   **SWO**

A late 18th/early 19thC Dutch satin birch, rosewood and satinwood crossbanded bureau.
45in (113cm) wide
$500-650   **BE**

A George III-style carved mahogany bureau, made by J.W. Varley, the fall enclosing a fitted interior of pigeon holes and ten small drawers, drawers below with Chippendale-style brass cast handles, labelled 'MADE APRIL 1928 BY J W VARLEY, BOUGHT BY MISS WRIGHT, ???GATE, WHITBY'.
41.75in (106cm) high
$1,300-1,900   **TEN**

A Regency burr yew, rosewood and mahogany cylinder bureau, with faux marble top, the doors centered by a convex glass panel reverse painted with game above a cylinder with an interior of six small drawer pigeon holes and writing slide.

28.75in (73cm) wide

$3,200-3,800   **CHOR**

A Louis XV-style burr chestnut bureau en pente, of bombé form with pierced brass gallery.

24.75in (63cm) wide

$3,200-3,800   **CHOR**

A French Louis XV-style Kingwood, walnut and floral marquetry bureau plat, inlaid with acanthus scrolls, flowers, Mother-of-pearl butterflies and various metals, minor losses and damage.

c1870   *50in (128cm) wide*

$5,000-6,500   **TEN**

A Louis XVI-style ormolu mounted rosewood cylinder bureau, with pull-out fitted interior.

39.5in (100cm) wide

$1,900-2,500   **BELL**

A 19thC and earlier Alpine marquetry inlaid walnut and fruitwood bureau, decorated with townscape scenes, on later stand.

40.5in (103cm) high

$3,200-3,800   **BELL**

A late 19thC Dutch rosewood, walnut and marquetry bureau, inlaid with flowering urns, birds and cornucopia, the bombé slant front opening to an interior fitted with drawers and pigeon holes.

41in (104cm) high

$3,800-5,000   **L&T**

FURNITURE

ESSENTIAL REFERENCE - DAVENPORTS

A Davenport is a type of desk or small writing cabinet developed in the late 18thC.

- The name comes from an entry found in the records of cabinetmakers Gillow that specified a desk order for Captain Davenport.
- The basic form, which consisted of a small chest-of-drawers and a desk compartment on top, changed very little during the 19thC.
- Women usually used Davenports in the 19thC.
- Davenports made between 1800 and 1820 are usually no larger than 18in (46cm) deep.
- In the 1830s, they were broadened to at least 24.5in (61cm) in width.
- Mahogany, rosewood, and burr walnut were the most popular choices of wood.
- The finest examples have concealed drawers.

A Regency burr walnut Davenport desk, on gadrooned feet with castors.

20.25in (51.5cm) wide

$1,500-1,900   CHOR

A Victorian burr walnut veneer piano-top Davenport, the superstructure with a fitted stationery compartment, the fall enclosing an interior with pull out adjustable rachetted leather inset writing surface, twin inkwells, pen tray, and two maple fronted drawers.

22.75in (58cm) wide

$1,500-2,500   BE

A Victorian walnut Davenport, the superstructure with a lidded fitted stationery compartment.

41in (104cm) wide

$500-650   BE

A 19thC walnut, inlaid and gilt-metal-mounted Davenport.

22in (56cm) wide

$250-320   WHP

A 19thC walnut and inlaid Davenport, with fitted inkwell, tooled leather surface, and an arrangement of four drawers.

21.5in (55cm) wide

$300-350   WHP

A late Victorian satin birch and parcel-gilt Davenport desk, with pen box above writing slope.

21in (53cm) wide

$900-1,300   CHOR

A satinwood Gillow-style Davenport, the fallfront enclosing fitted drawer, pen drawer to the side fitted with a pair of ink bottles.

c1900   *37.5in (95.5cm) high*

$1,600-2,300   HT

ESSENTIAL REFERENCE - CANTERBURIES

Thomas Sheraton (1751-1806) referred to two types of Canterbury in 'The Cabinet Dictionary' (1803): the music stand and the supper tray.

- He described the first as an open-topped rack, with slatted partitions meant for storing books or music sheets.
- It is thought that the Canterbury was named after the Archbishop of Canterbury, who commissioned the first example.
- The second type of Canterbury is described as a supper tray made to hold cutlery.
- It resembles a small table and is much taller than the music stand.
- Both types of Canterbury stood on castors so that they could be moved around easily.

An unusual George III mahogany Canterbury, on tall turned legs, ending in brass caps and castors.

c1800   *23.75in (60cm) high*

$1,000-1,250   **L&T**

An early 19thC mahogany Canterbury, with curved and slatted divisions and central carrying handle, on ring-turned tapered legs, terminating in brass cappings and castors.

19in (48.5cm) wide

$550-700   **BE**

A Regency mahogany Canterbury, the top shaped rail and sides of trellis design, the supports and drawer decorated with incised lines.

24in (61cm) wide

$2,300-2,800   **DN**

An Irish Regency mahogany Canterbury, by Gillington's Dublin, the drawer stamped 'Gillingtons 12773'.

18in (46cm) wide

$400-500   **BELL**

A late 19thC figured walnut Canterbury.

34.25in (87cm) high

$250-320   **WHP**

A large 19thC mahogany four-division Canterbury.

24.5in (62cm) deep

$550-650   **BELL**

An Edwardian mahogany three-tier Canterbury.

23.25in (59cm) wide

$80-150   **WHP**

A 19thC oak folio stand, with adjustable ratchet mechanism.

26.5in (67cm) wide

$1,100-1,400   **CHOR**

A George I giltwood pier glass, the frame carved with delicate leaf motifs, bell flowers and stylized shells, with punch work decoration, with the original divided beveled mirror plates.

83.5in (212cm) high

$19,000-25,000 DN

A George II mahogany and parcel-gilt mirror, with feathered and urn finial between swan-neck pediment, with shell pendant base flanked by brass candle holders.

c1740 *60in (152cm) high*

$3,800-5,000 ROS

A George II giltwood and gesso wall mirror, the cartouche-shaped frame decorated with flowerheads and scrolling acanthus and surmounted by a central female mask, the lowest section of surmount to one side is split and detached.

c1735 *77.25in (196cm) high*

$4,000-6,500 DN

An 18thC carved giltwood mirror, with scroll and floral carved surround and ho ho bird surmount, ho ho bird re-glued, chipping to paintwork at joints in places, later plate.

59in (150cm) high

$9,000-10,000 CHOR

A pair of George III carved giltwood mirrors.

56.25in (143cm) high

$9,000-10,000 TEN

An early George III Irish giltwood pier mirror, the later plate flanked by cluster columns and carved 'C' scrolls with floral garlands, with a basket of flowers surmount above a later cartouche carved with a Pegasus crest flanked by a pair of ho ho birds.

62in (157.5cm) high

$13,000-15,000 WW

A Regency gilt-framed convex wall mirror, with a mythological sea horse surmount and ball-mounted frame.

37in (94cm) high

$650-750 BELL

An early 19thC Regency gilt, gesso and ebonized convex wall mirror, with ball surmounted frame and reeded slip surmounted by cornucopias and an eagle.

43in (110cm) high

$2,500-3,200 TEN

A Regency satinwood wall mirror, the frame decorated with brass bosses, lacking mirror.

33in (84cm) high

$300-400 BRI

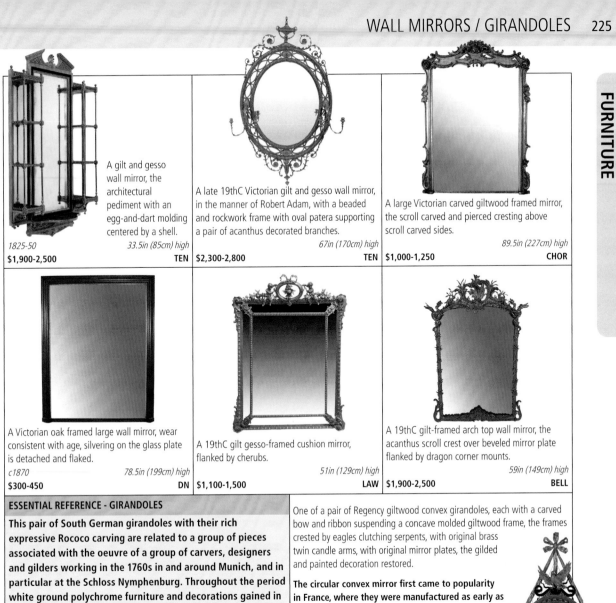

A gilt and gesso wall mirror, the architectural pediment with an egg-and-dart molding centered by a shell.

1825-50   33.5in (85cm) high

$1,900-2,500   TEN

A late 19thC Victorian gilt and gesso wall mirror, in the manner of Robert Adam, with a beaded and rockwork frame with oval patera supporting a pair of acanthus decorated branches.

67in (170cm) high

$2,300-2,800   TEN

A large Victorian carved giltwood framed mirror, the scroll carved and pierced cresting above scroll carved sides.

89.5in (227cm) high

$1,000-1,250   CHOR

A Victorian oak framed large wall mirror, wear consistent with age, silvering on the glass plate is detached and flaked.

c1870   78.5in (199cm) high

$300-450   DN

A 19thC gilt gesso-framed cushion mirror, flanked by cherubs.

51in (129cm) high

$1,100-1,500   LAW

A 19thC gilt-framed arch top wall mirror, the acanthus scroll crest over beveled mirror plate flanked by dragon corner mounts.

59in (149cm) high

$1,900-2,500   BELL

ESSENTIAL REFERENCE - GIRANDOLES

This pair of South German girandoles with their rich expressive Rococo carving are related to a group of pieces associated with the oeuvre of a group of carvers, designers and gilders working in the 1760s in and around Munich, and in particular at the Schloss Nymphenburg. Throughout the period white ground polychrome furniture and decorations gained in popularity. The Emperor Maximillian III was Prince-elector and Duke of Bavaria from 1745-1777, and it is under his guidance and artistic patronage that this taste became fashionable. He founded the Nymphenburg porcelain factory, and was a patron of François de Cuvilliés, a pioneer of the Rococo style. Another one of his circle was the musician Mozart. White porcelain, which had its roots in Chinese blanc-de-Chine, stylistically pervaded all areas of the decorative arts and the illustrated girandoles testify to the Emperor's influence in the sphere of the furniture.

A pair of 18thC painted German Rococo girandoles, with a polychrome foliate scroll, entwined with branches, flowers and buds.

44in (112cm) high

$5,500-7,000   DN

One of a pair of Regency giltwood convex girandoles, each with a carved bow and ribbon suspending a concave molded giltwood frame, the frames crested by eagles clutching serpents, with original brass twin candle arms, with original mirror plates, the gilded and painted decoration restored.

The circular convex mirror first came to popularity in France, where they were manufactured as early as 1756. In Sheraton's 'The Cabinet Dictionary' (1803), convex mirrors were said to 'strengthen the color and take off the coarseness of objects by contracting them'. Sheraton emphasized the new severer and more archeologically correct aspect of the classical spirit, which he had derived from French Directoire designs and from the work of Giovanni Battista Piranesi, Henry Holland, Charles Heathcote Tatham, and Thomas Hope. Sheraton included animal motifs such as lion masks or lion-shaped supports for chairs and tables. He also made use of dolphins and other marine motifs such as anchors, masts, oars, and sails in designs associated with Nelson's nautical victories.

52.5in (133cm) high

$9,000-10,000 pair   DN

A Regency giltwood convex girandole wall mirror, with twin scrolling candle arms to each side with cylindrical brass sconces, brass and glass drip pans and lusters, surmounted by twin dolphin terminals and ebonized carved wood eagle, some damage.

c1815   49in (124cm) high

$3,200-3,800   DN

A George III Irish giltwood overmantel mirror, attributed to Francis & John Booker.

57.25in (145.5cm) long

$6,500-7,500   WW

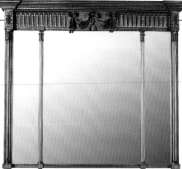

An early 19thC large Regency overmantel mirror, the frieze centered by drapery swags and quill tips.

60.25in (153cm) wide

$3,200-3,800   L&T

A Regency giltwood and gesso overmantle mirror, the frieze depicting Apollo in a chariot pulled by lions.

58.75in (149cm) wide

$1,500-2,000   L&T

A late 19thC gilt framed overmantel mirror, with open cartouche crest centered by songbirds.

84.75in (215cm) high

$1,500-1,900   BELL

A 19thC giltwood overmantel mirror, with a pediment of crossed quivers, birds, flowers, and leafage, above a laurel leaf and strapwork molded frame.

87.5in (222cm) high

$1,300-1,800   MOR

A 19thC Irish carved giltwood triple overmantel mirror, in the early George III style, the frame carved with C-scrolls, acanthus, architectural arches and flower garlands.

65.5in (166cm) long

$1,300-1,900   L&T

An early 19thC Anglo-Indian carved ebony cheval glass, bearing the family arms of Norton and Rose within reserves.

Research has confirmed the arms on one panel are the arms of George Norton, called to the bar in 1816, who in 1825 became Advocate-General in Bombay and from 1827-1854 was Advocate-General in Madras. The other panel to be those of the Rose family of Waddesdon, Buckinghamshire, possibly the family of George Norton's wife, whose father was John Rose, who was admitted to Grays Inn, in 1800, the second son of Thomas Rose of Winchendon, Buckinghamshire.

65.75in (167cm) high

$3,200-3,800   CHEF

A Victorian mahogany-framed cheval mirror.

36.5in (93cm) wide

$300-400   BELL

A Regency flame mahogany-veneered dressing table mirror, by William Wilkinson, the base stamped 'WILKINSON. LUDGATE HILL 14110'.

30.75in (78cm) wide

$750-900   **WW**

A mid-19thC French carved bone and ivory dressing table mirror, Dieppe, with satyrs, winged cherubs and other classical figures amongst foliage, surmounted by a crowned armorial shield, with frieze drawer fronted by lion mask handles, and on carved lion paw feet.

34in (86cm) high

$6,500-7,500   **DN**

A 19thC mahogany swing mirror.

32.25in (82cm) high

$80-100   **WHP**

A marquetry inlaid three-tier étagère, with three-quarter pierced brass gallery above a drawer.

20in (51cm) wide

$1,000-1,500   **CHOR**

A four-tier trellis veneered étagère.

14in (36cm) wide

$1,900-2,500   **CHOR**

A mid-18thC mahogany dumb waiter, with revolving dished tops and turned baluster column uprights.

$300-350   **BE**

A late 18thC George III mahogany dumb waiter, with a fluted and part wrythen support, raised on three flower carved cabriole legs with carved claw feet, formerly raised on castors, the top support split and repaired.

43.25in (110cm) high

$500-650   **TEN**

A set of George III mahogany hanging wall shelves, in Chinese Chippendale style.

58.75in (149cm) high

$1,500-1,900   **WW**

FURNITURE

A George III mahogany wine cooler, with a lead liner, with lion's mask handles, raised on semi-engaged reeded balusters applied to the body, on turned, tapered and reeded feet, with castors, the body has several splits.

28in (71cm) wide

$3,200-3,800　　　　　TEN

A George III oval brass-bound wine cooler, on a stand.

$1,900-2,500　　　　　CHOR

A George III mahogany and brass-bound wine cooler, with lion mask and ring handles to sides, on base, with zinc liner.

24in (61cm) high

$300-400　　　　　MART

A Regency burr elm wine cooler, of sarcophagus form, the lid surmounted by a spherical finial over bombé shoulders.

25.5in (65cm) high

$3,800-4,400　　　　　WHP

An early 19thC Scottish mahogany wine cooler, in the manner of James Mein, of sarcophagus form, on carved paw feet with later ceramic castors, the interior with a partial lead-lined interior.

31.5in (80cm) wide

$2,300-2,800　　　　　L&T

A George IV mahogany cellaret, of sarcophagus shape, with egg-and-dart moldings, the interior later fitted for tea with three lift-out and hinged canisters.

37in (93.5cm) wide

$900-1,000　　　　　WW

A William IV mahogany squat pagoda-shaped wine cooler, with lead liner, raised on hairy paw feet.

26in (66cm) wide

$950-1,100　　　　　BELL

A William IV Irish mahogany wine cooler, by Mack, Williams & Gibton, the front carved with vine leaves and grapes, on scroll-carved lion's paw feet and brass castors, stamped 'MACK, WILLIAMS & GIBTON DUBLIN'.

31.75in (80.5cm) wide

$1,000-1,500　　　　　WW

A 19thC George III-style mahogany cellaret, of Adam-style, carved with husk swags, rosettes, and satyr masks, with a lead-lined interior, with brass lion mask handles.

30in (76cm) wide

$1,500-2,300　　　　　L&T

A pair of George I giltwood and gesso torchères, in the manner of James Moore, with foliate motifs and lattice reserves, on triple S-shaped downswept legs with scroll terminals, some damage.

This model of torchère was popular during the first half of the 18thC and was often made ensuite with a pier mirror and table. James Moore has been recognized as the foremost maker using this gilt gesso technique, having supplied pieces to Hampton Court, Blenheim Palace and Boughton castle.

c1720   *46.5in (118cm) high*
$3,200-4,400   **DN**

A George III mahogany brass-mounted Hepplewhite torchère, with a pierced brass gallery over a ring-turned and part fluted column, on a tripod base carved with coin medallions.

c1780   *37.75in (96cm) high*
$1,800-2,500   **L&T**

A Venetian painted and gilded Blackamoor, the arm has been glued and there are small areas of retouching to the paint.

39in (99cm) high
$750-900   **CHEF**

A pair of 19thC ebonized and gilded stands, with blackamoor figural supports, on scrolling tripod bases.

36.25in (92cm) high
$500-650   **BELL**

A George III mahogany wig stand, with three drawers, supported by leaf carved supports and cabriole legs joined by a dished jug stand.

33.5in (85cm) high
$500-650   **CHOR**

A George III mahogany urn stand.

23.25in (59cm) high
$950-1,100   **CHOR**

An early 19thC burr yew teapoy, with four-lidded interior centered by a pair of mixing bowls.

18.5in (47cm) wide
$500-650   **BELL**

A Regency rosewood teapoy, with a fitted interior for canisters and mixing bowls.

30.75in (78cm) high
$250-400   **CHEF**

An early 19thC brass mounted mahogany plate bucket.

25in (64cm) high handle up
$950-1,100   **BELL**

A Regency black lacquer and gilt chinoiserie decorated tray, decorated with three pagodas amongst a rocky and foliate landscape, some deeper knocks to edges.

c1815   *30.5in (77cm) wide*

$800-950   **DN**

A mid-19thC Victorian papier mâché tray, by Jennens & Bettridge, the painted center depicting a 17thC interior scene, stamped maker's mark 'JENNENS & BETTRIDGE/ BIRMM & LONDON'.

25.25in (64cm) wide

$550-700   **L&T**

An early Victorian papier mâché tray table, painted with parrots amongst flowers and foliage, on a later folding stand.

30in (76cm) wide

$1,000-1,100   **WW**

A Victorian tôle peinte tray, painted with a steamer in full sail.

30.5in (77cm) wide

$250-320   **WW**

A Victorian papier mâché tray, by B Walton & Co., painted fountain and exotic bird, stamped 'B Walton & Co. Warranted and S & I Woolley, Picadilly'.

32.75in (83cm) wide

$300-400   **CHOR**

A Victorian 'The Larder Invaded' papier mâché tray, a frightened cat above a table of game with dog barking at the side, small chip to lower right.

31.5in (80cm) long

$950-1,100   **CHOR**

A rare Victorian papier mâché oval tray, of cricketing interest, painted with 'Cricket in the Artillery Ground', after Francis Hayman, mounted on a later stand to form a table.

The original painting by Francis Hayman can be found in the Marylebone Cricket Club Museum at Lords. It depicts an early game of cricket being played with a thin curved club and the wicket keeper believed to be William Hogarth who was a friend of Hayman. In the mid-18thC the Artillery Ground, Finsbury was the sport's focal point and home of the London Cricket Club.

29.75in (75.5cm) wide

$5,000-6,500   **WW**

A 19thC black papier mâché tray, by Jennens and Bettridge, painted with flowers, within Mother-of-pearl borders, impressed mark to reverse.

32.75in (83cm) wide

$400-450   **SWO**

A Victorian papier mâché tray, painted with a hunting scene.

26in (66cm) wide

$650-750   **SWO**

A 17thC oak tester bed, the paneled tester with arcaded and inlaid panels and carved terms, two moldings detached, later carved posts and evidence of alterations to the structure.

82.75in (210cm) deep

$2,800-3,500   CHEF

A George III Irish mahogany four-poster bed, with a carved leaf pelmet above Gothic carved cluster columns, with leaf capitals and leaf and flower carved baluster supports, with eight bolts.

94in (239cm) high

$4,400-5,700   WW

A mid-19thC satin birch four-poster bed, the molded cornice raised on bold octagonal fluted columns.

95in (241cm) high

$4,400-5,700   L&T

A Victorian walnut four-poster bed, with arched elaborately carved headboard, decorated with foliate swags and barleytwist uprights and footboard.

82.75in (210cm) deep

$650-750   ROS

An Edward VII mahogany four-poster bed, with reeded and leaf carved and turned posts, indented panel headboard.

87in (221cm) high

$2,800-3,500   MOR

A French late 19thC gilt wood three-paneled screen, the upper glazed section with foliate carving and rams head terminals above silk panels.

53.5in (136cm) wide

$400-500   PC

An early 20thC giltwood three-fold draught screen, embroidered with an urn of pomegranates, pears, apples and scrolling leafage, within a ovolu molded frame.

76.5in (194cm) high

$650-750   MOR

A cast iron hall stand, in the manner of Coalbrookdale, decorated with festoons of fruit, scrolling foliage and ivy leaves between twisted colonettes, with a diamond registration stamp to the back, dated.

This is reminiscent of the Coalbrookdale 'Midsummer Night's Dream' pattern.

1873   *69.75in (177cm) high*

$500-650   CHEF

An 18thC German Kingwood and brass-mounted tea chest, attributed to the workshop of Abraham Roentgen, the interior with three lift-out brass canisters, the central one with a domed lid and two divisions, flanked by a pair of rectangular caddies with star-decorated lids, above a secret base drawer.

Abraham Roentgen (1711-1793) was born in Müllheim, Germany. He learned cabinet-making in his father's workshop and was an apprentice in the Hague before settling in London in 1731. One of his most famous pieces is the Walderdorffer bureau now in the Rijksmuseum, Amsterdam.

8.75in (22cm) wide

$2,800-3,200　　　WW

ESSENTIAL REFERENCE - HISTORY OF TEA

Tea has been enjoyed in Britain for over 350 years.
- It first reached Europe during the first half of the 17thC.
- First advertised as a 'China Drink' in the 17thC, it was an expensive beverage.
- The East India Company was the main tea supplier to England. It shipped tea leaves from India and China on vessels called tea clippers from the mid-18thC.
- Drinking tea soon became an important social pastime in fashionable circles. This provided hosts with the opportunity to display their wealth.
- Due to its high price, tea was often kept in locked caddies to stop servants from pilfering.
- Heavy duty on tax encouraged smuggling. Despite this, tea still remained a relatively expensive commodity.
- Duty on tea was lifted in 1771. Tea gradually became more affordable.
- Tea rooms were very popular during the 19thC and became the place where women could meet with friends.
- Although tea remains a staple today, the ritual of taking afternoon tea or serving it in one's home has declined in popularity.

A George III inlaid mahogany tea caddy, with triple-lidded canister interior.

10.25in (26cm) wide

$750-900　　　BELL

A George III Gillows of Lancaster burrwood tea caddy, with two colored wood floral motifs, satinwood line inlay and edging, stamped to inside edge 'Gillows Lancaster' and to inside of lid 'J Bower 1800'.

6in (15cm) long

$2,500-3,200　　　TRI

A George III burr yew tea caddy, with twin-lidded interior centered by a mixing bowl.

11.5in (29cm) wide

$250-320　　　BELL

A George III mahogany tea caddy, with batswing patera to the cover, and oval patera to the front, with an ivory escutcheon.

7.25in (18.5cm) wide

$250-320　　　CHOR

A George III satinwood tea caddy, cross-banded and inlaid, shell and floral patera, the interior fitted twin-lidded compartments and bowl.

7.25in (18.5cm) wide

$550-700　　　CHOR

A George III satinwood and inlaid tea caddy, with boxwood stringing, the interior with two lidded canisters, very minor damage.

7.25in (18.5cm) long

$550-700　　　CHOR

A George III inlaid tea caddy, the hinged cover centered by a shell patera, the sides inlaid ovals and the corners inlaid as pilasters.

7.5in (19.5cm) wide

$700-800   **CHOR**

A George III satinwood barrel-front tea caddy, with tulipwood crossbanding and stringing, the cover with a foliate marquetry spray, with cast-brass handle, the lid warped.

11.25in (28.5cm) wide

$950-1,100   **PC**

A Regency rosewood sarcophagus tea caddy, the cover and front cross-banded, fitted two-lidded compartments to the interior.

7.75in (20cm) wide

$180-250   **CHOR**

A Regency yew wood sarcophagus tea caddy, with box wood stringing and ivory diamond shaped escutcheon, twin-lidded compartments to the interior.

9in (23cm) wide

$300-350   **CHOR**

A Regency rosewood sarcophagus tea caddy, fitted two compartments and central glass bowl.

13in (33cm) wide

$250-320   **CHOR**

An early 19thC Regency satinwood tea caddy, opening to fitted compartments and a later glass bowl.

14.75in (37.5cm) wide

$300-400   **L&T**

A Regency brass and bone inlaid rosewood tea caddy, with twin-lidded interior.

13.5in (34cm) wide

$150-190   **BELL**

An early 19thC rare painted wood teapot form tea caddy, parcel-gilt decoration with a fan patera on a mahogany brown ground, the hinged lid with turned finial to a foil lined interior.

7in (18cm) high

$3,200-3,800   **MART**

A 19thC rosewood sarcophagus tea caddy, inlaid with a brass shell with urn and floral scrollwork, with mixing bowl and inner caddies initialed 'B' and 'G'.

14.25in (36cm) wide

$650-750   **CHOR**

A George III green tortoiseshell twin-compartment tea caddy, with ivory borders.

6.5in (16.5cm) wide

$1,500-1,900   SWO

A George III green tortoiseshell single-compartment tea caddy, ivory borders and a white metal oval plaque within a piqué ware 'frame'.

4.5in (11cm) high

$1,500-1,900   SWO

A George III tortoiseshell tea caddy, with twin-lidded interior.

6.25in (16cm) wide

$500-650   BELL

A George III tortoiseshell single-compartment tea caddy, having a molded sunburst panel to the front, pewter stringing.

5in (13cm) high

$900-1,000   SWO

A George III tortoiseshell tea caddy, with silvered stringing, the interior with fitted triple-lidded compartment.

10in (25cm) long

$550-700   CHOR

A George III blonde tortoiseshell tea caddy, inlaid ivory lines and containing two lidded compartments, small area of restoration and area of tortoiseshell missing.

6.5in (16.5cm) wide

$1,000-1,500   CHOR

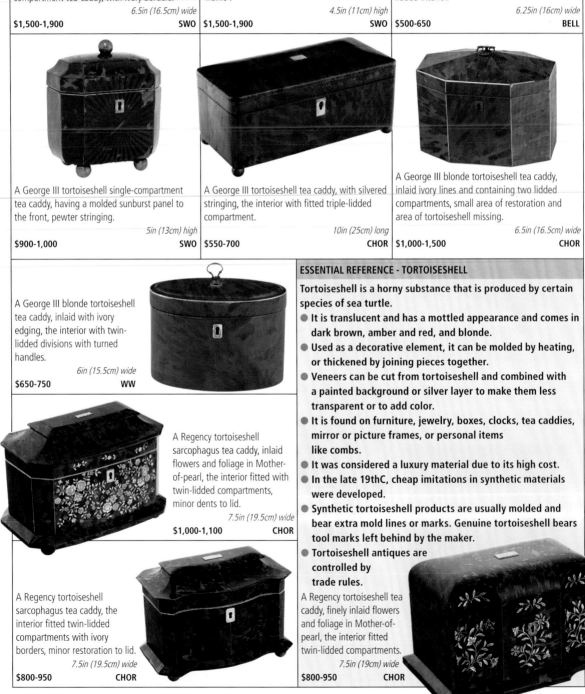

A George III blonde tortoiseshell tea caddy, inlaid with ivory edging, the interior with twin-lidded divisions with turned handles.

6in (15.5cm) wide

$650-750   WW

A Regency tortoiseshell sarcophagus tea caddy, inlaid flowers and foliage in Mother-of-pearl, the interior fitted with twin-lidded compartments, minor dents to lid.

7.5in (19.5cm) wide

$1,000-1,100   CHOR

A Regency tortoiseshell sarcophagus tea caddy, the interior fitted twin-lidded compartments with ivory borders, minor restoration to lid.

7.5in (19.5cm) wide

$800-950   CHOR

ESSENTIAL REFERENCE - TORTOISESHELL

Tortoiseshell is a horny substance that is produced by certain species of sea turtle.

- It is translucent and has a mottled appearance and comes in dark brown, amber and red, and blonde.
- Used as a decorative element, it can be molded by heating, or thickened by joining pieces together.
- Veneers can be cut from tortoiseshell and combined with a painted background or silver layer to make them less transparent or to add color.
- It is found on furniture, jewelry, boxes, clocks, tea caddies, mirror or picture frames, or personal items like combs.
- It was considered a luxury material due to its high cost.
- In the late 19thC, cheap imitations in synthetic materials were developed.
- Synthetic tortoiseshell products are usually molded and bear extra mold lines or marks. Genuine tortoiseshell bears tool marks left behind by the maker.
- Tortoiseshell antiques are controlled by trade rules.

A Regency tortoiseshell tea caddy, finely inlaid flowers and foliage in Mother-of-pearl, the interior fitted twin-lidded compartments.

7.5in (19cm) wide

$800-950   CHOR

A Regency tortoiseshell sarcophagus tea caddy, inlaid flowers and foliage in Mother-of-pearl, the interior fitted with twin-lidded compartments with ivory borders, some restoration.

7.5in (19cm) wide

$650-750   CHOR

A Regency tortoiseshell sarcophagus tea caddy, the interior fitted twin-lidded compartments and bowl within ivory lining, restoration to small areas.

11in (28cm) wide

$700-800   CHOR

A tortoiseshell tea caddy, with interior fitted basin, lidded compartments within ivory lining, minor abrasions.

7.5in (19.5cm) wide

$2,000-2,500   CHOR

CLOSER LOOK - A TORTOISESHELL TEA CADDY

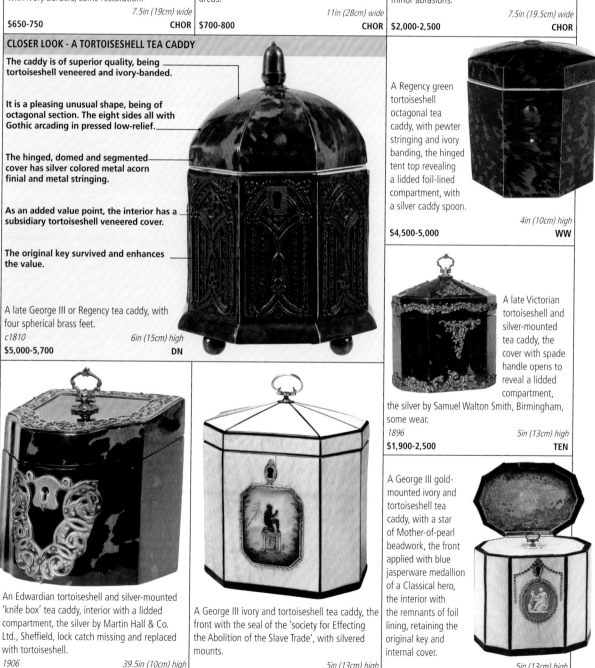

The caddy is of superior quality, being tortoiseshell veneered and ivory-banded.

It is a pleasing unusual shape, being of octagonal section. The eight sides all with Gothic arcading in pressed low-relief.

The hinged, domed and segmented cover has silver colored metal acorn finial and metal stringing.

As an added value point, the interior has a subsidiary tortoiseshell veneered cover.

The original key survived and enhances the value.

A late George III or Regency tea caddy, with four spherical brass feet.

c1810   *6in (15cm) high*

$5,000-5,700   DN

A Regency green tortoiseshell octagonal tea caddy, with pewter stringing and ivory banding, the hinged tent top revealing a lidded foil-lined compartment, with a silver caddy spoon.

4in (10cm) high

$4,500-5,000   WW

A late Victorian tortoiseshell and silver-mounted tea caddy, the cover with spade handle opens to reveal a lidded compartment, the silver by Samuel Walton Smith, Birmingham, some wear.

1896   *5in (13cm) high*

$1,900-2,500   TEN

An Edwardian tortoiseshell and silver-mounted 'knife box' tea caddy, interior with a lidded compartment, the silver by Martin Hall & Co. Ltd., Sheffield, lock catch missing and replaced with tortoiseshell.

1906   *39.5in (10cm) high*

$1,900-2,500   TEN

A George III ivory and tortoiseshell tea caddy, the front with the seal of the 'society for Effecting the Abolition of the Slave Trade', with silvered mounts.

5in (13cm) high

$2,500-3,800   DN

A George III gold-mounted ivory and tortoiseshell tea caddy, with a star of Mother-of-pearl beadwork, the front applied with blue jasperware medallion of a Classical hero, the interior with the remnants of foil lining, retaining the original key and internal cover.

5in (13cm) high

$3,800-4,400   DN

A Georgian ivory tea caddy, banded in tortoiseshell with silver ring handle and oval of Mother-of-pearl beads, the interior with lidded compartment, missing tortoiseshell stringing.

$1,500-2,000   CHOR

A George III ivory tea caddy, with a silver loop handle, escutcheon and navette shape plaque inscribed with initials 'F B', with tortoiseshell stringing and Mother-of-pearl decoration, with a foil-lined interior.

4.5in (11cm) high

$900-1,000   WW

A late 18th/early 19thC fruitwood apple tea caddy, with steel lock escutcheon and key, with much of the original foil lining.

4.75in (12cm) high

$2,300-2,800   DN

A late 18th/early 19thC fruitwood apple tea caddy, with much of the original foil lining.

4.75in (12cm) diam

$3,000-3,500   DN

Judith Picks

I have always had a passion for these seemingly quite plain fruitwood tea caddies. The fruit caddy, appropriately carved from fruitwood, boasts a wonderful, tactile shape and deep, lustrous patina. The fact that it is a pear, rather than the more common apple, also adds to its appeal. You can't quite imagine the culture: gourmet tea is still having a moment, but it's rare that as we sit down with our cup of Kusmi or TWG Tea, we worry, 'I must go and make sure the tea bags are safely locked away.' Conversely, if you'd lived in Britain from the mid-17th to late 18thC, and you were lucky enough to have tea (albeit loose-leaf rather than tea bags in those days), it would have been one of the first things on your mind.

An late 18th/early 19thC fruitwood apple tea caddy, with remains of its original foil lining.

5in (13cm) high

$2,500-3,200   DN

A Regency Mother-of-pearl tea caddy, the interior with lidded compartment, small area of foot molding and linings replaced

5.75in (14.5cm) high

$800-950   CHOR

A Victorian papier mâché tea caddy, painted and inlaid Mother-of-pearl flowers, the interior with fitted two-lidded compartments.

7.75in (20cm) long

$230-280   CHOR

A late 18th/early 19thC fruitwood pear tea caddy, retaining much of the foil lining.

4.5in (11cm) high

$3,800-4,400   DN

A Regency black japanned sarcophagus tea caddy, painted with fruit, flowers, stylized foliage, and Asiatic pheasants, the interior now with three fabric-covered compartments.

12in (30cm) long

$650-750   SWO

A mid-19thC French ebonized and brass inlaid decanter box, inlaid with Mother-of-Pearl and Kingwood, the interior with four cut glass decanters and stoppers and with apertures for twelve cigars, with key.

13.5in (34cm) high

$500-650

WW

A French Napoleon III burr walnut 'cave a liqueur', with boulle, brass and cross-banded inlay, with a removable tiered tray with gilt relief metal armature, with four etched glass decanters with balloon form stoppers and six cordial glasses.

c1870   14in (35.5cm) wide

$650-750

MART

A Victorian brass inlaid coromandel liqueur cabinet, with a fitted interior and plaque for 'Chapmans Patent No.101'.

12.5in (32cm) wide

$550-650

BELL

A Victorian oak decanter box, the lift top with Bramah lock.

8.75in (22cm) wide

$450-500

BELL

A 19thC satinwood decanter box, with a six-division interior.

11.5in (29cm) wide

$200-250

BELL

A Victorian rosewood brass inlaid dressing case, with silver fittings by W. Lund, London, the interior with a lift-out tray and fitted with silver-mounted glass jars and containers, bearing maker's stamps 'W. Lund Maker 24 Fleet St London' and no.17240.

1838   11.5in (29cm) wide

$650-750

L&T

A Victorian coromandel toilet box, with silver-mounted fittings, by Thomas Whitehead, London, with engraved brass, Mother-of-pearl, and abalone inlay and a Bramah lock, with a concealed mirror and stationery pocket, fitted with three cut glass bottles and two cylindrical jars, a tray with two small bottles, two circular and two rectangular jars and a seven-piece Mother-of-pearl handled and/or steel manicure set, a compartment beneath.

1849   12.5in (32cm) wide

$3,200-3,800

DN

A Victorian calamander dressing case, by Asprey, the interior with twelve 'hobnail' cut-glass vanity bottles, each of the silver fittings bear the maker's mark of Abraham Brownett and John Rose, and are hallmarked, with maker's mark of 'ASPREY. MANUFACTURER TO HER MAJESTY. 166 BOND ST W', hallmarked London.

1859   14in (36cm) wide

$5,500-7,000

DN

A 19thC French decanter box, the ebony and amboyna case with Mother-of-pearl and brass inlay, with four decanters and eight glasses.

10.5in (26.5cm) high

$400-500

CHEF

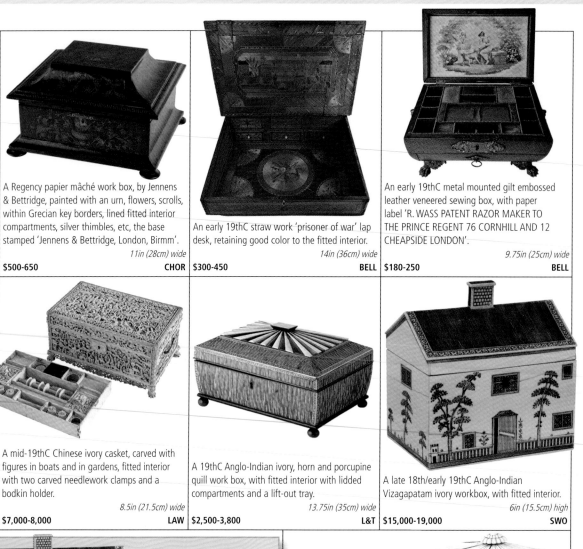

A Regency papier mâché work box, by Jennens & Bettridge, painted with an urn, flowers, scrolls, within Grecian key borders, lined fitted interior compartments, silver thimbles, etc, the base stamped 'Jennens & Bettridge, London, Birmm'.

11in (28cm) wide

$500-650   **CHOR**

An early 19thC straw work 'prisoner of war' lap desk, retaining good color to the fitted interior.

14in (36cm) wide

$300-450   **BELL**

An early 19thC metal mounted gilt embossed leather veneered sewing box, with paper label 'R. WASS PATENT RAZOR MAKER TO THE PRINCE REGENT 76 CORNHILL AND 12 CHEAPSIDE LONDON'.

9.75in (25cm) wide

$180-250   **BELL**

A mid-19thC Chinese ivory casket, carved with figures in boats and in gardens, fitted interior with two carved needlework clamps and a bodkin holder.

8.5in (21.5cm) wide

$7,000-8,000   **LAW**

A 19thC Anglo-Indian ivory, horn and porcupine quill work box, with fitted interior with lidded compartments and a lift-out tray.

13.75in (35cm) wide

$2,500-3,800   **L&T**

A late 18th/early 19thC Anglo-Indian Vizagapatam ivory workbox, with fitted interior.

6in (15.5cm) high

$15,000-19,000   **SWO**

A late 18th/early 19thC Anglo-Indian Vizagapatam ivory workbox, with fitted interior.

Vizagapatam on the northern Coromandel coast is a natural harbour midway between Calcutta and Madras. The British East India Company had an important trading station there and a tradition grew in Vizagapatam for the manufacture of objects and furniture of Western form, decorated in a distinctive manner, all being inlaid or veneered with black lacquer. The decoration was often drawn from Mogul culture, adapted to appeal to western taste. However here, on this rare box, the inspiration is from an English country cottage.

8.25in (21cm) wide

$18,000-23,000   **SWO**

An early 19thC Vizagapatam ivory work box, the interior fitted with a mirror and lidded compartments, thread spools, barrels, slight cracks to reeded sections of cover, lift-out tray has crack to base.

13in (33cm) wide

$3,800-4,400   **CHOR**

A Vizagapatam sarcophagus ivory work box, the interior with lift-out tray fitted with lidded compartments, some damage.

13in (33cm) wide

$1,000-1,200   **CHOR**

A 17thC chestnut writing box, with hinged lid above a fall-front applied with geometric moldings and concealing seven drawers, some lined with 17thC pomegranate design paper.

20.5in (52cm) wide

$1,300-1,800   **CHOR**

A George III walnut campaign writing box, brass-banded and with handles, fitted with seven compartments each with sliding cover, stationery compartments to each side and with lower tier of two compartments.

14in (36cm) wide

$650-750   **CHOR**

A mid-19thC coromandel writing box, the interior is satinwood lined with button release, letter rack and tray, with tablet by 'Wedgwood & Son, 9 Cornhill'.

14in (35.5cm) long

$800-950   **TRI**

A mid-19thC Victorian walnut writing slope, with an interior fitted for stationery and writing, with a drawer to the side, with abrass presentation plaque inscribed 'Gulielmo K. Maccrorie, A.M. / Coll: S. Petri. ap. Radley Socio / SUI GRATISSIMI / 1858'.

17in (43cm) wide

$900-1,000   **L&T**

A Victorian coromandel writing box, fitted with pen and ink compartments, a well over slope, letter and stationery compartments.

16in (40.5cm) wide

$400-450   **TRI**

A Victorian papier mâché writing box, painted with exotic birds and roses with fitted interior.

12.25in (31cm) wide

$300-350   **CHOR**

A rare 17thC Indian Gujarat casket, the brass frame applied with polished red stone and Mother-of-pearl plaques, some old damage and losses.

Some people believed that this casket could be provenanced to Clive of India. Its 17thC origins probably put it at a time when Gujarat was part of the Mughal Empire, before the era of the Hindu Maratah Empire from 1674. Certainly, the box conforms to the Islamic ban on figurative decoration and, as such, retained its appeal to the many Middle-Eastern buyers of Indian artefacts.

8in (20cm) wide

$45,000-50,000   **BE**

A 19thC Flemish red tortoiseshell fruitwood, ebony, and ivory table cabinet.

16in (41cm) wide

$2,500-3,200   **L&T**

A 19thC Russian bone-veneered table casket, probably Arkangel, on bracket feet.

9.75in (24.5cm) wide

$500-650   **L&T**

A large 19thC Italian Kingwood and tulipwood crossbanded casket, inset with pietra dura panels depicting birds, flowers and scrolls.

This large example was a good piece of early 19thC craftsmanship, but the main attraction was the pietra dura panels which had the look of the late 17th/early 18thC products of the Grand Ducal workshops in Florence. There was some debate about the age of the panels, but the general comment was that the plaques were c1800 in a moderately later box.

16.5in (42cm) long

$45,000-50,000   GORL

An early 19thC New England painted basswood dome lid box, with original sponge decorated surface with green and black trim.

26.25in (67cm) wide

$4,500-5,000   POOK

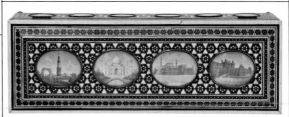

An Anglo-Indian inlaid mosaic ware box, with twenty watercolors of Indian buildings, the top comprising: Qutab Minar, Taj Mahal, Jami Masjid, and the Red Fort, others include the Golden Temple, Amritsar and Humayun's Tomb.

15.25in (39cm) wide

$2,800-3,300   SWO

An early 19thC Vizagapatam carved ivory box, the hinged lid and body with black stained borders of fruiting vines, opening to a void sandalwood lined interior.

8in (20cm) wide

$500-650   L&T

A silver mounted marble casket, the mounts by Storr & Mortimer and Rundell, Bridge & Rundell, London, the corner mounts and hinges by Paul Storr, the applied cast coat of arms, supporters, motto and baron's coronet by John Bridge.

The arms are those of Gray, Barons Gray probably for Francis, 14th Lord Gray (1765-1842), who succeeded to the title upon the death of his brother in 1807. He was married in 1794 to Mary Anne (d.1858), daughter of Colonel James Johnston, and had issue, one son and three daughters.

c1832   *11.75in (30cm) wide*

$4,500-5,000   MAB

A 19thC harewood and inlaid box, the cover centered by a painted roundel depicting a cherub, with oval inlays to the sides.

11in (28cm) wide

$450-550   CHOR

A red velvet covered casket, in Renaissance-style, possibly in part 16thC, the Cupid-handled key fitting into a combination lock flanked by Classical portrait ovals, with some losses, likely that it is mostly of 19thC construction.

7in (18cm) wide

$11,000-12,000   CHEF

A Louis XV-style gilt-metal mounted Kingwood casket, of bombé outline and plush lined interior, on four scroll feet.

15in (38cm) wide

$500-650   CHOR

ESSENTIAL REFERENCE - KNIFE BOXES

When cutlery was provided by the host, decorative cases, especially for the knives, were often left on display in the dining-room. Some of the most elegant and often ornate were in the styles of Robert Adam, George Hepplewhite and Thomas Sheraton. Occasionally flat-topped containers, they were most frequently either rod-shaped, or tall and narrow with a sloping top necessitated by a series of raised veins for exhibiting the handles of knives and the bowls of spoons. Mahogany and satinwoods were most common, occasionally inlaid with marquetry, or edged with boxwood which was resistant to chipping. These receptacles, often made in pairs, were often converted into stationery cabinets.

A pair of George III-style mahogany urn shaped knife boxes, with fitted interiors and decorated with bands of boxwood stringing.

c1900　　　　*25in (63cm) high*

$2,000-2,500　　　　**L&T**

A George III mahogany apothecary chest, with sixteen bottles and stoppers, including bottles labelled 'Tincture and Quinine', 'Fine Turkey Rhubarb' and 'spirit of Sal Volatile', two drawers and a concealed catch releasing a sliding section to the rear enclosing four poison bottles.

10.75in (27.5cm) high

$650-900　　　　**SWO**

A pair of George III mahogany knife boxes, inlaid with barber's pole stringing and Kingwood banding, the lids inlaid with a marquetry patera, the interior with a parquetry star above a matrix with thirty-seven apertures, with a gilt brass plaque with initials 'R H'.

15in (38cm) high

$2,500-3,200　　　　**WW**

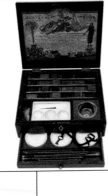

A Georgian artist's mahogany and satinwood-strung paint box, by Reeves and Inwood, the lift-out tray with watercolor tablets, glass water bowl, pottery mixing bowls, ivory palette, the frieze drawer containing six pottery mixing palettes and brushes.

9.5in (24cm) wide

$1,000-1,200　　　　**BE**

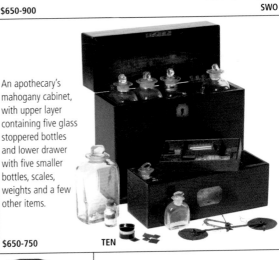

An apothecary's mahogany cabinet, with upper layer containing five glass stoppered bottles and lower drawer with five smaller bottles, scales, weights and a few other items.

$650-750　　　　**TEN**

A leather and brass-mounted cartridge magazine, with an oak and fitted interior, bearing the initials 'J.W.F.H.'.

16in (41cm) long

$500-650　　　　**WHP**

A Victorian-style yew wood country house pillar box, the door below the mouth of the post box with the postal rates of the day postered to one side of the key escutcheon.

15in (38cm) high

$750-900　　　　**CHEF**

An early 20thC 'McLean' Tartanware box, three-quarter lift-off lid.

7.5in (19cm) long

$50-60　　　　**MART**

A Regency tôleware chestnut vase, possibly Pontypool, of Classical urn shape, with lion mask ring handles to the sides.

Tôleware refers to items made out of tinplated sheet iron, which is covered with black asphaltum, and painted. It was produced in Pennsylvania in large quantities during the 18th and 19thC.

12.25in (31cm) high

$180-250   **CHOR**

An early Victorian painted tôleware peinte coal box and cover, decorated with floral sprays and with a lift-out liner.

25.5in (65cm) long

$500-650   **WW**

A pair of early 19thC red-lacquered papier mâché wine coasters, with gilt trailing flowering foliage.

6in (15cm) diam

$650-750   **SWO**

A pair of early 19thC black-lacquered papier mâché wine coasters, decorated in gilt with flowers and butterflies.

5.5in (13.5cm) diam

$400-450   **SWO**

A large Japanese black lacquer cutlery box, formed as an urn, decorated in Mother-of-pearl and gold, with exotic birds and flower sprays, with a rising cover revealing tiered compartments for knives.

c1800   *30in (76cm) high*

$5,500-6,500   **WW**

A pair of early 19thC japanned pewter chestnut urns and covers, transfer-printed and painted with chinoiserie scenes, with lion's mask ring handles, probably Dutch.

13in (33cm) high

$700-800   **WW**

ESSENTIAL REFERENCE - TUNBRIDGEWARE

Tunbridgeware is a form of decorative woodware.

- **It refers to a technique where patterns are created by gluing strips of wood together to form a block, which is then sliced transversely to reveal an intricate design. Identical patterns could be produced in this way and then applied to an item.**
- **Geometric or floral patterns, buildings or landscapes were popular.**
- **Colors were achieved by combining different types of wood.**
- **Some of the most commonly used were oak, sycamore, maple, and holly.**
- **The technique is thought to have originated in Tunbridge Wells, Kent, in the 17thC.**
- **Tunbridgeware became a popular souvenir with visitors to the town throughout the 18th and 19thC.**
- **Examples of Tunbridgeware were exhibited at the Great Exhibition of 1851.**

An early 19thC rare painted Tunbridgeware nutmeg grater, in the form of a Brighton Pavilion tower, painted with pairs of arched windows, tiles and geometric motifs, the circular box base fitted with a nutmet grater.

7.5in (19cm) high

$7,500-9,000   **BLEA**

An early 19thC rare painted Tunbridgeware spice box, incorporating a nutmeg grater, the interior with four radiating divisions with printed herb labels and centered by a wooden circular box with tin grater.

5.5in (14cm) diam

$16,000-20,000   **BLEA**

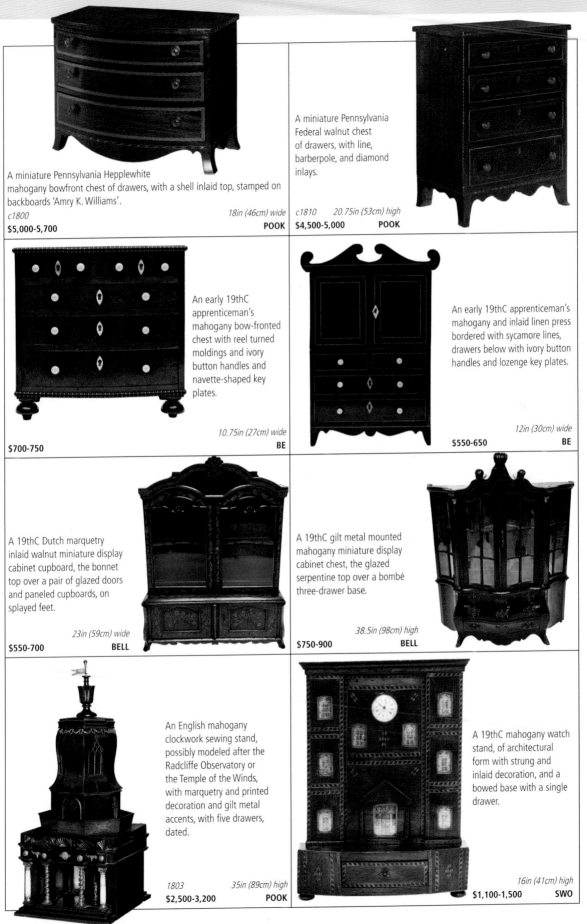

A miniature Pennsylvania Hepplewhite mahogany bowfront chest of drawers, with a shell inlaid top, stamped on backboards 'Amry K. Williams'.
c1800   18in (46cm) wide
$5,000-5,700   POOK

A miniature Pennsylvania Federal walnut chest of drawers, with line, barberpole, and diamond inlays.
c1810   20.75in (53cm) high
$4,500-5,000   POOK

An early 19thC apprenticeman's mahogany bow-fronted chest with reel turned moldings and ivory button handles and navette-shaped key plates.
10.75in (27cm) wide
$700-750   BE

An early 19thC apprenticeman's mahogany and inlaid linen press bordered with sycamore lines, drawers below with ivory button handles and lozenge key plates.
12in (30cm) wide
$550-650   BE

A 19thC Dutch marquetry inlaid walnut miniature display cabinet cupboard, the bonnet top over a pair of glazed doors and paneled cupboards, on splayed feet.
23in (59cm) wide
$550-700   BELL

A 19thC gilt metal mounted mahogany miniature display cabinet chest, the glazed serpentine top over a bombé three-drawer base.
38.5in (98cm) high
$750-900   BELL

An English mahogany clockwork sewing stand, possibly modeled after the Radcliffe Observatory or the Temple of the Winds, with marquetry and printed decoration and gilt metal accents, with five drawers, dated.
1803   35in (89cm) high
$2,500-3,200   POOK

A 19thC mahogany watch stand, of architectural form with strung and inlaid decoration, and a bowed base with a single drawer.
16in (41cm) high
$1,100-1,500   SWO

BOXES & TREEN

A 17thC carved pearwood snuff box, in the manner of Cesar Bagard of Nancy, decorated with a portrait bust, the body with leaves and flowers, some cracking.

3.5in (9cm) diam

$200-250   WW

A late 18thC bugbear flask, unmarked, the body carved with Masonic symbols including altar, sun, tools, house and bell, with silver ball eyes and stopper to terminal.

'Bugbear' coconut flasks were often carved by sailors on long sea voyages who had visited the Tropics and collected the 'green' nuts. Easier to carve whilst still young and fresh 'bugbears' have been collected originating from Mexico, South and North America, the French Polynesian Islands and Europe.

5in (13cm) long

$700-800   L&T

An early 19thC French carved coquilla nut hunchback snuff box.

2.5in (6cm) high

$500-550   WW

An early 19thC French carved coquilla nut snuff box, carved with Neptune riding three seahorses.

2.75in (7cm) wide

$180-230   WW

An 18thC yew wood snuff box, with carving of a village fayre, lifting by means of a yoke form thumbpiece to reveal a tortoiseshell interior, underside with chequer board weave design.

3.5in (9cm) wide

$450-500   MART

A 19thC chip-carved snuff box, in the form of a book with sliding cover.

5in (12.5cm) long

$230-280   LAW

An early 19thC French carved coquilla snuff box, with a bugbear end, carved with a winged cherub and palm trees.

3.5in (8.5cm) long

$250-320   WW

An early 19thC French carved coquilla nut snuff flask, with a white metal top, carved with a soldier and five horses, with a screw-off base.

2.5in (6cm) high

$250-320   WW

A Victorian treen and bone mounted snuff shoe, with a lift-off lid, inlaid with brass and Mother-of-pearl, with visible toenails.

4.75in (12cm) long

$400-450   WW

An early 20thC English carved boxwood snuff box, of Charles II-style, carved with the Royal arms, motto and supporters of Charles II of England, the reverse with the coat of arms for the Thornicroft family of Cheshire.

4in (10.5cm) long

$1,000-1,200   BELL

A late 17th/early 18thC rare treen lever-action nutcracker, carved as a bearded man above a fluted tapering handle, probably English.

See Edward H. Pinto, 'Treen and other Wooden Bygones', plate 74, for a similar nutcracker dated '1700' and with initials.

5.5in (13.5cm) long

$7,000-7,500 WW

A late 17th/early 18thC rare treen lever-action nutcracker, carved with the head of a man, with a flat face and engraved with owner's name 'Geoe Holt', probably English.

See Jonathan Levi, 'Treen for the Table', plate 12/11 and 12/13 for similar nutcrackers carved with the same flat faces.

6.5in (16.5cm) long

$7,500-9,000 WW

A late 17th/early 18thC treen lever-action nutcracker, carved with the head of a man with a flat face with stylized hair, with owner's initials 'W M' and with remains of red painted decoration.

6in (15.5cm) long

$4,500-5,000 WW

An 18thC pocket fruitwood screw-action nutcracker, of barrel shape.

See Owen Evan-Thomas, 'Domestic Utensils of Wood', pages 126-127, plate 49 for a similar nutcracker described as English 18thC, see also Jonathan Levi 'Treen for the Table', page 158, plate 12/7, for five similar nutcrackers; he describes them as 'being designed to slip into the pocket, just as some people eat popcorn in cinemas today, in the 18th and 19thC it was popular to eat hazlenuts at theatrical performances.'

3in (7.5cm) long

$3,200-3,800 WW

An early 19thC French boxwood screw-action nutcracker, carved with rondels.

See Owen Evan-Thomas, 'Domestic Utensils of Wood', pages 126-127, plate 49 for a similar nutcracker described as rare English 17thC. However also see Jonathan Levi 'Treen for the Table', page 156, plate 12/4 for three similar nutcracker which are attributed to France, Switzerland and Germany and dated to the early 19thC.

4.25in (10.5cm) long

$250-400 WW

A pair of 19thC treen yew wood nutcrackers, engraved decoration to the handles of a farmer and his dog, and all over with crude birds and trees.

7.5in (19cm) high

$1,500-1,900 BELL

A 19thC continental boxwood screw-action violin player nutcracker.

6.25in (16cm) high

$550-650 WW

A 19thC Swiss carved treen screw action nutcracker, of a gentleman sporting a hat.

7.75in (19.5cm) high

$180-250 WW

A George III mahogany cheese coaster, on roller castors.

17in (43cm) long

$450-500   SWO

A George III mahogany cheese coaster, wooden roller castors.

17.25in (43.5cm) long

$250-320   SWO

A George III walnut cheese dish, in the form of a galleon with a lion mask figurehead in front and a carved details of the captain's gallery behind, the coaster on a base with carved foliate decoration.

$1,900-2,500   DN

An early 19thC mahogany Lazy Susan, by John Earnshaw, the frieze with six turned knobs, a paper label to the underside reads 'John Earnshaw, Joiner, Cabinetmaker and Upholsterer, Borough Gate, Otley, most respectfully solicits a share of your favours'.

34in (86cm) diam

$750-900   SWO

A turned sycamore dairy bowl.

17.75in (45cm) diam

$450-500   WW

An unusual painted pine candlebox, with a fret-cut front over a drawer and a shaped base.

16.5in (42cm) high

$400-450   SWO

A turned wood treen goblet, probably 16thC, with traces of painted decoration.

4in (10cm) high

$300-400   WW

An 18thC lignum vitae wassail bowl, on a pedestal base, there is a new section to about 1/4 of the foot.

9in (23cm) diam

$1,900-2,500   CHOR

A Victorian softwood treen ladle, the terminal carved with an outstretched hand, with barley-twist shaft and crude shallow bowl.

17in (43.5cm) long

$250-400   BELL

A 16thC Continental coconut tankard, with three decorative cast straps, the lappet mounts engraved with repeating fleur-de-lys motifs, the rim with a frieze of arabesque floral scrolls and a central cartouche, inscribed 'ANNA SCHARNAGELIN', struck with 19thC Austro-Hungarian storage marks for Prague, probably German.

1570-80   *8.25in (21cm) high*

$7,000-7,500   **LAW**

A 19thC lignum vitae stringbox, in the form of a beehive.

4.75in (12cm) high

$90-110   **DW**

A mid-19thC pair of Victorian turned mahogany candlesticks, each with height-adjustable mechanism.

13.5in (34.5cm) high

$300-450   **BELL**

A Regency rosewood book carrier, inlaid Mother-of-pearl with drawer beneath on bun feet, the base is split and there are other veneer splits.

15.5in (39cm) wide

$1,300-1,800   **CHOR**

A George III mahogany cutlery box, with two-lidded compartments.

14.5in (37cm) long

$300-400   **SWO**

A pair of Irish Georgian mahogany buckets, one for peat and one for plates, the reeded brass-bound, coopered bodies, with brass carrying handles.

17in (43cm) high

$7,500-9,000   **DN**

An Elizabethan shoe horn, by Robert Hendart Mindum, incised and inked with a lady, flanked by hatched borders and 'THIS IS ROBART HEND / 1596 / ART MINDUM', below a band of scalework, suspension hole and curved terminal, dated.

This item forms an addition to the fascinating corpus of shoe horns by Robert (or 'Robart' as he invariably signed himself) Mindum, twenty-one of which are to be found cataloged online by Wayne Robinson, 'A catalogue of shoehorns made by Robert Mindum 1593-1613'. Apart from the horns themselves and one powder horn, nothing concrete is known of Mindum himself. It seems likely he was an amateur worker in horn; his name apparently does not appear on the rolls of the Horner's nor any other London company. Robinson speculates, given the similarities of the decoration on pamphlets and other printed matter of the period to that on the horns, that Mindum may have been a printer, used to working with woodblocks. He makes a case for the shoe horns having been bought by Mindum as 'blanks' from different sources.

1596   *5.75in (14.5cm) long*

$4,500-5,000   **MAB**

An early 19thC coquilla nut urn and stand, with a screw-off lid with swags of fruit and flowers above coats of arms with animal supporters, the screw-off base above a plinth carved with the fox and the crane from Aesop's Fables.

4.75in (12cm) high

$250-320   **WW**

A late 18th/early 19thC carved treen coquilla nut nutmeg grater, the screw-off acorn finial with a bone and steel grater with a compartment for nutmegs, the screw-off base also with a nutmeg compartment.

6in (15cm) high

$650-750   **WW**

BOXES & TREEN

ESSENTIAL REFERENCE - KNITTING STICKS

Knitting sticks were essential everyday objects in most British lower and working class families during the 17th, 18th and 19thC.

- **They were used to mend clothing items, or to make clothing that was sold to supplement a family's income.**
- **They were usually carved from wood by hand and were often decorated with a simple design or a person's initials.**
- **Some decorative designs are specific to certain areas.**

A late 18thC treen initialed and dated straight knitting stick, carved with floral motifs to the triangular top, naive-style cross-hatched and chip carving, initialed 'IH 1789', slight wear overall.

8.25in (21cm) long

$180-250   TEN

An 18thC treen peg knitting stick, with chip carved decoration including heart motifs and a star, inscribed 'IB 1766', several worm holes to front and back.

1766   *9in (22.5cm) long*

$400-500   TEN

A 19thC treen knitting stick, modeled as a hand with a pointed finger, with carved decoration to create a cuff, nails, palm and wrinkles to each knuckle, by 'H Lowerson', dated, some damage.

1882   *7.5in (19cm) long*

$550-650   TEN

A late 19th/early 20thC large wooden bird cage, in the form of a cathedral.

37.5in (95cm) high

$1,800-2,300   ROS

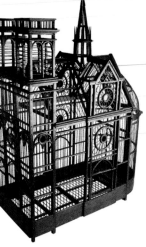

A 19thC carved pine articulated artist's mannequin, fully jointed, with detailed facial features, fingers, and toes.

69in (175.5cm) high

$19,000-25,000   POOK

A late 19thC Continental carved wooden artist's lay figure, life size.

The wooden figure, known affectionately as Mr Hogarth by the family he had been with for the past 100 years, was of a type made on the continent at the end of the 19thC. He is fully jointed with articulated fingers and naturalistically carved feet. His head had painted detail.

61.5in (156cm) high

$10,500-11,000   TS

An early 20thC French articulated walnut artist's model of a horse and rider, retailed by Lechertier Barbe, Jermyn Street, with jointed limbs set upon an adjustable steel spike and walnut base with applied retailer's plaque, some damage.

24in (61cm) wide

$2,800-3,500   BELL

A pair of 19thC giltwood wall appliqués, carved with crossed rake and pitchfork, with sheaves of wheat over birds nesting, emblematic of the seasons, some damage.

28.5in (72cm) high

$1,000-1,100   BELL

One of a pair of 19thC Continental hardwood panels, carved with dead game.

37.5in (95cm) high

$1,800-2,300 pair   DW

A pair of late 19thC Venetian-style carved and stained softwood wall brackets, each in the form of a Blackamoor in Medieval dress.

14in (36cm) high

$750-900   MOR

A late 15thC sculpted walnut model of Saint Peter, probably Limburg, Netherlands, the right forearm and hand are missing, the big toe of the right foot is also missing.

27.5in (70cm) high

$6,500-7,500 DN

A late 15thC German sculpted, polychrome painted and giltwood group, of Saint George and the Dragon, Swabia, the lance is a later replacement.

21.75in (55cm) high

$19,000-25,000 DN

A German sculpted, polychrome painted and parcel-giltwood group of Saint Anne -Anna Selbdritt, with the Virgin and Child, the painted surfaces have been refreshed, some damages.

c1520 *21.25in (54cm) high*

$6,500-7,500 DN

A late 16thC carved wood figure of a seated bagpipe player.

9.5in (24cm) high

$5,500-6,500 BE

A late 17thC Italian carved limewood figure of a winged mermaid, with polychrome decoration, signs of repair to right hand arm, tail with flaking paint work.

27in (69cm) high

$4,500-5,000 CHOR

A late 17thC Spanish carved decorated group of the Madonna Lactans, of wood and polychrome, with traces of gilt decoration.

17.75in (45cm) high

$700-800 WW

A late 17th/early 18thC European carved ivory figure of 'Winter', probably German, from a set of the seasons.

14.5in (37cm) high

$5,000-6,500 MOR

A late 17th/early 18thC German carved wood and polychrome decorated Corpus Christi.

15.5in (39.5cm) high

$1,300-1,800 WW

A 17th/18thC polychrome figure of Saint Francis, damage to right hand, there are two wire pegs on top of the book from where something is missing.

12.25in (31cm) high

$400-500 CHEF

A 19thC Anglo-Indian model of a palanquin, with a group of attendant figures.

20in (51cm) wide

$1,900-2,500   DN

A carved and painted group of two men chopping and sawing lumber, by George D. Wolfskill (1872-1940), Lancaster, Pennsylvania, inscribed 'Best take another before you go to bed'.

6.5in (16.5cm) high

$2,800-3,500   POOK

A 19thC Black Forest table centerpiece, carved as two bears carrying a dish, some wear to surface.

26.25in (67cm) wide

$2,500-3,200   CHOR

A Black Forest hat and stick stand, carved as an adult and cub bear at the foot of a tree with another cub seated at the top.

77.25in (196cm) high

$1,500-1,900   LAW

A late 19thC Black Forest bear tobacco box, with glass eyes and a hinged-head lid, the base with a musical movement.

11in (28cm) high

$900-1,000   WW

ESSENTIAL REFERENCE - BLACK FOREST CARVINGS

Black Forest describes the woodcarvings that originated in the Swiss village of Brienz.

● During the 1800s the wood carving industry flourished in the area.

● The term 'Brienzer ware' is also sometimes used to describe these carvings.

● Black Forest carvings were exhibited at the Great Exhibition of 1851, the Exposition Universelle in Paris in 1900, and at several American World Fairs.

● They were popular with wealthy Victorian travellers who bought them on their trips to decorate their homes.

● Fine examples can be found in Royal collections.

● They usually depict naturalistic or whimsical themes featuring forest or domestic animals, such as bears, stags, boars, eagles, and dogs.

● Carvings from the Huggler family are highly sought after.

● Most figures are not signed.

A Black Forest carved linden wood pedestal stand, in the form of a bear climbing a fir tree, on a shaped oval naturalistic base.

40.25in (102cm) high

$3,800-4,400   BE

A late 19thC Black Forest carved wood model of a mountain dog, with glass eyes.

9.5in (24cm) long

$1,300-1,800   WW

A 17thC walnut marquetry month-going longcase clock, by William Cattell in Fleet Street Londini fecit, the hood with later giltwood cresting above gilt pilasters, large outside countwheel to the six-pillar movement, five of which latched.

William Cattell is recorded by Britten as working 1664-90, apprenticed to Edward Stanton 1664, made a Freeman of the Clockmaker's Company in 1672.

100.5in (255cm) high

$13,000-15,000   **CHEF**

A late 17thC William and Mary marquetry longcase clock, by Evan Herbert, London, the eight-day movement striking on a bell.

82.25in (209cm) high

$4,400-5,700   **L&T**

A late 17thC walnut marquetry longcase clock, by Jacobus Goubert, the eight-day movement with anchor escapement rack striking on a bell.

81.5in (207cm) high

$4,500-5,000   **HT**

A walnut marquetry longcase clock, signed 'Rich Colston', London, four latched dial feet and six-knopped pillar movement, anchor escapement and outside countwheel striking on a bell, pediment with the caddy rebuilt, later finials, later barleytwist columns, in need of restoration.

Richard Colston is listed as working in London between 1682-1709. See Baillie (GH) 'Watchmakers & Clockmakers of the World', page 64.

c1700   *93in (236cm) high*

$7,500-9,000   **TEN**

A Dutch month-going ebony-veneered alarm longcase clock, signed 'Peter Klock', Amsterdam, five-pillar movement with four latched dial feet, anchor escapement, half-hour passing strike on a bell and striking the hours on a larger bell, hood rebuilt.

c1700   *93in (236cm) high*

$9,000-10,000   **TEN**

A mahogany eight-day quarter striking longcase clock, arch with rolling moonphase, triple weight-driven movement with anchor escapement, quarter striking on two bells and striking a further larger bell for the hours, signed 'Jno Clough, Manchester', small cracks, later feet.

c1750   *93.75in (238cm) high*

$8,000-9,500   **TEN**

An early 18thC walnut marquetry eight-day longcase clock, later marquetry with urn, floral, and bird decoration, five-pillar movement with anchor escapement and rack striking on a bell, case restored, hood with later columns.

85.5in (217cm) high

$4,000-4,800   **TEN**

An early 18thC walnut and marquetry longcase clock, with seconds and date dials and cherub spandrels, inscribed 'Brounker Watts, London'.

83in (211cm) high

$6,500-7,500   **SWO**

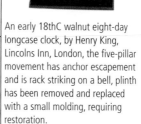

An early 18thC walnut eight-day longcase clock, by Henry King, Lincolns Inn, London, the five-pillar movement has anchor escapement and is rack striking on a bell, plinth has been removed and replaced with a small molding, requiring restoration.

86in (34cm) high

$1,800-2,300   **TRI**

A lacquered longcase clock, by John Lee, London, the eight-day duration, five-pillar movement, the green lacquered case with raised chinoiserie decoration, on replaced bracket feet, fifth pillar.

There were various makers named John Lee working in London at this time, with the most likely maker of the clock being either a John Lee who was apprenticed in 1719, becoming free of the clockmakers company in 1737 or another apprenticed in 1734 becoming free of the clockmakers company in 1745.

95.75in (243cm) high

$2,300-2,800   **BE**

A mid-18thC mahogany cased eight-day longcase clock, by John Ellicott, London.

John Ellicott (1702-1776) was the most famous member of a family who were amongst the finest clockmakers of the 18thC. He was the son of an eminent clockmaker, also John, who had been admitted to the Clockmaker's Company in 1696. When his father died in 1733, John took over the business. In 1738 he was elected a Fellow of the Royal Society. He showed a keen interest in all scientific matters and maintained an observatory at his home in Hackney. One of his most significant achievements was his work on the compensated pendulum. He also supplied clocks to the Spanish Royal Family. His son, Edward (d.1791), joined the business in 1760 and from then their joint clocks were simply signed 'Ellicott'.

18.75in (47.5cm) wide

$11,000-14,000   **L&T**

A mid-18thC walnut eight-day longcase clock, by Samuel Marshall, London, with subsidiary seconds and date aperture, engraved and signed, some splitting to the sides and later replacements.

81in (206cm) high

$1,900-2,500   **CHOR**

A mid-18thC Scottish George II mahogany longcase clock, by Thomas Hall, Cannongate.

95.25in (242cm) high

$1,300-1,900   **L&T**

A mahogany longcase clock, by Thomas Haley, London, the eight-day duration, five-pillar movement striking the hours on a bell.

Thomas Haley is quite possibly the maker who started his working life in north Walsham, Norfolk, leaving in 1742 to work in Norwich and then on to London after 1746 where he was known at Cold Field Baths in c1753 before moving to Oxford Street in c1781.

92in (234cm) high

$1,000-1,200   BE

A Philadelphia Chippendale mahogany case clock, the arch bonnet with applied spandrels enclosing an eight-day works, the arch bonnet broken, brass face inscribed 'Devereux Bowly London'.

c1770   *101in (256.5cm) high*

$7,000-8,000   POOK

A Chippendale walnut case clock, Reading, Pennsylvania, with an eight-day movement and a brass face, over a highly adorned case with an inlaid rooster, flowers, and insects, inscribed 'Valentin Urletig'.

1779   *98.75in (251cm) high*

$9,500-10,500   POOK

A mahogany eight-day longcase clock, William Kirk, Stockport, the door inlaid urn and floral decoration, arch with moonphase aperture, with four-pillar movement with anchor escapement and rack striking on a bell, signed, some damage.

c1780   *95.25in (242cm) high*

$13,000-15,000   TEN

A mahogany eight-day longcase clock, John Myers, London, five-pillar movement with anchor escapement and rack striking on a bell, signed, some damage.

c1789   *96in (244cm) high*

$3,200-3,800   TEN

A Bucks County, Pennsylvania Chippendale cherry tallcase clock, with an eight-day works, silvered dial face, inscribed with the owner's name 'Wm. Smith 1784', and signed by the maker, Aseph Warner.

Provenance: This clock was originally purchased by William Smith Jr. in 1784. It descended directly in the Smith family of Windy Bush Hill in Upper Makefield, Bucks County, Pennsylvania.

c1784   *98.5in (250cm) high*

$9,000-10,000   POOK

An 18thC George III mahogany longcase clock, by Richard Clark, London, dial with a subsidiary seconds dial, strike/silent dial, and date aperture.

93.25in (237cm) high

$3,200-3,800   L&T

A late 18thC George III mahogany longcase clock, by Wyke & Green, Liverpool, the eight-day movement striking a bell.

95in (234cm) high

$3,200-3,800   L&T

A late 18thC Northampton County, Pennsylvania Chippendale walnut tall case clock, the thirty-hour movement signed 'John Murphy'.

93in (236cm) high

$1,500-2,300   POOK

A late 18thC George III mahogany eight-day longcase clock, by Pollard, Exeter, with four-pillar rack-and-bell striking movement, on later paneled plinth base, signed.

82in (208cm) high

$900-1,100   DN

A late 18thC George III japanned tallcase clock, the eight-day works with a brass face, inscribed 'John Fletcher London'.

97.5in (248cm) high

$2,500-3,200   POOK

An 18thC green lacquered chinoiserie longcase clock, with a moon-and-sun phase dial with an automaton figure of Father Time, inscribed 'Wm Andrews, London', on an eight-day striking movement.

85.5in (217cm) high

$1,600-2,000   LAW

CLOSER LOOK - MUSICAL AUTOMATON CLOCK

This is a musical automaton clock, which makes it rare and desirable.

It plays six tunes, inscribed 'FAL LA LA, HOME SWEET HOME, MARCH IN ROB ROY, BLUE BELLS OF SCOTLAND, MARINERS HYMN, 104th PSALM'.

It has an eight day, six-pillar three-train movement with an anchor escapement and striking on a bell.

Unusually the arch is painted with a Georgian interior with figures playing instruments, with a lady at a harpsichord.

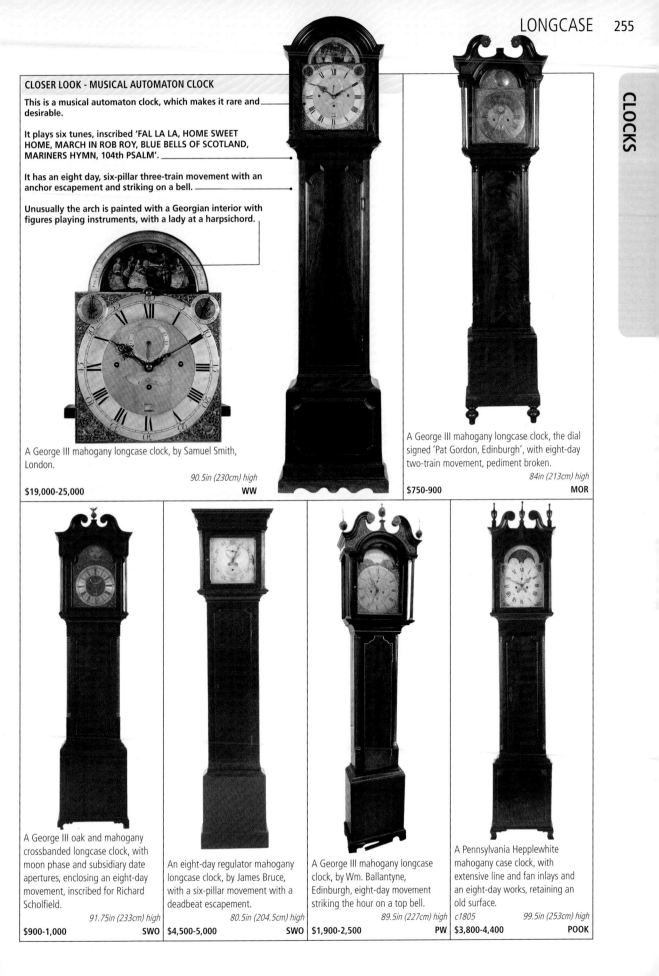

A George III mahogany longcase clock, by Samuel Smith, London.

90.5in (230cm) high

$19,000-25,000 **WW**

A George III mahogany longcase clock, the dial signed 'Pat Gordon, Edinburgh', with eight-day two-train movement, pediment broken.

84in (213cm) high

$750-900 **MOR**

A George III oak and mahogany crossbanded longcase clock, with moon phase and subsidiary date apertures, enclosing an eight-day movement, inscribed for Richard Scholfield.

91.75in (233cm) high

$900-1,000 **SWO**

An eight-day regulator mahogany longcase clock, by James Bruce, with a six-pillar movement with a deadbeat escapement.

80.5in (204.5cm) high

$4,500-5,000 **SWO**

A George III mahogany longcase clock, by Wm. Ballantyne, Edinburgh, eight-day movement striking the hour on a top bell.

89.5in (227cm) high

$1,900-2,500 **PW**

A Pennsylvania Hepplewhite mahogany case clock, with extensive line and fan inlays and an eight-day works, retaining an old surface.

c1805 *99.5in (253cm) high*

$3,800-4,400 **POOK**

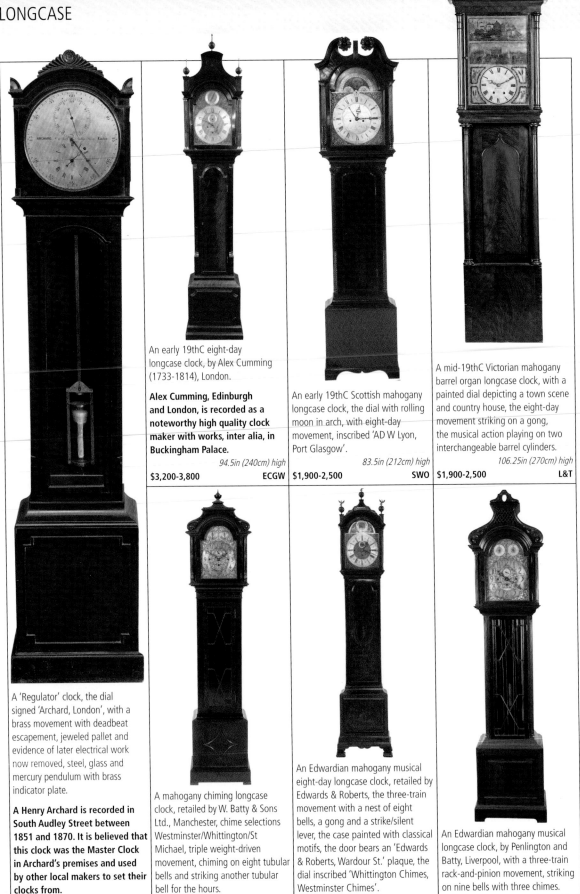

An early 19thC eight-day longcase clock, by Alex Cumming (1733-1814), London.

Alex Cumming, Edinburgh and London, is recorded as a noteworthy high quality clock maker with works, inter alia, in Buckingham Palace.

94.5in (240cm) high

$3,200-3,800   ECGW

An early 19thC Scottish mahogany longcase clock, the dial with rolling moon in arch, with eight-day movement, inscribed 'AD W Lyon, Port Glasgow'.

83.5in (212cm) high

$1,900-2,500   SWO

A mid-19thC Victorian mahogany barrel organ longcase clock, with a painted dial depicting a town scene and country house, the eight-day movement striking on a gong, the musical action playing on two interchangeable barrel cylinders.

106.25in (270cm) high

$1,900-2,500   L&T

A 'Regulator' clock, the dial signed 'Archard, London', with a brass movement with deadbeat escapement, jeweled pallet and evidence of later electrical work now removed, steel, glass and mercury pendulum with brass indicator plate.

A Henry Archard is recorded in South Audley Street between 1851 and 1870. It is believed that this clock was the Master Clock in Archard's premises and used by other local makers to set their clocks from.

74.5in (189cm) high

$11,000-13,000   LAW

A mahogany chiming longcase clock, retailed by W. Batty & Sons Ltd., Manchester, chime selections Westminster/Whittington/St Michael, triple weight-driven movement, chiming on eight tubular bells and striking another tubular bell for the hours.

c1890   95.5in (243cm) high

$3,200-3,800   TEN

An Edwardian mahogany musical eight-day longcase clock, retailed by Edwards & Roberts, the three-train movement with a nest of eight bells, a gong and a strike/silent lever, the case painted with classical motifs, the door bears an 'Edwards & Roberts, Wardour St.' plaque, the dial inscribed 'Whittington Chimes, Westminster Chimes'.

94.5in (240cm) high

$4,400-5,700   SWO

An Edwardian mahogany musical longcase clock, by Penlington and Batty, Liverpool, with a three-train rack-and-pinion movement, striking on nine bells with three chimes.

100in (254cm) high

$3,200-3,800   HW

A George III mahogany bracket clock, the brass eight-day repeating movement with verge escapement, chiming to a nest of four bells, striking to a single bell and inscribed 'Chas Blanchard / Bartletts Buildings / Holbourn London / Fecit August 1st / 1765 / Etatis Suce 78'.

1765   *17.5in (44cm) high*

$7,500-9,000   **LAW**

A George III mahogany bracket clock, by Eardley Norton, the twin-fusee eight-day movement striking on a bell.

Eardley Norton is listed as working at 49 St. John's Street, Clerkenwell between 1762 and 1794. He was a member of the Clockmakers Company and there are examples of his work in the Royal Collection. He is famous for his musical and astronomical clocks especially for the export market.

                          19in (48cm) high

$7,000-7,500   **WW**

An 18thC 'Boulle' striking bracket clock, signed 'Naudin, Paris', the case with floral, scroll, and figural mounts, twin-barrel movement now converted to anchor escapement, outside countwheel striking on a top-mounted bell, some tortoiseshell veneers missing.

                          33in (84cm) high

$2,300-2,800   **TEN**

A George III mahogany bracket clock, by John Ellicott, the twin-fusee movement marked for Thwaites, the shouldered plates signed 'Ellicott London', bell striking with pull repeat cord, the rear of the case stamped '931', with a later wall bracket.

John Ellicott (1706-1772) was one of the finest clockmakers of the 18thC. He was elected a Fellow of the Royal Society in 1738, serving on its council for three years. In 1760 he was joined in business by his son Edward and in 1762 he was appointed Clockmaker to the King. Thwaites supplied high quality movements to a number of clockmakers, including Allam and Clements, Henry Borrell, Dwerrihouse and Carter, Thomas Earnshaw, John Leroux, Francis Perigal and James Tregent.

                          17in (43cm) high

$13,000-18,000   **CHEF**

A mahogany bracket clock, the double-fusee movement striking the hours and half-hour on individual bells, inscribed for Thomas Best, London.

                          23.25in (59cm) high

$2,300-2,800   **SWO**

A George III inlaid mahogany bracket clock, the eight-day movement striking the hour, with a repeater, the dial and backplate inscribed 'Chancellor, London'.

                          18in (46cm) high

$3,800-5,000   **SWO**

A George III and later mahogany striking bracket clock, the twin-barrel, four-pillar movement striking on a bell, dial with female mask and inscribed 'William Jourdain, LONDON', with pendulum, winding key and door key.

                          17in (43.5cm) high

$1,500-2,000   **WW**

CLOCKS

A Regency mahogany bracket clock, with eight-day movement striking on a bell, grills in need of re-silking, face rubbed, complete with pendulum, no key.

$1,400-1,800   CHOR

A Regency brass-mounted mahogany bracket clock, the four-pillar twin-fusee bell striking movement with anchor escapement, unsigned.

19in (48cm) high

$1,300-1,900   DN

A late Regency mahogany and brass inlaid chiming bracket clock, with Egyptian terms surmounted by pyramidal corner finials, the eight-day quarter striking and chiming movement with a bell strike and playing and eight bells.

38in (97cm) high

$5,000-6,500   L&T

An early 19thC Swiss Neuchâtel bracket clock and bracket, verge escapement with silk suspension, quarter striking on two gongs, the rectangular movement with countwheel on the backplate and stamped 'P.G.'.

29in (74cm) high

$900-1,000   WW

A William IV Gothic Revival rosewood, inlay, and parcel-gilt chiming bracket clock, the eight-day double-fusee movement with hour gong strike and quarter chimes on eight bells, dial inscribed 'J. MacGregor / Charterhouse Square / London'.

c1835   *26in (66cm) high*

$1,300-1,900   L&T

A 19thC rosewood and brass inlaid bracket clock, the dial inscribed 'John Brock, 16 George Street, Portman Square, London', on a brass twin-fusee movement striking on a bell.

15.25in (38.5cm) high

$2,500-3,200   LAW

A Victorian Gothic oak bracket clock, by James Dann of Wisbech, eight day English carillon chiming movement, triple-fusee movement with anchor re-coil escapement, eight-day chiming octave bells and single hour gong.

26.5in (67.5cm) high

$1,100-1,500   MART

A Victorian oak musical bracket clock, the triple-fusee movement striking the hours on a bell and the quarters on either eight or ten bells, the dial signed 'Hamilton Crighton & Co., 41 George Street, Edinburgh', the backplate also signed.

33in (84cm) high

$4,000-4,800   **SWO**

ESSENTIAL REFERENCE - BOULLE

André-Charles Boulle (1642-1732) was a renowned French cabinetmaker.

● His talents were apparent early on in his life.

● A royal warrant allowed him to work in the lodgings of the Louvre.

● Boulle was exempted from strict guild regulations that usually prevented artisans specializing in more than one profession. He was allowed to make both furniture and works in gilt bronze.

● His furniture adorned the homes of the French elite.

● Louis XIV and his son, the Grand Dauphin, were some of his most important clients.

● His output included wardrobes, commodes, desks, and clock cases, all richly decorated with his signature style of gilt bronze ornaments.

● He mastered the art of metal and wood marquetry.

● His style has been widely copied by cabinetmakers.

● Boulle never signed any of his work.

A Victorian carved oak chiming bracket clock, the eight-day duration, triple-fusee movement striking the hours on a gong and the quarters on a further eight gongs, with chime/silent and chime on eight gongs/chime on four gongs.

22.75in (58cm) high

$1,500-1,900   **BE**

A mid-late 19thC French red boullework and gilt-brass mounted bracket clock and bracket, the caddy top with female warrior finial, with figures below, on gadrooned feet, the bracket with female mask corners.

63in (160cm) high

$7,000-8,000   **L&T**

An 19thC mahogany and inlaid bracket clock, with a twin-fusee striking movement.

18.5in (47cm) high

$1,100-1,500   **CHOR**

A mahogany bracket clock, by John Collett, London, the associated eight-day duration double-fusee movement striking the hours on a bell.

18in (46cm) high

$500-650   **BE**

An early 20thC small pad-top bracket clock, with an eight-day duration, single-fusee timepiece movement, signed 'Chas. Fox, Bournemouth', with plaque engraved 'An Affectionate Token, Rev. Canon H. Barton R.D. and Mrs Barton on Their Silver Jubilee from the Congregation of St Luke's Church Parkstone, March 1920-1945'.

11.75in (30cm) high

$1,200-1,400   **BE**

A late Louis XVI ormolu mantel clock, the silk suspension movement in a drum case flanked by two Turkish warriors, the case attributed to Nicolas Bonnet, the dial signed 'Gille L'aine a Paris'.

This is a good early date and a well styled piece.

18in (46cm) high

$4,500-5,000   WW

An early 19thC Empire gilt-bronze mantle clock, with an eight-day movement striking on a bell.

12.5in (31.5cm) high

$2,300-2,800   L&T

An early 19thC French Empire ormolu clock, by Le Clerc à Bruxelles, dial signed 'Le Clerc / a Bruxelles' with a relief panel depicting shepherdesses and sheep, flanked by a Classical youth holding a scroll inscribed with a quotation from 'Estelle' by Jean-Pierre Claris de Florian, and a dog and pastoral attributes, the eight-day movement striking a bell.

16.5in (42cm) high

$5,500-7,000   L&T

A Regency gilt-bronze mantel clock, with a striking French drum movement.

18in (46cm) high

$500-650   SWO

An early 19thC Louis XIV-style ormolu and white marble mantel clock, the dial detailed 'Allion Versailles', with a two-train movement, with pendulum.

10.25in (26cm) high

$500-650   BELL

An ormolu mantle clock, in the French taste, by John Peterkin.

c1820   *10.5in (27cm) high*

$700-800   ECGW

An early 19thC French porcelain mantel clock, dial detailed 'Hry Marc, Paris', with a French two-train movement.

15.5in (39cm) high

$900-1,000   BELL

An early 19thC Louis XVI-style ormolu striking mantel clock, dial detailed 'Lietaud a Paris', with a two-train movement also signed with makers name, key and pendulum.

$1,900-2,500   BELL

A 19thC Louis XIV-style ormolu mounted 'tête de poupée' mantel clock, with a two-train movement, with pendulum.

19.25in (49cm) high

$1,500-2,000   BELL

A mid-19thC French ormolu striking mantel clock, the case set with a figure of Apollo, with a two-train movement, the backplate signed 'steffenoni A Paris, Guyerdet' and numbered 1627.

19.5in (50cm) high

$700-800　BELL

A mid-19thC Empire ormolu striking mantel clock, by Charles Oudin, the dial signed 'Ch Oudin eleve de Bregnet', the twin-barrel movement with recoil anchor escapement, silk suspension and count wheel strike to bell.

14.5in (37cm) high

$900-1,000　BELL

A mid-19thC French gilt-metal and silvered mantel clock, the movement stamped 'Hy MARC A PARIS', with two-train movement.

21in (53cm) high

$650-750　MOR

A French Empire four-glass mantel clock, in gilt and patinated bronze, the French drum movement striking on a bell.

21in (53cm) high

$1,000-1,250　SWO

CLOSER LOOK - GILT BRONZE MANTEL CLOCK

This is an impressive mantel timepiece.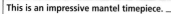

It is mounted with gilt bronze figures of Dawn and Dusk and surmounted by a figure of Lorenzo di Medici, after Michelangelo's tomb of Lorenzo II di Medici.

The sectional square-set clock with an enamel chapter ring enclosing a panel of lapis lazuli.

It is marked 'F. BARBEDIENNE. FONDEUR', with foundry mark - a sign of quality.

A 19thC French gilt-bronze and slate mantel clock.

29in (74cm) high

$3,200-3,800　L&T

A mid-19thC French gilt-brass mantel clock, the movement stamped 'F.Gautier & J.Albinet, Paris', with key and pendulum.

21in (53cm) high

$1,000-1,250　MOR

A 19thC French patinated and gilt-bronze mantle clock, the eight day movement striking a bell.

18in (46cm) high

$1,300-1,800　L&T

A 19thC tortoiseshell and brass boulle-type eight-day mantel clock, the movement striking on a gong, with bracket.

23.75in (60cm) high

$450-500　CHOR

A 19thC French porcelain mounted gilt-metal mantel clock, in a gilt-metal Rococo case, with porcelain plaques depicting Marie Antoinette, and a musical couple, the eight-day movement striking a bell.

15.75in (40cm) high

$1,400-1,900　L&T

A 19thC 'Gothic' lacquered brass mantel timepiece, with single-fusee movement, the dial marked 'W.H.Young, Swaffham'.

15in (38cm) high

$900-1,000 CHEF

A Napoleon III ormolu and champlevé enamel decorated onyx striking mantel clock, the twin-barrel movement with recoil anchor escapement and rack striking to bell.

c1870 *15.5in (39cm) high*

$550-700 BELL

A late 19thC French ormolu and porcelain-mounted eight-day mantel clock, the movement striking on a bell stamped 'Ducasse Claveau du Paris 9888'.

15in (38cm) high

$400-500 CHOR

A pendule d'officier mantel clock, the twin-barrel movement striking on a bell with back plate stamped '9464 3 3/4'.

11.25in (28.5cm) high

$750-900 HT

An ormolu and porcelain-mounted striking mantel clock, retailed by Agnew & Sons, Manchester and Paris, twin-barrel movement with outside countwheel striking on a bell, movement backplate stamped 'Raingo Freres' and numbered 2075.

c1880 *20in (51cm) high*

$1,400-1,900 TEN

A 19thC French gilt brass and porcelain mantle clock, the movement striking on a bell.

14.5in (36.5cm) high

$700-800 L&T

A late 19thC French Carrara marble and ormolu urn form clock, in the manner of Henry Dasson, with original ruby jeweled cylinder single-train movement.

13.5in (34cm) high

$1,500-2,000 L&T

A French ormolu and blue porcelain cased mantel clock, by Japy Frères, the twin-barrel movement striking on a bell and with backplate stamped 'GMF 329'.

8in (20.5cm) high

$1,000-1,100 HT

An ormolu and champlevé enamel striking mantel clock, twin-barrel movement striking on a bell, movement backplate stamped 'LeRoy & Fils A Paris' and numbered 10003.

c1880 *21in (53cm) high*

$2,000-2,500 TEN

A late 19thC French gilt-brass and champlevé enamel four-glass mantel clock, the eight-day movement striking on a gong, the backplate stamped 'A1 MADE IN FRANCE' and numbered '3427 4.11'.

16.5in (42cm) high

$1,300-1,500   WW

A French ormolu-mounted marble mantel clock, with drum movement with strike bell, the enamel dial signed 'Planchon, Paris'.

16.5in (42cm) high

$1,300-1,900   CHOR

A French black marble and ormolu mantel clock, the eight-day movement striking on a bell.

16.5in (42cm) high

$1,000-1,250   CHOR

A large French ormolu mantel clock, with an eight-day drum movement striking on a bell.

25in (62cm) high

$1,300-1,900   CHOR

A late 19thC French gilt-brass mantel clock, with key and pendulum.

22.5in (57cm) high

$500-650   MOR

A French ormolu mantel clock, by Bourdin, Paris, with two-train movement, dial inscribed 'Bourdin HER BTE Rue de la Paix 28 Paris', the movement stamped 'Bourdin a Paris No.4673', with key and pendulum.

14.25in (36cm) high

$900-1,100   MOR

A late 19thC ormolu-mounted brass and pewter inlaid boulle-work mantel clock, with two-train movement, with pendulum.

30in (76cm) high

$3,200-3,800   BELL

A Louis XV-style boulle mantel clock, movement stamped Ettienne Maxant striking to a gong, in a scrolling tortoiseshell and ormolu-mounted case.

18in (46cm) high

$1,300-1,500   LAW

A late 19thC French bronze, gilt and white marble mantel clock, the movement back plate stamped 'C.H-S PICKARD & AD PUNANT 771 PARIS', dial replaced.

12.75in (32.5cm) high

$950-1,100   BELL

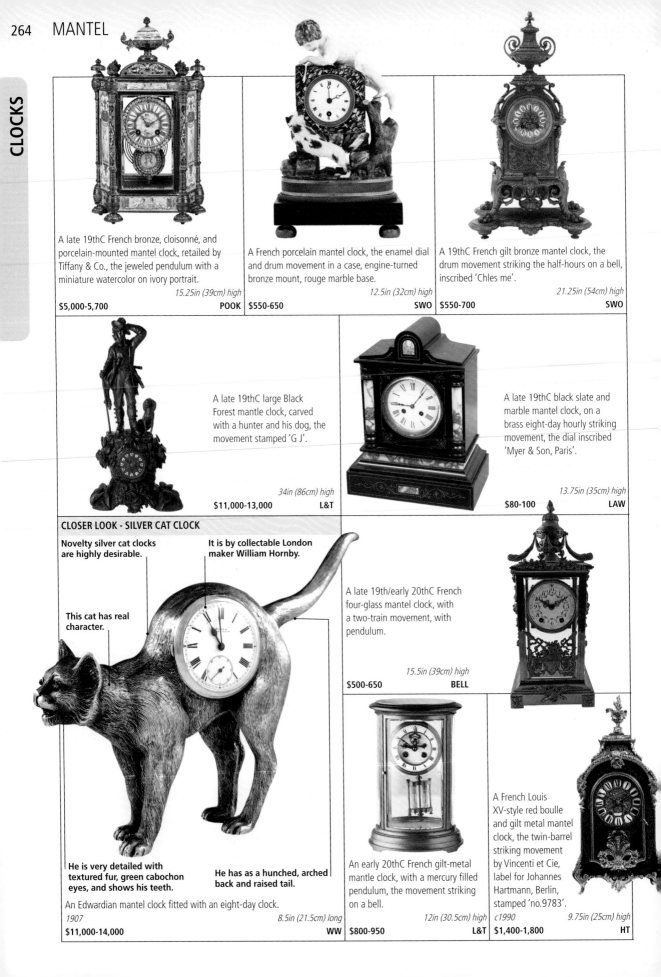

A late 19thC French bronze, cloisonné, and porcelain-mounted mantel clock, retailed by Tiffany & Co., the jeweled pendulum with a miniature watercolor on ivory portrait.

15.25in (39cm) high

$5,000-5,700   **POOK**

A French porcelain mantel clock, the enamel dial and drum movement in a case, engine-turned bronze mount, rouge marble base.

12.5in (32cm) high

$550-650   **SWO**

A 19thC French gilt bronze mantel clock, the drum movement striking the half-hours on a bell, inscribed 'Chles me'.

21.25in (54cm) high

$550-700   **SWO**

A late 19thC large Black Forest mantle clock, carved with a hunter and his dog, the movement stamped 'G J'.

34in (86cm) high

$11,000-13,000   **L&T**

A late 19thC black slate and marble mantel clock, on a brass eight-day hourly striking movement, the dial inscribed 'Myer & Son, Paris'.

13.75in (35cm) high

$80-100   **LAW**

CLOSER LOOK - SILVER CAT CLOCK

Novelty silver cat clocks are highly desirable.

It is by collectable London maker William Hornby.

This cat has real character.

A late 19th/early 20thC French four-glass mantel clock, with a two-train movement, with pendulum.

15.5in (39cm) high

$500-650   **BELL**

He is very detailed with textured fur, green cabochon eyes, and shows his teeth.

He has as a hunched, arched back and raised tail.

An Edwardian mantel clock fitted with an eight-day clock.

1907   *8.5in (21.5cm) long*

$11,000-14,000   **WW**

An early 20thC French gilt-metal mantle clock, with a mercury filled pendulum, the movement striking on a bell.

12in (30.5cm) high

$800-950   **L&T**

A French Louis XV-style red boulle and gilt metal mantel clock, the twin-barrel striking movement by Vincenti et Cie, label for Johannes Hartmann, Berlin, stamped 'no.9783'.

c1990   *9.75in (25cm) high*

$1,400-1,800   **HT**

TABLE 265

CLOCKS

A late 17thC ebony-veneered striking pull quarter repeating table clock, signed 'Jno Barrow, London', five-pillar twin-fusee movement with a verge escapement, later block feet, strike is not working correctly.

c1695   *15in (38cm) high*

$13,000-15,000   **TEN**

A Louis XIV table clock, the movement by Beltazar Martinot, with an outside wheel strike bell, the exterior within a tortoiseshell and brass mounted boullework case, needs restoration.

$3,200-3,800   **LOC**

An early 18thC table clock, by Joseph Windmills, London, the single-fusee movement with verge escapement.

32in (81.5cm) high

$9,000-11,500   **HT**

A Regency mahogany-inlaid table clock, of Miles Ludgate Street, London, twin-fusee movement with anchor escapement and striking on a bell, the dial has been repainted.

22.5in (57cm) high

$2,500-3,200   **TEN**

A mahogany cased table clock, by Brockbank & Atkins, London, the twin-fusee movement with anchor escapement striking on a bell, back plate numbered '2210'.

17.75in (45cm) high

$1,000-1,100   **HT**

A Victorian oak-cased table clock, the 'Winterhalder & Hoffmeier' three-train chiming movement striking on five gongs and eight bells, stamped 'No.195'.

28.5in (72.5cm) high

$1,900-2,500   **HT**

A French red 'boulle' and gilt-metal table clock and stand, by Le Roy et Fils, Paris, the twin-barrel movement striking on a gong, the backplate stamped 'C.F.17620', tortoiseshell veneered case with cherub surmount.

20.25in (51.5cm) high

$4,500-5,000   **HT**

A Victorian mahogany chiming table clock, the chime on Eight Bells/Westminster chimes, triple fusee movement with anchor escapement, quarter chiming on a nest of eight bells and four gongs and striking a larger gong for the hours.

c1890   *25.5in (65cm) high*

$2,000-2,500   **TEN**

A brass alarm carriage clock, single-barrel movement with a platform lever escapement, rack striking on a gong, alarm striking on a bell below the movement.

c1840　　　　　　　7.5in (19cm) high

$2,000-2,500　　　　　　TEN

A brass engraved malachite cabochon-set striking carriage clock, with Gothic-style case, twin-barrel movement with a platform cylinder escapement, stamped 'Roblin & Fils Freres A Paris' and numbered '0255'.

c1850　　　　　　6in (15.5cm) high

$1,900-2,500　　　　　TEN

A brass 'grande sonnerie' alarm carriage clock, by Webster, London, twin-barrel movement with a platform lever escapement, two hammers striking the quarters and hours, backplate stamped 'Roblin & Fils Freres A Paris' and numbered '887'.

c1880　　　　　　7in (17.5cm) high

$1,900-2,500　　　　　TEN

A brass porcelain-mounted carriage clock, signed 'Ollivant & Botsford, Manchester', the twin-barrel movement with platform lever escapement and striking on a blued-steel gong, some damage.

c1880　　　　　　7.5in (19cm) high

$1,300-1,800　　　　　TEN

A Swiss enameled miniature chinoiserie carriage clock, the keyless wind jeweled movement detailed 'Golay Fils & Stahl, Geneve'.

　　　　　　　1.5in (4cm) high

$650-750　　　　　　BELL

A blue enamel and ormolu dressing table clock, by Le Roy et Fils, 13 and 15 Palais Royal, Paris, Aiguilles, no.11516.

　　　　　　　3.5in (9cm) high

$2,500-3,200　　　　　CHOR

A late 19thC brass cased carriage clock, with push hour repeat, two-train movement.

　　　　　　　6in (15cm) high

$1,300-1,800　　　　　BELL

A striking repeating alarm carriage clock, twin-barrel movement with a platform lever escapement, striking on a gong, with travelling case.

c1890　　　　　7.75in (19.5cm) high

$4,500-5,000　　　　　TEN

A French gilt-brass gorge case grande sonnerie carriage clock, by Henri Jacot, with repeat mechanism, striking on two gongs, the movement numbered '8134', with original key.

c1890　　　　　　5.5in (14cm) high

$3,200-3,800　　　　　SWO

A brass and porcelain-mounted striking and repeating carriage clock, twin-barrel movement with a silvered platform lever escapement, the case back porcelain panel with a crack.

c1890   *7in (18cm) high*

$2,800-3,800   **TEN**

CLOSER LOOK - LE ROYS & FILS CARRIAGE CLOCK

The clock is by renowned maker Le Roys & Fils, 35 Avenue del Opera, Paris.

The decoration is particularly attractive.

The painted enamel dial decorated with cherubs in a river landscape with love birds.

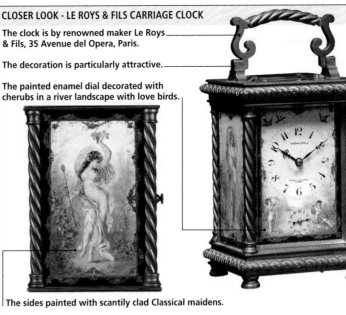

The sides painted with scantily clad Classical maidens.

A late 19thC French gilt-brass and enamel repeating carriage clock, with alarm, the platform lever escapement striking on a gong.

6in (15cm) high

$4,500-5,000   **WW**

A brass carriage clock, twin-barrel movement with a platform lever escapement and striking on a blued-steel gong.

c1890   *7.75in (19.5cm) high with handle*

$1,500-1,900   **TEN**

A brass champlevé enamel 'petite sonnerie' repeating carriage clock, retailed by Howell & James Ltd., London & Paris, twin-barrel movement with a later platform lever escapement, with maker's mark 'R&C' for Richard & Co., numbered '730'.

c1900   *7in (18cm) high*

$1,900-2,500   **TEN**

A brass and enamel striking repeating alarm carriage clock, retailed by Tiffany & Co., twin-barrel movement with a platform lever escapement, striking on a gong, the strike and alarm are not working.

c1900   *6in (15cm) high*

$2,000-2,500   **TEN**

A 20thC brass and four-glass carriage clock, with alarm and repeater on lever escapement.

4.75in (12cm) high

$300-400   **ECGW**

An early 20thC brass double-carriage clock and barometer, with compass and thermometer dial, by F. Vicker Regent Street, London, lacking mercury and glass.

6.75in (17cm) high

$250-400   **ECGW**

An early 20thC French gilt-brass hour repeating carriage clock, with a two-train movement.

5.75in (14.5cm) high

$800-950   **BELL**

CLOCKS

A 17thC brass striking lantern clock, unsigned, four-posted movement with a central verge escapement, inside countwheel striking on a top-mounted bell, the top finial later, alarm work missing, later weight.

c1680   *16.25in (41cm) high*

$3,800-4,400   **TEN**

A brass striking lantern clock, signed 'Wm Barlow, Lynn Regis', four-posted movement with anchor escapement and inside countwheel striking on a top-mounted bell, some parts later.

c1700   *15.5in (39.5cm) high*

$5,000-5,700   **TEN**

A mid to late 19thC Victorian brass lantern clock, unsigned, the five-pillar twin chain-fusee movement with anchor escapement and striking the hour.

16in (40.5cm) high

$650-750   **DN**

A Victorian brass lantern clock, fitted with an eight-day duration, single-fusee movement, engraved 'Thos. Moore, Melford', hammer missing.

14in (35.5cm) high

$500-650   **BE**

ESSENTIAL REFERENCE - JAMES CONDLIFF

James Condliff started his business at 32 Gerard Street, Liverpool in 1816, and is regarded as one of the finest English skeleton clockmakers of the 19thC, as well as being known for producing high quality regulators. Condliff's skeleton clocks were individually handcrafted and not one of his clocks were made exactly alike. He produced timepieces, striking clocks and chiming examples. These clocks incorporated five and six spoke wheel trains, maintaining power, balance and helical hairsprings, some used Condliff's lever form escapement, rack and snail striking. Only a small number of his clocks are still in existence today.

A brass skeleton striking mantel clock, twin chain-driven fusee movement with anchor escapement and rack striking on a gong, with a glass dome.

c1870   *14in (35.5cm) high*

$1,500-1,900   **TEN**

A Victorian Lichfield Cathedral brass skeleton clock, with a twin-fusee chain-driven movement, quarterly striking to a bell, hourly striking to a gong with repeater mechanism, with a glass dome.

14.25in (36cm) high

$2,800-3,500   **LAW**

A skeleton clock, attributed to James Condliff, Liverpool, prototype second series, beneath a glass dome.

c1840   *13in (33cm) high*

$25,000-32,000   **TEN**

A skeleton clock, the two-train chain fusee movement, with anchor escapement, striking on a gong, signed 'Rossi, Norwich', lacking dome.

16.25in (41cm) high

$2,500-3,200   **WW**

A Victorian twin-fusee brass skeleton clock, by G. Rossi, Norwich, with a glass dome.

11.5in (29cm) high

$2,000-2,500   **SWO**

A Junghans mystery or swinger clock, the spelter elephant with raised trunk suspending a pendulum, not in working order.

11.25in (28.5cm) high

$500-650   **CHOR**

A Junghans mystery or swinger clock, modeled as a pilot holding a propeller and a pendulum.

15in (38cm) high

$650-750   **CHOR**

A brass striking 'Eiffel Tower' mantel clock, twin-barrel movement striking on a bell, movement backplate stamped R&C.

c1889   *25.5in (65cm) high*

$650-750   **TEN**

A late 19thC French industrial windmill clock, fitted with later sails above the thermometer, barometer and clock dials.

16.25in (41cm) high

$2,300-2,800   **L&T**

A gilt metal striking cathedral clock, signed 'Dent, 82 The Strand', the twin-barrel movement with outside count wheel, backplate stamped 'Raingo Freres Paris' and numbered '3254'.

21.75in (55.5cm) high

$1,900-2,500   **HT**

A Black Forest musical cuckoo clock, triple weight-driven movement striking on a gong, small attached cylinder musical movement, some damage.

c1880   *39.5in (100.5cm) high*

$2,800-3,500   **TEN**

ESSENTIAL REFERENCE - JOSEPH KNIBB

Joseph Knibb moved to Oxford c1662, although his presence there was not welcomed by the local trade and it was not until 1668, upon payment of a fine, that he was allowed to work unhindered. The token served both as a temporary form of currency (value one farthing) and for advertising. Knibb moved to London in 1670.

A 20thC octagonal red marble veneered desk clock compendium, by Kutchinsky, comprising an orrery with a quartz movement, a time piece with quartz movement, a barometer, a hygrometer and thermometer.

11in (28cm) diam

$1,100-1,500   **BELL**

A 17thC trade token, by Joseph Knibb, a clockmaker based in Oxon, obverse is a Roman numeral chapter ring around the initials 'I K', either side of a single hand to the center.

c1670

$1,500-1,900   **HALL**

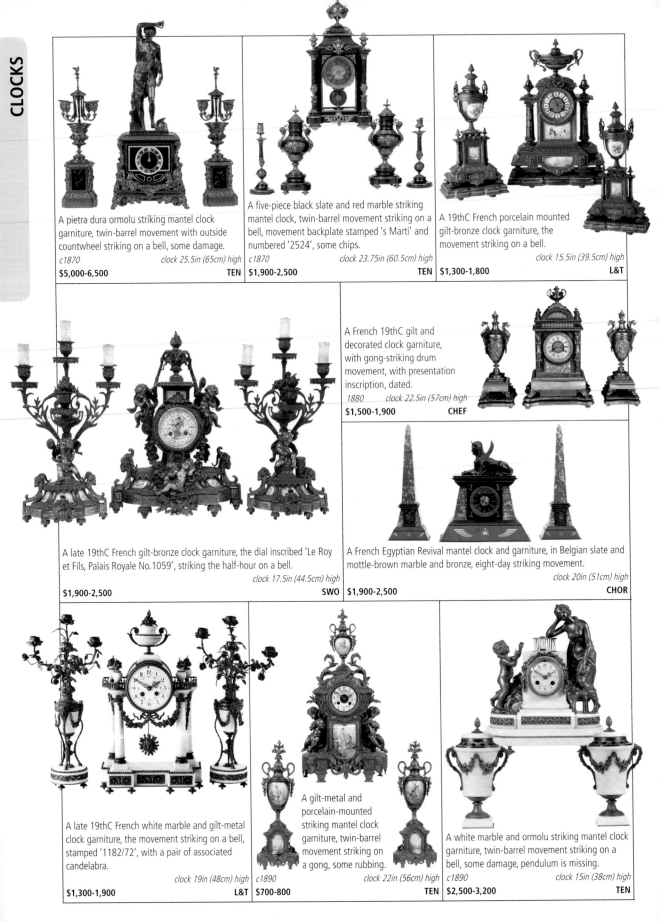

A pietra dura ormolu striking mantel clock garniture, twin-barrel movement with outside countwheel striking on a bell, some damage.
c1870   *clock 25.5in (65cm) high*
$5,000-6,500   **TEN**

A five-piece black slate and red marble striking mantel clock, twin-barrel movement striking on a bell, movement backplate stamped 's Marti' and numbered '2524', some chips.
c1870   *clock 23.75in (60.5cm) high*
$1,900-2,500   **TEN**

A 19thC French porcelain mounted gilt-bronze clock garniture, the movement striking on a bell.
clock 15.5in (39.5cm) high
$1,300-1,800   **L&T**

A late 19thC French gilt-bronze clock garniture, the dial inscribed 'Le Roy et Fils, Palais Royale No.1059', striking the half-hour on a bell.
clock 17.5in (44.5cm) high
$1,900-2,500   **SWO**

A French 19thC gilt and decorated clock garniture, with gong-striking drum movement, with presentation inscription, dated.
1880   *clock 22.5in (57cm) high*
$1,500-1,900   **CHEF**

A French Egyptian Revival mantel clock and garniture, in Belgian slate and mottle-brown marble and bronze, eight-day striking movement.
clock 20in (51cm) high
$1,900-2,500   **CHOR**

A late 19thC French white marble and gilt-metal clock garniture, the movement striking on a bell, stamped '1182/72', with a pair of associated candelabra.
clock 19in (48cm) high
$1,300-1,900   **L&T**

A gilt-metal and porcelain-mounted striking mantel clock garniture, twin-barrel movement striking on a gong, some rubbing.
c1890   *clock 22in (56cm) high*
$700-800   **TEN**

A white marble and ormolu striking mantel clock garniture, twin-barrel movement striking on a bell, some damage, pendulum is missing.
c1890   *clock 15in (38cm) high*
$2,500-3,200   **TEN**

A 19thC French onyx and gilt-bronze mounted clock garniture, the movement striking on a bell.

clock 19.25in (49cm) high

$750-1,000   **L&T**

A late 19thC French gilt-bronze and white marble clock garniture, the small two-barrel movement with platform lever escapement and rack striking to bell, with key.

clock 12.25in (31cm) high

$800-950   **BELL**

A late 19thC ormolu and porcelain mantel clock garniture.

clock 16.5in (42cm) high

$1,000-1,250   **BELL**

A late 19thC French gilt-bronze and porcelain clock garniture, the movement striking on a bell.

clock 15.5in (39.5cm) high

$1,900-2,500   **L&T**

A French white marble and bronze clock garniture, the eight-day duration movement striking the hours and half-hours on a bell with an outside countwheel and silk suspension.

$1,500-1,900

clock 18in (45.5cm) high

    BE

A late 19thC French champlevé enamel and gilt-brass three-piece clock garniture, the clock with twin-train movement striking a gong.

clock 18in (46cm) high

$5,000-6,500   **L&T**

A French 19thC clock garniture, visible escapement and an eight-day movement, within a black marble case.

18in (46cm) high

$180-250   **WHP**

A 19thC Cantonese ormolu-mounted striking mantel clock garniture, visible Brocot escapement, twin-barrel movement with outside countwheel striking on a bell, garniture vase bases have been drilled.

clock 25.5in (65cm) high

$2,500-3,200   **TEN**

A late 19thC French gilt bronze and porcelain clock garniture, the movement striking on a gong, stamped 'H. F & CIE/ PARIS'.

clock 20.5in (52cm) high

$1,000-1,250   **L&T**

A George III mahogany dial clock, by Thwaites and Reed, Clerkenwell, London, the eight-day chain and fusee movement with large tapering plates, with pendulum and key.

dial 12in (30.5cm) diam

$3,800-4,400 **SWO**

A Regency strung mahogany wall clock, by Geo. Wilkins, Frith Street, Soho, the two-train movement probably by Thwaites & Reed.

12.25in (31cm) square

$1,900-2,500 **SWO**

A 19thC eight-day wall clock, by Barwise, London, signed.

16in (40.5cm) diam

$1,500-1,900 **CHOR**

A wall clock, the backplate stamped '5460 Made by F W Elliott Ltd, England, 1938', the dial recently painted as an RAF sector clock.

dial 14in (35.5cm) diam

$900-1,000 **SWO**

A Regency mahogany wall clock, with eight-day fusee movement.

$500-650 **CHOR**

A mid-19thC mahogany single-fusee wall timepiece, by Jonas Priest, Harrogate, with pendulum and key.

Jonas Priest is listed in 'Yorkshire Clockmakers' by Brian Loomes as working in Harrogate and Knaresborough in the 1850s and 1860s.

18in (46cm) high

$1,900-2,500 **MOR**

A late 19thC French gilt-bronze cartel clock, of Louis XVI-style, the dial signed 'C.H.Dubret/ Dijon', the twin-barrel movement with recoil anchor escapement, rack striking to bell.

pendulum 21.75in (55cm) high

$650-750 **BELL**

A late 19thC Swedish carved and giltwood clock, by Robert Engstrom, the two train movement striking on a bell, some damage.

41.5in (105.5cm) high

$650-750 **ECGW**

A late 19thC German fusee dial clock, by Winterhalder & Hoffmeier, with retailers name 'smith Bros of Buckingham', with single-train fusee movement.

13in (33cm) diam

$300-450 **TRI**

A mahogany tavern clock, the painted dial inscribed 's Thorndike, Ipswich'.

case 38in (96.5cm) high

$7,000-7,500 SWO

An early Victorian weight-driven hook-and-spike wall clock, the dial inscribed 'Whitehurst, Derby'.

87in (221cm) high

$1,300-1,800 SWO

ESSENTIAL REFERENCE - GUSTAV BECKER

Gustav Becker was born in1819 and died in 1885. He initially worked as a clockmaker in the German region of Silesia before spending time in Vienna. On his return to the area he settled in Freiburg in 1847 and opened a small clock factory. Orders came flooding in following the Silesia Fair of 1852 and production rose to some 300,000 clocks per year by 1875. The Gustav Becker brand continued after his death following a merger in 1930 with the clockmaking company Junghans.

A Vienna regulator striking wall clock, by Gustav Becker, the eight-day duration weight-driven movement striking the hours on a gong and having adjustable pallets and a wood-rod pendulum with brass bob.

48in (122cm) high

$250-400 BE

A 19thC mahogany wall clock, with five-pillar movement with shaped plates.

67in (170cm) high

$1,000-1,200 SWO

A Continental walnut cased wall clock compendium, with a clock, thermometer and barometer.

c1900 *27in (68.5cm) high*

$180-250 BELL

A late 19thC Austrian single-weight Vienna regulator, the single-train movement has a solid deadbeat escapement.

67in (170cm) high

$950-1,100 TRI

A 19thC walnut and ebonized Vienna-type regulator wall clock.

72in (183cm) high

$750-900 WHP

A German Vienna regulator, of eight-day duration, the weight-driven movement with adjustable pallets and a wood-rod pendulum with brass bob.

49.5in (126cm) high

$200-250 BE

A small late 20thC Viennese-style burr walnut regulator wall timepiece, with a single weight, inscribed 'Josef Lorenz IN WIEN'.

16.5in (42cm) high

$650-750 WW

A late 17thC gold cased pocket watch, by Christopher Gould, the movement signed 'Chr. Gould, London' and numbered '555', glass missing.

By family repute this pocket watch belonged to Admiral Sir John Leake (1656-1720).

1.75in (4.5cm) diam

$2,500-3,200 **LAW**

A French gold and enamel open-face pocket watch, by Le Roy, Paris, no.98982, with verge fusee movement.

c1790 *1.5in (4cm) diam*

$3,200-3,800 **DN**

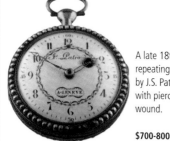

A French three-color gold open-face repeating pocket watch, by Joseph Bertrand, Paris, no.666, with verge fusee movement.

c1790 *2in (5cm) diam*

$1,000-1,250 **DN**

A late 18thC Swiss gold verge quarter repeating open-faced pocket watch, by J.S. Patron, the full plate movement with pierced balance bridge, fusee wound.

2in (5cm) diam

$700-800 **LAW**

An 18ct gold open-face erotica repeating automaton pocket watch, no.51292, with Swiss commercial verge fusee movement, three-armed steel undersprung balance, pierced and engraved balance cock, engraved 'Breguet A Paris', the sliding cover revealing an automated erotic scene.

c1800 *2.25in (5.5cm) diam*

$7,000-8,000 **DN**

ESSENTIAL REFERENCE - QUARTER REPEATING GOLD-CASED WATCH

It is likely that the watch originally belonged to William Harry Vane, first Duke of Cleveland of the second creation and third Earl of Darlington (1766-1842) of Raby Castle, County Durham. Further, that it was inherited by his second wife, Elizabeth Russell (d.1861), who was allowed to choose which of his possessions she wished on his death. She was daughter of Robert Russell of Newton, Yorkshire. The Duke was a notable sportsman and lived at Raby Castle for much of the year. He began to hunt his father's hounds in 1787. His hounds were divided into two packs, one of large breed and one of small, which he hunted on alternate days. He paid considerable sums to his tenants for the preservation of foxes and successfully opposed the first Stockton and Darlington railway in 1820 because in its course it encroached on a favorite covert.
The date hallmark of case obscured but with case maker's marks of 'sG' below a heart for Stephen Gillet, 12, Compton Street, London, stamp registered 13 May 1793, the case may have been updated at the requested of the original owner around 1800-1810.

A quarter repeating gold-cased watch, by Josiah Emery, London, no.1238, the movement with ruby cylinder escapement, chain fusee, bi-metallic compensated regulator, pierced and engraved balance cock with diamond end-stone, the movement dumb quarter repeating.

c1790 *2.25in (5.5cm) high*

$9,000-10,000 **LAW**

A French gold open-face pocket watch, by Esquivillon et Dechoudens, Paris, with verge fusee movement, case with foliate chased borders, set with ruby and turquoise decoration, missing a ruby from the bezel at 3 o'clock.

Esquivillon et Dechoudens are recorded in Baillie, G.H. 'Watchmakers & Clockmakers of the World Volume 1' as working in Paris from 1765-1830.

c1810 *1.5in (4cm) diam*

$900-1,000 **DN**

A George III 18ct gold open-faced pocket watch, the movement signed 'Brockbanks & Atkins', hallmarked for London, dated.

1817 *1.75in (4.5cm) diam*

$1,300-1,800 **LAW**

A Victorian triple-cased 'Turkish Market' pocket watch, by Edward Prior, London, with a verge escapement and a tortoiseshell mounted outer case, the case hallmarked.

1863 *2.25in (5.5cm) diam*

$650-750 **LAW**

A George IV 18ct gold cased pocket watch, with key-wind to 3 o'clock, the movement signed 'J.King, Market Place, Yarmouth, no.963', in an ebonized box.

$900-1,000 **CHOR**

A lady's 18ct gold cased, keyless wind, open-faced fob watch, London, the enameled dial with black Roman numerals, the case fitted to a gilt metal and bloodstone set chatelaine clip, having two pendant drops, comprising a spherical box, with a motto to the band, inscribed 'A SMILE FROM THEE IS A WORLD TO MEE', with a drop shaped box, with a threaded top.

1873

$1,500-1,900 **BELL**

A gentleman's 18ct gold cased, keyless wind, half-hunting cased pocket watch, the movement detailed 'Edwd Culver, Clerkenwell Road, London, No 2268, London'.

1881

$1,300-1,800 **BELL**

A large 18ct gold pocket watch, London, white enameled dial Roman numerals.

1888 *5.65oz*

$1,900-2,500 **HAN**

An 18ct gold-cased pocket watch, inscribed 'George Oram & Son, 10 & 18 Wilmington Square, London'.

$1,000-1,200 **TRI**

An 18ct gold-cased pocket watch.

$750-900 **TRI**

A lady's 18ct gold-cased keyless wind, half hunting cased fob watch.

$500-650 **BELL**

An 18ct gold full hunting cased pocket watch, engraved with a coat of arms to the front case.

2in (5cm) diam

$800-950   **LAW**

An 18ct gold gentlemen's pocket watch, by Butcher & Swann, Nottingham, with Swiss enamel dial and subsidiary dial.

$1,400-1,900   **HAN**

An 18ct gold open-faced keyless lever pocket watch, signed 'Patek Philippe & Co, Geneve, No.102707', the 'moustache' lever movement signed and numbered '102707', stamped 'pat Jan 13 1891', the case with surface scratches and small dents in parts.

c1898   *2in (5cm) wide*

$5,000-5,700   **TEN**

A 19thC enameled pocket watch, with silver dial and Roman numerals.

$550-700   **HAN**

An 18ct gold open-faced single push chronograph pocket watch, retailed by Barraclough, Thornton, Bradford, the karussel lever movement signed and numbered '152293', blued overcoil hairspring with a compensation balance, diamond endstone, the case with a London hallmark.

2.25in (5.5cm) wide

$5,000-5,700   **TEN**

A gentleman's 9ct gold cased keyless wind open-faced pocket watch, with a jeweled Swiss lever movement, Birmingham.

1925

$300-400   **BELL**

An Art Deco platinum and sapphire-set open-faced keyless pocket watch, signed 'Cartier', the 19-jewel lever movement signed 'EW & CCo Inc', with eight adjustments, with a Cartier fitted box.

c1925   *2in (5cm) wide*

$10,000-11,000   **TEN**

A 14ct gold full hunter keyless lever pocket watch, signed 'A Lange & Sohne, Deutsche Uhrenfabrikation, Glashutte I/SA, No.85809', back cover numbered '85809' and stamped 'Glashutte A Lange&Sohne' and '0.585'.

c1930   *2.25in (5.5cm) wide*

$3,800-4,400   **TEN**

A gentleman's 9ct gold cased Rolex wristwatch, the jeweled lever movement detailed 'Rolex Prima Timed 6 Positions For All Climates, Swiss Made', the milled screw-off caseback numbered '26975 678', import mark Glasgow 1929, with a brown leather strap.

$1,300-1,800 BELL

A rare 18ct gold Rolex single pusher chronograph bracelet wristwatch, ref. 2021, no.13372, chronograph movement, 17 jewels, monometallic split balance, overcoil balance spring, dial unsigned, case and movement signed, on an unsigned 18ct gold block link bracelet with fold over clasp, no box or paperwork.

c1937 *1.5in (4cm) diam*

$19,000-25,000 DN

ESSENTIAL REFERENCE - MILITARY GRANA W.W.W. WRISTWATCH

In the 1940s the Ministry of Defence acknowledged the requirement for a wristwatch that could be issued to army personnel. Strict specifications were set for a watch to be made that could stand up to every day military life. Swiss manufacturers were invited to build a watch that could meet these specifications. Twelve manufacturers were accepted and these were: Buren, Cyma, Eterna, Grana, Jaeger Le-Coultre, Lemania, Longines, IWC, Omega, Record, Timor and Vertex. Each company produced a different number of watches. Grana produced the fewest with an estimated production volume of between 1000-1500 watches. This is a very small production run compared to the 25,000 produced by Omega. Today collectors try to collect a watch from each of the twelve manufacturers. These collections are known as 'The Dirty Dozen'.

A Tiffany & Co. Oscar Heyman gem-set dress watch, rectangular platinum case and lugs set with RBC diamonds and two deep-purple rectangular step-cut amethysts in 18ct yg, diamonds approximately 86ct TW, amethysts approximately 11.0cts TW, double 18ct gold snake chain strap, Movado 17 jeweled Swiss movement, marked 'Tiffany & Co.' on dial, case interior, no.8277, Oscar Heyman cipher.

c1948 6.75in (17cm) high 1.2oz

$3,200-3,800 DRA

An 18ct gold wristwatch, signed 'Patek Philippe, Geneve, ref: 2516', the calibre 10-200 lever movement signed 'Patek Philippe & Co' and numbered '742084', stamped twice with a Geneva seal mark.

1954 *1.5in (4cm) high*

$6,500-7,500 TEN

A rare stainless steel British military Grana W.W.W. wristwatch, no.552421, with manual wind movement, 15 jewels, cal. K.F.320, engraved with the British government broad arrow property mark, above 'W.W.W.', above 'M 18883', the movement not functioning.

c1945 *1.5in (4cm) diam*

$7,000-8,000 DN

A duo time gold bracelet watch, inset with two Swiss 17 jeweled unadjusted mechanical movements by Wakmann, one dial trimmed with 22 RBC diamonds, approximately 1.10ct, the other dial with emeralds, unmarked.

c1960 *7in (18cm) long*

$7,000-8,000 DRA

A stainless steel automatic center seconds wristwatch, signed 'Rolex, Oyster Perpetual, model: Submariner, 660ft=200m, ref: 5512', the calibre 1530 lever movement signed and numbered '75415', later black dial and rotating bezel, screw back numbered inside '5512' and dated 'I.61', case serial number '662025', later Rolex stainless steel bracelet.

1961 *1.75in (4.5cm) wide*

$4,400-5,700 TEN

An Omega 9ct automatic Seamaster Deville wrist watch, on an after market strap and with original boxed black leather strap.

case 1.5in (4cm) diam

$650-750 TRI

A gentleman's 18ct gold International Watch Co. wristwatch, on a 9ct gold woven mesh link bracelet, with a foldover clasp, Birmingham.

1970

$1,100-1,500 BELL

A gentleman's stainless steel Rolex Oyster Perpetual Explorer wristwatch, with booklet dated 1973 and numbered '2986194', price-list and booklet for 1972, with case and box.

$7,500-9,000   HT

A gentleman's gold Longines wristwatch, on a brick link bracelet, with a foldover clasp, detailed '750'.

$1,900-2,500   BELL

A gentleman's stainless steel Rolex Oyster Perpetual Air-King-Date wristwatch, with a block link bracelet with foldover clasp, together with case, box and guarantee dated (Fattorini of Harrogate), with other paperwork.

1988

$1,500-2,000   HT

A platinum Jaeger LeCoultre Geographique wristwatch, no. 0094, ref. 169.6.92, with automatic movement, 36 jewels, adjusted to 4 positions, cal. 25Z6872, on a Jaeger LeCoultre alligator strap.

c1991   *1.5in (4cm) diam*

$7,500-9,000   DN

A lady's 18ct gold diamond-set wristwatch, signed 'Chopard, Geneve', model Happy Diamonds, with quartz movement, diamond-set bezels, with seven loose diamond-set collets, baguette diamond and cabochon set lugs, numbered '20/4846-21 327143 4113', on a 18ct gold bracelet.

c2000   *1in (2.5cm) wide*

$6,500-7,500   TEN

An 18ct gold tonneau-shaped triple calendar wristwatch, signed 'Franck Muller, Geneve, model: Master Calendar, ref: 7501MC', lever movement.

c2005   *1.5in (4cm)*

$5,500-6,500   TEN

An 18ct gold dual time-zone wristwatch, signed 'Patek Philippe, Geneve, model: travel time, ref: 5034J', lever movement, Patek Philippe strap with a PPCo 18ct gold buckle, with Patek Philippe box.

c2010   *1.5in (4cm) wide*

$8,000-9,500   TEN

A black ceramic Hublot, Big Bang Chronograph wristwatch, no. 761624, with automatic chronograph movement, 25 jewels, cal.4100.

c2010   *1.75in (4.5cm) diam*

$5,000-6,500   DN

A steel and gold automatic calendar chronograph wristwatch, signed 'Breitling, Chronographe Certifie Chronometre, model: Chronomat', lever movement, Breitling steel and gold bracelet with a deployant clasp.

c2013   *2in (5cm) wide*

$6,500-7,500   TEN

CLOSER LOOK - STICK BAROMETER

Ramsden (1731-1800) is known to be one of the greatest instrument makers of all time. His outstanding invention was a dividing machine for accurate scale division, and he was credited with adapting the tripod as a carrying case for the mountain barometer.

This barometer has a particularly nicely figured trunk.

The concealed mercury tube with a silvered single vernier dial which is signed.

Although the piece has some damage, it is of such quality that the value remains high.

A George III mahogany bow-fronted stick barometer, signed 'Ramsden, London'.

c1790   40.75in (103.5cm) high
$6,500-7,500   **TEN**

A George III mahogany cased stick barometer, by P. Caminuda Taunton.

38.5in (98cm) high
$250-320   **BELL**

A late George III mahogany stick barometer and thermometer, by J Somalvico and Son, Hatton Garden, London.

37in (94cm) long
$650-750   **BELL**

A Georgian stick barometer, by C. Trombetta, the mahogany case with satinwood edge molding, with a barometer gauge and an inset thermometer, engraved 'C. Trombetta, Ld Howe St, Bend, Norwich'.

Charles Trombetta, an Italian immigrant, married Mary Fisher at St Stephens Church, Norwich in 1797 and is recorded as working at Lord Howe Street, Benedict's Street c1800 and after.

38.25in (97cm) high
$650-750   **BE**

A mahogany stick barometer, the silvered brass dial inscribed 'W Fraser & Son London', with rack vernier.

This barometer originally came from the Nag's Head Public House, known locally as the Half Way House as it stood on the Ware Road, halfway between Hertford and Ware.

c1810   39in (98.5cm) high
$1,300-1,800   **SWO**

A mahogany stick barometer, with thermometer, silvered registers, the ebony-banded case with ivory urn finial and roundels, with molded circular cistern cover, signed 'Cooper, London'.

39.25in (100cm) high
$1,000-1,200   **HT**

An early 19thC mahogany marine stick-barometer, by Cary, London, with ring suspension above hinged panel enclosing silvered dials, dials with some damages.

William Cary (1759-1825) was a famous maker of barometers and other scientific instruments and, like Thomas Jones, had been a pupil of Jesse Ramsden. His two nephews retained the name of 'William Cary' when they took over the business upon his death in 1825.

38.25in (97cm) high
$1,000-1,300   **L&T**

An early 19thC mahogany stick barometer, by Thomas Jones, 62 Charing Cross, London, with arched ivory dial, hemispherical reservoir to base.

Thomas Jones (1775-1852) was a highly accomplished instrument-maker whose career flourished for over 50 years after his apprenticeship to the leading maker Jesse Ramsden. He was elected Fellow of the Royal Society in 1835.

37in (94cm) high
$1,300-1,800   **L&T**

A 19thC Scottish oak stick barometer, signed 'C. Crotchie, Inverness'.

39.5in (100cm) high
$550-700   **L&T**

A George III fruitwood stick wall thermometer, by Cary, with brass mounts and inscribed 'CARY LONDON'.

37.5in (95cm) high
$2,300-2,800   **WW**

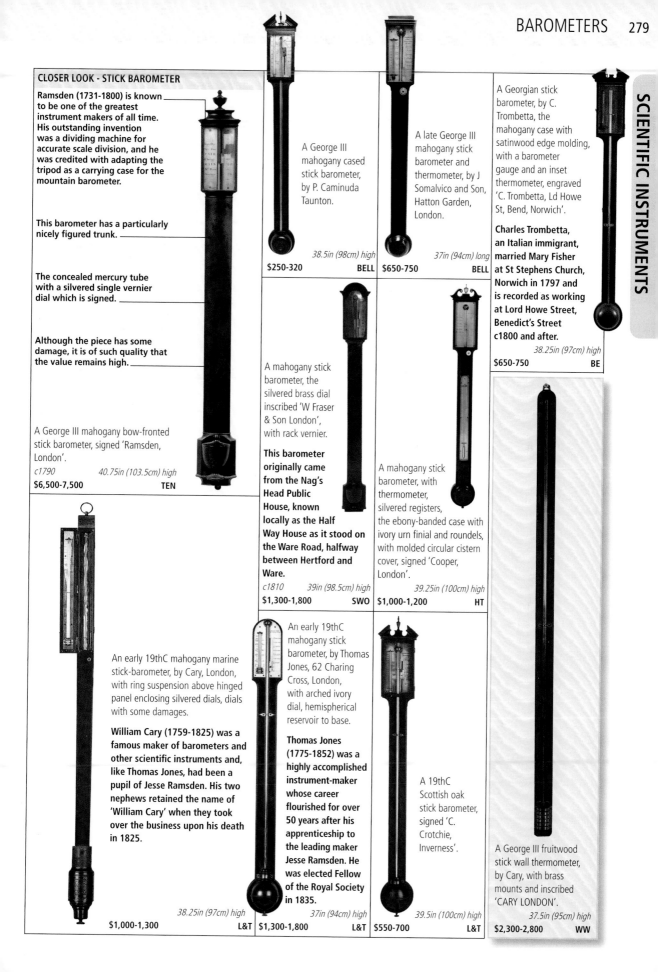

SCIENTIFIC INSTRUMENTS

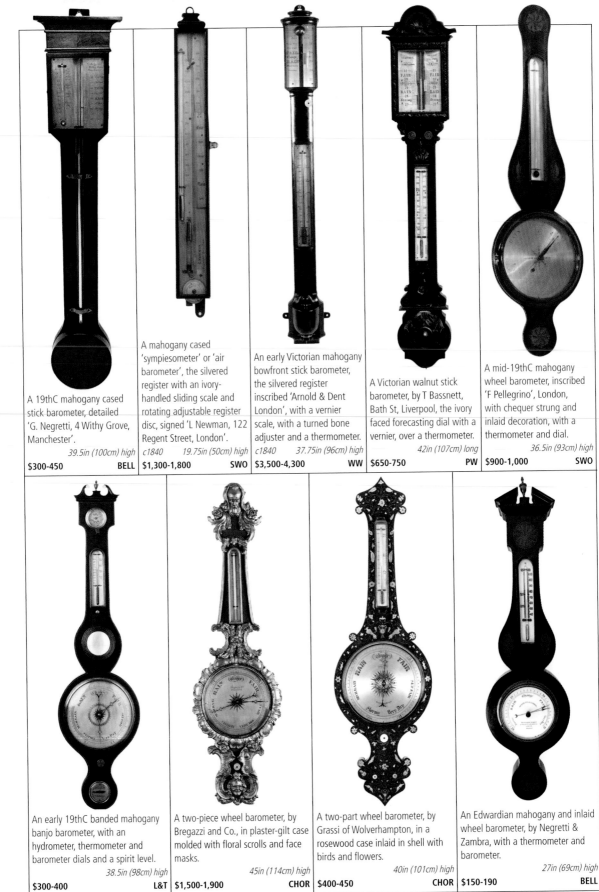

A 19thC mahogany cased stick barometer, detailed 'G. Negretti, 4 Withy Grove, Manchester'.
39.5in (100cm) high
$300-450 **BELL**

A mahogany cased 'sympiesometer' or 'air barometer', the silvered register with an ivory-handled sliding scale and rotating adjustable register disc, signed 'L Newman, 122 Regent Street, London'.
c1840   19.75in (50cm) high
$1,300-1,800 **SWO**

An early Victorian mahogany bowfront stick barometer, the silvered register inscribed 'Arnold & Dent London', with a vernier scale, with a turned bone adjuster and a thermometer.
c1840   37.75in (96cm) high
$3,500-4,300 **WW**

A Victorian walnut stick barometer, by T Bassnett, Bath St, Liverpool, the ivory faced forecasting dial with a vernier, over a thermometer.
42in (107cm) long
$650-750 **PW**

A mid-19thC mahogany wheel barometer, inscribed 'F Pellegrino', London, with chequer strung and inlaid decoration, with a thermometer and dial.
36.5in (93cm) high
$900-1,000 **SWO**

An early 19thC banded mahogany banjo barometer, with an hydrometer, thermometer and barometer dials and a spirit level.
38.5in (98cm) high
$300-400 **L&T**

A two-piece wheel barometer, by Bregazzi and Co., in plaster-gilt case molded with floral scrolls and face masks.
45in (114cm) high
$1,500-1,900 **CHOR**

A two-part wheel barometer, by Grassi of Wolverhampton, in a rosewood case inlaid in shell with birds and flowers.
40in (101cm) high
$400-450 **CHOR**

An Edwardian mahogany and inlaid wheel barometer, by Negretti & Zambra, with a thermometer and barometer.
27in (69cm) high
$150-190 **BELL**

A pocket globe, published by Richard Cushee, signed and inscribed in cartouche 'A New GLOBE of the Earth by R Cushee 1731', Australia half delineated and described as 'New Holland', Africa described as 'Negro Land', Northern Canada described as 'New Britain', with original shagreen case.

1731   *3in (7.5cm) diam*

$9,000-10,000   **CM**

An early 19thC pocket globe, by Aloriot, 65 New Bond Street London, in original leather case with internal star chart, dated, with some minor knocks, the cartouche is original.

1809

$6,500-7,500   **ECGW**

A pocket globe, by Newton Son & Berry, London, mounted within calibrated brass meridian with indicator and contained in fishskin-covered wooden case with horizon ring and celestial gores in lid.

c1835   *4in (10cm) diam*

$6,500-7,500   **CM**

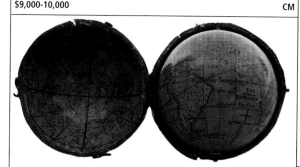

A Regency celestial globe, by Newton & Son, on a mahogany triform base.

40.5in (103cm) high

$550-700   **BELL**

A celestial library globe, by W. & A.K. Johnston, Edinburgh, with 12 hand-painted gores, mounted in original mahogany stand with signed compass stretcher and casters.

c1850   *42in (106.5cm)*

$3,200-4,400   **CM**

A pair of 19thC terrestrial and celestial table globes, by W. Bardon, each on mahogany stands, both globes damaged, one stand also damaged.

15in (38cm) high

$5,500-7,000   **TEN**

A Victorian terrestrial globe, inscribed 'CRUCHLEY's LATE CARY's NEW TERRESTRIAL GLOBE SHOWING THE LATEST DISCOVERIES SETTLEMENTS, IN AUSTRALIA, NEW ZEALAND, CALIFORNIA & THE NORTH POLE G.F. CRUCHLEY, MAP-SELLER, GLOBE MAKER AND PUBLISHER 81, FLEET STREET, LONDON Additions to 1853'.

10in (26cm) high

$1,000-1,250   **WW**

ESSENTIAL REFERENCE - JOHN BIRD

John Bird (1709-1776) worked in London for Jonathan Sisson but by 1745 had his own business in the Strand and was advised by the eminent clockmaker George Graham. Bird was commissioned to make a brass quadrant eight feet across for the Royal Observatory at Greenwich where it remains to this day. He also supplied the astronomer James Bradley with further instruments of such quality that the Commissioners of Longitude paid him the huge sum of £500 on condition that he take on a seven-year apprentice and produce in writing on oath a full account of his working methods. This was the origin of his two treatises 'The Method of dividing Instruments' (1767) and 'The Method of constructing Mural Quadrants' (1768).

An 18thC bronze sundial, by John Bird, London, the engraved scale with outer ring of Roman numerals, before/after the sun ring, calendar ring and compass points, with bronze gnomon, signed with the coat of Arms for the Buller family.

16.5in (42cm) diam

$3,800-4,400 **BE**

A rare desk model of the Lords calculator slide rule, by W.Wilson, London, the dials adjusted with three knurled brass knobs, mounted in it's original folding mahogany cabinet.

9in (23cm) long

$6,500-7,500 **DSA**

ESSENTIAL REFERENCE - MICROSCOPE

This simple brass microscope was made in 1774 by John Clark, a jeweller, goldsmith and optical instrument maker based in Edinburgh between 1749 and 1796. He first offered microscopes, made in silver, for sale in 1749, subsequently modifying their design in 1754, and ultimately advertising a brass instrument from 1773. In this pocket instrument, designed for the gentleman-amateur, Clark has managed to include all the fittings and accessories found in the much more substantial microscopes used in the contemporary drawing room. The entire instrument folds up and fits into its fishskin-covered case, allowing it to be taken out (in a pocket) into the field. Clark had at least three shops in his career: one at James Gilliland's Jeweller, at the upper-end of the Luckenbooths (1749); one at Parliament Close (1751-55); and one at Sir Isaac Newton's Head, a little above the Guard, north side of the High Street (1773-82).

A brass microscope, by John Clark, Edinburgh, the instrument brass fittings with a vertical pillar, folding concave mirror, focusing to the stage by a knurled knob and screw, below an adjustable platform with numbered scale (1-5) holding a wheel of five numbered objectives ranging sequentially in power.

1774 *microscope extended*
6in (15.5cm) high

$11,000-14,000 **L&T**

A lacquered brass sundial, by Henry Shuttleworth, London, engraved to a latitude of 55°, Newcastle or Londonderry, with finely worked sixteen-point compass rose, signed.

c1770 *10in (25.5cm) high*

$4,500-5,000 **CM**

A universal equinoctial ring dial, by Troughton & Simms, London, within original leather plush-lined case, with a set of period instructions, published by Frances West.

c1840 *8in (20.5cm) high*

$3,200-3,800 **CM**

A double theodolite, by Matthew Berge, London, in lacquered brass with silvered scales, bubble levels, compass with jeweled pivot, telescope with blanking nut, lower telescope mounted on separate axis, inscribed on the mainplate 'M. Berge, London/ Lord Dundas'.

Thomas, Lord Dundas (1741-1820) the educated and well-connected 'nabob of the north' was a hugely significant figure in Scottish and Northern English politics. From 1793 to 1813 he was the effective commander of the Yorkshire militia, and was Lord Lieutenant and Vice-Admiral of Orkney and Shetland between 1794 and 1820. As governor of the Forth and Clyde Navigation Company (1786-1816), he presided over the canal's completion and the creation of Grangemouth and Port Dundas. Matthew Berge succeeded Jesse Ramsden in 1800 and for a time signed his instruments 'Berge, Late Ramsden'.

c1805 *14.5in (37cm) high*

$11,000-12,000 **CM**

An oak cased barograph, by R. Stewart of Glasgow, with frieze drawer to the base.

c1900 *15in (38cm) high*

$700-800 **BELL**

Judith Picks

There is a fascination with the weird and wonderful inventions of the 19thC. This boxed set of 72 antique prosthetic eyes is a case in point. They come in various colors and sizes, from children's to adult's, and are very realistic, even to the bloodshot veins. The more realistic the better!

A mid to late 19thC cased set of eyes, German or French.

case 12.25in (31cm)

$1,900-2,500 **MART**

ESSENTIAL REFERENCE - CHRONOMETER

This chronometer was made by George Hornby & Son who were in business in Liverpool in the early 19thC. Chronometer makers sometimes signed the dials they supplied to clients, like this one supplied by John Penlington, who also started a business in the early 19thC at Parker Street in Liverpool. This chronometer was one of two early 19thC marine chronometers, 'A' and 'B', which were both made by Liverpool makers and were carried and used on board the Cunard Liner Queen Elizabeth II on her voyages from 16 December 1968 and 22 April 1970. A certificate confirming this issued and signed by Captain W.E.Warwick a Master of Q.E.2 dated 4 June 1970. It is understood the other chronometer used as chronometer 'A' was by Robert Roskell No.216/33501. This is at the National Maritime Museum, Greenwich.

An early 19thC mahogany one-day marine chronometer, by George Hornby & Son, Liverpool, no.857, spring detent escapement, free sprung helical hairspring, bi-metallic balance with weights and timing screws, diamond endstone.

c1815

8.25in (21cm) high

$5,000-6,500 TEN

An early 19thC mahogany cased marine chronometer, by Reid & Sons, Newcastle-upon-Tyne, with subsidiary seconds hand against a silvered dial plate, in a brass gimbal mount.

5.5in (14cm) wide

$400-500 BELL

A late 19thC Parkinson & Frodsham two-day marine chronometer, signed 'Parkinson & Frodsham, Royal Exchange, London', with a brass inlaid coromandel case with an incised bone plaque named 'Parkinson & Frodsham, London', all numbered '4184'.

7in (18cm) square

$3,800-4,400 SWO

A mahogany two-day marine chronometer, by John Parkes & Sons, 11 St George's Crescent, Liverpool, no.3917, two dials for seconds and 56-hour power reserve indication, single-chain fusee movement with a spring detent escapement, underside of the gimbal stamped 'H.S.broad arrow1'.

c1900

7.5in (19cm) high

$2,500-3,800 TEN

A World War II two-day marine chronometer, by Hamilton Watch Co., with fourteen jewels, spring detent escapement, Hamilton typical balance and helical spring, free-sprung, signed 'HAMILTON LANCASTER, PA., U.S.A., N4612, 1941', the dial plate numbered 'N1875', the backplate signed.

bezel 5in (12.5cm) diam

$1,200-1,500 WW

A mid-20thC two-day Hamilton model 21 marine chronometer, signed 'HAMILTON/LANCASTER. PA. U.S.A. ', with chain fusee with Earnshaw-type escapement with helical balance, with a later three-tier wooden box.

7.5in (19cm) square

$1,500-1,900 CM

A George III monocular telescope, the shagreen case with silver panel inscribed 'Nelson from Emma 1804'.

$5,000-6,500

BELL

A George III brass telescope, clad in shagreen, with a sealable brass eyepiece.

A rare 0.5in single-draw spyglass, attributed to Thomas Ribright, London, the tortoiseshell main tube with silver wirework and Rococo silver end pieces, eyepiece and main lens with dust slide, unsigned.

c1750

$13,000-15,000

5.5in (14cm) closed

CM

10.5in (26.5cm) high

$800-950

DN

A rare 2in four-draw telescope by Steinberg, London, main tube covered in baleen, signed on the draw tube Steinberg, 44 Cirencester Place, Fitzroy Square, London.

c1830   *12in (30.5cm) closed*

$1,900-2,500

CM

A Scrimshaw whale's tooth, carved with two scenes of naval battles and inscribed 'Commodore Oliver H Perry/Victory over the British Fleet/On Lake Erie on the/10th of September 1813'.

Family history suggests that a family member, Commander Thomas Henry Wilson, who had served in the Royal Navy, went to Canada in 1824 having obtained a grant of land on the terms prescribed for Half Pay Officers.

A late 19thC three-drawer brass and mahogany naval telescope, by Dolland, inscribed 'Dolland LONDON, Day or Night'.

closed 11.5in (29cm) long

$130-180

WW

7.75in (19.5cm) long

$5,000-5,700

LAW

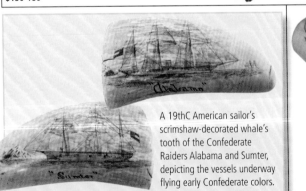

A 19thC American sailor's scrimshaw-decorated whale's tooth of the Confederate Raiders Alabama and Sumter, depicting the vessels underway flying early Confederate colors.

Both of these highly successful Confederate commerce raiders were commanded by the famous and hot-tempered Raphael Semmes. The dramatic action between Alabama and the U.S.S. Kearsage fought off the coast of France is one of the most gripping encounters of the American Civil War.

6in (15cm) high

$2,800-3,500

CM

A 19thC scrimshaw whale's tooth, scratch-carved with a British three-masted ship.

$400-500

5.5in (14cm) high

CHEF

A brass sextant with vernier scale, with no maker's mark, in mahogany case with additional parts.
$130-180 TEN

A 15.5in radius mahogany and boxwood fiducial octant, by Gregory London, the boxwood arc divided to 90°, with three removable shades and mirrors, signed.
c1765 *18in (46cm)*
$2,500-3,200 CM

ESSENTIAL REFERENCE - PORTRAIT FIGUREHEAD

The Emily Burnyeat, named for the wife of William Burnyeat, the founder of the eponymous Whitehaven firm, was a wooden brigantine of 128 tons which, with her consort barque Sarah Burnyeat, plied a steady trade for over thirty years. Both were built at Gowan's Yard, Berwick in 1861-62. The Emily Burnyeat found fame of a sort when, during an Atlantic crossing bound for the Mersey, a violent storm disabled all of her crew save the Master and a cabin boy of fourteen. In a remarkable feat of endurance, the Master (possibly a Captain Bale) managed, almost single-handedly, to navigate his ship to the Mersey. Unable to hove to for a pilot, he sailed on and ran the Emily Burnyeat aground on the Sloyne before collapsing from exhaustion. She disappears from the Lloyd's Register by 1896.

A portrait figurehead, from the Brigantine Emily Burnyeat, carved from laminated yellow pine, repainted, with a copy of Mariners' Market of 1961.
1862 *42in (106.5cm) high*
$23,000-28,000 CM

A figurehead, from the Royal Danish Navy corvette H.D.M.S. Najaden, carved from stained pine in the form of a three-quarter length depiction of Ceres.

The choice of Ceres is appropriate for a vessel used for voyages to the West Indies. The goddess of agriculture, she is associated with plenty and is usually depicted wearing a crown of corn and carrying a sheath of corn or cornucopia as here. In mythology, her daughter, Proserpine was abducted by Pluto causing Ceres to travel everywhere in search of her, during which time crops wouldn't grow.
1820 *72in (183cm) high*
$10,000-13,000 CM

A 12-bolt copper and brass diving helmet, by Siebe Gorman Co. Ltd., matched no.18648.
19in (49cm) high
$3,800-4,400 CM

A 19thC seaman's yellow pine chest, the lid painted inside with a trading ship inscribed 'As She Shone In The Light of Declining Day: Each Sail Was Set and Each Heart Was Gay'.
36in (91.5cm) long
$550-650 CM

A bronze Carpathia or Titanic medal, as issued by Tiffany, on behalf of the Titanic Relief Fund Committee, ribbon and later pin fitting removed.
1912
$2,300-2,800 CM

A leather bucket, from HMS Victory, with copper bound rim and copper rivets, painted with ship's name and 'GR' and '1803', carry handle missing.
10in (25.5cm) high
$1,900-2,500 W&W

A 19thC musical box, by Nicole Frères, playing eight airs, the comb having ninety-eight teeth, label to lid listing the airs and the retailer Wales & McCulloch of Ludgate Hill, no.45802.

22.5in (57.5cm) long

$700-800   **APAR**

A 19thC musical box, in a walnut case, playing twelve airs with chromium recorder to the side.

19in (48cm) wide

$1,000-1,250   **CHOR**

A 19thC Swiss mandolin-zither musical box, playing twelve airs with label.

24in (61cm) wide

$1,100-1,400   **CHOR**

A Swiss music box, with fifteen stop organ, playing six airs with two combs, lever-pull mechanism, in walnut case with inlay.

$900-1,000   **TEN**

A late 19thC Swiss music box, playing eight airs, with a six inch roller and applied ivory plaque detailed 'H D Scrine, 48 Dawes Road, Walham Green'.

17in (43cm) wide

$550-700   **BELL**

An antique Swiss musical box, with a three-air movement, with songsheet on the inside of the lid, with a winding key underneath.

5in (12.5cm) wide

$230-280   **LAW**

A Nicole Frères interchangeable cylinder music box on stand, no.52474, in an ebonized and burr walnut case, playing eight airs.

48in (122cm) wide

$5,000-6,500   **L&T**

A 19thC Symphonion musical box, with a quantity of discs and a winding handle, with a German-made movement stamped 'schutz Marke, Made in Germany, 266519'.

case 18in (46cm) wide

$1,900-2,500   **LAW**

A late 19thC German walnut cased polyphon, with coin-operated mechanical movement playing eleven inch steel discs, with winding key.

32.75in (83cm) high

$750-900   **BELL**

A Victorian walnut symphonium, the glass front enclosing the disc, two extra discs, sublime/harmony comb arrangement, with a penny slot.

33in (84cm) high

$2,500-3,200

SWO

A late 19thC polyphon music box and discs, serial no.26028, in a walnut case and base, with eighty-five 24.5in (62.5cm) discs.

77in (196cm) high

$10,000-13,000

L&T

A Swiss gilt and enamel singing bird box, the movement by Henri Metert, in the manner of Charles Bruguier, the cover enameled with a view of Lake Geneva, the fusee-driven movement with an eight-stack cam, signed 'H Metert Geneve' and signed 'R Burnett 1964'.

c1850

4in (10cm) long

$19,000-25,000

TEN

A Bontems-type spring-driven gilt-metal automaton 'singing Bird' musical box, decorated with foxes and birds.

4in (10cm) long

$1,900-2,500

SWO

A Continental singing bird musical automaton, gilt and decorated in enamels, the cover with a depiction of 'The Swing' after Jean-Honoré Fragonard, the moving, flapping and singing bird, the case stamped 'EB METAL'.

4in (10cm) long

$3,800-4,400

TEN

A 20thC caged bird musical automaton, the three birds singing and moving in their gilded cage.

24in (61cm) high

$1,900-2,500

CHOR

An early 20thC Swiss singing bird box, faux tortoiseshell-cased, marked 'RAYMY's Geneva' and numbered '523', in a fitted case.

4in (10cm) wide

$1,900-2,500

CHOR

An early 20thC silver singing bird automaton, with a spring-driven movement powering a turning, flapping and tweeting bird.

4in (10cm) wide

$2,500-3,200

TEN

A George II cast silver taper stick, with maker's mark '?E', London.

1729   *4.25in (10.5cm) high 3.9oz*

$450-550   **DN**

A pair of George II silver candlesticks, London, in the Rococo style with twisted square section stems, maker's mark 'I.I'.

1748   *10.25in (26cm) high 41oz*

$3,200-3,800   **TEN**

A pair of George II cast silver candlesticks, by Simon Jouet, London, light scratches and wear.

1749   *9in (23cm) high 48.45oz*

$3,200-3,800   **DN**

A pair of George II silver cast candlesticks, by William Gould, London.

1750   *7.5in (19cm) high 29.1oz*

$2,800-3,500   **LAW**

A pair of George II silver candlesticks, by John Cafe, London, the sconces unmarked, neither drip pan marked, one sconce has slight dent to rim.

1754   *8.75in (22cm) high 35oz*

$1,500-2,300   **CHOR**

A pair of George II silver candlesticks, probably by John Priest or John Perry, London.

1756, 1757   *9.75in (25cm) high 46.5oz*

$2,800-3,800   **WW**

A pair of George III cast silver taper sticks, by William Cafe, London, with spool-shaped capitals, ropework borders.

1763   *6.25in (16cm) high 13.4oz*

$3,800-5,000   **WW**

A George III silver taper stick, London, makers mark 'IH'.

1763   *6in (15cm) high 5.5oz*

$650-750   **WW**

A pair of George III silver candlesticks, by Ebenezer Coker, London, repair below lower knop on one of the stems.

1770   *10.5in (27cm) high 41.39oz*

$2,500-3,200   **CHEF**

A George III cast silver taper stick, by Ebenezer Coker, London.
1771   *6.25in (16cm) high 7.5oz*
$750-900   **WW**

A set of four George III silver candlesticks, London, in the Neo-classical style, with acanthus sockets and removable nozzles, maker's mark 'WA', with mahogany bases, some splits.
1772   *12.25in (31cm) high*
$2,000-2,500   **TEN**

A pair of George III cast silver pillar candlesticks, with pair of matching two-light candelabra branches, by John Schofield, London,.
1790, 1793   *candelabra 16.25in (41.5cm) high 95oz*
$9,000-10,000   **CAN**

A suite of George III silver candelabra and candlesticks, by Matthew Boulton, for M. Boulton & Plate Co., Birmingham, loaded sticks with following scratch weights: '10.6', '10.8', '10.10', '10.10'.
1797   *candelabra 16.5in (42cm) high 55oz*
$6,500-7,500   **MAB**

A pair of George III silver candlesticks, by John Green, Roberts, Mosley, and Co., Sheffield, engraved with a crest.
1800   *12in (30.5cm) high*
$2,300-2,800   **WW**

A pair of George III silver candlesticks, by John Roberts & Co., Sheffield, with gadrooned borders and detachable drip pans.
1810   *12.5in (31.5cm) high*
$750-900   **WW**

A pair of George III silver candlesticks, by John Roberts & Co., Sheffield, with detachable drip pans, one drip pan is plated.
1810   *12.25in (31cm) high*
$950-1,100   **WW**

A pair of Victorian silver taper sticks, by Henry Wilkinson and Co., Sheffield.
1839   *5.5in (14cm) high*
$450-550   **WW**

A Victorian silver four-light candelabrum, by Richard Hodd & Son, London, base and column loaded, one branch slightly drooped.
1892   *29in (74cm) high*
$1,600-2,300   **CHEF**

A Charles II silver chamber candlestick, maker's mark 'IC' with a mullet below in a heart-shaped punch, London, split near the handle.

See 'Jackson's', third edition, page 137, for this unknown maker's mark.

1673   *6in (15cm) long 4.1oz*
$3,800-4,400   **DN**

A James II silver chamber candlestick, London, on three bun feet, crest is slightly worn, light scratches.

1686 or 1688   *5.75in (14.5cm) long 6oz*
$1,300-1,900   **DN**

CLOSER LOOK - CHAMBER CANDLESTICK

The chamber candlestick is by the renowned maker Sampson Mordan & Gabriel Riddle, London.

It has a pleasing naturalistic form.

It has a calyx form capital on a leaf and flower spray stem.

The lobe bordered base has a cast flower and foliate rim.

A George IV silver chamber candlestick, light scratches, slight movement to stem.

1828   *3.5in (9cm) high 5.6oz*
$950-1,100   **DN**

A George II silver chamber stick, by William Gould, London, with a later associated sconce and conical snuffer.

c1740   *5.75in (14.5cm) diam 11oz*
$300-400   **WW**

A George II silver chamber stick, by James Gould, London, with a later snuffer, engraved with an armorial.

1743   *5.5in (14cm) diam 12.5oz*
$250-320   **WW**

A George IV Scottish silver chamber candlestick with snuffer, by Adam Elder, Edinburgh, engraved underneath 'To A.C. Bonar as a remembrance from her aunt Miss Bonar who died March 5, 1828'.

1827   *4.75in (12cm) diam 7.2oz*
$300-450   **DN**

A William IV silver chamber candlestick with snuffer, by Creswick & Co., Sheffield, engraved with a monogram and '1831' beneath, the snuffer with an acorn finial, marked, light scratches.

1830   *4.75in (12cm) across 4.35oz*
$300-400   **DN**

A William IV silver chamber candlestick, by James Charles, Edington, London.

1836   *6in (15cm) long 13oz*
$750-900   **DN**

A Victorian silver chamber candlestick and snuffer, by Robert Dicker, London, engraved with a cipher and a baron's coronet, light scratches and wear.

1876   *6in (15cm) long 8.1oz*
$300-400   **DN**

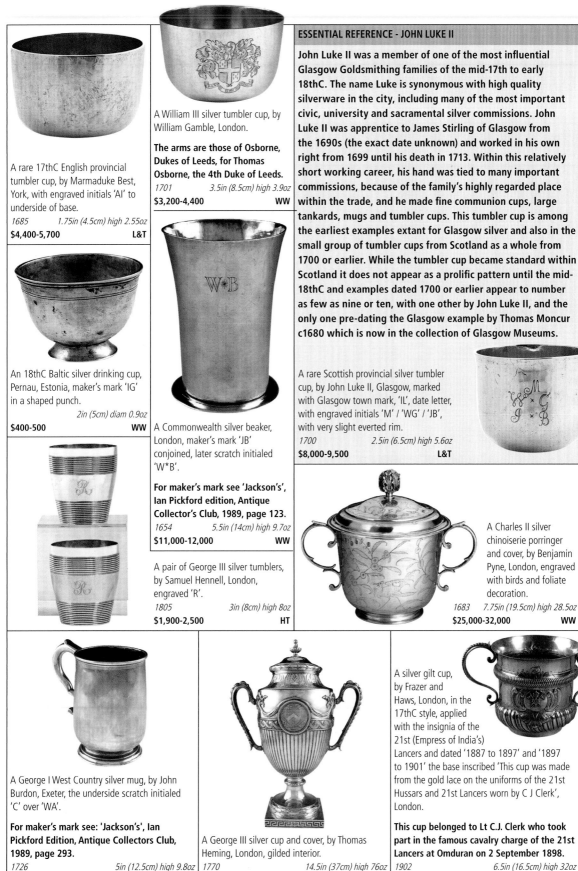

A rare 17thC English provincial tumbler cup, by Marmaduke Best, York, with engraved initials 'AI' to underside of base.

1685   1.75in (4.5cm) high 2.55oz

$4,400-5,700   **L&T**

A William III silver tumbler cup, by William Gamble, London.

The arms are those of Osborne, Dukes of Leeds, for Thomas Osborne, the 4th Duke of Leeds.

1701   3.5in (8.5cm) high 3.9oz

$3,200-4,400   **WW**

An 18thC Baltic silver drinking cup, Pernau, Estonia, maker's mark 'IG' in a shaped punch.

2in (5cm) diam 0.9oz

$400-500   **WW**

A Commonwealth silver beaker, London, maker's mark 'JB' conjoined, later scratch initialed 'W*B'.

For maker's mark see 'Jackson's', Ian Pickford edition, Antique Collector's Club, 1989, page 123.

1654   5.5in (14cm) high 9.7oz

$11,000-12,000   **WW**

A pair of George III silver tumblers, by Samuel Hennell, London, engraved 'R'.

1805   3in (8cm) high 8oz

$1,900-2,500   **HT**

ESSENTIAL REFERENCE - JOHN LUKE II

John Luke II was a member of one of the most influential Glasgow Goldsmithing families of the mid-17th to early 18thC. The name Luke is synonymous with high quality silverware in the city, including many of the most important civic, university and sacramental silver commissions. John Luke II was apprentice to James Stirling of Glasgow from the 1690s (the exact date unknown) and worked in his own right from 1699 until his death in 1713. Within this relatively short working career, his hand was tied to many important commissions, because of the family's highly regarded place within the trade, and he made fine communion cups, large tankards, mugs and tumbler cups. This tumbler cup is among the earliest examples extant for Glasgow silver and also in the small group of tumbler cups from Scotland as a whole from 1700 or earlier. While the tumbler cup became standard within Scotland it does not appear as a prolific pattern until the mid-18thC and examples dated 1700 or earlier appear to number as few as nine or ten, with one other by John Luke II, and the only one pre-dating the Glasgow example by Thomas Moncur c1680 which is now in the collection of Glasgow Museums.

A rare Scottish provincial silver tumbler cup, by John Luke II, Glasgow, marked with Glasgow town mark, 'IL', date letter, with engraved initials 'M' / 'WG' / 'JB', with very slight everted rim.

1700   2.5in (6.5cm) high 5.6oz

$8,000-9,500   **L&T**

A Charles II silver chinoiserie porringer and cover, by Benjamin Pyne, London, engraved with birds and foliate decoration.

1683   7.75in (19.5cm) high 28.5oz

$25,000-32,000   **WW**

A George I West Country silver mug, by John Burdon, Exeter, the underside scratch initialed 'C' over 'WA'.

For maker's mark see: 'Jackson's', Ian Pickford Edition, Antique Collectors Club, 1989, page 293.

1726   5in (12.5cm) high 9.8oz

$1,000-1,100   **WW**

A George III silver cup and cover, by Thomas Heming, London, gilded interior.

1770   14.5in (37cm) high 76oz

$7,000-8,000   **WW**

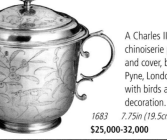

A silver gilt cup, by Frazer and Haws, London, in the 17thC style, applied with the insignia of the 21st (Empress of India's) Lancers and dated '1887 to 1897' and '1897 to 1901' the base inscribed 'This cup was made from the gold lace on the uniforms of the 21st Hussars and 21st Lancers worn by C J Clerk', London.

This cup belonged to Lt C.J. Clerk who took part in the famous cavalry charge of the 21st Lancers at Omduran on 2 September 1898.

1902   6.5in (16.5cm) high 32oz

$1,900-2,500   **MOR**

CLOSER LOOK - GEORGE II COMMUNION CUP

This is an early Scottish silver cup by a quality maker Charles Dickson, Edinburgh, and assay master Edward Penman.

The bowl is engraved 'The money for buying this Cup left in Legacy by John Smith of Smithfield and payed by John Edington his Executor and Successor on the fifteenth of February 1728'. This adds to its historical interest.

The cup is raised on a tapered knopped stem and domed spreading circular foot.

An early George II silver communion cup.
1727   9in (22.5cm) high 15oz
$5,000-6,500   **L&T**

ESSENTIAL REFERENCE - AYME VIDEAU

Ayme Videau was a Huguenot silversmith. In 1685 Louis XIV revoked the Edict of Nantes, which had given religious freedom to the French Protestants, or Huguenots. Many of the Huguenots were skilled artists, like silversmiths, and their influence on English silver of the period has long been recognized. The Huguenot contribution to silver made in England was responsible for the great flowering of style and technique in English silver between 1680 and 1760.

A George II silver cup and cover, by Ayme Videau, London, with scroll, rocaille and grapevine decoration, on a later wooden stand with a plaque, inscribed 'Anniversary Cup, Sandown, 1937, Won by Lord Hurst's Magnet'.
1745   12in (30.5cm) high off plinth 76oz
$9,000-10,000   **WW**

A near pair of Irish silver communion cups, probably by Richard Williams, Dublin, one with maker's mark, crowned harp struck twice and Hibernia struck twice.
c1772-76   8in (20cm) high 8oz each
$1,600-2,300   **CHEF**

A pair of Turkish silver goblets, of the Abdulhamid II period, with engine-turned decoration, on knopped stems, six-bracket feet.
1876-1909   5.5in (14cm) high 9.6oz
$500-650   **WW**

A pair of George III silver goblets, by Robert Hennell, London, with crests.
1792   6.5in (16cm) high 12oz
$3,800-5,000   **WW**

A silver cup and cover, by Robert Garrard, London, with double-dolphin handles, chased with two heads of Neptune with shell crest.
1869   15.5in (39cm) high 40oz
$1,000-1,200   **MOR**

A late 19thC German silver wager cup, by Neresheimer of Hanau, with import marks for Chester 1899, importer's mark of Berthold Muller.
10in (25.5cm) 11.5oz
$1,000-1,200   **WW**

A German silver pineapple cup and cover, by Neresheimer of Hanau, with import marks for Chester, dated, importer's mark of Berthold Muller, the stem modeled as a tree trunk and mounted with a figure playing bag-pipes.
1906   11.25in (28.5cm) 11oz
$450-500   **WW**

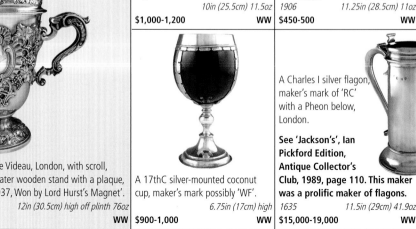

A 17thC silver-mounted coconut cup, maker's mark possibly 'WF'.
6.75in (17cm) high
$900-1,000   **WW**

A Charles I silver flagon, maker's mark of 'RC' with a Pheon below, London.

See 'Jackson's', Ian Pickford Edition, Antique Collector's Club, 1989, page 110. This maker was a prolific maker of flagons.
1635   11.5in (29cm) 41.9oz
$15,000-19,000   **WW**

A Charles II silver tankard, London, engraved with an armorial, scratch initialed 'E*B', '14lb 1731', maker's mark 'ID' conjoined.
1673   *6.75in (17cm) high 30oz*
$9,000-10,000   **WW**

A Charles II silver-gilt tankard, maker's mark of 'T.C' with a fish above, with later decoration, London.

The arms are those of Bertie, for those granted in 1550 to the father of Richard Bertie, MP for Lincolnshire, who married the daughter and sole heiress of Lord Willoughby de Eresby and widow of the Duke of Suffolk. His son's succession to the Willougby title was established and augmented in 1626 by the Earldom of Abingdon and in 1715 by the Dukedom of Ancaster and Kesteven.
1678   *6.75in (17cm) high 31.3oz*
$7,000-7,500   **WW**

ESSENTIAL REFERENCE - CHINOISERIE

This tankard forms part of a small group of silver dating from the last quarter of the 17thC with Chinese decoration in relief. This relief decoration makes the group stand out from the more common flat-chased chinoiserie decoration in vogue at the time. The flat-chased chinoiserie silver is of unquestionably English origin. However, recent research into the rare pieces with cast and chased decoration like this tankard has shown that some are Chinese and retailed in England. Some are hallmarked in England, for instance the tea pot of London 1682 from the estate of Samuel Wagstaffe (Christie's New York, 18 April 1989, lot 589), and some are made by London makers in imitation of Chinese examples. This tankard had a spectrographic analysis carried out by the London Assay Office which found the silver impurity levels consistent with it being of 16th-17thC age and of sterling (.925) standard, thus pointing to an English, rather than Chinese origin. The pieces now known to be of Chinese origin have been found to be made from a silver alloy of a higher standard.

A William III silver tankard, by Alexander Roode, London, later engraved with a coat of arms, with pricking 's, / I.G. / 1700'.
1699   *7in (18cm) high 25oz*
$3,800-5,000   **MAB**

A William III silver tankard, by John Sutton, London, prick-engraved with the initials 'M' over 'IM' to the handle, one side with a small erasure.
1699   *7.5in (19cm) high 29oz*
$5,000-6,500   **TEN**

A rare late 17thC silver parcel gilt small chinoiserie tankard, unmarked but with 1814-1893 Dutch tax/census marks (crowned V), engraved with Chinese-style flowers and foliage, the cover with a pheasant beneath a flowering bush, two birds flying above, the body with a pine tree and rockwork with a stag and hind.
c1685   *4.75in (12cm) high 17oz*
$60,000-70,000   **DN**

A George I silver tankard, by William Darker, London.
1720   *7.25in (18.5cm) 24.9oz*
$2,300-2,800   **WW**

An English provincial George II silver tankard, by John Langlands, Newcastle, with bold S-scroll handle with cast thumb strap work.
1747   *8.25in (21cm) high 29.5oz*
$6,500-7,500   **L&T**

A George II silver tankard, engraved coat of arms by John Payne, London.
1754   *8in (20cm) high 25.75oz*
$1,300-1,800   **LAW**

A silver tankard, by Thomas Wallis, London.
1773   *7.75in (19.5cm) high 26.5oz*
$1,300-1,800   **CHOR**

An Irish silver teapot, possibly by Henry Daniell, Dublin, of pear shape with fruitwood handle, crest beneath coronet to one side, small dent to side.
1715   *6in (15cm) high 12.3oz*
$11,000-14,000   **CHOR**

A George I silver bullet teapot, by Gabriel Sleath, London.
1723   *7.25in (18.5cm) long 9.5oz*
$1,600-2,000   **WW**

A Scottish provincial George II silver bullet teapot, by Robert Luke, Glasgow, marked 'RL' twice, 's', with town mark, swan spout and muscular handle.
                                    5in (12.5cm) high 15.5oz
$5,500-6,500   **L&T**

A George III silver teapot, possibly by Benjamin Mordecai, London, with bright-cut decoration, cover with an ivory pineapple finial.
1788   *10.5in (26.5cm) long 14oz*
$400-450   **WW**

A George III silver teapot, London, with a later foliate finial, engraved with two monograms, maker's mark worn.
1814   *11in (27.5cm) long 24.5oz*
$450-550   **WW**

A George III provincial silver teapot, by Barber and Whitwell, York.
1815   *11.25in (28.5cm) long 19.8oz*
$750-1,000   **WW**

A George III silver-gilt bachelor's teapot, by Charles Price, London, of fluted melon form.
1818   *6.5in (16cm) long 10.4oz*
$7,500-9,000   **WW**

A Victorian silver tea pot, by Benjamin Preston, London.
1858   *10in (25.5cm) long 22oz*
$400-450   **WW**

A Victorian silver bachelor's tea pot, by Alexander Macrae, London.
1863   *7in (18cm) long 8oz*
$300-450   **WW**

A George II silver coffee pot, by Gabriel Sleath, London, engraved with a contemporary coat of arms, base with scratch weight '26=4' and the initials 'P' over 'WA', small part of handle re-glued.

1734   9.5in (24cm) high 26oz

$3,200-4,400   TEN

An Irish provincial George II silver coffee pot, by George Hodder, Cork, with a later crest and motto, underside engraved with initial triangle 'D / P=M' and scratch weight '29=17'.

c1740   9.75in (24.5cm) high 31oz

$3,800-5,000   MAB

ESSENTIAL REFERENCE - JAMAICAN SILVER

Although 18thC Jamaican silver is rare, it is thought that at least twenty-three goldsmiths were working there in the mid-18thC. By this time there was concern that substandard articles were being produced. An act was passed, and accompanied by the introduction of an assay master. The first master was Charles Wood, who was replaced in 1749 by Anthony Danvers. Danvers is thought to have come from Liverpool, and it is thought he died in Kingston in 1772. The practice of assay marking appears to have stopped by about 1765. Geradus Stoutenburgh may have originally come from New York.

A Jamaican silver coffee pot, by Geradus Stoutenburgh, decorated in the Rococo manner with shells, scroll, maidens, and animals, above a castle, the body with two cartouches, each engraved with a later crest.

c1760   11in (27.5cm) high 40.7oz

$9,500-10,500   WW

A George II silver coffee pot, by Ayme Videau, London, chased foliate and scroll decoration, engraved with a crest.

1748   9in (23cm) high 27oz

$950-1,100   WW

A George III silver coffee jug, by David Whyte & William Holmes, London, engraved with the crest of Holden of Lancashire impaling Massenden of Helme, Lincolnshire.

1764   8.75in (22cm) high 14oz

$700-800   WW

A George II silver coffee pot, by Richard Guerney and Co., London, later engraved with the arms of Nathaniel Booth, 4th Baron Delamere of Dunham Massey, date letter worn.

Lady May Langham, only surviving child of the 2nd Langham Baronet married the Earl of Warrington. This family died out in the male line and some of the Dunham Massey silver came to the Langham family in the 18thC.

8.25in (21cm) high 25oz

$1,000-1,100   WW

A George II silver coffee pot, by Thomas Whipham, London, embossed foliate and scroll decoration, engraved with an armorial and later crest.

1755   11in (28cm) high 35.5oz

$1,900-2,500   WW

A George III silver coffee pot, by Charles Hougham, London.

1787   11.25in (28.5cm) high 23.5oz

$1,000-1,100   WW

An American silver coffee pot, by Howard and Co., New York, engraved with the ancient arms of Seymour of Langley, Buckinghamshire.

8.75in (22cm) high 33oz

$550-700   WW

An early 19thC German silver coffee pot, by Johaan Georg Friderich Welle, Arolsen, with lion mask spout, on a raised foot modeled as three mythical dolphins.

c1800   *8.75in (22cm) high 25.5oz*

$1,200-1,500   **WW**

A George III silver hot water jug, by Paul Storr, London, engraved with a crest and the initials 'DG', probably for Garrick or Gawler.

1795   *10.25in (26cm) high 23.9oz*

$2,500-3,200   **LAW**

A Queen Anne silver chocolate pot, probably by Samuel Lee, London, engraved with an armorial.

The arms are possibly those of Lille.

1703   *9.75in (24.5cm) high 22.5oz*

$5,000-6,500   **WW**

A George II West Country silver chocolate pot, by Samuel Willmott, of Plymouth, Exeter, the base scratch initialed 'MM' over 'ML' '1744', date letter partially rubbed.

For details of the maker see: Kent, T., West 'Country Silver Spoons and Their Makers, 1550-1750,' J.H. Bourdon-Smith Ltd., 1992, page 143.

1730   *9.5in (24cm) high 24.8oz*

$4,400-5,700   **WW**

A George II West Country silver chocolate pot, by Samuel Wilmot of Plymouth, engraved with a crest and underneath with the initials 'G.C', hallmarked Exeter.

1740   *9.5in (24.5cm) high 29.9oz*

$3,800-5,000   **LAW**

An American silver chocolate pot, the body with floral and foliate embossed decoration and raised on three pad feet, detailed 's Kirk & Son' and engraved 'From Caroline W. Astor 1883'.

9in (23cm) high

$500-650   **BELL**

A silver café-au-lait set, by William Gibson & John Langman, London, retailed by Goldsmiths & Silversmiths Company.

1892   *11.5in (29cm) high 26.3oz*

$400-500   **CHOR**

A silver kettle on stand, by J.B. Carrington, London, stand on four scroll legs with a burner.

1893   *11in (28cm) high 46oz*

$1,000-1,200   **WW**

A silver kettle on stand, by Harry Brasted, London, in mid-Georgian-style, with a long-handled flame extinguisher.

1898, 1905   *kettle 13.5in (34cm) high 56.45oz*

$1,500-1,900   **DN**

A George III silver four-piece tea and coffee service, the coffee pot, sucrier and cream jug London 1781, the tea pot London 1757.

teapot 12in (30.5cm) wide 87oz

$1,500-2,300   TRI

A Philadelphia silver tea and coffee service, bearing the touch of Joseph Richardson, all pieces monogrammed 'EM'.

c1800   *coffee pot 12.75in (32.5cm) high 72oz*

$3,800-4,400   POOK

A George IV four-piece silver tea set, by John Bridge, London, with chased Classical foliate decoration, engraved with the crest and motto of Glenorchy.

1825   *kettle 16.5in (42cm) high 209oz*

$6,500-7,500   WW

An oversized silver four-piece tea and coffee service, by Joseph Gloster Ltd., Birmingham.

1969, 1971, 1972   *coffee pot 12in (30cm) high 183.05oz.*

$3,800-5,000   DN

A George III silver cased set of tea caddies, initialed, by Edward Aldridge, London, the case with shagreen covering and silver mounts.

1766   *case 11.75in (29.5cm) long 31.5oz*

$7,000-8,000   LAW

A silver tea caddy, importer's mark of William Neal, London, decorated in the chinoiserie manner.

1900   *6in (15cm) high 13oz*

$700-800   WW

A silver tea caddy, by Neresheimer of Hanau, with import marks for Chester, importer's mark of Berthold Muller.

1901   *5.5in (13.5cm) high 5.5oz*

$400-450   WW

An American silver tea caddy, by Tiffany and Co., of the Charles Cook period, engraved with a monogram, with an interior cover.

c1902   *4in (10cm) high 11.4oz*

$500-650   WW

A silver tea caddy, by S. Blanckensee and Sons, Birmingham, in the George I manner.

1917   *5.5in (13.5cm) high 4.8oz*

$150-230   WW

An Elizabeth I silver Apostle spoon, St. Thomas, maker's mark 'W' within a Sun, or a fringed 'W', London, gilded finial, pierced nimbus.

1561   7in (18cm) long 1.8oz
$8,000-9,500   **WW**

An Edward VI silver seal-top spoon, London, the reverse of the bowl scratch initialed 'GH', with traces of gilding.

1552   6.25in (16cm) long 1.1oz
$13,000-19,000   **WW**

A pair of Elizabeth I silver Apostle spoons, The Master and St. Peter, maker's mark of a bird's claw, for Francis Jackson, London, the reverse scratch initialed 'sB' and 'MB', gilded finials, the nimbus with a dove.

6.75in (17.5cm) long 3.8oz
1562
$25,000-32,000   **WW**

An Elizabeth I silver Apostle spoon St. James the Less, maker's mark of a device, possibly a scallop, London, the reverse scratch initialed 'D.E', gilded finial, the nimbus with a dove.

1574   6.75in (17.5cm) long 1.7oz
$2,500-3,200   **WW**

A pair of Elizabeth I silver Maidenhead spoons, by Richard Orenge, Sherborne, with gilded finials.
c1580   6.5in (16.5cm) long 2.5oz
$11,000-14,000   **WW**

An Elizabeth I West Country silver seal-top spoon, by John Edes, Exeter, later crested.

The crest is that of many families including Brookman, Gatty, Petytand Shore.
c1580-1600   6.5in (16.5cm) long 1.4oz
$4,200-5,000   **WW**

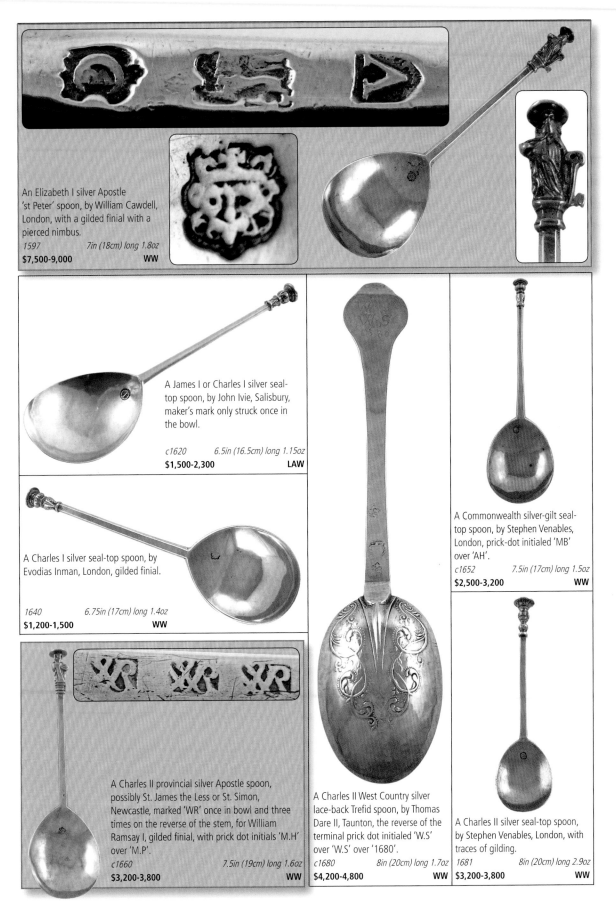

An Elizabeth I silver Apostle 'st Peter' spoon, by William Cawdell, London, with a gilded finial with a pierced nimbus.
1597   *7in (18cm) long 1.8oz*
$7,500-9,000   **WW**

A James I or Charles I silver seal-top spoon, by John Ivie, Salisbury, maker's mark only struck once in the bowl.
c1620   *6.5in (16.5cm) long 1.15oz*
$1,500-2,300   **LAW**

A Charles I silver seal-top spoon, by Evodias Inman, London, gilded finial.

1640   *6.75in (17cm) long 1.4oz*
$1,200-1,500   **WW**

A Charles II provincial silver Apostle spoon, possibly St. James the Less or St. Simon, Newcastle, marked 'WR' once in bowl and three times on the reverse of the stem, for William Ramsay I, gilded finial, with prick dot initials 'M.H' over 'M.P'.
c1660   *7.5in (19cm) long 1.6oz*
$3,200-3,800   **WW**

A Charles II West Country silver lace-back Trefid spoon, by Thomas Dare II, Taunton, the reverse of the terminal prick dot initialed 'W.S' over 'W.S' over '1680'.
c1680   *8in (20cm) long 1.7oz*
$4,200-4,800   **WW**

A Commonwealth silver-gilt seal-top spoon, by Stephen Venables, London, prick-dot initialed 'MB' over 'AH'.
c1652   *7.5in (17cm) long 1.5oz*
$2,500-3,200   **WW**

A Charles II silver seal-top spoon, by Stephen Venables, London, with traces of gilding.
1681   *8in (20cm) long 2.9oz*
$3,200-3,800   **WW**

ESSENTIAL REFERENCE - FROST FAIRS

Eight frost fairs were held on the Thames between 1607 and 1814; the first recorded frost fair was in the winter of 1607/08. The frost commenced in mid-December, and by 10-15 January the ice between Lambeth and Westminster was firm and thick enough to allow a large number of people to walk on it in perfect safety. Booths were set up for the sale of fruit, food, beer and wine, and shoemakers and barbers plied their trade on the ice.

People indulged in practically every sport including dancing, skating, sledging, bull-bating, bear baiting, fox-hunting, football and skittles... King Charles II and his family visited the frost fair and had their names printed on a quarto sheet of Dufra paper by 'G Groom on the ICE on the River Thames January 31st 1684'.

A rare late Charles II silver 'Frost Fair' souvenir laceback trefid spoon, scratched with the initials 'EW' on the terminal and inscribed 'This Spoon was bought upon the Frozen Thames January:28:1683/4', maker's mark 'PL' (script monogram), London.

1683   *7.75in (20cm) long 1.84oz*

$18,000-23,000   **LAW**

A rare George III silver 'Duty Drawback' Hanoverian-pattern teaspoon, by Hester Bateman, London.

The Duty Drawback mark was used on exported wares 1 December 1784 up to 24 July 1785.

1784   *4.75in (12cm) long 0.3oz*

$300-400   **WW**

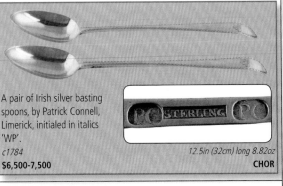

A pair of Irish silver basting spoons, by Patrick Connell, Limerick, initialed in italics 'WP'.

c1784   *12.5in (32cm) long 8.82oz*

$6,500-7,500   **CHOR**

A George III silver pierced caddy spoon, by Samuel Pemberton, Birmingham, engraved 'JEA'.

1803   *3.25in (8cm) long*

$400-450   **DN**

A George III silver flowerhead caddy spoon, of Old English pattern, Birmingham, with maker's mark 'TH'.

1809   *2.5in (6.5cm) long*

$250-320   **DN**

An Edwardian silvergilt fish caddy spoon, by T. Bradbury & Sons, Sheffield, now with an added pin for use as a pin.

1909   *3in (7.5cm) long 0.45oz*

$450-500   **LAW**

ESSENTIAL REFERENCE - LORD NELSON

Nelson, as a young naval officer of 27, met the newly-widowed Frances 'Fanny' Nisbet in the West Indies in 1785 and married her in 1787. Making their home with Nelson's father in rural Norfolk, a less than happy marriage ensued, with Nelson impatient for another command at sea, and Fanny longing desperately for the warmth and comparative luxuries of her former life in the Caribbean. When the French Revolutionary War began early in 1793, Nelson was recalled to sea and the couple did not see each other again for four years. As it was, he only came home then in order to recuperate from the loss of his right arm during the attack on Tenerife. Back in the Mediterranean in April 1798, the fleet put into Naples after the great victory at the Nile (1 August 1798) where Nelson met Emma, Lady Hamilton, and fell in love with her. Their passionate affair soon scandalized Europe and by the time Nelson returned to England with Emma in November 1800, his marriage to Fanny was over in all but name. Although they never met again, they never divorced either so that, after Nelson's death at Trafalgar, she retained the title of Viscountess Nelson and, somewhat surprisingly, continued to cherish her unfaithful husband's memory until her own death in 1831. This spoon is a fascinating relic of Nelson's legacy to his lawful wife who clearly ordered some additional cutlery just a few years after her husband's death.

A George III silver fiddle-pattern dessert spoon, by Eley, Fearn and Chawner, London, the terminal engraved with one of the variants of Admiral Lord Nelson's crests, namely the stern of the Spanish man-o'war San Josef, captured at the battle of Cape St. Vincent, and the chelengk, presented by the Ottoman Sultan after the battle of the Nile.

1811   *3in (7.5cm) long 1.3oz*

$700-800   **WW**

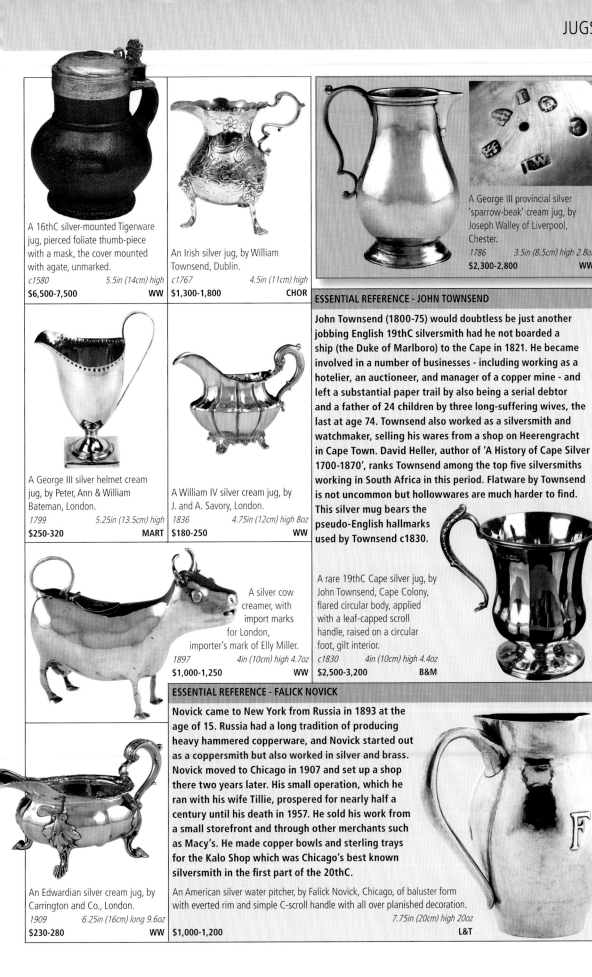

A 16thC silver-mounted Tigerware jug, pierced foliate thumb-piece with a mask, the cover mounted with agate, unmarked.
c1580   5.5in (14cm) high
$6,500-7,500   WW

An Irish silver jug, by William Townsend, Dublin.
c1767   4.5in (11cm) high
$1,300-1,800   CHOR

A George III provincial silver 'sparrow-beak' cream jug, by Joseph Walley of Liverpool, Chester.
1786   3.5in (8.5cm) high 2.8oz
$2,300-2,800   WW

A George III silver helmet cream jug, by Peter, Ann & William Bateman, London.
1799   5.25in (13.5cm) high
$250-320   MART

A William IV silver cream jug, by J. and A. Savory, London.
1836   4.75in (12cm) high 8oz
$180-250   WW

ESSENTIAL REFERENCE - JOHN TOWNSEND

John Townsend (1800-75) would doubtless be just another jobbing English 19thC silversmith had he not boarded a ship (the Duke of Marlboro) to the Cape in 1821. He became involved in a number of businesses - including working as a hotelier, an auctioneer, and manager of a copper mine - and left a substantial paper trail by also being a serial debtor and a father of 24 children by three long-suffering wives, the last at age 74. Townsend also worked as a silversmith and watchmaker, selling his wares from a shop on Heerengracht in Cape Town. David Heller, author of 'A History of Cape Silver 1700-1870', ranks Townsend among the top five silversmiths working in South Africa in this period. Flatware by Townsend is not uncommon but hollowwares are much harder to find. This silver mug bears the pseudo-English hallmarks used by Townsend c1830.

A silver cow creamer, with import marks for London, importer's mark of Elly Miller.
1897   4in (10cm) high 4.7oz
$1,000-1,250   WW

A rare 19thC Cape silver jug, by John Townsend, Cape Colony, flared circular body, applied with a leaf-capped scroll handle, raised on a circular foot, gilt interior.
c1830   4in (10cm) high 4.4oz
$2,500-3,200   B&M

ESSENTIAL REFERENCE - FALICK NOVICK

Novick came to New York from Russia in 1893 at the age of 15. Russia had a long tradition of producing heavy hammered copperware, and Novick started out as a coppersmith but also worked in silver and brass. Novick moved to Chicago in 1907 and set up a shop there two years later. His small operation, which he ran with his wife Tillie, prospered for nearly half a century until his death in 1957. He sold his work from a small storefront and through other merchants such as Macy's. He made copper bowls and sterling trays for the Kalo Shop which was Chicago's best known silversmith in the first part of the 20thC.

An Edwardian silver cream jug, by Carrington and Co., London.
1909   6.25in (16cm) long 9.6oz
$230-280   WW

An American silver water pitcher, by Falick Novick, Chicago, of baluster form with everted rim and simple C-scroll handle with all over planished decoration.
7.75in (20cm) high 20oz
$1,000-1,200   L&T

An Irish silver tazza, by Thomas Bolton, Dublin, with armorial, initialed beneath 'H'/GE, scratchweight under foot 10=14=12, crowned harp to stem.

1694-95   *8.25in (21cm) diam 11.11oz*

$5,500-6,500   **CHOR**

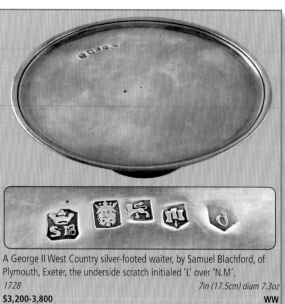

A George II West Country silver-footed waiter, by Samuel Blachford, of Plymouth, Exeter, the underside scratch initialed 'L' over 'N.M'.

1728   *7in (17.5cm) diam 7.3oz*

$3,200-3,800   **WW**

A large George III silver salver, by Robert Jones, London, with an armorial, on four gadroon paw feet.

1774   *15.5in (39cm) diam 49oz*

$1,900-2,500   **WW**

A pair of George III silver-gilt plates, by Andrew Fogelberg, London, engraved with an armorial and crest.

The arms are those of James Brydes, 3rd Duke Chandos (1711-1789), with Gamon in pretence for the Duke's 2nd Marriage (1777) to Anna Ekiza, widow of Roger Hope Ellerton.

1775   *9.5in (24cm) diam 30oz*

$3,500-4,300   **WW**

A George III silver salver, over-stamped with maker's mark, possibly of John Swift, London, with an armorial and motto, the underside scratch initialed 'G' over 'I.S', and with a later inscription.

The arms of Curtis Miranda Lampson (b.1806), a native of Vermont, USA who was naturalized a British subject in 1846. As a Director of the Atlantic Telegraph Company he displayed great perseverance on his achievement in laying the Atlantic Cable and was created a baronet in 1866 after these arms had been granted.

1776   *15in (38cm) diam 44.5oz*

$900-1,100   **WW**

A George III silver meat plate, by Paul Storr, London, engraved with a coat of arms, engraved '1A' to base and numbered '25', some scratches.

The arms are those of Pelham impaling Aufrere, for Charles Anderson Pelham, later 1st Baron Yarborough (1748-1823) and his wife Sophia, only daughter and eventual heiress of George Aufrere Esq. of Chelsea, whom he married in 1770.

1808   *21.5in (55cm) wide 120oz*

$4,400-5,700   **TEN**

A George III silver salver, by Paul Storr, London, crested, the reverse with an inventory 'N. 757'.

1812   *13.5in (34cm) diam 42.1oz*

$3,500-4,000   **LAW**

A George III silver salver, by Edward Edwards, London, the border with masks and foliate scroll decoration.

1817   *12.5in (32cm) diam 44oz*

$1,900-2,500   **WW**

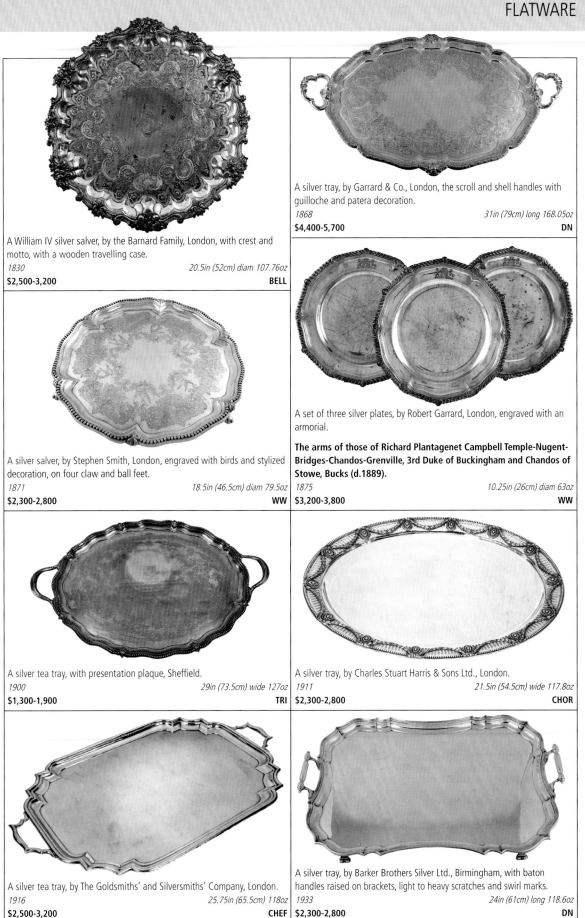

A William IV silver salver, by the Barnard Family, London, with crest and motto, with a wooden travelling case.
1830   *20.5in (52cm) diam 107.76oz*
$2,500-3,200   **BELL**

A silver salver, by Stephen Smith, London, engraved with birds and stylized decoration, on four claw and ball feet.
1871   *18.5in (46.5cm) diam 79.5oz*
$2,300-2,800   **WW**

A silver tea tray, with presentation plaque, Sheffield.
1900   *29in (73.5cm) wide 127oz*
$1,300-1,900   **TRI**

A silver tea tray, by The Goldsmiths' and Silversmiths' Company, London.
1916   *25.75in (65.5cm) 118oz*
$2,500-3,200   **CHEF**

A silver tray, by Garrard & Co., London, the scroll and shell handles with guilloche and patera decoration.
1868   *31in (79cm) long 168.05oz*
$4,400-5,700   **DN**

A set of three silver plates, by Robert Garrard, London, engraved with an armorial.

The arms of those of Richard Plantagenet Campbell Temple-Nugent-Bridges-Chandos-Grenville, 3rd Duke of Buckingham and Chandos of Stowe, Bucks (d.1889).
1875   *10.25in (26cm) diam 63oz*
$3,200-3,800   **WW**

A silver tray, by Charles Stuart Harris & Sons Ltd., London.
1911   *21.5in (54.5cm) wide 117.8oz*
$2,300-2,800   **CHOR**

A silver tray, by Barker Brothers Silver Ltd., Birmingham, with baton handles raised on brackets, light to heavy scratches and swirl marks.
1933   *24in (61cm) long 118.6oz*
$2,300-2,800   **DN**

A James II silver bleeding bowl, London, with maker's mark 'TO' with a fish above, handle scratch initialed 'H' over 'I.M'.

1688   *8in (20cm) long 7oz*

$3,800-4,400   **WW**

A William III silver Monteith bowl, by Francis Garthorne, London, lion mask drop-ring handles, engraved with an armorial.

1700   *11.75in (30cm) diam 55oz*

$5,500-6,500   **WW**

A George III silver punch bowl, by Daniel Smith and Robert Sharp, London, engraved with an armorial and a crest.

1761   *12.5in (32cm) diam 66.5oz*

$6,500-7,500   **WW**

A silver pedestal punch bowl, by Richard William Elliott, London, engraved 'Presented to Percy Warnford-Davis Esq, Chief representative of the London Chamber of Commerce by the delegates attending the 7th Congress of Chambers of Commerce of the Empire, held at Sydney, N. S. W. 1909'.

1842   *14.5in (37cm) diam 56.4oz*

$1,900-2,500   **DN**

An Edwardian silver punch/rose bowl, by William Henry Sparrow, Birmingham.

1903   *7in (18cm) high 39oz*

$1,000-1,500   **WHP**

A silver punch bowl, by the Barnards, London, with lion mask drop-ring handles, spot-hammered decoration.

1918   *11.5in (29cm) diam 44oz*

$1,300-1,800   **WW**

A Charles II silver porringer and cover, London, maker's mark 'PB' between crescents on shield shape, some repair.

1661   *9in (22.5cm) wide 25oz*

$12,000-14,000   **TEN**

ESSENTIAL REFERENCE - ROYAL CONNECTION

The inscription reads: 'shew not thy valientnesse in wine; for wine hath destroyed many. Can a man take fire in his bosome, and his clothes not bee burned? can one goe upon hote coles, and his feet not bee burned.'

This bowl is one from a set of thirty-four such vessels belonging to George IV's brother, Prince Frederick the Duke of York, each with a differing inscription. The Duke amassed an enormous collection of silver, much of it through the auspices of the maverick retailer, Kensington Lewis (c1790-1854). Although Prince Frederick took his official duties seriously, his extravagant lifestyle and gambling debts forced his executors to take the rare step of holding the exceptional Royal sale at Christie's in 1827.

The Prince's collection included a number of Farrell's extraordinary and somewhat eccentric designs. Kensington Lewis had encouraged Farrell to gain inspiration from early silver, leading the chaser and silversmith to become one of the earliest proponents of historicist silver.

A George IV silver-gilt bowl, by Edward Farrell, London, chased with panels containing the arms of James I and his emblems and the date '1610' below a Gothic inscription.

1824   *6.25in (16cm) diam 16oz*

$5,500-7,000   **MAB**

A George II Irish silver bowl and cover, by Thomas Walker, Dublin.

c1740   *6.5in (16.5cm) high 16.8oz*

$5,500-7,000   **WW**

An early 19thC Maltese silver sugar vase and cover, maker's mark 'GC', incuse 'M', stag's head above 'R', incuse 'M', 'GC', fairly crudely made, old silver solder repair in lower body.

The stag's head above 'R' stands for the Roman standard of 11 parts of silver to one part base metal. The 'GC' maker's mark could be for Giuseppe Cremona or Giuseppe Cousin.

5.5in (14cm) high 10.75oz

$2,500-3,200   **DN**

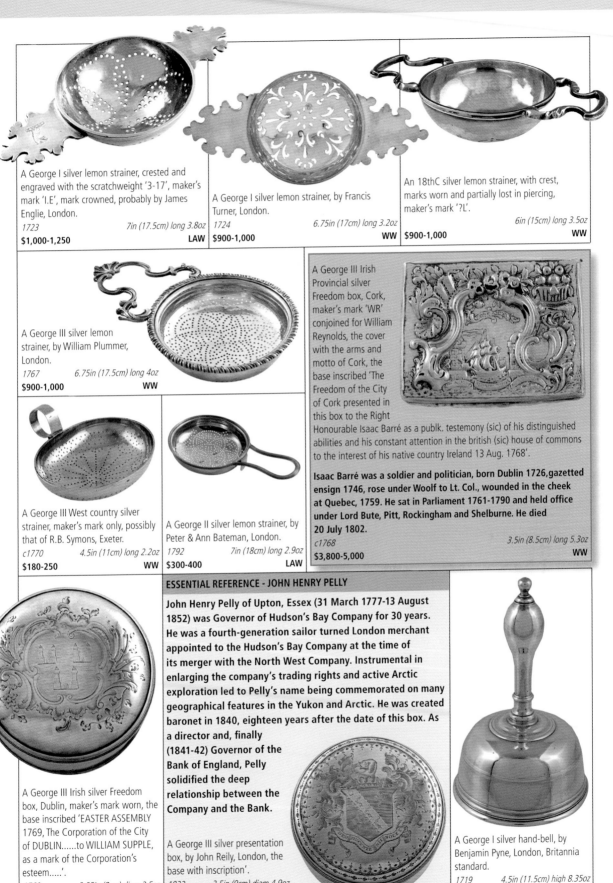

A George I silver lemon strainer, crested and engraved with the scratchweight '3-17', maker's mark 'I.E', mark crowned, probably by James Englie, London.
1723   *7in (17.5cm) long 3.8oz*
$1,000-1,250   **LAW**

A George I silver lemon strainer, by Francis Turner, London.
1724   *6.75in (17cm) long 3.2oz*
$900-1,000   **WW**

An 18thC silver lemon strainer, with crest, marks worn and partially lost in piercing, maker's mark '?L'.
6in (15cm) long 3.5oz
$900-1,000   **WW**

A George III silver lemon strainer, by William Plummer, London.
1767   *6.75in (17.5cm) long 4oz*
$900-1,000   **WW**

A George III West country silver strainer, maker's mark only, possibly that of R.B. Symons, Exeter.
c1770   *4.5in (11cm) long 2.2oz*
$180-250   **WW**

A George II silver lemon strainer, by Peter & Ann Bateman, London.
1792   *7in (18cm) long 2.9oz*
$300-400   **LAW**

A George III Irish Provincial silver Freedom box, Cork, maker's mark 'WR' conjoined for William Reynolds, the cover with the arms and motto of Cork, the base inscribed 'The Freedom of the City of Cork presented in this box to the Right Honourable Isaac Barré as a publk. testemony (sic) of his distinguished abilities and his constant attention in the british (sic) house of commons to the interest of his native country Ireland 13 Aug. 1768'.

Isaac Barré was a soldier and politician, born Dublin 1726, gazetted ensign 1746, rose under Woolf to Lt. Col., wounded in the cheek at Quebec, 1759. He sat in Parliament 1761-1790 and held office under Lord Bute, Pitt, Rockingham and Shelburne. He died 20 July 1802.
c1768   *3.5in (8.5cm) long 5.3oz*
$3,800-5,000   **WW**

ESSENTIAL REFERENCE - JOHN HENRY PELLY

John Henry Pelly of Upton, Essex (31 March 1777-13 August 1852) was Governor of Hudson's Bay Company for 30 years. He was a fourth-generation sailor turned London merchant appointed to the Hudson's Bay Company at the time of its merger with the North West Company. Instrumental in enlarging the company's trading rights and active Arctic exploration led to Pelly's name being commemorated on many geographical features in the Yukon and Arctic. He was created baronet in 1840, eighteen years after the date of this box. As a director and, finally (1841-42) Governor of the Bank of England, Pelly solidified the deep relationship between the Company and the Bank.

A George III Irish silver Freedom box, Dublin, maker's mark worn, the base inscribed 'EASTER ASSEMBLY 1769, The Corporation of the City of DUBLIN......to WILLIAM SUPPLE, as a mark of the Corporation's esteem.....'.
1769   *3.25in (8cm) diam 2.5oz*
$3,200-3,800   **WW**

A George III silver presentation box, by John Reily, London, the base with inscription'.
1822   *3.5in (9cm) diam 4.9oz*
$9,500-10,500   **WW**

A George I silver hand-bell, by Benjamin Pyne, London, Britannia standard.
1719   *4.5in (11.5cm) high 8.35oz*
$7,500-9,000   **DN**

SILVER & METALWARE

A George III silver sugar caster, crest engraved, London.
1767   *11.68oz*
$250-320   **BELL**

A Dutch silver inkstand, by Lambrecht Van Der Woord, Vlissingen, inkwell with a later hinged cover and a sander, with an armorial beneath a Marquess' coronet, lacking finial and scissor trimmers.
1785   9.25in (23.5cm) long 34oz
$6,500-7,500   **WW**

A Victorian cast silver owl ink well, by Henry Wilkinson & Co., Sheffield, the hinged head with glass eyes, with pen holders and pot.
1851   6in (15.5cm) high 20oz
$7,500-9,000   **WW**

A silver inkstand, London.
1905   11in (27.5cm) wide 27.87oz
$550-700   **BELL**

A silver eagle, on a wooden stand.
23.75in (60cm) high
$9,000-10,000   **SWO**

A pair of German silver models of a parrot and parakeet, with detachable heads and hinged wings, with import marks for Chester 1905, importer's mark of Samuel Landeck.
12in (30.5cm) high 35.5oz
$5,500-6,500   **WW**

A George IV silver swing-handled basket, by Robert Gainsford, Sheffield, engraved with coat of arms and French inscription 'Don de Dame Cathe Marchant Vve de Beauvior a Mademoiselle Matilde Priaulx'.
1824   13.75in (35cm) long 46.2oz
$2,500-3,800   **BELL**

An Irish George III silver dish ring, Dublin, maker's mark 'WH'.
1774   8in (20.5cm) diam 11oz
$2,500-3,200   **MAB**

A George III Irish silvergilt neo-classical épergne, maker's mark 'MH' or 'HW', Dublin, no date.
c1775   23.75in (60cm) wide 116oz
$7,000-7,500   **LAW**

A late George I silver sauce boat, by John Clifton, London, engraved with a crest.
1726   7.75in (19.5cm) long 14.1oz
$3,200-3,800   **LAW**

A George III silver-gilt wax jack, by Charles Aldridge and Henry Green, London, engraved with a crowned 'K'.
1770   5.5in (13.5cm) high 5.3oz
$1,900-2,500   **WW**

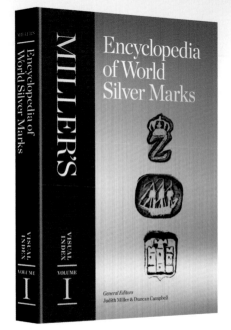
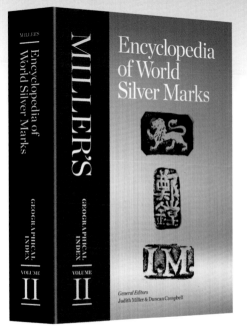
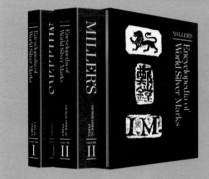

SILVER & METALWARE

ESSENTIAL REFERENCE - WINE LABELS

Although still made today, wine labels had their heyday in 1770-1860. These labels, also used for sauces, were typically made of silver or silver plate with materials such as enamel, pottery, porcelain, ivory, bone or Mother-of pearl also in common use.

- There are many approaches to the study of wine labels. Some collectors concentrate on the great variety of designs, others on the multiplicity of names on labels, on the silversmiths and other makers, or on the place of manufacture.
- Labels in the form of a single vine leaf were enormously popular from the 1820s into the Victorian period, but by the 1860s improvements in the production of wine enabled it to be served direct from the bottle while legislation permitted the sale of single bottles of wine with paper labels.
- More than 500 silversmiths are recorded as having made labels. Alongside the luxurious cast silver-gilt versions from the great London makers such as Paul Storr or Benjamin Smith, wine labels were produced by the jobbing silversmiths of regional England, Ireland and Scotland and in India and the Far East.

A George III silver armorial wine label, London, with Bacchanalian cherubs, incised 'CLARET', maker's mark only 'JC' or 'IC' script, possibly for James Clark, London.
c1770   *2.5in (6cm) long 0.7oz*
$160-200   WW

A George III silver-gilt wine label, by Samuel Meriton, maker's mark 's.M'.
c1780   *1.75in (4.5cm) long 0.3oz*
$500-550   WW

A George III provincial silver wine label, incised and blackened 'HOLLAND', maker's mark mis-struck, probably Exeter.
c1800   *1.75in (4.5cm) long 0.2oz*
$250-320   WW

A George III silver wine label, by Phipps and Robinson, London, incised 'ORANGE.WINE'.
1793   *1.75in (4.5cm) long 0.5oz*
$450-500   WW

A George III cast silver wine label, by Benjamin Smith, London, four leaf clover form, pierced 'TENERIFFE'.

This is a rare form.
1807   *2.25in (5.5cm) long 1.5oz*
$1,600-2,300   WW

Judith Picks

This is an interesting wine label for many reasons. It is Scottish which increases the value. It is an early 19thC label given as a prize with the inscription 'To Mrs Rhind for excellent Gooseberry Wine, from the Cal: Hort: Soc: 1814'. It also has the original handwritten recipe for gooseberry wine in a letter to Mrs Rind, dated 1808.

A George III Scottish silver 'prize' wine label, by William Peat, Edinburgh.
1814   *3in (8cm) long 1.55oz*
$900-1,000   LAW

A George III silver armorial wine label, London, marks partially lost in piercing, pierced 'CLARET'.

1815   *1.5in (4cm) high 0.7oz*
$900-950   WW

A George III silver wine label, by Edward Farrell, London, pierced 's. CHAMPAGNE'.
1817   *2.25in (6cm) long 0.6oz*
$650-700   WW

A George III silver wine label, by Edward Farrell, London, pierced 'ROUSSILLION'.
1819   *2.5in (6cm) long 0.6oz*
$500-550   WW

A George IV provincial silver wine label, by Barber and Whitwell, York, incised 'sHERRY'.

c1820   *2in (5cm) long 0.3oz*

$180-250   **WW**

An early 19thC silver 'Anti Corn Law League' wine label, by Mordan, embossed 'FREE', pierced 'MADEIRA'.

2in (5.5cm) long 0.2oz

$900-950   **WW**

An early 19thC Scottish provincial silver wine label, by Andrew Davidson, Arbroath, incised 's'.

c1835   *2in (5cm) long 0.4oz*

$700-800   **WW**

A silver wine label, pierced 'P', maker's mark partially lost in piercing 's?', London.

1837   *1.5in (4cm) long 0.7oz*

$180-230   **WW**

An early 19thC Scottish provincial silver wine label, by James Morrison, Fochabers, incised 'H. WHISKY'.

c1840   *1.5in (4cm) long 0.2oz*

$500-550   **WW**

A rare Victorian cast silver-gilt oak leaf wine label, by Rawlings and Sumner, London, engraved to the rear with the crest and badge.

This wine label has regimental interest. The Badge of the 22nd Regiment of Foot is engraved upon the reverse. The regiment was raised by the then Duke of Norfolk in 1689 and was able to boast an independent existence of over 300 years.

1855   *2.5in (6cm) wide 0.49oz*

$1,500-2,300   **L&T**

A pair of George III silver-mounted bottle coasters, London.

1799   *6in (15.5cm) diam*

$650-750   **BELL**

An early 19thC Sheffield plated decanter trolley, unmarked.

c1820   *13.75in (35cm) long*

$650-750   **WW**

A Victorian silver-plated decanter wagon, by Elkington & Co., numbered '3758' to back of wagon.

16.5in (42cm) long

$800-950   **TEN**

A German silver fox head stirrup cup, with import marks for London, importer's mark of Israel Segalov.

1925   *5.5in (14cm) high 6.8oz*

$950-1,100   **WW**

SILVER & METALWARE

An 18thC French provincial silver wine taster, probably Troyes, inscribed 'F.N. CHARDON', marks worn.

c1762   *4.5in (11.5cm) long 4oz*

$900–1,000   **WW**

A George III silver wine taster, London, maker's mark 'I'?, partially worn, inscribed 'James Brett, 1800'.

1800   *4.25in (10.5cm) diam 3.2oz*

$750–900   **WW**

A 19thC French silver wine taster, with maker's mark of 'AB', inscribed 'J. BARRAUD V'.

4.5in (11cm) long 2.6oz

$300–350   **WW**

A George III silver wine funnel, by Hester Bateman, London.

1781   *5in (12.5cm) high 2.7oz*

$450–500   **WW**

A George III Scottish silver wine funnel, with a matching circular wine funnel stand, Edinburgh.

1801   *5.5oz*

$750–800   **BELL**

A George III silver wine funnel, by G. McHattie, Edinburgh.

c1820   *5in (12.5cm) high 3.5oz*

$400–500   **L&T**

A West Country silver brandy pan, maker's mark three times 'TF' conjoined, for Thomas Foote, Exeter, the front with a crest, the underside scratch initialed 'M.V' over 'M.G', '1692'.

For details of the maker and a reference to this brandy pan see: Kent, T., 'West Country Silver Spoons and Their Makers, 1550-1750', J.H. Bourdon-Smith Ltd., 1992, page 89, M.48.

c1692   *12in (30cm) long 12.3oz*

$1,900–2,500   **WW**

A George II silver brandy saucepan, with a later wooden handle, the cover lacking, maker's mark 'J.E' for John Edwards II, London.

c1749   *21.48oz*

$750–800   **BELL**

A George III silver brandy pan, by Charles Wright, London.

1778   *12.5in (31.5cm) long 16.4oz*

$650–750   **WW**

A small Commonwealth silver wine cup, London, maker's mark partially worn.

1657   *2.25in (5.5cm) high 2.2oz*

$1,000–1,200   **WW**

An Old Sheffield plated honey skep, unmarked, possibly by Morton or Watson and Co.

c1790   *5.5in (14cm) high*

$650-700   **WW**

A George III old Sheffield plated cucumber slicer, unmarked.

This ingenious device is surprisingly 'modern', with a wooden turning handle that moves the cucumber toward the slicing blade.

c1800   *8.75in (22cm) long*

$1,500-2,000   **WW**

A Napier silver-plated coffee machine, by William Padley & Son of Sheffield, silver plating worn, the ivory knobs cracked and stained.

$400-500   **ECGW**

A Victorian silver-plated urn, with tap.

22in (56cm) high

$250-320   **TRI**

A Charles II pewter tankard, the lid with owner's initials 'W S' over 'C W', with maker's mark to interior 'L S'.

7.25in (18.5cm) high

$950-1,100   **WW**

A 17thC Continental pewter broadrim charger, with initials 'F R' and a stag head with two stars, the other dated and initialed 'D S C'.

1664   *17.5in (44cm) diam*

$900-1,000   **WW**

A pewter flagon, the late 17thC-style vessel, with inscription 'RB. IP. Wardens 1753'.

15.25in (39cm) high

$650-750   **CHEF**

A Regency bronze and marble inkstand, modeled as a hinged shell opening to ink and sand pots, on the back of a dolphin.

c1815   *4.75in (12cm) high*

$1,300-1,900   **L&T**

A 19thC Victorian copper and brass mash tun, tin-lined interior with brass side handles and tap.

38in (96cm) diam

$3,200-3,800   **L&T**

An 18thC set of six brass cylindrical measures, graded from a quarter gill to an imperial quart, engraved 'The Borough of Bewdley, Worcestershire'.

The historic engraving adds to its appeal. The town of Bewdley in the Wye Forest was made a borough and a weekly market by Edward IV in 1472 but lost it in the government reorganisation 502 years later.

$2,500-3,200   **BRI**

A Boston, Massachusetts pewter tankard, bearing the touch of Robert Bonnynge (Bonning or Bonynge).

c1750   *7.5in (19cm) high*

$22,000-23,000   **POOK**

A Philadelphia pewter tankard, bearing the touch of William Will.

c1780   *8in (20.5cm) high*

$19,000-25,000   **POOK**

A Philadelphia pewter tankard, attributed to William Will, with beaded bands and an engraved cartouche with a monogram.

This is an exceptional example of Philadelphia pewter and one of the finest American tankards extant.

c1780   *7.75in (20cm) high*

$32,000-38,000   **POOK**

A New York pewter tankard, bearing the touch of William Kirby.

c1780   *7in (18cm) high*

$5,000-5,700   **POOK**

An 18thC Boston IC-type pewter tankard.

6.75in (17cm) high

$7,500-9,000   **POOK**

A Hartford, Connecticut pewter tankard, bearing the touch of Thomas and Sherman Boardman.

c1840   *8in (20.5cm) high*

$1,000-1,200   **POOK**

A Philadelphia pewter sugar bowl, attributed to William Will.

c1780   *4.75in (12cm) high*

$3,200-3,800   **POOK**

A Castleton, Vermont pewter beaker, bearing the touch of Ebenezer Southmayd.

c1810   *4.25in (11cm) high*

$3,800-5,000   **POOK**

A Philadelphia pewter teapot, attributed to Johann Alberti.

c1765   *7in (18cm) high*

$13,000-15,000   **POOK**

A façon de Venise latticino wine glass, probably 17thC, with aventurine and opaque white decoration, on hollow swag-molded baluster stem.

7in (17.5cm) high

$1,300-1,900   TEN

A baluster wine glass, the funnel bowl on a knopped stem, with teardrop inclusion above a domed foot, the foot trimmed.

c1720   *5.5in (14cm) high*

$500-550   WW

An early 18thC wine glass, engraved with full Royal Armorial, on multi knop stem, the lower knop with twisted bubble inclusions.

7.5in (18.5cm) high

$3,200-3,800   L&T

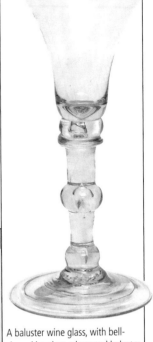

A baluster wine glass, with bell-shaped bowl on a knopped baluster stem above a folded foot.

c1730   *6.25in (16cm) high*

$400-500   WW

ESSENTIAL REFERENCE - JACOBITE

The word Jacobite comes from Jacobus, the Latin version of the name James, and the original Jacobites were supporters of King James II, usurped from the throne of England by his daughter Mary and her husband William of Orange in 1688. Later - even after James' death - it became a more general term for those who favored the restoration of the Stuart dynasty. The main emblem of the Jacobites is a white rose. It is widely believed that the rose signifies James Francis Edward Stuart (The Old Pretender). It is a common symbol on many Jacobite glasses, often in conjunction with two buds, representing James' sons. An open bud - generally to the left - alludes to his direct heir, Prince Charles Edward Stuart (Bonnie Prince Charlie - The Young Pretender). Other plants, insects and birds all appear on Jacobite glasses; bees signify undiminished loyalty to the royal lineage; moths, butterflies, dragonflies and beetles all pertain to fertility and rebirth; honeysuckle, carnations, pears, apples, vines are also often engraved, in addition to the rose. There are also Latin words and phrases: Fiat (let it come to pass), Redeat (it returns), Reviriscit (it flourishes), Audentior Ibo (I go more boldly) adorn glasses from which toasts to the enterprise would have been taken. The rejoinder to these toasts would have been 'to the King over the water'.

A mid-18thC Jacobite engraved airtwist wine glass, with engraved carnations, on a knopped airtwist stem.

6in (15cm) high

$1,500-2,300   L&T

A mid-18thC Jacobite wine glass, with engraved honeysuckle and a bee, on a swollen knopped plain stem.

5.75in (14.5cm) high

$750-1,000   L&T

A mid-18thC Jacobite wine glass, the pan top bowl with engraved floral border of rose and bud, carnation, corn flower and honeysuckle, on a swollen knopped air twist stem.

6in (15.5cm) high

$1,600-2,300   L&T

A mid-18thC Jacobite wine glass, with engraved rose head and buds with oak leaf and inscribed 'FIAT', above a tapered air twist stem.

6.5in (16.5cm) high

$2,500-3,200   L&T

A mid-18thC wine glass, the triple-knopped stem, with white, red and green enamel twist.

6.5in (16.5cm) high

$3,200-3,800   L&T

A color-twist wine glass, the rounded funnel bowl on a blue, red, green and white twist stem.
c1755   5.75in (14.5cm) high
$3,200-3,800   **TEN**

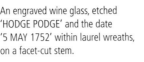

An engraved wine glass, etched 'HODGE PODGE' and the date '5 MAY 1752' within laurel wreaths, on a facet-cut stem.

This Glasgow club was founded in the 18thC and is still in existence. Records commenced on 5 May 1752 and Dr John Moore was a famous founding member. In its original form the club had a literary nature. They started out meeting monthly at seven but this was soon changed to five - 'the dinner hour among the better classes' - according to John Strang in his 1856 ' Glasgow and its clubs'. He continues 'with whist and conversation the evening passed till nine o'clock arrived'.
c1760   6.75in (17cm) high
$1,300-1,900   **L&T**

A Beilby enameled wine glass, the ogee bowl painted in white, with foliate swags on an opaque twist stem.
c1760   5.75in (14.5cm) high
$1,500-2,000   **TEN**

A mid/late 18thC Jacobite engraved airtwist stem wine glass, on a double-knobbed air twist stem, the domed foot engraved 'REDEAT'.
    6.25in (16cm) high
$1,900-2,500   **L&T**

An 18thC Newcastle armorial wine glass, with engraved Dutch armorial with supporters, on a multi-knopped stem, the lower knop with air bubble decoration.
    7.5in (19cm) high
$1,900-2,500   **L&T**

A wine glass, with bell-shaped bowl on a knopped stem, with double series opaque twist.
c1765   6in (15cm) high
$230-280   **WW**

A wine glass or champagne flute, engraved below with 'success to the Thwaite Colliery', the reverse with an armorial crest of a rearing bull above a ducal coronet, the monogram 'JS' below, the stem cut with facets.

This glass is thought to be the only 18thC one known to commemorate the opening of a colliery. Thwaite Colliery, about 4 miles outside Leeds between Hunslet and Rothwell, was owned by John Smyth, and the heraldic bull is his family crest. The mine was opened in 1780 and closed in 1796. The engineer who designed the main shafts was John Smeaton, better known for constructing the lighthouse now on Plymouth Ho. Smyth held various offices during his life being, MP for Pontefract, a Privy Councillor, a Lord of the Admiralty and the principal proprietorof the Aire and Calder Navigation Company which owned the mine.
c1780   6.5in (16.5cm) high
$2,800-3,500   **WW**

A color-twist wine glass, the bell shaped bowl on a stem with blue, brown and white twist.
c1770   6.5in (16.5cm) high
$5,500-6,500   **TEN**

An engraved color-twist wine glass, the ogee bowl decorated with tulip and moth, the stem with red, green and white twist.
c1770   5.75in (14.5cm) high
$1,900-2,500   **TEN**

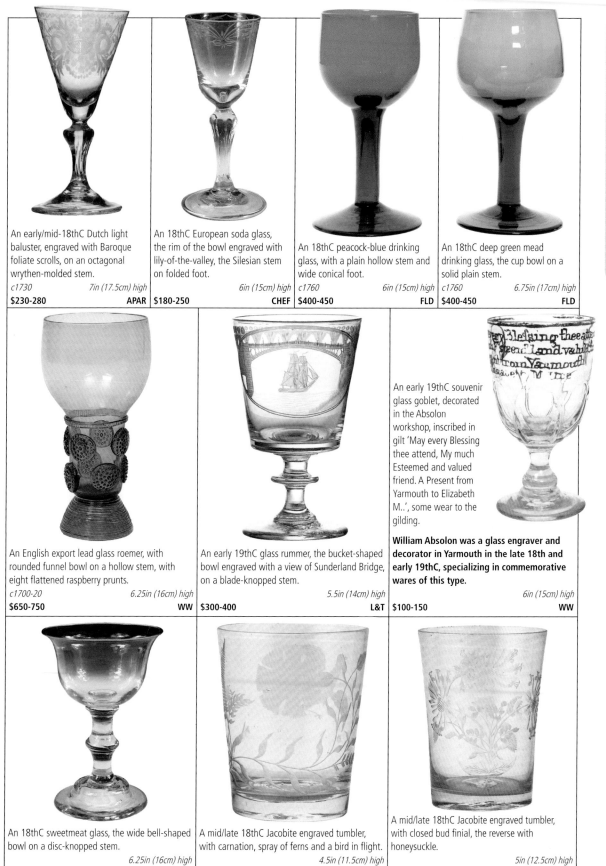

An early/mid-18thC Dutch light baluster, engraved with Baroque foliate scrolls, on an octagonal wrythen-molded stem.

c1730   *7in (17.5cm) high*

$230-280   **APAR**

An 18thC European soda glass, the rim of the bowl engraved with lily-of-the-valley, the Silesian stem on folded foot.

6in (15cm) high

$180-250   **CHEF**

An 18thC peacock-blue drinking glass, with a plain hollow stem and wide conical foot.

c1760   *6in (15cm) high*

$400-450   **FLD**

An 18thC deep green mead drinking glass, the cup bowl on a solid plain stem.

c1760   *6.75in (17cm) high*

$400-450   **FLD**

An English export lead glass roemer, with rounded funnel bowl on a hollow stem, with eight flattened raspberry prunts.

c1700-20   *6.25in (16cm) high*

$650-750   **WW**

An early 19thC glass rummer, the bucket-shaped bowl engraved with a view of Sunderland Bridge, on a blade-knopped stem.

5.5in (14cm) high

$300-400   **L&T**

An early 19thC souvenir glass goblet, decorated in the Absolon workshop, inscribed in gilt 'May every Blessing thee attend, My much Esteemed and valued friend. A Present from Yarmouth to Elizabeth M..', some wear to the gilding.

William Absolon was a glass engraver and decorator in Yarmouth in the late 18th and early 19thC, specializing in commemorative wares of this type.

6in (15cm) high

$100-150   **WW**

An 18thC sweetmeat glass, the wide bell-shaped bowl on a disc-knopped stem.

6.25in (16cm) high

$400-450   **CHEF**

A mid/late 18thC Jacobite engraved tumbler, with carnation, spray of ferns and a bird in flight.

4.5in (11.5cm) high

$1,000-1,100   **L&T**

A mid/late 18thC Jacobite engraved tumbler, with closed bud finial, the reverse with honeysuckle.

5in (12.5cm) high

$800-950   **L&T**

A wine bottle, of half-size onion shape, applied with a seal with the Prussian eagle of the Royal Arms of Brandenburg or Prussia, with inscription 'Ad Pavlt de Royal', the surface degraded, dated.

Possibly made for the court of the Friedrich William, The Great Elector of Brandenburg-Prussia 1640-88.

1664   *5.5in (14cm) high*
$2,500-3,200   **WW**

A late 17th/early 18thC mallet-shaped wine bottle, with kick-in base and short tapering neck, encrusted with barnacle.

6.5in (16.5cm) high
$180-230   **WW**

A freeblown English onion bottle, of flattened pancake form with string rim and base pontil.

c1700   *5.75in (14.5cm) high*
$300-350   **MART**

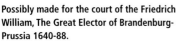

An English olive-green glass onion bottle, with an inscription 'DR. MARSHALL 1723'.

1723   *6.75in (17cm) high*
$4,400-5,700   **L&T**

An 18thC amethyst glass decanter, with a tapering neck and a squat globular body with six bands, with diamond-point engraving of vine, peacocks and flowers.

7in (18cm) high
$5,000-6,500   **WW**

A pair of 18thC Bristol Blue glass decanters, decorated in gilt with 'Rum' and 'Hollands'.

8in (20cm) high
$90-120   **LOCK**

An amethyst glass decanter, with stopper, perhaps American, molded with starburst designs and diamond banding.

c1820   *10.75in (27cm) high*
$130-180   **WW**

A pair of early 19thC-style 'Bristol Blue' ship's decanters and disc stoppers, with 'Sherry' and 'Port'.

9.5in (24cm) high
$350-400   **HW**

A mid-18thC Duke of Cumberland spirit flask, with naively engraved portrait of the Duke of Cumberland, above trophies of war and named above 'Duke William for ever', the reverse dated '1750'.

1750   *7in (18cm) high*
$1,900-2,500   **L&T**

ESSENTIAL REFERENCE - JACOBITE DECANTERS

The survival of Jacobite drinking glasses is well recorded. The survival of decanters however is much rarer. They follow the same designs as the glasses, using the same iconography and symbolism which would have been apparent to the Jacobite supporters. It is not clear why the survival of decanters is quite scarce, but it is thought that the larger stature of them may have been too much of a show of support for the cause and harder to disguise to the non-Jacobite community.

A mid-18thC pair of Jacobite glass decanters, engraved with rose head flanked by open and closed buds and to the reverse with chrysanthemum and buds.

10in (25cm) and 9.75in (24.5cm) high

$5,500-7,000   **L&T**

A late 18thC Irish 'Bushmills' decanter and stopper, engraved with 'Whiskey' flanked by shamrocks, inscribed above 'The Bushmills Old Distillery', and below 'Co Antrim Ireland'.

10.75in (27cm) high

$750-900   **L&T**

A silver-mounted glass claret jug, by John Figg, London, the mounts with masks and fruiting decoration.

1860   *11in (28cm) high*

$700-800   **WW**

A late Victorian claret jug, star-incised, with silver mount and hinged cover with thumb-piece, Sheffield.

1871   *9.25in (23.5cm) high*

$500-550   **TRI**

A pair of cut-glass decanters, attributed to Thomas Webb, with hobnail- and diamond-cut decoration, with original stoppers, finial missing.

15in (38cm) high

$2,300-2,800   **DN**

A 19thC Temperance wine bottle, engraved with a figure holding a banner titled 'Father Matthew For Ever', the reverse with fruiting grapevine.

Theobold Matthew (1790-1856) was an Irish Catholic temperance reformer credited with the establishment of the Cork Total Abstinence Society, from whence The Pledge originated. In 1849 he was welcomed in New York and spent two years spreading his message of teetotalism.

A Victorian silver-gilt mounted cut glass claret jug, by Finley and Taylor for Horace Woodward & Co., London.

1891   *11.75in (29.5cm) high*

$1,000-1,200   **WW**

An Edwardian silver-mounted glass claret jug, by Horace Woodward & Co. Ltd., London.

1907   *11.25in (28.5cm) high*

$700-800   **WW**

A beer jug, with initials above the date, with barley and hops, dated.

1773   *6.75in (17.5cm) high*

$800-950   **CHEF**

13.25in (33.5cm) high

$450-550   **WW**

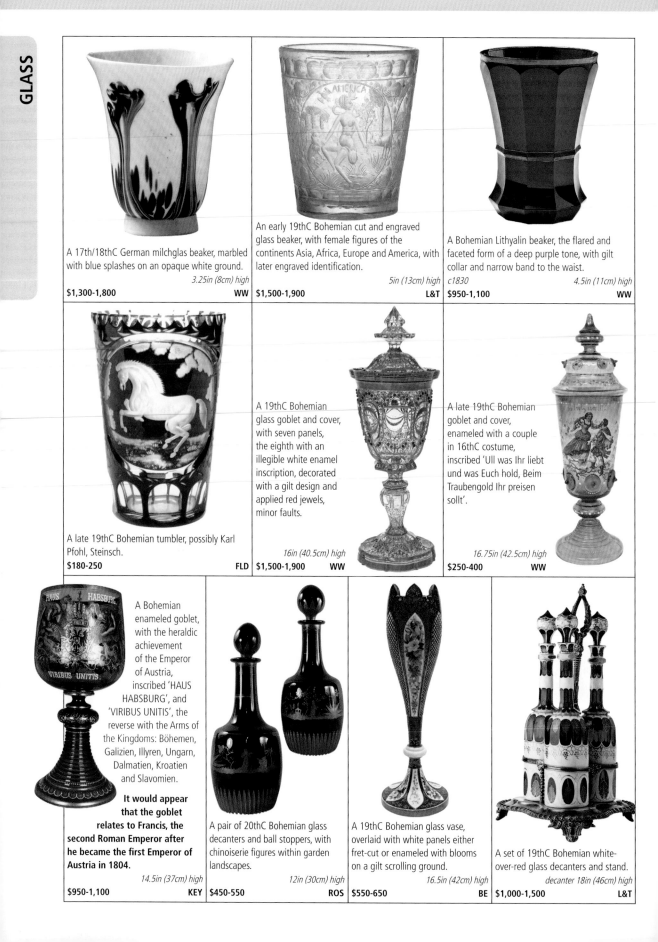

A 17th/18thC German milchglas beaker, marbled with blue splashes on an opaque white ground.

3.25in (8cm) high

$1,300-1,800   **WW**

An early 19thC Bohemian cut and engraved glass beaker, with female figures of the continents Asia, Africa, Europe and America, with later engraved identification.

5in (13cm) high

$1,500-1,900   **L&T**

A Bohemian Lithyalin beaker, the flared and faceted form of a deep purple tone, with gilt collar and narrow band to the waist.

c1830   *4.5in (11cm) high*

$950-1,100   **WW**

A late 19thC Bohemian tumbler, possibly Karl Pfohl, Steinsch.

$180-250   **FLD**

A 19thC Bohemian glass goblet and cover, with seven panels, the eighth with an illegible white enamel inscription, decorated with a gilt design and applied red jewels, minor faults.

16in (40.5cm) high

$1,500-1,900   **WW**

A late 19thC Bohemian goblet and cover, enameled with a couple in 16thC costume, inscribed 'Ull was Ihr liebt und was Euch hold, Beim Traubengold Ihr preisen sollt'.

16.75in (42.5cm) high

$250-400   **WW**

A Bohemian enameled goblet, with the heraldic achievement of the Emperor of Austria, inscribed 'HAUS HABSBURG', and 'VIRIBUS UNITIS', the reverse with the Arms of the Kingdoms: Böhemen, Galizien, Illyren, Ungarn, Dalmatien, Kroatien and Slavomien.

It would appear that the goblet relates to Francis, the second Roman Emperor after he became the first Emperor of Austria in 1804.

14.5in (37cm) high

$950-1,100   **KEY**

A pair of 20thC Bohemian glass decanters and ball stoppers, with chinoiserie figures within garden landscapes.

12in (30cm) high

$450-550   **ROS**

A 19thC Bohemian glass vase, overlaid with white panels either fret-cut or enameled with blooms on a gilt scrolling ground.

16.5in (42cm) high

$550-650   **BE**

A set of 19thC Bohemian white-over-red glass decanters and stand.

decanter 18in (46cm) high

$1,000-1,500   **L&T**

A George III silver two-bottle oil and vinegar stand, by R. Piercy, London, gadroon wirework frame.

The crest is that of Knatchbull, created baronets of Mersham Hatch, Kent in 1641. Most likely for Sir Edward Knatchbull (1704-1789), 7th Baronet, MP for Armagh.

1767 *9in (23cm) high 16oz*

$1,900-2,500 **WW**

A late 16th/early 17thC façon de Venise tazza.

6.25in (16cm) high

$2,000-2,500 **WW**

A 19thC cranberry glass epergne.

22in (56cm) high

$250-320 **LOC**

A late 19thC Moser glass vase, enameled with a capercaillie perched on fir trees, unmarked.

8in (20cm) high

$180-250 **FLD**

A late 19thC Continental glass vase, hand enameled with birds, insects, flowers and foliage, with internal air trap lattice pattern, unmarked.

10in (25cm) high

$50-60 **FLD**

A late 19thC cranberry glass bell, lacks clapper.

18.5in (47cm) high

$80-90 **FLD**

A late Georgian Nailsea miniature jug, decorated with white spotting over a sea-green ground.

4.5in (11cm) high

$500-550 **FLD**

A late Georgian Nailsea or Wrockwardine flask, with white splatter over the sea green ground.

c1800 *5.5in (14cm) high*

$300-400 **FLD**

A pair of 19thC Baccarat ormolu-mounted ruby glass vases.

13.5in (34cm) high

$2,500-3,200 **WW**

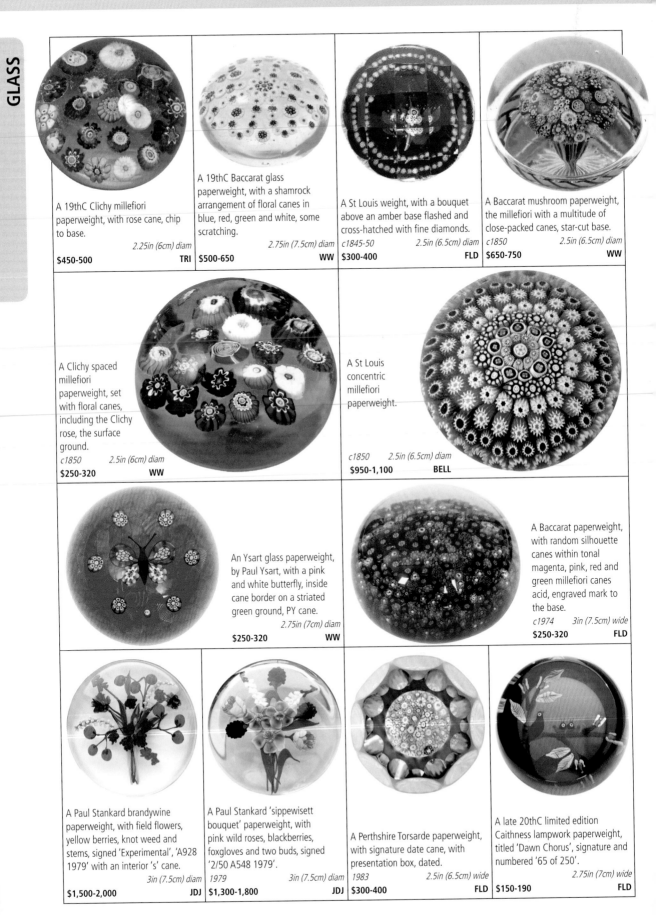

A 19thC Clichy millefiori paperweight, with rose cane, chip to base.

2.25in (6cm) diam

$450-500   **TRI**

A 19thC Baccarat glass paperweight, with a shamrock arrangement of floral canes in blue, red, green and white, some scratching.

2.75in (7.5cm) diam

$500-650   **WW**

A St Louis weight, with a bouquet above an amber base flashed and cross-hatched with fine diamonds.

c1845-50   2.5in (6.5cm) diam

$300-400   **FLD**

A Baccarat mushroom paperweight, the millefiori with a multitude of close-packed canes, star-cut base.

c1850   2.5in (6.5cm) diam

$650-750   **WW**

A Clichy spaced millefiori paperweight, set with floral canes, including the Clichy rose, the surface ground.

c1850   2.5in (6cm) diam

$250-320   **WW**

A St Louis concentric millefiori paperweight.

c1850   2.5in (6.5cm) diam

$950-1,100   **BELL**

An Ysart glass paperweight, by Paul Ysart, with a pink and white butterfly, inside cane border on a striated green ground, PY cane.

2.75in (7cm) diam

$250-320   **WW**

A Baccarat paperweight, with random silhouette canes within tonal magenta, pink, red and green millefiori canes acid, engraved mark to the base.

c1974   3in (7.5cm) wide

$250-320   **FLD**

A Paul Stankard brandywine paperweight, with field flowers, yellow berries, knot weed and stems, signed 'Experimental', 'A928 1979' with an interior 's' cane.

3in (7.5cm) diam

$1,500-2,000   **JDJ**

A Paul Stankard 'sippewisett bouquet' paperweight, with pink wild roses, blackberries, foxgloves and two buds, signed '2/50 A548 1979'.

1979   3in (7.5cm) diam

$1,300-1,800   **JDJ**

A Perthshire Torsarde paperweight, with signature date cane, with presentation box, dated.

1983   2.5in (6.5cm) wide

$300-400   **FLD**

A late 20thC limited edition Caithness lampwork paperweight, titled 'Dawn Chorus', signature and numbered '65 of 250'.

2.75in (7cm) wide

$150-190   **FLD**

A pair of William IV gilt and patinated-bronze candelabra, with cut-glass drops, on lion mask paw feet.

c1830 *18.25in (46cm) high*

$750-1,000 **BELL**

A pair of 19thC French gilt and patinated-bronze candelabra, after Clodion, on Sienna marble columns, signed 'Clodion'.

19in (48cm) high

$3,200-3,800 **L&T**

A pair of 19thC French gilt and patinated-bronze candlesticks, of standing Nubian boys holding torches, on Siena marble bases.

11in (28cm) high

$1,900-2,500 **WW**

A pair of Napoleon III ormolu and porcelain candelabra, in Louis XVI style.

25.25in (64cm) high

$1,000-1,100 **WW**

A pair of bronze and ormolu putto candlesticks, on red marble plinths.

16.5in (42cm) high

$1,900-2,500 **BELL**

A pair of 19thC Baccarat ceramic candlesticks, painted with ladies in medieval costume.

8.25in (21cm) high

$400-450 **TRI**

A pair of late 19thC French ormolu six-branch candelabra, each cupid figure holding a cornucopia of flowers.

25in (64cm) high

$2,100-2,500 **BELL**

A pair of 19thC Italian candelabra, with carved wood blackamoors, wearing gilt decorated tunics and ribbed pantaloons.

83in (211cm) high

$3,800-5,000 **CHOR**

A pair of late 19thC continental gilt-brass pricket candlesticks, in 17thC taste.

10in (52cm) high

$650-750 **DN**

A pair of late 19thC French gilt and patinated bronze candelabra, in Empire-style, with later faux candle light fittings.

18.5in (47cm) high

$1,900-2,500 **WW**

LIGHTING

ESSENTIAL REFERENCE - CHANDELIERS

Derived from the French word for candle, 'chandelle', which evolved from the Latin 'candere' meaning 'to shine or glow', the English word 'chandelier' didn't emerge until the 18thC. However, the artefacts it describes - ceiling-suspended light fittings with branches and holders for multiple sources of light - had been in use well before then. Wooden chandeliers of simple cross-like form had been employed since the early Middle Ages, while far more elaborate constructions in brass were developed during the Renaissance. Brass and other alloys have continued to be employed. Nevertheless, the medium the chandelier has been most closely associated with is glass, following the patenting in the late 17thC of lead oxide crystal which, being clearer and easier to cut, was particularly well suited to the refraction and reflection of light. Since then, innovations in the means of illumination candles, oil, gas and, finally, electricity - have been surpassed by the developments in design: from extravagant late Baroque, curvaceous Rococo, elegant Neo-Classical, and grand Empire, through the eclectic Victorian 'historical revivals', to sinuous Art Nouveau, geometrical Art Deco, and functional Modernism. Stylistically, there is much to choose from.

An 18thC Anglo-Dutch brass sixteen-light chandelier, with a tier of short scrolling arms terminating in flower heads.

29in (74cm) diam

$1,900-2,500   **L&T**

A late Louis XV gilt-bronze lantern, the finely cast frame with dividing mounts of scrolling brackets above trailing flowers, and surmounted by acorns.

30in (76cm) high

$8,000-9,500   **DN**

A George III brass lantern, the arched ogival supports above female term figures.

33in (84cm) high

$15,000-19,000   **DN**

An 18th/early 19thC Anglo-Dutch brass eight-light chandelier.

22in (56cm) high

$1,300-1,800   **L&T**

A Regency brass and cut-glass colza dish light, the colza oil reservoir in the form of a Classical vase, the rim of the dish surmounted by a pierced gallery with oak leaf decoration.

48in (122cm) high

$23,000-28,000   **DN**

One of a pair of Brighton Pavilion hanging lanterns, in the Brighton Pavilion style.

The Royal Pavilion, also known as the Brighton Pavilion, is a former royal residence. Beginning in 1787, it was built in three stages as a seaside retreat for George, Prince of Wales, who became the Prince Regent in 1811. It is built primarily in the Indo-Saracenic style prevalent in India for most of the 19thC. Between 1815 and 1822 the designer John Nash redesigned and greatly extended the Pavilion, and it is his work that is still visible today. The palace is striking in the middle of Brighton, for its Indo-Islamic exterior is unique. The fanciful interior design, primarily by Frederick Crace, was heavily influenced by both Chinese and Indian fashion (with Mughal and Islamic architectural elements). It is a prime example of the exoticism that was an alternative to more Classical mainstream taste in the Regency style.

$3,800-5,000 pair   **DN**

A Charles X tôle chandelier, with green and gilt decoration, with the original glass drip pans.

This is a high quality chandelier in outstanding original condition. It also has excellent provenance being owned by Queen Juliana of the Netherlands and from the Soestdijk Palace.

20in (50cm) high

$3,200-3,800   **DN**

A 20thC Louis XV-style birdcage sixteen-light chandelier, electrified.

46in (117cm) high

$3,800-5,000   **L&T**

A pair of ormolu five-branch wall lights, with lyre-shaped backs and mask head ribbon type surmounts.

55in (140cm) high

$1,900-2,500   CHOR

A pair of wall lights, of early 18thC style, with engraved and silvered glass with twin light fittings.

An 18thC pair was purchased by HRH The Duke of Gloucester, York House, St. James from Messrs. Phillips of Hitchin, May 1937. From these, a further four lights were reproduced, one pair going to HRH Duke of Gloucester, the other pair remaining with Messrs. Phillips of Hitchin and can be seen in Edward Wenham's 'Old Furniture for Modern Rooms', plate 4, published by Bell & Sons Ltd., 1939.

24.5in (62cm) high

$2,300-2,800   SWO

A pair of late 19thC bronze four-branch wall lights, each branch entwined with dragon-headed serpents.

By repute, these were removed from the Midland Grand Hotel at St Pancras, London which opened in 1873 and was designed by Sir George Gilbert Scott (1811-1878).

20in (50cm) deep

$1,300-1,900   SWO

A pair of Regency-style chinoiserie metal wall lanterns, the pagoda tops hung with bells, decorated with gold chinoiseries.

25in (63cm) high

$2,300-2,800   DN

Two of a set of four Restoration ormolu wall lights, each with a backplate decorated with a coat of arms and war trophies.

21in (53cm) high

$1,900-2,500 set   WW

A late 19thC Italian narwhal tusk and gilt-metal lantern, with an orb and cross finial above six glass panels, one with a hinged door above scroll leaf decoration, possibly Venetian.

To be sold with Cites Article 10 (nontransferable) License, No: 547080/01.

the lantern 70in (178cm) high

$3,200-3,800   WW

A late 19thC Deccan standard oil lamp, topped with a cockerel cast reservoir above a thirteen light tray.

78in (198cm) high

$650-1,250   CHOR

A pair of Venetian gondola-type tôle lanterns, each hexagonal lantern with coronet finial and glass panels.

89.75in (228cm) high

$1,000-1,250   CHOR

A Georgian garnet and gold pendant, the central locket compartment containing hair.

2in (5cm) long

$250-320　　　　　　　**LAW**

A Georgian rose-cut diamond-set Maltese Cross pin, in unmarked yellow and white metal.

1.25in (3cm) wide

$800-950　　　　　　　**ROS**

A Georgian diamond and amethyst-set pin, of cross form.

1.5in (4cm) wide

$1,300-1,800　　　　　**ROS**

A George III gold, diamond-set and white enameled urn mourning ring, the top reveals a locket compartment, detailed within the shank 'Henry Neve Ob 12'.

1768　　　　　size K 0.12oz

$5,500-6,500　　　　　**BELL**

A Georgian garnet and pearl cluster gold ring.

size N

$450-500　　　　　　　**LAW**

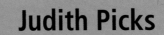

An early 19thC pendant, set with amethysts, hair locket compartment to the center, with a gold twin circular link neckchain, the pin fitting lacking.

$300-350　　　　　　　**BELL**

An early Victorian gilt-metal mounted eye miniature pin, engraved to the back 'M.RYE'.

$950-1,100　　　　　　**BELL**

A 19thC gold mounted ceramic pin, with a mountainous lakeside scene with buildings.

$130-180　　　　　　　**BELL**

Judith Picks

The provenance in this piece is all important - anything that is confidently linked to Lord Nelson is highly desirable. The hair sample included in this locket closely matches verified examples. As is well recorded, Emma was given all of Nelson's hair and was generous in presenting clips to well wishers. This locket may have been commissioned by Emma to give to an important well-wisher, or possibly a sympathetic admirer, both of whom thought it beyond reason to state its provenance.

A verre églomisé locket, depicting Emma Hamilton with a cage resting on a pediment inscribed 'NELSON' 'Obt21Octr', with probable lock of Nelson's hair to the reverse.

c1805-06　　2in (5cm) high

$2,500-3,200　　**CM**

A Victorian gold micromosaic pin, with a guard outside a gatehouse, in a fitted case.

1.75in (4.5cm) diam 0.92oz

$500-650　　　　　　　**BELL**

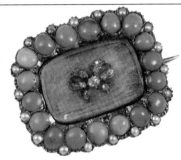

A Victorian turquoise and diamond pin, with small pearls.

1in (2.5cm) wide

$300-400   **LAW**

A Victorian enamel and pearl gold pin, with locket compartment to the reverse.

1.25in (3cm) diam

$250-320   **LAW**

A Victorian gold and seed pearl-set pin, the back glazed with a locket compartment.

0.27oz

$180-250   **BELL**

A 1900s diamond pin, set with cushion-shaped and circular diamonds, detachable pin fitting, one diamond deficient.

$1,300-1,900   **MAB**

A Victorian silver and gold pin, of flower head form, with graduated old brilliant-cut diamonds.

1in (2.5cm) wide

$1,900-2,300   **LAW**

A Victorian diamond and carbuncle garnet pin, with Faith, Hope, Charity and serpentine motifs.

$2,500-3,200   **BELL**

A Victorian pin, mounted with the carved coral portrait of a lady, with case.

$750-900   **BELL**

A Victorian pin, with cushion-shaped and rose-cut diamonds, with a detachable pin, hair ornament pin, fitted case.

$3,800-5,000   **BELL**

A 19thC boat-shape pin, with a cushion-shaped emerald within a gold openwork design, set with twelve graduated pear-shaped emeralds and sixteen old brilliant-cut or rose-cut diamonds.

2.5in (6.5cm) long

$7,500-10,000   **LAW**

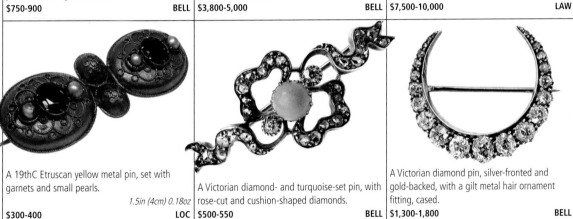

A 19thC Etruscan yellow metal pin, set with garnets and small pearls.

1.5in (4cm) 0.18oz

$300-400   **LOC**

A Victorian diamond- and turquoise-set pin, with rose-cut and cushion-shaped diamonds.

$500-550   **BELL**

A Victorian diamond pin, silver-fronted and gold-backed, with a gilt metal hair ornament fitting, cased.

$1,300-1,800   **BELL**

A late 19thC foil-backed emerald and rose diamond pin, probably Austro-Hungarian, with fitted case.
$750-900 BELL

A Victorian gold and amethyst-set pin.
c1850
$300-400 BELL

A Victorian silver pin, with a cut amethyst, in a border of collet-set Cairngorms and an amethyst.
4.25in (10.5cm) long
$650-750 L&T

A Victorian gold pin, with three carbuncle garnets, the center stone star set with a half-pearl.
$700-800 BELL

A Victorian silver and gold pin pendant, with emerald-cut peridot, set with old brilliant-cut diamonds.
1.5in (3.5cm) wide
$3,200-3,800 LAW

A Victorian pin, with cushion-shaped diamonds, with drops mounted with half-pearls and with enameled and half-pearl-set terminals, with case.
0.86oz
$450-500 BELL

A Victorian diamond and carbuncle garnet pendant pin, with a case detailed 'Hunt and Roskell'.
$4,500-5,000 BELL

A Victorian 14ct gold pin, with turquoise, pearls, garnets and pink tourmaline, opening to two photo reserves, unmarked.
c1890   *2.25in (6cm) wide 0.54oz*
$3,200-3,800 DRA

A Victorian diamond and garnet butterfly gold and silver pin.
4.25in (11cm) wide
$7,000-7,500 JDJ

A multi gemstone butterfly pin, set with emeralds, sapphires, rubies and diamonds.
This pin bears no hallmark, nor stamps, but in expert opinion it would test as silver and gold.
c1880   *1.25in (3cm) long 0.34oz*
$3,800-5,000 TEN

A French Japanesque gold cicada pin, with ruby eyes, with eagle mark for 18k, half struck and indistinct maker mark.
The cicada represents music and the sun and is a symbol of Provence, France.
c1890   *2in (5cm) long 0.37oz*
$4,500-5,000 DRA

An archaeological-revival gold pin, attributed to Melillo, designed in the 'Campana'-style, unsigned.
1.75in (4.5cm) wide 0.35oz
$1,000-1,500 DRA

A Belle Epoque sapphire and diamond pin.

1.5in (4cm) diam

$6,500-7,500   **LAW**

A late 19thC ruby and moonstone flower pin, later clasp.

1in (2.5cm) diam

$300-400   **MAB**

A Victorian yellow metal target pin, centered with a cushion-cut diamond in starburst setting.

1.25in (3cm) diam 0.54oz

$450-550   **APAR**

A Victorian gold, diamond-set and blue enameled pin, designed as a buckle and strap garter motif, with case.

$1,000-1,200   **BELL**

A 9ct Scottish dirk pin, set with amethyst, citrene and agate stones, unmarked, slight damage.

3in (8cm) long

$180-250   **FLD**

A Scottish Victorian pin, with a cut citrine at the center within an agate and engraved surround.

$400-450   **BELL**

A late Victorian silver and gold pin, with old brilliant-cut diamonds, with two rows of rose-cut diamonds.

2.5in (6.5cm) long

$650-750   **LAW**

A late 19thC gold, ruby and diamond, enameled and pearl pin, probably French.

2.25in (5.5cm) wide 0.67oz

$950-1,100   **BELL**

A Queen Victoria Diamond Jubilee gold and enamel pendant, with a profile of Queen Victoria within paste stones and a Masonic device.

2.5in (6.5cm) high

$180-250   **LAW**

A 19thC gold micromosaic pin, with foxgloves.

0.75in (2cm) wide 0.31oz

$900-1,000   **BELL**

A Victorian gold micromosaic pin, with a basket of flowers.

$180-250   **BELL**

A Tiffany & Co. 'Bonnet Baby' carved moonstone pin, rose-cut diamond bonnet with red enameled stripes, diamond bow, pearl pin, pearl replaced, marked 'Tiffany & Co.'.

c1890   1.25in (3cm) wide 0.23oz

$10,500-11,000   **DRA**

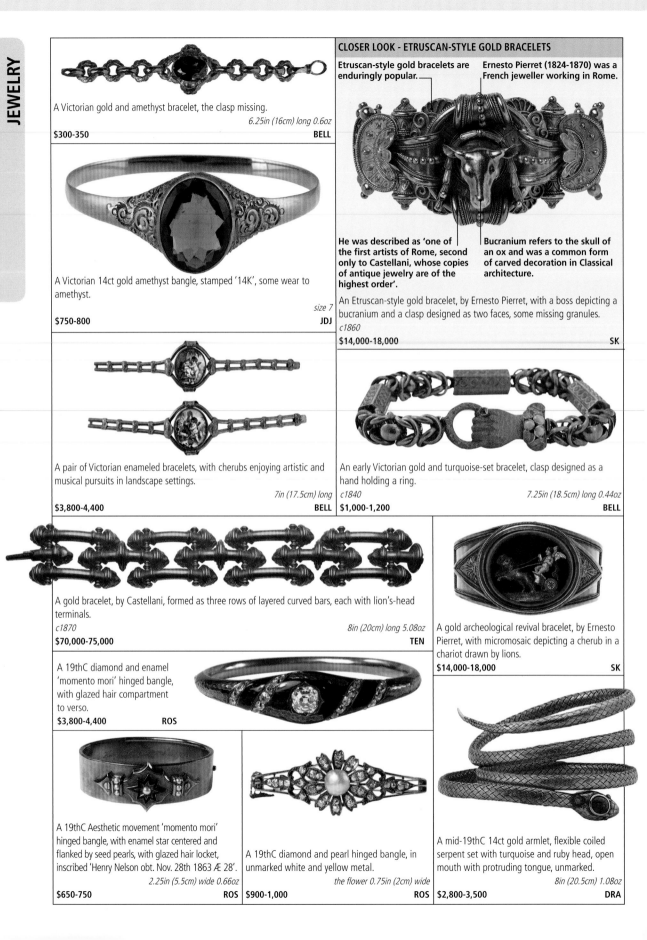

A Victorian gold and amethyst bracelet, the clasp missing.

6.25in (16cm) long 0.6oz

$300-350   BELL

A Victorian 14ct gold amethyst bangle, stamped '14K', some wear to amethyst.

size 7

$750-800   JDJ

A pair of Victorian enameled bracelets, with cherubs enjoying artistic and musical pursuits in landscape settings.

7in (17.5cm) long

$3,800-4,400   BELL

A gold bracelet, by Castellani, formed as three rows of layered curved bars, each with lion's-head terminals.

c1870

8in (20cm) long 5.08oz

$70,000-75,000   TEN

A 19thC diamond and enamel 'momento mori' hinged bangle, with glazed hair compartment to verso.

$3,800-4,400   ROS

A 19thC Aesthetic movement 'momento mori' hinged bangle, with enamel star centered and flanked by seed pearls, with glazed hair locket, inscribed 'Henry Nelson obt. Nov. 28th 1863 Æ 28'.

2.25in (5.5cm) wide 0.66oz

$650-750   ROS

A 19thC diamond and pearl hinged bangle, in unmarked white and yellow metal.

the flower 0.75in (2cm) wide

$900-1,000   ROS

CLOSER LOOK - ETRUSCAN-STYLE GOLD BRACELETS

Etruscan-style gold bracelets are enduringly popular.

Ernesto Pierret (1824-1870) was a French jeweller working in Rome.

He was described as 'one of the first artists of Rome, second only to Castellani, whose copies of antique jewelry are of the highest order'.

Bucranium refers to the skull of an ox and was a common form of carved decoration in Classical architecture.

An Etruscan-style gold bracelet, by Ernesto Pierret, with a boss depicting a bucranium and a clasp designed as two faces, some missing granules.

c1860

$14,000-18,000   SK

An early Victorian gold and turquoise-set bracelet, clasp designed as a hand holding a ring.

c1840

7.25in (18.5cm) long 0.44oz

$1,000-1,200   BELL

A gold archeological revival bracelet, by Ernesto Pierret, with micromosaic depicting a cherub in a chariot drawn by lions.

$14,000-18,000   SK

A mid-19thC 14ct gold armlet, flexible coiled serpent set with turquoise and ruby head, open mouth with protruding tongue, unmarked.

8in (20.5cm) 1.08oz

$2,800-3,500   DRA

A mid-19thC gold agate panel-link necklace, with agate bracelet, part of the clasp lacking, with a case, detailed 'Hunt & Roskell, Late Storr & Mortimer Jewellers and Goldsmiths to the Queen'.
$2,500-3,200   **BELL**

A mid-19thC gold archaeological-revival fringe necklace, with floral and pale links, with a hook shaped clasp.
14.25in (36cm) long 1.9oz
$2,500-3,200   **BELL**

A mid-19thC Mother-of-pearl, seed pearl and foil-backed amethyst collar necklace and pin, with a later fitted case.
$1,500-1,900   **BELL**

A Victorian gold and pearl necklet, one pearl missing.
15in (38cm) long
$400-450   **LAW**

A 19thC amethyst parure, with oval-cut amethyst necklace, hinged bangle and flower-head form pin, centered with a single pearl.
the necklace 17.75in (45cm) long
$8,000-9,500   **ROS**

A Victorian gold and garnet serpent's head necklace, with a heart-shaped pendant locket fitted to its mouth, on a serpentine link chain.
$1,900-2,300   **BELL**

A 15ct gold locket pendant, centered with an applied stellar motif set with diamonds and seed-cultured pearls, on gold bead chain necklace.
c1870-80   19.25in (49cm) long 1.7oz
$1,300-1,500   **APAR**

A late Victorian diamond and cultured pearl necklace, silver-fronted and gold-backed, on a cultured pearl necklace, original case.
$1,900-2,300   **BELL**

A late 19thC yellow and white metal diamond and pearl pendant/pin, with two principal stones, each approximately 0.50ct, above a silver lustrous pearl.
1.25in (3cm) long
$2,300-2,800   APAR

A gold, diamond, turquoise and seed pearl necklace, on a gold ropetwist link neck chain.
c1900
$750-900   **BELL**

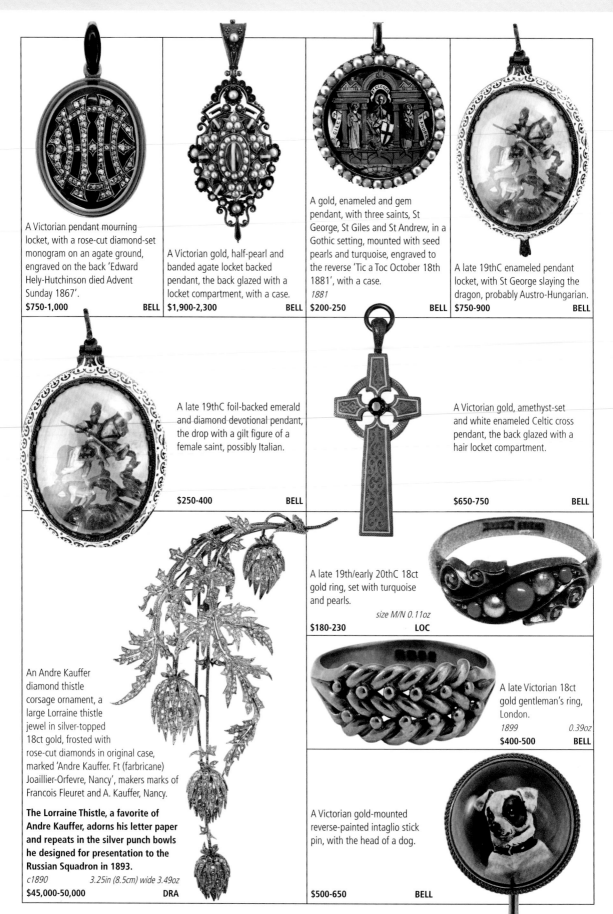

A Victorian pendant mourning locket, with a rose-cut diamond-set monogram on an agate ground, engraved on the back 'Edward Hely-Hutchinson died Advent Sunday 1867'.

$750-1,000 BELL

A Victorian gold, half-pearl and banded agate locket backed pendant, the back glazed with a locket compartment, with a case.

$1,900-2,300 BELL

A gold, enameled and gem pendant, with three saints, St George, St Giles and St Andrew, in a Gothic setting, mounted with seed pearls and turquoise, engraved to the reverse 'Tic a Toc October 18th 1881', with a case.
1881

$200-250 BELL

A late 19thC enameled pendant locket, with St George slaying the dragon, probably Austro-Hungarian.

$750-900 BELL

A late 19thC foil-backed emerald and diamond devotional pendant, the drop with a gilt figure of a female saint, possibly Italian.

$250-400 BELL

A Victorian gold, amethyst-set and white enameled Celtic cross pendant, the back glazed with a hair locket compartment.

$650-750 BELL

An Andre Kauffer diamond thistle corsage ornament, a large Lorraine thistle jewel in silver-topped 18ct gold, frosted with rose-cut diamonds in original case, marked 'Andre Kauffer. Ft (farbricane) Joaillier-Orfevre, Nancy', makers marks of Francois Fleuret and A. Kauffer, Nancy.

The Lorraine Thistle, a favorite of Andre Kauffer, adorns his letter paper and repeats in the silver punch bowls he designed for presentation to the Russian Squadron in 1893.
c1890   3.25in (8.5cm) wide 3.49oz
$45,000-50,000 DRA

A late 19th/early 20thC 18ct gold ring, set with turquoise and pearls.

size M/N 0.11oz
$180-230 LOC

A late Victorian 18ct gold gentleman's ring, London.
1899   0.39oz
$400-500 BELL

A Victorian gold-mounted reverse-painted intaglio stick pin, with the head of a dog.

$500-650 BELL

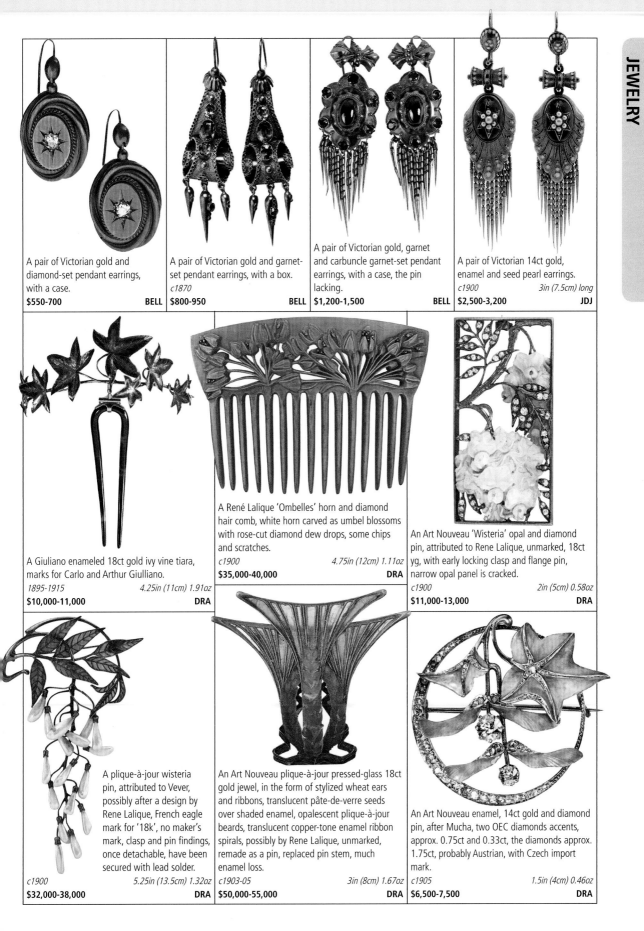

A pair of Victorian gold and diamond-set pendant earrings, with a case.
$550-700   **BELL**

A pair of Victorian gold and garnet-set pendant earrings, with a box.
c1870
$800-950   **BELL**

A pair of Victorian gold, garnet and carbuncle garnet-set pendant earrings, with a case, the pin lacking.
$1,200-1,500   **BELL**

A pair of Victorian 14ct gold, enamel and seed pearl earrings.
c1900   *3in (7.5cm) long*
$2,500-3,200   **JDJ**

A Giuliano enameled 18ct gold ivy vine tiara, marks for Carlo and Arthur Giulliano.
1895-1915   *4.25in (11cm) 1.91oz*
$10,000-11,000   **DRA**

A René Lalique 'Ombelles' horn and diamond hair comb, white horn carved as umbel blossoms with rose-cut diamond dew drops, some chips and scratches.
c1900   *4.75in (12cm) 1.11oz*
$35,000-40,000   **DRA**

An Art Nouveau 'Wisteria' opal and diamond pin, attributed to Rene Lalique, unmarked, 18ct yg, with early locking clasp and flange pin, narrow opal panel is cracked.
c1900   *2in (5cm) 0.58oz*
$11,000-13,000   **DRA**

A plique-à-jour wisteria pin, attributed to Vever, possibly after a design by Rene Lalique, French eagle mark for '18k', no maker's mark, clasp and pin findings, once detachable, have been secured with lead solder.
c1900   *5.25in (13.5cm) 1.32oz*
$32,000-38,000   **DRA**

An Art Nouveau plique-à-jour pressed-glass 18ct gold jewel, in the form of stylized wheat ears and ribbons, translucent pâte-de-verre seeds over shaded enamel, opalescent plique-à-jour beards, translucent copper-tone enamel ribbon spirals, possibly by Rene Lalique, unmarked, remade as a pin, replaced pin stem, much enamel loss.
c1903-05   *3in (8cm) 1.67oz*
$50,000-55,000   **DRA**

An Art Nouveau enamel, 14ct gold and diamond pin, after Mucha, two OEC diamonds accents, approx. 0.75ct and 0.33ct, the diamonds approx. 1.75ct, probably Austrian, with Czech import mark.
c1905   *1.5in (4cm) 0.46oz*
$6,500-7,500   **DRA**

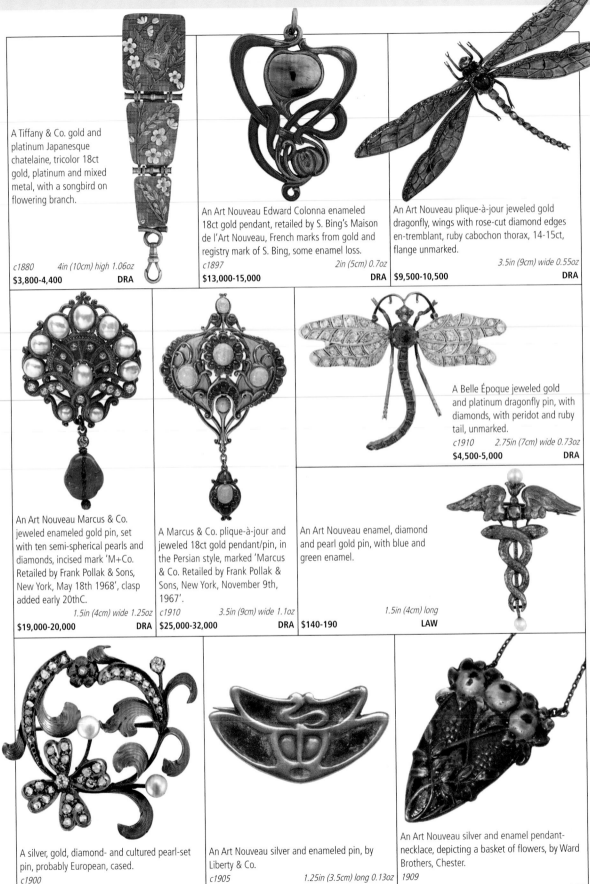

A Tiffany & Co. gold and platinum Japanesque chatelaine, tricolor 18ct gold, platinum and mixed metal, with a songbird on flowering branch.

c1880 4in (10cm) high 1.06oz
$3,800-4,400 **DRA**

An Art Nouveau Edward Colonna enameled 18ct gold pendant, retailed by S. Bing's Maison de l'Art Nouveau, French marks from gold and registry mark of S. Bing, some enamel loss.

c1897 2in (5cm) 0.7oz
$13,000-15,000 **DRA**

An Art Nouveau plique-à-jour jeweled gold dragonfly, wings with rose-cut diamond edges en-tremblant, ruby cabochon thorax, 14-15ct, flange unmarked.

3.5in (9cm) wide 0.55oz
$9,500-10,500 **DRA**

An Art Nouveau Marcus & Co. jeweled enameled gold pin, set with ten semi-spherical pearls and diamonds, incised mark 'M+Co. Retailed by Frank Pollak & Sons, New York, May 18th 1968', clasp added early 20thC.

1.5in (4cm) wide 1.25oz
$19,000-20,000 **DRA**

A Marcus & Co. plique-à-jour and jeweled 18ct gold pendant/pin, in the Persian style, marked 'Marcus & Co. Retailed by Frank Pollak & Sons, New York, November 9th, 1967'.

c1910 3.5in (9cm) wide 1.1oz
$25,000-32,000 **DRA**

An Art Nouveau enamel, diamond and pearl gold pin, with blue and green enamel.

A Belle Époque jeweled gold and platinum dragonfly pin, with diamonds, with peridot and ruby tail, unmarked.

c1910 2.75in (7cm) wide 0.73oz
$4,500-5,000 **DRA**

1.5in (4cm) long
$140-190 **LAW**

A silver, gold, diamond- and cultured pearl-set pin, probably European, cased.

c1900
$400-450 **BELL**

An Art Nouveau silver and enameled pin, by Liberty & Co.

c1905 1.25in (3.5cm) long 0.13oz
$400-500 **TEN**

An Art Nouveau silver and enamel pendant-necklace, depicting a basket of flowers, by Ward Brothers, Chester.

1909
$180-250 **LOC**

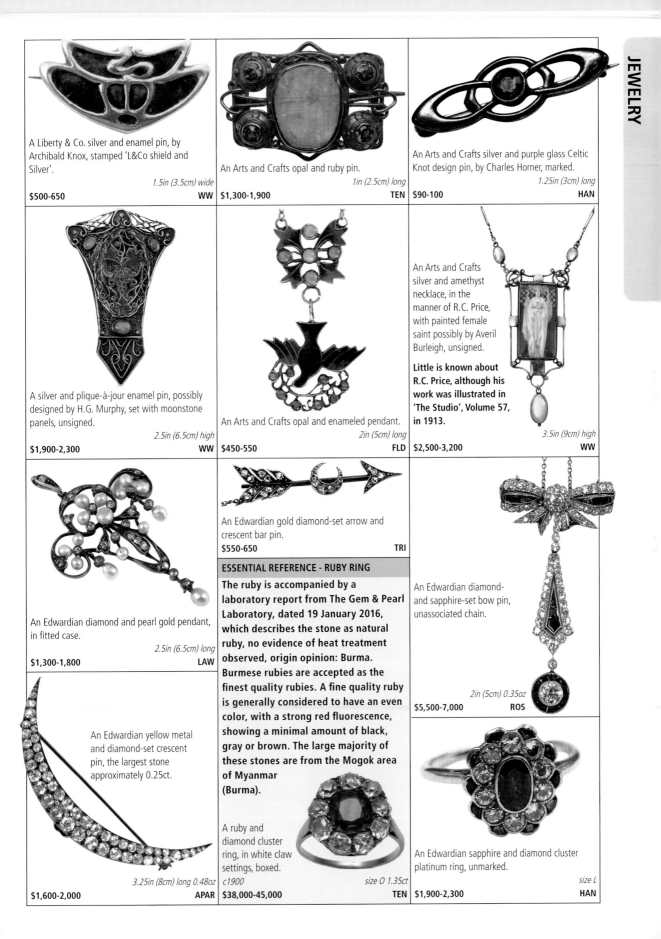

A Liberty & Co. silver and enamel pin, by Archibald Knox, stamped 'L&Co shield and Silver'.

1.5in (3.5cm) wide

$500-650   WW

An Arts and Crafts opal and ruby pin.

1in (2.5cm) long

$1,300-1,900   TEN

An Arts and Crafts silver and purple glass Celtic Knot design pin, by Charles Horner, marked.

1.25in (3cm) long

$90-100   HAN

A silver and plique-à-jour enamel pin, possibly designed by H.G. Murphy, set with moonstone panels, unsigned.

2.5in (6.5cm) high

$1,900-2,300   WW

An Arts and Crafts opal and enameled pendant.

2in (5cm) long

$450-550   FLD

An Arts and Crafts silver and amethyst necklace, in the manner of R.C. Price, with painted female saint possibly by Averil Burleigh, unsigned.

Little is known about R.C. Price, although his work was illustrated in 'The Studio', Volume 57, in 1913.

3.5in (9cm) high

$2,500-3,200   WW

An Edwardian diamond and pearl gold pendant, in fitted case.

2.5in (6.5cm) long

$1,300-1,800   LAW

An Edwardian gold diamond-set arrow and crescent bar pin.

$550-650   TRI

ESSENTIAL REFERENCE - RUBY RING

The ruby is accompanied by a laboratory report from The Gem & Pearl Laboratory, dated 19 January 2016, which describes the stone as natural ruby, no evidence of heat treatment observed, origin opinion: Burma. Burmese rubies are accepted as the finest quality rubies. A fine quality ruby is generally considered to have an even color, with a strong red fluorescence, showing a minimal amount of black, gray or brown. The large majority of these stones are from the Mogok area of Myanmar (Burma).

A ruby and diamond cluster ring, in white claw settings, boxed.

c1900   *size O 1.35ct*

$38,000-45,000   TEN

An Edwardian diamond- and sapphire-set bow pin, unassociated chain.

2in (5cm) 0.35oz

$5,500-7,000   ROS

An Edwardian yellow metal and diamond-set crescent pin, the largest stone approximately 0.25ct.

3.25in (8cm) long 0.48oz

$1,600-2,000   APAR

An Edwardian sapphire and diamond cluster platinum ring, unmarked.

size L

$1,900-2,300   HAN

JEWELRY

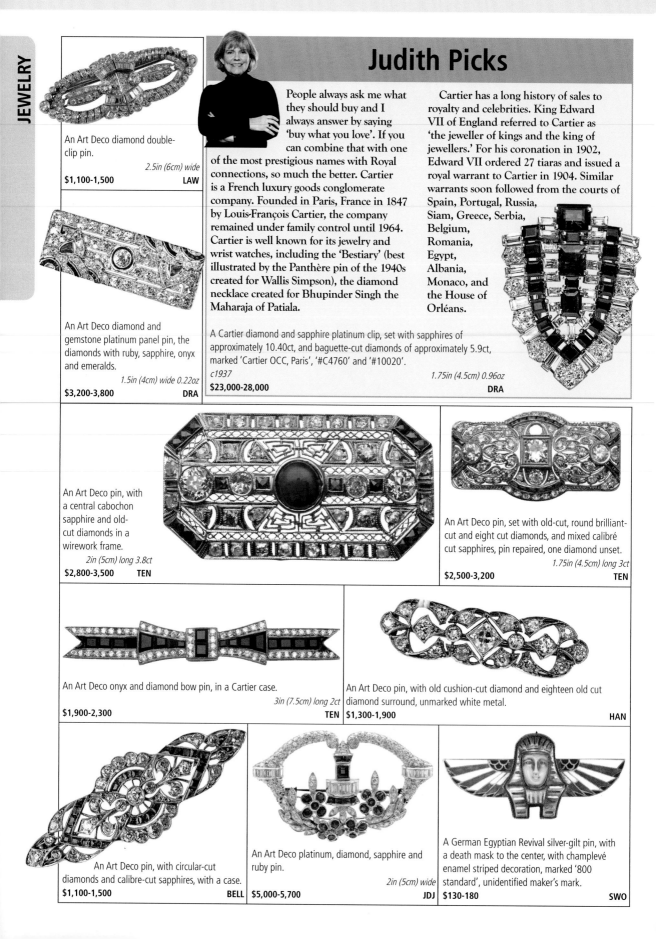

An Art Deco diamond double-clip pin.

2.5in (6cm) wide

$1,100-1,500　　LAW

An Art Deco diamond and gemstone platinum panel pin, the diamonds with ruby, sapphire, onyx and emeralds.

1.5in (4cm) wide 0.22oz

$3,200-3,800　　DRA

Judith Picks

People always ask me what they should buy and I always answer by saying 'buy what you love'. If you can combine that with one of the most prestigious names with Royal connections, so much the better. Cartier is a French luxury goods conglomerate company. Founded in Paris, France in 1847 by Louis-François Cartier, the company remained under family control until 1964. Cartier is well known for its jewelry and wrist watches, including the 'Bestiary' (best illustrated by the Panthère pin of the 1940s created for Wallis Simpson), the diamond necklace created for Bhupinder Singh the Maharaja of Patiala.

Cartier has a long history of sales to royalty and celebrities. King Edward VII of England referred to Cartier as 'the jeweller of kings and the king of jewellers.' For his coronation in 1902, Edward VII ordered 27 tiaras and issued a royal warrant to Cartier in 1904. Similar warrants soon followed from the courts of Spain, Portugal, Russia, Siam, Greece, Serbia, Belgium, Romania, Egypt, Albania, Monaco, and the House of Orléans.

A Cartier diamond and sapphire platinum clip, set with sapphires of approximately 10.40ct, and baguette-cut diamonds of approximately 5.9ct, marked 'Cartier OCC, Paris', '#C4760' and '#10020'.

c1937

$23,000-28,000

1.75in (4.5cm) 0.96oz

DRA

An Art Deco pin, with a central cabochon sapphire and old-cut diamonds in a wirework frame.

2in (5cm) long 3.8ct

$2,800-3,500　　TEN

An Art Deco pin, set with old-cut, round brilliant-cut and eight cut diamonds, and mixed calibré cut sapphires, pin repaired, one diamond unset.

1.75in (4.5cm) long 3ct

$2,500-3,200　　TEN

An Art Deco onyx and diamond bow pin, in a Cartier case.

3in (7.5cm) long 2ct

$1,900-2,300　　TEN

An Art Deco pin, with old cushion-cut diamond and eighteen old cut diamond surround, unmarked white metal.

$1,300-1,900　　HAN

An Art Deco pin, with circular-cut diamonds and calibre-cut sapphires, with a case.

$1,100-1,500　　BELL

An Art Deco platinum, diamond, sapphire and ruby pin.

2in (5cm) wide

$5,000-5,700　　JDJ

A German Egyptian Revival silver-gilt pin, with a death mask to the center, with champlevé enamel striped decoration, marked '800 standard', unidentified maker's mark.

$130-180　　SWO

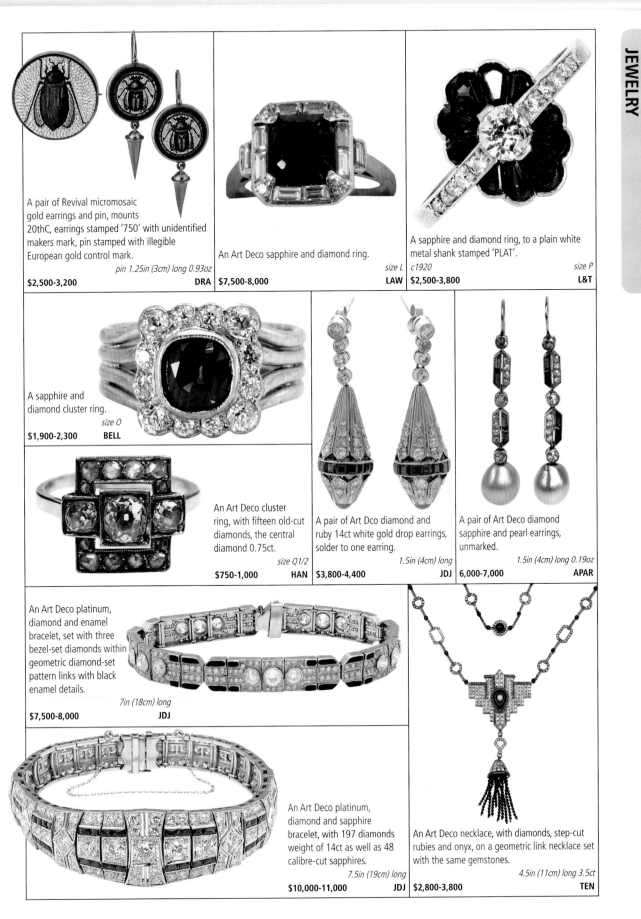

A pair of Revival micromosaic gold earrings and pin, mounts 20thC, earrings stamped '750' with unidentified makers mark, pin stamped with illegible European gold control mark.

pin 1.25in (3cm) long 0.93oz

$2,500-3,200   **DRA**

An Art Deco sapphire and diamond ring.

size L

$7,500-8,000   **LAW**

A sapphire and diamond ring, to a plain white metal shank stamped 'PLAT'.

c1920   *size P*

$2,500-3,800   **L&T**

A sapphire and diamond cluster ring.

size O

$1,900-2,300   **BELL**

An Art Deco cluster ring, with fifteen old-cut diamonds, the central diamond 0.75ct.

size Q1/2

$750-1,000   **HAN**

A pair of Art Dco diamond and ruby 14ct white gold drop earrings, solder to one earring.

1.5in (4cm) long

$3,800-4,400   **JDJ**

A pair of Art Deco diamond sapphire and pearl earrings, unmarked.

1.5in (4cm) long 0.19oz

6,000-7,000   **APAR**

An Art Deco platinum, diamond and enamel bracelet, set with three bezel-set diamonds within geometric diamond-set pattern links with black enamel details.

7in (18cm) long

$7,500-8,000   **JDJ**

An Art Deco platinum, diamond and sapphire bracelet, with 197 diamonds weight of 14ct as well as 48 calibre-cut sapphires.

7.5in (19cm) long

$10,000-11,000   **JDJ**

An Art Deco necklace, with diamonds, step-cut rubies and onyx, on a geometric link necklace set with the same gemstones.

4.5in (11cm) long 3.5ct

$2,800-3,800   **TEN**

ESSENTIAL REFERENCE - MARCUS & COMPANY

Marcus & Company (1892-1962), was founded by William Elder Marcus and later joined by George Marcus and their father, Herman, a German-born former employee of Tiffany & Co. It was located at 17th Street and Broadway in Manhattan. The designers used precious stones and gemstones such as zircons, chrysoberyls, tourmalines, opals, garnets, beryls, spinels, and peridots. The company was sold to Gimbels in 1941. It merged with Black, Starr & Frost in 1962.

An important platinum topped gold, Montana sapphire and diamond butterfly pin, by Marcus & Co.

0.63oz

$45,000-50,000 LH

A 1950s sapphire, topaz and citrine pin, accented with seed pearls, maker's mark 'C+F'.

$300-450 MAB

A gold, diamond- and ruby-set and enameled pin, designed as The Prince of Wales's feathers above a crown, detailed 'Ich Dien'.

$800-950 BELL

A T.B. Starr diamond and pearl platinum bow pin, pin stem marked 'T.B. Starr Inc. Retailed by Frank Pollak & Sons, New York, June 5th, 1968'.

2.5in (6.5cm) wide 0.58oz

$5,500-6,500 DRA

A 20thC Greek Zolotas 18ct gold octopus bracelet, with two octopodes with emerald eyes, central cabochon and round faceted sapphire 'bubbles', stamped 'Zolotus'.

6.5in (16.5cm) 2.2oz

$3,800-4,400 DRA

ESSENTIAL REFERENCE - GEORGES WEIL

Born in Vienna in 1938, the sculptor and jeweller Georges Weil studied at the St. Martin's School of Art in London. At the age of eighteen, he founded Georges Weil Jewellery Ltd. in Hatton Garden. Known for his use of textured gold combined with precious and semi-precious stones, from 1964 to 1972 he exhibited his collections in Tokyo, Israel, New York and at the Foyles Gallery and Jean Renet Gallery in London.

A French gold, emerald-set and enameled Siamese cat pin, detailed 'Depose'.

1.29oz

$900-1,100 BELL

A 1960s Georges Weil diamond and matrix organic pin, with red crystals within cells with three brilliant-cut diamonds, signed 'G. Weil'.

$2,500-3,200 MAB

A 1950s gold bracelet, the articulated brick link bracelet fastened with a flower head clasp.

7.5in (19cm) long 5.29oz

$2,300-2,800 MAB

A Robert Indiana 18ct gold 'LOVE' ring, attributed to Joan Kron, marks lost due to sizing, resized.

c1965-70 *size Q 1.2oz*

$3,800-4,400 DRA

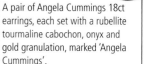

A pair of Angela Cummings 18ct earrings, each set with a rubellite tourmaline cabochon, onyx and gold granulation, marked 'Angela Cummings'.

c1990 *1in (2.5cm) wide*

$2,500-3,200 DRA

A 1940s Marcel Boucher rhodium-plated, rhinestone parure, including a necklace and earrings.
$850-900 GRV

A 1970s Chanel gold-plated metal and Gripoix glass necklace.
$2,500-3,200 GRV

A 1930s Ciro sterling silver and rhinestone pin.
$350-400 GRV

A Christian Dior gilt metal and paste necklace, by Mitchel Maer.

1952-56
$1,000-1,250 GRV

A pair of 1950s Christian Dior gold tone base metal and rhinestone earrings, possibly by Roger Scemama.
$550-600 GRV

A Christian Dior rhodium-plated, rhinestone parure, including a necklace, pin and earrings, by Mitchel Maer.
1952-56
$3,200-3,800 GRV

GEMMA REDMOND
VINTAGE

A 1980s Stanley Hagler gilt metal, glass, faux pearl and rhinestone parure, including a necklace and earrings.
$900-1,000 GRV

A 1960s Miriam Haskell gilt-metal and glass necklace.
$300-350　　　　　　　　　　　　**GRV**

A 1940s Miriam Haskell Japanese faux pearl, rhinestone and gilt-metal bracelet, by Frank Hess.
$350-400　　　　　　　　　　　　**GRV**

A 1940s pair of Joseff of Hollywood 'Russian gold' earrings.
$300-350　　　　　　　　　　　　**GRV**

A pair of Christian Lacroix gold tone base metal, plastic and rhinestone earrings.
1990s
$275-300　　　　　　　　　　　　**GRV**

A 1950s Mitchel Maer silver tone base metal and rhinestone pin.
$275-300　　　　　　　　　　　　**GRV**

A 1920s Max Neiger gilt-metal, faux jade and enamel pin.
$450-500　　　　　　　　　　　　**GRV**

A 1950s Elsa Schiaparelli gold tone base metal, rhinestone and paste bracelet.
$350-400　　　　　　　　　　　　**GRV**

A pair of 1950s Schreiner gold vermeil and rhinestone earrings.
$300-350　　　　　　　　　　　　**GRV**

A Trifari gold vermeil, glass and rhinestone necklace, designed by Alfred Philippe.
1944
$250-280　　　　　　　　　　　　**GRV**

A Trifari rhodium-plated, rhinestone and glass pin, by Alfred Philippe.
1941
$300-350　　　　　　　　　　　　**GRV**

A 1930s Trifari rhodium-plated, rhinestone pin, by KTF, sold by Asprey, in original box.
$650-700　　　　　　　　　　　　**GRV**

ESSENTIAL REFERENCE - VINAIGRETTES

By the 19thC a variety of perfume containers were being produced, including the vinaigrette, a gilded metal box with a pierced, decorated interior grille, used to hold sponges soaked in scented vinaigres de toilette (aromatic vinegar). The interiors were gilded to prevent the silver from staining. Perfume was also an exotic extravagance, so to be able to both afford perfume and then contain it within a decorative vinaigrette was a mark of social distinction and a display of grandeur and wealth.

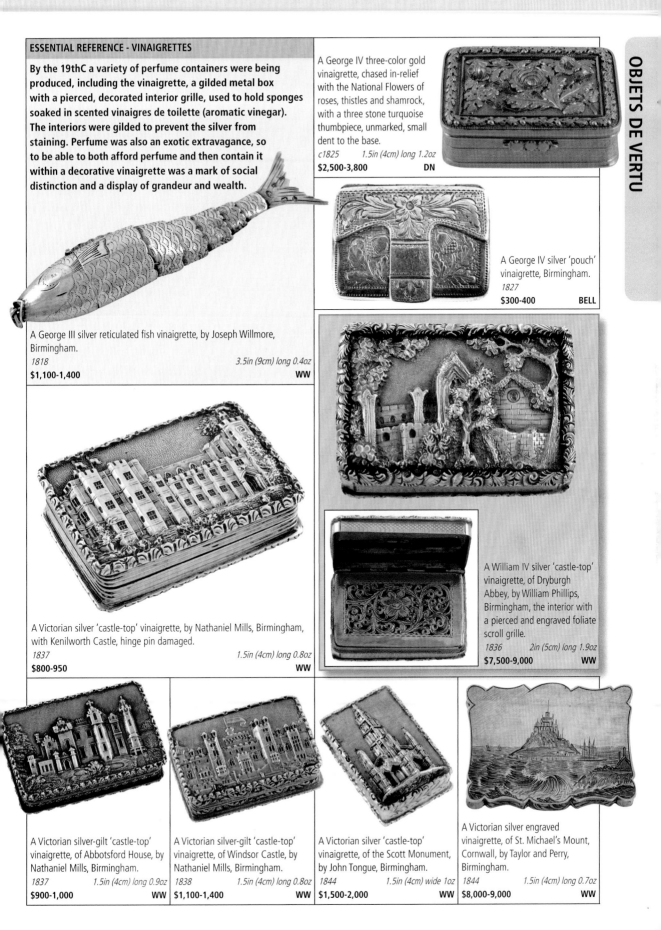

A George III silver reticulated fish vinaigrette, by Joseph Willmore, Birmingham.
1818 3.5in (9cm) long 0.4oz
$1,100-1,400 WW

A George IV three-color gold vinaigrette, chased in-relief with the National Flowers of roses, thistles and shamrock, with a three stone turquoise thumbpiece, unmarked, small dent to the base.
c1825 1.5in (4cm) long 1.2oz
$2,500-3,800 DN

A George IV silver 'pouch' vinaigrette, Birmingham.
1827
$300-400 BELL

A Victorian silver 'castle-top' vinaigrette, by Nathaniel Mills, Birmingham, with Kenilworth Castle, hinge pin damaged.
1837 1.5in (4cm) long 0.8oz
$800-950 WW

A William IV silver 'castle-top' vinaigrette, of Dryburgh Abbey, by William Phillips, Birmingham, the interior with a pierced and engraved foliate scroll grille.
1836 2in (5cm) long 1.9oz
$7,500-9,000 WW

A Victorian silver-gilt 'castle-top' vinaigrette, of Abbotsford House, by Nathaniel Mills, Birmingham.
1837 1.5in (4cm) long 0.9oz
$900-1,000 WW

A Victorian silver-gilt 'castle-top' vinaigrette, of Windsor Castle, by Nathaniel Mills, Birmingham.
1838 1.5in (4cm) long 0.8oz
$1,100-1,400 WW

A Victorian silver 'castle-top' vinaigrette, of the Scott Monument, by John Tongue, Birmingham.
1844 1.5in (4cm) wide 1oz
$1,500-2,000 WW

A Victorian silver engraved vinaigrette, of St. Michael's Mount, Cornwall, by Taylor and Perry, Birmingham.
1844 1.5in (4cm) long 0.7oz
$8,000-9,000 WW

A Scottish silver vinaigrette, with maker's mark 'AGW', for A.G. Wighton, the silver-gilt interior with thistle engraved grille.

c1850   *1.5in (4cm) wide*

$150-190   **CHOR**

A Victorian silver 'castle-top' vinaigrette, by Edward Smith, Birmingham, of St George's Hall, Liverpool.

1854   *2in (5cm) long 1.4oz*

$3,200-3,800   **WW**

A Victorian silver purse-form vinaigrette, by David Pettifer, Birmingham.

1864   *1.5in (4cm) long*

$400-500   **DN**

A Victorian silver horn vinaigrette or scent flask, by S. Mordan, London.

1872   *4.5in (11cm) long 2.3oz*

$450-500   **WW**

A Victorian silver bull's eye lantern combination vinaigrette and sewing étui, by Sampson Mordan & Co., London, the interior with a gold thimble, unmarked, with a turquoise bead and seed pearl border, and a spool holder with tape measure, the base with a scroll pierced grille.

1873   *2.5in (6.5cm) high*

$1,900-2,300   **DN**

A Victorian silver horn vinaigrette/scent bottle, by S. Mordan, London.

1873 3.25in (8cm) long 1.3oz

$450-500   **WW**

A Victorian silver horn-shaped combination scent bottle and vinaigrette, by Sampson Mordan & Co., London, with PODR mark for 21 June 1870, the scent end with a screw cap retained by a chain, marks are clear.

1875   *3in (8cm) long 1.7oz*

$500-650   **DN**

A 19thC gold watch vinaigrette, engine-turned decoration, the reverse opens to a photograph frame, unmarked.

1.25in (3cm) diam 1oz

$800-900   **WW**

A 19thC silver vinaigrette of articulated fish form, Birmingham, date letter illegible.

3.5in (8.5cm) long

$550-650   **CHOR**

A Victorian silver walnut vinaigrette, by Sampson Mordan, the grill inscribed 'Sampson Mordan London'.

c1880   *1.5in (4cm) 0.72oz*

$1,000-1,100   **CHEF**

A Victorian silver poppy head with stem vinaigrette, by Susannah Brasted, London, with pull-off cover.

1888   *3.5in (9cm) long 2.2oz*

$650-750   **WW**

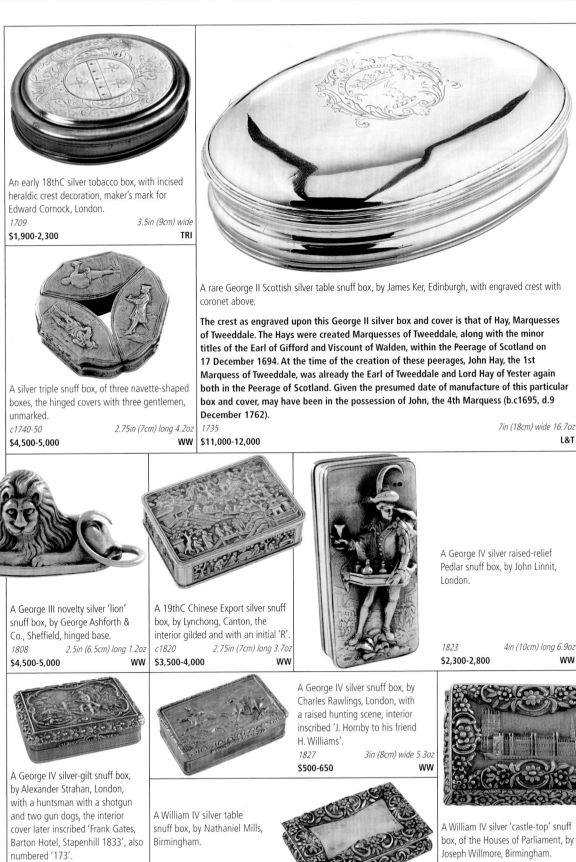

An early 18thC silver tobacco box, with incised heraldic crest decoration, maker's mark for Edward Cornock, London.

1709   *3.5in (9cm) wide*

$1,900-2,300   **TRI**

A silver triple snuff box, of three navette-shaped boxes, the hinged covers with three gentlemen, unmarked.

c1740-50   *2.75in (7cm) long 4.2oz*

$4,500-5,000   **WW**

A rare George II Scottish silver table snuff box, by James Ker, Edinburgh, with engraved crest with coronet above.

The crest as engraved upon this George II silver box and cover is that of Hay, Marquesses of Tweeddale. The Hays were created Marquesses of Tweeddale, along with the minor titles of the Earl of Gifford and Viscount of Walden, within the Peerage of Scotland on 17 December 1694. At the time of the creation of these peerages, John Hay, the 1st Marquess of Tweeddale, was already the Earl of Tweeddale and Lord Hay of Yester again both in the Peerage of Scotland. Given the presumed date of manufacture of this particular box and cover, may have been in the possession of John, the 4th Marquess (b.c1695, d.9 December 1762).

1735   *7in (18cm) wide 16.7oz*

$11,000-12,000   **L&T**

A George III novelty silver 'lion' snuff box, by George Ashforth & Co., Sheffield, hinged base.

1808   *2.5in (6.5cm) long 1.2oz*

$4,500-5,000   **WW**

A 19thC Chinese Export silver snuff box, by Lynchong, Canton, the interior gilded and with an initial 'R'.

c1820   *2.75in (7cm) long 3.7oz*

$3,500-4,000   **WW**

A George IV silver raised-relief Pedlar snuff box, by John Linnit, London.

1823   *4in (10cm) long 6.9oz*

$2,300-2,800   **WW**

A George IV silver-gilt snuff box, by Alexander Strahan, London, with a huntsman with a shotgun and two gun dogs, the interior cover later inscribed 'Frank Gates, Barton Hotel, Stapenhill 1833', also numbered '173'.

1824   *3in (8cm) long 5.9oz*

$500-650   **WW**

A George IV silver snuff box, by Charles Rawlings, London, with a raised hunting scene, interior inscribed 'J. Hornby to his friend H. Williams'.

1827   *3in (8cm) wide 5.3oz*

$500-650   **WW**

A William IV silver table snuff box, by Nathaniel Mills, Birmingham.

1830   *3.75in (9.5cm) long 6.5oz*

$800-950   **WW**

A William IV silver 'castle-top' snuff box, of the Houses of Parliament, by Joseph Willmore, Birmingham.

1834   *3.75in (9.5cm) long 8.6oz*

$6,500-7,000   **WW**

A silver presentation table snuff box, decorated with a six-wheeled locomotive engine, with inscription, by Nathaniel Mills, Birmingham.

Cumberland Pacquet of 22 January 1839 notes: 'The Arbroath and Forfar railway was opened to the public on Thursday. The first train, drawn by the Victoria engine, left Arbroath at half-past eight in the morning, carrying the directors and a large number of passengers. Great interest was excited among the spectators along the line as well as at Forfar, where there was a general turn-out. The trip was made in gallant style. The return of the engine to Arbroath at half-past eleven, was witnessed by hundreds of persons, who assembled at various points where a view of the railway could be obtained.'

1838   *3.5in (9cm) long 6.1oz*

$12,000-14,000   **LAW**

A rare Victorian silver 'castle-top' snuff box, of Old Colchester Town Hall, by Nathaniel Mills, Birmingham.

1844   *2.5in (6.5cm) long 2oz*

$14,000-16,000   **WW**

A George IV silver snuff box, by John Linnit, London, with a scene from Charles Dickens's 'Pickwick Papers', of Mr Pickwick addressing the club, dated.

Probably after the print by Seymour which formed the front-piece of the 'Pickwick Papers' printed in 1837.

1852   *3.75in (9.5cm) long 6.2oz*

$1,900-2,300   **WW**

A Victorian silver 'castle-top' snuff box, by Nathaniel Mills, Birmingham, of Durham Cathedral.

1840   *3in (8cm) wide 3.7oz*

$5,000-5,700   **WW**

ESSENTIAL REFERENCE - SNUFF BOX

It would seem likely that this was a diplomatic gift to King Sigcau. In 1886 the British segregated Xesibeland, traditionally part of Pondoland, a natural region on the South African shores of the Indian Ocean. It is located in the coastal belt of the Eastern Cape province. Armed Pondo people resisted the move by invading the territory, burning kraals and causing disorder. The segregation of Xesibeland was a first step prior to its annexation to the Cape Colony at the end of the same year. Finally Pondoland as well became a British protectorate and in 1894 the Pondos were forced to accept the annexation of their own region to the Cape Colony.

An early Victorian silver gilt snuff box, by Nathaniel Mills, Birmingham, engraved with a crown above Sigcau, King of Pondoland 1889, marks crisp.

1841   *4.5in (12cm) long 12.3oz*

$1,900-2,300   **DN**

A 19thC Chinese export silver table snuff box, by Wang Hing, engraved with a crest.

The crest is that of O'Callaghan, Viscount Lismore, of Shanbally Castle, Clogheen, Co. Tipperary.

4.5in (11cm) long 7oz

$2,500-3,200   **WW**

A commemorative silver snuff box, of Trafalgar interest, by the Pairpoint Brothers, London, engraved with a naval battle and inscribed 'Britons never, never shall be slaves, in Remembrance of the Battle in Oct 21st 1805'.

1922   *3.25in (8.5cm) long 2.4oz*

$400-450   **WW**

A gilt-metal-mounted lacquered snuff box, with a miniature chinoiserie painting, unmarked.

1800-20   *3in (7.5cm) long*

$800-900   **LAW**

A 19thC Continental gold and enamel snuff box.

3.25in (8.5cm) long 3.2oz

$2,500-3,200   **WW**

A Scottish silver-mounted ram's-head table snuff mull, by Crouch and Sons, Edinburgh.

1864   *16.25in (41.5cm) wide*

$3,800-4,400   **LOC**

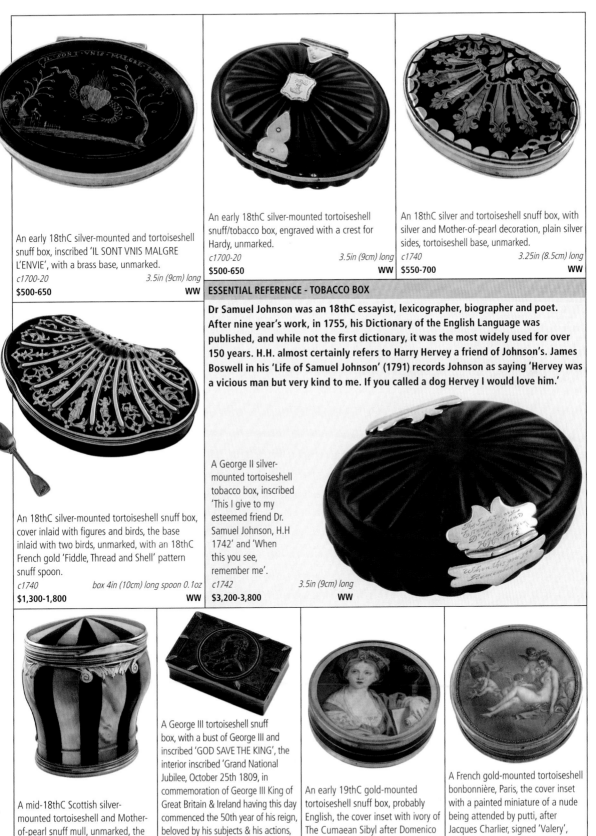

An early 18thC silver-mounted and tortoiseshell snuff box, inscribed 'IL SONT VNIS MALGRE L'ENVIE', with a brass base, unmarked.

c1700-20   *3.5in (9cm) long*

$500-650   **WW**

An early 18thC silver-mounted tortoiseshell snuff/tobacco box, engraved with a crest for Hardy, unmarked.

c1700-20   *3.5in (9cm) long*

$500-650   **WW**

An 18thC silver and tortoiseshell snuff box, with silver and Mother-of-pearl decoration, plain silver sides, tortoiseshell base, unmarked.

c1740   *3.25in (8.5cm) long*

$550-700   **WW**

ESSENTIAL REFERENCE - TOBACCO BOX

Dr Samuel Johnson was an 18thC essayist, lexicographer, biographer and poet. After nine year's work, in 1755, his Dictionary of the English Language was published, and while not the first dictionary, it was the most widely used for over 150 years. H.H. almost certainly refers to Harry Hervey a friend of Johnson's. James Boswell in his 'Life of Samuel Johnson' (1791) records Johnson as saying 'Hervey was a vicious man but very kind to me. If you called a dog Hervey I would love him.'

An 18thC silver-mounted tortoiseshell snuff box, cover inlaid with figures and birds, the base inlaid with two birds, unmarked, with an 18thC French gold 'Fiddle, Thread and Shell' pattern snuff spoon.

c1740   *box 4in (10cm) long spoon 0.1oz*

$1,300-1,800   **WW**

A George II silver-mounted tortoiseshell tobacco box, inscribed 'This I give to my esteemed friend Dr. Samuel Johnson, H.H 1742' and 'When this you see, remember me'.

c1742   *3.5in (9cm) long*

$3,200-3,800   **WW**

A mid-18thC Scottish silver-mounted tortoiseshell and Mother-of-pearl snuff mull, unmarked, the base inscribed, 'J. Bruce'.

c1750   *2.5in (6.5cm) high*

$4,500-5,000   **WW**

A George III tortoiseshell snuff box, with a bust of George III and inscribed 'GOD SAVE THE KING', the interior inscribed 'Grand National Jubilee, October 25th 1809, in commemoration of George III King of Great Britain & Ireland having this day commenced the 50th year of his reign, beloved by his subjects & his actions, the venration (sic) of all the world'.

2.5in (6.5cm) long

$500-650   **WW**

An early 19thC gold-mounted tortoiseshell snuff box, probably English, the cover inset with ivory of The Cumaean Sibyl after Domenico Zampieri, called Il Domenichino.

3in (7.5cm) diam

$3,200-3,800   **DN**

A French gold-mounted tortoiseshell bonbonnière, Paris, the cover inset with a painted miniature of a nude being attended by putti, after Jacques Charlier, signed 'Valery', splits to the gold mounts.

1809-19   *3in (7.5cm) diam*

$1,500-2,300   **DN**

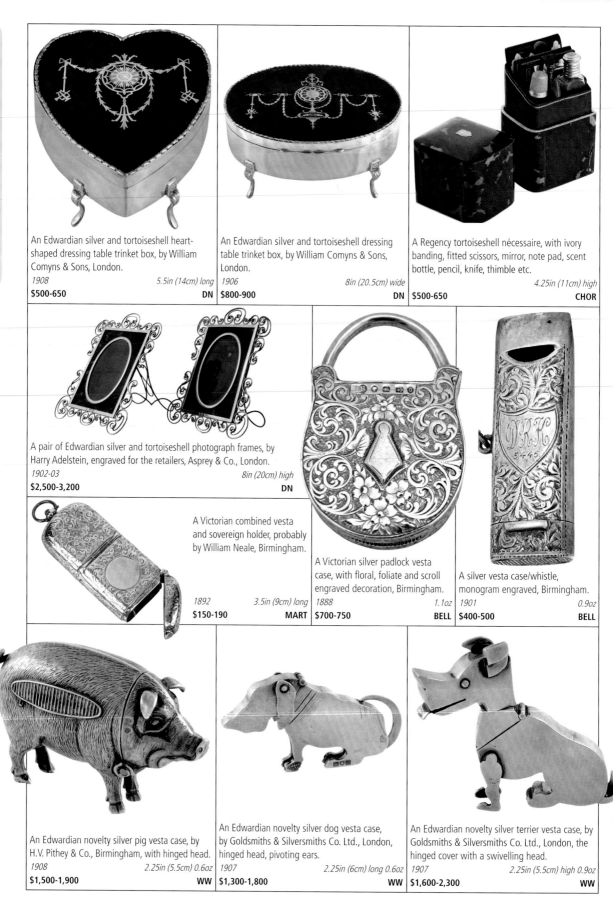

An Edwardian silver and tortoiseshell heart-shaped dressing table trinket box, by William Comyns & Sons, London.
1908   *5.5in (14cm) long*
$500-650   DN

An Edwardian silver and tortoiseshell dressing table trinket box, by William Comyns & Sons, London.
1906   *8in (20.5cm) wide*
$800-900   DN

A Regency tortoiseshell nécessaire, with ivory banding, fitted scissors, mirror, note pad, scent bottle, pencil, knife, thimble etc.
4.25in (11cm) high
$500-650   CHOR

A pair of Edwardian silver and tortoiseshell photograph frames, by Harry Adelstein, engraved for the retailers, Asprey & Co., London.
1902-03   *8in (20cm) high*
$2,500-3,200   DN

A Victorian combined vesta and sovereign holder, probably by William Neale, Birmingham.
1892   *3.5in (9cm) long*
$150-190   MART

A Victorian silver padlock vesta case, with floral, foliate and scroll engraved decoration, Birmingham.
1888   *1.1oz*
$700-750   BELL

A silver vesta case/whistle, monogram engraved, Birmingham.
1901   *0.9oz*
$400-500   BELL

An Edwardian novelty silver pig vesta case, by H.V. Pithey & Co., Birmingham, with hinged head.
1908   *2.25in (5.5cm) 0.6oz*
$1,500-1,900   WW

An Edwardian novelty silver dog vesta case, by Goldsmiths & Silversmiths Co. Ltd., London, hinged head, pivoting ears.
1907   *2.25in (6cm) long 0.6oz*
$1,300-1,800   WW

An Edwardian novelty silver terrier vesta case, by Goldsmiths & Silversmiths Co. Ltd., London, the hinged cover with a swivelling head.
1907   *2.25in (5.5cm) high 0.9oz*
$1,600-2,300   WW

A Victorian silver vesta case, with a 'flip' cover at each end, enameled with a fox-hunting scene, by Sampson Mordan & Co., London, dated.
1891   *2in (5cm) long 1.24oz*
$1,500-1,900   **LAW**

A silver and enamel vesta case, by Sampson Mordan & Co., London, painted with eight foxhounds, marks are clear.
1897   *1.75in (4.5cm) long*
$1,300-1,800   **DN**

An Edwardian silver vesta case, enameled with fox hunters and hounds jumping a ditch, maker's mark partially worn, possibly 'GB', Birmingham.
1905   *1.5in (4cm) long 0.8oz*
$1,000-1,100   **LAW**

An Edwardian silver vesta case, enameled with a pack of hounds waiting in a brick-paved yard, by Sampson Mordan & Co. Ltd., Chester.
1905   *2.5in (6cm) long 1.3oz*
$2,300-2,800   **LAW**

A Victorian silver and enamel novelty sentry box vesta case, by S. Mordan, London, enameled with a Coldstream Guardsman, the base with a striker.
1886   *2.25in (5.5cm) high 0.8oz*
$2,500-3,800   **WW**

A silver and enamel vesta case, of military interest, by Sampson Mordan & Co., London, painted with a Blues and Royals guard mounted on a horse.
1892   *2.25in (5.5cm) long*
$2,300-2,800   **DN**

A silver and enamel vesta case, by Howard James, Birmingham, enameled with a horse's head.
1890   *2.25in (5.5cm) long 1.1oz*
$300-450   **PC**

A Victorian silver and enamel erotica vesta case, by Sampson Mordan & Co., London, incuse-stamped 'Copyright', painted with a scantily clad young lady in silhouette.
1889   *2.25in (5.5cm) long*
$1,800-2,300   **DN**

A silver and shagreen double vesta box and covers, by AWH, London.
1923   *3.5in (9cm) wide*
$1,000-1,200   **MOR**

A silver vesta case, enameled with a flying flag and inscribed 'Miss Mollie - 1891', maker's mark 'TS', Birmingham.

Miss Mollie was a Clyde-built yacht, built on the Clyde in shipyard no. 7, by Alexander Robertson & Sons Ltd. in 1891.
1891   *2in (5cm) high 1.4oz*
$400-500   **LAW**

OBJETS DE VERTU

A Victorian silver and enamel vesta case, by Howard James, Birmingham, with a scene from Punch Magazine, with gilded interior.
1890   1.75in (4.5cm) long 0.9oz
$800-950   **WW**

A silver and enamel vesta case, by Saunders and Shepherd, Birmingham, with the King of Diamonds card, with a ring attachment.
1883   2in (5cm) long 0.8oz
$950-1,100   **WW**

An Austro-Hungarian silver cigarette case, enameled with fox hunting, by Georg Adam Scheid of Vienna, with English import marks for London, dated.
1897   3.5in (9cm) long 3.8oz
$950-1,100   **LAW**

A French Art Deco silver and guilloche enamel cigarette case, in a fitted case by Fattorini & Sons Ltd.
4.25in (11cm) high 5oz
$1,600-2,000   **HT**

A silver cigarette case, with enamel '19th hole' illustration to lid, with hallmarks for Birmingham, John Collard Vickery.
1913   3.25in (8.5cm) long
$1,100-1,400   **TEN**

A German silver and enamel stirrup shaped cigarette case, with maker's mark 'ALV', post-1886 sterling standard, some retouching, with a cabochon sapphire.
c1910   3.75in (9.5cm) long 5.2oz
$650-750   **DN**

A Continental silver and enamel cigarette case, stamped '900', probably German, painted with a half length portrait of a lightly clad maiden, the base plain.
c1910   3.5in (9cm) long 4.3oz
$700-750   **DN**

A Victorian silver and enamel cigar case, by George Heath, London, with two topless ladies having a duel, with four other ladies.

This case was originally part of a series of duel cases.
1889   5in (13cm) long 6.9oz
$1,300-1,500   **WW**

A Victorian silver and enamel cigarette case, by Howard James, Birmingham, with a Punch Magazine front cover.
1887   3.25in (8cm) long 3.6oz
$500-650   **WW**

A late 19thC German silver and enamel cigarette case, with a semi-nude lady holding an epee.
3.5in (8.5cm) long 2.5oz
$450-550   **WW**

A Birmingham enamel snuff box, painted with ducks, the sides with flowers.
c1760   3.25in (8cm) wide
$950-1,100   WW

A South Staffordshire enamel snuff box, with a figure flying a kite beside a seated lady, some restoration.
c1770   3in (7.5cm) long
$650-750   WW

A Bilston enamel snuff box, printed with the Ladies Amusement, the sides with putti emblematic of The Arts, the interior with a piper courting a maiden.
c1775   3.5in (9cm) wide
$1,900-2,300   WW

A Bilston enamel snuff box, with a figure driving a horse and cart, some restoration.
c1770-80   2.5in (6cm) wide
$650-750   WW

An English enamel snuff box, with a titled portrait of George Washington, with hinged metal mounts.
c1790   2in (5cm) long
$300-450   WW

A Staffordshire enamel étui, with courting couples, with scissors, a penknife, a snuff spoon and tweezers, some restoration.
c1770   4in (10cm) high
$1,900-2,300   WW

An English enamel étui with thimble, a small amount of cracking.
c1770   5in (13cm) long
$1,000-1,250   WW

An early 19thC English enamel and gilt metal étui, with figures in landscape, the interior with various implements.
     4in (10cm) high
$1,000-1,100   L&T

A Bilston enamel bonbonnière, with landscapes and hunting scenes.
c1780   1.5in (4cm) long
$700-800   CHOR

A Bilston enamel patch box, inscribed 'Parental Affection', enclosing a cracked mirror.
c1800   2.25in (5.5cm) wide
$1,000-1,200   CHOR

A late Victorian gold-mounted enamel scent bottle, by S. Mordan and Co., in a later case, unmarked, the neck engraved '16'.
     3in (8cm) high
$4,500-5,000   WW

A Bilston enamel portrait plaque, of Lady Harding.
c1765   3.5in (8.5cm) wide
$1,100-1,400   CHOR

OBJETS DE VERTU

ESSENTIAL REFERENCE - CARD CASES

In the late 18thC, among polite society, the practice emerged of presenting a 'calling card' (or carte-de-visite) at someone's house to request a visit or announce an impending arrival. Used extensively during 19thC, the convention of 'leaving one's card' fell into decline around the 1930s. Eminently collectable, most surviving cases date from the 1830s, and were fashioned from materials such as tortoiseshell, Mother-of-pearl, ivory, and silver (either plated over copper, or solid). Aside from exceptionally rare gold examples, solid silver had the most status and remains the most sought-after.

The main center of production for silver cases was Birmingham, and notable makers to look out for are Joseph Willmore, Taylor & Perry, Edward Smith, and especially Nathaniel Mills. It is in the decoration of silver cases, however, that collectors have most to choose from. The most sought-after are engraved or die-stamped with architectural views.

Collectively known as 'castle-tops', they depict well-known landmarks, such as Windsor, Kenilworth or Edinburgh castles, or Westminster Abbey, St. Paul's Cathedral, or Chatsworth House.

A silver engraved 'castle-top' card case, with the Holy Trinity Church, Hull, by Nathaniel Mills, Birmingham.
1844 *4in (10cm) long 2.3oz*
$7,500-9,000 **WW**

A 'castle-top' card case, of Windsor Castle, by Nathaniel Mills, Birmingham, inscribed 'To H. Arnot from her Sincere friend W.C. Smith, London, 3rd April 1846'.
1845 *4in (10cm) long 2.3oz*
$1,000-1,200 **WW**

A silver 'castle-top' card case, with Eddistone lighthouse, by Nathaniel Mills, Birmingham, the reverse with similar decoration.
1849 *4in (10cm) long 2.3oz*
$15,000-18,000 **WW**

A silver 'castle-top' card case, by Nathaniel Mills, Birmingham, with Osborne House from the water, inscribed 'Elizabeth'.
1847 *4in (10cm) high 2.6oz*
$1,000-1,200 **DN**

A silver embossed 'castle-top' card case, with the Tower of London with the Thames and traitor's gate, by David Pettifer, Birmingham.
1848 *4in (10cm) high 2oz*
$950-1,100 **LAW**

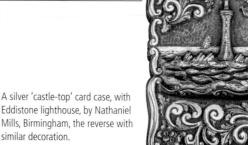

A silver engraved 'castle-top' card case, with Brighton Old Chain Pier, by Nathaniel Mills, Birmingham.
1851 *4in (10cm) long 2.1oz*
$1,900-2,300 **WW**

A silver embossed 'castle-top' card case, with the Scott Memorial, Edinburgh, initialed, by D. Pettifer, Birmingham.
1852 *4.25in (10.5cm) high 2.1oz*
$650-750 **LAW**

A silver 'castle-top' card case, with King's College, Cambridge, by Alfred Taylor, Birmingham, the reverse with similar decoration.
1854 *4in (10cm) long 2.2oz*
$3,500-4,300 **WW**

A silver embossed 'castle-top' card case, with King's College Chapel, Cambridge, by Hilliard & Thomason, Birmingham.
1858 *4in (10cm) high 2.1oz*
$2,500-3,200 **LAW**

A Victorian silver 'castle-top' card case, with Arundel Castle, by George Unite, Birmingham, with a cartouche engraved 'SD, from her father, Quebec August 21,1860'.

1858   *4in (10cm) long 2oz*

$15,000-18,000   **WW**

A silver engraved 'castle-top' card case, with Scarborough Esplanade and South Sands, maker's mark 'A&S', Birmingham 1859.

Taken from a print of 1846, engraved by W. Monkhouse.

4in (10cm) high 1.8oz

$5,500-6,500   **LAW**

A silver 'castle-top' card case, with The Post Office, Dublin, by Alfred Taylor, Birmingham, the reverse with similar decoration and engraved 'Helen'.

The crest is that used by a number of families including: Arthur, O'Fallon, O'Donovan, Marlay and Stratton.

1860   *4in (10cm) high 2.6oz*

$15,000-18,000   **WW**

An Irish 'castle-top' card case, of Trinity College, Dublin, by John Scriber, Dublin.

1864   *4in (10cm) long 2.1oz*

$11,000-14,000   **WW**

A Victorian silver 'castle-top' card case, by George Unite, Birmingham, with a scene of Osbourne House from the gardens.

1871   *3.75in (9.5cm) wide 2oz*

$650-750   **WW**

A Victorian 'castle-top' card case, by George Unite, Birmingham, with Newstead Abbey.

1875   *3.75in (9.5cm) high*

$800-950   **CHOR**

A late 19thC Chinese silver card case, with maker's mark, possibly that of Woshing.

3.5in (8.5cm) long 1.7oz

$700-800   **WW**

A Victorian tortoiseshell card case, side hinged button release lid, blonde shell to spine, with Mother-of-pearl floral inlay.

2in (5cm) wide

$180-250   **MART**

A Victorian tortoiseshell card case, with silvered motifs.

4.25in (10.5cm) high

$100-120   **BELL**

A Victorian tortoiseshell card case, inlaid with Mother-of-pearl.

4in (10cm) high

$150-190   **DW**

A silver nutmeg grater, London, engraved with a tulip, the base scratch initialed 'S*M', maker's mark 'TA' below a pellet, unascribed.

c1690   *2.5in (6.5cm) long 0.6oz*

$1,500-1,900   **WW**

A William and Mary silver nutmeg grater, maker's mark 'IA' for John Albright, London, engraved with a tulip.

c1690   *1.75in (4.5cm) long 0.9oz*

$2,500-3,200   **WW**

A silver rasp or grater, maker's mark only, 'AL', unascribed.

1680-1700   *2.75in (7cm) long 0.3oz*

$2,500-3,200   **LAW**

A silver nutmeg grater, by Samuel Meriton, London.

c1775   *1.75in (4.5cm) high 0.5oz*

$700-800   **WW**

A George III silver nutmeg grater, maker's mark 'I.P', possibly for James Phipps.

c1780   *2.75in (7cm) long 1.5oz*

$1,000-1,100   **WW**

A George III silver nutmeg grater, by Thomas Willmore, Birmingham.

1797   *1.5in (4cm) high 0.5oz*

$700-800   **WW**

A silver nutmeg grater/corkscrew, possibly by George Harris, London.

1810   *5in (13cm) long 2oz*

$7,000-7,500   **WW**

A George III silver nutmeg grater, by Thomas Phipps, Edward Robinson and James Phipps, London.

1812   *1.75in (5cm) long 1.6oz*

$500-550   **WW**

A silver nutmeg grater, by John Reily, London.

1823   *1.5in (4cm) long 1.2oz*

$2,800-3,500   **WW**

A silver nutmeg grater, by Taylor and Perry, Birmingham, of stylized melon form.

1836   *1.5in (4cm) long 0.9oz*

$1,300-1,500   **WW**

A silver nutmeg grater, London, of drop-shaped form.

1861

$400-450   **BELL**

ESSENTIAL REFERENCE - PEPPER POT

This design may be based on a story relating to Paul du Chaillu (1837-1903) an American 19thC explorer, who, in 1856 spent three and a half years exploring a large section of the Gabon coast. He was the first white man to see and hunt a gorilla. One story told was of a hunting expedition and a 'Killer Gorilla'. Du Chaillu was out with a group of local guides, they split in different directions and after a while he heard the 'tremendous roar of the gorilla... instinctively we made for the spot... the poor brave fellow who had gone off alone was lying on the ground in a pool of his own blood... beside him lay his gun, the stock broken, and the barrel bent almost double. In one place it was flattened, and it bore plainly the marks of the gorilla's teeth... this huge gorilla thought the gun was his enemy, so he had seized it and dashed it on the ground... not satisfied, had taken it up again and given it a tremendous bite...'.

A silver gorilla pepper pot, by Thomas, William, Henry and Louis Dee, London, the gorilla with a broken rifle, the pull-off head with glass eyes.

1861   *5in (12.5cm) high 8.5oz*
$6,500-7,500   **WW**

A silver owl cruet set, by Richards & Brown, London, leather cased.

1865 and 1867   *3in (7.5cm) high 5.5oz*
$6,500-7,000   **APAR**

A silver kitten condiment set, by Robert Hennell, London.

1875   *3.75in (9.5cm) long 13.5oz*
$7,000-7,500   **WW**

Judith Picks

Who doesn't remember summer holidays and the Punch and Judy show on the beach!

The Punch and Judy show has roots in the 16thC Italian 'commedia dell'arte'. The figure of Punch is derived from the Neapolitan stock character of Pulcinella. The figure who later became Mr Punch made his first recorded appearance in England on 9 May 1662. In the British Punch and Judy show, Punch is a hunchback whose hooked nose almost meets his curved, jutting chin. He carries a stick (called a slapstick) as large as himself, which he freely uses upon most of the other characters in the show. He speaks in a distinctive squawking voice, produced by a contrivance known as a 'swazzle'. There are many catchphrases associated with Punch. For example, Punch dispatches his foes with: 'That's the way to do it!', and the term 'pleased as Punch' is derived from his characteristic sense of gleeful self-satisfaction. What is particularly interesting in these pepper pots is that Judy is taking snuff. Very egalitarian!

A pair of Punch and Judy silver pepper pots, by Joseph Clarke, London.

1894   *2.25in (6cm) 4.2oz*
$2,500-3,200   **WW**

A silver pepper pot, modeled as a railway lamp, maker's mark of 'A' and 'B', Birmingham.

1900   *1.75in (4.5cm) high 1oz*
$300-350   **WW**

A pair of silver-cast budgerigar pepperettes, with red glass eyes and a hinged flap under their tails for filling, by George Brace, London.

1905   *4.5in (11.5cm) long 4.5oz*
$900-1,000   **LAW**

A silver teddy bear pepper pot, by J. Gloster Limited, Birmingham.

1909   *1.25in (3.5cm) high 0.3oz*
$300-400   **WW**

A silver drum mustard pot, by Charles and George Fox, London, with a blue glass liner.

1855   *3.25in (8.5cm) high 6.9oz*
$1,500-1,900   **WW**

A silver honey skep, by Thomas Hobbs and James Taylor, London.

1798   *4.75in (12cm) high 7.7oz*
$6,500-7,500   **WW**

CLOSER LOOK - SCENT BOTTLE

A rat is a quirky and interesting choice of form for a scent bottle.

The body is naturalistically engraved.

It has a sprung hinge, operated by pushing the tail.

It has the original Victorian internal glass phial.

A Victorian novelty rat scent bottle case, unmarked.

1.5in (4cm) long

$950-1,100 LAW

A desk seal, the terminal formed as a pug's head with paste set eyes, Birmingham.

1910 *2.5in (6cm) long*

$300-350 L&T

An early 20thC Continental white metal desk seal, formed as a lion sejant with a crowned heraldic shield, unmarked.

3.5in (9cm) long

$400-500 L&T

A novelty silver dog atomiser, by Thomas Johnson, London, the mechanism not working.

1876 *2.5in (6.5cm) high 2.3oz*

$1,900-2,300 WW

A Victorian silver-gilt mounted enamel horseshoe glass scent bottle, by Henry Dee, London, retailed by S.F. Schaffer, 27 Piccadilly, cover modeled as a jockey's cap.

1871 *3in (8cm) long*

$1,900-2,300 WW

A silver parcel-gilt posy holder, in the form of an Arum lily flower Zantedeschia Aetheopica, by E.H. Stockwell, London.

1877 *5.5in (14cm) long 3.6oz*

$1,300-1,900 LAW

A pair of silver-gilt grape scissors, by Charles Rawlings, London.

1827 *7.25in (18.5cm) long 4.9oz*

$400-450 WW

An Edwardian novelty pig paperweight, by Sampson Mordan & Co., Chester, with loaded base.

3.5in (9cm) long

$450-500 LAW

A novelty silver 'Johnnie Walker' whisky decanter, marked 'SILVER' to base.

9.25in (23.5cm) high 15oz

$550-700 WW

A novelty silver dog's head box, by E.H. Stockwell, London, in the form of a stirrup cup.

1877 *6.25in (16cm) long 16.5oz*

$10,000-11,000 WW

A silver butt marker, by John Banks, London, with eight numbered pegs.
1898   *1.75in (4.5cm) long 1.4oz*
$1,300-1,800   **WW**

A silver-gilt butt marker, by Charles and George Asprey, London, with eight numbered ivory pegs.
1907   *2.75in (7cm) high 1oz*
$950-1,100   **WW**

A silver butt marker, by Asprey and Co., Chester, with ten numbered ivory pegs.
1924   *1.75in (4.5cm) long 1.5oz*
$1,000-1,100   **WW**

A George III silver eye bath, by Hester Bateman, London.
1787   *1.75in (4.5cm) high 0.5oz*
$1,200-1,500   **WW**

A George III silver corkscrew, unmarked.
c1780-1800   *2.75in (7cm) long*
$300-400   **WW**

A George III silver pocket corkscrew, by Joseph Willmore, with Mother-of-pearl handle.
c1800-10   *3in (8cm) long*
$500-650   **WW**

A Dutch silver 'Beau Brummell' corkscrew, maker's mark 'PC', possibly for Pieter Cruyff, Amsterdam, marked with a 19thC tax mark.
c1784-1800   *2.25in (5.5cm) long*
$1,300-1,900   **WW**

A 19thC Hipkins Patent single-lever corkscrew.

With the rarest corkscrews making five-figure sums, there's always the chance of a gem. This Hipkins Patent Single Lever corkscrew was stamped 'G.F. Hipkins & Son', and was made to a patent taken out in 1879. Variations of Hipkins corkscrews have made up to $7,000 in the past but this one was not in great condition although it still has strong collector appeal.
$2,500-3,800   **BOL**

A 17thC Continental parcel-gilt silver pomander, with segments with covers engraved: 1 Ranel, Moscat (later), 3 Rosmarin, 4 Schlag, 5 Negelren, 6 Rosen, 7 Citron, and 8 Lavendel, wear to gilding.
c1640   *2.25in (5.5cm) high 1oz*
$9,500-10,500   **WW**

A novelty silver elephant table cigar lighter, by James Barclay Hennell, London, inscribed 'ALERT 1880', with a figure in Indian dress, ivory tusks.
1879   *3.25in (8cm) long 5oz*
$2,800-3,800   **WW**

A George II gold nécessaire, London, with the Parisian post-1838 warranty mark, and the French 1838 gold guarantee mark, with an ink well, gold mounted scissors, a gold folding knife, a gold mounted pencil, ear spoons, two pierced ivory leaves, the base with a secret compartment.
c1750   *4in (10cm) high*
$3,800-4,400   **BELL**

A combination stamp box, with stamp moisturiser and tank, London.
1898   *3.75in (9.5cm) long*
$750-900   **TRI**

A 19thC agate and gilt metal chatelaine hook, containing scissors, penknife etc, a tiger's eye locket and a heart-shaped pendant.
8.25in (21cm) long cased
$1,900-2,300   **CHOR**

An 18thC shagreen-cased drawing étui.
6in (15cm) long
$250-400   **CHOR**

An ivory and piqué-worked six-drawer opera glass, by W & J Jones, of 30 Holborn, London, in a case.
3.75in (9.5cm) open
$800-950   **SWO**

An 18thC bronze screw-action nutcracker, with a pipe tamper end.
3.25in (8cm) long
$1,500-1,900   **WW**

An 18thC steel screw action nutcracker.
3.75in (9.5cm) long
$1,900-2,300   **WW**

A set of four silver menu or place card holders, by Elkington & Co., London, with silhouettes of sporting scenes.
1908   *3.5in (8.5cm) wide*
$650-750   **TEN**

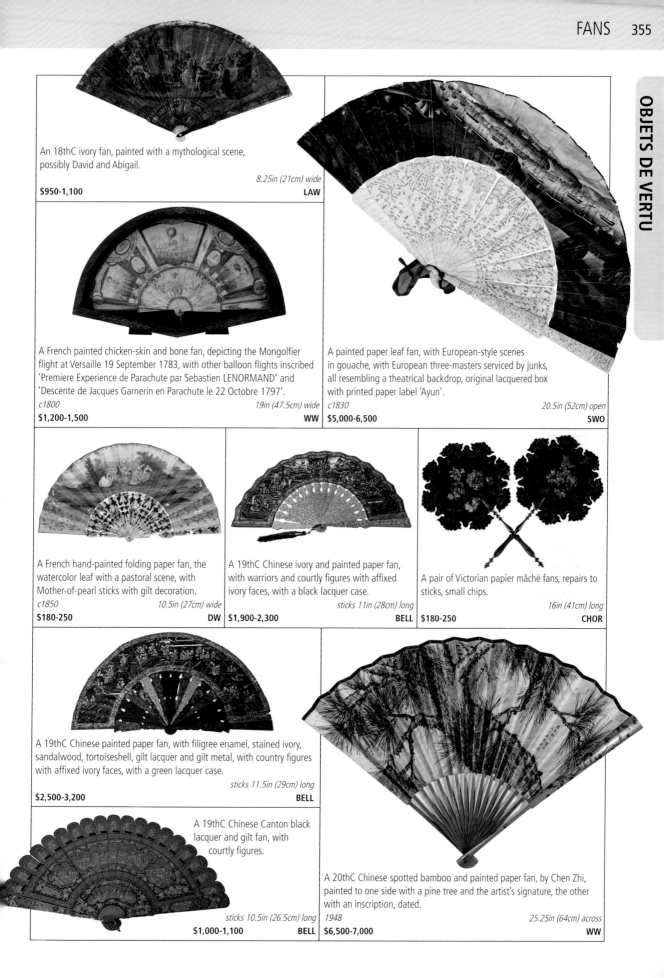

An 18thC ivory fan, painted with a mythological scene, possibly David and Abigail.

8.25in (21cm) wide

$950-1,100   **LAW**

A French painted chicken-skin and bone fan, depicting the Mongolfier flight at Versaille 19 September 1783, with other balloon flights inscribed 'Premiere Experience de Parachute par Sebastien LENORMAND' and 'Descente de Jacques Garnerin en Parachute le 22 Octobre 1797'.

c1800   *19in (47.5cm) wide*

$1,200-1,500   **WW**

A painted paper leaf fan, with European-style scenes in gouache, with European three-masters serviced by junks, all resembling a theatrical backdrop, original lacquered box with printed paper label 'Ayun'.

c1830   *20.5in (52cm) open*

$5,000-6,500   **SWO**

A French hand-painted folding paper fan, the watercolor leaf with a pastoral scene, with Mother-of-pearl sticks with gilt decoration.

c1850   *10.5in (27cm) wide*

$180-250   **DW**

A 19thC Chinese ivory and painted paper fan, with warriors and courtly figures with affixed ivory faces, with a black lacquer case.

sticks 11in (28cm) long

$1,900-2,300   **BELL**

A pair of Victorian papier mâché fans, repairs to sticks, small chips.

16in (41cm) long

$180-250   **CHOR**

A 19thC Chinese painted paper fan, with filigree enamel, stained ivory, sandalwood, tortoiseshell, gilt lacquer and gilt metal, with country figures with affixed ivory faces, with a green lacquer case.

sticks 11.5in (29cm) long

$2,500-3,200   **BELL**

A 19thC Chinese Canton black lacquer and gilt fan, with courtly figures.

sticks 10.5in (26.5cm) long

$1,000-1,100   **BELL**

A 20thC Chinese spotted bamboo and painted paper fan, by Chen Zhi, painted to one side with a pine tree and the artist's signature, the other with an inscription, dated.

1948   *25.25in (64cm) across*

$6,500-7,000   **WW**

A 17thC English silver thimble, the band inscribed 'EH', unmarked.

1in (2.5cm) high

$300-350   **BELL**

A 19thC silver thimble, with Brighton Pavilion, unmarked.

1in (2.5cm) high

$250-320   **BELL**

A 19thC tortoiseshell and gold 'Piercy's Patent' thimble, cased.

c1820   1in (2.5cm) long

$650-750   **APAR**

A Victorian 15ct gold and seed pearl set thimble.

1in (2.5cm) high

$180-250   **BELL**

A 19thC gold and enamel thimble, English or French, with the motto 'L'Industrie Ajoute A La Beaute', in a shagreen case.

1in (2.5cm) high 0.2oz

$900-1,000   **DN**

An 18ct gold and enamel thimble, marked '.750'.

0.75in (2cm) high

$150-190   **BELL**

A 15ct rose gold thimble, with white hardstone, hallmarked '.535 BH'.

1in (2.5cm) high

$100-150   **BELL**

A late 19thC Continental silver fish pin cushion, with import marks for London, and David Bridge, with later cushion.

1893   5.5in (13.5cm) long

$1,600-2,000   **WW**

A silver owl pin cushion, by S. Mordan and Co., London.

1894

$1,200-1,400

1.5in (3.5cm) long

WW

A silver camel pin cushion, by Levi and Salaman, Birmingham, with later cushion.

1903   4in (10cm) long

$1,000-1,200   **WW**

A hedgehog pin cushion, by Levi & Salaman, Birmingham.

1905   1.75in (4.5cm) long

$500-550   **LAW**

A silver tortoise pin cushion, by Saunders and Shepherd, Birmingham.

1906   2in (5cm) long

$1,000-1,100   **WW**

A silver camel pin cushion, by Adie and Lovekin Ltd., Birmingham, with later cushion.
1906   *2in (5cm) high*
$500-650   **WW**

A silver fox pin cushion, by Walker & Hall, Birmingham.
1906   *2.5in (6cm) long*
$800-950   **WW**

A silver frog pin cushion, by Adie and Lovekin Limited, Birmingham, with later cushion.
1907   *2.25in (6cm) long*
$500-550   **WW**

A silver polar bear pin cushion, by Cohen & Charles Birmingham.
1907   *2.75in (7cm) long*
$1,500-1,900   **WW**

A silver rabbit pin cushion, Birmingham, repaired.
1908   *2.25in (5.5cm) long*
$500-550   **WW**

A silver elephant pin cushion, possibly by Adie and Lovekin Limited, Birmingham, with later cushion.
1909   *2.5in (7cm) long*
$450-500   **WW**

A silver lion pin cushion, by Spurrier and Co., Birmingham, with later cushion.
1909   *3.5in (8.5cm) long*
$2,500-3,200   **WW**

A silver donkey pin cushion, by Robert Pringle, Birmingham.
1909   *2.5in (6cm) high*
$900-1,000   **WW**

A silver and hardstone hoof pin cushion, registration no. Rd190006.
2in (5cm) long
$400-500   **WW**

A silver owl pin cushion, by Levi and Salaman, Birmingham, set with red eyes.
1910   *4.5in (11.5cm) long*
$1,300-1,600   **WW**

A silver Humpty Dumpty pin cushion, by Levi and Salaman, Birmingham, with later cushion.
1910   *1.75in (4.5cm) high*
$900-1,000   **WW**

A silver cock pheasant pin cushion, Birmingham.
1913   *5.5in (14cm) long*
$800-950   **TRI**

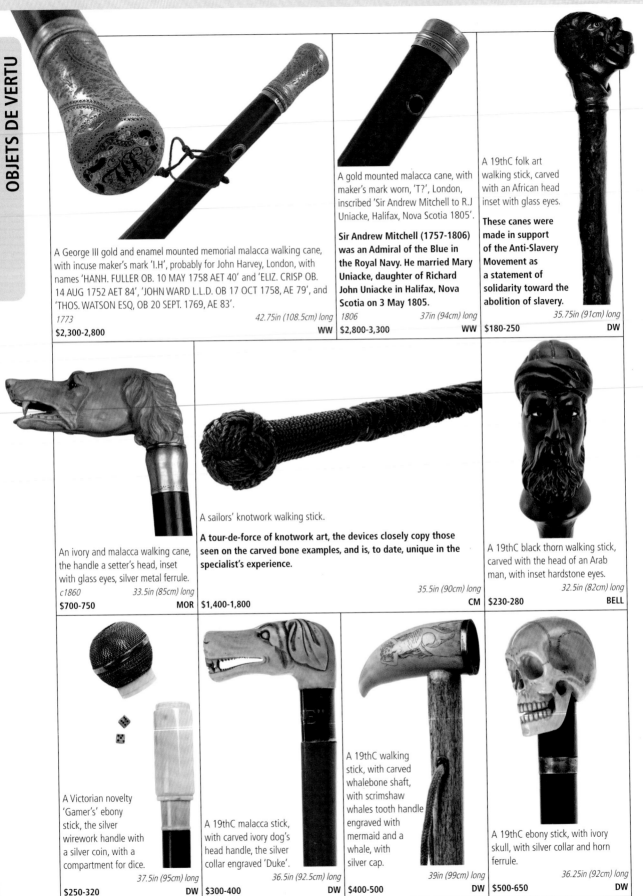

A George III gold and enamel mounted memorial malacca walking cane, with incuse maker's mark 'I.H', probably for John Harvey, London, with names 'HANH. FULLER OB. 10 MAY 1758 AET 40' and 'ELIZ. CRISP OB. 14 AUG 1752 AET 84', 'JOHN WARD L.L.D. OB 17 OCT 1758, AE 79', and 'THOS. WATSON ESQ, OB 20 SEPT. 1769, AE 83'.

1773   *42.75in (108.5cm) long*

$2,300-2,800   **WW**

A gold mounted malacca cane, with maker's mark worn, 'T?', London, inscribed 'Sir Andrew Mitchell to R.J Uniacke, Halifax, Nova Scotia 1805'.

Sir Andrew Mitchell (1757-1806) was an Admiral of the Blue in the Royal Navy. He married Mary Uniacke, daughter of Richard John Uniacke in Halifax, Nova Scotia on 3 May 1805.

1806   *37in (94cm) long*

$2,800-3,300   **WW**

A 19thC folk art walking stick, carved with an African head inset with glass eyes.

These canes were made in support of the Anti-Slavery Movement as a statement of solidarity toward the abolition of slavery.

     35.75in (91cm) long

$180-250   **DW**

An ivory and malacca walking cane, the handle a setter's head, inset with glass eyes, silver metal ferrule.

c1860   *33.5in (85cm) long*

$700-750   **MOR**

A sailors' knotwork walking stick.

A tour-de-force of knotwork art, the devices closely copy those seen on the carved bone examples, and is, to date, unique in the specialist's experience.

     35.5in (90cm) long

$1,400-1,800   **CM**

A 19thC black thorn walking stick, carved with the head of an Arab man, with inset hardstone eyes.

     32.5in (82cm) long

$230-280   **BELL**

A Victorian novelty 'Gamer's' ebony stick, the silver wirework handle with a silver coin, with a compartment for dice.

     37.5in (95cm) long

$250-320   **DW**

A 19thC malacca stick, with carved ivory dog's head handle, the silver collar engraved 'Duke'.

     36.5in (92.5cm) long

$300-400   **DW**

A 19thC walking stick, with carved whalebone shaft, with scrimshaw whales tooth handle engraved with mermaid and a whale, with silver cap.

     39in (99cm) long

$400-500   **DW**

A 19thC ebony stick, with ivory skull, with silver collar and horn ferrule.

     36.25in (92cm) long

$500-650   **DW**

ESSENTIAL REFERENCE - BLUE JOHN

Blue John is a semi-precious mineral found in Derbyshire and was used in France and England during the 18thC to manufacture decorative urns and objects with ormolu. Matthew Boulton (1728-1809) was a manufacturer based in Birmingham during the late 18thC who made works with this material and had success in selling vases to Queen Charlotte, wife of George III, which increased its popularity. See Ollerenshaw, Arthur and Harrison, Messrs R. J. and D., 'The History of Blue John Stone', second edition page 14, where illustrated and captioned: 'Collectors' specimens (part of the Ollerenshaw Collection)...Blue John and Ormolu urn attributed to Matthew Boulton c. 1780.'

A late 18thC ormolu-mounted Blue John urn, attributed to the Boulton workshop, with Neo-classical shouldered ovoid body.

16in (41cm) high 206.5oz

$33,000-38,000   **FELL**

A near pair of George III Blue John and gilt bronze urns, in the manner of Matthew Boulton, with pairs of satyr head handles.

9.5in (24.5cm) high

$6,500-7,500   **ROS**

A pair of late George III Derbyshire fluorspar Blue John, black slate, and gilt-metal mounted urns.

10.5in (27cm) high

$19,000-25,000   **APAR**

An early 19thC Derbyshire Blue John urn on stand, the body with deep purple inclusions, white and black marble mounted base.

13in (32cm) high

$7,500-10,000   **PC**

An 18thC George III Blue John and white marble sarcophagus, raised on lion's paw feet.

15.5in (39.5cm) wide

$19,000-25,000   **ROS**

An 18th/19thC Italian sienna marble and black marble tazza, in the manner of Benedetto Boschetti, with twin snake handles.

Benedetto Boschetti (fl.1820-1860) was based at no.74 Via dei Condotti, Rome and was known for selling carved works, after the antique, as well as micro mosaics and bronzes. He exhibited two 'mosaic tables' at the Great Exhibition of 1851 in Crystal Palace. Bonfigli's Roman Artistical Dictionary of 1856 lists Boschetti's shop and observes that 'The Establishment is particularly conspicuous for its great variety of marble works, bronzes, candelabra, table-tops, etc besides a rich collection of the best mosaics and shell engravings.'

13.5in (34cm) high

$8,000-9,000   **ROS**

A pair of 19thC French ormolu and white marble perfume burners, in Louis XVI-style, each with a lift-off lid with a cone finial.

13in (33cm) high

$650-750   **WW**

A pair of late 19thC French alabaster, enamel and gilt bronze urns.

18.25in (46.5cm) high

$1,900-2,300   **ROS**

A late 19thC novelty gilt brass inkstand, retailed by Ortner & Houle, London, the roof opening to a glass inkwell, with a vesta case and stamp box.

17in (43cm) wide

$1,000-1,500   **BELL**

OBJETS DE VERTU

A Dunhill 'Aquarium' table lighter, by Margaret Bennett, reverse painted with exotic and tropical fish, with brass fittings, cast 'Dunhill' and stamped 'made in England'.

4in (10cm) wide

$6,500-7,000 **WW**

A Dunhill 'Aquarium' table lighter, designed by Ben Shillingford, gilt metal and painted Perspex, with tropical fish amidst seaweed and rocks.

c1950 *2.75in (7cm) high*

$2,500-3,800 **BELL**

A 1950s Dunhill 'Aquarium' table lighter, with plated mounts and Lucite panels of fish, one panel cracked, stamped 'Made in England Patent No. 143752'.

2.75in (7cm) high

$1,500-2,000 **SWO**

A rare Dunhill 'Aquarium' table lighter, with chrome-plated mounts and a Perspex case, painted with a swan on one side and a goose on the other, marked 'Dunhill'.

3.75in (9.5cm) across

$11,000-14,000 **LAW**

A 9ct gold Dunhill petrol lighter, glazed with a mosaic of thirty miniature paintings, of floral and boating subjects, the lift arm detailed 'Dunhill', the body detailed 'London 1933'.

1.5in (4cm) high 1.1oz

$2,800-3,500 **BELL**

A 20thC silver plated Dunhill petrol lighter, with engine turned decoration, detailed 'Pat.No 390107', made in England.

$150-190 **BELL**

A Dunhill lacquered table lighter, with red flowers, inset Japanese bronze rectangular coins, 2 BU.

5.75in (14.5cm) high

$1,900-2,300 **L&T**

A rare Alfred Dunhill 9ct gold cigarette case unique lighter and integrated timepiece combination, by Bando (Matteo Cellini), stamped marks 'AD London 1929' and etched 'Bando'.

The name Bando first appeared in a Dunhill catalog as early as 1919 and Alfred Dunhill referred to Bando as 'These superb cases are the work of the renowned master craftsman in precious metal, Matteo Cellini, known familiarly as Bando. In beauty of design and perfection of craftsmanship they rival the famous craftsmen of old. Each bears the signature of the artist-craftsman, 'Bando'.

4in (10.5cm) wide

$7,000-8,000 **WW**

A Dunhill cased set of buttons, polished gilt frames, brushed white metal center, marked 'Dunhill Paris', in fitted case.

$250-320 **L&T**

A Russian silver-gilt and enamel bowl, Nemir-Kolodkin, Moscow, body cloisonné enameled with scrolling foliage.

1899-1908   *6in (15cm) wide*

$4,500-5,000   **MAB**

A Russian silver and enamel cauldron salt cellar, by Gustav Klingert, Moscow, 84 zolotniks.

1893   *1.75in (4.5cm) diam*

$300-450   **DN**

A Russian silver-gilt and enamel kovsch, bearing pseudo marks for Ovchinnikov, with vari-colored foliate scroll decoration, enameled blue bead border.

5in (12.5cm) wide 3.4oz

$950-1,100   **WW**

A Russian silver-gilt and cloisonné enamel beaker, with scroll foliate enamelling on a matted ground between turquoise borders, makers' marks 'IS', Moscow.

1889   *5.5in (14cm) high*

$3,800-4,400   **MAB**

ESSENTIAL REFERENCE - KOVSH

The Kovsh is a traditional drinking vessel or ladle. It was oval-shaped like a boat with a single handle and may be shaped like a water bird or a Norse longship. Originally the Kovsh was made from wood and used to serve and drink mead, with specimens excavated from as early as the 10thC. It is thought that many of the earliest silver examples, which date from the 16thC, were presented by the Tsars to loyal supporters or visiting dignitaries; they are sometimes engraved with the royal double-headed eagle and are inscribed around the rim with the name and an account of the recipient.

The vessels were usually made of silver and, until the 18thC, were of fairly simple design.

A Russian silver-gilt and shaded enamel kovsh, by Ivan Klebnikov, Kokoshnik mark, 88 zolotniks, painted with scroll foliage on a matted ground above a lobed band painted with flowers, two internal flakes to enamels within the cloisonnés.

1896-1908   *3.25in (8cm) long*

$1,900-2,300   **DN**

ESSENTIAL REFERENCE - ZOLOTNIK

The Russian silver standard is based on the zolotnik, a word derived from the Slavonic word for gold. The zolotnik was originally a gold coin circulating in Kievan Rus in the late 11thC, and was originally pegged to 1/96th of a Russian pound, which was later changed to 1/72nd of a Russian pound. One zolotnik is equal to 4,266g or 150oz.

By far the most common mark is '84', as with this purse. This degree of purity became the standard for every-day silver purity. In Russia the '84' was accompanied by several other punches: a regional or city punch, an assay master's punch, and a maker's punch are usually encountered. All but the maker's punch were required by law during the 18th and 19thC. This marking system remained in use until 1899. At that time the Kokoshnik (after a traditional headdress worn on the woman's head on the punch), was instituted.

A Russian silver gilt and enamel egg cup, by Nickolai Alexaey, Moscow, with Kokoshnik mark, 84 zolotniks, painted with Cupid kissing a putti, clear mark, some staining to the enamel.

1896-1908   *2.5in (6.5cm) high*

$1,000-1,200   **DN**

A Russian silver gilt and enamel jar and cover, by Gustav Klingert, Moscow, 84 zolotniks, decorated with scroll foliage on a matted ground, marks clear.

1896   *3.25in (8cm) high 5.57oz*

$1,900-2,300   **DN**

A Russian silver and enamel purse, by Alexander Yegorov or Egorov, Moscow, with Kokoshnik mark, 84 zolotniks, with a trellis panel bordered by a red band of shells and spirals, lower panels both flaked, some petals, leaves and scrolls flaked, case distorted, lining lacking.

1908-17   *4.75in (12cm) long*

$3,800-4,400   **DN**

RUSSIAN ANTIQUES

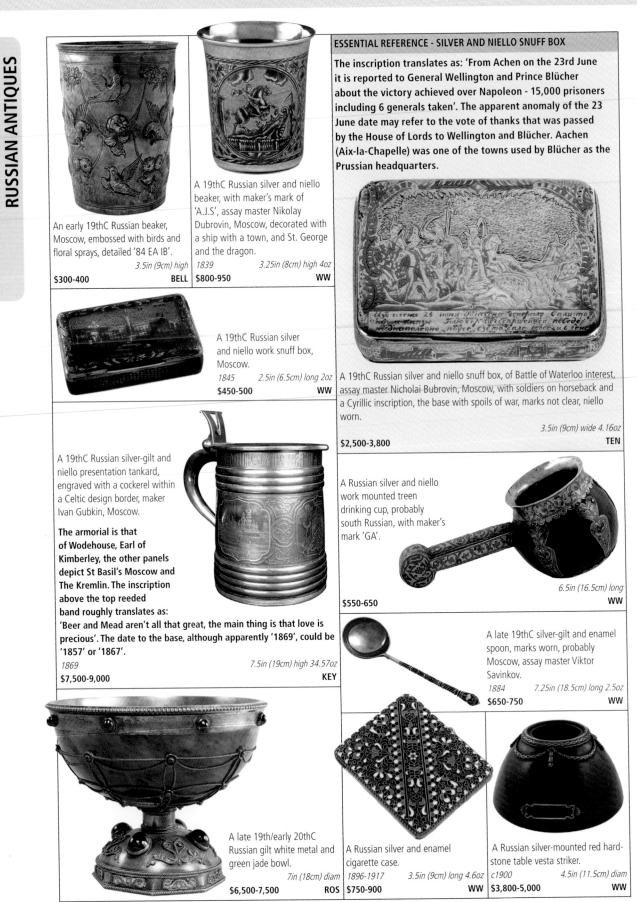

An early 19thC Russian beaker, Moscow, embossed with birds and floral sprays, detailed '84 EA IB'.

3.5in (9cm) high

$300-400 BELL

A 19thC Russian silver and niello beaker, with maker's mark of 'A.J.S', assay master Nikolay Dubrovin, Moscow, decorated with a ship with a town, and St. George and the dragon.

1839 3.25in (8cm) high 4oz

$800-950 WW

ESSENTIAL REFERENCE - SILVER AND NIELLO SNUFF BOX

The inscription translates as: 'From Achen on the 23rd June it is reported to General Wellington and Prince Blücher about the victory achieved over Napoleon - 15,000 prisoners including 6 generals taken'. The apparent anomaly of the 23 June date may refer to the vote of thanks that was passed by the House of Lords to Wellington and Blücher. Aachen (Aix-la-Chapelle) was one of the towns used by Blücher as the Prussian headquarters.

A 19thC Russian silver and niello work snuff box, Moscow.

1845 2.5in (6.5cm) long 2oz

$450-500 WW

A 19thC Russian silver and niello snuff box, of Battle of Waterloo interest, assay master Nicholai Bubrovin, Moscow, with soldiers on horseback and a Cyrillic inscription, the base with spoils of war, marks not clear, niello worn.

3.5in (9cm) wide 4.16oz

$2,500-3,800 TEN

A 19thC Russian silver-gilt and niello presentation tankard, engraved with a cockerel within a Celtic design border, maker Ivan Gubkin, Moscow.

The armorial is that of Wodehouse, Earl of Kimberley, the other panels depict St Basil's Moscow and The Kremlin. The inscription above the top reeded band roughly translates as: 'Beer and Mead aren't all that great, the main thing is that love is precious'. The date to the base, although apparently '1869', could be '1857' or '1867'.

1869 7.5in (19cm) high 34.57oz

$7,500-9,000 KEY

A Russian silver and niello work mounted treen drinking cup, probably south Russian, with maker's mark 'GA'.

6.5in (16.5cm) long

$550-650 WW

A late 19thC silver-gilt and enamel spoon, marks worn, probably Moscow, assay master Viktor Savinkov.

1884 7.25in (18.5cm) long 2.5oz

$650-750 WW

A late 19th/early 20thC Russian gilt white metal and green jade bowl.

7in (18cm) diam

$6,500-7,500 ROS

A Russian silver and enamel cigarette case.

1896-1917 3.5in (9cm) long 4.6oz

$750-900 WW

A Russian silver-mounted red hardstone table vesta striker.

c1900 4.5in (11.5cm) diam

$3,800-5,000 WW

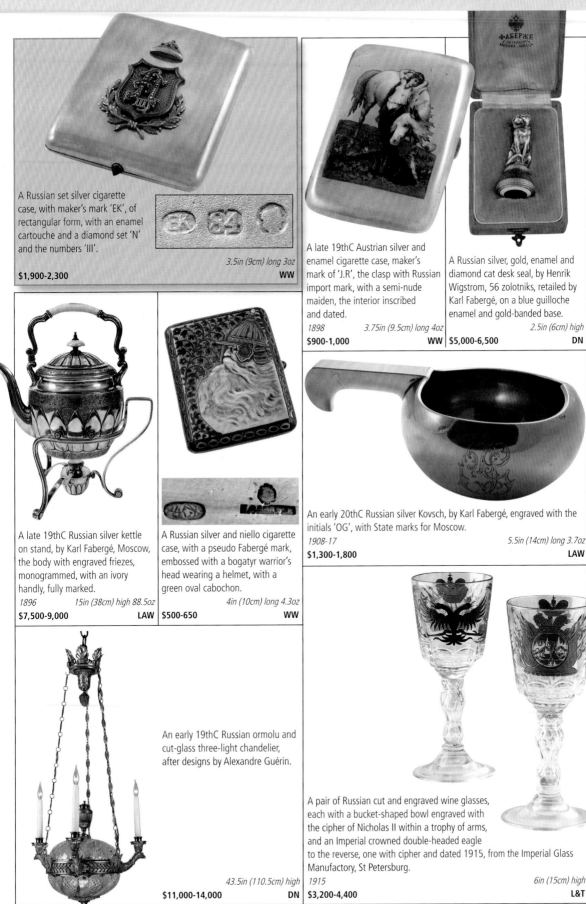

A Russian set silver cigarette case, with maker's mark 'EK', of rectangular form, with an enamel cartouche and a diamond set 'N' and the numbers 'III'.

3.5in (9cm) long 3oz

$1,900-2,300   **WW**

A late 19thC Austrian silver and enamel cigarette case, maker's mark of 'J.R', the clasp with Russian import mark, with a semi-nude maiden, the interior inscribed and dated.

1898   3.75in (9.5cm) long 4oz

$900-1,000   **WW**

A Russian silver, gold, enamel and diamond cat desk seal, by Henrik Wigstrom, 56 zolotniks, retailed by Karl Fabergé, on a blue guilloche enamel and gold-banded base.

2.5in (6cm) high

$5,000-6,500   **DN**

A late 19thC Russian silver kettle on stand, by Karl Fabergé, Moscow, the body with engraved friezes, monogrammed, with an ivory handly, fully marked.

1896   15in (38cm) high 88.5oz

$7,500-9,000   **LAW**

A Russian silver and niello cigarette case, with a pseudo Fabergé mark, embossed with a bogatyr warrior's head wearing a helmet, with a green oval cabochon.

4in (10cm) long 4.3oz

$500-650   **WW**

An early 20thC Russian silver Kovsch, by Karl Fabergé, engraved with the initials 'OG', with State marks for Moscow.

1908-17   5.5in (14cm) long 3.7oz

$1,300-1,800   **LAW**

An early 19thC Russian ormolu and cut-glass three-light chandelier, after designs by Alexandre Guérin.

43.5in (110.5cm) high

$11,000-14,000   **DN**

A pair of Russian cut and engraved wine glasses, each with a bucket-shaped bowl engraved with the cipher of Nicholas II within a trophy of arms, and an Imperial crowned double-headed eagle to the reverse, one with cipher and dated 1915, from the Imperial Glass Manufactory, St Petersburg.

1915   6in (15cm) high

$3,200-4,400   **L&T**

A 16thC central Russian polychrome painted and parcel-gilt icon, depicting Saint Nicholas and Scenes from his Life, the painted and gilded surfaces are rubbed.

39in (99cm) high

$19,000-25,000 DN

A late 17thC North Russian polychrome painted and parcel-gilt icon, depicting the Dormition of the Virgin, the Virgin on her deathbed surrounded by the Apostles, Christ standing behind her and holding a swaddled infant representing the soul of His mother, some damage.

23.25in (59cm) high

$3,200-3,800 DN

An 18thC Russian polychrome painted and parcel-gilt icon, depicting Saint Nicholas of Myra, significant overpainting overall.

14in (35.5cm) high

$900-1,300 DN

A late 18thC Russian polychrome painted and parcel-gilt icon, depicting Saint Zosima and Saint Savvati, with Christ portrayed in an arched recess some rubbing and repainting.

14in (35.5cm) high

$1,300-1,900 DN

A 19thC Russian icon, depicting St Dimitri slaying the pagan king, tempera on panel.

14.25in (36cm) high

$900-1,000 DN

A Russian icon, 'Our Lady of Kazan', in a silver, silver gilt and cloisonné enamel oklad, assay mark 'Anatoly Apollonovich Artsybashev, Moscow', maker's mark unclear, possibly Ivan Tarabrov, Moscow.

c1890 *11.75in (30cm) high*

$11,000-12,000 CHOR

ESSENTIAL REFERENCE - ICONOSTASIS

In Eastern Christianity an iconostasis is a wall of icons and religious paintings, separating the nave from the sanctuary in a church. Iconostasis also refers to a portable icon stand that can be placed anywhere within a church. The iconostasis evolved from the Byzantine templon, a process complete by the 15thC. A direct comparison for the function of the main iconostasis can be made to the layout of the great Temple in Jerusalem. That Temple was designed with three parts. The holiest and inner-most portion was that where the Ark of the Covenant was kept. This portion, the Holy of Holies, was separated from the second larger part of the building's interior by a curtain. Only the High Priest was allowed to enter the Holy of Holies. The third part was the entrance court. This architectural tradition for the two main parts can be seen carried forward in Christian churches and is still most demonstratively present in Eastern Orthodox churches where the iconostasis divides the altar, the Holy of Holies containing the consecrated Eucharist. In the Eastern Orthodox tradition only men can enter the altar portion behind the iconostasis.

A 19thC Russian portable iconostasis, the central panel simulating the Royal Doors, with the Evangelists and the Annunciation, the Last Supper, the Crucifixion and the Anastasis, on the top tier the Mother of God of the Sign flanked by two prophets, the three upper rows displaying portraits of saints, the apostles and prophets, tempera on panels.

56in (142cm) wide

$7,500-9,000 DN

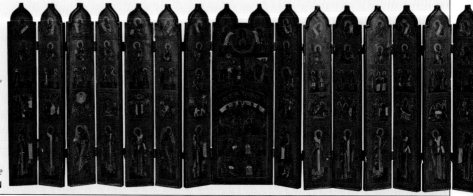

A pair of porcelain plates from the Tsar Nicholas I service, each with six cartouches displaying the Orders of St George, St Vladimir, White Eagle, St Stanislaus, St Alexander Nevsky and St Anne, enclosing the Order of St Andrew, with blue Imperial cipher for Nicholas I and gilt numerals, made at Imperial Porcelain Factory, St Petersburg.

1825-55   *9.75in (25cm) diam*

$18,000-23,000   **L&T**

A Russian porcelain military plate, the rim painted with a black Imperial eagle, the reverse inscribed in Cyrillic '15th Tversky Regiment of His Imperial Highness Grand Duke Nikolai Nikolaievich Senior, and the 16th Nizhegorodsky Regiment of His Royal Highness Virtembergsky by Kholshevnikov', green cipher mark and dated '75'.

9.75in (24.5cm) diam

$25,000-32,000   **PC**

A 19thC Russian transferware printed porcelain plate, and French transferware printed commemorative plate, the Russian plate decorated with a couple by the fountain in the park of Tsarskoye Selo, incised number 12, the French produced to commemorate the Tsar Nicholas II's visit to Paris in October 1896.

1896   *each 8in (21cm) diam*

$1,900-2,300   **L&T**

An early 20thC Lomonosov propaganda porcelain plate, painted with a clown in colorful costume, inscription 'from the drawing of L.V. copy 15' in Russian, manuscript no. 312/12, by the Imperial Porcelain factory, dated 1905, mark of Lomonosov factory 1922.

9in (23cm) diam

$9,000-10,000   **L&T**

A large Russian porcelain plate, from the Lomonosov Porcelain Manufactory, St Petersburg, painted with a castle being approached by a ship, titled in Russian with 'Struggle Breeds Heroes', painted mark and dated.

1921   *13in (33.5cm) diam*

$1,300-1,900   **PC**

An early 20thC Lomonosov porcelain covered Jug, green maker's marks.

5in (12.5cm) high

$500-650   **L&T**

A Soviet porcelain teapot, with an anthropomorphic sunflower head to one side and a stylized cockerel to the other, signed and dated to lid, body and underside, designed by Sergey Chekhonin, Comintern Porcelain and Faience Manufactory, Volkhov.

1923   *6in (15.5cm) high*

$13,000-18,000   **L&T**

ESSENTIAL REFERENCE - GARDNER PORCELAIN

Gardner first introduced the 'Glazier' model in the 1820s, perhaps as an addition to the popular street vendors from the Volshebnyi fonar (Magic Lantern) series. Although more commonly seen with a blue enameled coat, the figure was also produced in a variety of color-ways, such as a black coat or buff coat and trousers. For further comparable figures, see E. Ivanova, 'The Gardner Factory: Porcelain in Russia, 18th-19th Centuries', St. Petersburg, 2003, page 104.

A late 19thC/early 20thC Kuznetsov porcelain serving dish, decorated with the Imperial eagle, printed maker's marks and painted number 151, with a porcelain plate decorated with the gilt cipher for Napoleon III, with maker's marks.

dish 12in (24.5cm) wide

$250-400   **L&T**

A Russian Gardner Porcelain Manufactory figure of a glazier, with impressed factory mark, St. George and the number 8 and inscribed 'Nr.2/10', his coat originally white but later overpainted in blue.

1830s-40s   *7.25in (18.5cm) high*

$4,400-5,700   **MAB**

ESSENTIAL REFERENCE - GEORGE II CHIMNEYPIECE

The design for this magnificent statuary marble chimneypiece, which combines French influences with mid-18thC Georgian features in the 'picturesque' manner, is representative of the English Rococo period. The chimneypiece unites strong Palladian influences with the softer, more sinuous lines evolving in the middle of the 18thC and relates to the 'Basso Relievos' and monuments executed around 1750 by the celebrated sculptor Sir Henry Cheere (d.1781). The very fine carving of the morning glory and floral sprigs spreading out from the central 'pelta' scroll cartouche suggest themes of Dawn, Springtime, and the Feminine, while the bold corner pilasters with their Roman Ionic whorls, cartouches, and triumphal palms speak of the Masculine, drawing on Classicism and Palladian themes.

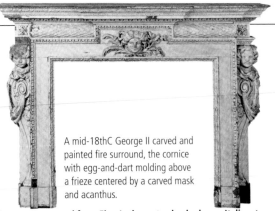

A mid-18thC George II carved and painted fire surround, the cornice with egg-and-dart molding above a frieze centered by a carved mask and acanthus.

By repute removed from Eigg Lodge, a twelve bedroom Italianate villa built as a Hebridean retreat by shipping magnate Sir Walter Runciman, 1st Baron Runciman in the 1920s. The Grade B listed house was only intermittently inhabited throughout the 20thC and gradually fell into disrepair from neglect.

8.25in (212cm) wide

$6,500-7,500   **L&T**

A late George II chimneypiece of statuary marble, inset with panels of verde antico.

c1750-1760   *83in (212cm) wide*

$45,000-50,000   **L&T**

An 18thC George III painted pine and gesso fire surround, ex-Westfield House, West Lothian, the frieze centered by a panel depicting a fox and hounds, flanked by thistles and urns.

87.5in (222cm) wide

$3,800-5,000   **L&T**

A George III Scottish pine and gesso chimney piece, the frieze centered with an eagle with thistles and flanked by panels of ribbon-tied swags of vine leaves, grapes and flowers.

69.25in (176cm) wide

$4,500-5,000   **WW**

A late 18thC Georgian pine and gesso chimney piece, frieze with composition tablet depicting a Classical figure scene.

69.25in (176cm) wide

$700-750   **HT**

A Regency statuary marble chimneypiece, the inverted breakfront marble over a frieze centered by an entablature carved with an urn.

c1810   *79in (201cm) wide*

$9,000-10,000   **L&T**

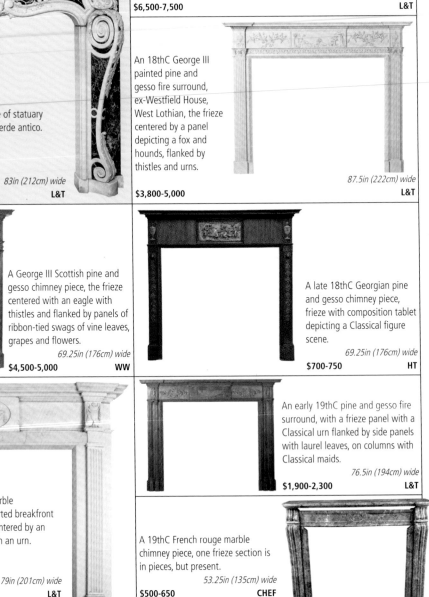

An early 19thC pine and gesso fire surround, with a frieze panel with a Classical urn flanked by side panels with laurel leaves, on columns with Classical maids.

76.5in (194cm) wide

$1,900-2,300   **L&T**

A 19thC French rouge marble chimney piece, one frieze section is in pieces, but present.

53.25in (135cm) wide

$500-650   **CHEF**

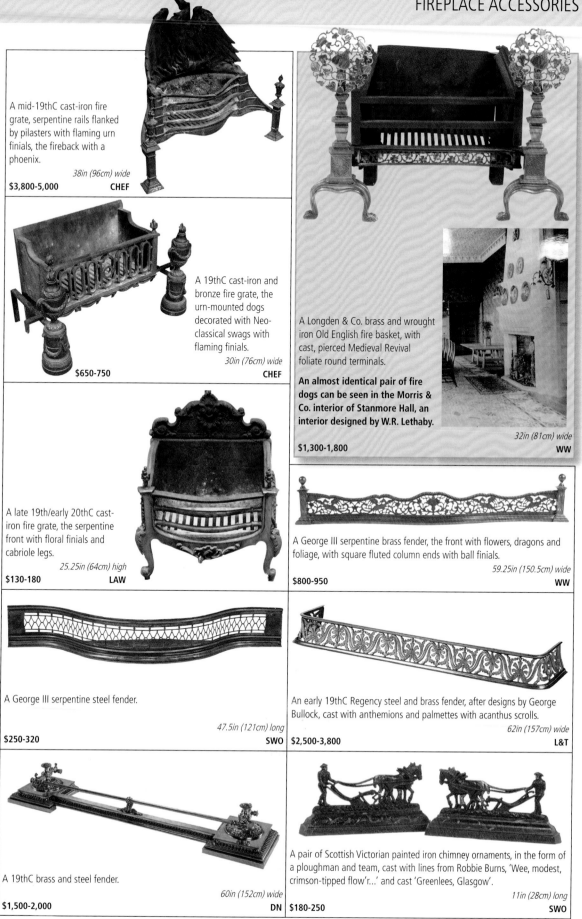

A mid-19thC cast-iron fire grate, serpentine rails flanked by pilasters with flaming urn finials, the fireback with a phoenix.

38in (96cm) wide

$3,800-5,000   **CHEF**

A 19thC cast-iron and bronze fire grate, the urn-mounted dogs decorated with Neo-classical swags with flaming finials.

30in (76cm) wide

$650-750   **CHEF**

A Longden & Co. brass and wrought iron Old English fire basket, with cast, pierced Medieval Revival foliate round terminals.

An almost identical pair of fire dogs can be seen in the Morris & Co. interior of Stanmore Hall, an interior designed by W.R. Lethaby.

32in (81cm) wide

$1,300-1,800   **WW**

A late 19th/early 20thC cast-iron fire grate, the serpentine front with floral finials and cabriole legs.

25.25in (64cm) high

$130-180   **LAW**

A George III serpentine brass fender, the front with flowers, dragons and foliage, with square fluted column ends with ball finials.

59.25in (150.5cm) wide

$800-950   **WW**

A George III serpentine steel fender.

47.5in (121cm) long

$250-320   **SWO**

An early 19thC Regency steel and brass fender, after designs by George Bullock, cast with anthemions and palmettes with acanthus scrolls.

62in (157cm) wide

$2,500-3,800   **L&T**

A 19thC brass and steel fender.

60in (152cm) wide

$1,500-2,000   **DN**

A pair of Scottish Victorian painted iron chimney ornaments, in the form of a ploughman and team, cast with lines from Robbie Burns, 'Wee, modest, crimson-tipped flow'r...' and cast 'Greenlees, Glasgow'.

11in (28cm) long

$180-250   **SWO**

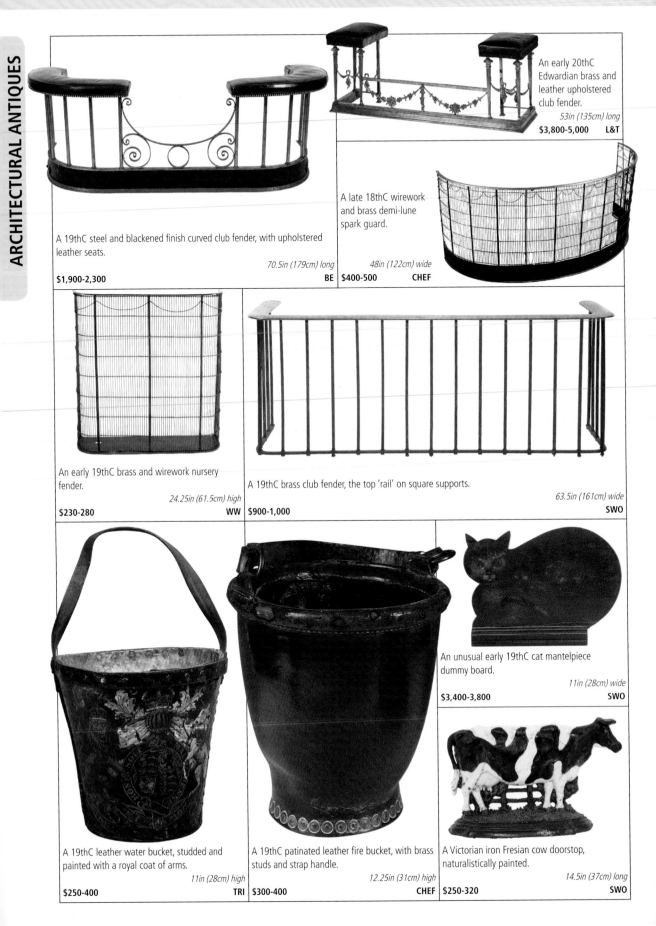

A 19thC steel and blackened finish curved club fender, with upholstered leather seats.

70.5in (179cm) long

$1,900-2,300 **BE**

An early 20thC Edwardian brass and leather upholstered club fender.

53in (135cm) long

$3,800-5,000 **L&T**

A late 18thC wirework and brass demi-lune spark guard.

48in (122cm) wide

$400-500 **CHEF**

An early 19thC brass and wirework nursery fender.

24.25in (61.5cm) high

$230-280 **WW**

A 19thC brass club fender, the top 'rail' on square supports.

63.5in (161cm) wide

$900-1,000 **SWO**

An unusual early 19thC cat mantelpiece dummy board.

11in (28cm) wide

$3,400-3,800 **SWO**

A 19thC leather water bucket, studded and painted with a royal coat of arms.

11in (28cm) high

$250-400 **TRI**

A 19thC patinated leather fire bucket, with brass studs and strap handle.

12.25in (31cm) high

$300-400 **CHEF**

A Victorian iron Fresian cow doorstop, naturalistically painted.

14.5in (37cm) long

$250-320 **SWO**

A Coalbrookdale 'Lily of the Valley' cast-iron garden seat, impressed 'C.B.DALE & Co.' and diamond registration mark for 8 February 1864, some damage.

1864   *73.75in (187cm) wide*

$5,500-7,000   CHEF

A white painted garden bench, in a variant of the 'Fern and Berry' pattern, by John Gray & Co., Glasgow.

1855-95   *41.25in (105cm) high*

$950-1,100   BELL

A pair of Victorian painted cast-iron garden benches.

46in (117cm) long

$1,900-2,300   L&T

A Coalbrookdale design fern and blackberry cast-iron garden bench.

44.5in (113cm) wide

$950-1,100   BELL

A Victorian Coalbrookdale design 'Fern' cast-iron garden bench, with wood slatted seat.

60in (152cm) wide

$650-900   CHEF

A Victorian Coalbrookdale 'Fern' cast-iron bench, with four conforming arm chairs.

$3,800-4,400   ROS

A late 19thC cast-iron and wood garden bench.

77.5in (197cm) long

$1,900-2,300   L&T

A set of eight 19thC cast-iron garden chairs, the heart-shaped backs enriched with leafy tendrils.

32in (81cm) high

$3,200-4,400   DN

An early 20thC painted cast-iron marble-top garden table and pair of chairs.

chairs 31.5in (80cm) high

$650-900   L&T

CLOSER LOOK - WARWICK VASE

The low campana form urn has entwined branch handles and is molded with relief masks.

The fireclay vase and stand is by renowned maker J & M Craig, Kilmarnock.

The plinth base is molded with rams' masks and seraphim.

The base is also molded with relief portraits of Robert Burns, which add to its desirability.

A mid-19thC Scottish Warwick vase and stand.

45in (114cm) high

$2,500-3,800   L&T

A mid-19thC Scottish fire-clay campana urn and pedestal, by Lindsay & Anderson, the base molded with lions' masks.

57in (145cm) high

$3,800-5,000   L&T

A pair of 19thC gritstone urns.

36.25in (92cm) high

$800-950   L&T

A Victorian white painted cast-iron urn or fountain, attributed to Andrew Handyside Foundry, with the portrait heads of Milton, Shakespeare, Scott, Stephenson, Watt, Wellington, Nelson and Peel.

This model appears as drawing No.27 in the 1874 catalog of Andrew Handyside who acquired the firm in 1848, formerly owned by Weatherhead and Glover 1818-1843, then Thomas Wright 1843-1848. He expanded the production to cover architectural, engineering and decorative wares such as garden vases and fountains.

49.25in (125cm) diam

$3,800-4,400   BELL

A pair of 19thC marble campana-shaped garden urns.

23.5in (60cm) high

$900-1,000   BELL

A pair of Victorian majolica ocher-glazed twin-handled urns.

40.5in (103cm) high

$550-650   BE

A pair of 19thC terracotta urns, impressed with woven trellis and floral spray.

52in (132cm) high

$3,200-3,800   CHEF

A pair of early 20thC lead urns, in the 17thC manner, the 'S' scroll handles with cherub head finials, the body with cherub mask.

19in (48.5cm) high

$900-1,100   HT

A pair of 20thC painted cast-bronze garden urns, the twin handles cast with opposing figural busts terminating in wild boar mounts.

39.5in (100cm) high

$950-1,100   BELL

A Victorian terracotta lion, with an alert expression, on rockwork base.

29in (74cm) high

$1,500-1,900 HT

A pair of early 20thC reconstituted stone greyhounds, weathered.

27.5in (70cm) long

$1,500-1,900 CHEF

One of a pair of 20thC reconstituted stone eagles for gate column finials.

41.25in (105cm) high

$1,000-1,200 pair CHEF

A 20thC carved stone garden statue of a lion.

43.5in (110cm) high

$650-750 WW

An early 20thC composite stone dog.

31.5in (80cm) wide

$250-400 ECGW

One of a pair of mid-19thC carved lime of Clipsham stone gargoyles.

By repute, these were removed during the restoration of The Palace Of Westminster following bomb damage in 1941 by an MP in the House of Commons.

41.25in (105cm) high

$3,800-5,000 pair BELL

A 19thC carved stone figure of a bulldog.

17.75in (45cm) high

$2,500-3,200 BELL

A 20thC cast stone figure of a hound.

27in (69cm) high

$450-550 L&T

A pair of 19thC Victorian lead garden figures, of a stag and doe.

40in (102cm) high

$2,500-3,200 L&T

A Victorian composition stone garden figure, of a Classical lady.

61.5in (156cm) high

$2,500-3,200   **WW**

A late 19thC T.C. Brown-Westhead, Moore & Co. garden seat, modeled as an Egyptian slave girl, with Egyptian motifs, impressed 'T.C. BROWN WESTHEAD MOORE & Co 25'.

The firm of T.C. Brown-Westhead, Moore & Co. worked in Cauldon Place Hanley from 1862-1904. They were formerly Bates Brown-Westhead & Moore and were subsequently Cauldon Ltd.

They were mentioned in The Potteries 1893 advertising and trade journal.

'The high merits of Messrs. T. C. Brown-Westhead, Moore and Co.'s productions have been duly recognized at a number of the world's great exhibitions, the most notable awards thus gained being at: London 1862, Lvons 1872, Cologne 1875, Philadelphia 1870, Paris 1878, Sydney 1879, Melbourne, 1880, Adelaide 1881, and the Grand Prix, Paris, 1889.'

'Their exhibit of 'Cauldon' china at Chicago is a very important one, the space occupied being 1,200 square feet. This space is crowded with the finest collection of table porcelain ever sent to any exhibition, and far exceeds the same firm's exhibit at Paris in 1889, where they secured the Grand Prix and two medals for collaborators'.

22in (56cm) high

$2,500-3,200   **TEN**

A pair of late 19thC red onyx marble columns.

39in (99cm) high

$3,800-4,400   **SWO**

A late 19thC French veined marble torchère, with gilt metal and champlevé enamel decoration.

34.5in (87.5cm) high

$3,200-3,800   **TRI**

A pair of 19thC carved marble corbel brackets, with scroll and leaf decoration.

33in (84cm) high

$900-1,000   **SWO**

A pair of 19thC gritstone staddle stones.

larger 33.5in (85cm) high

$700-800   **L&T**

A 19thC wirework conservatory stand.

30in (76cm) high

$750-900   **CHEF**

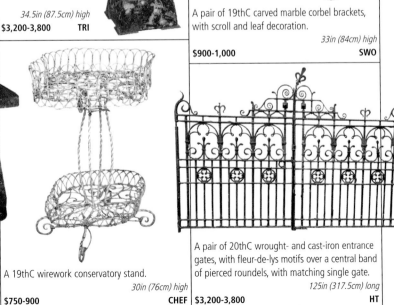

A pair of 20thC wrought- and cast-iron entrance gates, with fleur-de-lys motifs over a central band of pierced roundels, with matching single gate.

125in (317.5cm) long

$3,200-3,800   **HT**

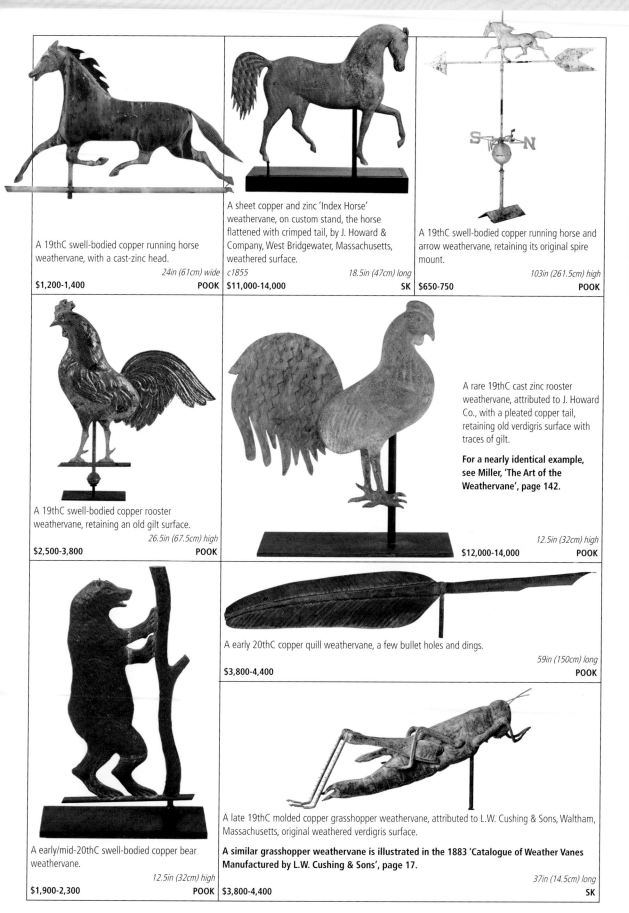

A 19thC swell-bodied copper running horse weathervane, with a cast-zinc head.

24in (61cm) wide

$1,200-1,400   POOK

A sheet copper and zinc 'Index Horse' weathervane, on custom stand, the horse flattened with crimped tail, by J. Howard & Company, West Bridgewater, Massachusetts, weathered surface.

c1855   *18.5in (47cm) long*

$11,000-14,000   SK

A 19thC swell-bodied copper running horse and arrow weathervane, retaining its original spire mount.

103in (261.5cm) high

$650-750   POOK

A 19thC swell-bodied copper rooster weathervane, retaining an old gilt surface.

26.5in (67.5cm) high

$2,500-3,800   POOK

A rare 19thC cast zinc rooster weathervane, attributed to J. Howard Co., with a pleated copper tail, retaining old verdigris surface with traces of gilt.

For a nearly identical example, see Miller, 'The Art of the Weathervane', page 142.

12.5in (32cm) high

$12,000-14,000   POOK

A early 20thC copper quill weathervane, a few bullet holes and dings.

59in (150cm) long

$3,800-4,400   POOK

A early/mid-20thC swell-bodied copper bear weathervane.

12.5in (32cm) high

$1,900-2,300   POOK

A late 19thC molded copper grasshopper weathervane, attributed to L.W. Cushing & Sons, Waltham, Massachusetts, original weathered verdigris surface.

A similar grasshopper weathervane is illustrated in the 1883 'Catalogue of Weather Vanes Manufactured by L.W. Cushing & Sons', page 17.

37in (14.5cm) long

$3,800-4,400   SK

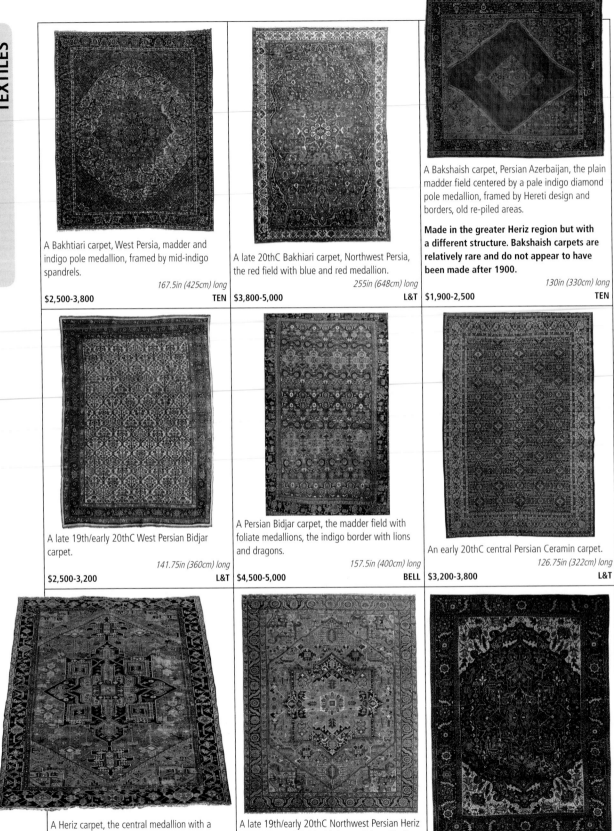

A Bakhtiari carpet, West Persia, madder and indigo pole medallion, framed by mid-indigo spandrels.

167.5in (425cm) long

$2,500-3,800   TEN

A late 20thC Bakhiari carpet, Northwest Persia, the red field with blue and red medallion.

255in (648cm) long

$3,800-5,000   L&T

A Bakshaish carpet, Persian Azerbaijan, the plain madder field centered by a pale indigo diamond pole medallion, framed by Hereti design and borders, old re-piled areas.

Made in the greater Heriz region but with a different structure. Bakshaish carpets are relatively rare and do not appear to have been made after 1900.

130in (330cm) long

$1,900-2,500   TEN

A late 19th/early 20thC West Persian Bidjar carpet.

141.75in (360cm) long

$2,500-3,200   L&T

A Persian Bidjar carpet, the madder field with foliate medallions, the indigo border with lions and dragons.

157.5in (400cm) long

$4,500-5,000   BELL

An early 20thC central Persian Ceramin carpet.

126.75in (322cm) long

$3,200-3,800   L&T

A Heriz carpet, the central medallion with a madder field decorated with foliage, some wear and damage.

138.5in (352cm) long

$2,500-3,800   DN

A late 19th/early 20thC Northwest Persian Heriz carpet, the pink field with large pink and indigo medallion.

139.5in (354cm) long

$3,200-3,800   L&T

A Heriz carpet.

c1930   *165in (419cm) long*

$3,800-4,400   POOK

A Heriz carpet.

221.75in (563cm) long

$1,500-1,900   BELL

A cental Persian Isfahan carpet, the mid-indigo field of palmettes and vines around a pale blue and ivory pole medallion.

c1950   142.25in (361cm) long

$3,200-4,400   TEN

An Isfahan rug.

172in (437cm) long

$5,000-5,700   SWO

A late 19th/early 20thC central Persian Kashan carpet, the indigo field with red and green medallion.

107in (271cm) wide

$3,800-5,000   L&T

A late 19th/early 20thC central Persian Kashan 'Mohtasham' rug.

54in (137cm) wide

$2,500-3,200   L&T

ESSENTIAL REFERENCE - KERMAN CARPETS

Kerman carpets (sometimes 'Kirman') are one of the traditional classifications of Persian carpets. They are named after Kerman, which is both a city and a province located in south central Iran. Kerman has been a major center for the production of high quality carpets since at least the 15thC. They have always been highly regarded partly because of the high quality of the wool from the region, known as Carmania wool.

Raver, or Lavar as it is called in the West, has had the reputation for the finest Kerman carpets. These so called Lavar Kerman may actually be made in a number of places in Kerman but the market calls them Lavar Kerman. Raver was a town 120 miles from the city of Kerman. Through the 20thC the Atiyehs were a major producer of Kerman carpets. After production stopped during the Islamic Revolution, it was shifted to China.

An early 20thC South Persian Lavar or Raver Kerman rug.

87.5in (222cm) long

$1,600-2,000   WW

A Kerman rug.

53in (134.5cm) long

$800-950   HT

A Mahal carpet, the ocher field and border decorated with boteh and meandering foliate branches, some wear.

120.5in (306cm) long

$1,100-1,400   DN

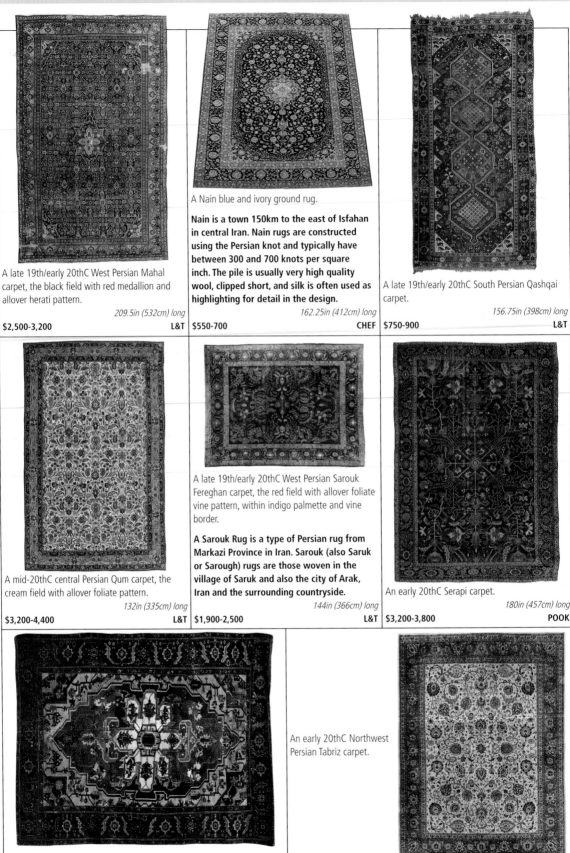

A late 19th/early 20thC West Persian Mahal carpet, the black field with red medallion and allover herati pattern.

209.5in (532cm) long

$2,500-3,200   L&T

A Nain blue and ivory ground rug.

Nain is a town 150km to the east of Isfahan in central Iran. Nain rugs are constructed using the Persian knot and typically have between 300 and 700 knots per square inch. The pile is usually very high quality wool, clipped short, and silk is often used as highlighting for detail in the design.

162.25in (412cm) long

$550-700   CHEF

A late 19th/early 20thC South Persian Qashqai carpet.

156.75in (398cm) long

$750-900   L&T

A mid-20thC central Persian Qum carpet, the cream field with allover foliate pattern.

132in (335cm) long

$3,200-4,400   L&T

A late 19th/early 20thC West Persian Sarouk Fereghan carpet, the red field with allover foliate vine pattern, within indigo palmette and vine border.

A Sarouk Rug is a type of Persian rug from Markazi Province in Iran. Sarouk (also Saruk or Sarough) rugs are those woven in the village of Saruk and also the city of Arak, Iran and the surrounding countryside.

144in (366cm) long

$1,900-2,500   L&T

An early 20thC Serapi carpet.

180in (457cm) long

$3,200-3,800   POOK

A Serapi carpet.

c1910   *156in (396cm) long*

$7,500-8,000   POOK

An early 20thC Northwest Persian Tabriz carpet.

156in (396cm) long

$1,300-1,900   L&T

An early 20thC Northwest Persian Tabriz 'Benlian' carpet, the field with palmettes, animals, trees, and foliate motifs, signature star to one corner.

164.5in (418cm) long

$3,200-4,400   **L&T**

A Persian Tabriz carpet, Azerbaijan, with scrolling vines, enclosed by ice blue borders of serrated leafy vines, one end with 1.25in (3cm) missing of outer plain guard.

151.25in (384cm) long

$1,300-1,800   **TEN**

A Persian Tabriz carpet, Azerbaijan, the madder field with palmettes and vines, with borders of turtle motifs, some damage.

143.75in (365cm) long

$1,300-1,900   **TEN**

ESSENTIAL REFERENCE - ZIEGLER AND CO.

In 1883, Ziegler and Co., of Manchester, England, established a Persian carpet manufactury in Sultanabad (now Arak), Iran. Their intention was to adapt traditional 16thC and 17thC Eastern carpet designs to satisfy more 'restrained' Western tastes, and they set about this by employing designers from some of the major Western department stores, such as B. Altman and Liberty of London, to rework standard Persian colors, patterns and motifs - palmettes, forked tendrils and rosettes. The new designs were produced using newly developed dying techniques in conjunction with Ziegler's 'modern' looms worked by highly skilful, locally recruited artisans, and the resulting rugs and carpets were characterized by bold, allover patterns with softer, more subtle palettes than their vibrant traditional Persian counterparts.

A Tabriz carpet, the madder field decorated with large flowerheads and meandering foliate branches, within navy borders.

174in (442cm) long

$9,000-10,000   **DN**

An early 20thC central Persian Veramin carpet, the field with blue rosette lattice pattern, with blue turtle border.

83.5in (212cm) wide

$2,500-3,200   **L&T**

A modern Ziegler Mahal design carpet, Iran.

197in (500cm) long

$1,900-2,500   **TEN**

An early 20thC Northwest Persian kelleh.

195.25in (496cm) long

$3,200-3,800   **L&T**

An early 20thC Northwest Persian runner, the indigo field with allover herati pattern, within red stylized palmette and vine border between bands.

203in (515cm) long

$1,300-1,800   **L&T**

An early 20thC Daghestan rug.

57in (145cm) long

$500-650　　WW

A Derbend rug, Caucasian, the madder and two indigo vertical panels with flowers and birds, a walnut flowerhead and leaf border.

76.75in (195cm) long

$500-650　　BELL

A 19thC South West Caucasian Karabakh carpet.

113.5in (288cm) long

$1,900-2,500　　WW

ESSENTIAL REFERENCE - TURKMEN RUGS

The original Turkmen rugs were produced by the Turkmen tribes who are the main ethnic group in Turkmenistan and are also found in Afghanistan and Iran. In the past, almost all Turkmen rugs were produced by nomadic tribes, almost entirely with locally obtained materials: wool from the herds and vegetable dyes, or other natural dyes from the land. They used geometrical designs that varied from tribe to tribe; most famous are the Yomut, Ersari, Saryk, Salor, and Tekke. More recently, large rug workshops in the cities have appeared. Since about 1910, synthetic dyes have been used along with natural ones. The size of nomadic rugs is limited to what can be done on a nomad's portable loom; larger rugs have always been produced in the villages, but they are now more common. Collectors love the irregularities of nomadic rugs. These were fairly common since natural materials varied from batch to batch and woollen warp or weft may stretch, especially on a loom that is regularly folded up for transport.

A Karabagh rug, South Caucasus, the field with a central panel of flowers flanked by two terracotta panels, with tribal devices.

107in (272cm) long

$950-1,100　　TEN

An early 20thC Kazak rug.

50in (127cm) long

$500-650　　BELL

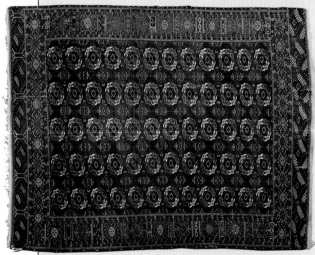

A late 19th/early 20thC Turkmenistan Tekke 'main' carpet.

115.5in (293cm) long

$1,300-1,900　　L&T

A Shirvan runner, Caucasian, the indigo field with five bold hooked diamonds.

52.75in (134cm) long

$400-500　　BELL

A red ground Turkish carpet.

161.5in (410cm) long

$750-1,000　　CHEF

An early 20thC Turkish Ushak carpet, West Antonia.

136.5in (347cm) long

$1,900-2,500   **WW**

A late 19th/early 20thC Turkish West Anatolian Ushak carpet.

269.75in (685cm) long

$1,900-2,500   **WW**

An Ushak carpet, decorated with abstract foliate motifs, some wear due to age, small holes, some areas of fading, losses and repairs.

252in (640cm) long

$6,500-7,500   **DN**

An Ushak carpet, decorated with palmettes and flowerheads, large areas of repair, faded colors, some wear.

126.5in (321cm) long

$1,900-2,500   **DN**

A late 19th/early 20thC West Anatolian large Ushak 'Turkey' carpet, the red field with columns of indigo palmettes and cruciform motifs.

277.5in (705cm) long

$2,500-3,200   **L&T**

A late 19thC West Anatolian Ushak carpet, the field with palmettes and central lozenge.

120in (306cm) long

$950-1,100   **L&T**

An early 20thC West Anatolian Ushak carpet, the field with brick-red and blue medallion, with turtle palmette and vine border.

234in (594cm) long

$1,300-1,800   **L&T**

A late 19th/early 20thC Ushak carpet, West Anatolia, the red field with allover stylized vine and cypress trees.

279.5in (710cm) long

$2,500-3,200   **L&T**

A Kurdish hamadan rug.

76in (193cm) long

$300-400   **CHOR**

A 19thC Chinese carpet, the field of Taoist symbols centered by a roundel enclosed by lotus flowers and wispy spandrels, some damage.

149.25in (379cm) long

$2,500-3,800   TEN

A Chinese Qing cut-velvet panel, decorated with a geometric floral design, with borders of key fret, lotus and dragons.

138.5in (352cm) long

$4,500-5,000   WW

A Chinese silk carpet, the terracotta field decorated.

118.25in (300cm) long

$1,900-2,500   TEN

A 20thC Chinese rug, the field with an Imperial dragon chasing a pearl, with four dragons enclosed by cloud borders.

73.25in (186cm) long

$450-550   TEN

A late 19th/early 20thC North Indian Agra carpet.

156.75in (398cm) long

$2,500-3,200   L&T

A modern Indian carpet, with a 'Shah Abbas' design of palmettes and flowerheads.

173.25in (440cm) long

$1,900-2,500   TEN

A 21stC Indian carpet, depicting a hunting scene, with borders of angels, exotic birds and vines.

238.25in (605cm) long

$2,300-2,800   TEN

An Aubusson-style woven carpet, in Louis XVI-style, decorated with a central medallion of flowers, with foliate borders and corner trophies.

165.75in (421cm) long

$1,500-2,300   WW

A full tiger skin rug with head mount, with Rowland Ward label to the reverse, visible wear and tear, teeth chipped and damaged, some claws missing.

This has rather charming provenance! It was purchased by the owner's grandfather. He states that he had his nappy changed upon the rug as an infant and he is now in his mid-60s.

c1930   *126.5in (321cm) long*

$650-900   CHEF

ESSENTIAL REFERENCE - BALTIMORE ALBUM QUILTS

Baltimore Album Quilts originated in Baltimore in the 1840s. The quilts are made up of a number of squares called blocks. Each block has been appliquéd with a different design. The designs are often floral, but many other motifs are also used, such as eagles and landmarks. Baltimore Album Quilts reflected the prosperous community of Baltimore, as most were made not from scraps, but with new fabric. Improvements in dying provided new colors.Many Baltimore Album quilts were signed. Many included blocks each made by a different person. The complexity of the designs of the blocks demonstrated the skill of the maker. Many hours were devoted to the creation of each of these quilts, and many were carefully preserved as family heirlooms.

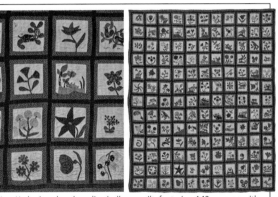

A New York pieced and appliqué album quilt, featuring 143 squares with animal and floral decoration, several of them titled 'Alegator', 'Rain Deer', 'Great Eagle', 'Indian Belt' and 'Tools', 'Elephant', etc.

88in (223.5cm) long

$14,000-18,000   POOK

A patchwork friendship quilt, Lancaster County, Pennsylvania, dated.

1856   88in (223.5cm) long

$1,500-1,900   POOK

A set of 15 mid-19thC Baltimore album quilt squares, mounted on a later red backing.

107in (272cm) long

$7,000-7,500   POOK

A pieced and appliqué quilt, Pennsylvania, with a tulip and diamond pattern and a vine border, inscribed 'Matilda Bower', dated.

1856   91in (231cm) wide

$2,500-3,800   POOK

A mid-19thC Pennsylvania 'Star of Bethlehem' patchwork quilt, with satellite stars.

80in (203cm) wide

$800-900   POOK

A late 19thC pineapple appliqué quilt, signed within the quilting 'Mary W. Fronheiser', Lancaster County, Pennsylvania.

88in (223.5cm) wide

$550-700   POOK

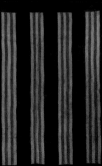

A late 19thC Amish split bars patchwork quilt, Lancaster County, Pennsylvania.

90in (228.5cm) wide

$800-950   POOK

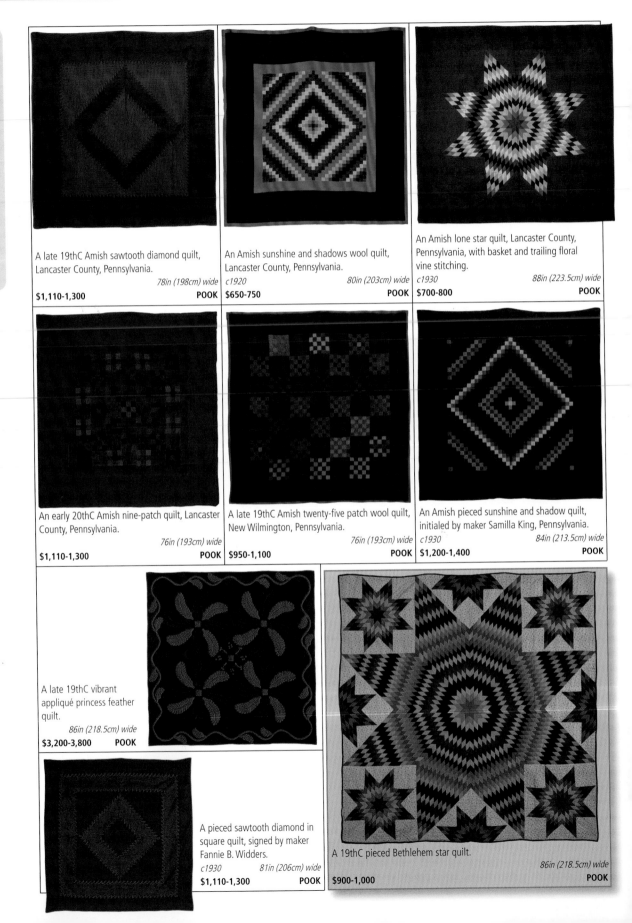

A late 19thC Amish sawtooth diamond quilt, Lancaster County, Pennsylvania.

78in (198cm) wide

$1,110-1,300 **POOK**

An Amish sunshine and shadows wool quilt, Lancaster County, Pennsylvania.

c1920 *80in (203cm) wide*

$650-750 **POOK**

An Amish lone star quilt, Lancaster County, Pennsylvania, with basket and trailing floral vine stitching.

c1930 *88in (223.5cm) wide*

$700-800 **POOK**

An early 20thC Amish nine-patch quilt, Lancaster County, Pennsylvania.

76in (193cm) wide

$1,110-1,300 **POOK**

A late 19thC Amish twenty-five patch wool quilt, New Wilmington, Pennsylvania.

76in (193cm) wide

$950-1,100 **POOK**

An Amish pieced sunshine and shadow quilt, initialed by maker Samilla King, Pennsylvania.

c1930 *84in (213.5cm) wide*

$1,200-1,400 **POOK**

A late 19thC vibrant appliqué princess feather quilt.

86in (218.5cm) wide

$3,200-3,800 **POOK**

A pieced sawtooth diamond in square quilt, signed by maker Fannie B. Widders.

c1930 *81in (206cm) wide*

$1,110-1,300 **POOK**

A 19thC pieced Bethlehem star quilt.

86in (218.5cm) wide

$900-1,000 **POOK**

A 17thC Aubusson tapestry, central France, woven in wool and silk, lacking original borders, some restoration, reduced in size.

101in (257cm) wide

$1,500-1,900   **TEN**

CLOSER LOOK - NEEDLEWORK HANGINGS

This is a rare pair of early tapestries.

They are embroidered in various stitches including chain and satin.

They are worked with a multitude of different figures and scenes, secular and biblical.

Figures include Elijah and the raven and St. Jerome and the lion, a North American Indian, a lady walking a young child, a Turk on horseback hunting, a maid milking a cow, figures brawling outside an inn, and many other animals.

A rare and fine pair of William and Mary needlework hangings.

c1700   *61in (155cm) high*

$25,000-32,000   **WW**

A late 17thC Aubusson tapestry, with an heron in a river landscape, the border with birds, flowers and panels, worn and repaired, backed.

98.5in (250cm) high

$950-1,100   **SWO**

A late 17thC Aubusson tapestry, depicting the marriage of Esther and Ahasuerus (King of Persia), some damage.

113in (287cm) wide

$3,800-4,400   **DN**

A Flemish tapestry, probably Brussels, in silk and wool, two ladies of the court with their attendants.

c1650-1700   *134in (340cm) wide*

$3,200-3,800   **LAW**

A 17thC 'verde dieu' Flemish tapestry panel, cut down and re-backed.

94in (239cm) high

$1,400-1,800   **BELL**

A 17thC Flemish tapestry, depicting figures in traditional dress in a panoramic rural landscape, restoration and old repairs.

214.5in (545cm) long

$3,800-5,000   **DN**

A 17th/18thC Flemish tapestry, in silk and wool, with figures harvesting fruits of the forest.

118.25in (300cm) high

$4,500-5,000
LAW

A late 17th/early 18thC Flemish verdure tapestry panel, with a grape collector and his companion.

51.75in (131cm) wide

$2,500-3,200
L&T

A late 17th/early 18thC Continental verdure wall tapestry, depicting an Old Testament scene of robed figures in a landscape, faded overall.

126in (320cm) wide

$2,500-3,200
DN

An early 18thC tapestry fragment, with a milkmaid in rocky landscape.

61in (155cm) high

$650-750
BELL

A late 19thC Swedish flat weave tapestry runner, with panels of geometric designs, figures, dated 1883 and with initials 'IK D', probably Scania.

Scania, also known by its local name Skåne, is the southernmost province of Sweden which consists of a peninsula on the southern tip of the Scandinavian Peninsula and some islands close to it. Scania was a province of Denmark in the early 18thC before becoming part of Sweden. Tapestry weaving textiles became general in Scanian peasant homes from c1750.

157in (399cm) long

$3,800-4,400
WW

A late 18thC Swedish Scania flat weave tapestry carriage cushion cover, with figures, birds, and vases of flowers.

40in (102cm) long

$2,500-3,200
WW

An early 18thC English petit-point needlework picture of a parrot, depicted in a chinoiserie taste tree.

10.5in (27cm) high

$500-650 **ROS**

A pair of George III framed silkwork pictures, depicting a lady within a floral border.

16in (41cm) high

$450-550 **L&T**

An early 19thC Philadelphia silk, chenille, and paint-on-silk embroidery, titled 'Palemon and Lavinia'.

26in (66cm) wide

$13,000-15,000 **POOK**

A Regency period sailor's woolwork picture, depicting the HMS Termagant.

15.25in (39cm) wide

$550-700 **BELL**

One of a pair of 19thC English silkwork and découpage pictures of English ladies and their suitors, framed and glazed.

14.25in (36cm) high

$2,800-3,500 pair **ROS**

A Victorian rosewood needlework firescreen, with a glazed wool and beadwork scene of a couple embracing.

c1840 *47in (120cm) high*

$300-450 **L&T**

A 19thC silk embroidered picture, with a warship offshore, a sailor with a telescope and figures walking toward a tower flying the Union flag.

14in (36cm) long

$500-650 **SWO**

A Louis XV beadwork altar frontal, embroidered with the monogram of Mademoiselle Louise, the daughter to Louis XV, surmounted by a coronet.

By repute this panel was worked by the Ladies in Waiting of Mademoiselle Louise, who took it to the Carmel of St Denis in 1769. When the Convent was disbanded during the French Revolution one of the nuns, Sister Mary Charlotte, brought it to England.

63in (159cm) wide

$900-1,000 **WW**

A late 19thC French paisley shawl, with central medallions and elongated botehs, with colored tassel ends.

121.25in (308cm) long

$250-320 WW

A square paisley shawl.

c1850 *67in (170cm) square*

$300-400 BELL

A Scottish silk and wool paisley shawl.

c1860 *126in (320cm) wide*

$900-1,000 PC

Judith Picks

Paisley pattern is a term in English for a design using the buta or boteh, a droplet-shaped vegetable motif of Persian (ie Iranian) origin. Its Western name derives from the town of Paisley, in West Scotland, a center for textiles where paisley designs were produced. Such designs became very popular in the West in the 18thC and 19thC, following imports of post-Mughal versions of the design from India, especially in the form of Kashmir shawls, and were then imitated locally.

From roughly 1800 to 1850, the weavers of the town of Paisley in Renfrewshire, Scotland, became the foremost producers of these shawls. Unique additions to their handlooms and Jacquard looms allowed them to work in five colors when most weavers were producing Paisley using only two. By 1860, Paisley could produce pattern shawls in up to 15 colors.

A European Paisley shawl, with black center and foliate border.

c1850 *71in (180cm) square*

$200-250 BELL

A set of early 19thC silk curtains, decorated with ribbon tied swags of flowers, cornucopiae, pairs of love birds, urns and trophies, comprising: five pelmets and five pairs of curtains.

curtains 107in (272cm) long

$3,800-4,400 WW

A 19thC Italian embroidered silk bed hanging, in 17thC Sicilian style, from either Rome or Sicily, with a copy of the original receipt.

Purchased 30 October 1901 from Jean Pallotti Antiquaire 3, Rue Rondinelli, Florence by Count Redmond Toler Clayton-Browne Clayton (1863-1937) to furnish his home: Villa La Punta, Cervara, Santa Margherita, Liguria, Italy.

88.25in (244cm) long

$2,500-3,800 WW

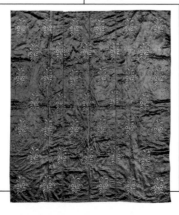

A late 19thC European embroidered silk panel, with repeating floral sprays in cream silks with metal threads, with cotton backing.

75.5in (192cm) high

$550-700 L&T

A mid-20thC oak concertina-action five-tier tabletop haberdashery cabinet, gilt stencil to the front, 'Clarks Anchor Stranded Cotton For Embroidery'.

22.5in (57cm) wide

$130-180 BELL

A George III needlework sampler, by Miss Mary Ann Bournes, centrally detailed with a beehive or skep over a landscape scene, rosewood veneered frame.

1791   *17.75in (45cm) long*

$1,500-1,900   **BELL**

A 19thC Welsh school sampler, worked by Mary Evans at Pwllhely School, with central verse worked in black cross stitch, within a floral embroidered oval cartouche, 'Wales is 180 miles long and 80 broad...' '...The Welch are Honest Brave and Hospitable', in a later ebonized frame, numerous holes, overall wear.

1812   *17.5in (44.5cm) long*

$1,000-1,100   **TEN**

A Pennsylvania silk on linen house sampler, wrought by Sarah Campion, with a large central rose-colored house above a lawn with trees, all within a floral vine and silk ribbon border.

1821   *23.5in (60cm) wide*

$5,000-6,500   **POOK**

A George IV needlework sampler, the work of Mary Atherton, aged 14 years, inscribed with a verse titled 'Prosperity and Adversity' and worked in wool with a man on horseback.

1827   *23in (58cm) high*

$650-750   **MOR**

An early 19thC needlework sampler, attributed to the Quaker School, Ackworth, worked with medallions with flowers, birds, letters, and numbers, in a later glazed wooden frame.

16.5in (42cm) long

$700-800   **WW**

A silk-on-linen sampler, with verse above central building flanked by flowers, trees and other designs, wrought by 'Hannah Wood 1835'.

14.5in (37cm) wide

$2,500-3,200   **PC**

A silk-on-linen sampler, with verse, baskets of fruit, trees, central brick house, and a young girl, by 'Eliza Haynes...done in her Ninth Years'.

13.25in (33.5cm) wide

$2,300-2,800   **PC**

A 19thC Adam and Eve sampler, the work of Sabina Joy Hebden, with a house and gardens, thought to be Sawley Hall, Adam and Eve, animals and flowering trees, within a Greek key border, together with an indenture recording the conveyancing of a property and land in Sawley, North Yorkshire to Mr John Hebden for £577, the sampler came from the property and was worked by a relative of Hebden.

1846   *23.25in (59cm) square*

$500-650   **MOR**

An early 18thC embroidered stomacher, decorated with a heart above entwined foliage and flowerheads.

$2,300-2,800   CHOR

A gentleman's waistcoat, in cream silk embroidered with pink and silver striped hot air balloons, with a gondola-style basket.

The waistcoat appears to be contemporary to the Montgolfier Brothers first hot air balloon flight in Annonay, Ardeche, France in 1783. It has been mentioned that the balloons resemble the gas balloons of Charles Green's Vauxhall balloon of 1836, which had a gondola basket, but the cut of the waistcoat predates this.

c1780

$2,000-2,500   TEN

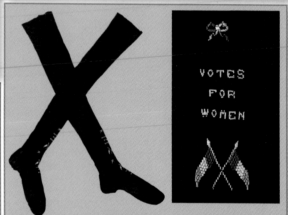

A mid-18thC cream silk sack-back lady's open robe, hand painted overall with pink peony-style bouquets, some damage.

$1,000-1,500   TEN

A platinum-palladium print, Cocoa Dress (Balenciaga), by Irving Penn, Paris, depicting the fashion model Lisa Fonssagrives, wearing a Balenciaga cocoa dress, signed, titled, dated and numbered '12 of an edition of 50' in pencil to the reverse, dated 1950, printed 1970.

By the end of the 1940s, Lisa Fonssagrives, a Swedish-born model based in New York, was one of the most coveted models in the industry, displaying an aristocratic elegance favored by both designers and photographers. Her subsequent marriage to Irving Penn, one of the most popular photographers at the time, led to some of the most iconic images in the history of fashion photography.

19.5in (49.5cm) high

$38,000-45,000   SWO

A rare pair of black Suffragette movement stockings, embroidered with flags and ribbons, tiny little bit of rubbing to toes and heels of stockings.

These stockings are in the colors of the movement - green, white and purple - with the words 'Votes for Women'. These would have been worn by suffragettes on marches and demonstration rallies.

c1908-10

$3,200-3,800   TEN

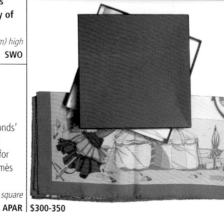

An early 20thC 'Grands Fonds' (Oceans Depths) silk scarf, designed by Annie Saivre for Hermès, in an orange Hermès box.

35.5in (90cm) square

$180-250   APAR

A Hermès scarf in original box, Charmes des Plages Normandes, by Loïc Dubigeon, Paris, unworn.

35.5in (90cm) square

$300-350   LAW

A vintage Chanel bag, quilted navy lambskin, gilt metal chain and lambskin entwined strap, Chanel decal to interior zip.

11in (28cm) wide

$750-900   MOR

A Chanel, 'Grand Shopping Tote GST' quilted black caviar leather purse, hologram number 9379981, Chanel guarantee card, paperwork and dust bag.

14in (35cm) wide

$3,800-4,400   DN

A vintage Chanel maxi flap bag, quilted white lambskin, gilt metal interlocking 'CCs' and chain strap entwined with lambskin, dark red leather, interior gilt stamped 'Chanel' and blind stitched with 'CC' logo, also stamped to hardware, with dust bag.

9.5in (24cm) wide

$900-1,100   MOR

A Christian Dior, 'Lady Dior Cannage', quilted leather tote, Christian Dior paperwork and dust bag.

12.5in (32cm) wide

$1,900-2,500   DN

A Dior, 'Lady Dior' tweed fringe purse, Christian Dior guarantee card and Dior dust bag.

13in (33cm) wide

$1,300-1,900   DN

A lady's Gucci purse, complete with key.

14.5in (37cm) wide

$400-500   APAR

A Gucci, 'Jackie' soft red python hobo purse, with interior wallet and suede interior lining, Gucci paperwork and dust bag.

15in (39cm) wide

$1,500-2,000   DN

Judith Picks

Wouldn't we all love an original Hermès Kelly bag! Designed in the 1930s by Robert Dumas as a spacious travel bag, it originally had a decidedly unglamorous name. 'Sac à dépêches' ... but that all changed in 1954 when costume designer Edith Head purchased it and other Hermès accessories for Alfred Hitchcock's film 'To Catch a Thief', starring Grace Kelly. By all accounts the glamorous Hollywood actress instantly fell in love with it, commissioned half-a-dozen in various colors, and within months of her 1956 marriage to Prince Ranier of Monaco was photographed using the bag to hide her pregnancy from paparazzi - a photograph that made the cover of 'Life' magazine. The bag immediately became known as the 'Kelly' bag, although it wasn't officially renamed by Hermès until 1977.

A lady's Hermès 'Trim' purse, in burgundy leather, the tab fastening with date code.

1976   *13in (33cm) long*

$450-500   FLD

An Hermès Kelly bag, in black calf leather with gilt hardware, with date code.

1955   *12.5in (32cm) high*

$1,500-2,000   CA

A Hermès purse, red lizard leather, metal hardware.

$10,000-11,000 ARTC

A Hermès, 'Birkin 40' black calf skin tote bag, yellow metal hardware lock and keys, a Hermès rain protector and dust bag.

c2003 *15in (40cm) wide*

$6,500-7,500 DN

ESSENTIAL REFERENCE - HERMÈS BAGS

As a rule-of-thumb, vintage purses by unknown or less well-known makers, regardless of age or rarity, don't generate nearly as much interest as bags made by the top brands, such as Hermès, Louis Vuitton, or Prada. However, condition is also very important. This 1960s Hermès 'Sac Malette' wouldn't have sold for nearly as much if it hadn't been in excellent condition - and that is equally applicable to even the most desirable, iconic, film star-connected bags of all, such as the Hermès 'Birkin', with pre-owned but near-pristine examples of the latter now commanding up to $120,000!

A 1960s Hermès black leather 'Sac Malette' jewelry bag, jewelry compartment to base, signed 'HERMES-PARIS'.

$3,800-5,000 L&T

A Hermès, 'Kelly Retourne 40', blue Jean Togo calfskin purse, blind stamp 'K' in a square 27Z, palladium fittings, padlock with keys, a Hermès dust bag, two rain protectors and a Hermès card box.

2007 *15in (40cm) wide*

$7,500-9,000 DN

An Hermès, 'Jypsiere Messenger', Etoupe, a taurillon Clemence leather bag, with a Hermès dust bag.

2008 *12.5in (32cm) high*

$3,200-3,800 DN

An Hermès, 'Birkin 40' black Togo leather purse, palladium fittings, pink stitching, padlock with keys a Hermès dust bag, rain protector and card box.

2013 *15in (40cm) wide*

$12,000-14,000 DN

A Mulberry graphite leather 'Bayswater' bag, with chrome mounts, chrome tag impressed '1259784', with dust bag, slight wear overall.

14.5in (37cm) wide

$1,000-1,100 TEN

A Prada, 'Struzzo' colbalt blue ostrich tote bag, ref.BN2606, Prada paperwork, a dust bag and card box.

12in (30.5cm) tall

$1,900-2,500 DN

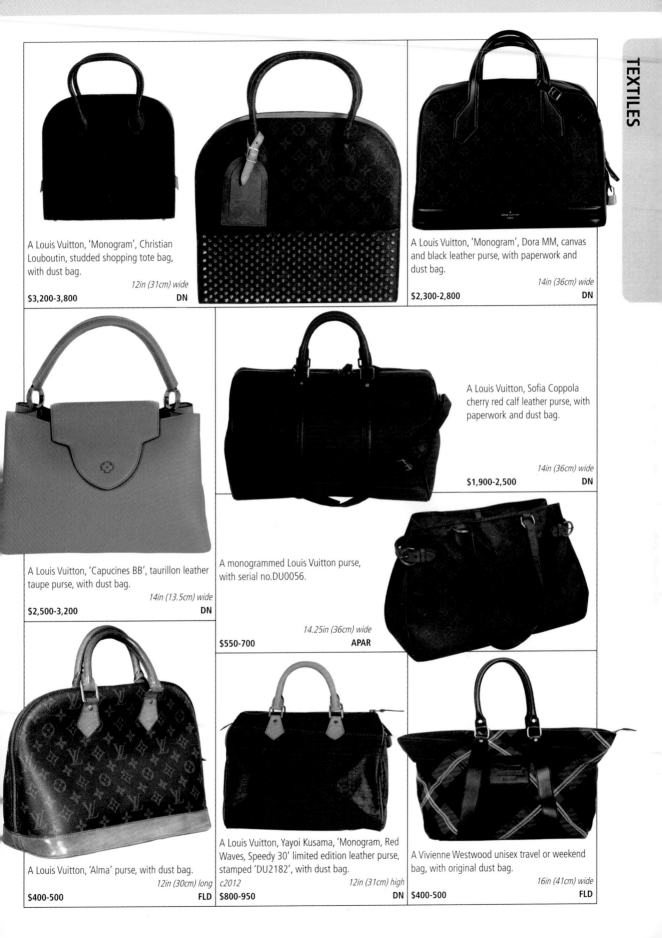

A Louis Vuitton, 'Monogram', Christian Louboutin, studded shopping tote bag, with dust bag.

12in (31cm) wide

$3,200-3,800 DN

A Louis Vuitton, 'Monogram', Dora MM, canvas and black leather purse, with paperwork and dust bag.

14in (36cm) wide

$2,300-2,800 DN

A Louis Vuitton, 'Capucines BB', taurillon leather taupe purse, with dust bag.

14in (13.5cm) wide

$2,500-3,200 DN

A Louis Vuitton, Sofia Coppola cherry red calf leather purse, with paperwork and dust bag.

14in (36cm) wide

$1,900-2,500 DN

A monogrammed Louis Vuitton purse, with serial no.DU0056.

14.25in (36cm) wide

$550-700 APAR

A Louis Vuitton, 'Alma' purse, with dust bag.

12in (30cm) long

$400-500 FLD

A Louis Vuitton, Yayoi Kusama, 'Monogram, Red Waves, Speedy 30' limited edition leather purse, stamped 'DU2182', with dust bag.

c2012   *12in (31cm) high*

$800-950 DN

A Vivienne Westwood unisex travel or weekend bag, with original dust bag.

16in (41cm) wide

$400-500 FLD

TEXTILES

A hard Louis Vuitton suitcase, in monogrammed canvas, the brass lock stamped 'no.1087262', with matching numbered keys, the interior lacking the tray, with 1.25in (3cm) split repaired to interior lid.

32in (81cm) wide

$1,600-2,300   DN

An early 20thC Louis Vuitton trunk, canvas with metal straps and ash straps, the brass studs stamped 'Louis Vuitton', with label and serial number '155780'.

43.25in (110cm) long

$4,400-5,700   L&T

A vintage Louis Vuitton briefcase, with brass catches, corners and lock stamped 'Louis Vuitton Made in France', with serial no.17623.

17in (43cm) wide

$1,000-1,100   DW

An early 20thC Louis Vuitton leather and ash steamer trunk, covered in monogram brown leather with leather straps, with paper trade label and serial number '734273'.

43.75in (111cm) long

$7,000-8,000   L&T

A George V leather artist's travelling paint case, by Brachers, the hinged top revealing a set of five concertina-action metal trays, stamped 'PATENT NO. 175202', with further Brachers stamps.

14.25in (36cm) wide

$500-650   WW

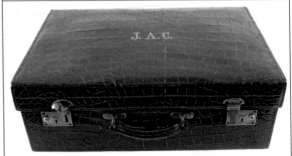

A gentleman's crocodile leather dressing case, with canvas outer cover and fitted ivory brushes, pots etc, initialed 'J.A.C'.

$500-650   CHOR

An early 20thC crocodile skin valise, fitted with ivory accessories and silver mounted bottles, hallmarked 'London 1924', with original canvas cover with initials 'P.D.C.'.

21.75in (55cm) wide

$750-900   L&T

A vintage crocodile skin attaché case, with nickel-plated catches and locks, with initials 'J.M.G'.

15.25in (38.5cm) wide

$180-250   DW

A pair of leather and brass-mounted trunks, bearing the Prince of Wales insignia.

22in (56cm) high

$750-1,000   WHP

'Book of Common Prayer', published by Robert Young, Edinburgh, small folio in eights, title-page in red and black, contemporary calf with decorative gilt stamps to covers and later red morocco gilt label to spine, bookplate of Robert John Archibald Steuart.
1637
$5,000-6,500   **L&T**

Albin, Eleazar, 'A Natural History of Birds', first editions (volumes I and II first issues, volume III a second issue), 3 volumes, 306 hand colored plates, 4to, printed for the Author and sold at William Innys, London.
1731-40   *11.5in (29cm) high*
$18,000-20,000   **L&T**

Aldin, Cecil and Byron, Mary 'Jack and Jill', first edition, pictorial title and 24 colored plates, 4to, published by Henry Frowde, Hodder and Stoughton, London.
c1919
$450-550   **LAW**

Annan, Thomas and Young, William, 'The Old Closes & Streets of Glasgow', published by James MacLehose and Sons, Glasgow, folio, 50 plates (49 of which are photogravures), original red cloth gilt, circulating library plate and ownership inscription of Bonhill and Alexandria St. Andrew's Royal Arch Lodge, no.321.
1900
$4,500-5,000   **L&T**

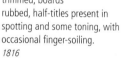

Austen, Jane, 'Emma', printed for John Murray, in three volumes, first edition, first volume with early manuscript ownership name at head, head trimmed, boards rubbed, half-titles present in spotting and some toning, with occasional finger-soiling.
1816
$10,000-11,000   **DW**

Baum, L. Frank, 'The Wonderful Wizard of Oz', with Pictures by W.W. Denslow, first edition, second state, Chicago & New York, 24 color plates including title, some slight soiling.
1900
$1,500-1,900   **DW**

Caroll, Lewis, 'Alice's Adventures in Wonderland', published by Macmillan, with forty-two illustrations by John Tenniel, sixth edition, yellow silk endpapers, upper and lower cover with depiction of the Mad Hatter and the White Rabbit onlaid in colored leathers respectively.
1872
$3,200-3,800   **DW**

ESSENTIAL REFERENCE - CHARLES CATTON

This is a first edition, marking the earliest use of aquatint for a work on natural history. This copy varies from others in having been bound in an upright rather than oblong format, the plates being mounted on contemporary blanks (watermarked 1794) and then framed within pen-and-ink and wash borders, with captions and numbering in ink. The son of the artist Charles Catton the Elder (1828-1798), coach painter to George III and founder-member of the Royal Academy, Charles Catton the Younger was taught by his father and admitted to the Royal Academy Schools in 1775. He worked as a landscape artist in England and Scotland, exhibiting some 37 paintings at the Royal Academy between 1775 and 1800. He emigrated to North America in 1805.

THE ROYAL TIGER.

Catton, Charles, the Younger, 'Animals drawn from Nature and Engraved in Aquatint', printed for the author and sold by I. and J. Taylor, London, 36 hand-colored aquatint plates.
1794   *16.5in (42.5cm) high*
$13,000-16,000   **L&T**

Chadwick, Philip George, 'The Death Guard', first edition, Hutchinson & Co., 52 pages, publisher's catalog at end, original black cloth, inscribed to front endpaper 'To Roy, Boom! Zuzzoo-oo! Not even Trenchmen could stop this other idea of yours! Philip'.
1939
$1,900-2,500   **DW**

Coleman Smith, Pamela, 'Widdicombe Fair', folio, no.401 of 500 copies only, 13 mounted pochoir plates, mounted sheet of music.
1899
$450-500   **LAW**

ESSENTIAL REFERENCE - CAPTAIN COOK'S FLORILEGIUM

The sumptuous binding incorporates a specimen of Banskia integrifolia in a panel inset into the front cover, this edition also has 42 plates, twelve more than the 'standard' edition of the same year which itself was limited to only 100 copies for subscribers. Both editions were fully subscribed long before publication date. The work is of importance as its publication reproduces for the first time some of the engraved plates of Australian plants made under the supervision of Sir Joseph Banks. Apart from a proof impression no prints were made from the plates selected here for publication, the original copper-engraved plates, the original drawings, the specimens used for the drawings and the proof impressions all being held by the British Museum. In the 1960s it was decided that the Royal College of Art should print a selection of the most beautiful plates.

Cook, Captain James, 'Captain Cook's Florilegium: Selection of Engravings from the Drawings of Plants collected by Joseph Banks and Daniel Solander on Captain Cook's first Voyage to the Islands of the Pacific, with Accounts of the Voyage by Wilfrid Blunt and of the Botanical Explorations and Prints by William T. Stearn', published by Lion and Unicorn Press, number 8 of 10 copies.
1973
$13,000-16,000   L&T

Darwin, Charles, 'On the Origin of Species', published by John Murray, London, second edition, 'fifth thousand' (second issue), 32 pages of adverts at rear, original green blind-stamped cloth with gilt tooling to spine, bookplate of James Whittle, 8vo.
1860
$3,800-5,000   L&T

Dickens, Charles, 'A Christmas Carol, in Prose, Being a Ghost Story of Christmas', with illustrations by John Leech, first edition, some spotting, toning and occasional marks, small 8vo.
$750-1,000   DW

Disney, Walt, 'Walt Disney's Sketch Book', published by Collins, twelve tipped-in color plates, signed to front endpaper 'Walt Disney -38', original cloth in pictorial dust jacket (not price clipped), slight fraying to edges and head of spine, 4to.
1938
$1,900-2,500   LOCK

Edwards, George, 'A Natural History of Birds; Gleanings of Natural History', printed for the author at the College of Physicians, 7 volumes, contemporary green morocco gilt by Charles Lewis, g.e., lavender endpapers, the William Gott copy with bookplates, 4to.
1743-64
$18,000-20,000   L&T

Judith Picks

To own your own special Fleming novel is not going to come cheap! Over $100,000 was paid in Sotheby's New York in 2004 for a copy of 'Moonraker', signed from Fleming to Raymond Chandler. Fleming and Chandler became friends after first meeting at a dinner in London in May 1955. It was inscribed by the author to Raymond Chandler: 'To / Field Marshall Chandler / from / Private Ian Fleming / 1955.' Fleming's admiring and deferential inscription did not divert Chandler from looking at Moonraker with a close or critical eye: at the end of Chapter 1, on page 18, he has written a big, underlined 'all Padding'.

Over $120,000 was paid at Sotheby's in 2012 for typescript 'Diamonds Are Forever'. This final typescript prepared by Fleming's secretary Ulrica Knowles, was checked by the publisher's reader and by the author, with autograph revisions to almost every page.

Over $65,000 was paid at Christies in 2002 for a First Edition 'Live and Let Die'. It was inscribed 'To Sir Winston Churchill / From whom I stole some / words! / from / The Author /1954'.

Fleming, Ian, 'Monraker', first edition, second impression, original cloth, spine a little toned with minor nick at head, 8vo.
1955
$1,300-1,900   DW

Fleming, Ian, 'From Russia With Love', first edition, original cloth, in bright condition, 8vo.
$1,900-2,500   DW

Fleming, Ian, 'Diamonds Are Forever', first edition, original cloth, 8vo, spines slighlty faded with small nicks and creases to ends, a few minor spots.
1956
$1,400-1,900   DW

Golding, William, 'Lord of the Flies', published by Faber & Faber, London, first edition, original red cloth, some damage, 8vo.
1954
$4,400-5,700   L&T

Grahame, Kenneth, 'The Wind in the Willows', fifth Edition, black and white frontispiece by Graham Robertson, bookplate of Ena Florence Sanderson, and with contemporary inscription.

The extremely rare first issue dustjacket in original, unrestored state, is identified by the price of 6/- to the upper panel.
1910
$28,000-35,000   DW

Hamilton, Patrick, 'Craven House', a rare original copy, first edition, published by Houghton Mifflin.
1927
$650-750   ECGW

Hamilton, Patrick, 'The Plains of Cement', first American edition, published by Little Brown.
1935
$250-400   ECGW

Hill, Reginald, 'A Clubbable Woman', signed by the author, with original dust jacket and added protective sleeve, published London, Collins.
1970
$500-650   ECGW

Hillerman, Tony, 'The Fly on the Wall', first edition, signed on half-title page, published by Harper & Row, New York.
1971
$230-280   ECGW

James, P.D., 'Cover Her Face', first edition, published by Faber & Faber, price-clipped, two small holes to lower joint, 8vo.
1962
$3,200-3,800   DW

ESSENTIAL REFERENCE - SIR JOSEPH DALTON HOOKER

Sir Joseph Dalton Hooker (1817-1911), one of the greatest British botanists and explorers of the 19thC, a close friend of Charles Darwin and one-time director of The Royal Botanic Gardens at Kew, was educated at Glasgow High School and Glasgow University. Walter Hood Fitch (1817-1892), born in Glasgow, was artist for all the Kew Garden Publications from 1841, and illustrated many botanical works including: William Hooker's 'A Century of Orchidaceous Plants' (1851) and James Bateman's 'A Monograph of Odontoglossum' (1864-74).

Hooker, Joseph Dalton, 'Illustrations of Himalayan Plants: the Plates Executed by W.H. Fitch', published by Lovell, Reeve, London, first edition.
1855   *19.5in (50cm) wide*
$15,000-19,000   L&T

King, Stephen, 'Salem's Lot', first UK edition, 8vo.
1976
$450-500   DW

Kipling, Rudyard, 'The Jungle Book' and 'The Second Jungle Book', first editions, black and white illustrations, both 8vo.
1894 and 1895
$1,900-2,500   DW

Latham, John, 'A General History of Birds', published by Jacob and Johnson, Winchester, first edition, 193 hand colored engraved plates, list of subscribers vol.1, modern half sheep and marbled boards, 11 volumes in 10, 4to.
1821-28
$5,500-6,500   **L&T**

Lewis, C.S., 'The Silver Chair', first edition, illustrations by Pauline Baynes, minor spots front and rear, spine faded with light stain, 8vo.
1953
$1,300-1,800   **DW**

McBain, Ed, 'King's Ransom', signed, first edition, first printing.
1959
$300-400   **ECGW**

ESSENTIAL REFERENCE - EADWEARD MUYBRIDGE

Eadweard Muybridge (1830-1904), a brilliant and eccentric photographer, gained worldwide fame photographing animal and human movement imperceptible to the human eye.

In 1872 former California Governor Leland Stanford asked Muybridge to determine through photography whether all four hooves of a galloping horse left the ground at the same time. By setting up multiple cameras to capture motion in stop-motion photographs, Eadweard Muybridge captured animals' movement in a way that had never been done before.

In the 1880s the University of Pennsylvania sponsored Muybridge's research using banks of cameras to photograph people in a studio, and animals from the Philadelphia Zoo to study their movement. In 1887 The University of Pennsylvania published 781 plates under the title Animal Locomotion in a series of volumes.

Milne, A.A., 'Winnie-The-Pooh', with decorations by Ernest H. Shepard, first edition, pictorial plan on end papers.
1926
$1,000-1,100   **BELL**

Milne, A.A., 'The House At Pooh Corner', with decorations by Ernest H. Shepard, first edition, pictorial end papers.
1928
$500-650   **BELL**

Muybridge, Eadweard, 'Animal Locomotion, Electro-Photographic Investigation of Consecutive Phases of Animal Movements', published in Philadelphia, large oblong folio, 95 collotypes, with letterpress title, plate number, copyright, and date in the margin, rebound in morocco-backed cloth, vellum corners, stamp of Museum of Edinburgh (Science and Art) to title page.
1887
$90,000-110,000   **L&T**

Orwell, George, 'Nineteen Eighty-Four', published by Secker & Warburg, London, first edition, modern green full morocco gilt, spine lettered in gilt with raised gilt banding, edges gilt, gilt doublures, 8vo.
1949
$700-800   **L&T**

Plath, Sylvia, 'Ariel', published by Faber, first edition, spine a little toned, 8vo.
1965
$500-650   **DW**

Potter, Beatrix, 'The Tailor of Gloucester', published by Strangeways, first edition, one of 500 copies privately printed for Potter, original pink boards with line drawing of mice to upper cover, colored frontispiece and 15 color plates, 12mo.
1902
$3,800-4,400   **L&T**

Potter, Beatrix, 'The Tale of Peter Rabbit', first privately printed edition, published by Strangeways, color frontspiece, woodblock engravings from the author's line drawings throughout, with contemporary inscription, 16mo.
1901
$25,000-32,000
DW

ESSENTIAL REFERENCE - BEATRIX POTTER

Only two of Beatrix Potter's works were bound in this style, the other - which is far more common - being 'The Tailor of Gloucester'. The author went to great trouble to find a suitable cloth in which to bind her books, obtaining numerous samples from her grandfather's firm, Edmund Potter & Co. of Dinting Vale, Manchester, one of the largest calico printers in Europe. After much deliberation Potter chanced upon a small packet of samples which she had overlooked, writing to the Warnes 'they are rather quaint, especially one like pansies'. This was the one settled upon, and the author referred to the two books as 'bound in flowered lavender chintz, very pretty' (Leslie Linder, 'A History of the Writings of Beatrix Potter', pages 138-140).

Rackham, Arthur, 'The Fairy Tales of Brothers Grimm', half-title, 40 tipped-in colored plates, 4to, published by Constable & Co., London, ends of spine slightly chipped.
1909
$750-900
LAW

Rendell, Ruth, 'A New Lease of Death', first edition, signed by the author to title, 8vo.
1967
$300-400
DW

Potter, Beatrix, 'The Tale of Squirrel Nutkin', first Deluxe edition, Frederick Warne, third issue, with 'Author of the Tale of Peter Rabbit', beneath the author's name on the title-page, color frontspiece and 26 full-page color illustrations, spine near-detatched, 16mo.
1903
$500-650
DW

Richards, J.M., 'High Street', published by Country Life Ltd., Curwen Press production, first edition, wood-engraved pictorial title illustration and 24 color lithographed plates by Eric Ravilious, spine fragile.
1938
$1,600-2,000
BELL

Roberts, David, 'The Holy Land, Syria, Idumea, Arabia, from Drawings Made on the Spot by David Roberts, R.A., with Historical Descriptions by the Revd. George Croly, L.L.D. 3 Volumes.

Without doubt one of the greatest travel books portraying the Middle East, based on nine months travel (August 1838-May 1839) in Egypt, Arabia and The Holy Land. The plates in this copy are exceptionally clean.
1842-49
25.5in (65cm) high
$21,000-23,000
L&T

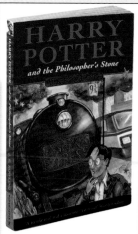

Rowling, J.K., 'Harry Potter and the Philosopher's Stone', published by Bloomsbury, London, first edition with 10-1 numberline.
1997
$3,800-4,400
L&T

Tolkien, J.R.R., 'The Hobbit', or 'There and Back Again', first edition, second impression, four color plates by the author, black and white illustrations, some damage, 8vo.
1937
$4,500-5,000
DW

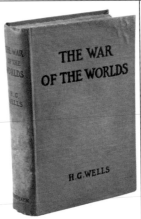

Waugh, Evelyn, 'Decline and Fall. An Illustrated Novlette', first edition, first issue, illustrations by the author, scattered light spotting, 8vo, with the names 'Martin Gaythorn-Brodie' and 'Kevin Saunderson' unchanged.
1928
$5,000-6,500   DW

Wells, H.G., 'War of the Worlds', first edition, first impression, published by William Heinemann, London.
1898
$500-650   ECGW

Wells, H.G., 'The Invisibile Man, A grotesque Romance', first edition, C. Arthur Pearson, front hinge split, spine faded, 8vo.
1897
$700-800   DW

Wodehouse, P.G., 'The Great Sermon Handicap', first edition, published by Hodder and Stoughton, London, dust-jacket, original imitation red leather gilt, small 8vo.
1933   5in (12.5cm) high
$1,300-1,900   L&T

Watkins, Dudley D., 'Oor Wullie' album, published by D.C. Thomson & Co., Ltd., Glasgow, London, Dundee, original paper wrappers showing Wullie through the months of the year, spine repaired with tape, 4to.
1953
$450-500   L&T

Judith Picks

A very rare copy of the first 'Oor Wullie' annual produced by Dundee publishers D.C. Thomson & Co. in October 1940 (priced 1s 6d). The annual has 96 pages, which became the standard number, consisting of a title page illustration, a poem/song and 94 cartoon strips reprinted from 'Sunday Post' Fun Sections. The creator of 'Oor Wullie', Dudley Dexter Watkins was born in Manchester on 27 February 1907. In 1925, he moved to Dundee to work for D.C. Thomson & Co. Ltd., the company founded by wealthy Tayside shipping boss William Thomson in 1905. In 1935 R.D. (Robert Duncan) Low, the Managing Editor and Head of Boys Story Papers at the time, asked Watkins to help him produced a new comic book for D.C. Thomson. Low was keen to give a degree of realism to the new characters and he encouraged Watkins to use real people as the basis for his cartoons. Many of the characters were based on Low's own family, Oor Wullie being modeled on his son Ron.

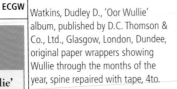

Watkins, Dudley Dexter, 'OOR WULLIE', no.1, illustrations, publisher's pictorial wrappers, 4to, original printed wrappers showing Wullie sat on his trademark bucket, some damage.
1940
$7,000-8,000   TEAR

Watkins, Dudley Dexter, 'THE BROONS', no.2, published by D.C.Thomson & Co. Ltd., illustrations throughout, publisher's pictorial wrappers, 4to.

The popularity of Watkins' cartoons grew to such an extent that in 1939 the first Christmas Annual was printed. 'The Broons' and 'Oor Wullie' annuals were then published in alternate years, starting with 'The Broons' in 1939. Watkins was also known for his early contributions to the comics 'The Beano' and 'The Dandy'. The early editions of these paperbound comic annuals are particularly rare.
1942
$3,800-5,000   TEAR

Albrizzi, Giovanni Battista, 'Carta Geografica Della America Meridionale', map of South America, Venice.

c1750   *17.5in (44.5cm) wide*

$400-500   **ALTE**

Cary, John, 'Cary's Actual Survey of the Great Post Roads between London and Falmouth' map, including a branch to Weymouth, first edition, some light spotting, contemporary half calf, rubbed, joints cracked.

1784

$3,200-3,800   **LAW**

Dower, John, 'A War Map of North West Italy', showing Sardinia, Piedmont, Savoy, Parma and Modena, London, original, lithograph.

1873   *17.25in (44cm) wide*

$90-100   **ALTE**

Dury, Andrew, 'A Collection of Plans of the Principal Cities of Great Britain and Ireland: with Maps of the Coast of the said Kingdoms; Drawn from the most Accurate Surveys' map, title inscribed 'Anna Maria Garbutt Walsham 1814'.

1764   *6in (15cm) wide*

$3,800-4,400   **LAW**

Honter, Johannes and Petri, Henri, a 16thC woodblock map of India, 'Cambaye Orissa Delli Decan', Basle, the map is surrounded by a Latin text description.

c1561

$400-450   **ALTE**

Juta, Jan Carel, 'Juta's Map of South Africa From the Cape to the Zambesi Compiled from the best available Colonial and Imperial Information Including the Official Cape Colony Map by the Surveyor General, Cape Town, Dr T. Hahn's Damaraland, and F.C. Selous' Journals & Sket' map, J.C. Juta & Co., & London, Edward Stanford.

Jan Carel Juta (1824-1886), of Dutch origin, settled in South Africa in 1853 with his wife Luisa (sister of Karl Marx) and became a successful publisher, creating a company which is now the oldest publishing house in South Africa. Although Luisa was embarrassed by her brother's socialism, Juta suggested that Karl could improve his finances by writing for the bilingual pro-Dutch newspaper De Zuid-Afrikaan in Cape Town: in 1854 the newspaper published Marx's 'The War in the East'.

1899   *50in (127cm) wide*

$750-1,000   **ALTE**

ESSENTIAL REFERENCE - CHART OF THE MEDITERRANEAN

Koeman described this as the 'most spectacular type of maritime cartography ever produced in 17thC Amsterdam: and the Mediterranean is the largest and most intricately decorated of the nine'. Mortier's motives in the production of this atlas was to flatter the Dutch king on the British throne since the Glorious Revolution of 1688, William III, to whom it is dedicated. The unprecedented size of the atlas and the use of artists such as de Hooghe were not cheap: Again, Koeman calls it the 'most expensive sea atlas' of the period, 'intended more as a show-piece than something to be used by the pilots at sea'. KOEMAN: M. Mor 5, and vol iv, page 424.

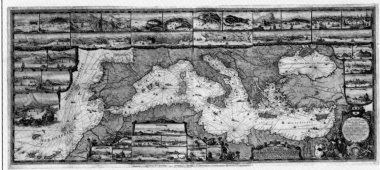

Hooghe, Romeyne de and Mortier, Pierre, the most famous chart of the Mediterranean Sea, 'Carte Nouvelle de la Mer Mediterranee ou sont Exactement Remarques Tous les Ports, Golfes, Rochers, Bancs de Sable &c.', Amsterdam.

54.75in (139cm) wide

$38,000-45,000   **ALTE**

Mallet, Alain Manesson, 'Nouveau Mexique et Californie' map, a miniature map of California as an island, colored, Paris.

1683   *6.25in (16cm) high*

$300-400   **ALTE**

Mercator, Gerard, 'The Ptolemaic British Isles on Mercator's Projection' map, Cologne.

The Ptolemaic British Isles, engraved by Mercator himself for his Ptolemaic atlas, which updated the maps to the projection named after him, but still keeping the famous east-west angle of Scotland.

1584   *16.25in (41cm) wide*
$900-1,000   **ALTE**

Munster, Sebastian, 'Londinum Feracis: Ang. Met', an early woodblock plan of London, derived from the Braun & Hogenberg map, surveyed c1560, German edition.

1614   *14.25in (36cm) wide*
$1,300-1,900   **ALTE**

Munster, Sebastian, 'Gallia IIII Nova Tabula' map, 16thC woodblock map of France, with a text giving the names of the cities in Latin and French, woodcut, Basle.

c1560   *13.5in (34cm) wide*
$400-450   **ALTE**

Munster, Sebastian and Basle, Henri Petri, a famous woodblock illustrating sea monsters, 'Deerwunder und seltzame Thier...', German text edition, derived from Olaus Magnus' 'Carta Marina' of 1539.

c1560   *13.5in (34cm) wide*
$1,300-1,900   **ALTE**

ESSENTIAL REFERENCE - MAP OF AMERICA

This map of America is one of the most important and influential maps of the continent published in the 16thC. This example has the pagination of the 1575 edition of the Theatrum erased, and the number of the 1579 edition added in old ink mss, the publishers were obviously using up the remainder of an old edition. It is printed from the first of three copper plates, all engraved by Frans Hogenberg, when the 1579 edition usually has the second, it comes from the third state, with the Azores now correctly named and the latitude number '230' erased.

ESSENTIAL REFERENCE - 15THC WORLD MAP

A fine example of the famous world map from the 'Nuremberg Chronicle', published a matter of months after Columbus' return to Spain after his first voyage to the New World, so including nothing of his discoveries. Appropriately for a history of the world, it takes a retrospective view, with the cartography that of Ptolemy, with a land-locked Indian Ocean with the island of Taprobana, but given a biblical theme by depicting the three sons of Noah in the borders; down the left are seven vignettes of mythological creatures, with a further fourteen on the reverse, taken from the works of Herodotus, Solinus and Pliny - these include figures with six arms, four eyes or a bird-neck - and a centaur, the text describing which parts of the world they inhabit.

Schedel, Hartmann D. and Koberger, Anton, world map, Nuremberg, Latin text edition, colored woodcut, very minor restoration to centerfold as usually found on this map.

1493   *2in (5cm) wide*
$16,000-19,000   **ALTE**

Ortelius, Abraham, 'The most famous map of the Americas, the cornerstone of any map collection' map, 'America Sive Novi Orbis Nova Descriptio', Latin text edition, original color, Antwerp.

1575   *19in (48cm) wide*
$3,800-5,000   **ALTE**

ESSENTIAL REFERENCE - LONDON UNDERGROUND

An early edition of Beck's revolutionary new 'electrical circuit' design, published within a year of the first edition in 1933. The interchange diamonds are now circles; the logo now refers to London Transport; the District Line no longer runs to South Harrow, replaced by the Piccadilly Line (October 1933); and a red box proclaims the 'Escalator Connection between Bank and Monument Stations'. However this edition does not mark the continuation of the Piccadilly Line to Uxbridge (23 October 1933) or the color of the Bakerloo Line changing from red to brown (1934). GARLAND: 'Mr Beck's Underground Map', an edition between his illustrations 18 & 19.

Seutter, Matthäus and Probst, J.M., a decorative 18thC map of Jamaica, Augsburg, shown divided into Precincts.

This unusual later issue of Seutter's large map of Jamaica was published by Johann Michael Probst, who had worked as an engraver for Seutter before becoming a publisher.

1770   *22in (56cm) wide*
$500-650   **ALTE**

Beck, Henry C., An early 1934 edition of Beck's iconic map of the London Underground, folded twice as issued.

1934   *8in (20cm) wide*
$900-1,000   **ALTE**

A late 19thC French porcelain 'fortune' doll, with a dress made of folded 'fortunes' inscribed in French, under a glass dome.

12.5in (32cm) high

$250-400   **SWO**

A 19thC wax doll, with a wax head and shoulder plate, with glass eyes and leather limbs and body, with contemporary clothing and undergarments.

25in (64cm) high

$750-900   **LAW**

A late 19thC porcelain-headed child doll, impressed '15.79 DEP', with brown sleeping eyes, pierced ears, brown wig and jointed composition body.

28in (71cm) high

$500-650   **KEY**

A late 19thC porcelain-headed child doll, stamped 'DEP', with blue lashed sleeping eyes, pierced ears, blonde mohair wig, jointed composition body.

15in (38cm) high with stand

$400-500   **KEY**

A bisque head doll, closed mouth and fixed blue eyes, kid body, original damask dress and later kid boots, unmarked.

c1880   *19.75in (50cm) high*

$750-900   **CHOR**

A late 19thC German bisque head doll, marked '350.II', large fixed brown eyes and pierced ears.

21.75in (55cm) high

$250-400   **CHOR**

A French bisque head character doll, marked 'SUB 2/0', painted face with fixed eyes, pierced ears, composition body in an original silk outfit and orange wig.

12.25in (31cm) high

$2,500-3,200   **CHOR**

A Bahr & Proschild doll, with weighted brown eyes, open mouth and pierced ears, marked '209', '16', 'Germany'.

31in (79cm) high

$450-500   **LAW**

A Heubach doll, shape 342.7, with open mouth, two teeth, sleep eyes, moving arms and legs.

22.75in (58cm) high

$150-230   **PW**

TOYS & MODELS

A Jumeau doll, model no.1907, with glass paperweight eyes, open mouth and pierced ears, marked.

1907   *12.25in (66cm) high*

$500-650   **LAW**

A Kaiser & Reinhardt/Simon & Halbig doll, shape no.80, open mouth with four teeth, sleep eyes, with articulated limbs, the body recently restrung and repainted.

30.75in (78cm) high

$300-400   **PW**

ESSENTIAL REFERENCE - JUMEAU

Jumeau was founded in the 1840s by Pierre-François Jumeau (1811-1895) and Louis-Desire Belton, just outside of Paris, France. The company designed and manufactured high-end bisque dolls, especially famous for their beauty and well-made clothing which mirrored fashions of the time. Louis-Desire Belton left the company in 1845. Jumeau's son Emile took over the company in 1874.

● In 1877, the company began producing Bébés, dolls in the form of little girls.

● Jumeau dolls won great critical acclaim. They were awarded medals at the 1849 Paris Exposition, the 1851 London Great Exhibition, and the 1878 Exposition Universelle.

● Damaged by competition from German markets, in 1899 the company joined the Société Française de Fabrication de Bébés et Jouets (S.F.B.J.) and remained a member until 1958.

● Jumeau dolls can fetch very high prices. In 2009, Theriault sold a 28-inch Jumeau Bébé Triste for $28,000.

A Kammer & Reinhardt closed-mouth 'Mein Liebling' doll, model no.117a, the head made by Simon & Halbig with weighted eyes and closed mouth, marked, 'K & R', 'Simon & Halbig', '117a'.

17.5in (44cm) high

$750-900   **LAW**

A Kestner doll, with weighted eyes and open mouth, with a bent limb composition body and voice box mechanism, marked '257', 'Made in Germany', '51'.

23in (59cm) high

$300-350   **LAW**

A Jumeau Triste doll and doll's trunk, the doll with fixed paperweight eyes, closed mouth, and applied ears, with a pin on her dress with the name 'Ethel', also with a dome-top dolls trunk, containing a variety of clothing and hats, original label on the inside, the doll with an impressed '10' mark on the neck.

doll 20in (50cm) high

$4,500-5,000   **LAW**

A Kestner doll, with weighted eyes, open mouth and bent limb body, marked 'JDK, 257', '51'.

21in (53cm) high

$180-250   **LAW**

A bisque shoulder-headed doll, German, probably Kling, with painted features, blonde molded hair, stuffed body, bisque limbs and heeled bar shoes.

17.25in (44cm) high

$100-130   **KEY**

A Leopold Lambert S.F.B.J. musical automaton figure, 'The Ballerina', on pointe, holding flowers which she lifts as she spins whilst moving her head and raising one leg, on a velvet box, the bisque headed doll stamped 'S.F.B.J./ 301/ PARIS'.

c1900   *23.5in (60cm) high*

$2,500-3,200   **L&T**

ESSENTIAL REFERENCE - ARMAND MARSEILLE

Armand Marseille was founded in Köppelsdorf in 1885. They manufactured and sold bisque doll heads from the 1880s to the 1930s.

- Armand Marseille (1856-1925) was the son of a Russian architect. He was born in St Petersburg, but moved to Germany in the 1860s.
- Armand Marseille specialized in doll heads. Between 1900 and 1930, they produced nearly 1,000 doll heads per day. The doll bodies were bought in from other manufacturers.
- The company merged with Ernst Heubach in 1919 but separated in 1932. Around this time, Armand Marseille ceased production.

A bisque head Armand Marseille girl doll, with brown sleeping eyes, an open mouth and fully jointed body, impressed 'A 6 1/2 M Germany'.

25in (63.5cm) high

$110-150 **BRI**

A Schuetzmeister & Quendt voice box doll, with weighted eyes and open mouth, the voice box making a 'crying' noise, marked 'SQ' monogram, '201', 'Germany'.

19in (49cm) high

$180-250 **LAW**

A late 19thC S.F.B.J. bisque head French boy doll, marked '2278 SFBJ', open mouth and fixed eyes, with a composition body.

19.25in (49cm) high

$250-400 **CHOR**

A Simon & Halbig doll, open mouth with four teeth, sleep eyes, with articulated limbs.

1909 *23.75in (60cm) high*

$130-180 **PW**

A Simon & Halbig bisque head doll, with weighted eyes, open mouth and pierced ears, marked 'Simon & Halbig', '1078', '15'.

32in (82cm) high

$450-500 **LAW**

A Simon & Halbig doll, no.117N, with weighted eyes, open mouth and sound mechanism, marked 'Simon & Halbig', '117n'.

17in (43cm) high

$500-550 **LAW**

A Simon & Halbig bisque head doll, mold number 10, with sleep eyes and jointed composite limbs.

c1900 *24.5in (62cm) high*

$150-190 **BELL**

A Sonja Henie English doll, with weighted glass eyes, open mouth, dimpled cheeks, a composition five-piece body, stamped 'SH'.

c1930 *15.75in (40cm) high*

$180-250 **KEY**

A Goss bisque shoulder-headed doll, stamped 'G8 - copyright as Act describes - W.H.Goss - Stoke on Trent...', stamped to the body 'British Toy Company', with painted eyes, mohair wig, cloth body, bisque arms, with original worn box.

28.75in (73cm) high

$400-500 **KEY**

An early 19thC large painted pine doll's house, with six rooms including hall, staircase and landing, dining room, kitchen, drawing room and bedroom, complete with fixtures, furniture and accessories, on an associated pine stand, dated.

1803

$9,000-10,000

49.25in (125cm) wide

BE

A mid-19thC open-fronted doll's house, 'The Spanish House', with four rooms retaining their original papers and finishes, the kitchen with original range, shelving and well, the fully furnished interior with Rock & Graner pieces comprising bed, armchair, sofa and jardinière with flowerpots, the numerous other pieces including an Erhard étagère and birdcage, a Gothic upright piano, probably by Sohlke, a fine Waltershausen sofa, whatnot and table and a framed 18thC enamel plaque, the well-equipped kitchen with a variety of interesting pieces, inhabited by six bisque or china-headed dolls.

38.75in (98.5cm) high

$2,500-3,800　　CHOR

An English 'Boxback' doll's house, with six rooms on three floors, all with fireplaces and grates, the kitchen with original range, dresser, sink, copper and towel roller, the fully furnished interior with tinplate Rock & Graner pieces comprising a fine half-tester bed, corner whatnot, pair of rare upholstered armchairs and round table, the seven pieces of Walterhausen including a bookcase and a writing desk, the gilt metal Erhard pieces including a rare love seat and standard lamp, Vienna wall clock, wall sconces and pictures, the other contents including a bone writing desk, German bedroom and dining room suites, two chandeliers and a lithophane fire screen, a family of seven Grödnertal dolls in original costume in residence.

c1870

$3,800-5,000

Dolls houses have been commercially made in London since the late 18thC. A rusticated lower storey with red or orange brickwork above, a plain orange finish to the sides and back and well appointed kitchens were common features. Many were retailed through well-known stores such as Gamages, Silber & Fleming and Hamleys.

36.25in (92cm) high

$3,800-5,000　　CHOR

A 19thC English rosewood cabinet doll's house, 'The Rosewood House', the upper storey divided into two rooms with original wall coverings, one in the French taste with faux panelling and double doors, the contents including a tinplate Rock & Graner bed, Dutch silver chandelier, pair of silver candlesticks, Waltershausen Gothic bookcase and eight other Waltershausen pieces, Erhard mantel clock, finely carved console table, red morocco trunk, a bisque-headed lady doll and numerous other items.

55in (140cm) high

$3,800-5,000　　CHOR

A 19thC pine dolls' house, with a brick effect facade, in original paint, with four internal rooms decorated in wallpaper.

43in (109cm) high

$550-700　　LAW

An early 20thC primitive-style pine doll's house chest of drawers, two drawers decorated with three glazed windows painted with curtains and window frames.

19.25in (49cm) high

$400-450　　TEN

A 20thC doll's house, modeled as a Tudor-style half-timbered house, divided into eight rooms and extensively furnished, to include kitchen, hallway, drawing room, nursery and two bedrooms.

41in (104cm) high

$1,900-2,500　　CHOR

A child's or doll's button back sofa.

32.25in (82cm) wide

$150-190　　LAW

A Victorian mahogany doll's half tester bed.

25in (63cm) high

$250-320　　PW

An early 20thC French cream and gray painted dovecote.

65in (165cm) wide

$1,000-1,100　　BELL

A gold Chiltern-type fully jointed teddy bear, with leather cloth pads.

$150-190   BRI

A Paddington bear, in original Dunlop red Wellington boots, brown overcoat and luggage label, design registration number '957892', brown hat and miniature teddy bear in pocket.

18.5in (47cm) high

$90-100   LOC

A 'Solomon' teddy bear, limited edition, made by Redmoor bears, bear 15 of 50, moveable limbs and padded paws, with tag certificate.

15in (38cm) high

$50-60   LOCK

A novelty Schuco perfume monkey, bottle/flask hidden inside the body.

c1930   4in (10cm) high

$90-100   MART

A Schuco 'Trip Trap' bear, with wheels on its feet, with a plastic label attached 'Schuco Trip Trap, Made in US Zone, Germany'.

9in (23cm) long

$200-250   LAW

A Steiff teddy bear, with boot button eyes, hand-stitched snout, plush golden fur, hump back, and jointed limbs.

c1910   16.5in (42cm) high

$2,500-3,200   BELL

A Steiff teddy bear, with boot button eyes, hand-stitched snout, plush orange fur, hump back, and jointed limbs.

c1910   12.25in (31cm) high

$150-190   BELL

A Steiff teddy bear, button in ear, some loss to fur, wear to the lower right paw.

c1910   7in (17.5cm) high

$650-750   LOCK

An early Steiff teddy bear, with black boot button eyes, elongated limbs and hump back, with a growler mechanism, an embroidered jacket and a Steiff Button in one ear, with a photograph of the original owner, the growler mechanism not working.

This Teddy Bear was purchased around 1912, after the birth of the vendor's father, Norman Keith William Bagley (1912-1986).

c1912   17in (43cm) high

$1,900-2,500   LAW

ESSENTIAL REFERENCE - STEIFF

Steiff was founded by Margarete Steiff (1847-1909) in Germany in 1880 and continues to manufacture soft toy animals today.

● Margarete's nephew Richard Steiff (1877-1939) joined the company in 1897. He is credited with helping to invent the iconic bear, and in 1902 designed his 'Steiff Bär 55 PB', the first soft toy bear with jointed arms and legs.

● Richard Steiff sold over 3,000 bears at his first fair, and the new 'Teddy' bear (after Theodore Roosevelt) became successful worldwide, especially in the USA.

● Today, although the market has softened, early 20thC Steiff bears can sell for upward of $30,000, with one record 1905 bear selling at Christie's in 1994 for over $130,000.

An early Steiff polar bear, with a jointed body and black boot button eyes, with a Steiff button in its ear.

14.25in (36cm) long

$3,200-3,800 **LAW**

An early English teddy bear, possibly by William J. Terry, with long limbs, glass eyes and hump back, growler mechanism not working.

17in (44cm) high

$1,000-1,100 **LAW**

A mid-20thC musical teddy bear, with orange glass eyes, hand-stitched snout, plush golden fur, with a winding key.

17.75in (45cm) high

$80-90 **BELL**

A late Victorian mechanical wind up bear, with gold faux fur, button eyes, wooden hands and feet, wind around arms in walking motion.

$150-230 **LOC**

A large early Steiff rabbit, with glass eyes and swivel head, and upright ears, with a Steiff button in one ear.

$450-500 **LAW**

An early Steiff donkey, with black boot button eyes, on metal wheels, with a pull chord and working sound mechanism, the saddle marked 'Steiff', and with a Steiff button in its ear.

14.5in (37cm) high

$500-750 **LAW**

An early 20thC Steiff peddling monkey, with golden fur and jointed limbs, on a wire work wooden mounted frame.

11in (28cm) long

$200-250 **BELL**

A Steiff mohair monkey, fully jointed with glass eyes and wire armature.

19in (48.5cm) high

$70-80 **BRI**

TOYS & MODELS

A large deluxe Carette Limousine, with beveled glass windows, three passengers in back seat, four original lamps, rubber tyres, some distress to tyres.

16in (40.5cm) long

$9,000-10,000   BER

A German Carette lithographed tin 'Tonneau No.50', closed rear entry model, headlamps, spoke wheels with rubber tyres, clockwork mechanism, wheels repainted.

c1914   *8in (20.5cm) long*

$2,300-2,800   BER

A 'CIJ Alfa Romeo P2 Racing Car', a scarce and early version of this large scale pressed steel racer, with working clockwork motor driving the rear wheels, all filler caps present, crazed effect to seats, restored.

c1930   *21in (53.5cm) long*

$4,500-5,000   BER

A German 'Three Man Cycle', colorful handpainted tin figures, clockwork driven, professionally restored.

8.5in (21.5cm) high

$8,000-9,500   BER

CLOSER LOOK - GUNTHERMAN SCULL

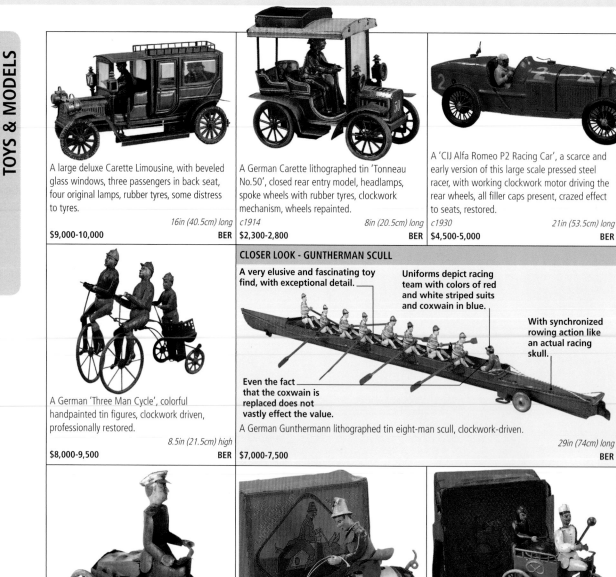

A very elusive and fascinating toy find, with exceptional detail.

Uniforms depict racing team with colors of red and white striped suits and coxwain in blue.

With synchronized rowing action like an actual racing skull.

Even the fact that the coxwain is replaced does not vastly effect the value.

A German Gunthermann lithographed tin eight-man scull, clockwork-driven.

29in (74cm) long

$7,000-7,500   BER

An early 20thC Lehmann clockwork tinplate toy, named 'Motor Rad Cycle', with Lehmann's patent details dates of 1903 (DR) and 1907 (USA), complete but worn.

$200-250   W&W

A boxed German Lehmann handpainted 'Paddy and the Pig', comical depiction of Irishman mounted on pig, tin Lehmann tag on blanket.

6.5in (16.5cm) high

$1,900-2,500   BER

A rare boxed German Lehmann 'Baker and Chimney Sweep', lithographed and handpainted tin, depicts baker driving while a chimney sweep attempts to hit him with broom, baker then turns and swipes at him with his spoon, clockwork action, tears to box and flaps.

c1900   *5.25in (13.5cm) long*

$5,000-6,500   BER

A German Lehmann lithographed tin 'Echo', well detailed toy cyclist on early spoke wheel model, clockwork driven, with box, reads 'Echo' on both sides.

6.5in (16.5cm) high

$11,000-14,000   BER

A French Fernand Martin handpainted tin 'Barber', toy depicts barber attempting to polish a bald man's head, clockwork driven, both heads repainted.

c1903   *7.75in (19.5cm) high*

$2,300-2,800   BER

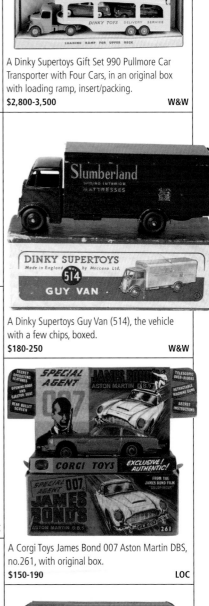

A second issue boxed set of six type 1 28/2 Dinky delivery vans, Marshes Sausages, Sharps Toffee, Kodak Film, Meccano, Oxo and Wakefield Castrol Motor Oil, in original box.

Dinky Toys are die-cast miniature vehicles that were produced by Meccano Ltd. They were made in England from 1934 to 1979, at a factory in Binns Road in Liverpool.
c1934
$23,000-28,000 TRI

An early Dinky Supertoys Foden DG Flat Truck with Tailboard 503, with early-style utility box with applied labels.
$4,500-5,000 W&W

A Dinky Supertoys Gift Set 990 Pullmore Car Transporter with Four Cars, in an original box with loading ramp, insert/packing.
$2,800-3,500 W&W

A Spanish Dinky Toys Renault 4L (518), boxed.
$90-110 W&W

A Dinky Supertoys Foden Flat Truck (902), light mottling to rear loadbed, minor chips only, boxed.
$150-190 W&W

A Dinky Supertoys Guy Van (514), the vehicle with a few chips, boxed.
$180-250 W&W

A Dinky Supertoys Bedford Pallet Jekta Van, with windows (930), boxed.
$160-210 W&W

A Corgi Toys Green Hornet Black Beauty, no.268, in original box, together with rear flying radar scanner.

Corgi Toys were introduced in the UK in July 1956 and were manufactured in Swansea, Wales, for twenty-seven years.
$130-180 LOC

A Corgi Toys James Bond 007 Aston Martin DBS, no.261, with original box.
$150-190 LOC

A Corgi Toys 214M Ford Thunderbird, boxed.
$130-180 WHP

A Corgi Toys Karrier Bantam Dairy Produce Van, no.435, boxed.
$250-320 BRI

A Corgi Toys Ford Consul Cortina Estate Golfing Set, no.440, boxed.
$140-190 BRI

A Scalextric C65 Alfa Romeo, racing no.2, French issue, boxed.
$500-650   WHP

A Scalextric E5 Aston Martin Marshal, boxed.
$180-250   WHP

A Scalextric tinplate Austin Healey C53, boxed.
$650-750   WHP

A Scalextric C99 Seat TC600, racing no.22, Spanish issue, boxed.
$400-450   WHP

A Scalextric Race-Tuned C84 Triumph TR 4A Sports, racing no.8, boxed.
$150-230   WHP

A Triang Minic clockwork double-decker bus, boxed.
$200-250   BELL

A Triang Minic clockwork Shell short bonnet petrol lorry, boxed.
$110-150   BELL

A boxed Japanese Ashi Toys black 'Imperial', features cream litho interior seating, a classic luxury auto, well appointed with nickel finish, with original box.
15in (38cm) long
$15,000-19,000   BER

A 1:18 scale Exoto Racing Legends Cobra Daytona Coupe, RN59, boxed with packing.
$150-190   W&W

A large scale surveillance vehicle, mounted on a World War II military 4-wheel Bedford QL chassis cab.
25in (63cm) long
$180-250   W&W

CLOSER LOOK - ROULETS ET DECAMPS BULLDOG

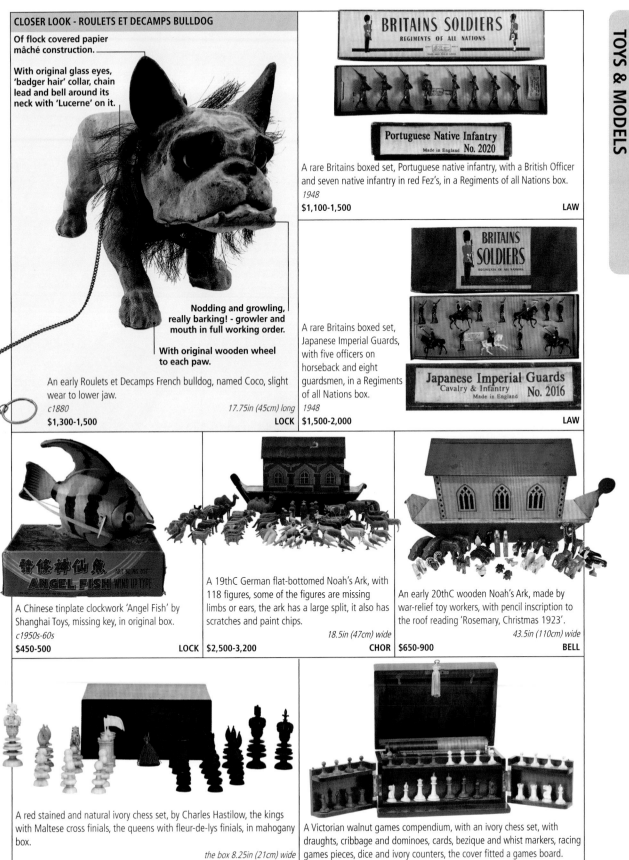

Of flock covered papier mâché construction.

With original glass eyes, 'badger hair' collar, chain lead and bell around its neck with 'Lucerne' on it.

Nodding and growling, really barking! - growler and mouth in full working order.

With original wooden wheel to each paw.

An early Roulets et Decamps French bulldog, named Coco, slight wear to lower jaw.

c1880   *17.75in (45cm) long*
$1,300-1,500   **LOCK**

A rare Britains boxed set, Portuguese native infantry, with a British Officer and seven native infantry in red Fez's, in a Regiments of all Nations box.
1948
$1,100-1,500   **LAW**

A rare Britains boxed set, Japanese Imperial Guards, with five officers on horseback and eight guardsmen, in a Regiments of all Nations box.
1948
$1,500-2,000   **LAW**

A Chinese tinplate clockwork 'Angel Fish' by Shanghai Toys, missing key, in original box.
c1950s-60s
$450-500   **LOCK**

A 19thC German flat-bottomed Noah's Ark, with 118 figures, some of the figures are missing limbs or ears, the ark has a large split, it also has scratches and paint chips.
18.5in (47cm) wide
$2,500-3,200   **CHOR**

An early 20thC wooden Noah's Ark, made by war-relief toy workers, with pencil inscription to the roof reading 'Rosemary, Christmas 1923'.
43.5in (110cm) wide
$650-900   **BELL**

A red stained and natural ivory chess set, by Charles Hastilow, the kings with Maltese cross finials, the queens with fleur-de-lys finials, in mahogany box.
the box 8.25in (21cm) wide
$2,800-3,500   **CHOR**

A Victorian walnut games compendium, with an ivory chess set, with draughts, cribbage and dominoes, cards, bezique and whist markers, racing games pieces, dice and ivory counters, the cover fitted a games board.
$650-750   **CHOR**

A pack of George III 'Monarchs of Europe' playing cards, by Rowley & Co., the suits the Kings and Queens of England, France, Spain and Russia, with their attendants as knaves, with a harewood card box.

c1775 *4in (10cm) high*

$500-650 **WW**

A 'The Wonderful Game of Oz' game, by Parker Brothers Inc., Springfield, four wooden playing pieces, 'W-I-Z-A-R-D' dice, and dice cup, tape repairs to rulebook.

1921

$900-1,300 **PC**

A 'Peter Rabbit Race' board game, published by Frederick Warne & Co., London, complete with board, die, rule sheet and cast metal figural counters depicting 'Nutkin', 'Jeremy Fisher', 'Peter Rabbit' and 'Jemima Puddleduck,' boxed.

c1925 *board 30in (75cm) wide*

$550-700 **BLO**

A game, 'The Tour of Doctor Syntax in Search of the Picturesque', with instructions, in the original box, the cover with a hand-colored illustration after Thomas Rowlandson.

c1830 *8.5in (27cm) wide*

$3,800-4,400 **LAW**

A Victorian magic set, with boxwood conjuring tools, including an Egg Vanisher, a Ball Vase, Grandma's Beads, Solomon's Pillars and the Secret Barrel, with mahogany box.

12.5in (31.5cm) wide

$700-800 **WW**

A World War I propaganda game 'Trench Football', with the goal guarded by The Kaiser, the German outfield players Count Zeppelin, Von Sanders, Von Der Goltz, Von Moltke, Enver Pasha, Von Hindenburg, Von Bulow, Little Willie, Von Terpitz & Von Kluck, printed instructions on a paper label.

c1915

$300-400 **GBA**

A croquet set in a pine box, with four mallets, two by Jaques, two by Spalding with six hoops, four balls and six posts.

$210-250 **WW**

An early 20thC pond yacht model 'Fleetwing', inscribed 'FLEETWING / SMYC'.

The pond yacht model, the 'Fleetwing' was built in the 1930s by John (Ian) Morrison, who was serving his apprenticeship with local yacht-builders James N. Miller in St Monans. In 1940 he joined the Royal Navy where he worked as a shipwright/carpenter, before he left to continue his career as a builder of both model and fishing boats in Scotland.

89in (226cm) high

$700-800 **L&T**

A 1940s green painted wooden portable Punch and Judy show, with puppets.

$250-320 **FLD**

An early 20thC carved and painted dapple gray rocking horse, by F.H. Ayres, with glass eyes and a leather bridle and saddle, the ash trestle base with stencil mark 'F.H. Ayres'.

42in (107cm) long

$450-550 WW

A rocking horse, made by Andrew Booth, on a pitch pine base.

c1920 *base 60in (152cm) long*

$500-650 LAW

An early 20thC Edwardian rocking horse, by G. & J. Lines, with horse hair mane and tail, glass eyes, leather saddle and mounted on bow rockers.

horse 60in (152cm) long

$2,300-2,800 L&T

An early 20thC painted rocking horse.

38in (97cm) long

$300-400 ECGW

An early 20thC painted rocking horse.

54.5in (138cm) long

$550-700 ECGW

A painted pine rocking horse.

37.75in (96cm) high

$1,000-1,200 LAW

A painted rocking horse with saddle and bridle, mounted on a painted wooden base, some repairs.

27in (69cm) high

$400-450 LAW

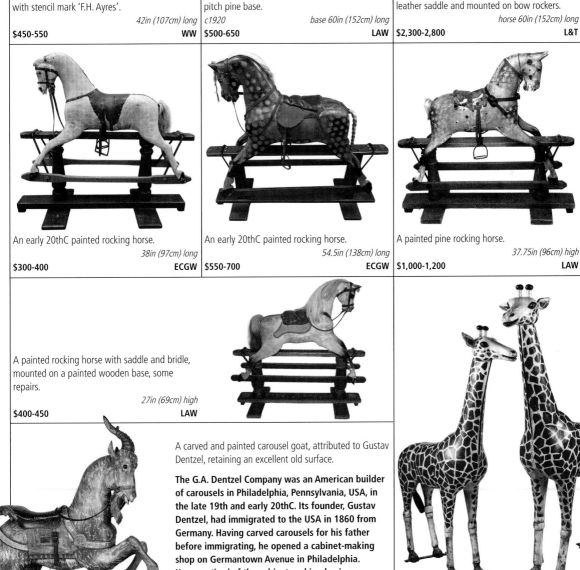

A carved and painted carousel goat, attributed to Gustav Dentzel, retaining an excellent old surface.

The G.A. Dentzel Company was an American builder of carousels in Philadelphia, Pennsylvania, USA, in the late 19th and early 20thC. Its founder, Gustav Dentzel, had immigrated to the USA in 1860 from Germany. Having carved carousels for his father before immigrating, he opened a cabinet-making shop on Germantown Avenue in Philadelphia. He soon tired of the cabinet-making business and decided to try his hand at building a small portable carousel that he could travel with around the country. After finding that people had a great enthusiasm for his carousel he decided to go into the carousel building business full-time in 1867.

c1900 *68in (173cm) high*

$38,000-45,000 POOK

A pair of 19thC French model giraffes, possibly made as fairground models, retaining the majority of their surface decoration.

67in (170cm) high

$8,000-9,500 DN

A static display model of 'H.M.S. Victory', as fitted after her 'Great Repair' of 1800-03, modeled by D. Patrick-Brown, 8ft:1in scale.

50in (127cm) long with case

$7,500-9,000   **CM**

A 1:64 scale static display model of 'H.M.S Victory', as fitted for action at Trafalgar, modeled by Y. Nefedov in fruit, box, teak and other woods, the framed hull with scaled copper sheathing.

71.5in (181.5cm) long

$25,000-32,000   **CM**

A prisoner-of-war-style bone model, for the 64-gun third rate ship 'Diadem', with planked and pinned hull, finely carved stern and full-length figurehead in the form of maiden proffering a crown (diadem).

1782   *20in (51cm) long*

$13,000-18,000   **CM**

A builder's waterline model for the turbine steamers 'Isle of Jersey' and 'Isle of Guernsey', built for the Southern Railway Company, by Denny Brothers, Dumbarton, glazed case and stand.

This pair of passenger ferries were ordered by Southern Railways for the Southampton to Channel Islands crossing in 1929. They were registered at 306ft in length and displaced 864 tons. The 'Isle of Jersey' became Hospital Ship No.3 during World War II, serving in Northern Waters and the Mediterranean, and also at the Normandy landings in June 1944. She returned to cross-channel service after the war and was sold to a Libyan buyer in 1960 before being scrapped in 1963. The 'Isle of Guernsey' also saw service as a hospital ship, including at Dunkirk, and later as a training vessel and landing ship. She was scrapped in 1961.

An early 19thC Napoleonic French boxwood and bone model, for the 90-gun second rate ship of the 'Line Union', the planked and pinned hull copper-sheathed below the waterline, standing and running rigging with blocks and tackle, with two fitted longboats.

26in (66cm) long

$11,000-14,000   **CM**

A builder's model for the 'S.S. Royal Emblem', built by J.L. Thompson for Hall Brothers.

1940   *60in (152.5cm) long with case*

$11,000-13,000   **CM**

1930   *90in (229cm) wide*

$15,000-19,000   **CM**

ESSENTIAL REFERENCE - WINCHESTER CASTLE

Built in 1930 by Harland & Wolff, Belfast, with a length of 656.5ft and a gross tonnage in excess of 20,000grt for the Union-Castle Line, the 'Winchester Castle' was the last 'Castle' to be upgraded to oil-fired boilers in 1938 when her twin funnels were replaced with a single raked funnel, as seen on this model. During World War II she served as a troop carrier, but was briefly used as the Allied Headquarters during the invasion of Vichy-held Madagascar as part of Operation Ironclad between May and November 1942. After the war, she was deployed as a UK-South Africa migrant ship before being scrapped in Japan in 1960.

A builder's model for the cargo ship 'S.S. Corsea', built by S.P. Austin & Son for Cory Colliers Ltd., model restored overall, with later case and stand.

1921   *54in (137cm) wide*

$9,000-10,000   **CM**

A Bassett-Lowke boardroom model of the 'R.M.M.V. Winchester Castle', as depicted after her 1938 refit.

94in (239cm) wide

$50,000-55,000   **CM**

A 1:48 scale builder's model of the collier 'S.S. Sir Johnstone Wright', built for the Central Electricity Authority by William Pickersgill & Sons Ltd., by the Sunderland Model Making Co., with original mahogany display case with ivorine plates, with a watercolor of the Sir Johnstone Wright, signed 'John Mortimer', and a leather photograph album showing the launch of the Sir Johnstone Wright.

1955   *50in (127cm) wide with case*

$9,500-10,500   **CM**

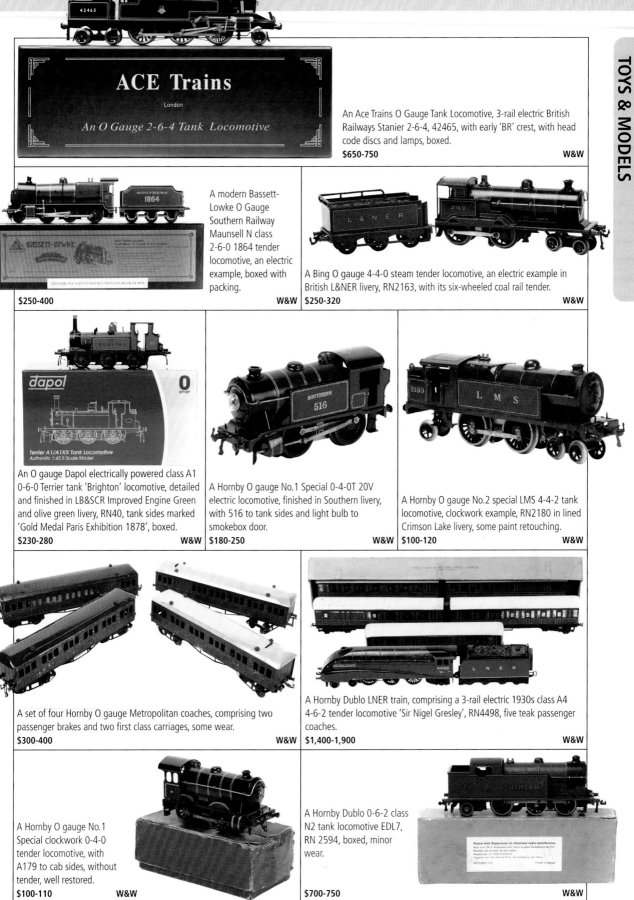

ACE Trains

London

An O Gauge 2-6-4 Tank Locomotive

An Ace Trains O Gauge Tank Locomotive, 3-rail electric British Railways Stanier 2-6-4, 42465, with early 'BR' crest, with head code discs and lamps, boxed.
$650-750 W&W

A modern Bassett-Lowke O Gauge Southern Railway Maunsell N class 2-6-0 1864 tender locomotive, an electric example, boxed with packing.
$250-400 W&W

A Bing O gauge 4-4-0 steam tender locomotive, an electric example in British L&NER livery, RN2163, with its six-wheeled coal rail tender.
$250-320 W&W

An O gauge Dapol electrically powered class A1 0-6-0 Terrier tank 'Brighton' locomotive, detailed and finished in LB&SCR Improved Engine Green and olive green livery, RN40, tank sides marked 'Gold Medal Paris Exhibition 1878', boxed.
$230-280 W&W

A Hornby O gauge No.1 Special 0-4-0T 20V electric locomotive, finished in Southern livery, with 516 to tank sides and light bulb to smokebox door.
$180-250 W&W

A Hornby O gauge No.2 special LMS 4-4-2 tank locomotive, clockwork example, RN2180 in lined Crimson Lake livery, some paint retouching.
$100-120 W&W

A set of four Hornby O gauge Metropolitan coaches, comprising two passenger brakes and two first class carriages, some wear.
$300-400 W&W

A Hornby Dublo LNER train, comprising a 3-rail electric 1930s class A4 4-6-2 tender locomotive 'Sir Nigel Gresley', RN4498, five teak passenger coaches.
$1,400-1,900 W&W

A Hornby O gauge No.1 Special clockwork 0-4-0 tender locomotive, with A179 to cab sides, without tender, well restored.
$100-110 W&W

A Hornby Dublo 0-6-2 class N2 tank locomotive EDL7, RN 2594, boxed, minor wear.
$700-750 W&W

A Craftsman Models OO SR 'Lord Nelson' class tender locomotive, Sir Francis Drake 851, boxed.
$100-120   W&W

A Millholme Models Goldcast Series OO SR 'Merchant Navy' class tender locomotive, un-rebuilt French Line C.G.T. 35019, boxed.
$100-110   W&W

A pair of RJH GWR non-corridor O gauge bogie passenger coaches, both second class brakes, boxed, minor wear.
$180-250   W&W

A Springside Models O gauge locomotive kit, comprising an electrically operated GWR 14xx class 0-4-2 tank locomotive and a D.J.R. Engineering GWR Auto-Coach as pulled-pushed by this locomotive, boxed, the Auto-Coach RN 206 in Chocolate & Cream livery, with 'GWR' and crest to coach sides, fully detailed.
$400-450   W&W

A scarce Trix OO gauge 3-rail tender locomotive, BR 4-6-2 Scotsman 60103 (1/540), boxed, trailing wheels and assembly detached but present, box with some wear/splitting to corners.
$100-120   W&W

A Trix OO gauge 3-rail model railway, BR 'Hunt' class 4-4-0 tender locomotive Pytchley 62750 (4/536), with 4 BR corridor coaches, including two passenger brakes, with a Pullman Car 'Trix Twin', all boxed, minor wear for age.
$130-180   W&W

A 5in gauge live steam Great Western 0-6-0 Pannier Tank Locomotive RN4612, fitted with a Modelworks International copper boiler, pressure system certificated to 18 July 2018, panniers marked 'Great Western', with certificate.
$2,800-3,500   W&W

A KGR 0-6-0 live steam tank locomotive, G scale, produced by Roundhouse Doncaster, with manufacturer's plate to side tanks 'Roundhouse Eng. Co. Ltd. Doncaster', boxed.
1.25in (3cm) long
$1,000-1,100   W&W

A mid-20thC Stanier '8F' 2-8-0 3.5in (9cm) working scale steam locomotive and tender, L.M.S. 8042.
49in (124cm) long
$2,800-3,500   BELL

A gauge brass and copper live steam 'Dribbler' 2-2-0 four wheeled two-cylinder locomotive, 'Speedwell' name plate to boiler sides, with soldering repairs.
3in (7.5cm) long
$150-190   W&W

A 1/10th scale Markie road locomotive showman's traction engine, designed by Tony Pearce, Hampshire, spirit fired, canopy with 'Albry Steam Traction Co.', named 'Millie', with original paperwork and certificate.
1989   23.25in (59cm) long
$2,500-3,200   CHOR

A Sammy Morfitt white England international rugby union shirt.

Sammy Morfitt played six times for England. The large style red rose badge dates it to 1894.

1894

$3,200-3,800   GBA

A Manchester United shirt, worn by captain Charlie Roberts in the Players' Union Match v Newcastle United at St James' Park 29 April 1908.

This shirt was worn by Charlie Roberts and is the only known surviving example from the game.

$7,500-9,000   GBA

A Manchester United shirt, worn by the captain Charlie Roberts during the club's first F.A. Cup Final appearance.

The 1909 F.A. Cup Final was played at the Crystal Palace on 24 April between Manchester United and Bristol City. Manchester United beat Bristol City 1-0, scored by Sandy Turnbull. This was the first of United's record eleven F.A. Cup titles to the present day.

$50,000-60,000   GBA

The Manchester United No.4 shirt, worn by John Anderson in the 1948 F.A. Cup Final.

John Anderson (1921-2006) was born in Salford and joined Manchester United in 1946. The midfielder helped United win the F.A. Cup in 1948 and scored one of the goals in the final during the 4-2 win over Blackpool.

$15,000-19,000   GBA

The red Liverpool No.8 jersey, worn by Roger Hunt in the 1965 F.A. Cup Final, the badge inscribed 'L.F.C., WEMBLEY, 1965'.

Liverpool beat Leeds United 2-1 in extra time in the 1965 F.A. Cup Final.

$7,000-8,000   GBA

An Eric Cantona signed match worn shirt, worn when at Manchester United, framed and double glazed to show the signature.

36.75in (93cm) high

$750-900   APAR

A David Beckham signed Manchester United shirt, from Beckham's final season at Manchester United, framed and glazed.

32.75in (83cm) high

$400-500   APAR

An F.A. Cup Final program and ticket stub for Cardiff City v Arsenal 23 April 1927, the program water damaged.

$1,000-1,100   GBA

A set of 32 used 1966 World Cup ticket stubs.

This is a rare set of every one of the tickets for all of the matches played at Wembley, White City, Goodison Park, Hillsborough, Villa Park, Old Trafford and the hard to find and very rare Ayresome Park & Roker Park tickets, including the Quarter-Finals, Semi-Finals, Play-off and Final.

$5,000-5,700   MART

A Billy Meredith Wales international cap, inscribed 'F.A.W. 1903'.

Manchester City's Meredith played in all the Home Championship matches in this season. England at Portsmouth (1-2), Scotland at Cardiff (0-1) and Ireland in Belfast (0-2). Billy Meredith was the greatest of the Wales pre-war players.
1902-03
$4,500-5,000   **GBA**

The England international debut cap of Billy Walker.

This match was played at Roker Park, Sunderland, 23 October 1920. England won 2-0 and Billy Walker scored on debut.
$1,100-1,400   **GBA**

A purple England cap, for the first international match played at Wembley Stadium, v Scotland, 12 April 1924, awarded to Charlie Spencer of Newcastle United.
$1,300-1,900   **GBA**

A red Charlie Spencer England v Wales international cap.
1924-25
$800-950   **GBA**

A green and red quartered England cap, awarded to Stanley Matthews for the 'Battle of Highbury' international v Italy.

The 'Battle of Highbury' was the name given to the football match between England and reigning World Champions Italy that took place on 14 November 1934 at Arsenal's ground. England won 3-2 in a hotly contested and frequently violent match. The 19-year-old Stanley Matthews, in only his second start for England, escaped unscathed but later said that it was singularly the most violent football match he had ever been involved in during his long career.
$23,000-28,000   **GBA**

The England international debut cap of Sir Geoff Hurst, made for the match v West Germany 23 February 1966.

In what was to prove to be a dress rehearsal for the 1966 World Cup Final, England's future hat-trick hero made his international debut in this friendly match played at Wembley Stadium. England won 1-0 through a Nobby Stiles goal. Geoff Hurst won a total of 49 England caps between 1966 and 1972.
$7,500-9,000   **GBA**

A Fred Keenor green Wales international cap, color fading.
1928-29
$1,000-1,200   **GBA**

An early gold F.A. Cup winner's medal, awarded to Bill Astley of Blackburn Olympic in 1883.
$15,000-19,000   **GBA**

A 15ct gold 1901 F.A. Cup winner's medal, inscribed '1901, TOTTENHAM HOTSPUR, WINNERS, TOM SMITH, FOOTBALL', with a repro photo of the Spurs 1901 Cup Winners.
$32,000-38,000   **GBA**

A 9ct gold 1930-31 Football League Championship medal, awarded to Jack Lambert of Arsenal, inscribed 'THE FOOTBALL LEAGUE, CHAMPIONS, DIVISION 1'.
$6,500-7,500   **GBA**

A 9ct gold Professional Footballers' Association 100 Football League Legend's Medal, awarded to Neville Southall in May 1999, in case.
$1,500-1,900   **GBA**

A Farlow patent lever, brass salmon reel with horn handle, no.348, engraved 'Patent Lever no.348, Cha. Farlow & Co. Makers, 191 Strand, London'.

4.25in (11cm) diam

$80-90 **BELL**

A Hardy brass plate wind reel, with 'Rod in Hand' and oval logos.

2.5in (6.5cm) long

$230-280 **FLD**

A Hardy 'The Silex Major' reel, with four setting check, ivorine side lever, stamped maker's mark and oval plaque inscribed 'Manton and Co. Made for Calcutta'.

4in (10cm) diam

$400-500 **APAR**

A Hardy alloy 'The Longstone' reel, with twin Bakelite handles, stamped marks and oval plaque inscribed 'Manton and Co. Made for Calcutta'.

5in (12.5cm) diam

$450-550 **APAR**

A Hardy brass face and alloy perfect reel, with 'Rod in Hand' logo and horn handle.

4in (10cm) diam

$900-1,000 **APAR**

A Hardy St George alloy trout fly reel, stamped 'D.W.' under spool.

3in (7.5cm) diam

$250-320 **BRI**

A Hardy trout fly reel, with ivorine handle, brass foot and strapped tension screw.

3.5in (9cm) diam

$80-90 **BRI**

A Hardy 'Perfect' fly reel, duplicated mark II, in leather case.

2.75in (7cm) diam

$250-320 **BRI**

A boxed Hardy 'Silex Major' reel, with twin black handles, ivorine brake handle, brass foot and stamped 'JD' under spool.

4.25in (11cm) diam

$210-250 **BRI**

A D & J patent brake reel, produced by Reuben Heatons Ltd., Birmingham, sea reel with mahogany drum, composition handles, knurled knut operated drag cork and composition clutch, signed.

c1925 *7in (18cm) diam*

$550-700 **BELL**

A leather fly wallet, 70 sea trout and trout wet flies.

$130-180 **BRI**

A Malloch's black fly tin, with three shelves for flies, containing 37 single sea trout flies.

$180-250 **BRI**

A Paris 1900 Olympic Games silver award plaque, designed by F. Vernon, inscribed 'CONCOURS D'EXERCICES MILITAIRES PREPARATOIRES', reverse inscribed 'REPUBLIQUE FRANCAISE, PARIS 1900, EXPOSITION UNIVERSELLE'.

$1,900-2,500　　　　GBA

A 1904 St Louis Olympic Games medal, by Dieges & Clust, New York, with shields of St Louis, France & USA on a background of ivy leaves.

The version of this medal presented to officials, etc has a loop at the top which was worn as a badge with the medal hanging from an inscribed ribbon suspended from a bar with Olympic legend, but this medal has no loop, or traces of a loop being removed, and therefore was originally presented to a participating athlete.

$19,000-25,000　　　　GBA

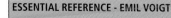

A 1908 London Olympic Games cased silver 'Comite-D'Honneur' medal, by Vaughtom, designed by Bertram Mackennal, case gilt stamped 'OLYMPIC GAMES, COMITE-D'HONNEUR, LONDON, 1908'.

2.12oz

$900-1,000　　　　GBA

A Paris 1924 Olympic Games silver prize medal, awarded to the British sailor Walter Riggs, designed by Andre Rivaud, struck by the Paris Mint in an edition of 304, half of the original fitted case preserved.

Walter Riggs was a crew member in the British eight meter class on board the yacht 'Emily'.

2.25in (5.5cm) diam

$4,500-5,000　　　　GBA

A Grenoble 1968 Winter Olympic Games gold winner's prize medal, awarded for Ice Hockey, in silver-gilt, by Roger Excoffon, inscribed 'HOCKEY SUR GLACE'.

2.25in (6cm) diam

$45,000-50,000　　　　GBA

A 1948 London Olympic Games bearer's torch, designed by Ralph Lavers, aluminum alloy, inscribed 'XIVth OLYMPIAD, 1948, OLYMPIA TO LONDON, WITH THANKS TO THE BEARER'.

$5,000-5,700　　　　GBA

ESSENTIAL REFERENCE - EMIL VOIGT

Emil Voigt was born in Manchester on 31 January 1883. The athlete won the four miles at the 1908 AAA Championships and Gold in the five miles at the London 1908 Olympic Games. Voigt later emigrated to Australia where he won further titles before retiring in 1914. In Australia he became one of the foremost pioneers of early radio, helping set up 2KY (now Sky Sports Radio) under the ownership of the Labour Council of New South Wales. Voigt returned to England in 1936, before finally settling in Auckland, New Zealand, in 1948, where he died aged 90 on 16 October 1973.

The London 1908 Olympic games Great Britain running vest badge, worn by the five miles gold medallist Emil Voigt, inscribed 'OLYMPIC GAMES 1908'.

$650-750　　　　GBA

ESSENTIAL REFERENCE - INNSBRUCK OLYMPICS

In 1976 the city of Innsbruck for the second time was hosting the Winter Olympic Games. As they received this honor last minute, because of the withdrawal of Denver, torches were also supplied last minute and had one important defect - they were never designed for the Torch relay ceremony. Even in Seefeld, site of the Nordic skiing event, for the welcome ceremony for the Olympic flame they used other simpler torches. This ceremonial torch is different from the normal torch. The 'XII' (on the standard torch) is written as '12' in the special torch. The legend on the base edge is manufactured with applied brass lettering, not stamped.

An Innsbruck 1976 Winter Olympic Games special ceremonial torch, in stainless steel and brass, lettered legend reading '12.OLYMPISCHE WINTERSPIELE INNSBRUCK 1967', with Olympic Rings.

29in (73.5cm) long

$38,000-50,000　　　　GBA

A rare Cortina 1956 Winter Olympic Games bearer's torch, based on Ralph Lavers's aluminum alloy design.

It is unrecorded how many torches were used during the 1956 Winter Games relay, but it was a moderately low figure.

$19,000-25,000　　　　GBA

An International Olympic Committee Tehran 1967 65th Session badge, partially gilt, with Persian archers either side of Olympic Rings.

$2,000-2,500　　　　GBA

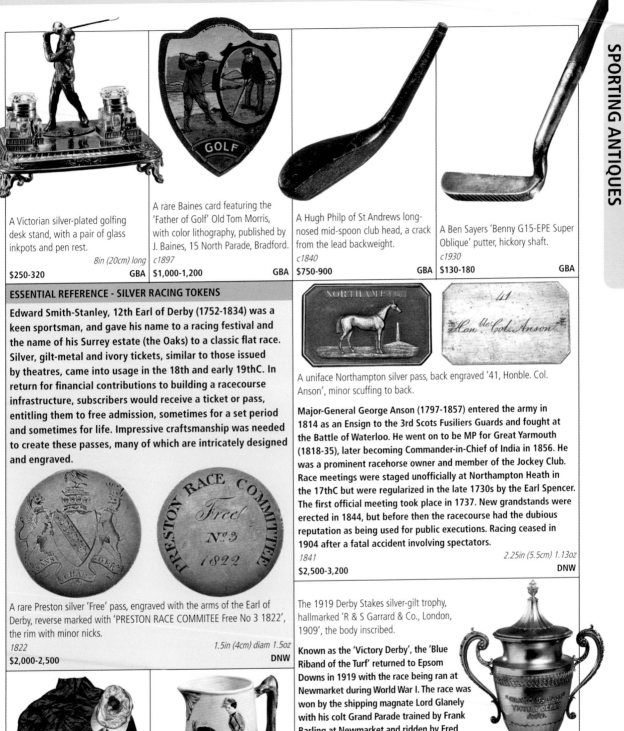

A Victorian silver-plated golfing desk stand, with a pair of glass inkpots and pen rest.

8in (20cm) long

$250-320 　　　　　　　　GBA

A rare Baines card featuring the 'Father of Golf' Old Tom Morris, with color lithography, published by J. Baines, 15 North Parade, Bradford.

c1897

$1,000-1,200 　　　　　GBA

A Hugh Philp of St Andrews long-nosed mid-spoon club head, a crack from the lead backweight.

c1840

$750-900 　　　　　　　GBA

A Ben Sayers 'Benny G15-EPE Super Oblique' putter, hickory shaft.

c1930

$130-180 　　　　　　　GBA

ESSENTIAL REFERENCE - SILVER RACING TOKENS

Edward Smith-Stanley, 12th Earl of Derby (1752-1834) was a keen sportsman, and gave his name to a racing festival and the name of his Surrey estate (the Oaks) to a classic flat race. Silver, gilt-metal and ivory tickets, similar to those issued by theatres, came into usage in the 18th and early 19thC. In return for financial contributions to building a racecourse infrastructure, subscribers would receive a ticket or pass, entitling them to free admission, sometimes for a set period and sometimes for life. Impressive craftsmanship was needed to create these passes, many of which are intricately designed and engraved.

A uniface Northampton silver pass, back engraved '41, Honble. Col. Anson', minor scuffing to back.

Major-General George Anson (1797-1857) entered the army in 1814 as an Ensign to the 3rd Scots Fusiliers Guards and fought at the Battle of Waterloo. He went on to be MP for Great Yarmouth (1818-35), later becoming Commander-in-Chief of India in 1856. He was a prominent racehorse owner and member of the Jockey Club. Race meetings were staged unofficially at Northampton Heath in the 17thC but were regularized in the late 1730s by the Earl Spencer. The first official meeting took place in 1737. New grandstands were erected in 1844, but before then the racecourse had the dubious reputation as being used for public executions. Racing ceased in 1904 after a fatal accident involving spectators.

1841 　　　　　　　　　　*2.25in (5.5cm) 1.13oz*

$2,500-3,200 　　　　　　　　　　DNW

A rare Preston silver 'Free' pass, engraved with the arms of the Earl of Derby, reverse marked with 'PRESTON RACE COMMITEE Free No 3 1822', the rim with minor nicks.

1822 　　　　　　*1.5in (4cm) diam 1.5oz*

$2,000-2,500 　　　　　　　　DNW

The 1919 Derby Stakes silver-gilt trophy, hallmarked 'R & S Garrard & Co., London, 1909', the body inscribed.

Known as the 'Victory Derby', the 'Blue Riband of the Turf' returned to Epsom Downs in 1919 with the race being ran at Newmarket during World War I. The race was won by the shipping magnate Lord Glanely with his colt Grand Parade trained by Frank Barling at Newmarket and ridden by Fred Templeman. A highly successful owner, Lord Glanely owned winners of all five English Classics including two wins in the St Leger.

14in (36cm) high

$4,500-5,000 　　　　　　　GBA

The red silk jacket worn by Sim Templeman when winning The Oaks at Epsom in 1847 aboard Sir Joseph Hawley's 'Miami'.

$1,900-2,500 　　　　　　GBA

A Staffordshire Prattware pottery jug, portraying the jockey Fred Archer, inscribed 'F.ARCHER'.

c1886 　　　　　　*7in (18cm) high*

$300-350 　　　　　　　GBA

A polo ball, signed by H.R.H. Charles Prince of Wales, with a color photograph of Charles on the polo field, with a certificate of authenticity.

$280-320 　　　　　　　GBA

SPORTING ANTIQUES

ESSENTIAL REFERENCE - HENRY COOPER'S GLOVES

Cooper and Clay met at Wembley Stadium, London in what was billed as 'An eliminating contest for the Heavyweight Championship of the World'. In the final moments of the fourth round Cooper famously dropped Clay with his trademark left hook, known as 'Enry's 'Ammer'. Clay stood up and started slowly toward Angelo Dundee who - in violation of the rules - guided him into the corner. At first Dundee talked and slapped Clay's legs, but after a still-dazed Clay misunderstood and tried to get off the stool Dundee used smelling salts in a serious violation of the rules. Dundee has since claimed to have opened a tear in one of Clay's gloves and told the referee that his fighter needed new gloves. Cooper always insisted that this delay denied him the chance to knock Clay out while he was still dazed. Cooper started the fifth round aggressively, but a recovered Clay effectively countered and Cooper was hit high on the face with a hard right which opened a severe cut under his eye. Referee Tommy Little was ultimately forced to stop the fight due to Cooper's excessive bleeding, with Clay declared the winner by TKO. The case plaque mistakenly listed the fight date as 17 June, rather than 18 June.

A pair of boxing gloves, by Baily's of Glastonbury, mounted in the case in which the gloves were displayed at the famous Thomas A Beckett pub in the Old Kent Road, London, inscribed 'THE GLOVES THAT DID NOT SPLIT; USED BY HENRY COOPER, IN HIS FIGHT WITH CASSIUS CLAY, HENRY IS THE FIRST MAN TO PUT CLAY DOWN, WEMBLEY STADIUM, 17.6.63'.

16in (40.5cm) high

$120,000-130,000   **GBA**

A matched pair of Victorian Staffordshire pottery figures of cricketers.

These figures are thought to represent famous cricketers of the Victorian period, the batsman is believed to be Julius Caesar who played for Surrey, the bowler is believed to be George Parr who played for Nottinghamshire.

14in (35.5cm) high

$1,500-1,900   **WW**

A pair of bronze figures of cricketers, after Joseph Durham, signed 'J.Durham'.

The original series of five cricketers was exhibited at the Royal Academy in 1864.

15.5in (39cm) high

$5,000-6,500   **WW**

A mid-1880s racket, with heavy strings, primitive rounded grip, convex wedge displaying a deep engraving of a '£' (?) sign and 'A', some breaks in strings.

$450-550   **GBA**

ESSENTIAL REFERENCE - 'THE ORIGINALS'

The Original All Blacks, also simply known as 'The Originals', were the first New Zealand national rugby union team to tour outside Australasia. They toured the British Isles, France and the USA during 1905-06. Their opening game was against Devon on 16 September 1905; they won 55-4. Such was the surprize that some British newspapers printed that Devon had scored 55 points, not the All Blacks. They went on to defeat every English, Scottish and Irish side they faced. Their only loss was 3-0 with Wales at Cardiff Arms Park.

The 1905 All Blacks tour of Britain went on to achieve legendary status within the rugby world and New Zealand in particular. They scored 976 points and conceded only 59. The tour also saw the first use of the All Blacks nickname with the black shirt becoming an international sporting icon.

Ernest Booth, nicknamed 'General' after the founder of the Salvation Army, played at full-back or as a three-quarter. He was selected for 16 of the Originals' matches on the tour. He also played for Kaikorai and represented Otago, before moving to Sydney where he captained Newtown and represented New South Wales. He later became a rugby journalist and during World War I served in the Australian forces as secretary of the YMCA. Ernest Edward Booth died in Christchurch 18 October 1935, aged 59.

A 'Ball-Tail' Paragon lawn tennis racket, by George Gibson Bussey, Peckham, London, a couple of broken strings.

c1910   *27in (68.5cm) long*

$750-900   **GBA**

A Roger Federer match-used tennis racket, customized to Federer's preferences with shorter grip, the 19x16 stringing pattern laid out differently to the commercial version, strings have been replaced, re-gripped but with the original Wilson grip beneath.

2006

$750-900   **GBA**

A Continental alpaca cigarette case, with an enamel portrait of a gentleman tennis player.

3.5in (9cm) wide

$500-650   **GBA**

A historic New Zealand 'Original All Blacks' shirt, worn by Ernest Booth during the tour of the British Isles and France in 1905-06.

$38,000-45,000   **GBA**

A Bamana antelope headdress, Chi wara, the head horizontally aligned with carved geometric motifs and pair of spiral twisted horns, on small body.

This 'horizontal' headdress form was the third of three categories of headdresses. Most Bamana sculptures are carved from a single piece of wood, but these works are usually carved as two separate units - the head and the body - which are subsequently joined together with iron staples, or nails.

28.5in (72cm) wide

$1,500-1,900   ROS

A large Bamana kono zoomorphic elephant mask, Mali, with ears and horns projecting from head.
37in (94cm) long
$900-1,000   ROS

A large Bamana kono zoomorphic mask, Mali, in the form of a stylized head of an elephant with human features, heavily encrusted.
37.75in (96cm) long
$3,200-4,400   ROS

A Dan-Ngere carved wood Kagle mask, Guinea Coast, of highly stylized human form with domed projecting forehead, cheeks and nose, and with flat protruding mouth carved with two holes to the upper lip.
8.75in (22cm) long
$900-1,000   ROS

A Dogon Tellem carved wood figure, Mali, with arms stretched above the head, good patina throughout and some encrustations, particularly between the legs.
15.5in (39cm) high
$1,400-1,900   ROS

Judith Picks

Dan masks have a typically high forehead, pouting mouth and pointed chin. They may also have scarification marks and are carved in wood and stained with a brown dye. Dan masks are sacred objects and are used for protection and as a channel for communication with the spirit world. The Dan believe that their world is split into two domains: the human domain which is represented by the village and its people, and the spiritual domain which is represented by the forest and its spirits. When a dancer wears a Dan mask he becomes the spirit of that mask. Dan masks are guarded by the Go master, the head of the secret Society of the Leopard who are responsible for the initiation rites of young men into adulthood.

A Dan carved wood mask, with slightly inverted face at eyes, the open mouth with three metal teeth, on metal stand.
8in (20cm) long
$2,300-2,800   ROS

A Dogon human dance mask, with stylized rectangular face and recessed rectangular eyes, large pair of ears and horns projecting from head.
26.5in (67cm) long
$500-650   ROS

A Lega (or Warega) people Congo ivory ancestor figure, carved as a stylized woman with hands by her sides, her body incised and decorated with concentric circles, on Perspex base.
6in (15cm) high
$1,300-1,900   ROS

An early 20thC carved wood fire-spitting mask, from Waniugo, Senufo, Ivory Coast, West Africa.
21in (53cm) long
$750-900   SWO

A late 19thC Ivory Coast carved wood horse and rider, Senufo, carved as an over-sized rider on stylized horse.
7.5in (19cm) high
$1,110-1,300   ROS

A Senufo carved wood guardian figure of a hornbill, the long beak curving to meet a protruding abdomen, with rectangular wings.

31in (79cm) high

$2,500-3,200   ROS

A Senufo female figure, her head surmounted with a jar and cover, her knees slightly bent with pronounced rear.

22.25in (56.5cm) high

$2,300-2,800   ROS

A large Senufo Ivory Coast guardian figure, carved as a hornbill, with powerful head and beak curving to meet the protruding chest.

with base 56.75in (144cm) high

$2,800-3,500   ROS

A 19thC tribal mask, Senufu, Ivory Coast, with raised bird coiffure and traces of original pigmentation.

31in (79cm) high

$400-500   APAR

A Sepik bark painting, painted in black white and pink with a stylized human figure.

41.75in (106cm) high

$650-750   ROS

A Sepik suspension hook, carved as a stylized man with his hands held behind his back, the eyes set with shell fragments.

31.5in (80cm) high

$650-900   ROS

A pair of Yoruba tribe 'Offering' figures, carved as a female and infant holding a chicken which is a lidded box.

19in (48cm) high

$750-900   DW

A 19thC Zulu chieftan's knobkerrie, with rounded head, shaft with copper wire chevron decoration and leather wrist strap.

24.5in (62cm) long

$450-550   HT

An African ceremonial stick having carved figurehead motif mounted with an animal.

This African hardwood stick or staff is carved by a craftsman known as the Baboon Master. Not much is known about him. He was active in the 1880s and 1890s in South Africa and Mozambique. He was possibly Zulu or a member of the Tsonga people. It is speculated that he carved these items to sell to soldiers stationed in the area since there is no history of indigenous walking staffs in late 19thC south-east Africa.

40in (103cm) long

$10,000-11,000   PFW

A 19thC ivory pipe, St Lawrence Island, Alaska, engraved with caribou, geese, walrus hunting scenes and whale flukes, as well as celebratory figures.

Eskimo engravers quickly realized that Europeans were eager to own engraved ivories. Around the Bering Strait and to the North, an ivory carving industry developed, and many of the engraved scenes found on bag handles and drill bows were transferred onto non-functional ivory pipes.

8.5in (21.5cm) long

$3,200-3,800   WAD

A late 19thC Eskimo ivory carving, of a polar bear head and torso and engraved with a walrus hunting scene and a rifleman hunting elk.

5.5in (13.5cm) long

$3,200-3,800   ROS

An early 20thC Eskimo marine ivory faceted pipe, engraved with figures in boats hunting walrus, dogs pulling a sleigh.

16.5in (42cm) long

$900-1,000   ROS

An early 20thC Eskimo walrus tusk cribbage board, Chukchi people, engraved and colored with whaling scenes, inscribed 'Coonea'.

20.5in (52cm) long

$800-950   ROS

ESSENTIAL REFERENCE - KAROO ASHEVAK

Karoo Ashevak is perhaps the most internationally recognized Canadian Inuit sculptor. Very few works prior to 1970 have been discovered, his main body of work being created in four short years before his untimely death in 1974. His work brought him great joy. Karoo's sister, Eeteemunga remembered 'seeing him working on huge pieces. He was also so proud of himself. He would pause and study a piece that he was working on... thinking or meditating. Sometimes he would put it aside... and glance at it from a distance... When he finished he would be pouring with sweat and looking joyful and exuberant!' Like many of Karoo's works there is a not-so-hidden narrative behind his carving. This work shows two opposing faces, the first with a joyous expression and a prominent toothy grin, the second (not shown) expressing distress conveyed humorously as a top tooth is pulled out by a piece of thread (traditional sinew has been used here). Exhibiting many characteristics that indicate his most developed and mature artistic phase, this work is dated c1973-74.

A 19thC Eskimo carved wood mask, with domed forehead, diminutive eyes, flattened nose and pronounced cheeks, traces of red and blue pigment.

10in (25cm) high

$4,500-5,000   ROS

A stone figure, 'Bird Spirit', by Kaiwak Ashoona O.C. R.C.A., Cape Dorset, Kingait, signed in syllabics.

Kiugak created a series of impressive 'bird spirit' carvings over his career. He made it clear that these sculptures depicted the bird shaman, Natturalik (Golden Eagle). Natturalik comes from a story about an eagle that abducts a young woman and takes her to his cliff top nest where she becomes his wife. Kiugak described the beginning of the story as involving two girls playing together. They pretended to have husbands, using the bones of a bowhead whale. One of the bones turned into an eagle: Natturalik.

1988   18in (45.5cm) high

$6,500-7,500   WAD

A stone figure, 'Mother Cradling Her Swaddled Child', by Siasie Kakangak Angutigirk, Sugluk, Salluit, disc number inscribed.

c1956   12.75in (32.5cm) high

$3,200-3,800   WAD

A stone figure, 'Midwives With Baby', by Ennutsiak, Frobisher Bay, Iqaluit.

c1958   7.75in (19.5cm) high

$5,000-6,500   WAD

'Spirit Faces' (Tooth Pull), by Karoo Ashevak, Spence Bay, Taloyoak, in whalebone, carved to both sides with shaman or spirit faces, highlighted by antler, stone and bone inlaid eyes and with inset bone teeth, the tattooed face grinning with a prominent third eye and the opposing face with crossed eyes, mouth agape and a removable tooth attached by sinew, signed in syllabics.

c1973-74   19in (48.5cm) wide

$100,000-110,000   WAD

A stone figure, 'Bird of Spring', by Abraham Etungat, Cape Dorset, Kingait, signed in syllabics.

12.25in (31cm) wide

$2,500-3,800 **WAD**

A stone figure, 'Playful Mother and Child', by John Kavik, Rankin Inlet, Kangiqlining, inscribed to underside with 'Kaverk, Rankin Inlet, N.W.T.'.

8.5in (21.5cm) high

$3,200-3,800 **WAD**

A figure, 'Dancing Polar Bear', by Pauta Saila, R.C.A., Cape Dorset, Kingait, with inset ivory teeth, signed in syllabics.

c1985 *13in (33cm) high*

$18,000-23,000 **WAD**

A stone figure, 'Mother With Child', by Mathewsie Sakiagak, George River, Kangiqsualujjuaq, signed in syllabics and inscribed with disc number.

c1956 *13.5in (34.5cm) high*

$1,900-2,500 **WAD**

A stone figure, 'Mother Chewing A Kamik With Child In Amaut', by Davidee Saumik, Port Harrison, Inukjuak, disc number inscribed.

c1960 *13.25in (33.5cm) high*

$3,200-3,800 **WAD**

A stone, ivory, thread and plastic figure, 'Hunter Carrying Pack, Bow and Gun', by Joe Talirunili, Povungnituk, Puvirnituq, signed in Roman.

c1960 *7in (18cm) high*

$1,500-2,500 **WAD**

A 1980s stone, bone, antler and musk ox horn figure, 'Flying Demon', by Charlie Ugyuk, Spence Bay, Taloyoak, signed in syllabics.

Ugyuk has created the effect of a demon or devil taking flight by constructing a vertical support for the intricately carved demon to sit atop.

17in (43cm) high

$19,000-25,000 **WAD**

A stone, antler and musk ox horn figure, 'Shaman With Helping Spirits', with inset moveable eyes, by Judas Ullulaq, Gjoa Haven, Uqsuqtuuq.

c1988 *20.75in (52.5cm) high*

$19,000-25,000 **WAD**

A stone, sinew and ivory figure, 'Mother Sewing', by Miaiji Uitangi Usaitaijuk, Sugluk, Salluit.

c1956 *9.75in (24.5cm) high*

$3,200-4,400 **WAD**

A stonecut, 'Complex of Birds', by Kenojuak Ashevak C.C. R.C.A., Cape Dorset, Kingait, framed, 20/50.
1960   *26in (66cm) wide*
$10,000-11,000   **WAD**

A stonecut, 'Night Hunter', by Kenojuak Ashevak C.C. R.C.A., Cape Dorset, Kingait, framed, signed, 50/50.
1969   *27in (68.5cm) wide*
$3,800-5,000   **WAD**

A stonecut, 'Thoughts of Birds', by Kellypalik Mangitak, Cape Dorset, Kingait, unframed, 33/50.
1959   *22.75in (58cm) high*
$2,500-3,800   **WAD**

A framed stonecut, 'People of the Inland', by Jessie Oonark O.C. R.C.A., Baker Lane, Qamani'tuaq, 42/50.
1961   *19.5in (49.5cm) high*
$1,900-2,500   **WAD**

A stonecut, 'Big Woman', by Jessie Oonark, Baker Lake, Qamani'tuaq, framed, 40/46.
1976   *33in (84cm) high*
$1,900-2,500   **WAD**

ESSENTIAL REFERENCE - BOB BOYER

Bob Boyer is Métis with a cultural background influenced by the Assiniboine and Sioux. His works, broadly, speak of a dual cultural perspective of his Native heritage and Western traditions of Abstract and Contemporary art. Though he worked in a variety of media throughout his career, Boyer is perhaps best-known for his series of blanket paintings completed between 1983 and 1995. Boyer elected to use a blanket as his substrate rather than a traditional canvas to address the political issues of First Nations people. Martin comments that blankets are symbolic of a gift that North American Aboriginal peoples hold in high regard. Boyer also stated, 'the blanket to me is a symbol of all things that are comforting in the world.' Thus Boyer juxtaposes the traditional sense of the domesticity associated with a blanket against a vocabulary of modern Western techniques. This work is composed with blazing hues on a subversively soft and yielding material which turns the blanket, an object from which one should derive comfort, into something aggressive. The incongruity of its formal qualities reinforces the already compromised idea of the blanket as it relates to Aboriginal populations, which were decimated in alarming numbers by the deliberate spread of the Smallpox virus using contaminated blankets in the 19thC.

A stonecut, 'Another Time', by Parr, Cape Dorset, Kingait, unframed, 21/50.
1964   *26.25in (66.5cm) wide*
$2,500-3,800   **WAD**

A stonecut, 'Vision of Caribou', by Egevadluq Ragee, Cape Dorset, Kingait, framed, 5/50.
1960   *24.75in (63cm) wide*
$3,800-5,000   **WAD**

A mixed media blanket, 'Dropping Atom Bombs', by Bob Boyer, signed, dated 'Spring '88' on the reverse, title faded.
91in (231cm) high
$6,500-7,500   **WAD**

A pair of late 19thC Apache hide high-top moccasins, beaded with geometric and circular devices, minor bead loss.

17in (43cm) high

$5,000-5,700   SK

A mid- to late 19thC Arapaho beaded hide pipe bag, with a bar design using multicolored seed beads.

with tabs 25in (63.5cm) long

$13,000-18,000   SK

A pair of late 19thC Arapaho pictorial beaded hide moccasins, hide seemingly oiled.

10in (25.5cm) long

$3,800-4,400   SK

A pair of late 19thC Arapaho fully beaded hide moccasins, tear to one cuff.

9.5in (24cm) long

$5,500-6,500   SK

A pair of Assiniboine beaded hide moccasins, with red trade cloth cuffs.

Provenance: Collected by Galen C. Cline, M.D., 'taken when on duty as a surgeon, U.S Army, Fort Assiniboine, Montana, 1876'.

c1870s   *10.5in (26.5cm) long*

$2,500-3,200   SK

A late 19thC pair of Blackfeet beaded buffalo hide man's moccasins, with geometric and cross devices.

10.5in (26.5cm) long

$3,800-4,400   SK

A late 19thC Blackfeet beaded buffalo dag sheath.

16.75in (42.5cm) long

$14,000-18,000   SK

A late 19thC Blackfoot beaded hide pipe bag.

26in (66cm) long

$3,200-3,800   SK

A pair of Cheyenne buffalo hide moccasins, beaded with classic Cheyenne designs.

c1870s   *11in (28cm) long*

$6,500-7,000   SK

A Cheyenne beaded buffalo hide flap belt pouch, the ends with geometric designs, a buffalo hide strap sewn across the back.

Collected in 1864 from the Cheyenne by James B. Beard, who worked on the construction of the Union Pacific Railroad and hauled lumber to Denver in the 1860s.

c1860   *flap 4in (10cm) long*

$19,000-25,000   SK

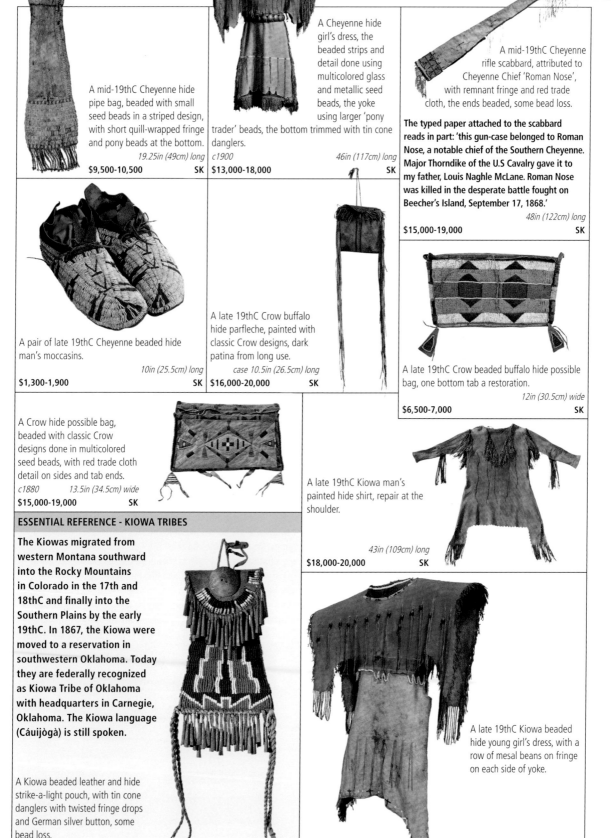

A mid-19thC Cheyenne hide pipe bag, beaded with small seed beads in a striped design, with short quill-wrapped fringe and pony beads at the bottom.

19.25in (49cm) long

$9,500-10,500   SK

A Cheyenne hide girl's dress, the beaded strips and detail done using multicolored glass and metallic seed beads, the yoke using larger 'pony trader' beads, the bottom trimmed with tin cone danglers.

c1900   *46in (117cm) long*

$13,000-18,000   SK

A mid-19thC Cheyenne rifle scabbard, attributed to Cheyenne Chief 'Roman Nose', with remnant fringe and red trade cloth, the ends beaded, some bead loss.

The typed paper attached to the scabbard reads in part: 'this gun-case belonged to Roman Nose, a notable chief of the Southern Cheyenne. Major Thorndike of the U.S Cavalry gave it to my father, Louis Naghle McLane. Roman Nose was killed in the desperate battle fought on Beecher's Island, September 17, 1868.'

48in (122cm) long

$15,000-19,000   SK

A pair of late 19thC Cheyenne beaded hide man's moccasins.

10in (25.5cm) long

$1,300-1,900   SK

A late 19thC Crow buffalo hide parfleche, painted with classic Crow designs, dark patina from long use.

case 10.5in (26.5cm) long

$16,000-20,000   SK

A late 19thC Crow beaded buffalo hide possible bag, one bottom tab a restoration.

12in (30.5cm) wide

$6,500-7,000   SK

A Crow hide possible bag, beaded with classic Crow designs done in multicolored seed beads, with red trade cloth detail on sides and tab ends.

c1880   *13.5in (34.5cm) wide*

$15,000-19,000   SK

A late 19thC Kiowa man's painted hide shirt, repair at the shoulder.

43in (109cm) long

$18,000-20,000   SK

ESSENTIAL REFERENCE - KIOWA TRIBES

The Kiowas migrated from western Montana southward into the Rocky Mountains in Colorado in the 17th and 18thC and finally into the Southern Plains by the early 19thC. In 1867, the Kiowa were moved to a reservation in southwestern Oklahoma. Today they are federally recognized as Kiowa Tribe of Oklahoma with headquarters in Carnegie, Oklahoma. The Kiowa language (Cáuijògà) is still spoken.

A Kiowa beaded leather and hide strike-a-light pouch, with tin cone danglers with twisted fringe drops and German silver button, some bead loss.

c1860   *10.5in (26.5cm) long*

$6,500-7,000   SK

A late 19thC Kiowa beaded hide young girl's dress, with a row of mesal beans on fringe on each side of yoke.

31in (78.5cm) long

$60,000-80,000   SK

A Kiowa beaded leather and hide strike-a-light pouch, tin cone danglers with red dyed twisted fringe drops from the corners, beaded with classic Kiowa designs.

c1870   pouch 10in (25.5cm) long
$12,000-14,000   SK

A late 19thC Kiowa beaded cloth and hide model cradle, the canvas and rawhide cover beaded with bold concentric crosses, with a pair of miniature moccasins hanging off the side, hide fringe at bottom and cotton print lining, some restoration to the beadwork.

24in (61cm) long
$32,000-38,000   SK

A pair of late 19thC Kiowa beaded hide man's moccasins, with red trade cloth cuffs.

10in (25.5cm) long
$28,000-38,000   SK

A Lakota beaded hide pictographic coat, with European cut and fringed at the edge and seams, with equestrian figures, minor stiffness to hide. **This is from the famous Adirondack Camp: 'Kamp Kill Kare' owned by Ms Mabel Brady Garvan. For a photograph of the coat in situ, see Harvey H. Kaiser, 'Great Camps of the Adirondacks', page 179; for a similar coat, see George P. Horse Capture, 'A Song for the Horse Nation', 2006.**

c1890   41in (104cm) long
$110,000-120,000   SK

A pair of Lakota beaded buffalo hide moccasins, with beaded bifurcated tongues and multicolored geometric designs.

c1870   10.5in (26.5cm) long
$4,500-5,000   SK

A late 19thC Lakota beaded hide child's dress, the fully beaded yoke with classic geometric and cross devices, the bottom with painted triangles, beaded lanes and tin cone danglers.

43in (109cm) wide
$50,000-55,000   SK

A late 19thC Lakota beaded hide cradle, with geometric designs.

22in (56cm) long
$9,500-10,500   SK

ESSENTIAL REFERENCE - NAVAJO WEAVING

Navajo textiles were originally utilitarian blankets for use as cloaks, dresses, and saddle blankets. Toward the end of the 19thC, weavers began to make rugs for tourism and export. Typical Navajo textiles have strong geometric patterns. They are a flat tapestry-woven textile produced in a fashion similar to kilims of Eastern Europe and Western Asia, but with some notable differences. In Navajo weaving, the slit weave technique common in kilims is not used, and the warp is one continuous length of yarn, not extending beyond the weaving as fringe.

A Navajo 'Yei' rug, woven with natural and synthetic dyed homespun wool, small repair.

71in (180cm) long
$3,800-4,400   SK

A Navajo 'third phase' chief's blanket.

65in (165cm) long
$2,500-3,200   POOK

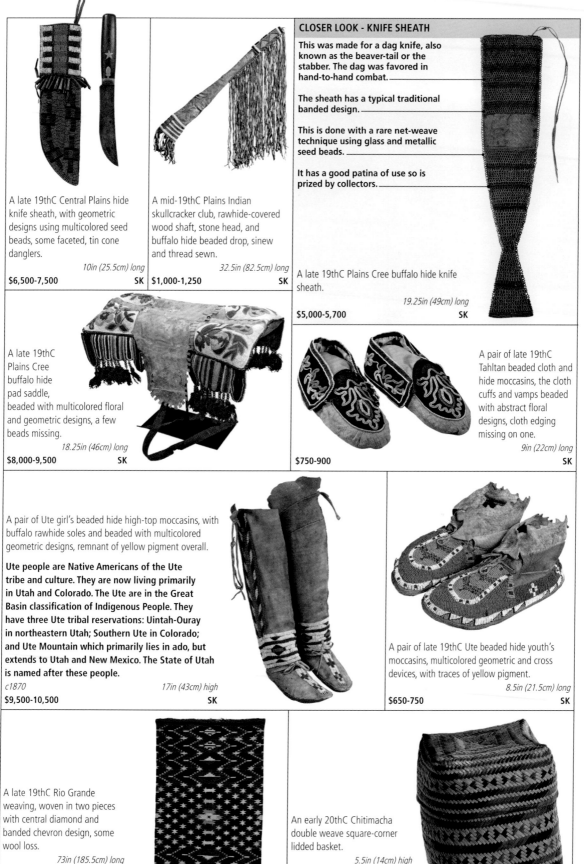

A late 19thC Central Plains hide knife sheath, with geometric designs using multicolored seed beads, some faceted, tin cone danglers.

10in (25.5cm) long

$6,500-7,500   SK

A mid-19thC Plains Indian skullcracker club, rawhide-covered wood shaft, stone head, and buffalo hide beaded drop, sinew and thread sewn.

32.5in (82.5cm) long

$1,000-1,250   SK

CLOSER LOOK - KNIFE SHEATH

This was made for a dag knife, also known as the beaver-tail or the stabber. The dag was favored in hand-to-hand combat.

The sheath has a typical traditional banded design.

This is done with a rare net-weave technique using glass and metallic seed beads.

It has a good patina of use so is prized by collectors.

A late 19thC Plains Cree buffalo hide knife sheath.

19.25in (49cm) long

$5,000-5,700   SK

A late 19thC Plains Cree buffalo hide pad saddle, beaded with multicolored floral and geometric designs, a few beads missing.

18.25in (46cm) long

$8,000-9,500   SK

A pair of late 19thC Tahltan beaded cloth and hide moccasins, the cloth cuffs and vamps beaded with abstract floral designs, cloth edging missing on one.

9in (22cm) long

$750-900   SK

A pair of Ute girl's beaded hide high-top moccasins, with buffalo rawhide soles and beaded with multicolored geometric designs, remnant of yellow pigment overall.

Ute people are Native Americans of the Ute tribe and culture. They are now living primarily in Utah and Colorado. The Ute are in the Great Basin classification of Indigenous People. They have three Ute tribal reservations: Uintah-Ouray in northeastern Utah; Southern Ute in Colorado; and Ute Mountain which primarily lies in ado, but extends to Utah and New Mexico. The State of Utah is named after these people.

c1870   *17in (43cm) high*

$9,500-10,500   SK

A pair of late 19thC Ute beaded hide youth's moccasins, multicolored geometric and cross devices, with traces of yellow pigment.

8.5in (21.5cm) long

$650-750   SK

A late 19thC Rio Grande weaving, woven in two pieces with central diamond and banded chevron design, some wool loss.

73in (185.5cm) long

$1,900-2,500   SK

An early 20thC Chitimacha double weave square-corner lidded basket.

5.5in (14cm) high

$750-900   SK

A late 19thC Apache polychrome basketry Olla, with black and red geometric and cross designs.

Provenance: Purchased from Charles Eagle Plume in 1962.

18in (45.5cm) diam

$9,000-10,000 SK

An Acoma painted pottery Olla, with red bottom and inner rim, decorated with an abstract design, restoration at rim, some paint wear.

c1900 *12.25in (31cm) diam*

$2,500-3,200 SK

A Cochiti figure of a storyteller, by Helen Cordero, depicted seated in traditional attire and with eight grandchildren.

This is accompanied with a photograph of Cordero holding this figure, signed 'Helen Cordero Cochiti, N. Mex.'.

c1985 *7.75in (19cm) high*

$3,800-5,000 SK

An early 20thC Hopi pottery bowl, by Nampeyo, painted with an abstract feather design, the sticker on the bottom reads 'Made by Nampeyo, Hopi'.

10in (25.5cm) diam

$6,500-7,500 SK

A Hopi carved wood doll, representing Shalako Kachina, the case mask with horns, square snout and popeyes, fur collar and painted detail overall, some minor wood loss.

15.5in (39.5cm) high

$13,000-15,000 SK

A late 19thC Maidu coiled basketry bowl, with stepped geometric designs, minor stitch loss at rim.

8in (20.5cm) diam

$1,900-2,500 SK

A late 19thC Pomo coiled gift basket, decorated with beads, shell discs, feather tufts and topknots, some restoration near rim.

11in (28cm) diam

$10,000-11,000 SK

An early 20thC San Ildefonso polychrome pottery jar, with abstract geometric and checkered design.

10.75in (27cm) diam

$4,500-5,000 SK

A late 19thC Zuni pottery jar, with an abstract rainbird design, small crack at rim.

12.5in (30.5cm) diam

$5,500-7,000 SK

A rare collection of three Aboriginal gorgets or king plates.
$32,000-38,000 SWO

An early 19thC Austral Islands wood paddle, with carved geometric designs, the top with eight stylized heads, wood loss.
56.5in (143.5cm) high
$5,000-6,500 SK

An Aboriginal carved wood figure of a man, Dalawongu people, his body painted with two snakes.
31in (79cm) high
$1,900-2,500 ROS

A 19thC Austral Islands ceremonial ladle, carved with incised geometric designs, the handle with ten stylized heads, with three birds perched at the top of the large scoop.

An example in The British Museum has the accompanying legend, 'ladle for serving out of the Poi Haari or coconut pudding to the Royal Party in the King's house.' Their careful carving supports such possible ceremonial use.
59.25in (150.5cm) long
$32,000-38,000 SK

ESSENTIAL REFERENCE - MOAI KAVAKAVA

'Moai Kavakava', translated simply as 'image with ribs', are perhaps the best-known of the wooden sculptures created by the (now extinct) Rapa Nui culture of Easter Island. 19thC examples do survive in many important collections, but this figure was cataloged as a recent copy from the second half of the 20thC. It was part of the estate of Jan Krugier (1928-2008), the Polish-born Swiss dealer. Despite the unambiguous cataloguing, there was clearly a belief among some who viewed it online that this richly patinated figure was more than just a tourist souvenir. It was sold to a buyer from Australia.

A late 19th/early 20thC 'Moai Kavakava' figure, with turned head, elongated arms framing the torso showing ribs, eyes inset with obsidian and shell eye, glyph on the top of the head, two holes to bottom of feet for attachment to stand.
17.75in (45cm) high
$150,000-190,000 DN

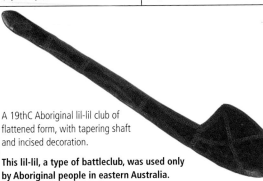

A 19thC Aboriginal lil-lil club of flattened form, with tapering shaft and incised decoration.

This lil-lil, a type of battleclub, was used only by Aboriginal people in eastern Australia.
24.75in (63cm) long
$6,500-7,500 SWO

A 19thC Fiji Islands carved wood kava bowl.
16in (40.5cm) diam
$1,900-2,500 SK

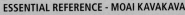

A Maori wooden vessel, carved with Tiki masks, on a lined and beaded ground, base missing.

4.75in (12cm) high

$3,800-4,400   MOR

A late 19thC Maori carved wood staff, one end with a male head showing tattoo designs.

16in (40.5cm) long

$1,900-2,500   SK

A 19thC New Zealand Maori taiaha, the Janus head with carved eyebrows and slanting eyes bearing traces of original Mother-of-pearl inlay.

66in (168cm) long

$800-950   TEN

A late 19thC Maori carved wood treasure box.

15.5in (39cm) long

$1,200-1,400   SK

ESSENTIAL REFERENCE - JADE TIKIS

Tiki or heitiki are traditional ornaments created by Maori, the Polynesian first settlers of New Zealand. The material they are most commonly made from is nephrite, a stone related to jade, found in several places in New Zealand's South Island. It is called pounamu in Maori. The Maori name for the South Island, Te Wai Pounamu, refers to the stone. There are traditional accounts for the creation of the stone which relate it to the children of Tangaroa. It is a very hard stone and is laborious to work, especially so with the basic grinding tools available to the Neolithic Maori.

A Maori carved wood Janus figure, with opposing male figures, shell inlaid eyes, one eye replaced.

12in (30.5cm) high

$2,800-3,500   SK

A Maori carved wood dance paddle, with stylized face on blade.

25.5in (62cm) long

$1,600-2,000   SK

A pair of 19thC Maori jade tiki pendants, both with red inlaid eyes.

larger 3.25 (8cm) high

$2,500-3,200   SK

A 19thC Maori carved wood billhook hand club, Waika, concentric arch design on blade, recumbent tiki on the inside, grotesque face at handle end.

14.75in (37.5cm) long

$14,000-18,000   SK

A 19thC Maori carved whale bone fiddle hand club, from Kotiate, New Zealand, the neck terminating in a Tiki head finial.

Provenance: Collected by Rev Alfred Fairbrother, Baptist minister to the Maoris, 1882-85.

13in (33cm) long

$5,000-5,700   SK

A 19thC Maori carved wood long club, from Taiaha, New Zealand, the shaft with Janus head finial, carved scrolls on protruding tongue and about the head, two remaining haliotis shell inlaid eyes.

Provenance: Collected by Rev. Alfred Fairbrother, Baptist minister to the Maoris, 1882-85.

63.5in (161cm) long

$3,800-4,400   SK

A late 18th to early 19thC Marquesas Islands iron wood war club, U'U, with stylized head with relief-carved tiki head eyes, and fine incised stylized lower panel, some wood loss.

55in (139.5cm) long

$55,000-60,000   SK

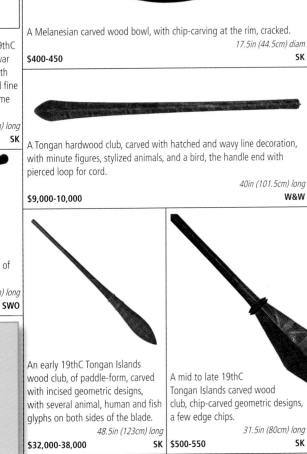

A Melanesian carved wood bowl, with chip-carving at the rim, cracked.

17.5in (44.5cm) diam

$400-450   SK

A Tongan hardwood club, carved with hatched and wavy line decoration, with minute figures, stylized animals, and a bird, the handle end with pierced loop for cord.

40in (101.5cm) long

$9,000-10,000   W&W

A Polynesian paddle club or pakipaki, probably Tongan, with four sets of horizontal carved details, losses.

46.75in (118.5cm) long

$800-950   SWO

An early 19thC Tongan Islands wood club, of paddle-form, carved with incised geometric designs, with several animal, human and fish glyphs on both sides of the blade.

48.5in (123cm) long

$32,000-38,000   SK

A mid to late 19thC Tongan Islands carved wood club, chip-carved geometric designs, a few edge chips.

31.5in (80cm) long

$500-550   SK

A late 18thC Tongan dense ironwood spear-club, carved with geometric designs, with over twenty-five glyphs representing birds, turtle, fish, and human figures.

Provenance: Collected by Captain William Trotter (1769-1822) in 1796, 'when his ship, the 'Susan', stopped in the Friendly Islands for provisions and the king presented Trotter with 'curiosities'.' Trotter was born in England and emigrated to Providence, Rhode Island, at the age of nineteen, having first been apprenticed as a cabin boy at the age of nine. After a lucrative globe-spanning career at sea, Trotter retired to Attleboro, Massachusetts, later settling in Bradford, Vermont. See Maryanne Tefft Force, 'Eighteenth Century Global Trade, The Logs of Captain William Trotter', Honolulu, Hawaii, 2012.

96in (244cm) long

$50,000-60,000   SK

A Solomon Islands feather money, from Tevau, Santa Cruz, carved wood with red feathers from the Scarlet Honeyeater, with shell attachments.

15in (38cm) diam

$25,000-32,000   SK

A pair of George II crested and silver-mounted walnut holster pistols, by Peter Gandon, London, stamped with London proof marks, the steel lock plates inscribed 'GANDON', the silver mounts with grotesque mask terminals and with trophies engraved with the arms of 'MURRAY', hallmarked for London, one has been cracked and repaired through the stock.

James Gandon, the celebrated English and Irish architect, responsible for among others, the Custom House, Dublin was the son of Peter Gandon (b.1713) gunmaker. The latter's father, also Peter, was a Huguenot refugee.

1742   *barrels 9.75in (25cm) long*
$9,000-10,000   DN

A pair of English flintlock duelling pistols, by Robert Wogdon, London, engraved 'WOGDON / CHARING CROSS LONDON'.

Robert Wogdon, gun maker (1737-1813) was a renowned maker of duelling pistols. He tuned his barrels so that they were accurate at twelve paces and this caused many more deaths of duellists than had previously been the case. His fame for his duelling pistols was written as a stanza by an Irish volunteer - 'Hail Wogdon patron of that leaden death'. His shop was at Number 2 Haymarket, near Charring Cross, London. He formed a partnership with John Barton in 1794.

c1770   *barrels 10in (25cm) long*
$9,500-10,500   L&T

An 18thC British flintlock long sea service pistol, the barrel with Ordnance view and proof marks, the lock plate with 'TOWER', crowned 'GR' and crowned 2 marks.

barrel 12in (30cm) long
$2,500-3,200   TEN

A pair of 18thC flintlock pistols, by Richards, The Strand, London, each with brass cannon barrels, the walnut stocks with brass butt caps, cast with grimacing masks, one with cracked hammer.

barrels 8in (20.5cm) long
$7,500-9,000   MOR

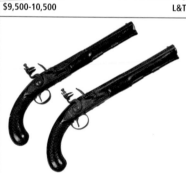

A pair of flintlock duelling pistols, by Durs Egg, London, signed 'D. Egg, London', stepped beveled locks, the walnut stocks with pineapple chequering, one walnut stock cracked, one ramrod damaged.

c1780-90   *barrels 9in (23cm) long*
$9,000-10,000   MOR

An 18thC 'Queen Anne' flintlock overcoat pistol, with rounded banana shape lockplate, walnut full stock.

barrel 5in (13cm) long
$650-750   TEN

A pair of early 19thC officer's holster percussion pistols, by Hamburger & Co., the spur of one hammer broken off, the case containing the ball mold, cleaning rod and clamp.

case 18in (45.5cm) wide
$3,800-5,000   TRI

A pair of officer's 16 bore holster pistols, with percussion breech drum conversions from flintlock, engraved 'W. Bond, 59 Lombard St, London', the locks retaining hints of original color hardening, one hammer screw missing, both hammer noses chipped.

c1820   *14in (35.5cm) long*
$1,900-2,500   W&W

A 41 Colt no.1 all metal single shot pistol, the rotating barrel stamped 'Colts PT.F.A. M.F.G. co Hartfort CT USA, no.1', serial no.2452.

c1870   *5in (12.5cm) long*
$950-1,100   BELL

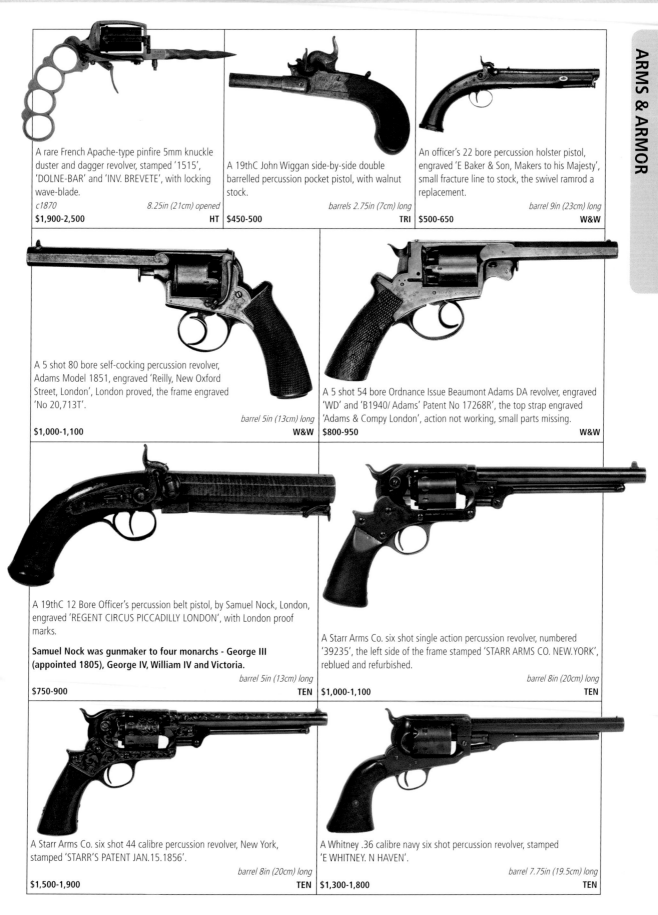

A rare French Apache-type pinfire 5mm knuckle duster and dagger revolver, stamped '1515', 'DOLNE-BAR' and 'INV. BREVETE', with locking wave-blade.

c1870   *8.25in (21cm) opened*

$1,900-2,500   **HT**

A 19thC John Wiggan side-by-side double barrelled percussion pocket pistol, with walnut stock.

barrels 2.75in (7cm) long

$450-500   **TRI**

An officer's 22 bore percussion holster pistol, engraved 'E Baker & Son, Makers to his Majesty', small fracture line to stock, the swivel ramrod a replacement.

barrel 9in (23cm) long

$500-650   **W&W**

A 5 shot 80 bore self-cocking percussion revolver, Adams Model 1851, engraved 'Reilly, New Oxford Street, London', London proved, the frame engraved 'No 20,713T'.

barrel 5in (13cm) long

$1,000-1,100   **W&W**

A 5 shot 54 bore Ordnance Issue Beaumont Adams DA revolver, engraved 'WD' and 'B1940/ Adams' Patent No 17268R', the top strap engraved 'Adams & Compy London', action not working, small parts missing.

$800-950   **W&W**

A 19thC 12 Bore Officer's percussion belt pistol, by Samuel Nock, London, engraved 'REGENT CIRCUS PICCADILLY LONDON', with London proof marks.

Samuel Nock was gunmaker to four monarchs - George III (appointed 1805), George IV, William IV and Victoria.

barrel 5in (13cm) long

$750-900   **TEN**

A Starr Arms Co. six shot single action percussion revolver, numbered '39235', the left side of the frame stamped 'STARR ARMS CO. NEW.YORK', reblued and refurbished.

barrel 8in (20cm) long

$1,000-1,100   **TEN**

A Starr Arms Co. six shot 44 calibre percussion revolver, New York, stamped 'STARR'S PATENT JAN.15.1856'.

barrel 8in (20cm) long

$1,500-1,900   **TEN**

A Whitney .36 calibre navy six shot percussion revolver, stamped 'E WHITNEY. N HAVEN'.

barrel 7.75in (19.5cm) long

$1,300-1,800   **TEN**

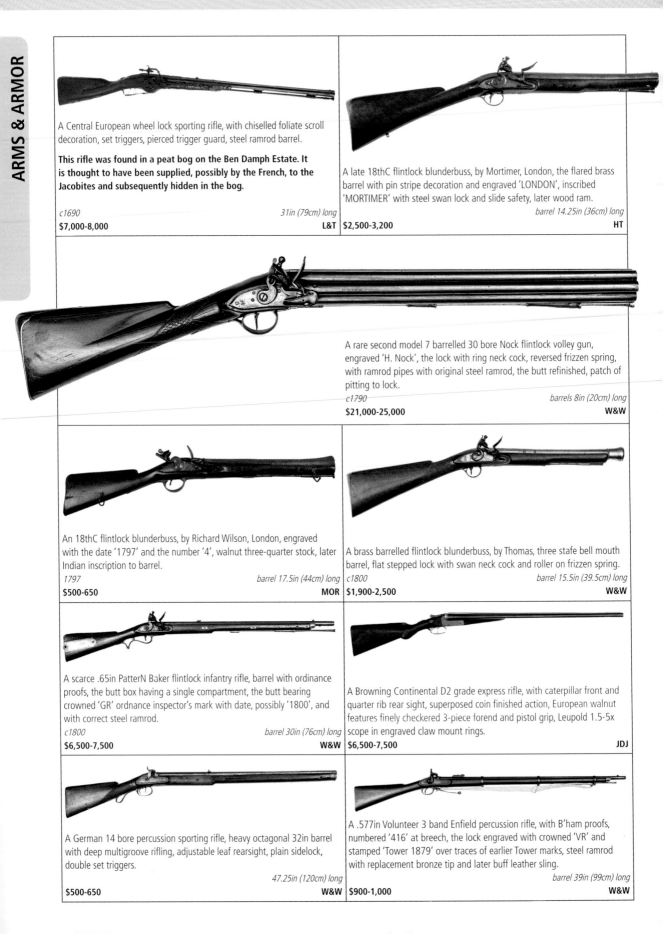

A Central European wheel lock sporting rifle, with chiselled foliate scroll decoration, set triggers, pierced trigger guard, steel ramrod barrel.

This rifle was found in a peat bog on the Ben Damph Estate. It is thought to have been supplied, possibly by the French, to the Jacobites and subsequently hidden in the bog.

c1690   *31in (79cm) long*
$7,000-8,000   L&T

A late 18thC flintlock blunderbuss, by Mortimer, London, the flared brass barrel with pin stripe decoration and engraved 'LONDON', inscribed 'MORTIMER' with steel swan lock and slide safety, later wood ram.

barrel 14.25in (36cm) long
$2,500-3,200   HT

A rare second model 7 barrelled 30 bore Nock flintlock volley gun, engraved 'H. Nock', the lock with ring neck cock, reversed frizzen spring, with ramrod pipes with original steel ramrod, the butt refinished, patch of pitting to lock.

c1790   *barrels 8in (20cm) long*
$21,000-25,000   W&W

An 18thC flintlock blunderbuss, by Richard Wilson, London, engraved with the date '1797' and the number '4', walnut three-quarter stock, later Indian inscription to barrel.

1797   *barrel 17.5in (44cm) long*
$500-650   MOR

A brass barrelled flintlock blunderbuss, by Thomas, three stafe bell mouth barrel, flat stepped lock with swan neck cock and roller on frizzen spring.

c1800   *barrel 15.5in (39.5cm) long*
$1,900-2,500   W&W

A scarce .65in PatterN Baker flintlock infantry rifle, barrel with ordinance proofs, the butt box having a single compartment, the butt bearing crowned 'GR' ordnance inspector's mark with date, possibly '1800', and with correct steel ramrod.

c1800   *barrel 30in (76cm) long*
$6,500-7,500   W&W

A Browning Continental D2 grade express rifle, with caterpillar front and quarter rib rear sight, superposed coin finished action, European walnut features finely checkered 3-piece forend and pistol grip, Leupold 1.5-5x scope in engraved claw mount rings.

$6,500-7,500   JDJ

A German 14 bore percussion sporting rifle, heavy octagonal 32in barrel with deep multigroove rifling, adjustable leaf rearsight, plain sidelock, double set triggers.

47.25in (120cm) long
$500-650   W&W

A .577in Volunteer 3 band Enfield percussion rifle, with B'ham proofs, numbered '416' at breech, the lock engraved with crowned 'VR' and stamped 'Tower 1879' over traces of earlier Tower marks, steel ramrod with replacement bronze tip and later buff leather sling.

barrel 39in (99cm) long
$900-1,000   W&W

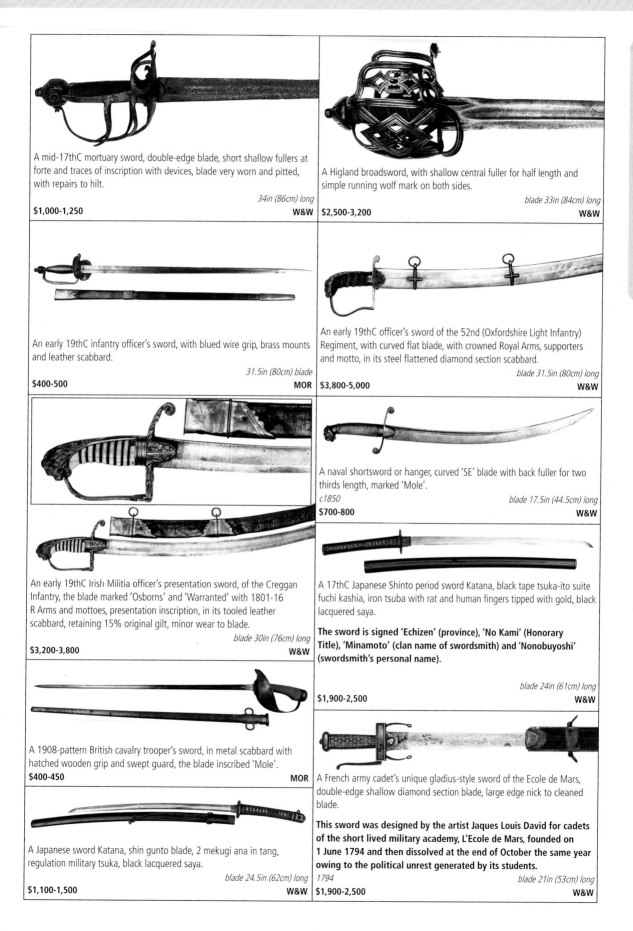

A mid-17thC mortuary sword, double-edge blade, short shallow fullers at forte and traces of inscription with devices, blade very worn and pitted, with repairs to hilt.

34in (86cm) long

$1,000-1,250 **W&W**

A Higland broadsword, with shallow central fuller for half length and simple running wolf mark on both sides.

blade 33in (84cm) long

$2,500-3,200 **W&W**

An early 19thC infantry officer's sword, with blued wire grip, brass mounts and leather scabbard.

31.5in (80cm) blade

$400-500 **MOR**

An early 19thC officer's sword of the 52nd (Oxfordshire Light Infantry) Regiment, with curved flat blade, with crowned Royal Arms, supporters and motto, in its steel flattened diamond section scabbard.

blade 31.5in (80cm) long

$3,800-5,000 **W&W**

A naval shortsword or hanger, curved 'SE' blade with back fuller for two thirds length, marked 'Mole'.

c1850   *blade 17.5in (44.5cm) long*

$700-800 **W&W**

An early 19thC Irish Militia officer's presentation sword, of the Creggan Infantry, the blade marked 'Osborns' and 'Warranted' with 1801-16 R Arms and mottoes, presentation inscription, in its tooled leather scabbard, retaining 15% original gilt, minor wear to blade.

blade 30in (76cm) long

$3,200-3,800 **W&W**

A 17thC Japanese Shinto period sword Katana, black tape tsuka-ito suite fuchi kashia, iron tsuba with rat and human fingers tipped with gold, black lacquered saya.

The sword is signed 'Echizen' (province), 'No Kami' (Honorary Title), 'Minamoto' (clan name of swordsmith) and 'Nonobuyoshi' (swordsmith's personal name).

blade 24in (61cm) long

$1,900-2,500 **W&W**

A 1908-pattern British cavalry trooper's sword, in metal scabbard with hatched wooden grip and swept guard, the blade inscribed 'Mole'.

$400-450 **MOR**

A French army cadet's unique gladius-style sword of the Ecole de Mars, double-edge shallow diamond section blade, large edge nick to cleaned blade.

This sword was designed by the artist Jaques Louis David for cadets of the short lived military academy, L'Ecole de Mars, founded on 1 June 1794 and then dissolved at the end of October the same year owing to the political unrest generated by its students.

A Japanese sword Katana, shin gunto blade, 2 mekugi ana in tang, regulation military tsuka, black lacquered saya.

blade 24.5in (62cm) long

$1,100-1,500 **W&W**

1794   *blade 21in (53cm) long*

$1,900-2,500 **W&W**

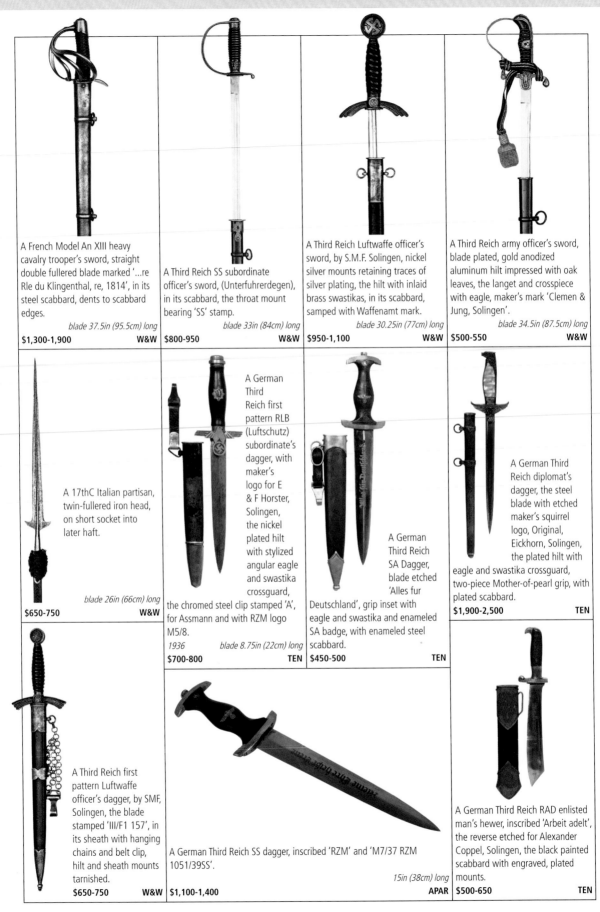

A French Model An XIII heavy cavalry trooper's sword, straight double fullered blade marked '...re Rle du Klingenthal, re, 1814', in its steel scabbard, dents to scabbard edges.

blade 37.5in (95.5cm) long

$1,300-1,900   W&W

A Third Reich SS subordinate officer's sword, (Unterfuhrerdegen), in its scabbard, the throat mount bearing 'SS' stamp.

blade 33in (84cm) long

$800-950   W&W

A Third Reich Luftwaffe officer's sword, by S.M.F. Solingen, nickel silver mounts retaining traces of silver plating, the hilt with inlaid brass swastikas, in its scabbard, samped with Waffenamt mark.

blade 30.25in (77cm) long

$950-1,100   W&W

A Third Reich army officer's sword, blade plated, gold anodized aluminum hilt impressed with oak leaves, the langet and crosspiece with eagle, maker's mark 'Clemen & Jung, Solingen'.

blade 34.5in (87.5cm) long

$500-550   W&W

A 17thC Italian partisan, twin-fullered iron head, on short socket into later haft.

blade 26in (66cm) long

$650-750   W&W

A German Third Reich first pattern RLB (Luftschutz) subordinate's dagger, with maker's logo for E & F Horster, Solingen, the nickel plated hilt with stylized angular eagle and swastika crossguard, the chromed steel clip stamped 'A', for Assmann and with RZM logo M5/8.

1936   *blade 8.75in (22cm) long*

$700-800   TEN

A German Third Reich SA Dagger, blade etched 'Alles fur Deutschland', grip inset with eagle and swastika and enameled SA badge, with enameled steel scabbard.

$450-500   TEN

A German Third Reich diplomat's dagger, the steel blade with etched maker's squirrel logo, Original, Eickhorn, Solingen, the plated hilt with eagle and swastika crossguard, two-piece Mother-of-pearl grip, with plated scabbard.

$1,900-2,500   TEN

A Third Reich first pattern Luftwaffe officer's dagger, by SMF, Solingen, the blade stamped 'III/F1 157', in its sheath with hanging chains and belt clip, hilt and sheath mounts tarnished.

$650-750   W&W

A German Third Reich SS dagger, inscribed 'RZM' and 'M7/37 RZM 1051/39SS'.

15in (38cm) long

$1,100-1,400   APAR

A German Third Reich RAD enlisted man's hewer, inscribed 'Arbeit adelt', the reverse etched for Alexander Coppel, Solingen, the black painted scabbard with engraved, plated mounts.

$500-650   TEN

ESSENTIAL REFERENCE - HIGHLAND DIRK

The Scottish dirk (Scottish Gaelic: Biodag) is the traditional and ceremonial sidearm of the officers of Scottish Highland regiments. The traditional Scottish dirk developed in the second half of the 18thC, when it became a popular item of military equipment in the Jacobite Risings. The 78th Fraser Highlanders, raised in 1757, wore full highland dress uniform; their equipment was described by Major-General James Stewart in 1780 as including a 'musket and broadsword, to which many soldiers added the dirk at their own expense.' The modern development of the Scottish dirk into a ceremonial weapon occurred during the 19thC. The shape of the grip developed from the historical, more cylindrical form to a shape intended to represent the thistle. Fancier fittings, often of silver, became popular shortly after 1800. The hilts of modern Scottish dirks are often carved from dark colored wood such as bog oak or ebony. Hilts and scabbards are often lavishly decorated with silver mounts and have pommels set with cairngorm stones. When worn, the dirk normally hangs by a leather strap known as a 'frog' from a dirk belt, which is a wide leather belt having a large, usually ornate buckle, that is worn around the waist with a kilt. Many Scottish dirks have a smaller knife and fork which fit into compartments on the front of the sheath, and a smaller knife known as a 'sgian dubh' is also worn tucked into the top of the hose when wearing a kilt.

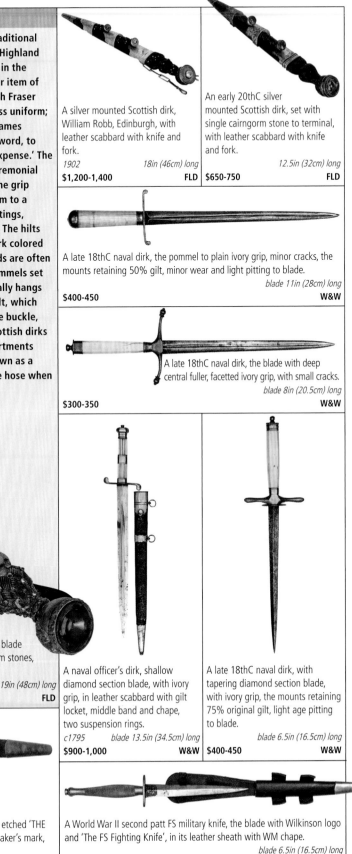

A silver mounted Scottish dirk, William Robb, Edinburgh, with leather scabbard with knife and fork.

1902   *18in (46cm) long*
$1,200-1,400   **FLD**

An early 20thC silver mounted Scottish dirk, set with single cairngorm stone to terminal, with leather scabbard with knife and fork.

12.5in (32cm) long
$650-750   **FLD**

A late 18thC naval dirk, the pommel to plain ivory grip, minor cracks, the mounts retaining 50% gilt, minor wear and light pitting to blade.

blade 11in (28cm) long
$400-450   **W&W**

A late 18thC naval dirk, the blade with deep central fuller, facetted ivory grip, with small cracks.

blade 8in (20.5cm) long
$300-350   **W&W**

A naval officer's dirk, shallow diamond section blade, with ivory grip, in leather scabbard with gilt locket, middle band and chape, two suspension rings.

c1795   *blade 13.5in (34.5cm) long*
$900-1,000   **W&W**

A late 18thC naval dirk, with tapering diamond section blade, with ivory grip, the mounts retaining 75% original gilt, light age pitting to blade.

blade 6.5in (16.5cm) long
$400-450   **W&W**

A late 19thC white metal mounted Scottish dirk, the etched blade with St Andrew and a Highlander, the grip set with cairngorm stones, with leather scabbard with knife and fork.

19in (48cm) long
$1,600-2,000   **FLD**

A Fairbairn Sykes, first pattern fighting knife, the steel blade etched 'THE F-S FIGHTING KNIFE', and 'Wilkinson Sword Co.', London maker's mark, blade tip with shortened tip.
$1,300-1,800   **TEN**

A World War II second patt FS military knife, the blade with Wilkinson logo and 'The FS Fighting Knife', in its leather sheath with WM chape.

blade 6.5in (16.5cm) long
$1,000-1,200   **W&W**

A scarce Georgian officer's tent cap, black beaver sides with gilt oak wreath lace headband.
$800-950   **W&W**

An officer's 1828-pattern helmet, of the South Salopian Yeomanry, the helmet plate bearing crowned 1816-37 Royal Arms and supporters on Prince of Wales's feathers.
$2,800-3,500   **W&W**

l. A Georgian officer's blue cloth tent cap, of the 8th The King's Royal Irish (Light) Dragoons (Hussars).
$1,300-1,800
c. An other rank's 'Hummel' bonnet, of the 71st (Highland) (Light Infantry). *c1830*
$1,500-2,000
r. A Georgian cavalry officer's blue cloth tent cap, with paper label of 'Furlong & Co. Hatters and Cap Makers, 15 New Bond Street, Joining Longs Hotel'.
$1,300-1,800   **W&W**

An officer's gilt helmet, of the 6th Dragoon Guards (Carabiniers) pattern, leather lining, worn and detached, regilt overall.
1834-43
$5,500-6,500   **W&W**

An officer's helmet, of Prince of Albert's Own Corps of Norfolk Yeomanry, retaining much original gilt, some service wear overall.
1843-49
$3,200-3,800   **W&W**

l. An OR's pattern quilted shako, of The Monmouthshire Rifle Volunteers.
1861
$700-800
r. A Victorian officer's peaked forage cap, of The Devonshire Regiment, with gilt logo of 'Hawkes & Co., 14 Piccadilly, London'.
$1,300-1,800   **W&W**

A 12th Lancer Officer's lance cap, the gilt cap plate mounted with silver Royal Coat of Arms and battle honors for Egypt, Peninsula, Waterloo, Sevastopol and Central India.
$5,000-5,700   **HT**

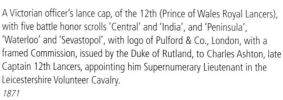

A Victorian officer's lance cap, of the 12th (Prince of Wales Royal Lancers), with five battle honor scrolls 'Central' and 'India', and 'Peninsula', 'Waterloo' and 'Sevastopol', with logo of Pulford & Co., London, with a framed Commission, issued by the Duke of Rutland, to Charles Ashton, late Captain 12th Lancers, appointing him Supernumerary Lieutenant in the Leicestershire Volunteer Cavalry.
1871
$4,500-5,000   **W&W**

A Victorian 1871-pattern trooper's brass helmet, of the 5th Dragoon Guards, with leather tongued liner.
$750-900   **TEN**

A late 19thC cork patent officers spiked helmet, by Hawkes & Co. inscribed 'Scottish Kings Own Borderers', in a vintage tin hat box.
$750-900   **APAR**

An officer's lance cap, of the Bedfordshire Imperial Yeomanry.
1901
$4,500-5,000   **W&W**

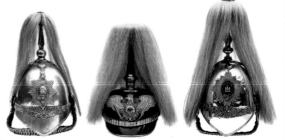

l. A trooper's white metal helmet, of the Montgomeryshire Imperial Yeomanry. *c1905*
$750-900
c. A Prussian M1895 Garde Infantry Reservist officer's parade pickelhaube.
$2,500-3,200
r. An officer's 1871-pattern helmet, of the 6th (Inniskilling) Dragoons.
$1,900-2,500   **W&W**

An Edwardian officer's 1878-pattern home service blue cloth helmet, of the East Yorkshire Regiment, in a black japanned tin.

$650-750   TEN

A World War I British tank driver's splatter face mask, of leather covered steel, with chain mail nose and mouth protector, cut-out eye slits, original fabric ties.

$1,900-2,500   TEN

A Prussian M1899 helmet, of an officer of the Garde du Corps or Garde Kürassier Regiment, of tombak, with silver plated mounts and trim.

$9,000-10,000   W&W

An Imperial German officer's pickelhaube, with large winged emblem inscribed 'Suun Cuique', stamped 'E.R.3. 1903'.

1903

$900-1,000   APAR

A Third Reich Waffen SS Panzer officer's peaked cap, the lining with maker's celluloid label 'Preisgekronte Pekuro Mutze Stirndruckfrei Deutsches Perchs Patent'.

$1,900-2,500   W&W

A German Third Reich EM/NCO's visor cap, possibly Panzer division, leather sweatband and brown liner stencilled '53'.

$300-400   TEN

A World War II German Afrika Korps tropical helmet, the leather sweat band with maker's initial 'JHS'.

$400-450   W&W

A German Third Reich Waffen-SS M35 double decal helmet, with original apple green paint, stamped 'SF64', and '3866'.

$1,900-2,500   TEN

A World War II German M35 steel helmet, with sand color camouflage and Afrika Korps decal.

12in (30cm) long

$400-450   HW

A mid-17thC Dutch lobster tail helmet.

$2,500-3,200   W&W

A French dragoon officer's helmet, gilt skull with leopard skin turban, in the front a Medusa head finial, and a grenade.

c1840-45

$5,500-6,500   W&W

A French Cuirassier brass and nickel mounted officer's helmet, stamped 'B. Franck & Ses Fils, Aubervilliers' with replaced comb and feather adornment, in an associated tin.

$500-650   APAR

ESSENTIAL REFERENCE - WELSH FUSILIERS

This gorget was undated but evidence suggests it was worn by a Welsh Fusiliers officer in America from 1775-81. Once a key element of armor, gorgets were introduced as decorative items to British Army uniforms in the mid-18thC and abandoned in 1830. The earlier ones bore the Royal Coat of Arms, as did this one, until the arms were replaced by the royal cipher in 1796. The north Wales regiment, founded in 1689, fought in virtually every British battle from the Boyne to Kohima and in every engagement bar one in the American War of Independence.

A Royal Welch Fusiliers 23rd Regiment brass gorget.
$5,000-5,700   H&H

l. A Victorian officer's full dress embroidered blue cloth sabretache, of the Derbyshire Yeomanry, with velvet lined bad weather cover.
12.5in (32cm) long in cover
$1,500-1,900

r. A Victorian officer's full dress embroidered scarlet cloth sabretache, of the 15th (the King's) Hussars.
13in (33cm) long
$1,900-2,500   W&W

An officer's full dress sabretache, of the 16th (the Queen's) Lancers.
1834-55   14.5in (37cm) long
$1,600-2,300   HT

Judith Picks

This is a very rare ivory Gunners' Rule. The maker has managed to mark more than 2,500 letters, numerals, etc on every available surface and to give instruction on the loading weights of powder and shot for various sizes of 'Brafs and Iron Guns, Musquets, Carbine, Pistol, Wall Pieces, Small Arms, Brafs and Iron Morters, Brafs Howits, Carronades' (all sic). Also included is the formula 'To find the No of shot in a Sq.r or Obl.g Pile...'

There is also reference that states 'In the Table of brafs guns G.D. signifies Gen. I Desaguliers'. This refers to Major General Thomas Desaguliers and may give a guide to dating the rule. Thomas was born in 1721 to John Theophilus Desaguliers who had fled to England at an early age to escape the French persecution of the Huguenots. His father was obviously a very learned man for at the age of 31 he was made a Member of the Royal Society, was an assistant to Isaac Newton and a distinguished scientist, inventor, hydraulic engineer, priest and a noted Freemason, becoming the Grand Master of the Grand Lodge of England in 1719. So it was hardly surprising that his son Thomas went on to follow his father in becoming a scientist and inventor, and as a military man applying his talents to various improvements in ordinance, especially cannons and their carriages. He was made Chief Fire Master at the Royal Arsenal at Woolwich in 1748 and was Superintendent when he died in 1780.

The Gunners Rule.
$6,500-7,500   DSA

A 20thC Korean military uniform, the helmet with a tall jade enameled and horsehair finial and with gilt dragon and phoenix appliqués and a fur-lined cowl, the red fabric tunic embellished with brass, studs and further gilt metal appliqués, with felt boots and a black lacquered fitted case.

$320,000-380,000   WW

An ERII painted tenor drum, of The Royal Marines, with the regimental badge with 'Gibraltar' and motto 'Per Mare ad Terram'.
$750-900   W&W

ESSENTIAL REFERENCE - FENIAN RIOTS

The Fenian Rising (1867) was a rebellion against British rule in Ireland.

● They were organized by the Irish Republican Brotherhood, who demanded an independent Republic of Ireland.

● In February and March 1867 there were risings in County Kerry, Cork, Tallaght and Dublin, but these were suppressed by the Irish police force.

● The rebellion was poorly coordinated and most of the leaders were arrested.

● Various attempts were made to free the Fenian leaders from prisons in Chester, Manchester and London. These were unsuccessful and several of the leaders were executed.

● This sparked riots and insurrections throughout Britain in 1867-68.

A Victorian blackened truncheon, painted 'M.S.D./ 1868', issued during the Fenian riots, Military Stores Department, Royal Arsenal, Woolwich.
17.5in (44.5cm) long
$250-320   W&W

An OR's universal pattern shako plate, interlaced 'GR' cipher, stitching holes to rim.
1812
$500-550   **W&W**

A Sutlej medal, for SOBRAON 1846, awarded to Sepoy Jubbar, Khan 3th L.I.
1846
$400-450   **TEN**

An Indian Mutiny medal, awarded to J. O'Conner, 1st Batallion, 5th Fusiliers, with two clasps 'Lucknow' and 'Defence of Lucknow', set in that order.
1857-59
$1,300-1,800   **TEN**

A City of London/Guildhall medal, with head of Queen Victoria with 'Inaugurated Nov 6 1869', with the crest of the City of London, with views of Holborn Viaduct and Blackfriars Bridge, reverse engraved 'William Ferneley Allen Esq. Alderman'.

William F. Allen became Lord Mayor of London in 1867. He became the subject of some satirical cartoons when he preferred his private carriage to the Lord Mayor's coach for his procession as the latter gave too much of a jolting ride!
$180-250   **W&W**

An Ashantee medal, with coomassie clasp, awarded to 'W. BUNT, PY.OFFR.1CL: H.M.S. ARGUS. 73-74', together with the miniature.
1873-74
$1,300-1,800   **TEN**

A D.C.M. George V issue, to 15136 Pte R.M. Laverick, 9/ North'd Fus.

Robert Makepeace Laverick, killed in action 16 April 1918 and commemorated at the Tyne Cot Memorial. DCM London Gazette 28 March 1916: '15136 Private R M Laverick 9th Battalion Northumberland Fusiliers. For conspicuous gallantry during a bomb attack by the enemy. He knelt on the parapet and kept up a continuous fusilade of grenades into the enemy's trench at 20 yards distance.'
$900-1,000   **W&W**

A set of four World War I medals, comprising George V first type (96537 Cpl G. Riley, RFA), 1914-15 star, British War Medal and Victory medal with MID leaf, with photocopies of service papers.

This soldier served with Bell Brothers munitions at Middlesbrough, 27 March 1916; mentioned in dispatches 15 June 1916; military medal awarded 11 October 1916.
$550-700   **W&W**

A Liverpool silver Shipwreck and Humane Society's Marine medal, awarded 'TO FREDERICK LINDSAY. FOR GALLANT SERVICE. 10/12/47', hallmarks for Birmingham.
1946   *1.5in (3.5cm) wide*
$180-250   **TEN**

A group of five World War I medals, for Sgt W.H. Rench, including Meritorious Service Medal, Territorial Force Efficiency Medal and Territorial War Medal for Voluntary Service Overseas, with ribbons and bar.
$750-900   **MOR**

A Third Reich early-type gold German Cross, with ten rivets to back and shorter pin than later types.
$1,400-1,900   **W&W**

A rare Third Reich Panzer Assault badge, for 100 engagements, with gilt wreath and silvered tank.
$950-1,100   **W&W**

ESSENTIAL REFERENCE - ROMAN GLASS

Glass vessels were produced in Egypt and Mesopotamia as early as the 15thC BC, but it was Ancient Rome which revolutionized glass production. Early Roman glass was thick, expensive and nearly opaque. However, this changed with the invention of glass-blowing in the 1stC BC and the development of the glass-blowing furnace in the 1stC AD. Glass was blown into carved molds, creating vessels with thinner, translucent bodies and a wider range of shapes. Glass became cheaper and therefore more common in everyday life, used for cups, bottles, ornaments, jewelry, mosaic tiles and even windows. Many vessels that were clear in Roman times now appear opaque or mottled: centuries buried underground have weathered the surfaces, causing iridescence. This can create a rainbow effect on the surface of the glass.

A Roman glass jar, with thread design, green glass handles and conforming decoration.

4th-5thC AD   3.25in (8cm) wide

$400-500   **LOCK**

A Roman bottle, with tapering body.

1st-3rdC AD   4in (10cm) high

$80-90   **LOCK**

A Roman glass container, with blue irridescent body.

1st-3rdC AD   5in (13cm) high

$100-110   **LOCK**

A Roman glass vessel.

1st-3rdC AD   4.75in (12cm) wide

$300-400   **LOCK**

A tall Roman glass vase.

46in (117cm) high

$230-280   **LOCK**

A Roman pale green glass bottle, with wide loop handle.

1st-3rdC AD   9.5in (24cm) high

$800-950   **ROS**

A Roman pale green glass flask, with octagonal body, cylindrical neck and everted folded rim with applied broad strap handle.

3rdC AD   8.25in (21cm) high

$800-950   **ROS**

A Roman yellow tinted glass jug, with applied blue glass strap handle.

1st-3rdC AD   6in (15cm) high

$650-750   **ROS**

A Roman pale green glass jug, with broad loop handle.

2nd-4thC AD   6in (15.5cm) high

$650-750   **ROS**

A Roman mold-blown olive green glass flask, of flattened form with a mask head to each side and simple loop handle, face encrustation and iridescence.

1st-2ndC AD

$550-700   **BE**

A Roman bronze saddled foot, the toes naturally modeled wearing a Classical caliga.

c2ndC AD   *9.5in (24cm) high*

$16,000-19,000   **ROS**

A large Roman mosaic, possibly Anatolian, depicting a leaping deer against a cream ground with stylized plants.

2nd-3rdC AD   *69in (175cm) wide*

$28,000-35,000   **L&T**

A late 3rdC Roman mosaic, possible Anatolian, the circular reserve depicting a peacock in full display with fanned tail feathers.

52.5in (133cm) diam

$6,500-7,500   **L&T**

A South Arabian limestone stele, modeled as a face with open eyes and square jaw.

c3rdC BC   *15.75in (40cm) high*

$4,400-5,700   **ROS**

A late 5th/4thC BC Egyptian faience shabti, the inscription identifies the owner as 'Nes-Ba-neb-djed', the name being only part of the inscription.

The shabti comes from a tomb found at Mendes, the capital of a province in the Nile delta, which was found in 1902. The shabti is carrying a pick and a hoe in his hands and a basket on his back, indicating that his function in a burial was to do any agricultural labor that might be required of the owners of the tomb by the gods.

6.75in (17cm) high

$1,900-2,500   **APAR**

A Boeotian terracotta Pappades archaic figure, wearing patterned peplos and painted with linear design.

Boeotian means characteristic of the ancient Greek region of Boeotia.

c550 BC   *6in (15cm) high*

$300-400   **ROS**

A Corinthian pottery alabastron, depicting a winged panther with rosettes, tongues and dots on the neck and rim.

This vessel would have been used for oils and perfumes.

c6thC BC   *6.75in (17cm) high*

$4,500-5,000   **CA**

An Apulian red-figured pottery kantharos, Greek South Italy, face masks on the handle on the rim, decorated with two figures of Eros, small rim chip, one handle has a touched-up repair, various firing cracks.

late 4thC BC   *10.5in (26.5cm) high*

$3,800-5,000   **DN**

An Attic red-figured owl skyphos of two handled form, restored.

Red-figure painting is one of the most important styles of figural Greek vase painting. It developed in Athens around 520 BC and remained in use until the late 3rdC BC. It replaced the previously dominant style of black-figure vase painting within a few decades. Its modern name is based on the figural depictions in red color on a black background, in contrast to the preceding black-figure style with black figures on a red background. The most important areas of production, apart from Attica, were in Southern Italy. The style was also adopted in other parts of Greece. Etruria became an important center of production outside the Greek World.

c5th-4thC BC   *3in (7.5cm) high*

$500-650   **BELL**

A violin, by Giovanni Battista Granchino II, Milan, in case, labelled 'Giouanni Grancino in Controda Largha di Milano al segno della Corona 17**'.

1715　　　*14in (35.5cm) long*
$200,000-250,000　　　**HAY**

A violin, by Tomasso Balestrieri, Mantura, labelled 'Thomas Balestrieri Cremonensis Fecit Mantuae. Anno 1788', with the certificate of J. & A. Beare, London, dated 12 April 2005.

1788　　　*13.75in (35cm) long*
$380,000-440,000　　　**HAY**

A violin, by Ferdinando Gagliano, Naples, with case, with original fingerboard, saddle and varnish, with original label reading 'Ferdinandus Gagliano Filius Nicolai fecit Neap. 1789'.

Purchased by a Neapolitan noblewoman at the end of the 18thC, the violin has belonged to the Cafisi family for over 200 years. Its first owner was the Marquis Giuseppe Cafisi, a wealthy landowner of Ferrara and patron of the arts. Upon his death in 1844, the violin passed into the hands of his nephew Ignazio, a clergyman. He, in turn, died without an heir and bequeathed the violin to his relative Maria Cafisi, who married Baron John Micciché. It has since passed down the male line of the Micciché family, who have carefully preserved it until the present day.
$230,000-280,000　　　**HAY**

A 'cigar box' violin, made from Winston Churchill's cigar box, inscribed on the label 'Sir Winston Churchill', branded on the front 'Made in Havana - Cuba' and on the back 'Selección Privado, Fabrica Tabacos Don Joaquin, Habana'.

This violin was made by William Robinson from a cigar box once owned by Sir Winston Churchill. A news article in the Toledo Blade from 31 October 1958 reads: 'William Robinson, a violin maker, always wanted to make a fiddle from one of Sir Winston Churchill's cigar boxes'. The violin was played by virtuoso Yehudi Menuhin in a radio broadcast to America in April 1958. Robinson, a former master saddler from Avebury, spent his childhood converting empty boxes into rustic violins. Self-taught, he went on to make over 400 violins, 40 violas and 16 cellos.
1956　　　*12.5in (32cm) long*
$9,000-10,000　　　**HAY**

A rare Irish George III upright square piano or camerachord, by William Southwell of Dublin.

William Southwell (1736/7-1825) was an Anglo-Irish inventor and musical instrument maker who made pianos for the nobility and the wealthy elite. He is most well known for the production of a demi-lune piano which when closed appeared as a very fashionable Adam-style pier table. The design for this piano was patented in 1798. It is number 22, which points it to being an early example made between 1798 and 1800.

62in (157cm) wide
$25,000-32,000　　　**WW**

A mahogany and satinwood inlaid Bechstein grand piano.

This piano was featured in the popular television show The Forsyte Saga and has been well restored.
78.75in (200cm) long
$4,500-5,000　　　**APAR**

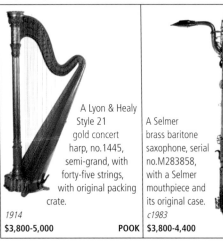

A Lyon & Healy Style 21 gold concert harp, no.1445, semi-grand, with forty-five strings, with original packing crate.

1914
$3,800-5,000　　　**POOK**

A Selmer brass baritone saxophone, serial no.M283858, with a Selmer mouthpiece and its original case.

c1983
$3,800-4,400　　　**POOK**

A set of silver and ivory mounted Scottish bagpipes, possibly Macpherson, hallmarks for Birmingham 1973, with accessories, cased, with CITES A10 non-transferable license no.541622/01.

$1,500-1,900　　　**TEN**

A Fender Stratocaster electric guitar, made in USA, serial no.2xxx6, three-tone sunburst finish, with hard case.

1958

$15,000-19,000 GHOU

A late 1970s Fender Telecaster electric guitar, made in USA, serial no.S831877, pot codes date to 1976, with contemporary hard case, imperfections to edges of neck, head and fretboard, mild wear to frets.

$1,900-2,500 GHOU

A Gibson J45 acoustic guitar, made in USA, overspray to a small section of the table on the bass side of the lower bout, with Gibson hard case.

This guitar was used for the illustration on page 39 of Tony Bacon and Paul Day, 'The Ultimate Guitar Book'.

1946

$5,500-7,000 GHOU

A Gibson B.B. King 'Lucille' model electric guitar, made in USA, serial no.00335706, within the original Gibson case.

The Album 'B.B. King & Friends: 80' was a celebration of B.B. King's 80th birthday and comprised a series of duets with the signatories on the guitar. B.B. King used this guitar for the session with Mark Knopfler. It was played by B.B. King during the recording of 'B.B. King & Friends: 80' in 2005. The body of the guitar is signed by B.B. King (and dated '4-18-05'), Eric Clapton, Van Morrison, Mark Knopfler, Billy Gibbons, Roger Daltrey, Glenn Frey, Sheryl Crowe, Gloria Estefan and Bobby Bland. The guitar comes with the pen used for signing and the pick used by B.B. King to play the instrument.

2005

$9,000-10,000 GHOU

A Gibson ES-345TD Stereo Varitone hollow body electric guitar, made in USA, with PAF bridge pickup, serial no.66347, some blemishes, no electric output from the neck pickup, later Bigsby vibrato installed.

This guitar was purchased in 1964 for a band called 'Southbeats' from Bognor Regis, West Sussex. The band came fifth in the 'All Britain Beat Contest'. They played locally for ten years in and around Devon.

1964

$6,500-7,500 GHOU

A Gretsch Nashville 6120-1960 electric archtop guitar, made in Japan, serial no.JT03xxxxx9, with hard case.

2003

$1,400-1,800 GHOU

A Martin 000-28LD Lonnie Donnegan King of Skiffle signature acoustic guitar, made in USA, no.56 of a limited run of 72, east Indian rosewood back and sides.

2002

$1,900-2,500 GHOU

A Parker Fly Delux electric guitar, made in USA, serial no.27xxxxBP, with original gig bag, manual and accessories, with original purchase receipt for the sum of £1,750.

1996

$1,500-1,900 GHOU

A 1960s Teisco SD4L electric guitar, with soft case, imperfections to finish on the body sides and back of neck.

This guitar is documented as being one of Ry Cooder's preferred instruments for playing slide.

$1,000-1,200 GHOU

DECORATIVE ARTS MARKET

As with many areas of collecting, Decorative Arts pieces have seen a rise in sales and prices of high-end items and stagnation of mid-to-low-end goods.

Many Doulton wares are quite simply unfashionable. Demand for the Royal Doulton figures has fallen dramatically and only the prototypes, limited production and rare colorways are fetching good money. Also demand for works by the Barlows, Eliza Simmance, Frank Butler, has been very sluggish. The opposite is true of the Doulton pieces with experimental glazes - especially anything unusual that is lustered or flambéd.

Moorcroft and Martin Brothers have continued to be strong in the marketplace. A rare Martin Brothers stoneware jar and cover, of a grotesque 'Birdman' beast, by Robert Wallace Martin, dated 1907, sold at Phillips for $95,000 (£75,400). Clarice Cliff will command high prices if the pattern and shape are rare.

Wedgwood Fairyland lustre ceramics have still been on a roll, particularly in the USA, Canada and Australia. Rare patterns, unusual colorways and experimental or trial pieces are highly contested.

The Ohio school, meanwhile, including Rookwood and Roseville, has had a quiet year, with few exciting pieces coming onto the market. However an early Lorelei vase 1902 by Van Briggle, from Colorado, sold at Rago's in January 2017 for $43,750 (£34,700).

George Ohr continues to excite the market with a large vase with ribbon handles fetching $87,500 (£69,500) at Rago's January 2017 sale of the collection of Dr. Martin Eidelberg.

20thC silver has continued to sell well, especially pieces by Charles Robert Ashbee and Omar Ramsden, as are rare and unusual Liberty pieces, particularly those designed by Archibald Knox.

In Art Nouveau glass, it is the big names that continue to sell: Lalique, Gallé, Tiffany, Loetz and Daum. James D. Julia sold a Tiffany dragonfly table lamp for $142,000 (£112,700) and a Lalique 'Sirenes Avec Bouchon' stoppered vase for $17,775 (£14,000).

Bronze and ivory figures by Demêtre Chiparus, Bruno Zach and Ferdinand Preiss have performed extremely well.

The sale of early 20thC furniture has been unspectacular - although when something fresh and with very good provenance appears so do the collectors. Charles Rennie Mackintosh continues to have a strong following.

Top Left: A rare bronze and ivory figure of a dancer, 'Le Grande Escart Respecteux' (The Respectful Splits), cast from a model by Paul Phillipe, modeled gracefully holding the splits pose, on polished black marble base, signed with R & M foundry mark in the cast

11in (28cm) wide

$9,000-10,000　　　　　　**WW**

Above: A large early 20thC French Gallé vase, decorated with trumpet flowers, multi-layered acid-etched cameo glass, signed 'Gallé' on the body, polished bubble or chip to top of rim done in the making of, a few minor scuffs to body

13.5in (34cm) high

$7,500-9,000　　　　　　**DRA**

A Carlton Ware 'Sketching Bird' pattern baluster vase, printed factory marks and inscribed pattern no.3889.

6.25in (16cm) high

$230-280   SWO

A Wiltshaw and Robinson Carlton Ware vase, decorated in a gilt chinoiserie pattern, printed mark.

12.75in (32.5cm) high

$80-100   FLD

A Carlton Ware 'Babylon' vase, model no.4126, printed and painted marks.

10.5in (26.5cm) high

$500-650   WW

A Carlton Ware Rouge Royale 'New Stork' tomb jar and cover, with modeled Dog of Fo finial, with wading herons and trees on a riverbank, printed factory marks, original paper label.

13.75in (35cm) high

$180-250   WW

A Carlton Ware 'Paradise Bird and Tree' vase and cover, pattern no.3144, printed and painted marks, professional restoration to rim.

7.75in (19.5cm) high

$250-400   WW

A rare Carlton Ware 'Chinaland' Temple ginger jar and cover, pattern no.3705, the cover with gilt lion finial and internally decorated with 'Chinaland' mon, printed and painted marks.

12.5in (31.5cm) high

$1,900-2,500   WW

A 1930s Carlton Ware 'Falling Flower and Leaf' jug, gilt transfer and enamel decorated with abstract flowers and foliage over a Rouge Royale ground.

7.75in (20cm) high

$400-500   FLD

A 1930s Carlton Ware 'Barge' pen stand, with enamel and gilt chinoiserie decoration, with an affixed black pen holder, with original Parker sticker to the back, printed script mark.

6.75in (17cm) long

$100-130   FLD

Two Carlton Ware novelty teapots, in the form of ballroom dancing gollies.

9in (23cm) high

$110-150   WHP

A Carlton Ware figure, modeled as a golly riding a bicycle, limited edition 23/50.

10in (25cm) high

$50-60   WHP

A Clarice Cliff Bizarre 'Bonjour' shape sugar sifter, decorated in the 'Aurea' pattern, black printed marks.

c1935   *5in (12.5cm) high*
$250-320   **BELL**

A Clarice Cliff Fantasque Bizarre wall plaque, 'Red Autumn' pattern, printed factory mark, impressed date code.

1931   *13in (33.5cm) diam*
$1,900-2,500   **WW**

A Clarice Cliff 'Orange Autumn' preserve pot, Bizarre marks.

$250-320   **HAN**

A Clarice Cliff conical sugar sifter, 'Applique Avignon' pattern, handpainted with a stylized garden scene, handpainted Applique and Bizarre mark.

c1931   *5.5in (14cm) high*
$3,800-5,000   **FLD**

A Clarice Cliff conical sugar sifter, 'Bridgewater Orange' pattern, handpainted with a stylized landscape, Bizarre mark.

c1934   *5.5in (14cm) high*
$900-1,000   **FLD**

A 1930s Clarice Cliffe Bizarre vase, 'Capri' pattern, shape no.268, printed marks.

7.75in (20cm) high
$180-250   **HW**

A Clarice Cliff Bizarre side plate, 'Circus - Art in Industry' pattern, designed by Dame Laura Knight, highlighted in gilt printed factory marks.

6.75in (17cm) diam
$550-700   **WW**

A Clarice Cliff 'Crocus' 'Athens' jug, Bizarre marks.

$250-320   **HAN**

A Clarice Cliff Bizarre teapot and cover, '8 o'clock' ware, of Bonjour shape, one side decorated with a clock dial, printed marks.

c1936   *5in (13cm) high*
$950-1,100   **BELL**

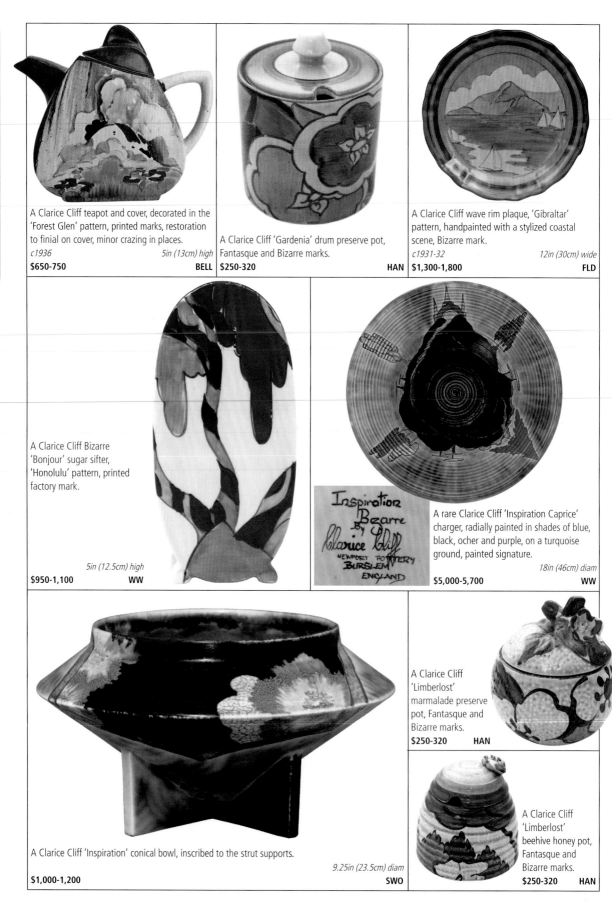

A Clarice Cliff teapot and cover, decorated in the 'Forest Glen' pattern, printed marks, restoration to finial on cover, minor crazing in places.
c1936   *5in (13cm) high*
$650-750   **BELL**

A Clarice Cliff 'Gardenia' drum preserve pot, Fantasque and Bizarre marks.

$250-320   **HAN**

A Clarice Cliff wave rim plaque, 'Gibraltar' pattern, handpainted with a stylized coastal scene, Bizarre mark.
c1931-32   *12in (30cm) wide*
$1,300-1,800   **FLD**

A Clarice Cliff Bizarre 'Bonjour' sugar sifter, 'Honolulu' pattern, printed factory mark.
5in (12.5cm) high
$950-1,100   **WW**

Inspiration Bizarre By Clarice Cliff NEWPORT POTTERY BURSLEM ENGLAND

A rare Clarice Cliff 'Inspiration Caprice' charger, radially painted in shades of blue, black, ocher and purple, on a turquoise ground, painted signature.
18in (46cm) diam
$5,000-5,700   **WW**

A Clarice Cliff 'Limberlost' marmalade preserve pot, Fantasque and Bizarre marks.
$250-320   **HAN**

A Clarice Cliff 'Inspiration' conical bowl, inscribed to the strut supports.
9.25in (23.5cm) diam
$1,000-1,200   **SWO**

A Clarice Cliff 'Limberlost' beehive honey pot, Fantasque and Bizarre marks.
$250-320   **HAN**

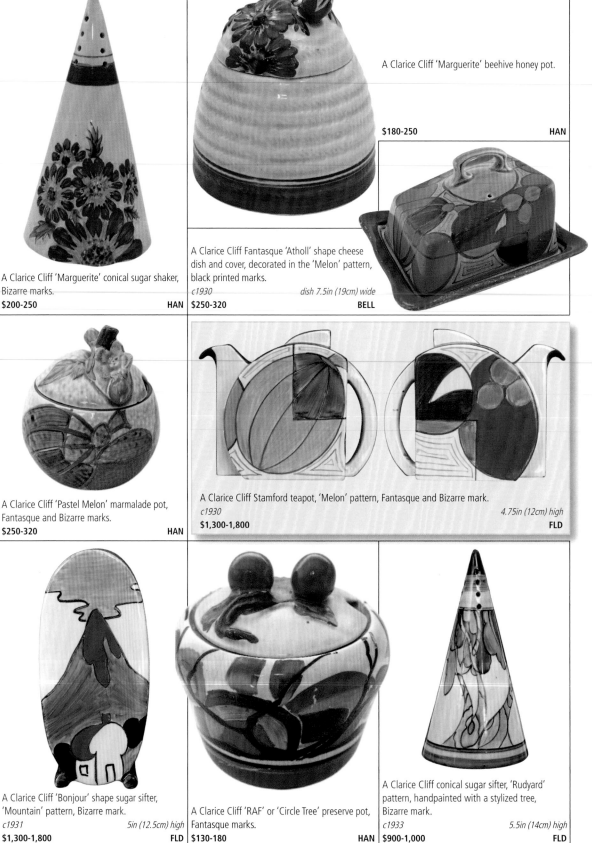

A Clarice Cliff 'Marguerite' beehive honey pot.

$180-250   HAN

A Clarice Cliff 'Marguerite' conical sugar shaker, Bizarre marks.

$200-250   HAN

A Clarice Cliff Fantasque 'Atholl' shape cheese dish and cover, decorated in the 'Melon' pattern, black printed marks.

c1930   *dish 7.5in (19cm) wide*

$250-320   BELL

A Clarice Cliff 'Pastel Melon' marmalade pot, Fantasque and Bizarre marks.

$250-320   HAN

A Clarice Cliff Stamford teapot, 'Melon' pattern, Fantasque and Bizarre mark.

c1930   *4.75in (12cm) high*

$1,300-1,800   FLD

A Clarice Cliff 'Bonjour' shape sugar sifter, 'Mountain' pattern, Bizarre mark.

c1931   *5in (12.5cm) high*

$1,300-1,800   FLD

A Clarice Cliff 'RAF' or 'Circle Tree' preserve pot, Fantasque marks.

$130-180   HAN

A Clarice Cliff conical sugar sifter, 'Rudyard' pattern, handpainted with a stylized tree, Bizarre mark.

c1933   *5.5in (14cm) high*

$900-1,000   FLD

A Clarice Cliff Bizarre 'Bonjour' shape sugar sifter, 'Secrets' pattern, black printed marks.
c1935   5in (13cm) high
$400-450   **BELL**

A Clarice Cliff teapot and cover, of Stamford shape, 'Sunshine' pattern, printed marks.
c1937   4.5in (11.5cm) high
$700-800   **BELL**

A Clarice Cliff 'Teepee' novelty teapot and cover, 'Greetings From Canada' pattern, printed marks.
     7in (17.5cm) high
$400-500   **WW**

A Clarice Cliff Stamford teapot, 'Tennis' pattern, handpainted in an abstract net and line design, Bizarre mark.
c1930   4.75in (12cm) high
$2,500-3,200   **FLD**

A Clarice Cliff conical sugar sifter, 'Tropic' pattern, handpainted with a stylized tree and cottage landscape, Fantasque and Bizarre mark.
c1934   5.5in (14cm) high
$1,500-1,900   **FLD**

A Clarice Cliff vase, 'Applique Windmill' pattern, shape no.280, handpainted with a stylized landscape with large blue windmill, printed Applique and Bizarre mark.
c1930   6in (15.5cm) high
$2,500-3,200   **FLD**

A Clarice Cliff single-handled Isis vase, 'Xanthic' pattern, Bizarre mark.
c1932   9.5in (24.5cm) high
$1,900-2,500   **FLD**

A Clarice Cliff Bizarre pattern vase, painted in orange, green and blue, impressed '268' mark, backstamp rubbed and faint.
     7.75in (20cm) high
$300-400   **ECGW**

A William De Morgan charger, on Davis blank, painted with a galleon at full sail, the foreground with a Classical dolphin, in ruby luster, the reverse painted with stylized foliage impressed mark.

12in (30.5cm) diam

$2,800-3,500   WW

A late 19thC William De Morgan ruby luster earthenware dish, painted with a prowling lioness, faint impressed numeral.

14.5in (37cm) diam

$5,000-6,500   BELL

A Persian-style dish, by William De Morgan (1839-1917), decorated with a panel of flowers within a floral band.

c1885   *8in (20cm) diam*

$3,200-3,800   L&T

A William De Morgan pottery charger, painted with a bird fighting a serpent, unmarked, restored.

14in (36cm) diam

$1,900-2,500   WW

A William De Morgan vase, painted in ruby with fish before stylized foliate palmettes, unsigned, restored neck and foot rims.

This vase is a rare example of a De Morgan vase which has not received its final luster firing.

12.5in (32cm) high

$500-650   WW

A William De Morgan 'Sunset and Moonlight' suite vase, by Fred Passenger, painted with columns of scaly fish amongst waterweed and flowers, painted 'FP' monogram.

10in (25.5cm) high

$10,000-11,000   WW

A William De Morgan pottery vase, painted with flower and foliage, the knop with a frieze of birds, unmarked, restoration to top rim.

13.5in (34cm) high

$1,900-2,500   WW

A William De Morgan 'Sunset and Moonlight' pedestal bowl, by Fred Passenger, painted with a mythical crested bird inside a border of clawed creatures, painted 'FP' monogram.

8.75in (22cm) diam

$7,500-9,000   WW

A William De Morgan 'Cavendish' two-tile panel, set inside turquoise border tiles.

panel 20.75in (53cm) wide

$650-750   WW

A rare William De Morgan watercolor design for a mosaic, on paper, 'Angel with Dove', framed.

See William Gaunt and M.D.E Clayton-Stamm, 'William De Morgan', Studio Vista, page 87, plate 64, for an illustration of the mosaic panel. The mosaic is held in the Kensington & Chelsea Borough collection, given by William De Morgan to the library in 1896. Born in London in 1865, Anna Maria Diana Wilhelmina Pickering (later Stirling) was the younger sister of Evelyn De Morgan and the sister-in-law of William De Morgan.

18in (45.5cm) wide

$1,600-2,000   WW

A large 19thC Doulton Lambeth vase, decorated by Hannah Barlow and Eliza Simmance, with incised deer, 'HB' and 'ES' monograms incised to base, with 'BN Bessie Newbury', with incised numbers '235' and '466.R'.

21.25in (54cm) high

$1,400-1,900 **TRI**

A pair of Doulton Lambeth ponies stoneware vases, by Hannah Barlow, impressed mark and date, incised monograms for Barlow and Elizabeth Fisher.

1887 *8in (20.5cm) high*

$750-900 **HT**

A late 19thC Doulton Lambeth vase, by Frank Butler, incised 'M.M.C.G 1888', impressed mark, incised monogram.

I.E.G. stands for the International Exhibition (of Science, Art and Industry) Glasgow, held in 1888. It is noted that one of the main commercial exhibitors was Doulton & Co.

9.75in (25cm) high

$450-500 **FLD**

A 19thC Doulton Lambeth oil lamp, with a Messengers Patent Duplex No.2 burner, with chimney and frosted glass shade, on a weighted brass plinth.

26.75in (68cm) high

$400-650 **FLD**

A Doulton Lambeth salt-glazed 'Merry Musician' figure, by George Tinworth, impressed factory mark 'DOULTON LAMBETH ENGLAND', 'G.T' monogram to back, instrument and hand restored.

A photographic record survives of the original clay models for fifty-five different figures (including two conductors) playing thirty-seven different instruments. The pieces were in production from the 1880s onward. They were molded and then individually finished.

4.25in (11cm) high

$500-650 **TEN**

A 19thC Doulton Lambeth oil lamp, with a Hinks & Sons No.2 burner, with chimney and frosted glass shade, impressed mark with monogram for Eliza Bowen, dated.

1882 *24.5in (62cm) high*

$400-650 **FLD**

A late 19thC Doulton Lambeth plate, by Edith D. Lupton, incised monogram, impressed mark, dated.

1876 *11.25in (28.5cm) diam*

$450-550 **FLD**

A 19thC Doulton & Co. 'The Lion of the East' wall mask, by Richard Garbe A.R.A., of glazed ivory porcelain, fully marked, limited edition 19/100, impressed '849 41034' and '8', incised '19'.

12.5in (32cm) high

$950-1,100 **TEN**

ESSENTIAL REFERENCE - CHARLES NOKE

Charles John Noke (1858-1941) started at the Doulton Burslem works in 1889 and is credited with turning the company into the leading art manufacturer of the period. For over eighteen months he worked on the magnificent Columbus vase, at almost six feet high and topped by a similar model of the navigator, as well as a few individual 'vellum ware' figures, for the company's pavilion at the Chicago 'World Columbian Exposition' in 1893. A few other figures were added to the range in the following years, but none of these early vellum figures were ever produced in large numbers. Unknown until recently, the free-standing version of the Columbus figure is particularly rare.

A 'vellum' ware Christopher Columbus figure oil lamp, designed by Charles Noke for Doulton & Co., Burslem, original lamp fittings later converted to electricity, crowned Doulton Burslem green mark (used 1891-1902) and painted in red with Robert Allen studio number for January to November 1892, 'RA1286'.

c1892 *24.75in (63cm) high*

$3,200-3,800 **MAB**

DECORATIVE ARTS

A Doulton Art Pottery jug, molded with fish and water lilies.

8.25in (21cm) high

$100-110   **ECGW**

A Doulton stoneware jug, probably by Mark V. Marshall, on pierced Art Nouveau flower stem foot, the handle a dragon modeled climbing the side, unmarked.

9in (22.5cm) wide

$2,500-3,200   **WW**

A Doulton Lambeth stoneware washing line post finial, 'Ship', designed by Gilbert Bayes, made for the St Pancras Housing Association flats, unsigned, chips and repair to finial.

1937   *17in (43cm) high*

$5,000-6,500   **WW**

CLOSER LOOK - 'CHRISTMAS TREE'

This rare stoneware washing post finial, 'Christmas Tree', was designed by Gilbert Bayes, for St Nicholas' Flats.

It is modeled as a tree decorated with baubles and candles, with inscribed banner 'Peace on Earth Good Will to Men'.

It is glazed in colors and signed in the cast Bayes.

Even with old restoration to the banner, its rarity and desirability underpin the value.

A Doulton Lambeth washing post finial.

1937   *21.25in (54cm) high*

$10,000-11,000   **WW**

A Doulton Lambeth stoneware washing-line post finial, 'Thistle', designed by Gilbert Bayes, made for the St Pancras Housing Association Flats, unsigned, minor chips.

1937   *13in (33cm) high*

$2,500-3,200   **WW**

A Doulton Lambeth stoneware washing-line post finial, 'Rose', designed by Gilbert Bayes, with Yorkshire and Lancashire roses, unsigned, minor chips.

13.75in (34.5cm) high

$2,500-3,200   **WW**

A 1930s Doulton Lambeth goat garden ornament, modeled by Francis Pope, impressed factory marks.

9.5in (24cm) high

$1,300-1,800   **TRI**

A 1930s Doulton Lambeth terracotta owl garden ornament, designed by Francis Pope, impressed factory marks.

19.5in (49.5cm) high

$3,200-3,800   **TRI**

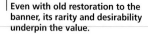

A rare Doulton Lambeth stoneware fountain, 'The Water Baby', by Gilbert Bayes for his own garden, modeled as a young boy holding a large fish, signed 'Gilbert Bayes', restoration to neck.

Provenance: Gilbert Bayes' garden at Boundary Road, late 1920s. See Louise Irvine and Paul Atterbury, 'Gilbert Bayes Sculptor 1872-1953', Richard Dennis/Fine Art Society 1998, page 32, for a contemporary photograph of the fountain in situ at Boundary Road; see page 146 for a version of the stoneware fountain (1927) and page 148 for a bronze maquette for a sculpture of this subject, 1928.

19.5in (49cm) high

$16,000-20,000   **WW**

A Royal Doulton 'A Moorish Minstrel' figure, no.HN34, after the model by Charles Noke, printed mark, impressed numbers and painted with the title 'C.J. Noke Sc., Potted by Doulton &. Co' and 'H.N:34'.

c1920   *13.5in (34.5cm) high*

$700-800   **MAB**

A Royal Doulton 'Carpet Vendor' figure, modeled by Charles Noke, no.HN350, inscribed and numbered '163'.

                              6in (15cm) high

$1,110-1,300   **SWO**

A Royal Doulton 'Pretty Lady' trial figure, the base marked 'Potted by Doulton D.Co'.

This 'Pretty Lady' figure is a prototype for a range of 'Pretty Ladies' made between 1916 and 1938, designed by H. Tittensor. For each figurine developed by Royal Doulton, a few prototypes were made. These would be painted in different colors and shown to the company's design team for consideration. If approved, the model joined the HN collection. Several different versions of the 'Pretty Lady' figure went on to be produced: HN69, 70, 302, 330, 361, 384, 565, 700, 763 and 783. These are decorated in a variety of colors, including blue, gray, and yellow and green. Interestingly, none of the final 'pretty lady' figures were decorated in pink as this trial figure is. The closest example is the red HN384.

                              9.5in (24cm) high

$500-650   **LOC**

A rare Royal Doulton 'Mephisto' figure, no.HN722, printed marks to base, inscribed 'Potted by Doulton & Co', with impressed marks '11 25', minor flaking to the paint on hat, a small chip to the rim of cape's collar.

                              6.75in (17cm) high

$2,500-3,200   **APAR**

A Royal Doulton 'Captain' figure, no.HN778, with printed marks to base, inscribed 'Potted by Doulton & Co', with initials 'FW', impressed marks '7.26', two small chips to the rim of the hat.

                              7in (18cm) high

$650-750   **APAR**

A Royal Doulton figurine, 'Lido Lady', by Leslie Harradine, no.HN1220, printed and painted marks.

c1930   *7in (18cm) high*

$300-400   **HAN**

A Royal Doulton figurine, 'Lady Jester', by Leslie Harradine, no.HN1221, printed and painted marks.

1927-38   *7in (18cm) high*

$1,000-1,200   **HAN**

A Royal Doulton Art Deco figure, 'Ko Ko', by Leslie Harradine, no.HN1286, modeled as an Oriental figure with fan, printed and painted marks.

                              5in (13cm) high

$400-450   **HAN**

A Royal Doulton figurine, 'Sleepyhead', by Peggy Davies, no.HN2114, painted marks.

1952   *5in (13cm) high*

$800-950   **HAN**

A Royal Doulton prototype figure, 'Young Lady with a Fishing Basket', modeled bare breasted, printed with Royal Doulton Prototype mark.

                              9.5in (24cm) high

$650-750   **WW**

A Royal Doulton 'Tower of London' mantel clock, gilt metal frame by Cooper & Sons Norwich, printed green Royal Doulton mark, minor glaze chip.

11.5in (29.5cm) high

$2,500-3,200   WW

A pair of Royal Doulton Lambeth stoneware vases, by Frank A. Butler, with incised monogram signature to the base, no.495.

13.5in (34cm) high

$400-450   APAR

A Royal Doulton stoneware jardinière on stand, by Mark V. Marshall, incised 'M.V.M 918', impressed factory mark and 'X6034' on stand and 'X6084' on jardinière, some damage.

50.75in (129cm) high

$1,500-2,000   TEN

A Royal Doulton loving cup, commemorating King George and Queen Elizabeth, no.737/2000, with certificate.

10.25in (26cm) high

$250-320   PW

A Royal Doulton loving cup, commemorating King George V and Queen Mary, no.565/1000, without certificate.

10.25in (26cm) high

$150-230   PW

A Royal Doulton flambé tiger, designed by Charles Noke, black printed factory mark and signed 'Noke'.

14in (36cm) long

$800-950   TEN

A Royal Doulton flambé elephant, modeled with trunk curled down with two ivory colored tusks signed 'Noke' to one foot, minor chip.

12.5in (32cm) high

$700-800   PW

A Royal Doulton flambé vase, decorated with landscapes, impressed '7163', minor chip to the foot.

12.25in (31cm) high

$130-180   PW

A 1920s Royal Doulton 'Sung' landscape vase, factory marks to base, signed 'Sung and Noke'.

6.75in (17cm) high

$550-700   TRI

A 1910s Fulper early Vasekraft vessel, with Café au Lait flambé glaze, with rectangular ink stamp, short glazed-over firing line to base.

This vessel has a 1915 San Francisco Exposition label to body, and also remnants of the original Fulper paper label.

12.25in (31cm) high
$6,500-7,500 DRA

A 1910s Fulper urn, with mirror black glaze, with vertical racetrack ink stamp, a few minor grinding chips around edge of base.

12in (30.5cm) high
$750-900 DRA

A 1910s Fulper vase, with blue mat flambé glaze, with rectangular ink stamp, one minor stilt pull to edge of base, some burst glaze bubbles.

13in (33cm) high
$750-900 DRA

A 1910s Fulper vase, with fine mission verde or leopard skin crystalline glaze, with vertical racetrack stamp, a few minor grinding chips.

12in (30.5cm) high
$1,000-1,250 DRA

A Fulper melon vase, with green mat crystalline glaze, with raised racetrack mark.

1915-20 *14in (35.5cm) high*
$7,500-9,000 DRA

A Fulper famille rose vase, with famille rose glaze, with raised racetrack mark, with original Vasekraft paper label, professional restoration to rim.

1915-20 *13.5in (34.5cm) high*
$2,500-3,200 DRA

A Fulper vase, with copperdust crystalline glaze, with raised racetrack mark.

1915-20 *11.5in (29cm) high*
$1,900-2,500 DRA

A Fulper urn, with mission verde glaze, with raised racetrack mark, a few light scratches to rim.

1915-20 *11in (28cm) high*
$1,000-1,250 DRA

A Fulper vase, with cat's-eye flambé glaze, with raised racetrack mark, grinding chips, one small one visible from side, several small bubbles.

1915-20 *9in (23cm) high*
$650-750 DRA

A Fulper vase, with copperdust crystalline and green flambé glaze, incised racetrack mark, three grinding chips, none showing from exterior.

1915-20 *10in (25.5cm) wide*
$1,600-2,000 DRA

ESSENTIAL REFERENCE - GEORGE OHR

George Ohr (1857-1918) called himself the 'Mad Potter of Biloxi'. He dug his own clay from the banks of the Tchoutacabouffa River and created unconventional pieces. Ohr folded, dented, crumpled and squashed the clay to give his 'mud babies' an asymmetrical and abstract appearance. He was known for being an eccentric owing to his unusual pottery style, his distinctive appearance and the strange engravings on some of his pieces. One reads 'Mary had a little Lamb & Ohr has a little Pottery.' He was known to sign himself 'George Ohr, MD' - 'MD', he said, standing for 'Mud Dauber'. His experimental pieces now usually fetch over $12,000 and often well over $90,000.

A large crumpled vase, by George Ohr, fine gunmetal and aventurine hare's-fur glaze, stamped 'G.E. OHR Biloxi, Miss.'.
c1900   *5in (12.5cm) high*
$16,000-19,000   **DRA**

A dimpled vase, by George Ohr, with ruffled rim, brown, green, and gunmetal glaze, stamped 'G.E. OHR Biloxi, Miss.'.
c1900   *6.5in (16.5cm) high*
$13,000-16,000   **DRA**

A crumpled and torn vessel, by George Ohr, brown and ocher speckled glaze, stamped 'G.E. OHR Biloxi, Miss.', two glazed-over firing lines.
c1900   *5in (12.5cm) high*
$13,000-18,000   **DRA**

A bowl, by George Ohr, with in-body twist, raspberry, green, ocher and gunmetal sponged-on glaze, stamped 'GEO. E. OHR BILOXI, MISS'.
1895-96   *6.5in (16.5cm) high*
$10,000-11,000   **DRA**

A vase with ruffled rim, by George Ohr, with ocher and brown speckled glaze, stamped 'G.E. OHR Biloxi, Miss'.
c1900   *4.25in (11cm) high*
$4,500-5,000   **DRA**

A vase with ruffled rim, by George Ohr, with raspberry glaze, stamped 'G.E. OHR Biloxi, Miss.', incised 'MOBILE ALABAMA CLAY', professional restoration around rim.
c1900   *4in (10cm) high*
$4,500-5,000   **DRA**

A cup with double ear handle, by George Ohr, gunmetal over green and ocher glaze, with script signature.
1898-1900   *4.5in (11.5cm) high*
$3,200-3,800   **DRA**

A bisque vessel, 'Progeny', by George Ohr, with thirteen ear handles, script signature, illegible handwriting to most handles, one handle broken and reglued, some restoration.
c1900   *10.5in (26.5cm) high*
$21,000-25,000   **DRA**

A large vase, by George Ohr, with ruffles, in-body twist, and pedestal base, green, brown and gunmetal speckled glaze, stamped 'G.E. OHR Biloxi, Miss.'.
c1900   *6.5in (16.5cm) high*
$10,000-13,000   **DRA**

A Goldscheider pottery figure of an exotic dancer, by Rose, model no.5513, impressed and printed marks, signed in the case 'Rose'.

5.5in (14cm) high

$650-750   **WW**

A Goldscheider pottery model of a dancer, designed by Josef Lorenzl, model no.7195, printed and impressed marks, facsimile signature, professional restoration to the hands.

15in (38cm) high

$1,100-1,400   **WW**

A Goldscheider pottery model of a dancer, designed by Josef Lorenzl, model no.6227, impressed marks, facsimile signature.

13in (33cm) high

$1,600-2,300   **WW**

A Goldscheider pottery figure of a woman in a butterfly dress, cast from a model by Josef Lorenzl, model no.5715, impressed and printed marks, facsimile signature to hem of dress, minor professional restoration to one hand.

15.25in (39cm) high

$2,500-3,200   **WW**

A Goldscheider pottery figure, 'The Captured Bird', cast from a model by Josef Lorenzl, model no.5230, impressed and printed marks, minor professional restoration to tips of fingers.

18.5in (47cm) high

$2,500-3,200   **WW**

A Goldscheider pottery model of a dancer, by Stefan Dakon, model no.5625, impressed and printed marks, signed Dakon in the cast on the vase of flowers, professionally restored arms and neck.

18.5in (47cm) high

$1,900-2,500   **WW**

Judith Picks

This figure embodies the style and the modernism of the Art Deco movement. This dancer was a thoroughly modern girl - the 'bob' hair cut, the revealing dress with spider webs and butterflies. Lorenzl was born on 1 September 1882 in Vienna, Austria and died there on 15 August 1950. He started his career working at a foundry at the Vienna Arsenal where he learned the techniques of bronze casting, and produced many bronze and ivory sculptures. He was captivated by the female form and was known for his shapely dancing girls with long, elegant legs and closed eyes. They were often signed 'Lor', 'Renz', 'Enzl'. The large majority of Lorenzl's figurines were attached to Brazilian green onyx plinths. As here, Lorenzl's talents also extended to being a gifted ceramicist, producing many pieces for Goldscheider. This 'The Butterfly Girl' was modeled after the famous dancer Niddy Impekoven from the 1920s.

A Goldscheider pottery figure, 'The Butterfly Girl', modeled by Josef Lorenzl, with printed marks, labelled and impressed '5960-560-16'.

15.5in (39.5cm) high

$2,500-3,200   **SWO**

A Goldscheider pottery figure, 'The Captured Bird', by Josef Lorenzl, printed and incised marks, fingers restored.

18.25in (46.5cm) high

$2,800-3,500   **SWO**

A Goldscheider pottery figure of a Venetian lady, designed by Joseph Lorenzl, model no.6557, with a borzoi by her side, impressed mark, incised numbers '6557/45/11'.

c1931   *12in (30.5cm) high*

$500-650   **MAB**

A Goldscheider pottery model of a woman with a setter dog, designed by Stefan Dakon, model no.6756, impressed marks, minor glaze chips, hairline to hind-leg.

See Ora Pinhas, 'Goldscheider', Richard Dennis, page 132, for a color variation of this figure suggested to be Marlene Dietrich.

12in (30.5cm) high

$1,600-2,000   **WW**

A Goldscheider Art Deco earthenware figure, with stamped and impressed maker's marks.

c1930   *12.25in (31cm) high*

$700-800   **L&T**

A Goldscheider pottery model of a 'Ballet Girl', by Josef Lorenzl, with gilt-metal lamp base fitting, impressed factory marks and Lorenzl signature, small chips.

10.75in (27cm) high

$1,300-1,900   **WW**

A Goldscheider table lamp, designed by E. Tell, modeled as a nude maiden holding a clam shell tray, glazed mat green impressed factory mark.

See Ora Pinhas, 'Goldscheider, A Catalogue of Selected Models', Richard Dennis, model no.2046, c1898, artist E. Tell, for an example of the model.

22in (56cm) high

$650-750   **WW**

A Goldscheider model of an Oriental lady feeding a fawn, designed by Marcel Goldscheider, impressed marks, numbered '386', heavily restored.

10.25in (26cm) high

$400-500   **CHEF**

A Goldscheider bust of an Arab woman, by D.Rochella, model no.1340, impressed '1340/41/40 REPRODUCTION RESERVEE FRIEDRICH GOLDSCHEIDER WEIN', some rubbing.

c1900   *19.75in (50cm) high*

$2,300-2,800   **TEN**

A Goldscheider pottery wall mask, 'Girl with a Fan', model no.6542, impressed and with printed marks.

10.25in (26cm) high

$500-650   **WW**

A 1930s Goldscheider pottery wall mask, depicting an Art Deco female bust holding a yellow mask, indistinctly marked.

11in (28cm) high

$400-500   **BELL**

A Goldschieder glazed terracotta bust of Eva, by Rudolf Knörlein (1902-1988), printed and incised maker's marks 'GOLDSCHIEDER/ WIEN/ MADE IN AUSTRIA/ 6305'.

c1931   *9.5in (24cm) high*

$1,000-1,250   **L&T**

ESSENTIAL REFERENCE - GRUEBY FAIENCE COMPANY

William Henry Grueby (1867-1925) began working at the Low Art Tile Works in Chelsea, Massachusetts. In 1894 Grueby started the Grueby Faience Company in Boston, MA. Grueby developed his own glazes and created a mat finish very different to the glossy glazes popular at the time. The pottery was reorganized and incorporated in 1897. Pottery was made by hand and decorations were added or modeled mainly by young girls. The company made two types of

pottery - architectural tiles and art pottery. In 1907 Grueby Pottery Company was incorporated. In 1909, Grueby Faience went bankrupt. Then Grueby founded the Grueby Faience and Tile Company. The Grueby Pottery closed about 1911 while the tile company burned in 1913 but was rebuilt and worked until 1920.

A Grueby vase, with ruffled rim and yellow buds, glazed-over circular stamp, partial paper label, professional restoration to rim.
c1905 8in (20.5cm) high
$1,900-2,500 DRA

A Grueby vase, with yellow buds, with circular 'Faience' stamp, incised 'N' inside circle, one chip to base, some crazing lines around rim.
c1905 10.75in (27.5cm) high
$7,000-7,500 DRA

A Grueby early floor vase, with leaves and buds, with partial circular 'Faience' stamp, professional restoration to chip at rim.
c1905 23in (58.5cm) high
$10,000-11,000 DRA

An early Grueby bulbous vase, carved with leaves, with circular 'Faience' stamp '152' and artist cipher, drill hole to base.
c1900 12in (30.5cm) high
$3,800-4,400 DRA

A Grueby gourd vase, with leaves, with circular pottery stamp '224' and artist's initials.
c1905 7.75in (19.5cm) high
$6,500-7,000 DRA

A Grueby vase, with leaves, with circular pottery stamp, incised 'ERF 4-6'.
c1905 8.5in (21.5cm) high
$2,500-3,200 DRA

A Grueby cabinet vase, with leaves, with glazed-over mark, a few flecks.
c1905 4in (10cm) high
$1,900-2,500 DRA

A 1910s Grueby framed trivet, decorated in cuerda seca with penguins, in brass frame, tile monogrammed 'O.C.'.
tile 4in (10cm) wide
$3,200-3,800 DRA

A Grueby copper trivet, tile decorated in cuenca with seagulls, probable mark obscured by mount.
c1905 4in (10cm) wide
$1,100-1,400 DRA

DECORATIVE ARTS

ESSENTIAL REFERENCE - LENCI

Lenci was founded in Turin, Italy, in 1919, by Helen Konig Scavini and her husband Enrico. The name 'Lenci' is an acronym for the company's motto 'Ludus Est Nobis Constanter Industria' ('Play is Our Constant Work'). It is also thought to be a variation on Konig Scavini's nicknames 'Lenchen' and 'Helenchen'. The factory manufactured dolls from 1919, adding ceramic figurines to their range in 1928. Lenci stylized Art Deco figurines typified the Art Deco style. They were much admired by Walt Disney, who allegedly tried to persuade Konig Scavini to work for him. The company was taken over in 1937. Ceramic production ceased in 1964. The factory closed in 2002. Lenci figurines can now fetch very high prices. One 1930 Lenci figurine sold at Christies in 2005 for $48,400.

A Lenci pottery figure, 'Colpo il Vento', designed by Helen Konig Scavini, model no.363, modeled as a sophisticated woman with a hat caught in the wind, painted marks, professional restoration to back of dress.

15in (38cm) high

$9,000-10,000 WW

A Lenci pottery figure, 'Me ne Infischio - La Studentessa', designed by Helen Konig Scavini, the young girl modeled perched on a book shelf, painted marks, impressed signature, professional restoration to head.

15in (38cm) high

$9,500-10,500 WW

A Lenci figure, 'Nella', by Helen Konig Scavini, modeled as a girl seated on a bench beside an open book, a frog seated behind, incised to the reverse, inscribed 'Lenci Made in Italy 11-4?1'.

9in (23cm) high

$6,500-7,500 SWO

A Lenci pottery figure, 'Capri', designed by Fanni Giuntoli, modeled as a young girl, painted marks, remains of paper retail label, professional restoration to legs.

13.25in (33.5cm) high

$4,500-5,000 WW

A Lenci pottery figure group, 'Amanti sul Tronco', designed by Giovanni Grande, modeled as two young lovers embracing, painted marks, dated '4-4-30'.

12.5in (31.5cm) high

$5,000-5,700 WW

A 1930s Lenci figure, 'Nuda con Uccellino su Piatto', by Helen Konig Scavini, modeled as a young nude kneeling with a small bird in her hair, on a platter dish, marked 'Lenci' to the base, Torino 7-1396-XIV, with original Lenci sticker.

12.5in (32cm) high

$4,500-5,000 FLD

A Lenci pottery figure, 'Maternita', designed by Helen Konig Scavini, painted marks, impressed signature, minor professional restoration.

12.25in (31cm) high

$2,300-2,800 WW

A Lenci earthenware figure, modeled as a young girl, with an open bag and bird at her feet, signed 'Lenci TORINO ITALIA', restored.

15in (38cm) high

$300-450 TEN

A Joseph Holdcroft majolica model of a pug, minor restoration to the ears.
1850-99   *11.5in (29cm) high*
$1,300-1,900   **WW**

ESSENTIAL REFERENCE - MINTON MAJOLICA

In 1851, Herbert Minton and his French ceramic chemist, Leon Arnoux, presented 'majolica' at the Great Exhibition at the Crystal Palace in London. The richly colored majolica inspired Minton artists to develop art revival styles similar to those of the Renaissance, Palissy design, Gothic revival and medieval styles, 'naturalism' (by far the most prolific), Oriental and Islamic styles, and figural pieces, both human and mythological. The shapes, such as cache pots, urns, fountains and umbrella stands were made for the garden or conservatory. The Victorian dinner table highlighted the growing interest in a vast variety of shapes and foods; oyster, crab and lobster plates and fish platters were popular. There were also game designs illustrating the contents of the game dish, humorous and bizarre tea pots, cheese bells with cows as finials while pitchers of every size and every naturalistic design poured water, milk and cream.

A George Jones majolica salmon fish tureen and cover, impressed registration lozenge.
c1871   *19.25in (49cm) long*
$700-800   **DN**

A George Jones majolica mackerel oval fish tureen and cover, impressed registration lozenge, light wear to top of fish.
c1871   *15in (38.5cm) long*
$500-650   **DN**

A late 19thC Minton majolica teapot and cover, with a snail finial above the monkey-formed handle, clutching reins around the cockerel-formed spout, impressed 'MINTON/ 624', with a year cipher.
9in (23cm) wide
$2,500-3,200   **L&T**

A Minton's majolica teapot and cover, humorously modeled as a portly Oriental gentleman.
5.25in (13.5cm) high
$500-650   **WHP**

A pair of Minton majolica toby jugs, 'The Barrister' and his companion 'Lady with Fan', impressed marks, model nos.1139/40 and year ciphers.
11.25in (28.5cm) high
$700-800   **MAB**

A Minton majolica game pie tureen and cover, molded with game birds and foliage, with stamped marks.
c1865   *12.25in (31cm) wide*
$650-750   **BELL**

A Minton majolica game pie dish, cover and liner, the cover with a hound on a gun, the tureen with game, impressed marks, with date code.
1861   *16.5in (42cm) wide*
$950-1,100   **TEN**

A Minton majolica rabbit and lettuce-leaf comport, impressed marks, shape no.1451, hairline firing faults, date code.

1861

$3,800-4,400 DN

A Minton majolica crab tureen and cover, with molded seaweed handle, impressed 'M' to base, with year cipher mark.

1859 *15.75in (40cm) wide*

$2,500-3,200 BELL

A Minton majolica jardinière, with six vertical straps with lion ring masks terminating in paw feet, damaged.

14.25in (36cm) high

$140-190 WHP

A Minton majolica oyster stand, model no.636, impressed marks, small rim chip and some surface cracks, stand and metal fitting a bit rickety.

c1860 *12.25in (31cm) high*

$3,800-5,000 DN

A Sarreguemine majolica humorous figure of a monkey, seated on a curved edition of Darwin's 'Origin of Species', impressed marks to base, no.213.

7.5in (19cm) high

$300-400 APAR

A 19thC Villeroy & Boch majolica dish, with two dachshund puppies playing tug of war with a slipper, printed mark.

8.75in (22cm) wide

$350-400 WW

A pair of early 20thC majolica cheese domes and stands, typically modeled with leaves and floral sprays, one with a matching stand, the other with an associated stand.

8.75in (22cm) high

$300-400 L&T

An early 20thC majolica elephant planter, trunk restored.

11.5in (29cm) high

$180-250 BE

An Art Deco majolica figure group of a woman with deer, signed in the cast, Polbert.

20.75in (53cm) wide

$80-90 HAN

Judith Picks

'When you enter the shop... you find yourself in a dim-lit passage with crowded shelves of stoneware jugs carved into leering, laughing, grinning and ogling heads, jostling with the most impossible, and most fascinating, pot birds with strangely anthropological expressions...'

This is how Holbrook Jackson described his first visit to a small pottery situated in Brownlow Street, Holborn in 1910. Just like Mr Jackson, I find myself captivated by the eccentric creations of the four Martin Brothers.

Production began in 1873 with a kiln at the family home in Fulham and expanded in 1877 with a move to a disused soap works on the canal on Havelock Road in Southall, where production continued until 1923. Eldest brother Robert Wallace modeled the figures, Walter fired the kiln, mixed the glazes and threw the pots, Edwin was chiefly the decorator, while youngest brother Charles ran the City shop. He was wildly eccentric, and hated to part with the pots, hiding the best under the floorboards and turning away many a prospective customer. Eventually, the shop burned down and the brothers lost their stock.

'The Potter', a portrait color photograph on artist board, of Walter Martin, modeled throwing a large pot in the studio, framed applied title label to reverse and annotated 'Southall'.

11.25in (28.5cm) wide

$900-1,000 WW

A Martin Brothers double bird glazed stoneware jar and cover, modeled by Robert Wallace Martin, one bird with its wing on the other and looking into each other's eyes, inscribed '11.12.1914' and 'R W Martin & Bro. Southall'.

1914 *6.25in (16cm) high*

$32,000-38,000 SWO

CLOSER LOOK - WALLY BIRD

It is modeled by Robert Wallace Martin who had worked as an architectural sculptor.

He is modeled with a very disgruntled look - much admired by collectors.

It is a saltglaze stoneware, a high-temperature firing method where salt was thrown into the kiln, in order to fuse with the clay.

He has a shaved feather pate and broad pointed beak, with particularly large talons.

A Martin Brothers stoneware 'Monk' bird jar and cover, incised 'Martin Bros London & Southall 2.1895' to head and 'Martin Bros London & Southall', small chip to underside of eyebrow.

1895 *12.5in (32cm) high*

$50,000-60,000 WW

A salt-glazed stoneware 'Brother Jonathan' and 'John Bull' jug, by R. W. Martin & Brothers, incised with '5-1899/ R.W. Martin + Bros/ London + Southall'.

1899 *10in (25.5cm) high*

$32,000-38,000 PHI

A Martin Brothers stoneware face jug, modeled in relief with a smiling face, the reverse a similar smiling face, incised 'R W Martin & Bros London & Southall'.

5.5in (13.5cm) high

$3,200-3,800 WW

A Martin Brothers stoneware face jug, modeled to one side with a merry smiling face, the reverse with a debauched expression, base incised 'R W Martin & Bros London & Southall'.

This is accompanied with a letter describing the jug and the two distinct faces and quoting 'If Sinners Entice Thee Consent Thou Not'.

9in (23cm) high

$8,000-9,500 WW

A Martin Brothers stoneware spoon warmer, by Robert Wallace Martin, the ovoid body with large gaping mouth, carved snout and eyes, its tail rolled back to form a loop handle, incised 'R W Martin London & Southall 79'.

It is believed that this grotesque was purchased directly from the Martin Brothers.

1879 *5.75in (14.5cm) high*

$19,000-25,000 WW

A Martin Brothers stoneware grotesque spoon warmer, depicting a reptile creature, marked 'R W Martin Bros., London & Southhall, 190', some repairs to handle.

This example is particularly unusual as it has two lower teeth.

9.75in (25cm) long

$7,500-9,000 LOCK

A Martin Brothers stoneware grotesque jug, by Robert Wallace Martin, with rodent head with gaping mouth, incised 'Martin 1880, London' and unusual impressed 'Martin' mark, applied paper collection label, small repair to one foot.

1880   *4.5in (11.5cm) high*
$4,400-5,700   **WW**

A Martin Brothers stoneware Toby jar and cover, by Robert Wallace Martin, incised to neck 'Southall 2-1890', applied paper collection label.

1890   *5.75in (14.5cm) high*
$28,000-35,000   **WW**

A Martin Brothers stoneware gourd vase, by Edwin and Walter Martin, incised '11-1905 Martin Bros London & Southall'.

1905   *10.25in (26cm) high*
$1,110-1,300   **WW**

A Martin Brothers glazed stoneware vase, the body with a tube-lined glaze, incised '8.1904 Martin Bros London and Southall'.

1904   *9in (23cm) high*
$2,500-3,200   **SWO**

A Martin Brothers stoneware vase, by Edwin and Walter Martin, incised with finches perched on blackberry stems, incised '9-1899 Martin Bros London & Southall'.

1899   *9.75in (24.5cm) high*
$3,200-3,800   **WW**

A Martin Brothers stoneware bird vase, by Edwin and Walter Martin, incised '3 - 1898 Martin Bros London & Southall', small chip to rim.

1898   *8.25in (21cm) high*
$3,200-4,400   **WW**

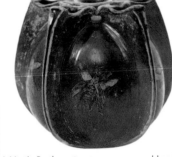

A Martin Brothers stoneware poppy seed-head vase, by Edwin and Walter Martin, incised with flying insects, incised '2 - 1900 Martin Bros London & Southall', applied paper collection label.

1900   *5.5in (14cm) high*
$7,000-7,500   **WW**

A Martin Brothers stoneware vase, by Robert Wallace Martin, incised with a grotesque dragon, incised '8-1889 R W Martin & Bros London & Southall'.

8in (20cm) high
$3,800-4,400   **WW**

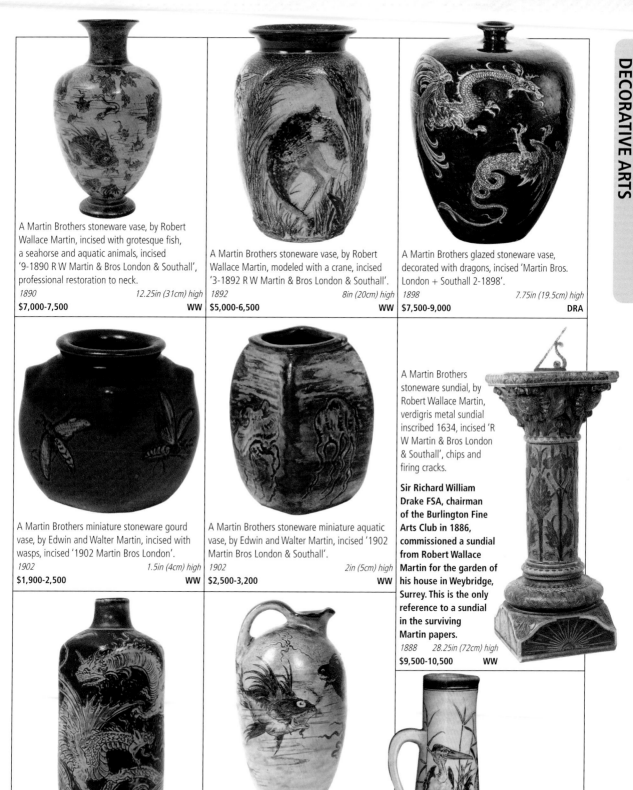

A Martin Brothers stoneware vase, by Robert Wallace Martin, incised with grotesque fish, a seahorse and aquatic animals, incised '9-1890 R W Martin & Bros London & Southall', professional restoration to neck.
1890   *12.25in (31cm) high*
$7,000-7,500   **WW**

A Martin Brothers stoneware vase, by Robert Wallace Martin, modeled with a crane, incised '3-1892 R W Martin & Bros London & Southall'.
1892   *8in (20cm) high*
$5,000-6,500   **WW**

A Martin Brothers glazed stoneware vase, decorated with dragons, incised 'Martin Bros. London + Southall 2-1898'.
1898   *7.75in (19.5cm) high*
$7,500-9,000   **DRA**

A Martin Brothers miniature stoneware gourd vase, by Edwin and Walter Martin, incised with wasps, incised '1902 Martin Bros London'.
1902   *1.5in (4cm) high*
$1,900-2,500   **WW**

A Martin Brothers stoneware miniature aquatic vase, by Edwin and Walter Martin, incised '1902 Martin Bros London & Southall'.
1902   *2in (5cm) high*
$2,500-3,200   **WW**

A Martin Brothers stoneware sundial, by Robert Wallace Martin, verdigris metal sundial inscribed 1634, incised 'R W Martin & Bros London & Southall', chips and firing cracks.

Sir Richard William Drake FSA, chairman of the Burlington Fine Arts Club in 1886, commissioned a sundial from Robert Wallace Martin for the garden of his house in Weybridge, Surrey. This is the only reference to a sundial in the surviving Martin papers.
1888   *28.25in (72cm) high*
$9,500-10,500   **WW**

A Martin Brothers stoneware ewer, by Edwin and Walter Martin, incised with dragons fighting, incised '2-1895 Martin Bros London & Southall'.
1895   *6.5in (16.5cm) high*
$3,800-5,000   **WW**

A Martin Brothers stoneware jug, by Edwin and Walter Martin, incised with grotesque fish, octopus, eels and other water creatures, incised '6-1897 Martin Brothers London & Southall', professionally restored.
1897   *10.25in (26cm) high*
$3,800-5,000   **WW**

A Martin Brothers stoneware bird jug, by Edwin and Walter Martin, incised '10 1903 Martin Bros London & Southall'.
1903 8.25in (21cm) high
$7,500-9,000   **WW**

A Minton's 'Cloisonné' fan vase, designed by Dr Christopher Dresser, painted with a crab, a butterfly, below tube vases with peacock feathers, 'T Goode' retailers mark.

6.5in (16.5cm) high

$7,000-8,000 WW

A Minton's Art Pottery studio plaque, by Henry Stacey-Marks, one from the series of 'The Seven Ages of Man' based on Shakespeares's character Jaques in 'As You Like It', impressed Mintons and inscribed monogram and '26' and date code for 1874.

1874 *20.25in (51.5cm) wide*

$2,500-3,200 SWO

A pair of Minton pâte-sur-pâte vases, by Lawrence Birks, one signed with the monogram 'LB' in green, gilt marks, impressed mark to one, some restoration.

Lawrence Birks was apprenticed to Marc Louis Solon at Minton from 1877 and stayed at the factory until 1894. He was one of few artists at Minton allowed to sign his work.

c1880-90 *15.5in (39.5cm) high*

$2,500-3,200 WW

An early 20thC Minton parian pâte-sur-pâte plaque 'Tribute to Love' by Louis Marc Emmanuel Solon (1835-1913), signed 'L. SOLON'.

10.5in (27cm) high

$6,500-7,000 DN

A pair of Minton Secessionist vases, marked, Minton printed factory 'No 8 H', one with chip to the rim.

9.75in (25cm) high

$650-750 ECGW

A Minton's Secessionist floor vase, designed by John Wadsworth and Leon Solon, impressed marks.

18.5in (47cm) high

$750-900 WW

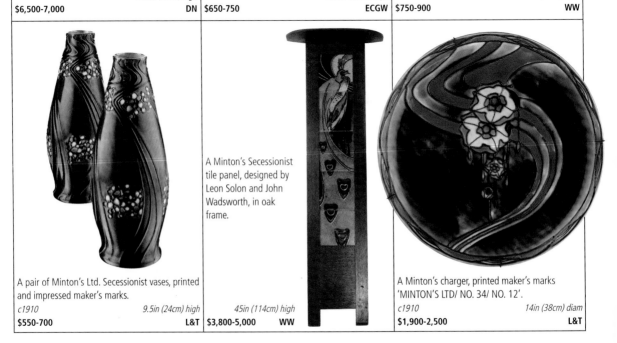

A pair of Minton's Ltd. Secessionist vases, printed and impressed maker's marks.

c1910 *9.5in (24cm) high*

$550-700 L&T

A Minton's Secessionist tile panel, designed by Leon Solon and John Wadsworth, in oak frame.

45in (114cm) high

$3,800-5,000 WW

A Minton's charger, printed maker's marks 'MINTON'S LTD/ NO. 34/ NO. 12'.

c1910 *14in (38cm) diam*

$1,900-2,500 L&T

ESSENTIAL REFERENCE - MOORCROFT

William Moorcroft (1872-1945) studied at the Royal College of Art, London. In 1897 he began to work for Staffordshire pottery manufacturers James Macintyre & Co. Ltd. and within a year was in charge of the company's art pottery studio. His early designs included the distinctive 'Florian' ware, decorated with bright flower blossoms, foliage and peacock feathers. He founded W. Moorcroft Ltd. in 1913. His famous patterns include 'Pansy', 'Moonlit Blue', 'Hazeldene' and many others. His work is distinctive for his use of 'tube-lining', piping thin lines of clay to create relief patterns to be filled in with glaze. His pottery was sold by Liberty of London, Harrods and Tiffany & Co., and in 1928 he was appointed 'Potter to H.M. The Queen'. On William's death in 1945, his son Walter took over the company. Moorcroft is still open today and operates from the same factory in Stoke-on-Trent where the company was founded over 100 years ago.

A Moorcroft Macintyre 'Florian' ware minature vase, in 'Alhambra' pattern, minor wear to gilding.
c1903   *2.5in (6.5cm) high*
$700-800   TEN

A Moorcroft Macintyre 'Green and Gold Florian' vase, printed mark, painted green signature.
8.75in (22cm) high
$500-650   WW

A Moorcroft Macintyre 'Florian' ware vase.
5in (12.5cm) high
$800-950   SWO

A Moorcroft 'Florian' ware vase, in 'Lilac' pattern, brown printed marks and a green signed mark.
c1902   *9in (23cm) high*
$650-750   BELL

A Moorcroft vase, in 'Revived Cornflower' pattern, green painted signature, impressed factory marks and 'Burslem 73', pin head to top rim, crazed all over.
c1913   *13.25in (33.5cm) high*
$3,200-4,400   TEN

A Moorcroft vase, in 'Revived Cornflower' pattern, green painted signature, impressed '57', crazed all over.
c1912   *12.5in (32cm) high*
$9,500-10,500   TEN

A Moorcroft Macintyre vase, in 'Revived Cornflower' pattern, printed mark and signed in green.
10.25in (26cm) high
$1,500-2,300   FLD

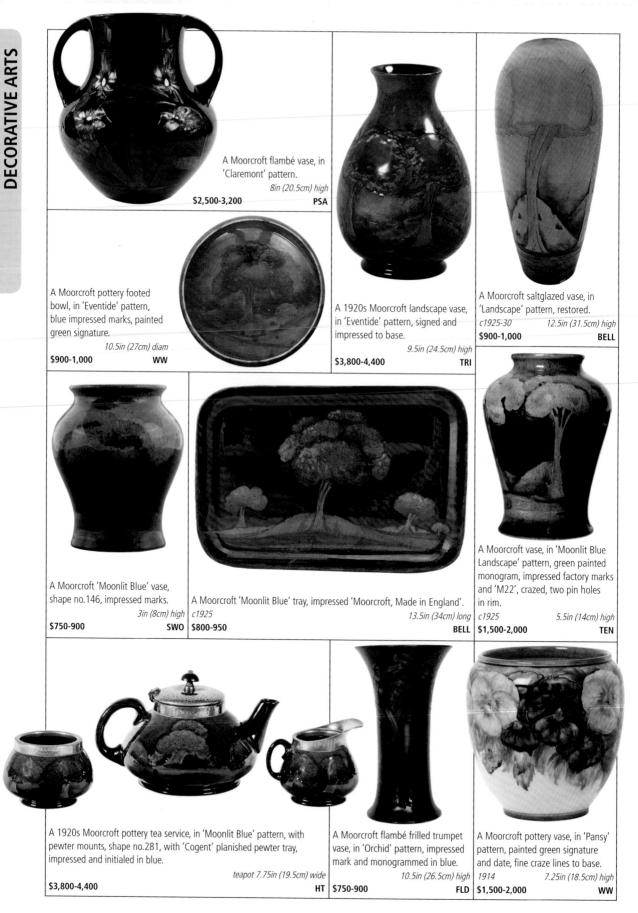

A Moorcroft flambé vase, in 'Claremont' pattern.

8in (20.5cm) high

$2,500-3,200   PSA

A Moorcroft pottery footed bowl, in 'Eventide' pattern, blue impressed marks, painted green signature.

10.5in (27cm) diam

$900-1,000   WW

A 1920s Moorcroft landscape vase, in 'Eventide' pattern, signed and impressed to base.

9.5in (24.5cm) high

$3,800-4,400   TRI

A Moorcroft saltglazed vase, in 'Landscape' pattern, restored.

c1925-30   *12.5in (31.5cm) high*

$900-1,000   BELL

A Moorcroft 'Moonlit Blue' vase, shape no.146, impressed marks.

3in (8cm) high

$750-900   SWO

A Moorcroft 'Moonlit Blue' tray, impressed 'Moorcroft, Made in England'.

c1925   *13.5in (34cm) long*

$800-950   BELL

A Moorcroft vase, in 'Moonlit Blue Landscape' pattern, green painted monogram, impressed factory marks and 'M22', crazed, two pin holes in rim.

c1925   *5.5in (14cm) high*

$1,500-2,000   TEN

A 1920s Moorcroft pottery tea service, in 'Moonlit Blue' pattern, with pewter mounts, shape no.281, with 'Cogent' planished pewter tray, impressed and initialed in blue.

teapot 7.75in (19.5cm) wide

$3,800-4,400   HT

A Moorcroft flambé frilled trumpet vase, in 'Orchid' pattern, impressed mark and monogrammed in blue.

10.5in (26.5cm) high

$750-900   FLD

A Moorcroft pottery vase, in 'Pansy' pattern, painted green signature and date, fine craze lines to base.

1914   *7.25in (18.5cm) high*

$1,500-2,000   WW

A Moorcroft pottery vase, in 'Peacock Feathers' pattern, painted blue signature, professionally restored rim.

8in (20.5cm) high

$650-750   WW

A pair of early 20thC Moorcroft vases, in 'Pomegranate' pattern, signed and stamped 'Made for Liberty & Co'.

8.25in (21cm) high

$4,500-5,000   TRI

A 1930s Moorcroft pottery vase, in 'Pomegranate' pattern, with impressed maker's marks 'MOORCROFT BURSLEM', signed in green 'W. MOORCROFT'.

10.25in (26cm) high

$550-700   L&T

A Moorcroft vsdr, for Liberty & Co., in 'Spanish' pattern, printed mark and signed in green, restored.

6.5in (16.5cm) high

$900-1,000   FLD

A pair of Moorcroft vases, in 'Tudor Rose' pattern, green painted signature, green printed 'MADE FOR LIBERTY & Rd No 431157', one with chip to rim.

5.5in (14cm) high

$1,500-1,900   TEN

A rare Moorcroft flambé vase, decorated in the 'Warratah' design, minor restoration to rim.

7.5in (19cm) high

$5,000-6,500   PSA

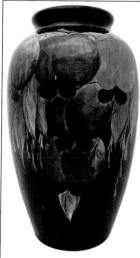

A Moorcroft vase, in 'Wisteria' pattern, impressed 'Moorcroft', blue painted signature and dated.

1927   *20.25in (51.5cm) high*

$3,200-3,800   BELL

A Moorcroft 'After the Storm' pattern vase, numbered 146/200, signed by Walter Moorcroft.

This was produced for the 1997 Centenary.

1996   *20.75in (53cm) high*

$1,900-2,500   CHEF

A Moorcroft 'Carp' pattern vase, by Sally Tuffin, limited edition, signed by John Moorcroft, numbered 60/100, with painted 'S.T Des.' mark, dated '21.8.92', some crazing.

1992   *26in (66.5cm) high*

$2,500-3,200   CHEF

A Moorcroft 'Lamia' pattern vase, designed by Rachel Bishop, signed by John Moorcroft, numbered 52/100, also marked 'R.J.B Des. 13.10.95'.

1995   *20.5in (52cm) high*

$1,300-1,900   CHEF

DECORATIVE ARTS

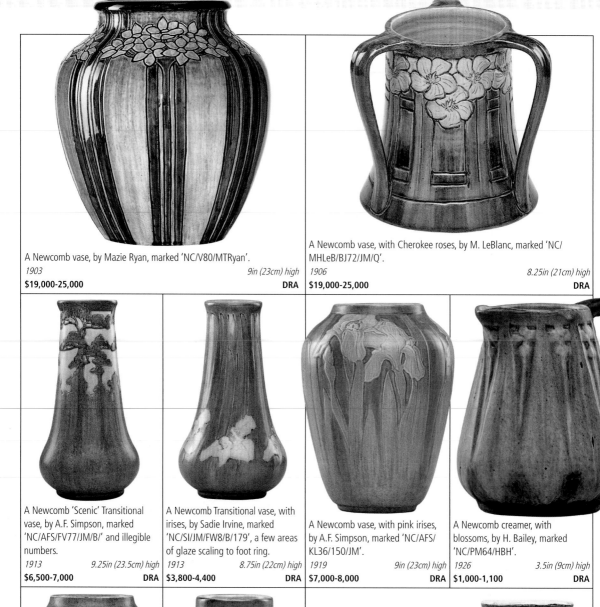

A Newcomb vase, by Mazie Ryan, marked 'NC/V80/MTRyan'.
1903　　　　　　　　　　*9in (23cm) high*
$19,000-25,000　　　　　　　　　　**DRA**

A Newcomb vase, with Cherokee roses, by M. LeBlanc, marked 'NC/MHLeB/BJ72/JM/Q'.
1906　　　　　　　　　　*8.25in (21cm) high*
$19,000-25,000　　　　　　　　　　**DRA**

A Newcomb 'Scenic' Transitional vase, by A.F. Simpson, marked 'NC/AFS/FV77/JM/B' and illegible numbers.
1913　　　*9.25in (23.5cm) high*
$6,500-7,000　　　　　**DRA**

A Newcomb Transitional vase, with irises, by Sadie Irvine, marked 'NC/SI/JM/FW8/B/179', a few areas of glaze scaling to foot ring.
1913　　　*8.75in (22cm) high*
$3,800-4,400　　　　　**DRA**

A Newcomb vase, with pink irises, by A.F. Simpson, marked 'NC/AFS/KL36/150/JM'.
1919　　　*9in (23cm) high*
$7,000-8,000　　　　**DRA**

A Newcomb creamer, with blossoms, by H. Bailey, marked 'NC/PM64/HBH'.
1926　　　*3.5in (9cm) high*
$1,000-1,100　　　　**DRA**

A Newcomb vase, with jonquil, by A.F. Simpson, marked 'NC/RD10/JH/AFS/148'.
1928　　　*8.75in (22cm) high*
$3,200-3,800　　　　**DRA**

A Newcomb 'Scenic' vase, with live oaks and Spanish moss, by Sadie Irvine, marked 'NC/SI/4/RS51'.
1929　　　*5.5in (14cm) high*
$1,900-2,500　　　　**DRA**

A Newcomb vase, by Elizabeth Villere, marked 'NC/E.M.V./Z69/JM/U'.

H. Sophie Newcomb Memorial College was a woman's art school founded in New Orleans, LA, in 1886, to instruct young Southern women in the liberal arts. Under the tuition of art professors such as William Woodward, Ellsworth Woodward and Mary Given Sheerer, the Newcomb College potters produced a range of outstanding Arts and Crafts pottery until production ceased in 1940. Its many designers included Sadie Irvine and A.F. Simpson.

1903　　　*7.5in (19cm) high*
$4,500-5,000　　　　**DRA**

A Pilkington's Lancastrian luster vase, by Richard Joyce (1873-1931), decorated with deer and trees, impressed maker's marks, painted artist's monogram and date cipher.
1907 8in (20cm) high
$5,000-6,500 **L&T**

A Royal Lancastrian vase, by Gordon Forsyth (1879-1952), decorated with lions and apple trees, impressed 'P symbol/2437/X/ENGLAND', glazed artist cipher, incised 'x'.
1910 14in (35.5cm) high
$5,000-6,500 **DRA**

A Pilkington's Lancastrian vase, by William S. Mycock, painted with wild poppies, impressed mark, painted artist cipher and date code.
1913 11.75in (29.5cm) high
$1,900-2,500 **WW**

A Pilkington's Lancastrian vase, by William S. Mycock, painted with a galleon, impressed mark, painted artist cipher and date mark, paper label.
1914 7.5in (19cm) high
$2,300-2,800 **WW**

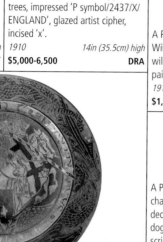

A Pilkington's Lancastrian charger, designed by Walter Crane, painted by William S. Mycock, painted with St George mounted on a rearing horse, holding a lance, piercing the head of a ferocious dragon, inscribed 'Un Chevalier Sans Peur et Sans Reproche', ('The Knight without Fear and Beyond Reproach'), painted date mark and artists' ciphers.

See Greg Smith Walter Crane, 'Artist Designer and Socialist', Lund Humphries, page 145, plate K12, for a smaller example painted by Richard Joyce, from the Whitworth Gallery, Manchester.
1918 19in (48.5cm) diam
$23,000-28,000 **WW**

A Pilkington's flambé and luster charger, by William S. Mycock, decorated with mythical winged dog-like creatures, with Latin script 'Frangas non flectes, lutum nisi tundatur non fit urceus' ('Bend not break, unless you pound the clay, you get no jar'), impressed and painted marks, dated.
1919 18.75in (47.5cm) diam
$3,200-3,800 **FLD**

A Pilkington's Lancastrian luster vase, by William S. Mycock, with flowering foliage, impressed maker's marks, painted artist's monogram, dated.
1926 10.25in (26cm) high
$4,500-5,000 **L&T**

A Pilkington's Lancastrian 'Pegasus' moon flask, designed by Walter Crane and painted by William S. Mycock, the reverse with heraldic coat of arms for Manchester and motto Concilio et Labore, impressed mark, painted Crane and Mycock ciphers and date code.

It is believed that this example combining the Pegasus image and the Manchester coat of arms is unique.
1932 10.75in (27cm) high
$9,000-10,000 **WW**

A Pilkington's Lancastrian luster bowl, by Walter Crane, decorated by William S. Mycock with a band of lions, impressed maker's mark, painted artist's and decorator's monograms, dated.
1932 7.5in (19cm) wide
$3,200-3,800 **L&T**

A Pilkington's Royal Lancastrian luster vase, decorated with trees and antelopes, boar's head mark, impressed '212B XII'.
7.75in (19.5cm) high
$1,900-2,500 **SWO**

ESSENTIAL REFERENCE - POOLE POTTERY

Poole Pottery began as Carter and Co. in Poole, Dorset in 1873, but did not produce the colorful artistic wares it has become known for until after World War I. In 1921, owners Owen and Charles Carter formed a partnership with Harold and Phoebe Stable and John and Truda Adams, to create Carter Stabler & Adams, renamed Poole Pottery in 1963. From the 1920s, the company produced distinctive Art Deco pottery wares, often characterized by vibrant colors and decorated with stylized plants and animals. Carter Stabler & Adams combined traditional hand-throwing techniques and modern decoration. Their patterns included the 1920s 'Handcraft' range, defined by bright colors on pale grounds, Truda Adams's traditional handmade 'Twintone' range in the 1940s, and the 1960s-70s 'Delphis' range, developed by Robert Jefferson and Guy Sydenham, where decorators created a unique design for each piece.

The Poole factory closed in 2006, but the brand continues as part of Lifestyle Holdings, based at the Royal Stafford factory in Stoke-on-Trent.

A rare Carter Stabler & Adams Poole Pottery 'Holly' vase, designed by Truda Carter, painted by Ann Hatchard, pattern 'LG', shape no.949, impressed and painted marks.

Sue Lunt, 'Age of Jazz: British Art Deco Ceramics', National Museums of Liverpool, page 128, catalog number 136, for a comparable vase illustrated.

13.5in (34cm) high

$5,500-6,500   WW

A Carter Stabler & Adams Poole Pottery vase, probably designed by Truda Carter, shape no.435, impressed mark, incised '435'.

11in (28cm) high

$650-750   WW

A Carter Stabler & Adams Poole Pottery 'Bluebird' vase, designed by Truda Adams, painted by Anne Hatchard, pattern NE, shape no.901, impressed and incised marks, painted marks and artist cipher.

9.25in (23.5cm) high

$180-250   WW

A pair of Carter's Poole Pottery tiles, 'The Chase', designed by Edward Bawden, painted with two foxes and a pack of four fox hounds, impressed marks painted 'CS4' and 'CS6'.

c1922   *5in (12.5cm) wide*

$700-800   WW

A 1930s Art Deco Poole Pottery 'Leaping Gazelle' vase, pattern 'TZ', decorated by Marian Heath, shape no.966.

10in (25.5cm) high

$500-650   TRI

A Poole Pottery 'Free-Form' carafe, designed by Guy Sydenham and Alfred Read, shape no.698, marked 'X/PRB'.

15in (38.5cm) high

$250-400   SWO

A Poole Pottery 'Delphis' charger, shape no.5, painted with a geometric abstract design, printed and painted marks.

14in (36.5cm) diam

$230-280   WW

A rare Poole Pottery 'Atlantis' vase, by Guy Sydenham, modeled with a stylized face, impressed 'Poole' mark 'Guy Sydenham' monogram.

This is believed to be one of only six such vases produced.

12.5in (32cm) high

$6,500-7,500   WW

ESSENTIAL REFERENCE - ROOKWOOD

Rookwood was founded in 1880 in Cincinnati, Ohio. Originally the hobby of a wealthy young lady, Maria Longworth Nichols, Rookwood soon became one of the most important potteries in the USA. The factory employed a range of talented artists, chemists and technicians. These include Artus Van Briggle (1869-1904), who worked with Rookwood before setting up his own pottery, and artist Laura Fry (1857-1943), who developed the 'Standard' glaze, where color is applied with an atomizer to create a gradient effect. The Japanese ceramicist Kataro Shirayamadani (1865-1947) worked with Rookwood from 1887 until his death. Early Rookwood wares were heavily potted, slip-cast or thrown and painted with naturalistic and often Oriental decoration. Rookwook suffered heavily during the Depression and filed for bankruptcy in 1941. It continued for two decades after this, with production ceasing in 1967.

A Rookwood 'Standard' glaze portrait vase, by unidentified artist, with flame mark '614C', restoration to rim, a few scratches.
1896   *12in (30.5cm) high*
$700-800   **DRA**

A Rookwood 'Standard' glaze pitcher, with cherries and silver overlay, by Sadie Markland, with flame mark '639D/W/SM', silver stamped 'GORHAM MFG CO. R1786'.
1893   *6.5in (16.5cm) high*
$1,400-1,800   **DRA**

A Rookwood 'Standard' glaze pitcher, with dogwood and silver overlay, by Mary Perkins, with flame mark '669/L/W/MLP', silver stamped 'GORHAM MFG. CO. R958', a few splits and some lifting to silver.
1892   *6.25in (16cm) high*
$1,900-2,500   **DRA**

A Rookwood 'Tiger Eye' vase, by K. Shirayamadani, decorated with cherry blossoms, flame mark '35DD/P' and artist cipher, Buffalo and Paris exposition labels to base, fine crazing.

Exhibited: Universal Exposition Paris, France 1900 and Pan-American Exposition Buffalo, NY 1901.
1896   *7in (18cm) high*
$9,500-10,500   **DRA**

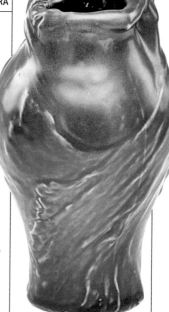

A Rookwood proto-'Lorelei' vase, designed by Artus Van Briggle, incised 'A. Van Briggle 1898', with 'Paris Exposition Universelle 1900' label, one minor glazed-over firing line.
1898   *7.5in (19cm) high*
$200,000-250,000   **DRA**

A Rookwood 'Sea Green' glaze vase, with poppies, by Constance Baker, with flame mark 'III/900C/G/CAB', overall crazing, several long scratches to body.
1903   *8in (20cm) high*
$1,200-1,400   **DRA**

A Rookwood Iris Glaze vase, designed by William McDonald (1882-1931), decorated with water lilies, flame mark 'III/787B/WPM'.
1903   *14.75in (37.5cm) high*
$9,000-10,000   **DRA**

A Rookwood Z-line vase, designed by Harriet Wilcox (1869-1943), decorated with chrysanthemums, flame mark 'III/381Z/HEW'.
1903   *7.5in (19cm) high*
$4,500-5,000   **DRA**

A Rookwood banded 'Vellum' vase, with crow on a branch, by K. Shirayamadani, with flame mark 'IX/952E/V' and artist cipher, crazing, minor peppering around rim.
1909   *7.75in (19.5cm) high*
$1,400-1,900   **DRA**

DECORATIVE ARTS

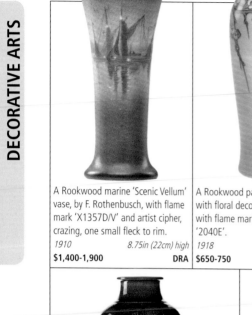

A Rookwood marine 'Scenic Vellum' vase, by F. Rothenbusch, with flame mark 'X1357D/V' and artist cipher, crazing, one small fleck to rim.

1910   *8.75in (22cm) high*

$1,400-1,900   **DRA**

A Rookwood painted 'Mat' vase, with floral decoration, by Sara Sax, with flame mark, date, numbered '2040E'.

1918   *8in (20cm) high*

$650-750   **DRA**

A Rookwood 'Turquoise Blue' vase, by Arthur Conant, with flame mark, date, number and artist cipher, restored.

1920   *8in (20cm) high*

$750-900   **DRA**

A squat Rookwood vase with flowers, by K. Shirayamadani, with flame mark 'XXIV/2760', artist cipher, minor scratches to body.

1924   *7in (18cm) wide*

$1,400-1,900   **DRA**

A Rookwood jewel porcelain vase, by Edward T. Hurley (1869-1950), decorated with birds, flame mark 'XXVI/2373', one restored drill hole.

1926   *16.5in (42cm) high*

$10,000-11,000   **DRA**

A Rookwood 'Sang-de-boeuf 'Production' vase, with fish, with flame mark 'XXIX', one grinding chip to base.

1929   *11.5in (29cm) high*

$950-1,100   **DRA**

A Rookwood decorated 'Mat' vase with wild roses, by K. Shirayamadani, with flame mark 'XXXVI/6184C/' and artist cipher, stilt pulls.

1936   *9.25in (23.5cm) high*

$1,110-1,300   **DRA**

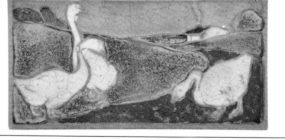

A rare 1900s Rookwood faience tile, with geese in landscape, impressed 'Rookwood FAIENCE 13967', one small chip, a few chips along top and bottom edges on back of tile.

8.75in (22cm) wide

$1,300-1,900   **DRA**

A Rockwood faience five-tile frieze, decorated in cuenca with cottage in a landscape, framed, one small hairline crack.

Removed from a Plymouth Park residence in St Louis, Minnesota, originally built in 1912 for the president of Lowell Bank, William Koeneman.

1910   *59.5in (151cm) wide*

$7,500-9,000   **DRA**

A Rookwood glazed ceramic tile, with stylized irises, impressed 'Rookwood 1749Y', a few chips, crazing.

c1915   *9in (23cm) high*

$950-1,100   **DRA**

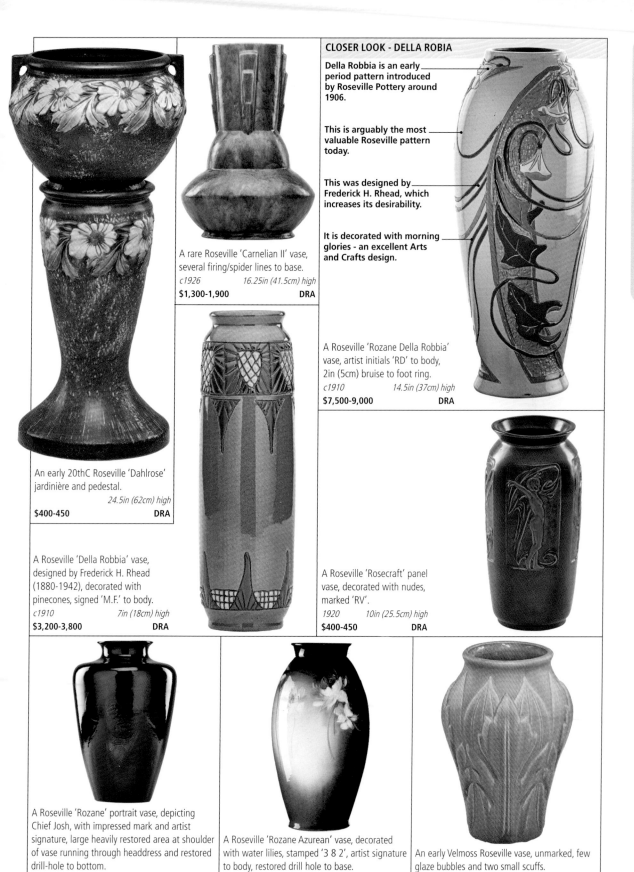

An early 20thC Roseville 'Dahlrose' jardinière and pedestal.

24.5in (62cm) high

$400-450 **DRA**

A rare Roseville 'Carnelian II' vase, several firing/spider lines to base.

c1926 *16.25in (41.5cm) high*

$1,300-1,900 **DRA**

CLOSER LOOK - DELLA ROBIA

Della Robbia is an early period pattern introduced by Roseville Pottery around 1906.

This is arguably the most valuable Roseville pattern today.

This was designed by Frederick H. Rhead, which increases its desirability.

It is decorated with morning glories - an excellent Arts and Crafts design.

A Roseville 'Rozane Della Robbia' vase, artist initials 'RD' to body, 2in (5cm) bruise to foot ring.

c1910 *14.5in (37cm) high*

$7,500-9,000 **DRA**

A Roseville 'Della Robbia' vase, designed by Frederick H. Rhead (1880-1942), decorated with pinecones, signed 'M.F.' to body.

c1910 *7in (18cm) high*

$3,200-3,800 **DRA**

A Roseville 'Rosecraft' panel vase, decorated with nudes, marked 'RV'.

1920 *10in (25.5cm) high*

$400-450 **DRA**

A Roseville 'Rozane' portrait vase, depicting Chief Josh, with impressed mark and artist signature, large heavily restored area at shoulder of vase running through headdress and restored drill-hole to bottom.

1961 *16in (40.5cm) high*

$400-500 **DRA**

A Roseville 'Rozane Azurean' vase, decorated with water lilies, stamped '3 8 2', artist signature to body, restored drill hole to base.

1902 *14in (35.5cm) high*

$400-500 **DRA**

An early Velmoss Roseville vase, unmarked, few glaze bubbles and two small scuffs.

c1895 *10in (25.5cm) high*

$250-400 **DRA**

A pair of Royal Dux Art Nouveau porcelain vases, artist's signature 'F. OTTO', impressed mark '1512', pink triangle mark with inscription 'ROYAL DUX BOHEMIA/ E'.

c1890   *27.5in (69.5cm) high*
$650-750   **L&T**

A Royal Dux spill vase, modeled as a maiden, pink triangle to base.

15in (38.5cm) high
$180-250   **ECGW**

A Royal Dux figural group, by Alois Hampel, modeled as a pair of lovers.

26.5in (67cm) high
$180-250   **LOC**

A Royal Dux figure of a Classical lady, applied and impressed marks.

18in (46.5cm) high
$180-250   **CHEF**

A Royal Dux centerpiece, modeled as a mother and two young children, red seal marked 'royal dux bohemia', with impressed number '1573'.

17in (43cm) high
$80-90   **LOCK**

A Royal Dux Art Nouveau porcelain tazza, molded as a maiden picking apples, applied pink triangle mark reading '1821'.

c1900   *20.5in (52cm) high*
$300-400   **L&T**

A Royal Dux porcelain figural group, of a young woman, child and kid, printed and molded pink triangular marks.

13in (33cm) wide
$180-250   **HW**

A pair of Royal Dux porcelain pierrot bookends.

10.5in (27cm) high
$400-500   **ECGW**

A Royal Dux model of a flamenco dancer, applied pink triangle, with impressed marks.

14.5in (37cm) high
$400-500   **WW**

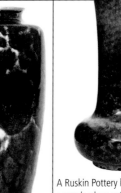

A Ruskin Pottery high fired vase, in a streaked lavender, with green copper spotting over a deep red ground, with impressed oval West Smethwick mark, dated, restored.
1906   *7in (18cm) high*
$700-800   **FLD**

A Ruskin Pottery high fired stoneware vase, by William Howson Taylor, in a mottled mint green glaze, impressed Ruskin roundel mark and date.
1907   *13in (33cm) high*
$1,000-1,100   **WW**

A Ruskin pottery high fired barrel vase, with a fissured sang-de-boeuf and a sweeping lavender glaze, impressed mark, dated, restored.
1913   *10in (25cm) high*
$1,900-2,500   **FLD**

A Ruskin Pottery high fired vase, in a purple glaze, with copper green speckling, marks removed.

The owner purchased this vase in the 1950s at Portobello market. He was sold this as a highly desirable Chinese flambé vase with the Ruskin oval mark being scratched out!
                        8.75in (22cm) high
$750-900   **FLD**

A Ruskin Pottery high fired vase, with a sang-de-boeuf glaze with a mottled sweeping lavender glaze, with copper green spotting to the neck, impressed mark, dated.
1913   *12.5in (32cm) high*
$1,900-2,500   **FLD**

A Ruskin Pottery high fired sang-de-beouf vase, with sweeping red glaze over a gray ground with lavender spotting, impressed mark, dated.

1913   *10.25in (26cm) high*
$950-1,100   **FLD**

A Ruskin Pottery vase, by William Howson Taylor, painted with a band of clover leaf, impressed marks, dated.
1916   *9.75in (25cm) high*
$400-500   **WW**

A Ruskin Pottery vase, by William Howson Taylor, in a strawberry pink luster glaze streaked with sky blue, impressed marks, dated.
1917   *9.5in (24cm) high*
$1,000-1,100   **WW**

A Ruskin Pottery 'Kingfisher Blue' luster glaze rolling vase, with impressed mark, dated, restored rim chip.
1920   *10.5in (26.5cm) high*
$180-250   **FLD**

A Saturday Evening Girls ceramic bowl, decorated in cuerda seca with turtle and hare, incised 'THE RACE IS NOT TO THE SWIFT', signed '352.10.10/S.E.G./IG'.

In 1899, librarian Edith Guerrier set up a Saturday Evening Club in Boston to educate poor young women in the liberals arts. With assistance from Edith Brown and Helen Storrow, this became the Paul Revere Pottery Club in 1908. The aim was to provide struggling young women with a safe and skilled way to earn a living. Saturday Evening Girls pottery is clean and simple in design; their patterns are decorated in cuerda seca (Spanish for 'dry cord'), where thin lines of grease prevent colored glazes from running.

1910   *5.5in (14cm) diam*
$1,500-2,000   **DRA**

A Saturday Evening Girls ceramic milk pitcher, decorated in cuerda seca with turtle and hare, incised 'SLOW BUT SURE', signed '333 6/10 S.E.G./R.B.'.
1910   *5in (12.5cm) high*
$3,200-3,800   **DRA**

A Saturday Evening Girls ceramic trivet, decorated in cuerda seca with lake scene, signed 'AM/11-10/S.E.G.', one small chip to top edge.
1910   *5.5in (14cm) diam*
$2,500-3,200   **DRA**

A Saturday Evening Girls ceramic mug, decorated in cuerda seca with roosters, incised 'If I sing faithfully, sonorously & if long after me & long after that in every farmyard its cock sings faithfully sonorously I truly believe there will'.
1911
$9,500-10,500   **DRA**

A Saturday Evening Girls ceramic mug, decorated in cuerda seca with ships and monogram 'C.R.S.', signed 'AM/224-4-12/S.E.G.'.
1912   *5.5in (14cm) high*
$3,800-4,400   **DRA**

A Saturday Evening Girls vase, decorated in cuerda seca with daffodils, by Fannie Levine, signed 'FL S.E.G. 12-13', overcoated, extensive professional restoration.
1913   *10.5in (26.5cm) high*
$1,900-2,500   **DRA**

A Saturday Evening Girls vase, decorated in cuerda seca with daffodils, signed '5-15/S.E.G./S.G.', extensive professional restoration.
1915   *10.75in (27.5cm) high*
$2,500-3,200   **DRA**

A Saturday Evening Girls vase, decorated in cuerda seca with wooded landscape, by Sara Galner, signed 'SEG 21-17/S.G.', a few burst glaze bubbles.
1917   *10in (25cm) high*
$3,800-4,400   **DRA**

A Saturday Evening Girls ceramic bowl, decorated in cuerda seca with 'The Midnight Ride of Paul Revere', by Paul Revere, inside incised 'A VOICE IN THE DARKNESS A KNOCK AT THE DOOR AND A WORD THAT SHALL ECHO FOREVER MORE', base signed 'LS/P.R.P./6-41'.
1941
$1,500-2,000   **DRA**

ESSENTIAL REFERENCE - VAN BRIGGLE

Artus Van Briggle (1869-1904) worked at Avon Pottery and Rookwood and traveled widely in the USA and Europe, before settling in Colorado in 1899 due to poor health. There he and his wife Anne, also an artist, founded the Van Briggle Art Pottery in Colorado Springs. They made slip-cast ceramic vessels, finished with Chinese-inspired colored mat glazes, which were sprayed on using an atomizer. Van Briggle vases were often embossed with stylized flowers or Native American designs. After Artus's death from Tuberculosis in 1904, the quality of Van Briggle pottery began to suffer. Anne sold the factory in 1912. The pottery is still open today, mainly producing copies of original Artus Van Briggle work.

A Van Briggle vase, with roses, with variegated green glaze, incised 'AA Van Briggle 1903/III', stamped '61', two chips to foot, tight hairlines to rim.

1903   12.75in (32.5cm) high
$1,900-2,500   DRA

A Van Briggle vase, with stylized flowers, celadon and green glaze, incised 'AA Van Briggle 1904 V', stamped '149'.

1904   4in (10cm) high
$950-1,100   DRA

A Van Briggle vase, with poppy pods, with mocha glaze, incised 'AA Van Briggle 1902/III'.

1902   3.75in (9.5cm) high
$1,500-2,000   DRA

A Van Briggle vase, with blossoms, with variegated green glaze, incised 'AA Van Briggle 172/1904/V', short T-shaped line to rim.

1904   12in (30.5cm) high
$2,500-3,200   DRA

A Van Briggle vase, with celadon green glaze, incised 'AA Van Briggle 1/2 1905', stamped '426', one short firing line to base.

1905   9in (23cm) high
$1,000-1,200   DRA

A Van Briggle vase, with leaves, with green glaze, incised 'AA Van Briggle Colo. Spgs. 699'.

1908-11   11in (28cm) high
$1,500-2,000   DRA

A 1920s Van Briggle 'Lorelei' vase, in mat black glaze, marked 'AA Van Briggle COLO SPGS Z', few surface scratches at base.

10.5in (26.5cm) high
$450-550   DRA

A 1920s Van Briggle 'Despondency' vase, marked 'AA Van Briggle COLO SPGS Z', one 2in (5cm) scratch.

16.25in (41.5cm) high
$550-700   DRA

A 1930s Van Briggle vase, with columbines, 'Persian Blue' glaze, signed 'AA Van Briggle USA'.

16.25in (41.5cm) high
$800-950   DRA

ESSENTIAL REFERENCE - DAISY MAKEIG-JONES

Daisy Makeig-Jones was born in 1881. After studying at Torquay School of Art, she became a tableware painter and designer at Wedgwood in 1909. She started her 'Fairyland lustre' series in 1915. She decorated these distinctive wares with colorful scenes of magical kingdoms, featuring pixies, goblins and sprites, painted and printed in gold and luster glazes. This line was hugely popular during and immediately after World War I, but fell out of fashion and was discontinued in 1929. Makeig-Jones was said to be difficult to work with and was asked to retire from Wedgwood in 1931. She died in 1945. Fairyland lustre pieces are now highly sought after, particularly the rarer patterns.

A Wedgwood Fairyland lustre K'ang Hsi bowl, by Daisy Makeig-Jones, the interior in the 'Garden of Paradise' pattern, the exterior in 'Woodland Bridge Variation 1', with printed Portland Vase mark.

7.25in (18.5cm) diam

$2,500-3,200   **FLD**

A Wedgwood Fairyland flame lustre bowl, by Daisy Makeig-Jones, the interior in the 'Woodland Elves V' pattern, with four printed 'MJ' monograms and a mermaid roundel, the exterior in the 'Poplar Trees' pattern, printed Portland Vase mark.

9.5in (24cm) diam

$3,200-3,800   **FLD**

A Wedgwood Fairyland lustre bowl, designed by Daisy Makeig-Jones, the exterior in the 'Woodland Bridge Variation 1' pattern, the interior in 'Picnic by a River' printed and painted marks.

8in (20.5cm) diam

$1,900-2,500   **WW**

A Wedgwood Fairyland lustre 'Octagon' bowl, designed by Daisy Makeig-Jones, printed to the exterior in the 'Castle on a Road' pattern, the interior 'Bird in a Hoop', printed factory marks.

7in (18cm) diam

$2,800-3,500   **WW**

A Wedgwood 'Fairy in a Cage' Fairyland lustre bowl, designed by Daisy Makeig-Jones, the exterior with the 'Woodland Elves VII-Toadstool' pattern.

9in (23cm) diam

$5,000-6,500   **WW**

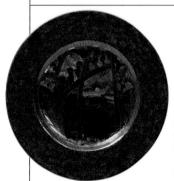

A Wedgwood Fairyland lustre Lincoln plate, 'Imps on a Bridge - Tree House', designed by Daisy Makeig-Jones, printed factory mark.

10.75in (27cm) diam

$3,800-5,000   **WW**

A Wedgwood Fairyland lustre 'Firbolgs' pattern vase and cover, designed by Daisy Makeig-Jones, printed Portland Vase mark to base, no.Z5247 shape no.2410.

9.75in (25cm) high

$2,800-3,300   **ECGW**

A Wedgwood 'Lahore' luster vase, by Daisy Makeig-Jones, factory marks and pattern no.Z5266.

c1925 *7.5in (19cm) high*

$2,500-3,200 **HT**

A Wedgwood 'Sycamore Tree' Fairyland flame lustre vase, designed by Daisy Makeig-Jones, shape no.3150, printed and painted with Feng Hwang, Bridge and Ship and Tree, printed and impressed marks, small glaze frit to rim.

8in (20.5cm) high

$1,300-1,800 **WW**

A Wedgwood Fairyland lustre vase, decorated in 'Imps on a Bridge' pattern, with Portland vase, 'Wedgwood Made in England', and gold scrolled medallion with an 'H' and 'Z5360'.

This pattern has green imps crossing a bridge and a blue Roc bird flying above along with a large serpent climbing a tree nearby, all against a flame luster sky.

11.75in (30cm) high

$5,500-6,500 **JDJ**

A Wedgwood Fairyland lustre vase, decorated in 'Pillars' pattern, signed with Portland vase mark 'Wedgwood Made In England Z4968'.

14in (35.5cm) high

$11,000-14,000 **JDJ**

A Wedgwood Fairyland lustre malfrey pot, decorated in the 'Sycamore Tree' pattern, the lid is decorated with a fairy caught in a spider web, signed with Portland vase mark 'Wedgwood Made In England Z-4968'.

10in (25.5cm) high

$15,000-18,000 **JDJ**

A Wedgwood Fairyland 'Rainbow' and 'Bifrost' lustre vase, designed by Daisy Makeig-Jones, shape no.3149, printed and painted marks.

8.5in (21.5cm) high

$2,500-3,200 **WW**

A Wedgwood Fairyland lustre footed bowl, possible restoration.

4.25in (10.5cm) diam

$500-650 **CHOR**

A Wedgwood Fairyland lustre melba bowl, decorated on exterior in 'Garden of Paradise' pattern, the interior with 'Jumping Faun' pattern, signed with Portland vase mark 'Wedgwood Made In England', professional restoration.

8in (20.5cm) diam

$3,200-3,800 **JDJ**

A Wedgwood Fairyland lustre '2357' vase, by Daisy Makeig-Jones, decorated in the 'Candlemas' pattern, printed Portland Vase mark.

8.75in (22cm) high

$3,200-3,800 **FLD**

DECORATIVE ARTS

A Wedgwood black basalt vase, designed by Keith Murray, impressed and printed marks, facsimile signature.

Keith Murray (1892-1981) was born in New Zealand but trained as an architect in Britain. From 1932, he designed ceramics, glass and metalware for Wedgwood. He combined traditional methods with modern bodies and glazes, to create bold, simple, modernist designs. His pieces were often lathe-turned and slip-glazed with mat glazes of green, straw yellow or 'moonstone'. He also designed the Wedgwood Barlaston factory, which opened in 1940.

c1934   7.75in (20cm) high
$1,000-1,100   WW

A Wedgwood glazed earthenware 'moonstone' vase, by Keith Murray, shape no.3801, marked to the base.

6in (15.5cm) high
$150-190   APAR

A Wedgwood 'The Panther' ceramic figure, by Allen Best, covered in a celadon glaze, impressed mark 'WEDGWOOD'.

c1930   11.5in (29.5cm) high
$2,500-3,200   L&T

A Wedgwood 'Travel' series plate, designed by Eric Ravilious, printed marks.

9in (23cm) diam
$180-250   SWO

A Wedgwood 'Garden Implements' lemonade set, designed by Eric Ravilious in 1939, reissued 1968 in an edition of 250.

$900-1,000   SWO

Judith Picks

If you ask any collector what they regret, it is rarely something they bought but rather things they didn't buy, and for me (along with the Murano birds by Pianon - but more of that later!) it is the ceramics of Eric Ravilious. Eric William Ravilious (22 July 1903 - 2 September 1942) was an English painter, designer, book illustrator and wood engraver. He grew up in East Sussex, and is particularly known for his watercolors of the South Downs. He served as a war artist, and died when the aircraft he was in was lost off Iceland.

Ravilious engraved more than 400 illustrations and drew over 40 lithographic designs for books and publications during his lifetime. In 1936, he was commissioned by Wedgwood to create ceramic designs. His work for them included a commemorative mug to mark the abortive coronation of Edward VIII; the design was revized for the coronation of George VI. Other popular Ravilious designs included the Alphabet mug of 1937, and the china sets, 'Afternoon Tea' (1938), 'Travel' (1938), and 'Garden Implements' (1939), plus this 'Boat Race Day' in 1938. Production of Ravilious' designs continued into the 1950s, with the coronation mug design being posthumously reworked for the coronation of Elizabeth II in 1953.

A Wedgwood urbanware 'Boat Race' bowl, by Eric Ravilious, the interior decorated with Piccadilly Circus at night, the sides with scenes from the Oxford and Cambridge Boat Race, and a mermaid with oars.

c1938   12in (31cm) diam
$3,800-4,400   DW

A Wedgwood 'Zodiac' bull, designed by Arnold Machin, with the star signs over the body, printed and impressed marks, 'Wedgwood', 'Barlaston', 'England'.

15.75in (40cm) long
$550-700   LAW

A mid-20thC Wedgwood figure of 'Ferdinand the Bull', by Arnold Machin, painted with floral decoration, marked under left forefoot 'WEDGWOOD, BARLASTON, ENGLAND/ CKH 6408. M'.

12.5in (31.5cm) long
$250-400   L&T

ESSENTIAL REFERENCE - WELLER POTTERY

Weller Pottery was founded by Samuel A. Weller in 1872 in Fultonham, Ohio. Weller started producing tiles and plain pots but soon expanded. In 1888 the company relocated to Zanesville and in 1893 launched a new art pottery line with William A. Long as art director. Weller's significant designers and artists include Charles Babcock Upjohn, who introduced the Weller 'Dickensware' line from 1895, Frederick Hurten Rhead, who developed 'Jap Birdimal', and Jacques Sicard, who designed the 'Sicardo' range from 1901 to 1907. Sicard worked with metallic glazes, creating distinctive wares colored in blues, crimsons and purples. Other popular Weller patterns included 'Louwelsa', 'Aurelian' and 'Etna'. After World War I, commercial 'Production ware' began to replace hand-decorated art pottery. Samuel Weller died in 1925. The pottery closed shortly after the end of World War II.

A Weller gourd vase, with blossoms, by Jacques Sicard, signed 'Weller Sicard', base incised '12'.

1903-17   5.5in (14cm) high

$950-1,100   DRA

A Weller floriform vase, by Jacques Sicard, stamped 'Weller', with raised '45' to base, overall scratches to body.

1903-17   15in (38cm) high

$2,300-2,800   DRA

A Weller lidded vase, with mistletoe, by Jacques Sicard, signed 'Sicard Weller', stamped '2'.

1903-17   8.5in (21.5cm) wide

$1,000-1,100   DRA

A Weller 'Dickensware II' vase, with English street scene and David Copperfield quote, impressed 'Dickensware Weller 11 808'.

c1900   11in (28cm) high

$300-400   DRA

A Weller 'Dickensware II' vase, with revolutionary scene, 8in (20.5cm) hairline radiating from rim.

c1900   16in (40.5cm) high

$300-400   DRA

A Weller 'Louwelsa' floor vase, decorated with tulips, by Albert Haubrich, signed and impressed, some chips to rim, three 1in (2.5cm) bruises to base.

1896-1924   24in (61cm) high

$300-400   DRA

A Weller 'Dickensware II' vase with golfer, stamped 'DICKENSWARE Weller W/6/X', professional restoration to rim.

1897-1905   9.25in (23.5cm) high

$450-550   DRA

A 'Hudson Floral' Weller vase, by Hester Pillsbury, with blue Weller 'WARE' stamp, artist signature.

1917-34   9.5in (24cm) high

$650-750   DRA

A Weller vase with silver overlay hunt scene, marked, one nick to base.

9in (23cm) high

$400-450   DRA

A 1920s Weller 'Coppertone' vase, restoration to base.

18in (45.5cm) high

$300-400   DRA

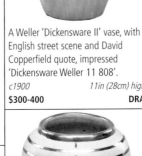

A rare Wemyss 'Thistles' sleeping pig, impressed mark 'WEMYSS', restored ear.

c1900 6.25in (16cm) long

$6,500-7,500 L&T

A Wemyss 'Cabbage Roses' pig, painted and impressed mark 'WEMYSS'.

c1900 6.25in (16cm) long

$1,000-1,200 L&T

A late 19thC rare Wemyss large pig, probably decorated by Karel Nekola, painted with flowering clover.

17.5in (44cm) long

$10,000-11,000 L&T

A near pair of Wemyss pottery cats, with glass eyes, painted with pink roses, painted marks.

c1900 13in (33cm) high

$1,500-2,000 TEN

A Wemyss 'Plumb' pattern Tulip vase, marked 'Wemyss', stamp for retailer T. Goode & Co., 2in (5cm) long hairline crack.

14.5in (37cm) high

$1,500-2,000 ECGW

A rare Wemyss Drummond flower pot, decorated with daisies, aquilegia, bluebells, dog roses, clover, and forget-me-nots, painted with a ribbon and the inscriptions 'INNOCENCE.', 'RESOLUTION.', 'SUBMISSION.', 'SIMPLICITY.', 'THINK OF ME.', and 'TRUE LOVE.', impressed marks 'R.H.&S.' and 'WEMYSS WARE', printed retailer's mark.

c1900 8.75in (22.5cm) diam

$3,800-5,000 L&T

An early 20thC Wemyss ware small 'Apples' loving cup, impressed mark 'WEMYSS WARE' and 'R.H.&S.', printed retailer's mark.

4in (10cm) high

$500-650 L&T

A Wemyss 'White Broom' teacup and saucer, decorated by David Grinton, painted and impressed marks 'WEMYSS'.

c1900 saucer 5in (12.5cm) diam

$500-650 L&T

A Wemyss 'Stag and Hind' teacup, with printed retailer's mark.

c1900 2.25in (6cm) high

$650-750 L&T

A Wemyss 'daisies' tray, impressed mark 'WEMYSS WARE/ R.H.&S'.

c1900 11.75in (30cm) long

$1,110-1,300 L&T

ESSENTIAL REFERENCE - ZSOLNAY

The Zsolnay factory was established by Miklós Zsolnay (1800-1880) in Pécs, Hungary, in 1853, to produce stoneware and other ceramics. In 1863, his son, Vilmos Zsolnay (1828-1900) joined the company and became its manager and director. He led the factory to worldwide recognition by demonstrating its innovative products at World Fairs and International Exhibitions, including the 1873 World Fair in Vienna and the 1878 World Fair in Paris, where Zsolnay received a Grand Prix. Many Zsolnay ceramics are noted for the use of the eosin process that was introduced in 1893. The process results in a light red iridescence of the first prepared hue, hence the term eosin (Greek eos, flush of dawn). Different eosin colors and processes were developed over time. The eosin-based iridescence became a favorite of Art Nouveau and Jugendstil artists.

A Zsolnay vase, by Jozsef Rippl-Ronai (1861-1927), with stylized night-time landscape, eosin glaze, impressed '5282/21' with raised five churches seal.
c1898   12.75in (32.5cm) high
$23,000-28,000   **DRA**

A Zsolnay vase, by Sandor Apati Abt (1870-1916), with stylized flowering vine, eosin glaze, impressed '8191/6/48' with raised five churches seal.
c1908   11.75in (30cm) high
$25,000-32,000   **DRA**

A Zsolnay tulip vase, eosin glaze, impressed 'ZSOLNAY PECS 5495/1/12/M' with five churches mark, a few minor scratches.
c1900   13.25in (33.5cm) high
$18,000-23,000   **DRA**

A Zsolnay bowl, by Tade Sikorski (1852-1940), with apple trees, eosin glaze, impressed 'ZSOLNAY PECS 4669/3/36/22' with five churches mark, minor light wear and scratches.
c1898   9in (23cm) diam
$20,000-25,000   **DRA**

A rare large Zsolnay koi center bowl, by Mihaly Kapas Nagy (1864-1943), eosin glaze, impressed '6801/35' with raised five churches seal and original paper label 6801, firing line to base, professional restoration to hairline from rim to foot.
c1902
$50,000-55,000   **DRA**

A Zsolnay bowl, by Mihaly Kapas Nagy (1864-1943), decorated with dragons and koi fish, eosin glaze, impressed '5790/36' with raised five churches seal.
c1900   12in (30.5cm) long
$15,000-19,000   **DRA**

A Zsolnay figural centerpiece, with three Art Nouveau partially nude female figures, signed with disc and five steeples mark.
11in (28cm) diam
$7,500-9,000   **JDJ**

A rare Zsolnay 'Serpent' ewer, base with green circular seal mark and impressed 'M 6081'.

Hungarians are keen to buy back their ceramics heritage at the moment, including Art Nouveau wares from the Zsolnay factory.

11.5in (29cm) high
$15,000-19,000   **CLV**

An Amphora Art Nouveau vase, decorated foot with iris buds and leaves, the lip of vase made up of large iris petals, an Art Nouveau maiden resting against an iris flower, unsigned.

21.5in (54.5cm) high

$3,200-3,800   JDJ

An Ault pottery 'Propeller' vase, designed by Christopher Dresser, unmarked.

8.25in (21cm) high

$150-190   FLD

A rare Beswick Pottery 'Duchess with flowers' Beatrix Potter Figure, printed 'BP2' gilt backstamp.

1955-72   *3.75in (9.5cm) high*

$1,000-1,500   L&T

A Boch 'Keramis' vase, designed by Charles Catteau, model no.D.943, enameled with deer, printed and painted marks, with facsimile signature.

13.5in (34cm) high

$750-900   WW

A Boch Freres 'Keramis' vase, designed by Charles Catteau, pattern 'D.750', painted with stylized flowerheads, impressed and printed marks, with facsimile signature.

13.75in (35cm) high

$300-400   WW

An early 20thC 'Barum' jug, by C.H. Brannam, modeled as a grotesque frog, incised mark, dated.

1909   *9.75in (24.5cm) long*

$300-400   FLD

A large late 19thC Bretby stick stand, modeled as a rustic tree trunk with a standing brown bear cub to the side, impressed mark, shape no.1248, restored.

26in (66cm) high

$650-750   FLD

An early 20thC Burmantofts Art Pottery vase, impasto decorated with monkey cradling its young, impressed mark.

13.5in (34cm) high

$250-320   FLD

A Burmantoft's faience 'Anglo Persian' vase, by Leonard King, design no.23, impressed and painted marks to base.

19.5in (49cm) high

$5,500-7,000   WW

An 1880s Burmantofts faience vase, tubelined with fish, impressed marks to base 'BURMANTOFTS', 'FAIENCE', '2123', 'ENGLAND', and '11', with painted mark 'COL. NO. 80/ 2', the rim with later silver mount by Adrian Hope, hallmarked.

12.5in (32cm) high

$700-800   L&T

A Burmantofts faience jardinière and stand, the jardinière decorated with peacocks, makers marks 'BURMANTOFTS FAIENCE ENGLAND' and number '2115' or '2116'.

c1910   *40in (104cm) high*

$3,800-5,000   L&T

A French glazed stoneware Symbolist vase, by Alphonse Voisin-Delacroix (1857-93) and Pierre-Adrien Dalpayrat (1844-1910), depicting a maiden and bat, oxblood drip glaze, base marked 'VD'.

c1892

$120,000-130,000   DRA

A Della Robbia vase, by Charles Collis, incised with tulips, with monogram 'E.L.L.', painters mark 'G.W.', possibly George Warhurst, shape no.265, factory marks and 'BrHead' to base.

13.25in (33.5cm) high

$1,900-2,500   PW

A Della Robbia Pottery Moorish vase, by Cassandra Annie Walker, incised factory marks and 'ELL' monogram and painted 'CW' monogram.

10.25in (26cm) high

$1,300-1,900   WW

A Della Robbia Pottery plaque, 'The Apple Gatherer', by Cassandra Annie Walker, painted 'CAW 1900' to bottom right, incised numbers to reverse, restored.

1900   *22.75in (57.5cm) high*

$6,500-7,500   WW

A late 19thC Della Robbia vase, Birkenhead, incised and painted with a frieze of foliage, incised maker's mark to base with painted initial 'A' and incised initial 'F'.

The painted mark 'A' is often ascribed to an 'Agnes *', an early decorator. The simple incised 'F' on earlier pieces is ascribed to clay decorator Harry Fletcher. However the more cursive 'F' on this example suggests it was decorated by John Fogo.

10.5in (27cm) high

$1,500-2,500   L&T

An Ewenny Pottery model of a pig, incised 'Y Mochyn Bach Tew', based etched 'Ewenny Pottery'.

6in (16cm) wide

$1,000-1,200   WW

A Gray's Pottery 'Paris' shape jug, designed by Susie Cooper, printed mark, inscribed '8071' pattern code.

4.25in (11cm) high

$180-250   SWO

A Gray's Pottery 'Cubist' bowl, designed by Susie Cooper, printed Liner mark and 'Cubist' pattern name.

8.75in (22.5cm) diam

$450-500 — WW

A Bauhaus Hamelner Topferei vase, designed by Gertrud Kraut, painted design by Anni Rawitzer, impressed mark to base, chips to foot rim.

The H.T. Hamelner Topferei pottery was founded in Hameln, Germany in 1922 by Gertrud Kraut and Dr Georg Rawitzer - who were both members of the Deutsche Werkbund. This vase was designed in 1924 and made c1930.

15.75in (40cm) high

$500-650 — WW

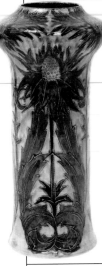

A Hancock & Sons Morris Ware vase, designed by George Cartlidge, model no.C17-25, printed and painted marks, facsimile signature.

11.5in (29.5cm) high

$1,900-2,500 — WW

A pair of Hancock & Sons Morris Ware candlesticks, designed by George Cartlidge, model no.C64-7, printed and painted marks, facsimile signature.

8.5in (21.5cm) high

$1,500-1,900 — WW

A Hancock & Sons Morris Ware vase, designed by George Cartlidge, model no.C14-9, slip, printed and painted marks, painted facsimile signature.

$1,200-1,500 — WW

A Keeling and Co. Losol ware vase, probably painted by C.B. Brown, with leopards at the water's edge, printed marks, crazing, minor oxidization to darker enamels.

Keeling & Co. was an earthenware and blue printed ware manufacturer at the Dale Hall Works, Longport, Burslem, Stoke-on-Trent. In 1905 the ceramics designer Charlotte Rhead was employed as an enameller.

c1920   *29.25in (74cm) high*

$1,500-2,000 — PW

A rare French Keller & Guérin glazed ceramic gourd vase, by Louis Majorelle, base signed 'K&G Lunéville Majorelle', one collapsed glaze bubble, small glaze loss between tendril and body of vase.

c1900   *11.75in (30cm) high*

$25,000-32,000 — DRA

An Art Nouveau porcelain vase, by Charles Korschann, with a panel of a child, on gilt bronze mount, with Louchet Paris seal, signed 'Pl Alp'.

7.5in (19cm) high

$1,300-1,900 — WW

A Linthorpe pottery vessel, by Christopher Dresser, based upon a Peruvian Chimu vessel, impressed signature mark alongside Henry Tooth monogram and shape number '330', restored.

4.25in (11cm) high

$500-650   FLD

A 1910s Marblehead vase, with trees, by Arthur Hennessey, impressed ship mark, incised 'HT', overcoated, professional restoration.

7in (18cm) high

$2,300-2,800   DRA

A Marblehead ship tile, stamped ship mark.

1904-36   4.5in (11.5cm) wide

$550-650   DRA

A 1910s Marblehead vase with geometric design, impressed ship mark 'MP', incised 'HT'.

6in (15.5cm) high

$3,200-3,800   DRA

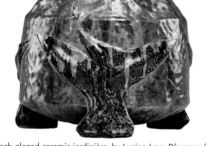

A rare French glazed ceramic jardinière, by Lucien Levy-Dhurmer (1865-1953) and Clement Massier (1844-1917), with butterflies and bird feet, base signed 'L. Levy/Clement', factory drill-hole plugged with cork, professional restoration to two feet.

c1890

$20,000-25,000   DRA

ESSENTIAL REFERENCE - DUCHESS OF SUTHERLAND

The Duchess of Sutherland Cripple Guild was founded in 1900 by Millicent, Duchess of Sutherland. The guild aimed to provide medical treatment and education for the children of the Staffordshire Potteries, many of whom had been injured or disabled by their work. In 1902, Francis Arthur Edwards began to teach the children metalwork. They made copper, silver and silver-plated items, which were sold locally and at a showroom in London. The guild closed in 1922.

An Arts and Crafts flambé glazed mazer bowl, the silver mounts stamped 'D.S.C.G' for the Duchess of Sutherland Cripple Guild, bowl signed 'BM' for Bernard Moore.

1907   11in (27.5cm) diam

$1,200-1,400   WW

ESSENTIAL REFERENCE - JOHN PEARSON

John Pearson (fl.1885-1910) was a master craftsman of the Newlyn School and Guild of Handicrafts. Together with Charles Robert Ashbee, he was a founding member of the Guild of Handicraft at Whitechapel, London, in 1888. John Pearson left the Guild of Handicraft in 1892 and went to Newlyn, Cornwall where he worked in the recently established industrial school. Pearson was greatly influenced by William De Morgan (1839-1917) and there is some evidence that he worked in some capacity at De Morgan's workshop decorating tiles and pottery and making associated metalwork, for example tile mounts. In addition to his time with De Morgan, Pearson worked on his own account as a metalworker and decorating pottery.

A late 19thC Arts and Crafts John Pearson charger, decorated with a squirrel, the reverse with a dragon, initialed 'JP'.

12in (30.5cm) diam

$950-1,100   FLD

An Art Deco earthenware figural group by Primavera, modeled as an embracing couple, factory marks and incised number '8328'.

8.75in (22.5cm) high

$300-400   ECGW

A set of Ridgway Potteries 'Homemaker' dinner wares, with six plates, four side plates, five dessert bowls, one sauce boat and two tureens with covers, with printed marks.

plates 10in (25cm) diam

$180-230   SWO

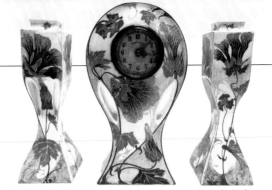

A Rozenburg Den Haag porcelain clock garniture, marks and artist's monogram for Sam Schellink, some cracks and chips.

Sam Schelling (1876-1958) worked as a decorator for Rozenburg from 1892 until bankruptcy in 1914, overseeing some of the firm's most admired designs in the Art Nouveau idiom. Unlike the factory's more robust wares in pottery, Rozenburg's medal-winning porcelain was so delicate as to be almost beyond use.

clock 8.5in (22cm) high

$7,500-9,000   GTH

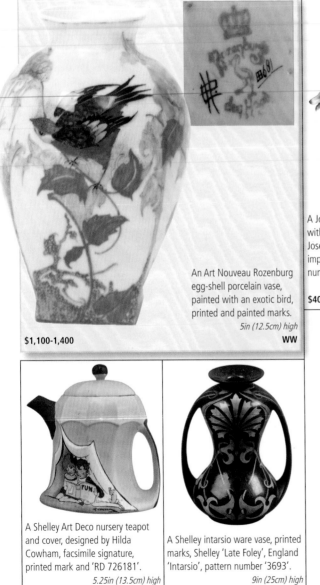

An Art Nouveau Rozenburg egg-shell porcelain vase, painted with an exotic bird, printed and painted marks.

5in (12.5cm) high

$1,100-1,400   WW

A Joesef Schuster model of a lady with a Borzoi, probably designed by Josef Lorenzl, printed, painted and impressed marks, including model number '8155 264'.

14in (35cm) high

$400-500   CHEF

A Sèvres porcelain vase, by Alexandre Sandier (1843-1916), with crystalline glaze, base marked 'S1905', silver lip is possibly a later addition, one burst glaze bubble and one scratch to body.

1905

$6,500-7,500   DRA

A Shelley Art Deco nursery teapot and cover, designed by Hilda Cowham, facsimile signature, printed mark and 'RD 726181'.

5.25in (13.5cm) high

$300-350   SWO

A Shelley intarsio ware vase, printed marks, Shelley 'Late Foley', England 'Intarsio', pattern number '3693'.

9in (25cm) high

$250-320   MOR

A large Sunflower Pottery vase, by Sir Edmund Elton, in a crackled gold luster glaze, painted Elton mark, minor professional restoration to rim.

20in (51cm) high

$400-500   WW

A 1910s buttressed Teco vase, impressed 'Teco 269'.

11in (28cm) high

$1,800-2,300   **DRA**

A reticulated Teco vase, stamped 'Teco', professional restoration to several leaves.

c1910   *11.75in (30cm) high*

$1,300-1,800   **DRA**

A Teco Aventurine vase, stamped 'Teco', incised 'X', restoration to several small chips.

c1910   *14.75in (37.5cm) high*

$550-700   **DRA**

A Troika wheel lamp base, designed by Alison Brigden, painted marks.

10.75in (27cm) high

$250-320   **CHEF**

A Troika wheel vase, molded and textured with geometric molding in high relief, signed and artist monogram to underside.

13in (33cm) high

$650-750   **HAN**

A textured Troika cube vase, by Tina Doubleday.

3.5in (9cm) square

$130-180   **HAN**

A rectangular Troika vase, signed to base.

9in (22.5cm) high

$450-500   **LOCK**

A Chelsea pottery figure, 'Autumn Leaves', by Charles Vyse, on an ebonized wooden plinth, incised marks to the side 'C. VYSE', 'CHELSEA', dated.

1929   *9.5in (24cm) high*

$2,500-3,200   **L&T**

A Chelsea pottery figure, 'The Balloon Woman', by Charles Vyse, painted marks 'CV', 'CHELSEA' and '1021', dated.

1921   *8.75in (22.5cm) high*

$1,300-1,900   **L&T**

DECORATIVE ARTS

CLOSER LOOK - CHARLES VYSE

This is a rare figure group.

Charles Vyse (1882 Staffordshire-1971 Deal, Kent), was an English studio potter, noted for producing colorful figurines of characters seen on London streets.

This figure is modeled as a man in a striped suit, his dog by his side and holding two puppies in his hands.

The sentimentality of the group adds to its appeal.

A Chelsea pottery figure, 'Club Row Sunday Morning', by Charles Vyse, wooden plinth base, incised mark to side 'C. VYSE', 'CHELSEA'.

c1937   *13in (33cm) high*

$7,500-9,000   **L&T**

A pottery figure of a gypsy lady, by Wiener Kunstkeramische Werkstätten Busch and Ludescher, impressed marks and painted 'TB' initials.

16in (41cm) high

$500-650   **CHEF**

A pottery figure of a lady, by Wiener Kunstkeramische Werkstätten Busch and Ludescher, impressed factory marks and numbers '13729-24-4', her head has been off and repaired.

9.5in (24cm) high

$250-320   **CHEF**

A Royal Worcester porcelain ginger jar and cover, with eight panels painted with figures in a lakescape, printed marks and numbered '2825'.

c1930   *6.5in (16.5cm) high*

$500-550   **BELL**

A Wileman Foley intarsio vase, designed by Frederick Rhead, painted with geese, professional restoration to a handle.

12in (30cm) high

$450-550   **ECGW**

A Royal Worcester Sabrina ware porcelain jardinière, with relief-molded verse 'While ye may gather ye roses', printed mark with date code, some damage.

1926   *10.25in (26cm) diam*

$300-350   **FLD**

A Royal Worcester Sabrina ware vase, with a stork wading through grass, initialed 'AS' for Albert Shuck, faint green mark.

5.5in (14cm) high

$300-400   **FLD**

A pair of Royal Worcester Crownware vases, G42 shape, decorated with a gilt luster landscape, printed marks, with date code.

1926   *8.75in (22cm) high*

$1,300-1,900   **BELL**

A late 19th/early 20thC Howard & Son mahogany and ebonized table, with a marquetry block decorated with birds, stamped underside 'Howard & Sons'.

25.75in (64.5cm) high

$3,800-4,400   **TRI**

A Morris & Co. Arts and Craft oak two-tier center table, stamped to underside of table top.

25in (63.5cm) high

$800-950   **TRI**

Judith Picks

Possibly it is because I'm Scottish, but I think Charles Rennie Mackintosh designs are unsurpassed and still have a very 'modern' look.

Mackintosh had produced versions of the traditional ladderback chair before, first for David Gauld in 1893, and then as a bedroom chair at Windyhill in 1901. This understated and deceptively simple design of 1903, for Miss Cranston's new Willow Tearooms in Sauchiehall Street, is his most successful treatment of this vernacular form. The dark wood against the pale walls and tablecloths of the tearoom interiors accentuating the striking lines of this, one of Mackintosh's most recognisable chairs.

A Charles Rennie Mackintosh ebonized oak 'ladderback' chair, for Miss Cranston's Willow Tearooms, with later oak-framed drop-in seat and rushing.

c1903   41in (104.5cm) high

$32,000-38,000   **L&T**

CLOSER LOOK - SHAPLAND & PETTER BOOKCASE

Made by one of the top Arts and Crafts makers - Shapland & Petter.

It is a classic design - the raised spindled gallery has a shaped shelf and inset embossed copper panel.

With the medieval inspired glazed and leaded doors, with copper hinges.

Bearing the inscription 'VITA SINE LITEREIS MORS EST' ('Life without literature is death').

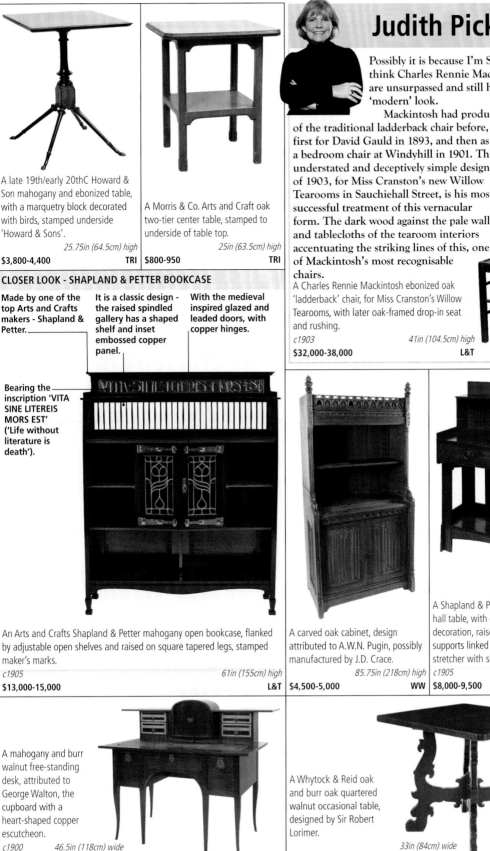

An Arts and Crafts Shapland & Petter mahogany open bookcase, flanked by adjustable open shelves and raised on square tapered legs, stamped maker's marks.

c1905   61in (155cm) high

$13,000-15,000   **L&T**

A carved oak cabinet, design attributed to A.W.N. Pugin, possibly manufactured by J.D. Crace.

85.75in (218cm) high

$4,500-5,000   **WW**

A Shapland & Petter inlaid oak hall table, with chequer inlaid decoration, raised on planked supports linked by a lower platform stretcher with slatted back.

c1905   48.5in (123cm) high

$8,000-9,500   **L&T**

A mahogany and burr walnut free-standing desk, attributed to George Walton, the cupboard with a heart-shaped copper escutcheon.

c1900   46.5in (118cm) wide

$5,500-6,500   **SWO**

A Whytock & Reid oak and burr oak quartered walnut occasional table, designed by Sir Robert Lorimer.

33in (84cm) wide

$5,000-6,500   **WW**

A walnut breakfront display cabinet, designed by Edward Barnsley, made by Charles Bray, inlaid with ebony banding and chequer banding, turned ebony handles.

1932   *87in (221cm) wide*

$13,000-15,000   **WW**

A Mother-of-pearl inlaid walnut dressing table mirror, by Sidney Barnsley, losses to the Mother-of-pearl.

                                    21.25in (54cm) high

$6,500-7,500   **WW**

A rosewood wall mirror, by Sidney Barnsley, probably made for Kenton & Co., the frame with holly and ebony borders, inset with Mother-of-pearl and abalone roundel panels and tesserae borders.

c1903   *29.5in (75cm) high*

$28,000-35,000   **WW**

An oak coffer, by Sidney Barnsley, chip carved heart and diamond motif to front, with wrought iron furniture.

                                    47.25in (120cm) wide

$10,000-11,000   **WW**

An Arts and Crafts chestnut dresser, designed by Sir Ambrose Heal, with an ivorine label 'HEAL & SON MAKERS LONDON, W'.

c1914   *72in (183cm) long*

$9,000-10,000   **SWO**

An oak wall shelf, by Sir Robert Lorimer KBE.

This was almost certainly made for the Early of Moray's new dairy at Kinfauns Castle, Perthshire in 1928. Lorimer designed a similar pair for the cottage kitchen at Earlshall Castle in Fife for R.W. Mackenzie in 1899.

                                    48.5in (123cm) wide

$800-950   **SWO**

A Stow single oak wardrobe, by Gordon Russell, with exposed pegged joints.

c1920s   *35.5in (90cm) wide*

$2,300-2,800   **CHOR**

An elm and cedar wood chest, by Gordon Russell, design no.266, cabinet maker H. Bellman, dated '12/6/26', label under drawer.

1926   *39in (99cm) wide*

$7,000-8,000   **CHOR**

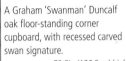

A Graham 'Swanman' Duncalf oak floor-standing corner cupboard, with recessed carved swan signature.

73.5in (186.5cm) high

$1,300-1,900   **TEN**

A 20thC oak refectory table, the adz plank top with pegged biscuit joints, with carved oak leaf decoration.

This table was probably made by David Langstaff, one of the Yorkshire Critters, formerly from the Robert 'Mouseman' Thompson of Kilburn workshop.

90in (229cm) long

$1,300-1,800   **BELL**

ESSENTIAL REFERENCE - ROBERT 'MOUSEMAN' THOMPSON

Robert Thompson (1876-1955) was a Yorkshire cabinetmaker who specialised in handcrafted, traditionally made furniture. He took over the family business in 1895 and by the 1930s employed thirty men and provided furniture for several schools and churches, including York Minster. His furniture was made from plain, English oak and shaped with an adze, giving it a rippled surface. Thompson signed each piece with a distinctive carved mouse. This signature may have originated in his early career when he described himself as being 'as poor as a church mouse'.

Several craftsmen who trained under Thompson went on to set up their own businesses. Like him, they signed their works with distinctive carved animals. These include Malcolm 'Foxman' Pipes, Wilf 'Squirrelman' Hutchinson and Graham 'Swanman' Duncalf.

Robert Thompson's Craftsmen Ltd. continues to make handcrafted furniture today.

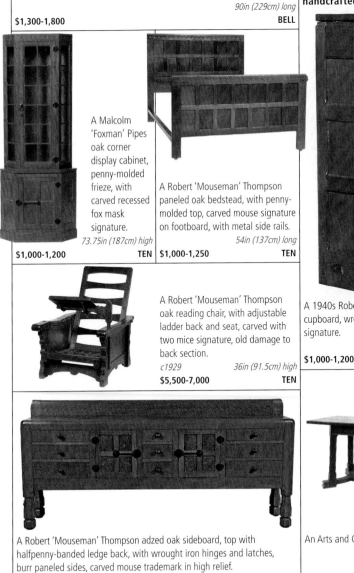

A Malcolm 'Foxman' Pipes oak corner display cabinet, penny-molded frieze, with carved recessed fox mask signature.

73.75in (187cm) high

$1,000-1,200   **TEN**

A Robert 'Mouseman' Thompson paneled oak bedstead, with penny-molded top, carved mouse signature on footboard, with metal side rails.

54in (137cm) long

$1,000-1,250   **TEN**

A Robert 'Mouseman' Thompson oak reading chair, with adjustable ladder back and seat, carved with two mice signature, old damage to back section.

c1929   *36in (91.5cm) high*

$5,500-7,000   **TEN**

A 1940s Robert 'Mouseman' Thompson paneled oak hanging corner cupboard, wrought-iron hinges and latch, with recessed front paw mouse signature.

27.75in (70.5cm) high

$1,000-1,200   **TEN**

A Robert 'Mouseman' Thompson adzed oak sideboard, top with halfpenny-banded ledge back, with wrought iron hinges and latches, burr paneled sides, carved mouse trademark in high relief.

91in (231cm) wide

$32,000-38,000   **HT**

An Arts and Crafts oak center table.

54.25in (138cm) long

$900-1,000   **SWO**

A German Secessionist ash wardrobe, with brass lock plates with shaped handles and hinges.

79.75in (205.5cm) high

$2,500-3,200   **SWO**

A Gustav Stickley sideboard, no.814, branded, with original finish and original patina to hardware.

Gustav Stickley founded his own company in 1898 in Eastwood, New York, after leaving Stickley Brothers. He filed for bankruptcy in 1915.

c1912   66in (168cm) wide

$4,500-5,000   DRA

An early Gustav Stickley server, red decal, cleaned and recolored.

c1902-03   59.5in (151cm) wide

$9,000-10,000   DRA

A Gustav Stickley leather-top lamp table, with stacked stretchers, wax build-up to original color.

c1904   41in (104cm) wide

$6,500-7,000   DRA

A Gustav Stickley oak side table, with pegged joints, stamped red mark.

27.5in (70cm) high

$650-750   WW

A Gustav Stickley willow settle, original finish, several areas of wear, small breaks.

c1912-15   88in (223.5cm) wide

$2,500-3,200   DRA

A Gustav Stickley drop-arm spindled Morris chair, old refinish, replaced leather cushions, repair to sling seat.

c1905   40.75in (103.5cm) high

$3,200-3,800   DRA

A Gustav Stickley double-door bookcase, with keyed tenons, branded, back panel reglued, hairline crack to side of one pane of glass.

c1905   56.25in (143cm) high

$3,800-4,400   DRA

A Gustav Stickley china cabinet, red decal, original finish, with key and partial paper label, the door slightly dragging on the bottom edge.

c1908   59.25in (150.5cm) high

$3,800-4,400   DRA

A Gustav Stickley chalet desk, large red decal, old refinish, skinned and oiled.

c1901   46in (117cm) high

$1,500-2,300   DRA

An L. & J.G. Stickley settle, in original color, possibly overcoated finish, pencil-marked '#221', original springs with older leather re-upholstery.

Leopold and John George Stickley were brothers of Gustav Stickley. They founded L. & J.G. Stickley in 1904 in Fayetteville, New York. In 1974 L. & J.G. Stickley was purchased by Alfred and Aminy Audi and continues today as Stickley's.

c1910   *60.5in (153.5cm) wide*
$4,500-5,000   **DRA**

An L. & J.G. Stickley paneled even-arm settle, unmarked, wax build-up to original finish, extensive wear to the original leather seat.
c1905   *84in (213cm) wide*
$8,000-9,000   **DRA**

An L. & J.G. Stickley bent-arm settle, handcraft decal, original color, original oilcloth cushion.
c1905   *77.25in (196cm) wide*
$3,200-3,800   **DRA**

An L. & J.G. Stickley drop-arm Morris chair, unmarked, overcoat to dark original finish, replaced leather seat and back cushion.
c1907   *42in (107cm) high*
$2,500-3,200   **DRA**

An L. & J.G. Stickley rocker, 'The Work Of...' decal, original seat cushion reupholstered, back pillow replaced.
1912   *36in (91.5cm) high*
$1,500-2,300   **DRA**

An L. & J.G. Stickley sideboard, 'The Work Of...' decal, missing loop to right-hand door.
c1915   *60in (152.5cm) wide*
$5,500-6,500   **DRA**

An L. & J.G. Stickley double-door bookcase, hairline crack to one pane of glass.
c1907   *55.5in (141cm) high*
$4,500-5,000   **DRA**

An L. & J.G. Stickley magazine stand, 'The Work Of...' decal, original finish and color.
c1912   *42in (106.5cm) high*
$1,500-2,000   **DRA**

An L. & J.G. Stickley dining table, with drop-down legs stored under the top and fold down when the table is extended.
c1907   *54in (137cm) wide*
$2,500-3,200   **DRA**

An L. & J.G. Stickley trestle table, 'The Work Of...' decal, some light scratches.
c1912   *48in (122cm) wide*
$1,300-1,800   **DRA**

DECORATIVE ARTS

A Stickley Brothers server, with hammered copper details, some minor staining to top and lower shelf.

Stickley Brothers was founded in 1883 by Albert, Gustav and Charles Stickley. By the 1890s it was the largest furniture manufacturer in New York State. After Gustav left the company, Albert moved Stickley Brothers to Grand Rapids, Michigan. He retired in 1927 and the company continued until 1947.

c1905   *54.25in (138cm) wide*
$5,500-6,500   DRA

A Stickley Brothers sideboard, with hammered copper details, original finish and color, one loop missing from drawer pull.

c1905   *70in (178cm) wide*
$7,500-9,000   DRA

A Stickley Brothers sideboard, stencilled '8216', original finish, several dark stains to top.

c1910   *54in (137cm) high*
$1,300-1,900   DRA

A Stickley Brothers quarter-sawn oak bookcase, with leaded slag-glass panels, some water marks to top, some filled holes to rails of sides.

c1915   *60in (152.5cm) high*
$1,300-1,900   DRA

A Stickley Brothers china cabinet, with hammered copper details, original finish, one replaced piece of glass to the side, some wear to color.

1905   *74in (188cm) high*
$9,000-10,000   DRA

A Stickley Brothers dining table, with hammered copper details, leaves quarter sawn, some wear to top.

c1905   *53in (134.5cm) wide*
$7,000-8,000   DRA

A Stickley Brothers dining table, paper label, original finish to base, new finish to top, leaves replaced.

c1910   *54in (137cm) wide*
$2,500-3,200   DRA

A Stickley Brothers diminutive writing desk, retailer paper label, light wear and stains to top.

c1905   *30in (76cm) high*
$1,300-1,900   DRA

A Stickley Brothers drop-arm quarter-sawn oak settle, overcoat to original finish, some moisture rings to arms.

c1915   *72in (183cm) wide*
$1,100-1,500   DRA

A rare Byrdcliffe wall-hanging cabinet, decorated with carved lily, branded.

Woodstock Byrdcliffe Guild is a regional center for the arts based in Woodstock, New York, USA. It was founded in 1902 and is still operational.

c1909   39.5in (100cm) wide

$7,000-8,000   DRA

A pair of Harden wavy-arm rockers, Camden, New Jersey, original finishes, older vinyl on original springs, the arm of one rocker slightly pulled away from rear leg.

c1908   36in (91.5cm) high

$3,200-3,800   DRA

A Lifetime drop-arm settle, partial paper label, 'Paine Furniture' metal distributor tag, stencilled model number, minor fading to original color, old leather reupholstery to cushion.

c1910   75.5in (192cm) wide

$1,900-2,500   DRA

A Limbert china cabinet, with paper label, refinished or cleaned and overcoated, some color loss, missing the third shelf.

Charles P. Limbert founded Limbert Furniture Company in 1894 in Grand Rapids, Michigan. The factory closed in 1944.

c1904   57.75in (146.5cm) high

$3,200-3,800   DRA

A Limbert cut-out side table, professional refinish, the corners seemingly rounded post-manufacture.

c1905   36in (91.5cm) wide

$1,900-2,500   DRA

A Limbert drop-front desk, professionally refinished, missing original pull to drop-front, filled screw holes on drop-front from original hardware.

c1905   54in (137cm) high

$8,000-9,500   DRA

A hall chair, by Charles Rohlfs (1853-1936), original ebonized finish with thin partial overcoat, finials professionally replaced to original specifications, professional repair to rear leg.

c1904   57in (145cm) high

$20,000-25,000   DRA

A dinner bell, by Charles Rohlfs (1853-1936), with original finish, carved with 'R' cipher, one replaced handle peg, some wear to handles.

Charles Rohlfs designed and worked in Buffalo, New York, USA.

c1902   31in (78.5cm) high

$5,500-7,000   DRA

A Charles Rohlfs bench, branded signature, dated, wear on overcoat to original finish.

1903   30in (76cm) wide

$11,000-15,000   DRA

A Roycroft magazine stand, with orb and cross mark, several circular stains to shelves.

c1905   63.75in (162cm) high

$11,000-12,000   DRA

A Victorian Gothic oak overmantel, with carved end finials and frieze of seventeen finials.

65.25in (166cm) wide

$750-900

CHOR

A late 19thC Japanesque walnut cabinet, decorated with contemporary Japanese panels, relief carved and inlaid with ivory and Mother-of pearl depicting a variety of birds, the interior fitted with three pigeonholes, the integral stand with carved foliate scroll apron.

69in (175cm) high

$1,300-1,800

SWO

An Aesthetic Movement ebonized side table, designed by E.W. Godwin.

34in (86.5cm) long

$3,200-3,800

SWO

A rosewood table, designed by E.W. Godwin, fitted with brass caps and castors, stamped 'Collinson & Locke London 6442 5'.

40.25in (102cm) diam

$15,000-20,000

SWO

An Aesthetic Movement ebonized cherry side cabinet, by Kimbel and Cabus, New York, with elaborate brass hinges, the ebonized surface incised and gilded, panels painted with birds, plants and animals.

A corner chair by Kimbel and Cabus, held in the Brooklyn Museum, shows the same characteristics as this cabinet (Accession no.1992.9).

c1875   *61in (155cm) high*

$1,900-2,500

L&T

An Aesthetic Movement ebonized corner cabinet, attributed to Daniel Cottier, centered with a painted panel and enclosed by further shelves.

c1870   *75in (191cm) high*

$3,200-3,800

L&T

A Gallé Art Nouveau marquetry étagère, by Emile Gallé, France, signed, with 'Ombelle' floral decoration and marquetry, some minor cosmetic restoration to back.

c1900   *62.5in (159cm) high*

$7,500-9,000

JDJ

An Art Nouveau marquetry display cabinet, by Louis Majorelle, with floral marquetry panel, the back case panel with marquetry landscape signed 'L. Majorelle Nancy', with some original polished surfaces and now professionally repolished.

c1900   *68in (173cm) high*

$9,000-10,000

JDJ

A bed and two bedside tables, by Louis Majorelle, of carved nutwood, in clematis pattern, with different kinds of inlaid exotic wood, poppy flowers and capsules.

c1900   *bed 78.75in (200cm) long*

$20,000-25,000 set

QU

An Art Deco walnut cocktail cabinet, with a mirrored interior.

49.5in (125.5cm) high

$750-900   **SWO**

An Art Deco walnut cocktail cabinet, the bottom section converted to take a television.

61.75in (157cm) high

$500-650   **MOR**

A 1920s German two-piece cocktail cabinet, nickel-plated rectangular steel, polished, blockboard handpainted by an artist in oil.

65in (165cm) high

$9,000-10,000   **QU**

An Art Deco burr maple cocktail cabinet, with ivory handles, with an illuminated interior with glass shelves and pull out mirrored slide for drinks.

c1930   *68in (173cm) high*

$7,000-8,000   **L&T**

An Art Deco walnut cabinet, with sunburst inlaid cupboard.

30.5in (77.5cm) high

$400-500   **SWO**

An Art Deco cabinet, by Alfred Chambon, mounted in oriental-style gilt-bronzes.

Alfred Chambon (1884-1973) established his workshops in Brussels in 1925 with his father, the architect Alban Chambon. Alfred developed a unique style, drawing inspiration from the simplified lines of Bauhaus and the elegance of oriental motifs. He infused drama into his pieces with rich and exotic veneers such as burr walnut, rosewood, mahogany and ebony to which he applied elaborate gilt-bronze mounts.

57in (145cm) high

$4,500-5,000   **DN**

An Art Deco coromandel sideboard, designed by Serge Chermayeff, for Waring and Gillow Ltd., labelled and stamped and numbered '93224' to the back.

60.25in (153cm) wide

$2,500-3,200   **SWO**

A walnut veneered 'Alarm Clock' side display cabinet, with label.

49.5in (126cm) high

$500-650   **FLD**

An Art Deco maple and beech occasional table, with ebony and rosewood banding.

23in (58.5cm) wide

$400-500   **HT**

An Art Deco maple table.

23.75in (60.5cm) high

$500-650

HT

An Art Deco walnut crossbanded metamorphic side table.

25in (64cm) high

$500-750

MOR

An Art Deco coromandel three-part dining table, designed by Serge Chermayeff, for Waring and Gillows.

87in (221cm) deep

$2,500-3,800

SWO

An Art Deco walnut upholstered ottoman, with taseled ends on brass castors.

59in (150cm) wide

$500-650

MOR

One of a pair of Art Deco armchairs, veneered in calamander, each with a cast white metal handle on the back with a stylized design of islands amongst waves.

31.5in (80cm) wide

$4,400-5,700 pair

DN

An Art Deco Seymour sitting room radio.

29.5in (75cm) high

$100-130

SWO

ESSENTIAL REFERENCE - MARCEL BREUER

The Wassily Chair, also known as the Model B3 chair, was designed by Marcel Breuer in 1925-1926 while he was the head of the cabinet-making workshop at the Bauhaus, in Dessau, Germany. A champion of the modern movement and protégé of Bauhaus founder Walter Gropius, Marcel Breuer is equally celebrated for his achievements in architecture and furniture. Breuer was an outstanding student and subsequently a master carpenter at the Bauhaus in the early 1920s. His entire body of work embodies the Bauhaus objective to reconcile art and industry. While at the Bauhaus, Breuer revolutionised the modern interior with his tubular-steel furniture collection - inspired by the techniques of local plumbers. His first designs, including the Wassily, remain among the most identifiable icons of the modern furniture movement and Modernism itself.

An Art Deco burr maple headboard, with downswept ends incorporating bedside cabinets.

110in (279.5cm) wide

$750-900

HT

A Gebrüder Thonet 'Wassily' Club Chair Model B3, by Marcel Breuer (1902-1981), chromed tubular steel and canvas.

designed 1925

30in (77cm) wide

$5,000-6,500

L&T

ESSENTIAL REFERENCE - GABRIEL ARGY-ROUSSEAU

Gabriel Argy-Rousseau (1885-1953) began his career as a ceramicist but soon became interested in glass. After exhibiting at the 1914 Exposition du Salon des Artistes Français, his fame and success grew. In 1921, he established the Société Anonyme des Pâtes de Verre d'Argy-Rousseau with Gustave Moser-Millot. The firm produced a range of small, richly colored Art Nouveau and Art Deco pieces, many of which were made using pâte-de-verre, an ancient method of casting powdered glass in molds, then firing in a kiln to melt and shape the glass. Argy-Rousseau wares are often decorated with stylized flowers, insects, animals and depictions of the female form. The partnership between Moser-Millot and Argy-Rousseau ended in 1929 but Argy-Rousseau continued producing until World War II.

A Gabriel Argy-Rousseau pâte-de-verre speckled leaves vase, with leaves that changed to deep green when illuminated, molded 'G. Argy-Rousseau' signature on side, molded '11244' on underside.

6.5in (16.5cm) high

$9,500-10,500   **JDJ**

A Gabriel Argy-Rousseau 'Alpine Thistles' pâte-de-verre bowl, cast signature 'G Argy-Rousseau'.

4in (10cm) high

$2,500-3,200   **WW**

A Gabriel Argy-Rousseau pâte-de-verre poppies vase, signed on the side 'G. Argy Rousseau' and 'France' on underside.

7.25in (18.5cm) high

$11,000-14,000   **JDJ**

A Gabriel Argy-Rousseau pâte-de-verre bowl, Paris, signed 'G. ARGY-ROUSSEAU', with nickel-plated metal mounting, marked with remains of a maker's mark '283'.

1930   *7.75in (20cm) diam*

$6,500-7,500   **QU**

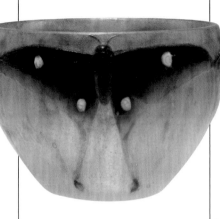

A Gabriel Argy-Rousseau pâte-de-verre 'Papillon' bowl, signed 'G. ARGY-ROUSSEAU'.

1915   *4.75in (12cm) diam*

$5,000-5,700   **QU**

A square pâte-de-verre pendant, by Gabriel Argy-Rousseau, molded with a reddish brown pine cone, molded mark 'G.A.R'.

1921   *2.25in (6cm) wide*

$700-800   **BELL**

A polychrome enamel Gabriel Argy-Rousseau scent bottle, depicting a bird in a cage.

c1921   *7in (18cm) high*

$1,000-1,250   **M&DM**

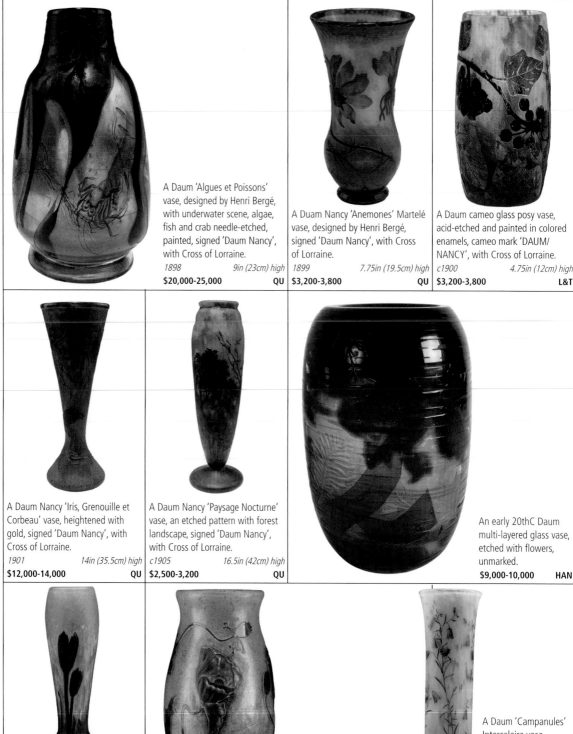

A Daum 'Algues et Poissons' vase, designed by Henri Bergé, with underwater scene, algae, fish and crab needle-etched, painted, signed 'Daum Nancy', with Cross of Lorraine.

1898   *9in (23cm) high*

$20,000-25,000   **QU**

A Duam Nancy 'Anemones' Martelé vase, designed by Henri Bergé, signed 'Daum Nancy', with Cross of Lorraine.

1899   *7.75in (19.5cm) high*

$3,200-3,800   **QU**

A Daum cameo glass posy vase, acid-etched and painted in colored enamels, cameo mark 'DAUM/ NANCY', with Cross of Lorraine.

c1900   *4.75in (12cm) high*

$3,200-3,800   **L&T**

A Daum Nancy 'Iris, Grenouille et Corbeau' vase, heightened with gold, signed 'Daum Nancy', with Cross of Lorraine.

1901   *14in (35.5cm) high*

$12,000-14,000   **QU**

A Daum Nancy 'Paysage Nocturne' vase, an etched pattern with forest landscape, signed 'Daum Nancy', with Cross of Lorraine.

c1905   *16.5in (42cm) high*

$2,500-3,200   **QU**

An early 20thC Daum multi-layered glass vase, etched with flowers, unmarked.

$9,000-10,000   **HAN**

A Daum cameo crocus vase, signed with cameo signature 'Daum Nancy', with the Cross of Lorraine.

12in (30.5cm) high

$11,000-12,000   **JDJ**

A Daum wheel-carved cameo poppy vase, with rich green cameo leaves, stems and buds, signed with carved signature 'Daum Nancy', with Cross of Lorraine.

12.75in (32.5cm) high

$12,000-14,000   **JDJ**

A Daum 'Campanules' Intercalaire vase, designed by Henri Bergé, pattern etched and enameled, bell flowers and field flowers, signed 'Daum Nancy', with engraved Cross of Lorraine.

1910   *19in (48.5cm) high*

$32,000-38,000   **QU**

A Daum cameo glass vase, signed 'Daum Nancy'.

4.75in (12cm) high

$1,300-1,900 ECGW

A Daum glass vase, shaded purple with gold foil inclusions, signed 'Daum Nancy/ France and Croix de Lorraine'.

c1925 26in (66cm) high

$1,000-1,100 MAB

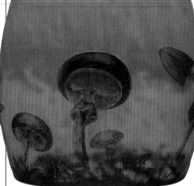

A Daum mushroom pillow cameo vase, wheel-carved and enameled decoration, signed with engraved signature 'Daum Nancy', with Cross of Lorraine.

4.75in (12cm) high

$7,500-9,000 JDJ

A Daum Art Nouveau cameo glass scent bottle, decorated with a dragonfly flying above water-lily flowers and pads, etched Daum Nancy mark, minor nicks.

c1900 5.25in (13.5cm) high

$5,000-6,500 WW

A Daum cameo glass footed vase, with a blue and clear glass body, with yellow and russet overlay, acid-etched with autumnal chestnut leaves, signed 'Daum Nancy'.

6.75in (17cm) wide

$1,000-1,100 WW

A yellow and black hot applied 'Jade' vase, signed 'Daum Nancy'.

c1920

$750-1,000 M&DM

A green 'Jade' bowl and lid, with orange knob, signed 'Daum Nancy'.

c1920 3in (7.5cm) high

$650-750 M&DM

An orange 'Jade' box and cover, with gold inclusions, signed 'Daum Nancy'.

c1920 5in (12.5cm) high

$750-1,000 M&DM

ESSENTIAL REFERENCE - 'PASSION FLOWER' VASE

This is an important Art Nouveau exhibition art glass vase, created for the Exposition Universelle de Paris, 1900, as a one off example of Galle's glass-making expertise and innovative design. The vase would have been displayed among other similar examples. It uses a pâte-de-verre type technique to create the mixture of contrasting colors. Galle's botanical training and interest in horticulture is evident in the design of this piece. The 1900 exhibition vases normally represented accurate and unusual species; in the same year which Galle attended the International Botanical Conference in Paris, presenting a paper on orchid varieties. The poem etched around the lower section of the vase talks about the passion and turbulence of life, symbolic of Galle's own sentiments in his writings: 'we know well that the eloquence of a flower, thanks to the mysteries of its organism and its destiny, thanks to the synthesis of the plant symbol evoked by the artist's pencil, exceeds sometimes the intense suggestive power of the human face'.

An Emile Gallé 'Passion Flower' vase, acid-etched and engraved with a naturalistic passion flower, with a verse by Marceline Desbordes Valmore 'O vie, o fleur d'orage, O menace, O mystere, O songe aveugle et beau', incised to the socle 'Galle, Expo 1900'.

20in (51cm) high

$55,000-60,000 HAN

An early Art Nouveau Gallé scent bottle and stopper, designed by Emile Gallé, enameled with a riverscape to one side, the reverse with a nude female figure, etched 'E Galle Nancy', repaired neck.

4.25in (11cm) high

$1,000-1,200 WW

A Gallé 'Sabot de Vénus et coprins' enameled vase, made in Meisenthal, etched inside and out, signed 'Emile Gallé delt ft' (delineavit et fecit) and 'Série C déposé.

1892 *14.25in (36cm) high*

$5,500-7,000 QU

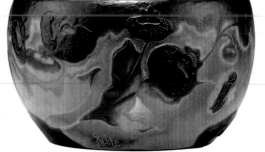

A Gallé 'Orchidées' bowl, with cut and engraved wild orchids at dusk, parts of ground martelé cut, signed 'GALLÉ'.

1895-1900 *8in (20.5cm) diam*

$6,500-7,500 QU

A Gallé 'Lys Tigré' vase, with etched tiger lily pattern, signed 'Gallé'.

1900-04 *19.25in (49cm) high*

$7,500-9,000 QU

An Emile Gallé cameo glass vase and cover, overlaid with amethyst glass and acid etched with a design of clematis, cameo mark 'GALLÉ'.

c1900 *4.75in (12cm) high*

$1,500-2,300 L&T

A Gallé mold-blown vase, with plums and leaves descending from lip, in cameo 'Gallé', light grind marks to foot, possibly from factory.

5.5in (14cm) high

$13,000-15,000 JDJ

A Gallé vase, with mold-blown decoration of figs, with leaves and vines encircling body of vase, signed in cameo 'Gallé'.

12in (30.5cm) high

$7,500-9,000 JDJ

A Gallé 'Primevères Roses' Intercalaire vase, with primroses in frost and fog, signed 'Gallé'.

c1902   *5.25in (13.5cm) high*

$19,000-23,000   **QU**

A Gallé vase, with cameo penguins, with shaded white and blue icebergs, signed in cameo 'Gallé'.

8.25in (21cm) high

$50,000-55,000   **JDJ**

A Gallé cameo glass vase, cut with a fruiting berry bough, cameo Gallé star mark to the body.

5in (13cm) high

$1,300-1,800   **FLD**

An early 20thC French Gallé vase, decorated with hibiscus, acid-etched cameo glass, signed 'Gallé' on body, some minor unevenness to rim.

10.75in (27cm) high

$7,500-9,000   **DRA**

A Gallé vase, with mold-blown decoration of long brown spiked leaves and stems with hyacinth flowers, signed in cameo 'Gallé'.

11.5in (29cm) high

$18,000-20,000   **JDJ**

A 1920s Gallé 'Laurier Rose' vase, etched with oleander at sunset, buds highlighted through etching on the inside, signed 'Gallé'.

16.75in (42.5cm) high

$6,500-7,500   **QU**

A 1920s Gallé 'Oléandre' vase, signed 'Gallé'.

21in (53.5cm) high

$5,500-6,500   **QU**

A Gallé cameo glass vase, the body with pink and green inclusions, overlayed in blue with iris, signed.

12.25in (31cm) high

$1,100-1,500   **MOR**

A Lalique vase, in the 'Albert' pattern, no.958, the handles as stylized birds of prey heads to the topaz glass body, engraved mark.

6.75in (17cm) high

$900-1,000   **FLD**

A Lalique 'Bacchantes' vase, of clear molded glass, blue patina, engraved signature 'R. Lalique France'.

1927   *9.75in (24.5cm) high*

$7,000-7,500   **QU**

A Lalique 'Ceylan' vase, no.905, with budgerigars picked out with opalescence, engraved marks.

9.5in (24cm) high

$5,000-6,500   **FLD**

A Lalique 'Druide' - 'Gui de chêne' - opalescent vase, signed 'R.LALIQUE'.

1924   *6.75in (17cm) high*

$1,100-1,500   **QU**

A Lalique vase, in the 'Fougeres' pattern, no.923, relief-molded with bands of stiff leaves with gray stain, engraved signature.

6in (15cm) high

$1,000-1,200   **FLD**

A Lalique opalescent glass 'Laurier' vase, no.947, molded with fruiting foliage.

designed 1922   *7in (18cm) high*

$550-700   **BELL**

A Lalique 'Oranges' frosted and enameled glass vase, model no.964, molded 'R. LALIQUE', small polished chip and a couple of minor flecks to rim.

designed 1926   *12in (30cm) high*

$25,000-32,000   **DRA**

A Lalique 'Perruches' clear, frosted and opalescent glass bowl, with blue staining, with a frieze of budgerigars, stencil etched 'R. LALIQUE FRANCE'.

9.5in (24cm) diam

$3,500-4,000   **TEN**

A Lalique 'Sophora' vase, amber glass with white patina, etched 'Lalique France No. 977'.

designed 1936   *11in (28cm) wide*

$8,000-9,500   **DRA**

A 1920s Lalique crystal bottle and cover, 'Tourterelles', with two love birds, script engraved 'R.Lalique' signature to base.

11.5in (29cm) high

1929

$3,200-3,800   FLD

A Lalique 'Calendal' flaçon, for Molinard, sandblasted signature 'MOLINARD PARIS FRANCE', in original box.

1929   4.5in (11.5cm) high

$1,110-1,300   QU

A Lalique glass scent bottle and stopper, 'Houbigant 7 la Belle Saisons', designed by Rene Lalique, with original presentation box, with silk lining and silk rope pull and tassels, cast mark 'R Lalique Made in France', etched stopper.

designed 1920   4.25in (10.5cm) high

$2,500-3,200   WW

A Lalique glass and metal mounted 'Le Parisien' atomiser, for Molinard, decorated in the 'Figurines et Guirlandes' pattern, with molded marks.

c1923   6.25in (16cm) high

$250-320   BELL

A Lalique black glass Flaçons perfume bottle and stopper, 'Ambre D'Orsay', molded with classical maidens, marks 'Lalique' and 'Ambre D'Orsay', some damage.

c1913   5.25in (13.5cm) high

$550-700   BELL

A Lalique glass car mascot 'Cinq Chevaux', no.1122, later colored irradiated blue, molded and etched mark 'R.LALIQUE FRANCE'.

c1925   6in (15cm) wide

$2,800-3,500   BELL

A Lalique 'Chrysis' clear frosted car mascot, signed 'LALIQUE FRANCE'.

5in (13cm) high

$400-500   TRI

A pair of Lalique 'Amour' clear and frosted glass bookends, modeled as cupids, wheel engraved 'R.LALIQUE FRANCE', some chips.

8in (20.5cm) high

$1,400-1,800   TEN

A René Lalique 'Lausanne' no.2479 amber glass plafonnier, molded with fruit and leaves, molded 'R.LALIQUE FRANCE', some nicks and scratches.

15in (38cm) diam

$1,100-1,400   TEN

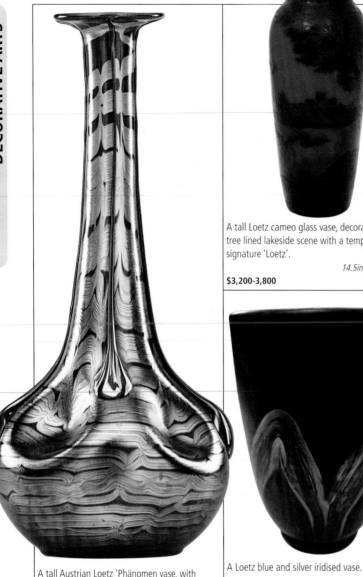

A tall Loetz cameo glass vase, decorated with a tree lined lakeside scene with a temple, cameo signature 'Loetz'.

14.5in (36.5cm) high

$3,200-3,800   **WW**

An Art Nouveau Loetz 'Papillon' glass water-dropper vase, in a blue-green lustrous finish, unsigned.

$650-750   **WW**

A tall Austrian Loetz 'Phänomen vase, with applied decoration, etched 'Loetz Austria', a few scuffs to body.

c1900   *19in (48cm) high*

$10,000-11,000   **DRA**

A Loetz blue and silver iridised vase.

This is from the company's less successful Art Deco lines.

c1925   *7in (18cm) high*

$650-750   **M&DM**

A Loetz iridescent glass fish bowl, molded with a tree lined lake scene, engraved signature to the base.

9in (23cm) wide

$4,400-5,700   **FLD**

An early 20thC Loetz 'Ausfuehrungen 237' vase, unmarked.

4.25in (10.5cm) high

$250-400   **FLD**

An early 20thC Loetz 'Creta Rusticana' posy vase.

5in (13cm) high

$90-110   **FLD**

A pair of Loetz opalescent on pale pink freeform handled vases.

8in (20.5cm) high

$1,300-1,500   **M&DM**

A Loetz glass coupe, by Michael Powolny (1871-1954).

c1930   *5.25in (13.5cm) wide at rim*

$300-400   **L&T**

A 20thC Monart glass vase, with gilt inclusions against a blue and green body.

7in (18cm) high

$150-230   **BELL**

A Monart shape 'JB Coupe' vase, pale blue glass with air bubble inclusions, unsigned.

8.75in (22cm) high

$500-650   **WW**

A 1930s Monart shape 'RD Stoneware' vase, decorated with a red stoneware effect, decorated with random murrine millefiori canes, polished pontil, retains original paper sticker to base.

9.5in (24cm) high

$1,300-1,900   **FLD**

A 1930s Monart shape 'C' vase, decorated with an amber/yellow luster over an opal base, with silver vertical stripes.

6.75in (17cm) high

$1,000-1,100   **FLD**

A 1930s Monart shape 'F' vase, decorated in red and orange with brown swirls and speckling, polished pontil, retains original paper sticker to base.

11.75in (30cm) high

$450-550   **FLD**

A Monart shape 'UA' vase, retains original paper label.

11.75in (30cm) high

$300-400   **FLD**

A rare Monart glass ginger jar and cover, mottled blue and white cased in clear, unsigned.

7in (18cm) high

$250-400   **WW**

A 1930s Monart shape 'X' bowl.

9.5in (24cm) diam

$1,000-1,100   **FLD**

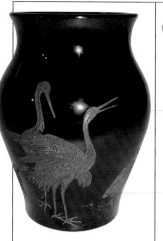

A Moser hyalith oroplastic crane vase, 'Mit Goldplastik', by Rudolf Wels, signed in gold 'RW' and 'Moser'.
1922   8in (20.5cm) high
$3,200-3,800   **M&DM**

A Moser oroplastic vase, in the 'Fipop' pattern, depicting battling amazons, probably designed by Leo Moser, signed.
c1925   8in (20.5cm) high
$550-700   **M&DM**

A Moser cobalt blue 'Animor' vase, designed by Rudolf Wels, depicting jungle scene with elephants, palm trees and birds, signed 'Rudolf Wels' twice.
1926   11in (28cm) high
$2,300-2,500   **M&DM**

A Moser scent bottle, designed by Heinrick Hussmann, signed.
1929   6in (15cm) high
$500-750   **M&DM**

A Moser six sided atomiser, designed by Rudolf Eschler, signed.

This atomiser is in Alexandrit - a color that changes between pink and purple depending on the lighting. These stylized pieces were made in a variety of sizes and colors and in three, four and six sided vessels.
1936   5in (12.5cm) high
$450-550   **M&DM**

A Moser bowl, designed by Heinrick Hussmann, in Alexandrit, signed.
c1929   10in (25.5cm) diam
$650-950   **M&DM**

A 'Functionalist' large Moser 'square' dressing table set, in eldor, designed by Rudolf Eschler, including scent bottle, atomiser and lidded box, signed, replacement puffer to atomiser.
1936   scent bottle 11in (28cm) high
$1,900-2,300   **M&DM**

A Moser lidded box, designed by Heinrick Hussmann, in Radion (uranium green), signed.
6in (15cm) high
$500-750   **M&DM**

A tall S.A.I.A.R. Ferro Toso & C. vase, designed by Guido Balsamo-Stella, with engraved depiction of a naiad, engraved 'GBS'.

c1928   *22.75in (57.5cm) high*

$1,300-1,900   QU

A Barovier & C. 'Aventurina' vase, designed by Ercole Barovier, with aventurines.

1929-30   *11.5in (29.5cm) high*

$1,500-1,900   QU

ESSENTIAL REFERENCE - FULVIO BIANCONI

Fulvio Bianconi (1915-1996) was born in Padua and studied at the Carmini School in Venice. He was apprenticed early as a glass decorator in the Murano furnaces, but spent much of his career as a graphic designer and cartoonist. While working at the publisher Garzanti after World War II, he operated as a freelance glasswork designer, first for GI.VI.M and later for Venini & C. The financial independence granted by his day job as a graphic designer allowed him greater artistic freedom in the Murano furnaces, where he would design and create a range of different glass objects. His wares are distinctive for their striking individuality, unusual forms and unique designs.

A Venini & C. 'Ventaglio' vase, designed by Fulvio Bianconi, unsigned.

c1948   *7.25in (18.5cm) high*

$3,200-3,800   QU

A Barovier & Toso/Ferro Toso 'Crepuscolo' vase, designed by Ercole Barovier.

1935-36   *11.5in (29.5cm) high*

$2,500-3,200   QU

A Barovier & Toso 'Lenti' iridescent vase, designed by Ercole Barovier.

c1940   *9.5in (24cm) high*

$3,800-4,400   QU

A Venini & C. 'Incamiciato' cased glassvase, designed by Tomaso Buzzi, base of white glass gather, maker's paper label, inscribed '346(...)', faintly acid stamped 'venini murano ITALIA'.

1932-33   *15.5in (39.5cm) high*

$3,800-5,000   QU

A Venini & C. 'Donna' cased glass vase, designed by Fulvio Bianconi, slightly iridescent, acid stamped 'venini murano MADE IN ITALY'.

c1949   *9.75in (25cm) high*

$14,000-18,000   QU

A Venini & C. 'Foglia' cased glass bowl, designed by Tyra Lundgren, acid stamped 'venini murano MADE IN ITALY'.

c1937   *14.25in (36cm) long*

$3,200-3,800   QU

A Venini & C. cased glass tomato, designed by Napoleone Martinuzzi, red with green iridescent seedhead, maker's label, acid stamped 'venini murano'.

1926-30　　　*3.5in (9cm) diam*

$1,900-2,500　　　**QU**

ESSENTIAL REFERENCE - CARLO SCARPA

Carlo Scarpa (1906-1978) was born in Venice and trained as an architect at the Academy of Fine Arts. He was the artistic director of Venini & C. from 1934 to 1947, before returning to a successful career in architecture. He introduced several significant decorative techniques and designs to Venini & C., including 'sommerso', cased glass with a transparent colored core enclosed by further transparent layers of glass, with a colorless outer later. He also created 'sommerso a bollicine', cased glass with gold inclusions, and 'mezze filigrana', glass with spiralling stripes.

A Seguso Vetri d'Arte 'Pulegoso' vase, designed by Flavio Poli, clear foam glass, burst gold foil to foot and handles, short tears to the handles.

c1936　　　*13.25in (33.5cm) high*

$1,000-1,100　　　**QU**

A Venini & C. 'a bollicine' bowl, designed by Carlo Scarpa, bubbly amber glass, acid stamped 'venini italia'.

c1932-33　　　*4in (10cm) high*

$2,100-2,500　　　**QU**

A Venini & C. 'Sommerso a bollicine' cased glass vase, designed by Carlo Scarpa, bubble layer, with gold foil, acid stamped 'venini murano'.

c1934-36　　　*4.25in (11cm) high*

$1,800-2,300　　　**QU**

A Venini & C. 'Mezza filigrana' vase, designed by Carlo Scarpa, acid stamped 'venini murano'.

c1934　　　*8.5in (21.5cm) high*

$1,900-2,500　　　**QU**

A Fratelli Toso 'Rosso e Nero' vase, deep purple glass with fused burst metal foils, the base, shoulder, handles and rim in red glass gather 'Pasta vitrea'.

c1930　　　*7.75in (19.5cm) high*

$1,300-1,800　　　**QU**

A Venini & C. 'Holbein' vase, designed by Vittorio Zecchin, emerald green glass, acid stamped 'venini italia', faint crack to the lower edge of one handle.

1922-26　　　*20in (50.5cm) high*

$1,900-2,500　　　**QU**

An M.V.M. Cappellin vase, designed by Vittorio Zecchin, light brown glass with eight applied drops, with red rim.

c1924　　　*12.5in (32cm) high*

$2,300-2,800　　　**QU**

An M.V.M. Cappellin vase, attributed to Vittorio Zecchin, blue glass with six applied drops.

c1925　　　*10.75in (27.5cm) high*

$1,000-1,250　　　**QU**

An iconic Schneider 'Jades' jug, in orange and white, with ornate stylized black handle, signed.

c1919   *7in (18cm) high*

$650-750   **M&DM**

A small Schneider 'Jades' vase, with applied handles and foot, signed.

c1920   *5in (12.5cm) high*

$900-1,000   **M&DM**

A Schneider 'Machine' cameo vase, purple and green over mottled orange, with tricolor candy cane, signed.

c1919   *6in (15cm) high*

$650-750   **M&DM**

A Schneider black footed hot applied 'Jades' tazza, in purple and white, signed.

c1921   *8in (20.5cm) high*

$900-1,100   **M&DM**

A 1920s 'Le Verre Francais' cameo glass footed bowl, cut back with bell-shaped flowers, amethyst glass foot.

11.5in (29cm) diam

$500-650   **MOR**

A tall Schneider 'Le Verre Francais' cameo glass vase, decorated with red overlay pendulous berried fronds, etched to foot 'Le Verre Francais'.

15.25in (39cm) high

$1,500-1,900   **WW**

A tall Schneider 'Orchidées' cased glass vase, signed 'Le Verre Français'.

1924-27   *19in (48.5cm) high*

$4,500-5,000   **QU**

A large 1920s Schneider 'Le Verre Francias' cameo glass vase, acid cut with toadstools, engraved signature to the foot.

24.75in (63cm) high

$2,500-3,200   **FLD**

A Schneider Charder cameo glass vase, acid etched with pendulous flowers and foliage, cameo Charder signature to side.

10.25in (26cm) diam

$1,900-2,500   **WW**

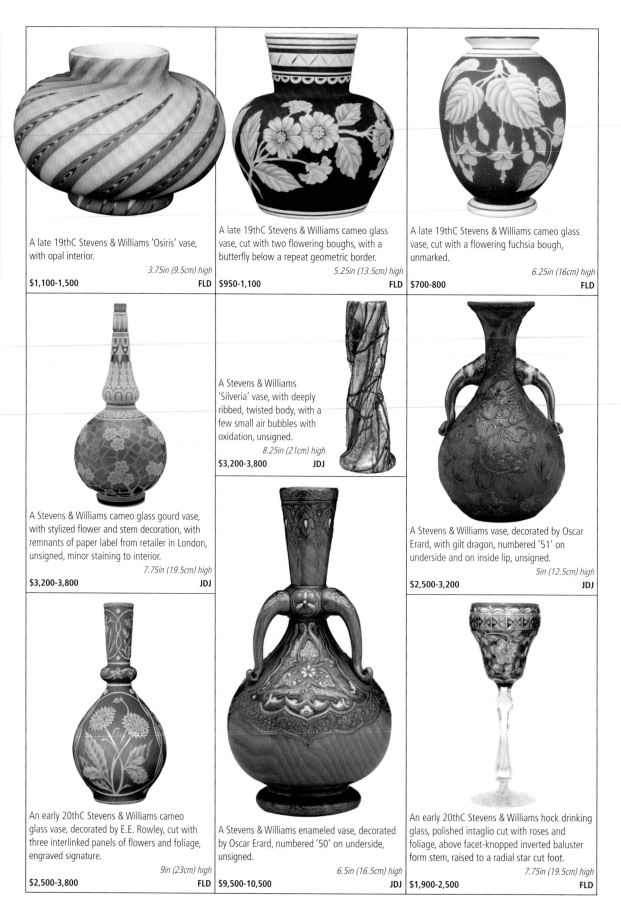

A late 19thC Stevens & Williams 'Osiris' vase, with opal interior.

3.75in (9.5cm) high

$1,100-1,500　　　　FLD

A late 19thC Stevens & Williams cameo glass vase, cut with two flowering boughs, with a butterfly below a repeat geometric border.

5.25in (13.5cm) high

$950-1,100　　　　FLD

A late 19thC Stevens & Williams cameo glass vase, cut with a flowering fuchsia bough, unmarked.

6.25in (16cm) high

$700-800　　　　FLD

A Stevens & Williams cameo glass gourd vase, with stylized flower and stem decoration, with remnants of paper label from retailer in London, unsigned, minor staining to interior.

7.75in (19.5cm) high

$3,200-3,800　　　　JDJ

A Stevens & Williams 'Silveria' vase, with deeply ribbed, twisted body, with a few small air bubbles with oxidation, unsigned.

8.25in (21cm) high

$3,200-3,800　　　　JDJ

A Stevens & Williams vase, decorated by Oscar Erard, with gilt dragon, numbered '51' on underside and on inside lip, unsigned.

5in (12.5cm) high

$2,500-3,200　　　　JDJ

An early 20thC Stevens & Williams cameo glass vase, decorated by E.E. Rowley, cut with three interlinked panels of flowers and foliage, engraved signature.

9in (23cm) high

$2,500-3,800　　　　FLD

A Stevens & Williams enameled vase, decorated by Oscar Erard, numbered '50' on underside, unsigned.

6.5in (16.5cm) high

$9,500-10,500　　　　JDJ

An early 20thC Stevens & Williams hock drinking glass, polished intaglio cut with roses and foliage, above facet-knopped inverted baluster form stem, raised to a radial star cut foot.

7.75in (19.5cm) high

$1,900-2,500　　　　FLD

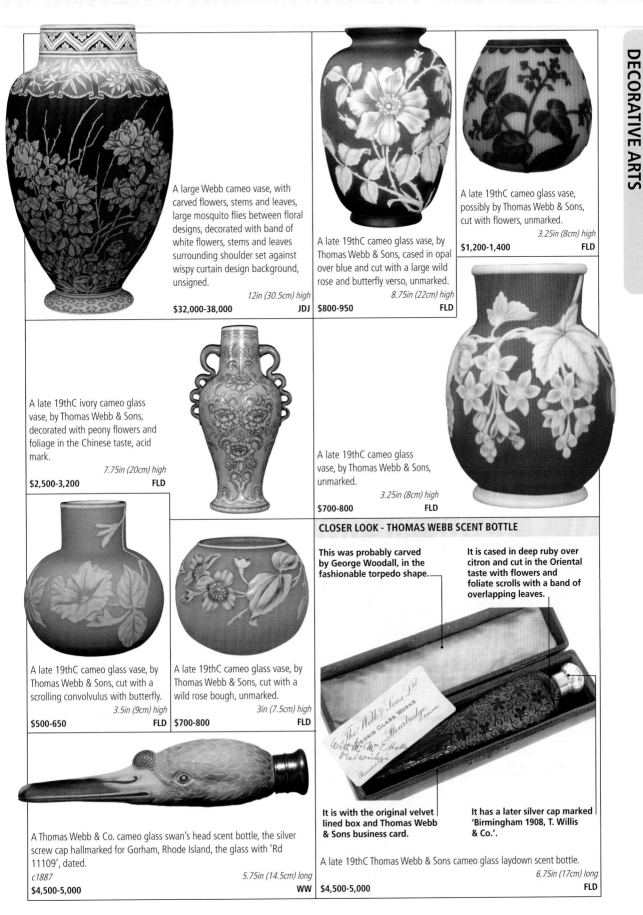

A large Webb cameo vase, with carved flowers, stems and leaves, large mosquito flies between floral designs, decorated with band of white flowers, stems and leaves surrounding shoulder set against wispy curtain design background, unsigned.

12in (30.5cm) high

$32,000-38,000 JDJ

A late 19thC cameo glass vase, by Thomas Webb & Sons, cased in opal over blue and cut with a large wild rose and butterfly verso, unmarked.

8.75in (22cm) high

$800-950 FLD

A late 19thC cameo glass vase, possibly by Thomas Webb & Sons, cut with flowers, unmarked.

3.25in (8cm) high

$1,200-1,400 FLD

A late 19thC ivory cameo glass vase, by Thomas Webb & Sons, decorated with peony flowers and foliage in the Chinese taste, acid mark.

7.75in (20cm) high

$2,500-3,200 FLD

A late 19thC cameo glass vase, by Thomas Webb & Sons, unmarked.

3.25in (8cm) high

$700-800 FLD

A late 19thC cameo glass vase, by Thomas Webb & Sons, cut with a scrolling convolvulus with butterfly.

3.5in (9cm) high

$500-650 FLD

A late 19thC cameo glass vase, by Thomas Webb & Sons, cut with a wild rose bough, unmarked.

3in (7.5cm) high

$700-800 FLD

CLOSER LOOK - THOMAS WEBB SCENT BOTTLE

This was probably carved by George Woodall, in the fashionable torpedo shape.

It is cased in deep ruby over citron and cut in the Oriental taste with flowers and foliate scrolls with a band of overlapping leaves.

It is with the original velvet lined box and Thomas Webb & Sons business card.

It has a later silver cap marked 'Birmingham 1908, T. Willis & Co.'.

A late 19thC Thomas Webb & Sons cameo glass laydown scent bottle.

6.75in (17cm) long

$4,500-5,000 FLD

A Thomas Webb & Co. cameo glass swan's head scent bottle, the silver screw cap hallmarked for Gorham, Rhode Island, the glass with 'Rd 11109', dated.

c1887

5.75in (14.5cm) long

$4,500-5,000 WW

ESSENTIAL REFERENCE - 'JACK IN THE PULPIT'

'Jack in the Pulpit' vases were inspired by a small American woodland flower (Arisaema triphyllum). They were made from iridescent favrile glass, which Tiffany patented in 1894. The term favrile, Tiffany's trade name for iridescent wares, derived from fabrile, an 'old English' word meaning handmade or belonging to a craftsman.

The iridescent colors of Tiffany's glass were inspired by those found on excavated antique Syrian and Roman glass. Jack in the pulpit vases were made in different sizes and color combinations. The colors were achieved by dissolving salts of rare metals in molten glass and keeping them in an oxidised state in the kiln to produce chemical reactions. Sometimes, the pieces were also sprayed with chloride, which made the surface break up into fine lines that picked up the light. Today, blue versions are among the rarest. Tiffany's iridescent glass was much imitated long after Tiffany ceased making 'Jack in the pulpit' vases in the late 1920s.

A gold Tiffany favrile 'Jack in the Pulpit' vase, with subdued gold iridescence with platinum and pink highlights, numbered 'W7733', unsigned.

8.25in (21cm) high
$4,500-5,000 JDJ

A gold Tiffany 'Jack in the Pulpit' vase, bright gold iridescence with strong pink, green and blue highlights on the face of the jack, signed on the underside 'L.C. Tiffany - Favrile 5970G'.

20.25in (51.5cm) high
$13,000-15,000 JDJ

A gold Tiffany favrile glass 'Jack in the Pulpit' vase, etched 'L.C.T. 1010A', heavy mineral deposits /dirt to interior bottom, stem lacking finish.

c1906　19.25in (49cm) high
$9,000-10,000 DRA

A Tiffany Studios gold favrile vase, blown and wheel-carved glass with vine pattern, etched '1535 6947K L.C. Tiffany - Favrile'.

c1916　13.5in (34.5cm) high
$1,500-1,900 DRA

A 1920s Tiffany Studios favrile pulled-feather vase, blown glass with acid-etched gilt-bronze, the glass etched 'LCT Favrile', the bronze stamped 'TIFFANY STUDIOS NEW YORK 1043' and etched 'Ladies Aid Society/M.E. Church'.

14.5in (37cm) high
$1,300-1,800 DRA

An early 20thC Tiffany Studios favrile glass vase, blown glass with bronze base, stamped 'LOUIS C. TIFFANY FURNACES INC. 158,' glass etched 'L.C.T. Favrile', minor flecks to base of glass insert.

17.25in (44cm) high
$1,300-1,500 DRA

A Tiffany Studios floriform favrile glass vase, etched 'L.C.T. Y7474', one burst bubble to inside of coupe in making of.

c1905　11.75in (30cm) high
$4,500-5,000 DRA

A 1900s Tiffany Studios floriform vase, favrile glass with patinated bronze base stamped 'TGDCO. TIFFANY STUDIOS NEW YORK 1743', one short scratch to patina on stem.

13in (33cm) high
$1,100-1,400 DRA

A Tiffany Studios gold favrile blown glass center bowl, with flower frog, heart and vine pattern, etched '5567L L.C. Tiffany - Favrile', some light wear.

c1917　9.5in (24cm) wide
$1,000-1,100 DRA

A Tiffany favrile cameo vase, of clear frosted glass, with wheel-carved cameo design of leaves, vines and berries, signed in polished pontil 'L.C. Tiffany-Favrile 6461C'.

11.75in (30cm) high

$9,500-10,500   **JDJ**

A Tiffany flower form vase, with translucent gold iridescence shading to orange at top, signed on underside 'L.C.T.'.

13in (33cm) high

$6,500-7,000   **JDJ**

A Tiffany favrile blown glass vase, etched 'Louis C. Tiffany 16160', some wear around shoulder, some scratches to body.

c1900   *15in (38cm) high*

$5,000-5,700   **DRA**

A Tiffany Studios 'Cypriote' favrile glass, etched '2066N L.C. Tiffany - Favrile'.

c1919   *6.25in (16cm) high*

$7,500-9,000   **DRA**

A Tiffany Studios red favrile glass vase, etched '1155-5386M L.C. Tiffany Inc. - Favrile', some scratches to the body.

c1918   *10in (25.5cm) high*

$5,000-5,700   **DRA**

A Tiffany aquamarine vase, with water lilies rising from bottom to lily pads, signed on underside 'L.C. Tiffany-Favrile 5792G', some light scratches to the bowl.

7.25in (18.5cm) high

$32,000-38,000   **JDJ**

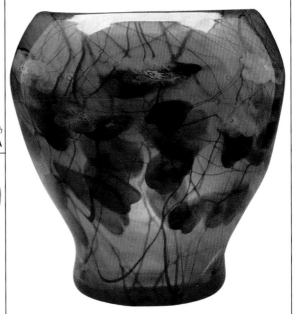

A Tiffany paperweight vase, with millefiori flowers encircling top portion of vase with wispy white flower petals, the interior of vase showing flashes of blue iridescence behind leaves, signed on underside in script 'Louis C. Tiffany U4011', large crack encircling bottom of vase.

Louis Comfort Tiffany (1848-1933), the son of Charles Lewis Tiffany, the founder of New York's famous jewelry and silversmithing business, was a leading American Art Nouveau designer and interior decorator. Initially trained as a painter, he turned to the decorative arts in 1878 and a year later set up a New York firm of interior decorators which won many prestigious clients including the American writer Mark Twain. It was his work in glass, however, from stained glass windows and lamp shades to beautiful floriate vases, that was to bring international fame.

10.5in (26.5cm) high

JDJ

A Tiffany paperweight glass vase, decorated with dogwood blossoms, etched 'L.C.T. Louis C. Tiffany ? 5979', some scratches to the body.

c1906   *5.75in (14.5cm) wide*

$10,000-11,000   **DRA**

$9,500-10,500   **JDJ**

DECORATIVE ARTS

A Baccarat glass vase, of rock crystal type, engraved in Japonesque style with exotic birds, silvered cast brass mounts in 'Chinese' taste.

c1880   *13in (33.5cm) high*
$3,200-3,800   **MAB**

A cameo vase, by Désiré Christian, the lime green ground etched with flowers, etched 'Désiré Christian Meisenthal, Loth'.

7.25in (18.5cm) high
$650-750   **SWO**

ESSENTIAL REFERENCE - JAMES COUPER & SON OF GLASGOW

James Couper & Sons was founded in Kyle Street, Glasgow, in 1855. It produced a range of glassware, usually blown, with decorative elements etched or engraved. The glassworks was best known for its 'Clutha' wares, designed by Dr Christopher Dresser (1834-1904) and produced from 1888 to 1905. 'Clutha' takes is name from the Celtic word for the river Clyde. The vessels were made from blown glass and were fluid, organic and often asymmetrical in shape. Most 'Clutha' vessels were made in pale green, yellow or amber transparent glass, with bubbles or swirls of color within. The company closed in 1922.

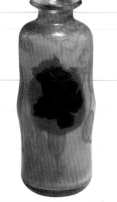

A Désiré Christian 'Courgettes' Marqueterie vase, with a pumpkin branch, signed.

1904-05   *6in (15.5cm) high*
$7,000-7,500   **QU**

A late 19thC 'Clutha' glass vase, by James Couper & Sons, Glasgow, acid etched stamp mark 'CLUTHA'.

9.25in (23cm) high
$1,000-1,100   **L&T**

A 'Clutha' glass vase, by James Couper & Son, Glasgow, designed by Christopher Dresser, the green glass body with milky inclusions.

c1880   *16.5in (42cm) high*
$3,200-3,800   **L&T**

A Degué cameo glass vase, cut with pendant flowering leaves on a frosted ground, signed 'Degué'.

c1905   *9.75in (24.5cm) high*
$400-500   **MOR**

A French Degué cameo glass vase, with blue fading to pink foliage and flowerheads, engraved signature to rim 'Degué'.

c1930   *11.75in (30cm) high*
$750-900   **MAB**

An Andre Delatte enameled vase, in orange with black and white enamelling, signed.

c1920
$500-750   **M&DM**

An Andre Delatte metal mounted blown glass vase, internally decorated with silver, acid etched 'A De Latte Nancy' to rim.

5.75in (14.5cm) high

$500-650   WW

A Dubarry 'A Toi' Depinoix perfume bottle and stopper, designed by Julien Viard, the frosted glass stopper molded as a Pierrot.

Depinoix et Fils was a glassworks and trading glass company established in 1846 at 7 rue de la Perle, Paris by Theophile Cœnon (1815-1888) and Constant Depinoix (1854-1936). They had an early involvement in the perfume bottle production and design, greatly expanded due to association with London-based International Bottle Company.

c1920   *5in (12.5cm) high*

$700-800   BELL

A French Devez cameo glass vase, decorated with flowers and insects, signed in cameo.

c1910   *14in (35.5cm) high*

$650-750   TRI

A Marcel Goupy black and blue enameled bowl, signed.

c1925   *3in (7.5cm) high*

$180-250   M&DM

A 1930s Haida 'Scorpion tail' vase, amber cut to clear.

12in (30.5cm) high

$450-550   M&DM

A Haida vase, by Carl Metzler, ruby cut to clear.

c1935   *10in (25.5cm) high*

$750-950   M&DM

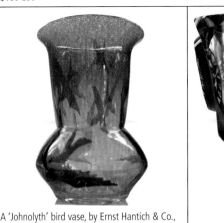

A 'Johnolyth' bird vase, by Ernst Hantich & Co., Haida.

The vase is unsigned but research has found it in a Hantich advert.

c1935   *9in (23cm) high*

$650-750   M&DM

A flashed and cut to clear vase, by Josephinenhutte.

c1930   *8in (20.5cm) high*

$650-750   M&DM

A Kosta glass vase, by Vicke Lindstrand, model no.LH 1592, of teardrop form, aubergine glass with threaded design, cased in clear, etched marks to base.

8in (20.5cm) high

$250-400   WW

ESSENTIAL REFERENCE - KRALIK GLASS

Wilhelm Kralik Söhne was one of the largest Bohemian art glass producers in the early 20thC. By the mid-19thC, Wilhelm Kralik operated seven glassworks collectively under the name Meyr's Neffe, which had been founded by his great-uncle Josef Meyr in 1815. After Wilhelm Kralik's death in 1877, the company was divided between his four sons. Karl and Hugo Kralik continued to trade as Meyr's Neffe, while Heinrich and Johann formed Wilhelm Kralik Söhne. Meyr's Neffe merged with Moser in 1922. Wilhelm Kralik Söhne continued until World War II. Wilhelm Kralik Söhne used martelé (hammered) or swirled glass, often decorated with flowers or spiral rigaree trails. The wide range of glassware produced and its similarity to Tiffany and Loetz makes Wilhelm Kralik Söhne wares hard to identify.

A Kralik cameo vase, purple to clear depicting stylized leaves.

One of the few surviving Kralik design pages depicts this range of cameo vases.

c1935   *9in (23cm) high*
$650-750   **M&DM**

A large Kralik beehive 'Bambus' vase, with original silver label marked 'Bambus', in brown on cream.

The 'Bambus' range employed latitudinal cut glass canes which resembled bamboo leaves.

11in (28cm) high
$750-1,000   **M&DM**

A stepped Kralik vase, mold blown, decorated with cross sectional glass canes.

c1930   *9in (23cm) high*
$400-500   **M&DM**

A pair of large Kralik ball vases, in orange and blue black.

c1930   *8in (20.5cm) high*
$1,100-1,400   **M&DM**

A deep green stylized Legras acid-cut vase, signed 'Legras'.

c1930   *8in (20.5cm) high*
$750-950   **M&DM**

An early 20thC Legras cameo vase, etched with a tree and river landscape.

14in (35.5cm) high
$550-700   **SWO**

A Legras et Cie cameo glass vase, with gilt flowering chestnut sprays, gilt banded rim, underside with Mont Joye mark.

c1900   *22in (56cm) high*
$500-650   **MAB**

A French Legras et Cie cameo glass vase, with enamel painted violets, gilt rim, with Mont Joye mark.

c1900   *22in (56cm) high*
$800-950   **MAB**

A dark green cut vase, made by Meyr's Neffe, signed 'WW' (Wiener Werkstrasse).

c1910   *6in (15cm) high*
$650-750   **M&DM**

A wine glass, designed by Otto Prutscher for Meyr's Neffe, with a green cased and ladder cut stem, with conical bowl flash cut.

See Essential Reference on p530.

c1906   *8.25in (21cm) high*
$3,200-3,800   **FLD**

A wine glass, designed by Otto Prutscher for Meyr's Neffe, with a pink cased and ladder cut stem, with pink cased conical bowl flash cut.

c1906   *8.25in (21cm) high*
$3,200-3,800   **FLD**

A Muller Frères 'Aquatique, poissons et algues' vase, decorated with etched and enameled patterns and an underwater scene with fish, signed 'MULLER FRES LUNÉVILLE'.

1910-15   *6.75in (17cm) high*
$1,300-1,500   **QU**

ESSENTIAL REFERENCE - MULLER FRÈRES

Muller Frères was founded by Henri Muller in 1895 in Lunéville, near Nice. Henri Muller had previously worked for Gallé and was now joined in his new business by his sister and four brothers. Muller Frères went on to become a leading French maker of cameo glass. The company made high-quality vases and lampshades, often decorated with landscapes. Production ceased in 1933 and the factory closed in 1936.

A Muller cameo glass vase, with a fallen tree at side of river and two birds, laced with bubbles, signed 'Muller Fres Luneville'.

9.25in (23.5cm) high
$10,000-11,000   **JDJ**

A handmade Paul Nicolas bowl, signed 'Paul Nicolas Nancy'.

This was a gift for his brother, with family provenance.

c1935   *15in (38cm) diam*
$1,900-2,500   **M&DM**

A Paul Nicolas cameo vase, red over orange, signed 'Chicks waiting to be fed'.

c1925   *5in (12.5cm) high*
$1,500-1,900   **M&DM**

An Orrefors glass 'Graal' fish vase, by Edward Hald, painted with fish and seaweed, etched signature, numbered '778'.

4.5in (11.5cm) high
$550-700   **SWO**

An Orrefors 'Graal' vase, by Edward Hald, decorated with fish and waterweed, etched marks and signature.

6.25in (16cm) high
$400-500   **WW**

A James Powell & Sons, Whitefriars glass 'Tear' vase, designed by James Hogan, with six emerald green tailed prunts, unsigned.

10in (25.5cm) high

$250-400   **WW**

A 1930s Whitefriars ribbon-trailed vase, by James Hogan, decorated with a blue spiral over sea green ground, pattern no.8975.

9.75in (25cm) high

$230-280   **FLD**

An early 20thC Whitefriars decanter, designed by Harry Powell, pattern no.2091, in sea green.

This is based upon a Roman jug held in the British Museum.

8.5in (21.5cm) high

$300-400   **FLD**

A vivid red Riedel blown and cut vase, with gilding in the Secessionist style.

The wreath on the front is taken directly from the decoration on the Secessionist building in Vienna.

c1905   *6in (15cm) high*

$500-650   **M&DM**

ESSENTIAL REFERENCE - STEUBEN

Steuben Glassworks was established in Corning, New York in 1903, by Thomas G. Hawkes and English glassmaker and chemist Frederick Carder (1863-1963). Steuben produced several artistic glassware lines, including 'Aurene', a range of iridescent glass made from 1904 to 1933. Other popular designs included 'Intarsia', 'Moss', and 'Agate'. In 1918, Steuben was purchased by the Corning Glass Works. Carder stayed on as managing director of the Steuben Division. In 1932, Steuben developed '10M', a high-quality, colorless crystal glass. From then on, colored glass was phased out of Steuben, with an increasing focus on clear crystal. Steuben continues today as part of Corning Inc.

A pair of gilded Riedel vases, in the Secessionist style.

c1905   *4in (10cm) high*

$400-500   **M&DM**

A Steuben 'millefiori' vase, with gold iridescent leaf and vine decoration, signed 'Aurene 550', a few scratches.

3.25in (8cm) high

$1,500-1,900   **JDJ**

A Steuben 'Aurene' vase, with gold iridescent heart, leaf and vine decoration, interior of mouth with gold iridescence, signed on underside 'Aurene 275'.

11.5in (29cm) high

$2,500-3,200   **JDJ**

A Steuben vase, shape no.6299, with leaf and vine decoration, signed 'Steuben Aurene 6299', with a 'Steuben Glassworks, Corning, NY' sticker, a few scratches.

6.25in (16cm) high

$2,000-2,500   **JDJ**

A Stuart amber enamel bowl, with freeform brown fronds decorated in flowers and insects, signed.

c1933   11in (28cm) diam
$650-750   **M&DM**

ESSENTIAL REFERENCE - AMALRIC WALTER

Victor Amalric Walter (1870-1959) studied at the Sèvres porcelain factory, France. As a student and then a decorator, he experimented with the pâte-de-verre technique. In 1903, he exhibited his pieces at the Paris Salon with his tutor Gabriel Lévy. This brought him to the attention of Antonin Daum, for whom he worked for the next ten years. After World War I, Amalric Walter founded his own workshop. He initially focused on pâte-de-verre pieces, but moved to Art Deco as pâte-de-verre lost popularity. The workshop closed in 1935.

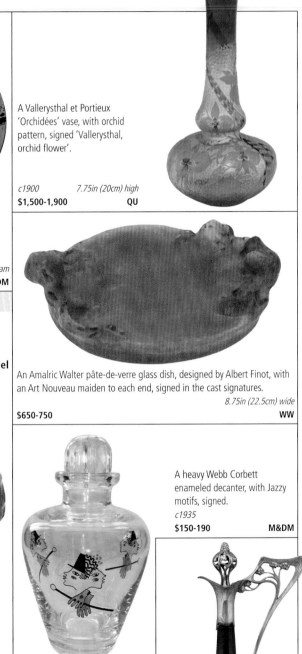

A Vallerysthal et Portieux 'Orchidées' vase, with orchid pattern, signed 'Vallerysthal, orchid flower'.

c1900   7.75in (20cm) high
$1,500-1,900   **QU**

An Amalric Walter pâte-de-verre glass dish, designed by Albert Finot, with an Art Nouveau maiden to each end, signed in the cast signatures.

8.75in (22.5cm) wide
$650-750   **WW**

An Amalric Walter pâte-de-verre coupe, designed by Henri Berge, modeled with pine cones, signed in the cast 'A Walter, Nancy H Berge Sct', small chip to top rim.

4in (10cm) high
$1,900-2,500   **WW**

A heavy Webb Corbett enameled decanter, with Jazzy motifs, signed.
c1935
$150-190   **M&DM**

A pair of Webb Corbett mosaic enamel vases, signed.
c1935   9in (23cm) high
$650-750   **M&DM**

A WMF 'Ikora' fish.
c1935   12in (30.5cm) long
$750-1,000   **M&DM**

An Art Nouveau WMF silver-plated and green glass claret jug and stopper, stamped marks.
15in (38cm) high
$950-1,100   **SWO**

A Tudric pewter and enamel clock, designed by Archibald Knox (1864-1933) for Liberty & Co., the enameled dial with gilt numerals, with a stylized plant design and two enamel ovals under the dial, stamped marks, 'Rd. 463015' and model no. '0608'.

c1903   *5.5in (14cm) high*

$5,000-6,500   **SWO**

A Tudric pewter clock, designed by Archibald Knox for Liberty & Co., the enameled dial with copper chapter ring, impressed 'Z English Pewter Made By Liberty & Co. 0761'.

8in (20.5cm) high

$5,000-6,500   **SWO**

A Liberty & Co. Tudric pewter and enamel mantle clock, model no.0367, the shaped front cast in low relief with foliate panels, set with green and blue enamel panel, the rectangular copper dial stamped in low relief with Arabic numerals, stamped marks.

6.5in (16.5cm) high

$2,500-3,200   **WW**

A Liberty & Co. pewter, copper and abalone mantel clock.

c1900   *9.75in (25cm) high*

$7,000-7,500   **L&T**

A Liberty & Co. 'Tudric' pewter and enamel carriage clock, London, by Archibald Knox, underside stamped '0721/ ENGLISH PEWTER MADE BY LIBERTY & CO'.

1900   *4.5in (11.5cm) high*

$2,500-3,800   **L&T**

An Art Deco Omega chrome-plated and enamel mantel clock, with eight-day, hand wound Swiss movement, marked 'OMEGA / 8DAYS', numbered to the reverse '7549337', maker's marks 'OMEGA/ SWISS MADE/ FABRIACTION SUISE'.

c1925   *16in (41cm) wide*

$1,100-1,500   **L&T**

An Art Deco continental silver and enamel mantel clock, model no.58843, the octagonal face and sides enameled coral red, the dial enameled in black with Arabic figures, with Swiss movement, engine-turned stem and hinged back, on stepped black slate base, stamped marks 'HASK (?)Geneve, 0935', stamped import marks 'GS (George Stockwell), London, 1929'.

7in (18cm) high

$3,200-3,800   **WW**

An Art Deco marble and onyx clock garniture, with a square silvered dial.

18.5in (47cm) wide

$250-320   **SWO**

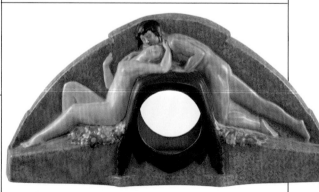

A French Art Deco D'Argyl ceramic figural clock case, with two nude lovers, signed to base.

20.75in (53cm) wide

$180-250   **ECGW**

A French Menneville Art Deco clock, on a stepped marble and slate case, with a patinated spelter figure.

c1930   *25in (63.5cm) long*

$650-750   **L&T**

An Art Deco marble-faced clock, with two spelter models of alsatians.

26.75in (68cm) wide

$250-400   **PC**

An Art Deco hardstone eight-day mantle clock garniture, with cast bronze deer to top.

17.25in (44cm) wide

$180-250   **PC**

An Art Deco Asprey red leather and chrome eight-day travel clock, designed by Le Coultre, the dial with fluorescent baton markers.

4.25in (10.5cm) long closed

$180-250   **HAN**

An Art Deco onyx and black slate mantel clock garniture, with a patinated metal swallow surmount.

9.5in (24cm) high

$130-180   **BELL**

An Art Deco mantle clock, by Ferdinand Preiss, with carved ivory figures, onyx and black marble casing, with brass dial face, base marked 'F. Preiss', clock casing slightly retouched.

c1920   *9.5in (25cm) wide*

$9,000-9,500   **QU**

A 1930s Art Deco figural clock, black lacquered base mounted with a female nude bronze, by Josef Lorenzl, with a green mirrored circular panel with integral clock, the figure signed to the base.

14.75in (37.5cm) high

$2,000-2,500   **FLD**

A General Electric Art Deco alarm clock, 'Circe', model 7H92, with stylized floral medallion to reverse-painted arched glass face, on stepped chrome base, die-stamped marks.

8in (20.5cm) wide

$650-750   **PC**

A pair of Newlyn copper candlesticks, with embossed fish decoration over a domed foot, with a beaten finish, stamped 'Newlyn'.

8.25in (21cm) high

$450-500   **BELL**

A pair of copper, brass and wooden candlesticks, to a design by Dr Christopher Dresser, possibly by Benham & Froud.

7.5in (19cm) high

$180-230   **CHOR**

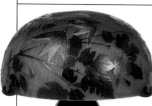

An Edwardian silver-plated oil lamp, with an etched shade, Hinks No. 2 lever, cut glass reservoir.

31.75in (81cm) high including chimney

$550-650   **SWO**

ESSENTIAL REFERENCE - QUENTIN BELL

Quentin Bell was the son of Clive and Vanessa Bell and nephew of Virginia Woolf. He moved to Charleston, in Lewes, East Sussex, when he was six years old. There he grew up within the heart of the Bloomsbury Group. Quentin Bell initially trained in fine art but moved to Stoke-on-Trent at the age of twenty-five to study pottery. He continued to work with clay for the rest of his life alongside his writing and painting. He created the pottery at Charleston during World War II. His work is in the Victoria and Albert Museum, London.

A Fulham pottery figural lamp base and painted shade, by Quentin Bell, painted by Cressida Bell, the central column with a King and Queen, with mermaids and mermen between, around the base reads 'Her Pacific Majesty rules the Children of Anger, He rules hers', the hand painted shade initialed internally with Quentin's initials, there is a crack through the base of the lamp.

32.5in (78cm) high

$5,500-6,500   **CHEF**

A Fulham pottery figural lamp base and painted shade, by Quentin Bell, the central column with two Spanish women, the base divided into panels with bull masks, the handpainted shade initialed internally, would need re-wiring if intending to use.

26in (66cm) high

$5,500-6,500   **CHEF**

A Gallé cameo glass mushroom table lamp-top with base, signed with original paper label on underside.

13.5in (34.5cm) high

$15,000-19,000   **POOK**

An Art Nouveau Gallé cameo glass table lamp and shade, designed by Emile Gallé, decorated with butterflies flying amongst pendulous lilac flowers, cameo signature to shade and base.

11.75in (30cm) high

$1,000-1,500   **WW**

A four-color cameo Gallé lamp, with cameo decoration of flowers, both base and shade are signed in cameo 'Galle', base is fitted with brass three-arm spider and single socket.

23.5in (59.5cm) high

$50,000-55,000   **JDJ**

A rare French Gallé Allium table lamp, the glass brown, acid-etched and wheel-polished, patinated metal, not electrified, no socket, shade signed 'Gallé' twice.

See 'Decorative Arts 1900: Highlights from Private Collections in Detroit, The Detroit Institute of Art', 1994, page 73, no.86; and Bloch-Dermant, 'Le Verre en France: D'Emile Gallé à Nos Jours; Les editions de l'Amateur', 1986, page 38.

c1900   *30in (76cm) high*
$45,000-50,000   **DRA**

CLOSER LOOK - DAUM LAMP

Lamps are particularly popular as they perfectly display the cameo scene.

This is an exceptionally good subject matter with decoration of barren trees rising from an enameled snow covered ground.

The trees are enameled in shades of brown and patches of white enameled snow cling to them.

The matching cameo shade rests on a forged iron collar and a single socket incorporates a socket illuminating the inside of base.

A Daum winter scene lamp, signed 'Daum Nancy', with cross of Lorraine.

16.5in (42cm) high
$23,000-28,000   **JDJ**

An Austrian/French Gallé table lamp with shade, by Peter Tereszczuk (1875-1963), patinated bronze, cameo glass, two sockets, the shade associated to base on added ring, base signed 'P. Tereszczuk', rewired.

c1910
$4,500-5,000   **DRA**

A rare Daum 'Epine vinette' table light, so-called 'Plaquettes', shade and foot signed 'DAUM NANCY', with engraved Cross of Lorraine, wrought-iron mounting.

1910   *17in (43cm) high*
$13,000-19,000   **QU**

A Daum cameo scene lamp, decorated with desirable rain scene on shade and base, signed with black 'Daum Nancy', 'D' and Cross of Lorraine, minor wear to metal shade arms and collar, rewired.

14.25in (36cm) high
$25,000-32,000   **JDJ**

A Loetz art glass lamp, the papillion blue iridescent stem with brass riser supporting four-socket cluster and brass shade ring, with Formosa pinched shade, unsigned.

29in (73.5cm) high
$6,500-7,500   **JDJ**

A Loetz black bottom candlestick, in 'Phaenomen Genre 358', with bronze band around foot as well as bronze collar, candle cup and bobeche, unsigned.

7.5in (19cm) high
$6,500-7,500   **JDJ**

An Austrian Art Nouveau lamp, with cast bronze base of two snakes around iridescent pottery bowl, with iridescent Loetz shade with amber oil spot, base and shade are unsigned, bowl is signed 'Hellosino Ware, Austria', with incised numbers 'V 21074'.

28.5in (72.5cm) high
$13,000-18,000   **JDJ**

DECORATIVE ARTS

A table light, by Otto Prutscher, manufactured by Wiener Werkstätte metal workshop and Elisabeth glassworks, of silvered bronze, stamped rose mark 'WIENER WERK STÄTTE' and 'OP', shade with mat petrol luster.

c1910   *22.75in (58cm) high*
$19,000-25,000   QU

A Lalique 'Grand Depot' shade, clear and frosted glass, on a later composite glass base.

designed 1928   *20.5in (52cm) high*
$1,300-1,800   BELL

A Sabino opalescent table lamp, modeled as a nude inside a shell, holding a pearl, unmarked, mold lines around base, minor nicks on edges of shell.

          10.5in (27cm) high
$550-700   TEN

A 'Suzanne au Bain' opalescent glass lamp, by Marius-Ernest Sabino (1878-1961), the molded figure raised on a black Vitrolite glass base, fitted for electricity.

c1920   *9in (24cm) high*
$3,200-3,800   L&T

An Art Deco lamp, the painted metal base with a nude figure in front of a frosted glass, some chips and spotting to paint.

          13in (33cm) high
$250-320   ECGW

A 1920s 'Parachutist' gilded bronze table light, by Richard W. Lange for Rosenthal & Maeder, the head, neck and hands of carved ivory, base marked 'GERMANY, R. W. Lange R.u.M'.

          27.25in (69.5cm) high
$7,500-9,000   QU

A Monart glass table lamp, the shade and base in mottled green and orange with gold aventurine inclusions, wood and brass light fittings, with a torn label and numbered 'VI.A 384'.

          15.25in (39cm) high
$1,000-1,200   SWO

A WMF 'Ikora' fish light.

The metal fitted lamp is set between the fins and lights the inside of the fish.

c1935   *8in (20.5cm) long*
$750-1,000   M&DM

A pair of Art Deco aluminum Egyptian mask wall lights.

          8in (20cm) high
$450-550   SWO

CLOSER LOOK - DRAGONFLY TABLE LAMP

This style is considered to be the most desirable of the dragonfly patterns.

The leaded glass shade with nine dragonflies surrounding bottom edge of shade with heads and wings creating irregular border.

Each dragonfly wing is made of shaded red, green and yellow glass which is covered on the exterior with acid etched veining.

The tree trunk base and shade are fully marked 'Tiffany Studios New York' and '1507'. The cap is a rare authentic Tiffany cap.

A Tiffany Studios drophead dragonfly table lamp, re-wired with appropriate cloth cord.

32.5in (82.5cm) high

$125,000-200,000   **JDJ**

A Tiffany Studios Peony table lamp, on a rare mosaic base, no.355, set with eight green turtleback tiles, shade topped with original acid etched cap, base stamped '1', signed on the underside 'Tiffany Studios New York', the shade signed 'Tiffany Studios New York 1505-25', one tile replaced.

shade 22in (56cm) diam

$400,000-500,000   **JDJ**

A Tiffany Studios patinated bronze table-lamp, with a leaded glass poinsettia shade, the shade signed and numbered '556', the base signed and numbered '534'.

22in (56cm) high

$25,000-32,000   **POOK**

A Tiffany Studios banded 'Dogwood' table lamp, signed on interior rim 'Tiffany Studios New York 1554', with bronze base, signed on underside 'Tiffany Studios New York 68546'.

22.5in (57cm) high

$19,000-25,000   **JDJ**

A Tiffany favrile glass bellflower shade on 'jeweled' base, patinated bronze, leaded slag glass, three sockets, base stamped 'TIFFANY STUDIOS NEW YORK S216/437', metal tag to shade reading 'TIFFANY STUDIOS NEW YORK', rewired, tight cracks to glass.

c1900   *24.25in (61.5cm) high*

$20,000-25,000   **DRA**

A Tiffany Studios 'Geranium' table lamp, signed to interior rim 'Tiffany Studios New York', with Tiffany Studios bronze decorated library base, with an authentic Tiffany pierced slip cap, signed on underside 'Tiffany Studios New York 362 S175', re-wired with appropriate cloth cord.

22.5in (57cm) high

$90,000-110,000   **JDJ**

A 1900s Tiffany patinated bronze 'Peony' table lamp, with three sockets, base stamped 'TIFFANY STUDIOS NEW YORK 859/S173', shade stamped 'TIFFANY STUDIOS NEW YORK 1475', rewired, sockets replaced, short cracks to several pieces of glass.

25in (63.5cm) high

$60,000-70,000   **DRA**

A Tiffany Studios 'Apple Blossom' table lamp, on a rare adjustable patinated bronze base, tag reading 'TIFFANY STUDIOS NEW YORK 1555', base stamped 'TIFFANY', rewired.

c1900

$20,000-25,000   **DRA**

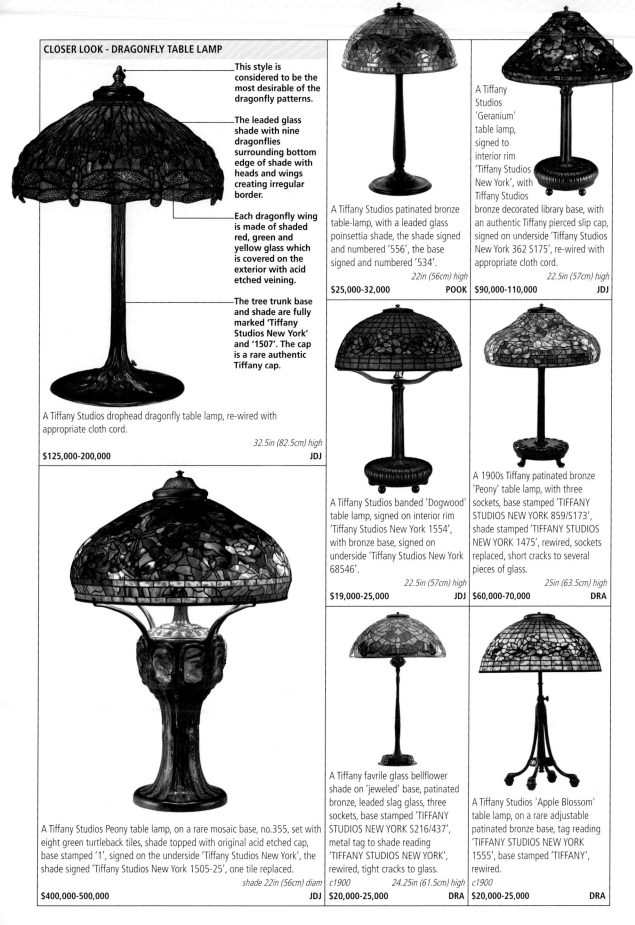

A Tiffany Studios Moorish table lamp, with bronze foot and shoulder, six arms extending to support a shade ring with ball chain tassels, opalescent favrile glass shade, signed 'Tiffany Studios New York 1433' with Tiffany Glass & Decorating logo, original oil burner replaced with electrified burner.

14.5in (37cm) diam

$15,000-19,000   **JDJ**

A Tiffany Studios kerosene lamp, with enameled bronze base, with electrified duplex burner, base and font are marked 'Tiffany Studios New York D826', with Tiffany Glass & Decorating Co. logo, the shade with pulled feather design, numbered 'o2815', shade unsigned.

19.25in (49cm) high

$32,000-38,000   **JDJ**

A Tiffany Studios nautilus desk lamp, the foot set with Mother-of-pearl cabochon jewels, decorated with cast bronze stylized leaves, signed 'Tiffany Studios New York 25892' with Tiffany Glass & Decorating Co. logo, re-wired with appropriate cloth cord.

13.5in (34.5cm) high

$7,500-9,000   **JDJ**

A Tiffany counter-balance patinated bronze desk lamp, the shade favrile glass with wave pattern, base stamped 'TIFFANY STUDIOS NEW YORK 416', shade etched 'L.C.T. Favrile'.

c1900   14in (35.5cm) high

$10,000-11,000   **DRA**

A pair of Tiffany Studios torchières, with cast bronze base, the shades topped with cast bronze cap with open work stylized flower, the bases signed 'Tiffany Studios New York', the shades signed 'Tiffany Studios New York'.

64in (162.5cm) high

$32,000-38,000   **JDJ**

A Tiffany Studios patinated bronze counter-balance floor lamp, with a damascene shade, the base signed and numbered '468', the shade signed 'L.C.T. Favrile'.

56in (142.5cm) high

$11,000-13,000   **POOK**

A Tiffany Studios 'Lily' desk lamp, patinated bronze with favrile glass shades, signed, marked, stamped 'TIFFANY STUDIOS NEW YORK 9911', one shade repaired.

c1900   13.5in (34.5cm) high

$2,500-3,200   **DRA**

A Tiffany favrile patinated bronze turtleback tile chandelier, with six sockets, metal tag reading 'TIFFANY STUDIOS NEW YORK', some cracks to ten pieces of glass, hardware replaced.

c1900   45in (114.5cm) high

$32,000-38,000   **DRA**

A Dirk van Erp hammered copper mica table lamp, with an open windmill stamp, with three sockets, rewired, mica likely replaced.

Dirk van Erp (1860-1933) was a Dutch American artisan craftsman and metalsmith based in San Franciso, California.

1915-1929   19in (48cm) high

$7,000-8,000   DRA

An early 20thC Roycroft hammered copper table lamp, by Victor Toothaker, with two sockets, unmarked, replaced bottom plate and added short spacer below shade.

Victor Toothaker (d.1932) was a Roycroft designer specializing in metalwork and painting. Roycroft was a community of artists and craft workers based in East Aurora, New York. It was founded in 1895 and was part of the Arts and Crafts Movement.

18.5in (47cm) high

$6,500-7,000   DRA

A 1920s Roycroft hammered copper mica table lamp, with a single socket, orb and cross mark, newer associated finial.

17.5in (44.5cm) high

$3,200-3,800   DRA

ESSENTIAL REFERENCE - GUSTAV STICKLEY

Gustav Stickley (1858-1942) is best known today as the creator of Craftsman furniture. He was a visionary American proponent for the Arts and Crafts philosophy in design, literature and life. He was based in Eastwood, New York. At the height of his career, his furniture was sold throughout the USA, Craftsman houses were built in many areas, and 'The Craftsman' magazine widely read. After bankruptcy in 1915, Stickley was mostly forgotten until the 1970s, when his importance as a designer was rediscovered by a new generation.

A hammered copper Gustav Stickley chandelier, with five sockets, the shades hand-blown uranium yellow glass, probably 1990s replacements by Michael Adam's workshop.

c1905   38in (96.5cm) high

$15,000-19,000   DRA

A Duffner & Kimberly double dome chandelier, of stippled caramel glass, with a border oak leaf design.

26in (66cm) diam

$10,000-11,000   JDJ

A Duffner & Kimberly Wisteria floor lamp, with cast bronze base which supports large leaded glass wisteria shade, both are unsigned.

70in (178cm) high

$50,000-55,000   JDJ

A Gorham gilt-bronze table-lamp, with a leaded glass shade, unmarked.

27.5in (70cm) high

$20,000-25,000   POOK

A Handel patinated metal chandelier, acid-etched obverse-painted glass decorated with gingko leaves, with four sockets, shades signed 'HANDEL 2910', a few chips to fitters.

c1910s-20s   20in (51cm) high

$7,500-9,000   DRA

ESSENTIAL REFERENCE - THE HANDEL COMPANY

The Handel Company began in 1885 as 'Eydam and Handel', founded in Meriden, Connecticut, by Philip J. Handel and Adolph Eydam. Handel later bought out his partner and the firm became The Handel Company from 1903. Handel is best known for its distinctive reverse-painted glass lampshades. These were typically hemispherical in shape, with a frosted finish on the exterior. The interior was painted or enameled with flora or scenic views, often featuring butterflies, leaves and flowers or depicting landscapes or seascapes. On Philip J. Handel's death in 1914, the company passed to his wife Fannie and then to his cousin William H. Handel. The Handel Company ceased production in 1936. Today, Handel lampshades vary in price, but rare designs have seen a strong increase in value recently.

A Handel nautical scene table lamp, with reverse painted fishing boats coming into harbour at sunset, exterior is done in chipped ice, signed on interior rim 'Handel Co. 7034' and artist initial 'M', shade rests on original Handel base with Oriental-style openwork foot, unsigned, re-wired with appropriate cloth cord.

lamp 23.5in (59.5cm) high
$4,400-5,700   JDJ

A Handel table lamp, with reverse painted Venetian harbour scene with sail boats with brightly colored sails and gondola signed on interior 'Handel 5935', with original Handel base, signed with impressed block letters 'Handel', re-wired with contemporary plastic cord.

22.5in (57cm) high
$6,500-7,500   JDJ

A Handel Exotic Bird table lamp, the birds in flight among exotic vegetation and flowers, all against a black background, exterior is finished in chipped ice, signed interior rim 'Handel 7026' and artist signature 'PAL', shade rests on original Handel base, re-wired with contemporary plastic cord.

23in (58.5cm) high
$7,500-9,000   JDJ

A Handel leaded table lamp, with eight panels of stylized red flowers, unsigned, with original Handel base, with tight hairline in corner of one large slag glass panel, re-wired with contemporary plastic cord.

25.5in (65cm) high
$6,500-7,000   JDJ

A Handel table lamp, the reversed painted shade with Venetian harbour scene, the exterior of the shade finished in chipped ice, signed 'Handel 6757' and artist initial 'R', on a Handel base, signed with a affixed 'Handel' plate.

23.5in (59.5cm) high
$8,000-9,000   JDJ

A Handel table lamp, the reverse painted shade with brightly colored macaw parrots with lush jungle foliage, the exterior of shade finished in chipped ice, signed 'Handel 6874' and with artist initials 'H.B.', on original Handel Oriental-style base, unsigned, re-wired with contemporary plastic cord.

22in (56cm) high
$10,000-11,000   JDJ

A Handel table lamp, with reverse painted with colorful jungle birds in dense jungle foliage, exterior finished in chipped ice, signed 'Handel 70(or 6)25', on an original Handel base, re-wired with contemporary plastic cord.

23.5in (59.5cm) high
$11,000-12,000   JDJ

A Moe Bridges lamp, the reverse painted shade with orange poppies, unsigned, on Moe Bridges base, signed 'Moe-Bridges Milwaukee', base possibly refinished, re-wired with cloth cord.

The Moe Bridges Company was founded in 1919 in Milwaukee, Wisconsin. The firm made lamps with patinated iron bases and reverse painted shades, often decorated with landscapes or flowers. Moe Bridges was purchased by the Electric Sprayit Co. in 1934.

23.5in (59.5cm) high
$2,300-2,800   JDJ

A Pairpoint table lamp, the 'Chesterfield' shade decorated in 'Garden of Allah' pattern, with Middle Eastern gentlemen resting near two camels, signed 'The Pairpoint Corp', on original Pairpoint base signed 'Pairpoint MFG Co.' with Pairpoint logo and 'B3065', re-wired with contemporary plastic cord.

23.5in (59.5cm) high

$5,000-5,700   JDJ

A Pairpoint table lamp, the 'Carlisle' shade with reverse painted decoration of jungle birds, signed 'The Pairpoint Corp'n', on an original Pairpoint base, signed 'Pairpoint' with Pairpoint logo and 'D3053', re-wired with contemporary plastic cord.

20in (51cm) high

$3,200-3,800   JDJ

A Pairpoint table lamp, the 'Carlisle' shade with reverse painted tropical scene of palm trees along shore line, with sailing ships, unsigned, on an original Pairpoint base signed 'Pairpoint' with Pairpoint logo and 'D3070', old cloth cord is fraying.

22in (56cm) high

$1,000-1,200   JDJ

A Pairpoint 'Puffy' bouquet table lamp, on an original Pairpoint base, signed 'Pairpoint MFG Co.' with Pairpoint logo and '3093', shade has some oxidation to paint, wired with old plastic cord which is cracking.

22in (56cm) high

$6,500-7,000   JDJ

A Pairpoint 'Puffy' apple tree table lamp, shade unsigned, on an original Pairpoint tree trunk base, signed 'Pairpoint MFG Co.' with Pairpoint logo and '3092', re-wired with cloth cord.

25in (63.5cm) high

$18,000-20,000   JDJ

A Pairpoint 'Puffy' rose table lamp, signed 'The Pairpoint Corp'n', on Pairpoint base signed 'Pairpoint MFG Co.' with Pairpoint logo and '3052', re-wired with plastic cord.

21in (53.5cm) high

$9,500-10,500   JDJ

A Somers Stained Glass Studio 'Peony' table lamp, decorated with peonies and leaves, on a contemporary cast bronze base, the shade signed, interior rim with applied tag 'Original Somers Stained Glass Deer Park N.Y.'.

28in (71cm) diam

$7,000-7,500   JDJ

A Wilkinson table lamp, the leaded glass shade with red and pink granite glass trumpet flowers, unsigned, on an original Wilkinson cast metal base with original locking cap, base signed 'Wilkinson Co. Brooklyn, NY' and numbered '517', re-wired with plastic cord.

25in (63.5cm) high

$5,500-6,500   JDJ

A Wilkinson leaded glass 'Poppy' table lamp, shade unsigned, on an original Wilkinson base, with original locking heat cap, base signed 'Wilkinson Co, Brooklyn N.Y.' and numbered '2756', original cloth cord is frayed.

26.5in (67.5cm) high

$7,000-7,500   JDJ

ESSENTIAL REFERENCE - LIBERTY & CO.

The world renowned department store Liberty was originally founded in 1875 as a furniture and drapery shop in Regent Street, London and was known as East India House. The business was established by Arthur Lazenby Liberty (1843-1917). As the original name of the shop suggests, there was a strong emphasis on Oriental and Moorish objects, furniture and fabrics as well as more traditional European items. The shop also sold Japanese objects. East India House was one of the first major shops to stock extensively products of the Arts and Crafts movement. Goods subsequently produced for Liberty showed both Oriental and Arts and Crafts influence. In 1884 Liberty opened a costume department and in 1885 a wallpaper department. Liberty commissioned leading designers of the time to create carpets, ceramics, clothing, furniture, silver and wallpaper exclusively for them.

Liberty registered their own silver hallmark in 1894, and in 1899 released a range of gold and silver objects under the name 'Cymric', an Art Nouveau interpretation of the Celtic style. They were made by the Birmingham-based company W.H. Haseler. Many were designed by Archibald Knox. Knox's designs owe much to the work of C.R. Ashbee and his Guild of Handicraft in particular. The characteristics include expanses of plain metal, concentrated fluid ornament and monochrome enamel work. Knox and his colleagues, the fellow designers at the Silver Studio, had moved the Arts and Crafts stylistic principles forward and created a distinctive British version of Art Nouveau.

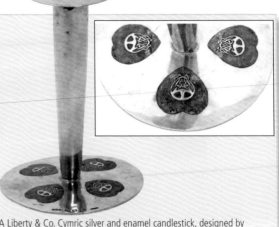

A Liberty & Co. Cymric silver and enamel candlestick, designed by Archibald Knox, model no.25, the base cast in low-relief, with four entwined entrelac enameled blue and green in heart-shaped green enamel panel, stamped marks, Birmingham.

See Stephen A. Martin, 'Archibald Knox', Artmedia, page 221, for a comparable pair of candlesticks with a similar enamel roundel.

1901   *6.25in (16cm) high*

$1,400-1,900   WW

A Liberty 'Cymric' silver ink stand, by Archibald Knox, Birmingham, model no.5106, the double rising lid embossed with celtic knot decoration and inset with oval cabochon turquoise, opening to reveal a glazed pottery ink well.

1902   *5in (12.5cm) square 15.07oz*

$13,000-15,000   MAI

A Liberty & Co. Tudric pewter and glass coupe, designed by Archibald Knox, model no.0276, the glass liner by Powell, stamped marks.

In 1903 a range of pewter of similar design to 'Cymric' was released under the name 'Tudric'. Apart from its interesting designs, Tudric pewter differed from other pewter as it had a high silver content. It was produced for Liberty by William Haseler of Birmingham.

c1903-05   *5.25in (13.5cm) high*

$1,000-1,100   BELL

An early 20thC Liberty Tudric pewter bowl, by Archibald Knox, the rim cast with stylized honesty and raised upon four open 'propellor' type supports, with green glass liner, stamped 'Tudric Pewter', 'Made In England', 'Made by Liberty & Co.' and '0319'.

5in (12.5cm) diam

$750-900   HT

A pair of Liberty Tudric pewter candelabra, by Archibald Knox, with removable sconces supported on column with openwork leaves and berries, the pierced base embellished with variegated leaves, stamped '5' and '0530', with registration marks.

c1905   *11in (28cm) high*

$3,200-3,800   L&T

A pair of Liberty pewter Tudric candlesticks, designed by Archibald Knox, stamped 'Tudric 0725'.

12.75in (32cm) high

$6,500-7,000   DRA

A Liberty & Co. Tudric pewter and enameled vase, designed by Archibald Knox.

c1905   *11.5in (29cm) high*

$2,500-3,200   PC

A Liberty & Co. silver and enameled rectangular lidded box, mounted with an enameled plaque, depicting a bridge scene with trees.

1909 5.5in (14cm) long

$1,500-2,300 **BELL**

An Arts and Crafts Liberty & Co. five-piece silver tea service, with a chased stylized stiff leaf rim within a faux rivetted border on a planished ground, comprising teapot and hot water jug, sugar basin, tongs and milk jug.

c1912 teapot 9.25in (23.5cm) wide 33oz

$750-900 **HT**

A Liberty & Co. English pewter and enamel jewelry box, with lakeside enamel by Charles Fleetwood Varley, the interior and fitted tray lined with green silk, stamped marks, enamel signed 'Varley'.

8.25in (21cm) long

$650-750 **WW**

A Liberty & Co. English pewter and enamel champagne bucket, designed by Archibald Knox, model no.0706, cast in low-relief with whiplash foliage sprays, with blue enameled heart-shaped leaves, stamped marks.

7.5in (19cm) high

$1,300-1,900 **WW**

An early 20thC Liberty pewter butter dish, by Archibald Knox, with three open triangular lug handles, the exterior cast with stylized honesty with lilac enamelling, with original green glass liner, stamped 'English Pewter', 'Made by Liberty & Co.' and '0162'.

1.25in (3cm) high

$1,400-1,900 **HT**

An early 20thC Liberty pewter vase, by Archibald Knox, with three open panels and loop handles beneath embossed berries and stylized leaves, with green liner, stamped to the base 'English Pewter 0957'.

8.5in (21.5cm) high

$450-500 **FLD**

A Liberty Tudric pewter organic vase, with band of blue and green enameled oval cabochons and two whiplash handles, stamped 'Tudric/029/4'.

9.75in (25cm) high

$1,300-1,900 **DRA**

A Danish silver grape pattern bowl or comport, designed by Georg Jensen, 264A, with a spiral-fluted stem with pendant grape clusters, stamped 'GEORG JENSEN 1921 264 GI 925 S', 'C.F.Heisse' assay master mark, Copenhagen mark for 1921 and import marks for London 1921.

1918 *10.75in (27.5cm) high*

$5,000-6,500 **TEN**

A Danish silver grape pattern oval serving dish with cover, designed by Georg Jensen, 408B, the cover with grape and leaf finial, stamped 'GEORG JENSEN 408 B GI 925 S', 'C.F.Heisse' assay master mark, Copenhagen mark for 1926 and import marks for London 1926.

1921 *11.5in (29cm) wide*

$5,000-6,500 **TEN**

A Danish silver grape pattern pitcher, designed by Georg Jensen, 407B, with applied fruiting grape vines, with part ebonized handle with pendant grape terminal, stamped 'GEORG JENSEN STERLING 407 B DENMARK GI 925 S', with import marks for London 1928.

1925 *8.75in (22.5cm) high*

$6,500-7,500 **TEN**

Judith Picks

Of the many designers to work with Georg Jensen through the years, Henning Koppel was among the most highly regarded. His designs played an important role in influencing the signature look of Georg Jensen, particularly in the second half of the 20thC. He had trained as a sculptor before turning his attention to jewelry, hollowware and cutlery. The pitcher is one of his most famous pieces and was first made in 1952. Characterised by fluid lines and sinuous curves, Koppel's work is a blend of the biomorphic and the sculptural.

A Georg Jensen water pitcher, designed by Henning Koppel, design no.1052.

c1950s *12in (30cm) high*

$13,000-19,000 **PC**

A Georg Jensen silver inkwell, with integral stand, the domed cover with pierced finial.

8.25in (21cm) diam

$1,900-2,500 **CHOR**

A Georg Jensen silver centerpiece bowl, by Johan Rohde, with lightly hammered surface, the whole raised on a circular stepped base, stamped maker's marks under base 'DESSIN', '925.S', 'DENMARK', 'STERLING' and '196'.

c1916 *11.25in (28.5cm) diam*

$3,200-3,800 **L&T**

A Georg Jensen bowl, designed by Henning Koppel, design no.980.

1950s *15in (38cm) diam*

$13,000-19,000 **PC**

A late Victorian Aesthetic silver tea service, maker Sibray & Hall, London, bright-cut engraved with cranes and bamboo, teapot handle with ivory stops.
1887   *teapot 9.5in (24cm) wide 39oz*
$400-500   HT

CLOSER LOOK - CANE HANDLE

It is modeled as a nude nymph tacked through torso and one draped wing, the other wing folded beneath her body.

This is an extremely rare object designed by one of Art Nouveau's greatest designers - René Lalique.

In such a small object the detail is extraordinary - her countenance expressing ecstatic agony.

Even with damage - the cane is missing and the wing has been restored - the rarity factor and the quality ensure the value.

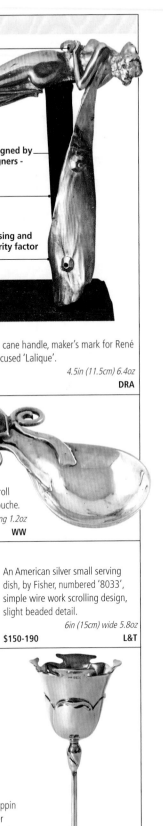

A René Lalique dragonfly woman gold cane handle, maker's mark for René Lalique, French eagle mark for 18ct, incused 'Lalique'.
c1900   *4.5in (11.5cm) 6.4oz*
$60,000-80,000   DRA

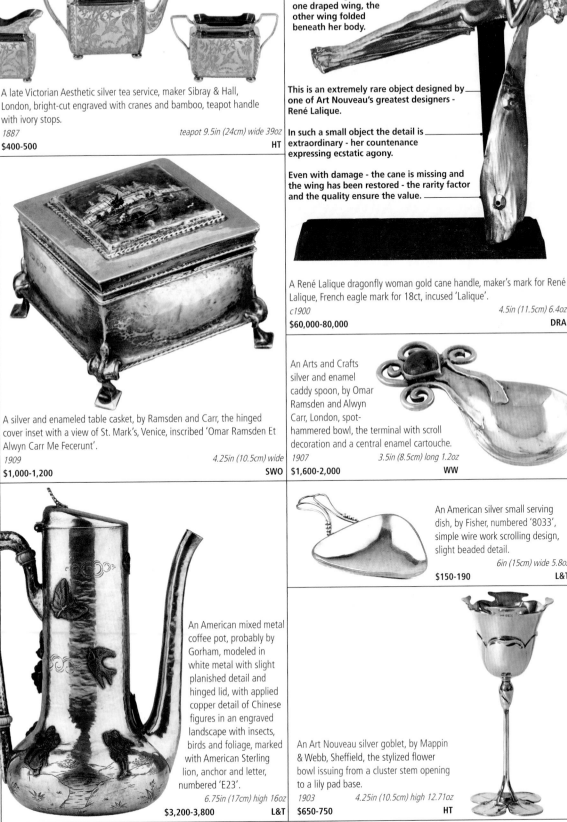

A silver and enameled table casket, by Ramsden and Carr, the hinged cover inset with a view of St. Mark's, Venice, inscribed 'Omar Ramsden Et Alwyn Carr Me Fecerunt'.
1909   *4.25in (10.5cm) wide*
$1,000-1,200   SWO

An Arts and Crafts silver and enamel caddy spoon, by Omar Ramsden and Alwyn Carr, London, spot-hammered bowl, the terminal with scroll decoration and a central enamel cartouche.
1907   *3.5in (8.5cm) long 1.2oz*
$1,600-2,000   WW

An American silver small serving dish, by Fisher, numbered '8033', simple wire work scrolling design, slight beaded detail.
6in (15cm) wide 5.8oz
$150-190   L&T

An American mixed metal coffee pot, probably by Gorham, modeled in white metal with slight planished detail and hinged lid, with applied copper detail of Chinese figures in an engraved landscape with insects, birds and foliage, marked with American Sterling lion, anchor and letter, numbered 'E23'.
6.75in (17cm) high 16oz
$3,200-3,800   L&T

An Art Nouveau silver goblet, by Mappin & Webb, Sheffield, the stylized flower bowl issuing from a cluster stem opening to a lily pad base.
1903   *4.25in (10.5cm) high 12.71oz*
$650-750   HT

An Art Nouveau Walter Scherf & Co. 'Osiris' silvered pewter toilet mirror, design attributed to Fredrich Alder, cast with two peacocks, stamped 'ISIS OSIRIS 521'.

11.75in (30cm) high

$800-950　　　　　　　　　　TEN

An Art Nouveau electroplated strut mirror, by WMF 'Wurttembergische' Metallwarenfabrik, the frame cast with flowers and an Art Nouveau maiden, stamped marks 'WEPCO/ EP/ IO/ OX'.

Wurtemberg [sic] Electo Plate Co. (WEPCO) was a division of WMF for the English-speaking export market.

c1900　　　　14.25in (36cm) high

$750-900　　　　　　　　　　L&T

A silver-plated cocktail shaker, 'The Thirst Extinguisher', by Asprey & Co., with recipes for eight cocktails on the base, stamped 'A & Co., Asprey London, Made in England 3212, regd. no. 833773'.

c1932　　　　15in (38cm) high

$2,500-3,200　　　　　　　SWO

A chrome 'rocket' table lighter, inscribed 'G.E.L. 1950-1960', with stamped details.

11in (27.5cm) high

$150-190　　　　　　　　　SWO

ESSENTIAL REFERENCE - GUILD OF HANDICRAFT

Charles Robert Ashbee founded the Guild and School of Handicraft in 1888. Based on the model of the medieval workshop, the Guild operated as a co-operative. Style and aesthetics followed the Art and Crafts movement and the Guild produced leather, furniture, metalwork, jewelry and books, with much of the work based on Ashbee's designs. Revival of traditional techniques, education of working people and encouraging satisfaction through work were key principles of the Arts and Craft movement and the Guild. In 1902, the Guild (150 people, the Guildsmen and their families) moved from East London to Chipping Campden. Ashbee believed that living a simple, collective life in rural surroundings would add to the health and well-being of the craftsmen and consequently the work they produced. Although the work of the Guild was widely exhibited, increasing financial difficulties from 1905 eventually resulted in the voluntary liquidation of the Guild in 1908.

A table lighter, in the form of a jet fighter, mounted on a ball joint, inscribed 'Gala-Sonic'.

10in (25cm) long

$130-180　　　　　　　　　SWO

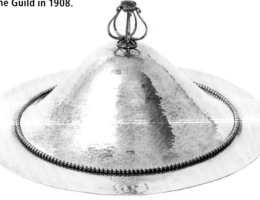

A Guild of Handicrafts electroplated metal muffin dish and cover, by Charles Robert Ashbee, the hammered conical dome cover with silver wirework finial set with moonstone, stamped 'Guild of Handicrafts Ltd', mark to cover and base.

9in (23cm) diam

$4,500-5,000　　　　　　　WW

A WMF silver-plated and green-glass biscuit barrel.

9.5in (24cm) high

$180-250　　　　　　　　　MOR

A Secessionist silver-plated and etched glass biscuit barrel and cover.

8.75in (22cm) high

$250-320　　　　　　　　　MOR

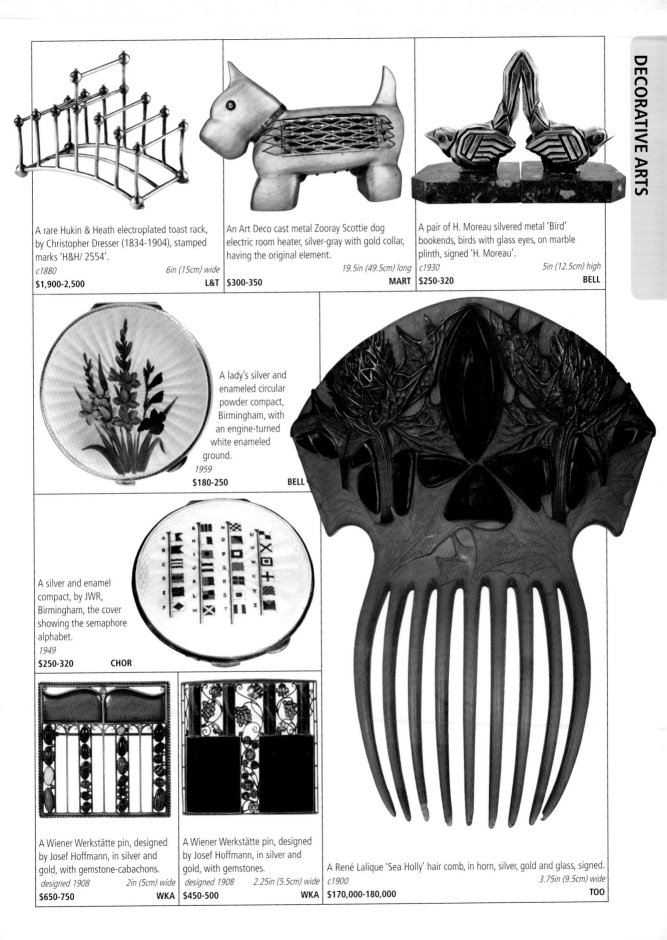

A rare Hukin & Heath electroplated toast rack, by Christopher Dresser (1834-1904), stamped marks 'H&H/ 2554'.

c1880   6in (15cm) wide

$1,900-2,500   **L&T**

An Art Deco cast metal Zooray Scottie dog electric room heater, silver-gray with gold collar, having the original element.

      19.5in (49.5cm) long

$300-350   **MART**

A pair of H. Moreau silvered metal 'Bird' bookends, birds with glass eyes, on marble plinth, signed 'H. Moreau'.

c1930   5in (12.5cm) high

$250-320   **BELL**

A lady's silver and enameled circular powder compact, Birmingham, with an engine-turned white enameled ground.

1959

$180-250   **BELL**

A silver and enamel compact, by JWR, Birmingham, the cover showing the semaphore alphabet.

1949

$250-320   **CHOR**

A Wiener Werkstätte pin, designed by Josef Hoffmann, in silver and gold, with gemstone-cabachons.

designed 1908   2in (5cm) wide

$650-750   **WKA**

A Wiener Werkstätte pin, designed by Josef Hoffmann, in silver and gold, with gemstones.

designed 1908   2.25in (5.5cm) wide

$450-500   **WKA**

A René Lalique 'Sea Holly' hair comb, in horn, silver, gold and glass, signed.

c1900   3.75in (9.5cm) wide

$170,000-180,000   **TOO**

A Guild of Handicrafts patinated copper and enamel box, with riverscape scene, probably by Charles Fleetwood Varley, cedar lined, unsigned.

5in (12.5cm) wide

$1,110-1,300   WW

A copper box, by John Pearson, embossed with peacocks beneath a fruit tree, loop lock, monogrammed 'J.P', dated, shows signs of age.

1907   12.25in (31cm) wide

$900-1,000   TEN

A pair of wrought iron fire dogs, designed by Ernest Gimson, made by Alfred Bucknell, the circular terminal with pierced heart-shaped motif, unsigned.

These fire dogs have great provenance. They were owned by Sidney Barnsley and given by Edward Barnsley to Nic Antonini (Sidney's great-grandson).

22in (56cm) high

$5,500-6,500   WW

A William Hutton pewter ewer, designed by Kate Harris, model no.0616, the handle cast with an Art Nouveau maiden with flowing hair, above a turquoise ceramic stone, stamped marks.

12in (30.5cm) high

$900-1,000   WW

A pair of wrought iron chenets, after a design by Edgar Brandt, modeled as stylized peacocks.

19.25in (49cm) high

$1,000-1,250   SWO

A Kayserzinn pewter decanter, designed by Hugo Leven, model no.4433, modeled as an auk, stamped marks.

See Paul Carter Robinson, '20th Century Pewter Art Nouveau to Modernism', Antique Collector's Club, page 49, catalog no.1.89. This actual jug was illustrated on the front cover.

11.5in (29cm) high

$500-650   WW

A polished steel candlestick, designed by Ernest Gimson, probably made by Alfred Bucknell, stamped with simple bands of decoration, on three faceted ball feet, unsigned.

9.5in (24cm) high

$2,500-3,200   WW

A rare W.A.S Benson fire screen, the copper stylized flowerhead screen with brass center, on rise and fall central stem with loop carry handle terminal, unmarked.

29.25in (74cm) high

$13,000-18,000   WW

ESSENTIAL REFERENCE - FRANZ BERGMAN

Franz Bergman (1838-1894) was born in Bohemia and worked as a metalwork finisher before founding a bronze factory in Vienna in 1860. After his death, the factory passed to his son, also named Franz Bergman (1861-1939). Although Bergman junior was not a sculptor himself, his factory produced numerous patinated and cold painted bronze sculptures, chiefly Oriental, animal or erotic figures. Bergman bronzes are notable for their impressive attention to detail and their vibrant colors. The bronzes were stamped with a capital 'B' within a twin-handled urn and often inscribed 'Geschutzt', meaning 'copyrighted'. The more erotic figures were sometimes stamped 'Namgreb' - Bergman in reserve.

A figurative Franz Bergman painted bronze table light, with maker's mark 'GESCH', 'AUSTRIA'.
c1900 17in (43.5cm) high
$7,000-8,000 QU

A good large 19thC Franz Bergman cold painted bronze figural group, depicting two Arabic huntsman upon an elephant, with a fallen tiger upon its back.
10in (25.5cm) wide
$9,500-10,500 HANN

A Franz Bergman cold painted bronze figure group, cast as four Arabic boys, seated and standing on a palm tree, cast maker's marks '4888'.
c1910 *9.75in (25cm) wide*
$3,200-3,800 L&T

A Franz Bergman cold painted bronze figure of an Arab carpet seller, stamped to base 'B Gesch' within an urn.
c1900 *4.5in (11.5cm) high*
$800-950 TRI

An Art Nouveau Franz Bergman bronze watch stand, in the form of a young lady and lily pads, stamped Bergman mark, also marked 'Geschützt' and '5070' verso.
6.75in (17cm) high
$1,000-1,100 ECGW

A Franz Bergman cold painted model of a Native American, modeled crouched with a shield, with impressed marks, numbered '3605'.
4in (10cm) high
$950-1,100 BELL

An erotic Franz Bergman patinated and cold painted bronze harem dancer, signed in the cast 'Namgreb'.
10.5in (26.5cm) high
$1,900-2,500 WW

A metamorphic erotic bronze study of an owl and nude, by Franz Bergman, the owl with sprung door, opening to reveal a gilt-bronze nude, signed 'Namgreb' in the bronze, stamped 'B' within urn symbol.

7.75in (19.5cm) high

$5,000-6,500   **ROS**

A late 19thC/early 20thC Austrian cold painted bronze Orientalist group of an Arab on a camel, by Bergman, previously with a lion attacking the camel, stamped with a 'B' in a vase, 'GESCHUTZT 4374'.

8.5in (21.5cm) high

$1,500-2,000   **WW**

An Austrian cold painted bronze model of a carpet seller, attributed to Franz Bergman, double stamped 'Austria' to underside, some paint loss to his turban.

8.25in (21cm) high

$1,500-1,900   **CHEF**

An early 20thC Austrian cold painted bronze and ivory figure of a court jester, on a marble plinth, unsigned.

8.5in (21.5cm) high

$400-500   **BELL**

A 19thC Austrian cold painted bronze figure, modeled as an Arab standing barefoot on a carpet, apparently unmarked.

6in (15cm) high

$650-750   **HT**

A late 19th/early 20thC cold painted bronze model of a Marabou stork, with her five chicks.

3.75in (9.5cm) high

$450-550   **L&T**

A late 19th/early 20thC Austrian cold painted bronze model of a bulldog, in the manner of Franz Bergman.

7.25in (18.5cm) long

$700-800   **WW**

An Austrian cold painted bronze pin tray, decorated with a pheasant, signed and inscribed 'Austria', with factory stamp to underside.

3.75in (9.5cm) wide

$250-400   **ROS**

A late 18th/early 19thC bronze statue of a lion, 'A Walking Lion', by Antoine-Louis Barye, signed 'Barye' and inscribed 'F Barbedienne Fondeur Paris' and incised underneath 'F36', '11188T' and '1141'.

The original model was in the Place de la Bastille, Paris

15.75in (40cm) long

$4,500-5,000   **CHOR**

A bronze and marble study of a panther, 'Panthère en Marche', by Maurice Prost, signed 'M Prost' and inscribed with foundry mark 'Susse Frères Editeurs Paris'.

c1930   *25.25in (64cm) wide*

$23,000-28,000   **HICK**

A bronze and marble study of a striding panther, 'Panthère', by André-Vincent Becquerel, the animal modeled grooming his outstretched front leg, signed 'A Becquerel'.

c1920   *26.75in (68cm) wide*

$23,000-28,000   **HICK**

A bronze study of a 'Striding Panther', by Louis-Albert Carvin, Paris, modeled in a stretched pose widening its mouth to roar, signed 'L Carvin' and engraved 'Etling'.

c1920   *24.5in (62cm) wide*

$3,800-4,400   **HICK**

A bronze study of a panther, 'Panthère Tournant', by Irénée René Rochard, signed 'Rochard', on a marble plinth.

c1930   *15.75in (40cm) wide*

$3,800-4,400   **HICK**

A cold painted bronze and stone group of a warrior, 'The Call', by Charles Charles, Le Verrier Foundry, holding the reins of an energetic horse, representative of the horses of San Marco in Venice, inscribed 'MARCO', the bronze signed 'C Charles'.

c1940   *19.25in (49cm) high*

$5,000-5,700   **HICK**

A pair of 19thC patinated bronze Marley horses, after the original by Coustou.

15in (38cm) high

$700-800   **TRI**

A 19thC bronze figure of two horses, 'L'Accolade', by Pierre-Jules Męne.

These were first exhibited in 1852, the two horses 'Tachiani' and 'Nedjébé' both appear in separate models.

26.75in (68cm) wide

$6,500-7,500   **CHOR**

A 19thC bronze pug dog, with a white marble plinth.

4.25in (11cm) long

$300-400 SWO

A bronze group of two retrievers, by Emmanuel Fremiet, France, signed 'E. FREMIET', numbered '238'.

9.75in (24.5cm) high

$1,300-1,500 WW

A 1930s bronze figure of a stretching Borzoi, by Armand Lemo, raised to a stepped veined marble plinth, with incised signature.

19.25in (49cm) long

$1,300-1,800 FLD

A late 19th/early 20thC gilt-bronze owl, by Edouard-Marcel Sandoz, signed 'Ed. M. Sandoz, Susse Fr. Edn. Paris', on a marble plinth.

4.5in (11cm) high

$1,110-1,300 SWO

A French bronze owl, 'Hibou', by Antoine-Louis Barye, French, signed 'BARYE, F. Barbedienne'.

3.5in (9cm) high

$1,300-1,800 ECGW

A bronze figure of a mouse attempting to eat an alabaster egg, by Clovis Edmond Masson, on a rouge marble plinth, signed 'C Masson'.

4in (10cm) high

$950-1,100 SWO

A bronze study, 'Leaping Antelope', by Raoh Schorr, signed 'Schorr' and stamped 'Bronze'.

c1930 *10.5in (27cm) wide*

$1,000-1,100 HICK

A bronze figure, Study for 'L'action enchainee', by Aristide Maillol, signed with monogram, numbered '3/6', Alexis Rudier foundeur, with Paris stamp.

c1906 *6.5in (16.5cm) high*

$15,000-19,000 FLD

A bronze portrait study of Fanny Moscovici, 'La Roumaine', by Emile Antoine Bourdelle, numbered 'VII', with Valsuani foundry stamp, dated.

1927 *20in (51cm) high*

$7,500-9,000 FLD

A bronze figure of a young girl, holding a puppy whilst it licks her face, signed 'A. Bolle'.

29.25in (74cm) high

$3,200-3,800   **SWO**

A large late 19thC/early 20thC bronze figure of Mephistopheles, by Jacques Louis Gautier, signed 'J. GAUTIER'.

33.75in (85.5cm) high

$2,500-3,800   **WW**

ESSENTIAL REFERENCE - PIERRE-JULES MÊNE

P.J. Mêne lived and worked in Paris. He was one of the pioneer animalière or animal sculptors of the 19thC. He was largely self-taught, spending many hours sketching in the Jardin des Plantes. He was one of the most prolific sculptors of his time, with the reputation of producing high quality work. He was awarded the Cross Legion d'Honneur for his contribution to art in 1861 and First Class Medals at the London Exhibitions of 1855 and 1861. Despite his reputation, he declined all offers of large public works and specialised in small bronzes. His work was influenced by the artists Carle Vennet and Landseer, which can be seen particularly in these Scottish pieces. 'Ecossais Montrant un Renard a son Chien' was orginally cast in 1861 and 'Valet de Chiens' in 1864.

A pair of patinated bronze figures, by Pierre-Jules Mêne, 'Ecossais Montrant un Renard a son Chien' and 'Valet de Chiens Tenant deux Griffons Ecossais', depicting a Scottish huntsman lifting a dead fox and a Ghillie with his deerhounds, signed in the bronze.

19.75in (50cm) high

$7,000-8,000   **CHEF**

A mid-20thC bronze figure of a nymph, 'Nymph Emblematic of Summer', after Auguste Moreau for Tiffany & Co., signed 'Tiffany & Co.', pitting in areas, split to circular base at back.

37.5in (95cm) high

$1,000-1,250   **CHOR**

A bronze and ocher marble group, by Charles Theodore Perron (1862-1934), the lady reaching for a chain of flowers.

39in (99cm) high

$3,200-3,800   **CHEF**

A bronze group, by Jean Sul-Abadie, modeled as a lady, holding a bow and arrows confiscated from Cupid, who stands below, signed and with founders mark.

38.25in (97cm) high

$1,900-2,500   **CHEF**

ESSENTIAL REFERENCE - GIO PONTI

Gio Ponti (1891-1979) was poet, painter, artist and architect, referred to as the 'Godfather of Italy's post-war design renaissance'. He trained as an architect; his most famous building being the Pirelli Tower in Milan built in 1958. However Ponti also designed furniture, flatware, vases and sculptures, set designs at La Scala, and was editor of the influential Domus magazine. His daughter Lisa wrote that he could regularly work an 18-hour day. His sculpture 'Letizia', meaning 'Happiness', was a design from the 1920s and is typical of his more lyrical style of that era.

A patinated bronze figure of a cloaked maiden, 'Letizia', by Gio Ponti, modeled with musical instruments and vessels to her feet, unsigned, lacks definition, likely a later casting.

24in (61cm) high

$1,300-1,900   **CHEF**

A late 19thC patinated bronze model of Hercules, draped in a lion skin and with club in hand, unsigned.

22.5in (57cm) high

$3,800-4,400   **BELL**

A late 19th/early 20thC patinated bronze figure, depicting Milo of Croton, unsigned.

28.75in (73cm) high

$2,500-3,200   **BELL**

ESSENTIAL REFERENCE - DEMÉTRE CHIPARUS

Demétre Chiparus (1886-1947) was born in Romania, studied in Italy and ultimately settled in Paris. There he worked for Etling and the Les Neveau de J. Lehmann foundry, chiefly as a designer and sculptor of chryselephantine (bronze and ivory) figures.

He depicted exotic women, often dancers, and his sculptures show Mexican, Inca, Aztec and Mayan influences. His figures were extremely detailed and the bases often elaborate. He almost always signed his work, usually as 'D. H. Chiparus' or 'D. Chiparus'. Early pieces often also bear the inscription 'ETLING.PARIS'.

A bronze and ivory 'Shimmer' figure, cast and carved from a model by Demétre Chiparus, on a marble base, unsigned, two toes chipped off, minor chips to base.

15in (38cm) high

$19,000-25,000   **WW**

A green patinated bronze figure, 'Equilibrium', by Demétre Chiparus, modeled as a nude wearing a headdress, holding three hoops, on a banded agate plinth, signed 'D Chiparus'.

18in (46cm) high

$9,500-10,500   **TEN**

A gilt-bronze and ivory figure of an elegant lady, 'Winter', by Demétre Chiparus, on an alabaster plinth, inscribed 'Chiparus'.

12.5in (32cm) high

$5,000-6,500   **SWO**

A bronze and ivory figure, 'Water Carrier with Child', by Demètre H. Chiparus, signed 'D. H. Chiparus', on marble base.

c1920   *21.75in (55.5cm) high*

$15,000-18,000   **QU**

A bronze and ivory 'Indiscreet' figure, cast and carved from a model by Demétre Chiparus, signed to the base 'Chiparus', loses to the right hand, chips to base.

17.25in (44cm) high

$9,000-10,000   **WW**

A patinated bronze model of a dancer, 'A Dancer of the Ganges' (Chain Dancer), cast from a model by Demétre Chiparus, on a marble base, etched 'Chiparus' to base top.

11.5in (29cm) high

$3,800-5,000   **WW**

An Art Deco bronze and ivory 'Innocence' figure, by Demétre Chiparus, on an alabaster base, signed on the base 'D Chiparus', with a repair to the foot.

9.5in (24cm) high

$2,300-2,800   **LAW**

ESSENTIAL REFERENCE - ERTÉ

Romain de Tirtoff (1892-1990) was born in St Petersburg. He moved to Paris in 1910 and began working under the pseudonym 'Erté', after his initials R.T., to avoid embarrassment for his family, who disapproved of his choice of profession. He worked as a designer in a range of fields, from graphics to sculpture, from costume to interior design. He was a fashion illustrator for magazines such as Harper's Bazaar, Vogue and Cosmopolitan, and designed costumes and sets for ballets, operas and theatrical revues. His reputation lessened after World War II, but the Art Deco revival of the 1960s brought a renewed interest in his work. He began a new career, re-creating his previous designs into limited edition prints, art jewelry and bronze figures. He died in New York, aged 97, and was still working until two years before his death.

A cold painted Erte bronze group of 'The Three Graces', inspired by 'Beauty', 'Charm' and 'Elegance' in mythology, heightened with gilding, signed, numbered '41/375', dated, inscribed 'Fine Art Acquisitions' and stamped with the Meisner foundry logo.

1987   *15.25in (39cm) high*
$9,000-10,000   **HICK**

An Art Deco cold painted bronze group, 'Two Vamps', by Erté, signed, dated, numbered and stamped with the SevenArts copyright foundry mark.

This has the original Certificate of Authenticity signed by Erté. In Erté's own words, 'These are two of my six Vamps, the Seductress and the Pretentieuse. Pretention often precedes seduction.'

c1990   *19in (48cm) high*
$6,500-7,500   **HICK**

A 20thC cold painted bronze figure of a young woman, 'Starstruck', modeled in a glamorous fitted gown, with a theatrical head dress representing a constellation of stars, signed 'Erté', dated, numbered '87/375', with Meisner foundry mark.

1987   *22in (56cm) high*
$6,500-7,500   **HICK**

An Art Deco cold painted bronze figure of a young beauty, 'L'Amour', modeled wearing a flamboyant costume depicting the violent movements of her passionate dance, signed 'Erté', numbered '105/375', inscribed 'Fine Art Acquisitions' for the publisher, dated.

1985   *20.75in (53cm) high*
$5,000-5,700   **HICK**

A cold painted bronze figure, representing the 'Firebird' and the numeral 'Five', by Erté, signed, dated, stamped and numbered '25/250'.

'This bronze sculpture represents a fantastic creature half-woman half-bird. It is inspired by the numeral five of my lithograph series The Numerals. I always like to use fantastic images as subjects for my sculptures. I don't like realism in my art. As a child I was always fascinated by the mythical creature called 'the Firebird' in Russian fairy tales. My love for it got stronger when I heard Stravinsky's wonderful music for the ballet The Firebird, produced by Diaghilev for the Ballets Russes. My sculpture and numeral Five were inspired by this poetic creature of the imagination.'
Erté

1980   *16.5in (42cm) high*
$4,500-5,000   **HICK**

A cold painted bronze figure of a young lady, 'Belle du Bal', modeled in striking theatrical costume, raised on a base, signed 'Erté', numbered '109/500', dated, stamped with foundry mark 'Seven Arts Ltd. London'.

1990   *17.75in (45cm) high*
$5,000-5,700   **HICK**

ESSENTIAL REFERENCE - LORENZL

Josef Lorenzl (1892-1950) was a designer and sculptor for a number of Austrian manufacturers, including Vienna Arsenal and Goldscheider. He worked in ceramics and metal and produced a range of figures in bronze, ivory and occasionally chryselephantine. His sculptures were typically small and depicted single female figures, usually dancers, often nudes, with the bobbed hair and slender figures fashionable in the 1920s-30s. He used patinated silver or gilt finishes on his figures, giving them a distinctive metallic appearance. The bases were typically plain green or black onyx or marble. Lorenzl usually signed his work, either as 'Lorenzl', 'Lor' or 'Renzl'. See page 465 for his ceramics.

A cold painted gilt-bronze figure of a 'Scarf Dancer', by Josef Lorenzl, on a Brazilian green onyx plinth, signed 'Lorenzl'.

c1930   *27.25in (69cm) high*

$16,000-17,000   **HICK**

A silvered bronze model of a dancer, cast from a model by Josef Lorenzl, on black veined marble base, signed 'Lorenzl'.

12.5in (32cm) high

$1,500-2,000   **WW**

A patinated bronze figure of a lady, by Josef Lorenzl (1892-1950), modeled holding a fan and wearing a short dress, on a plinth, signed 'Lorenzl' to her shoes.

14in (35.5cm) high

$5,500-7,000   **SWO**

A bronze and ivory figure, of a lady holding her billowing dress, by Josef Lorenzl, on an onyx plinth, signed.

8.75in (22.5cm) high

$3,200-3,800   **SWO**

An Art Deco silvered and patinated bronze figure of a nude female dancer, 'Vivian', after Josef Lorenzl, on a onyx plinth with bronze brackets, stamped 'Real Bronze, Made in Austria'.

14in (35.5cm) high

$1,300-1,900   **HT**

An Art Deco silvered and patinated bronze figure of a nude female, after Josef Lorenzl, fixed onto an onyx column and plinth, stamped 'R. Lor'.

13.5in (34.5cm) high

$1,900-2,500   **HT**

A 1920s bronze and ivory figure, 'Dancer', by Josef Lorenzl, on onyx base.

9.75in (25cm) high

$1,300-1,800   **QU**

A patinated bronze model of a dancer, cast from a model by Josef Lorenzl, on an onyx base, signed in the cast 'Lorenzl'.

7.75in (20cm) high

$550-700   **WW**

ESSENTIAL REFERENCE - FERDINAND PREISS

Ferdinand Preiss (1882-1943) was a German sculptor who specialised in chryselephantine and ivory figures. After an apprenticeship with his uncle, the ivory carver Philipp Willmann, Preiss traveled throughout Europe, working as a designer and modeller. After he met Arthur Kassler, the pair founded Preiss & Kassler in Berlin in 1906. The foundry began with small ivory figures, typically children or classical nudes. From 1910 onward, Preiss also made chryselephantine figures of bronze and ivory on onyx or marble bases. Early Preiss chryselephantine figures feature classical maidens. His later figures depict women in sporting, dancing or theatrical poses. Preiss figures usually bear the monogram 'PK' and the signature 'F.Preiss'.

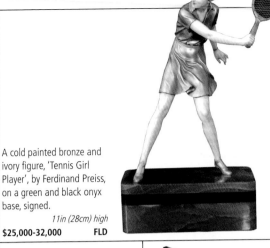

A cold painted bronze and ivory figure, 'Tennis Girl Player', by Ferdinand Preiss, on a green and black onyx base, signed.

11in (28cm) high

$25,000-32,000   FLD

A Ferdinand Preiss ivory and bronze sculpture of 'Diana the Archer', on an onyx and marble base, signed 'F Preiss', arrow missing.

10.5in (27cm) high
TRI

$15,000-19,000

An Art Deco silvered bronze and ivory figure, modeled as a Grecian-style girl dancing, in the manner of Ferdinand Preiss, unsigned, repaired hairline crack inverted 'v' on back of neck, one hand damaged, one foot detached.

9.75in (25cm) high
ECGW

$2,500-3,800

A silver-plated bronze figure, 'Gymnast', by Ferdinand Preiss, cast by Preiss & Kassler, Berlin, marked 'Mark of Preiss & Kassler', base is of onyx and black marble, base marked 'F. Preiss'.

c1920   *14in (35.5cm) high*
QU

$19,000-25,000

A 1920s silvered bronze figure, 'Discus Thrower', by Ferdinand Preiss, base is of onyx and black marble, marked 'F. Preiss'.

14.75in (37.5cm) high
$15,000-19,000   QU

A bronze and ivory 'Skater' figure, cast and carved from a model by Ferdinand Preiss, model no.1149, on an onyx and black base, incised 'F Preiss' to base, losses to right hand, chips to base.

13.25in (33.5cm) high
$11,000-13,000   WW

A miniature carved ivory figure, 'Woman Contemplating', by Ferdinand Preiss, on a green onyx base, unsigned.

2.25in (5.5cm) high
$1,100-1,400   WW

An Art Deco bronze and ivory figure of a nude dancer, by Louis Barthélemy, France, on an alabaster plinth, signed 'Barthelemy'.

9in (23cm) high

$1,900-2,500 SWO

A gilt-bronze sculpture, 'Snake Dancer', cast from a model by H. Calot, on marble base, signed in the cast 'H Calot'.

23.25in (59cm) high

$1,000-1,250 WW

A bronze and ivory figure of a young lady, 'Off to Market', by Dominique Alonzo, signed 'Alonzo', impressed 'Etling, Paris'.

c1920 *9in (23cm) high*

$2,300-2,800 SWO

A gilt and cold painted bronze figure of an Art Deco 'Sun Dancer', by Claire J.R. Colinet, modeled in full costume, signed 'Cl J R Colinet'.

c1925 *20.5in (52cm) high*

$6,500-7,000 HICK

A cold painted and silvered bronze and ivory figure, 'Pierrot', by Dorothea Charol, on a marble plinth, signed 'D. Charol'.

c1930 *15in (38cm) high*

$900-1,000 BELL

A gilt-bronze figure, 'Theban Dancer', by Claire Jeanne Roberte Colinet, modeled as a semi-nude female wearing an exotic costume, on a marble base inset with a bas-relief of Egyptian figures and hieroglyphics, signed 'CL J R Colinet', stamped in the cast 'D80', some restoration.

12in (30.5cm) wide

$3,800-5,000 TEN

A cold painted bronze figure of a young flapper, 'Cloaked Dancer', by Stefan Dakon, on a Brazilian green onyx plinth, signed 'Dakon'.

c1930 *8.25in (21cm) high*

$1,800-2,300 HICK

A cold painted bronze and ivory study of a dancer, 'Sylvia', by Stefan Dakon, on a Brazilian green onyx base, signed 'Dakon'.

c1930 *12.25in (31cm) high*

$3,200-3,800 HICK

A hand carved ivory figure of a young woman, 'Flower Lady', by Joseph Descomps, modeled hiding her modesty with a flower garland, on an onyx plinth, signed 'Descomps'.

c1920   10.25in (26cm) high

$5,000-5,700   **HICK**

A patinated bronze and ivory figure of a female musician, cast from a model by Joe Descomps, on alabaster base, etched 'Joe Descomps' signature.

19.5in (49.5cm) high

$2,500-3,200   **WW**

A French carved ivory figure, by Joseph Jules Emmanuel Cormier, base signed 'Joe Descomps', with its Boucheron gold-mounted pedestal, the neck mount with carnelian bosses and lapis lazuli drops, mount signed 'Boucheron, Paris', 18ct gold mark and maker's mark.

Joseph Jules Emmanuel Cormier is also known as Joe Descomps. In fact his work is usually found as Joe Descomps, although the sculptor and goldsmith also went by (and sometimes signed with) his Cormier name. Known for his female nudes in bronze and ivory, he trained in the Falguière studio, exhibited regularly at the Salon des Artistes Francais between 1891-1937 and, as the Musée d'Orsay notes, also worked with the famous Parisian jewellers Boucheron.

c1915   9in (23cm) high

$9,500-10,500   **MAB**

A 20thC bronze and ivory nude, by Josef Dorls, with a robe over one shoulder and slave bangles to her arms, signed 'DORLS fec.', on a marble plinth, finger missing.

19.5in (49.5cm) high

$3,800-5,000   **SWO**

A cold painted bronze and ivory study of an 'Exotic Dancer', by Gerda Iro Gerdago, modeled in theatrical costume, on an onyx base, signed 'Gerdago'.

c1935   12.25in (31cm) high

$11,000-13,000   **HICK**

A Hagenauer polished chrome figure of a tennis player, stamped 'Hagenauer Wien, Made in Austria, Handmade'.

17.75in (45cm) high

$700-800   **SWO**

A Hagenauer silvered bronze model of a javelin thrower, modeled mid-throw, on an oval base, stamped marks.

9in (23cm) high

$550-650   **CHEF**

An Art Deco spelter and marble group, modeled as a man running between two lionesses, inscribed 'G Limosin'.

24in (60.5cm) long

$700-800   **SWO**

A bronze and ivory figure of a Classical lady throwing a discus, by Ferdinand Lugerth, on a marble plinth, signed 'F Lugerth', with foundry stamp.

c1900   *10.5in (27cm) high*

$1,900-2,500   **SWO**

CLOSER LOOK - 'GIRL AND TERRIER'

The figure group is by the acclaimed sculptor Charles Henri Molins and is in excellent original condition.

This is a charming subject with the girl teaching her cheeky terrier new tricks.

The girl has delicate hand-carved ivory head and hands.

The group is raised on a Brazilian green onyx plinth.

A cold painted bronze figure, 'Girl and Terrier'.

c1930   *6.75in (17cm) high*

$3,800-4,400   **HICK**

A hand carved ivory and bronze figure, 'The Archer', by Charles Henri Molins, modeled as a young athletic woman in a striking stylized pose with her bow, on a Brazilian green onyx plinth.

c1938   *16.5in (42cm) high*

$9,000-9,500   **HICK**

An Art Deco enameled bronze and ivory figure of a dancing girl, by J.P. Morante, on a marble base, signed to the marble 'Morante'.

12.25in (31cm) high

$3,200-3,800   **SWO**

A cold painted gilt-bronze and hand carved ivory figure of a young woman in a ball gown, 'Coquette Violetta', by Rafael Nannini, on an onyx plinth, signed 'R Nannini'.

This was possibly inspired by Violetta in Verdi's opera 'La Traviata'.

c1920   *11.75in (30cm) high*

$5,000-5,700   **HICK**

A 1920s bronze and ivory figure, 'Shadow Player', by Roland Paris, engraved signature 'ROLAND PARIS', marble base.

7.25in (18.5cm) high

$2,500-3,200   **QU**

A cold painted enamel and gilt-bronze figure, 'Exotic Dancer', by Otto Poertzel, on a marble plinth, signed 'Prof. Poertzel'.

c1925   *14.5in (37cm) high*

$9,000-9,500   **HICK**

A bronze and ivory figure, modeled as a snake dancer, by Otto Poertzel (1876-1963), signed 'Prof. Poertzel', light patination, fingers restored.

c1924   *11.75in (30cm) high*

$11,000-14,000   **QU**

An early 20thC Italian Eduardo Rossi bronze and ivory figure, of a female castanet dancer, on onyx base, signed in the bronze 'Rossi', numbered '7399'.

17in (43cm) high

$1,900-2,500   MAB

A hand carved ivory and gilt-bronze figure of 'Salome', by Louis Sosson, modeled in lavish Eastern costume, on an onyx plinth, signed 'L.Sosson'.

Salome (c14 AD to 62-71 AD) was the daughter of Herod II and Herodias. According to Flavius Josephus's 'Jewish Antiquities', Salome was first married to Philip the Tetrarch of Ituraea and Trakonitis. After Philip's death in 34 AD she married Aristobulus of Chalcis and became Queen of Chalcis and Armenia Minor. They had three children. Salome is often identified with the dancing woman from the New Testament depicting her as an icon of dangerous female seductiveness, notably in regard to the dance iconised as the Dance of the Seven Veils. A similar motif was struck by Oscar Wilde in his Salome, in which she plays the role of femme fatale.

c1920   *10.25in (26cm) high*

$5,000-5,700   HICK

An enameled bronze and ivory figure of a harlequin dancer, by Theodor Ullmann, on an alabaster plinth, signed 'Th. Ullmann'.

Theodor Ullmann (fl.1920-1930) was an Austrian sculptor. His work was characteristically playful and inventive, taking influence from the naturalism of Art Nouveau and the stylized look of Art Deco. He worked at the Arthur Rubenstein Foundry. His figures are usually signed 'Th. Ullmann.'

c1920   *12.5in (31.5cm) high*

$9,500-10,500   SWO

A cold painted bronze figure of a young woman, 'Kokette Frau', by Bruno Zach, modeled in a sensuous pose, on a Brazilian onyx plinth, signed 'Zach' to bronze.

c1925   *15.75in (40cm) high*

$12,000-13,000   HICK

A cold painted bronze figure, by Bruno Zach, the girl with a fringed skirt and gartered stockings, on a marble plinth, signed in the bronze 'B. ZACH'.

c1920   *15.25in (39cm) high*

$3,200-4,400   L&T

A 1920s silvered bronze figure, 'Dancer', by Bruno Zach, on onyx base, signed 'B. Zack (!)'.

18in (46cm) high

$5,500-6,500   QU

A bronze and ivory figure of a Classical lady dancing, on a marble plinth.

13in (33cm) high

$1,900-2,500   SWO

MODERN MARKET

Where other areas have faltered financially, interest in and prices for outstanding post-World War II design has in many cases quadrupled. Design in this period was totally international and, with the added impetus of the internet, so is the collecting market. Moreover, many pieces are found in large numbers and are consequently relatively affordable, making this area accessible to younger buyers. The styles are also in tune with a younger taste.

While the seeds of Mid-century Modern lay in the Scandinavian 'Soft Modernism' of the 1930s, the designers who started working during and after World War II were excited by the possibilities of new materials and the demands of an enthusiastic consumer class. Designers such as Charles and Ray Eames in the USA said their mission was 'getting the most of the best to the greatest number of people for the least amount of money'. Of course many of the Eames' original pieces can no longer be purchased for 'the least amount of money' as they are now highly prized as icons of design.

The designs of Paul Evans continue to excite collectors: a unique and important cabinet, designed in 1977 sold in January 2017 at David Rago's sale for $382,000 (£300,000).

The Modern Movement is by its very nature diverse. It covers the great studio craftsmen, such as furniture maker George Nakashima. The work of George Nakashima continues to gain followers. In March 2017 Freemans in Philadelphia sold a hanging wall case for $62,500 (£49,600). Potters such as the Natzlers and Peter Voulkos continue to achieve record prices.

It also covers 1960s plastic and Postmodern pieces by designers such as Joe Colombo and Ettore Sottsass. There is something in this area to suit all tastes and pockets.

Glass from the 20thC greats - the designers and factories of Scandinavia and Murano - continues to sell really well. Buyers like the vibrant colors and modern forms. Big names are another plus factor and prices for the work of luminaries, such as American designer Dale Chihuly, have quadrupled in recent years. Other glass artists who have pioneered new techniques in the US include Mary Ann 'Toots' Zynsky. A Murano 2002 Cosmos vase by Yoichi Ohira fetched $43,750 (£34,700) at Rago's January sale.

A newcomer to the growing 20thC glass stable is Post-War Czech glass, triumphed by my friend and colleague Mark Hill in his book 'High Sklo Low Sklo'. His new book 'Berànek & Skrdlovice: Legends of Czech Glass' is a must for collectors. Currently, the low end of the market is the most popular. As people get more comfortable with the unusual names of the designers, this market seems set to rise. To prove this point, in January 2017 a small 'Green Eye of the Pyramid' (1997) by Stanislav Libensky and Jaroslava Brychtova sold at David Rago's for $43,750 (£34,700)!

Top Left: A contemporary padded cameo glass vase, 'The Fall', designed by Allister Malcolm and Helen Millard, internally with gold aventurine and externally with fourteen cameo glass leaves, signature to base.

16.5in (42cm) high

$3,200-3,800 **FLD**

Above A 'Peacock' lounge chair, by Verner Panton for Plus-linje, Copenhagen.

c1960 *37.5in (95cm) diam*

$6,500-7,500 **QU**

MODERN DESIGN

A 'Capri' steel and fabric settee, by Johannes Andersen for Trensum, newly upholstered.

1958   *88.25in (224cm) wide*

$3,200-3,800   QU

A plywood and cognac leather 'Sgarsul' rocking chair, by Gae Aulenti for Poltronova, with maker's label.

1962   *43in (109cm) long*

$800-950   QU

A unique wooden 'Bildbank' bench, by Andres Bally, marked 'Andres Bally 2009'.

2009   *52.25in (133cm) wide*

$2,500-3,200   QU

A 1960s hardwood and chrome-plated extending dining table, in the manner of Milo Baughman, with a single removable leaf, the top veneered in rosewood and other hardwood stripes.

                          78in (198cm) long

$950-1,100   HT

A table, 'The Diana Willow Table', by John Barnard, the yew wood top with an organic base 'growing' through the top surface before reconnecting with the top.

The original table and design by John Barnard was commissioned as a wedding gift to H.R.H. The Prince and Princess of Wales from the Royal County of Norfolk; the young Princes, William and Harry, did their homework on the table. John Barnard continues to make limited editions of the table by commission, including this example. John Barnard studied furniture making, following the designs and tradition of the Arts and Crafts movement. He opened his first workshop in 1971. The Diana Willow table is designed to echo the form of a weeping willow tree. Hundreds of hours are taken to achieve the form of and finish on the table.

58.75in (149cm) wide

$2,800-3,500   CHEF

A 'Cab 415' couch, by Mario Bellini for Cassina, of tubular steel and black leather.

1977   *61in (155cm) wide*

$1,300-1,900   QU

A beechwood and glass Unicum 'Dreirund' coffee table, by Max Bill for Horgen Glarus, the glass mosaic professionally and elaborately restored.

c1950   *42.75in (108.5cm) wide*

$4,500-5,000   QU

A 'Canada' plywood easy chair, by Osvaldo Borsani for Tecno, with maker's label.

1965   *35in (89cm) long*

$1,000-1,100   QU

A tubular metal 'D 70' sofa bed, by Osvaldo Borsani for Tecno, with maker's badge.

1954   *75.25in (191cm) wide*

$3,200-3,800   QU

A European walnut and American black walnut dining table and chairs, by Matthew Burt, with ten Coopered high back chairs, with red padded seats, stamped 'Matthew'.

table 91in (231cm) long

$3,800-5,000

WW

A sideboard, by Pierre Cardin, manufactured by Frankreich, the wooden construction with white plastic laminate, chrome-plated sheet metal, marked with facsimile signature.

Pierre Cardin's costumes were used for the first time in 'La Belle et la Bête', 1946, by Jean Cocteau.

c1970   *74in (188cm) long*

$5,000-5,700

QU

A glass and nickle-plated steel desk, by Raymond Cohen.

c1970   *43.25in (110cm) wide*

$9,000-10,000

QU

ESSENTIAL REFERENCE - JOE COLOMBO

Joe Colombo, born Cesare Colombo (1930-1971) was an Italian designer. He studied painting at the Academy of Fine Arts in Milan, then went on to study architecture. Attracted by the possibilities of materials such as plastics, he gave up his painting and sculpting career in the late 1950s to focus on design. He created innovative designs for furniture, lighting, wristwatches and glassware. He was interested in adaptable and space-saving furniture systems, which prompted designs such as his Tube chair. This chair can be carried in a duffel bag and easily assembled in a variety of ways, providing a range of different sitting positions. Over the course of his career, Colombo designed products for Alessi, Bieffe, Flexform, Oluce, Kartell and many more.

A white PVC and fabric 'Tube chair', by Joe Colombo for Flexform.

1969   *39in (99cm) long*

$5,500-6,500

QU

A '4801/5' plywood easy chair, by Joe Colombo for Kartell, Noviglio, Milan.

1965   *28in (71cm) wide*

$1,900-2,500

QU

ESSENTIAL REFERENCE - TOM DIXON

Tom Dixon (b.1959) was born in Tunisia and moved to England at the age of four. Despite no formal training, Dixon's fame as a designer grew in the mid-1980s. He gained notice for his avant-garde chairs, made from scrap metal and displayed at the London nightclub Titanic. His first commercial success was his 'S' chair, designed for Cappellini in 1988. He was Creative Director of Habitat from 1998 to 2008. In 2004, he also became Creative Director for Artek. He received an OBE in 2000 and in 2002 established the brand 'Tom Dixon' with David Begg. Dixon remains the Creative Director today. The brand specialises in furniture, lighting, and accessories. Its products are sold in over fifty countries.

A polychromatic glass 'Trompe l'oeil S0002' mirror, by Lorenzo Forges Davanzati for Barovier & Toso, with maker's badge.

c1988   *33.75in (86cm) high*

$1,300-1,800

QU

An Oregon pine plywood prototype chair, by Nanna Ditzel for Poul Christiansen.

1962   *28.25in (72cm) high*

$7,500-9,000

QU

A cast iron and leather 'S' chair, by Tom Dixon for Cappellini, marked 'CAPPELLINI'.

1988   *40.25in (102cm) high*

$900-1,000

QU

MODERN DESIGN

A plywood and leather '670' lounge chair with '671' ottoman, by Charles Eames for Vitra, rosewood veneer retouched.
1956 *chair 31.5in (80cm) wide*
$5,000-6,500 QU

A red wickerwork 'E 19' bench, by Egon Eiermann for Heinrich Murmann.
1956 *56.75in (144cm) high*
$10,000-11,000 QU

A pair of brown leather 'Skater - FK 710' chairs, by Preben Fabricius and Jörgen Kastholm for Alfred Kill, marked 'Qualität aus Baden Württemberg'.
1968 *27.5in (70cm) high*
$4,500-5,000 QU

An armchair, by Martin Grierson for Arflex, of cast aluminum and tubular steel, with mustard yellow leather, dark brown piping.
c1962 *33.5in (85cm) wide*
$7,000-8,000 QU

One of a pair of 1930/40s beech bentwood 'H 269' armchairs, by Jindrich Halabala for Spojene UP Zavody.
34.25in (87cm) deep
$4,500-5,000 pair QU

A 'Sexy Relaxy' carbon fibre easy chair, by Richard Hutten, one of only three examples constructed by hand, with certificate of authenticity.
This design was inspired by the memorable scene with Sharon Stone in Paul Verhoeven's blockbuster movie 'Basic Instinct'.
2005 *30in (76.5cm) long*
$7,500-9,000 QU

A mirror on a brass frame, by Georges Jouve for Marcel Asselbur, with four ceramic coat hooks.
c1950 *20.5in (52cm) high*
$1,300-1,900 ECGW

Two of a set of four mid-20thC 'Spade' teak-framed open-arm easy chairs, probably by Finn Juhl.
$2,500-3,200 set BELL

A rosewood veneer sideboard, by Bodil Kjaer for E. Pedersen & Søn, Denmark, with oak veneer inside, chrome-plated rectangular steel.
c1959 *67in (170cm) long*
$9,500-10,500 QU

A 'Capitello Ionico' tubular metal and plywood chair, by Piero Fornasetti, no.20/30 of the 1999 edition, maker's label, maker's mark 'No. 20 di 30/99'.

designed 1980   *37.5in (95cm) high*

$4,500-5,000   QU

A 1990s 'Sole' tubular metal and plywood chair, by Piero Fornasetti, painted with sun motif, with maker's label.

This was one of a small edition, due to a production fault: the Sun was inadvertently painted looking angry.

37.5in (95.5cm) high

$4,500-5,000   QU

A sheet metal 'Casa con colonne' umbrella stand, designed by Piero Fornasetti in the 1950s/60s, marked 'FORNASETTI MILANO MADE IN ITALY Nr. 42 93'.

1993   *22.5in (57cm) high*

$2,000-2,500   QU

A 1950s 'Strumenti Musicali' sheet metal umbrella stand, by Piero Fornasetti, remains of a maker's label.

25.5in (65cm) high

$1,900-2,500   QU

A 1950s/60s 'Firenze' umbrella stand, by Piero Fornasetti.

22.75in (57.5cm) high

$1,000-1,300   QU

A center table, designed by Piero Fornasetti, the center with a lacquered architectural design, labelled 'Fornasetti, Milano'.

39.75in (101cm) diam

$1,000-1,250   SWO

A wood 'Gran Coromandel' screen, by Piero Fornasetti, with brass hinges.

1958   *55in (140cm) high*

$5,500-6,500   QU

A unique 1990s 'Architettura' counter, by Barnaba Fornasetti, with maker's mark.

This item is one of a kind from a boutique in Verona. Barnaba Fornaseti continues to create objects, furniture and fashion items under the brand founded by his late father, the 20thC surrealist designer Piero Fornasetti.

89in (226cm) wide

$19,000-25,000   QU

MODERN DESIGN

A 'PK-41 PK-91' steeel and leather folding stool, by Poul Kjaerholm for Kold Christensen.
1961   *23in (58.5cm) wide*
$3,800-4,400   **QU**

A 'How high the Moon' easy chair, by Shiro Kuramata for Vitra, of nickel-plated expanded metal, with maker's label.
designed 1986   *37.5in (95cm) wide*
$3,800-4,400   **QU**

A pair of chrome-plated steel and leather 'PLR 1' easy chairs, by Ross Franklin Littell for ICF Cadsana.
1968   *29in (73.5cm) high*
$3,800-4,400   **QU**

A marble 'M' dining table, by Angelo Mangiarotti for Skipper.
1969   *51.25in (130cm) wide*
$3,800-5,000   **QU**

A Merrow Associates leather chaise longue, with chrome supports.
66in (168cm) long
$1,900-2,500   **SWO**

A brass 'Thinking Man's Chair', by Jasper Morrison for Cappellini, with metal badge reading 'THINKING MAN'S CHAIR LIMITED 50/99'.
1986   *37.75in (96cm) long*
$2,000-2,500   **QU**

A 'Djinn' armchair, by Olivier Mourgue for Airborne International, Montreuil-sous-Bois.
1965   *31.5in (80cm) wide*
$1,300-1,600   **QU**

A 'Gadames' chipboard dresser, by Paolo Navone for Alchimia, laminated in plastic, with plate glass on drawers.
1980   *59.5in (151cm) high*
$7,500-9,000   **QU**

A bent ply and leather 'Rio' lounge chair, by Oscar Niemeyer for Fasem International Srl.
c1970   *68in (173cm) wide*
$3,200-3,800   **QU**

One of a pair of 'Ari' chairs and stools, by Arne Norell, with leather and steel, labelled to underside 'Norell, Made in Sweden', one stool re-covered.
$1,300-1,900   **BELL**

A 'Rainbow' polychromatic polymethylmethacrylate chair, by Patrick Norguet for Cappellini.
2000   *31.5in (80cm) high*
$6,500-7,500   **QU**

ESSENTIAL REFERENCE - VERNER PANTON

Verner Panton (1926-1998) was a Danish furniture and interior designer. He trained at the Royal Danish Academy of Fine Art and worked at the architectural firm Arne Jacobsen before founding his own studio in 1955. His designs were innovative and unconventional. In 1960, he designed a house made entirely of plastic. His designs for chairs often had no distinctive back and legs. He used steel wire frames and carefully molded curved plastic to create new and experimental designs. He worked with a range of manufactures, including Plus-linje and later Vitra, with whom he shared a long collaboration from the 1960s onward. His aim to design the world's first single-component plastic chair resulted in his best-known design, the Panton Chair, introduced by Vitra in 1967.

A 'Bikini' chair, designed by Hans Olsen for Frem Rojle, stamped.
designed 1968
$1,500-1,900   **SWO**

A pair of 'Cone' chairs, by Verner Panton for Nehl, Bünde, of sheet steel, part chrome-plated.
1958   *33in (84cm) high*
$1,100-1,400   **QU**

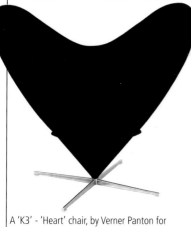

A 'K3' - 'Heart' chair, by Verner Panton for Plus-linje.
                    40.5in (103cm) wide
$2,500-3,200   **QU**

A wooden and aluminum sideboard, by Ico and Luisa Parisi for Mobili Italiani Moderni.
1959   *34in (86.5cm) high*
$1,900-2,500   **QU**

A pair of plywood and veneer sideboards, by Ico Parisi for Mobili Italiani Moderni, black patina, one lock lost.
1959   *56.25in (143cm) wide*
$6,500-7,000   **QU**

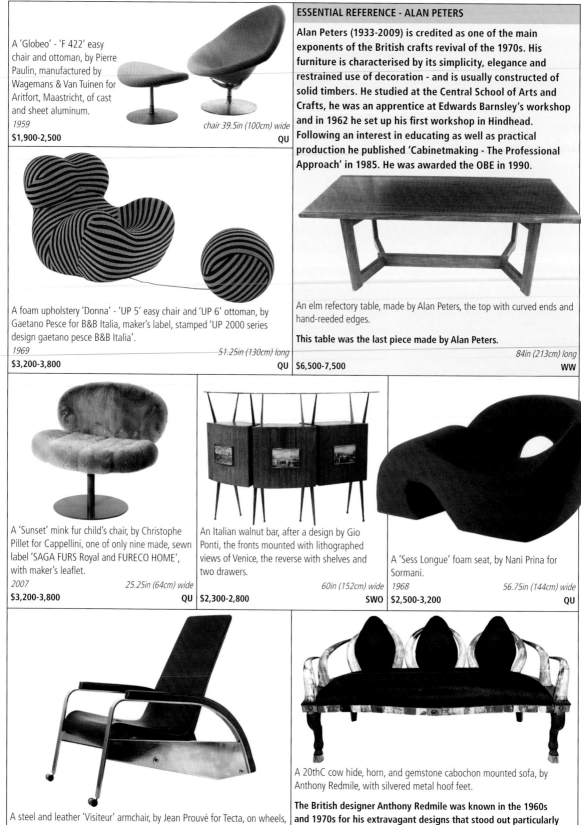

A 'Globeo' - 'F 422' easy chair and ottoman, by Pierre Paulin, manufactured by Wagemans & Van Tuinen for Aritfort, Maastricht, of cast and sheet aluminum.
1959
$1,900-2,500

chair 39.5in (100cm) wide
QU

ESSENTIAL REFERENCE - ALAN PETERS

Alan Peters (1933-2009) is credited as one of the main exponents of the British crafts revival of the 1970s. His furniture is characterised by its simplicity, elegance and restrained use of decoration - and is usually constructed of solid timbers. He studied at the Central School of Arts and Crafts, he was an apprentice at Edwards Barnsley's workshop and in 1962 he set up his first workshop in Hindhead. Following an interest in educating as well as practical production he published 'Cabinetmaking - The Professional Approach' in 1985. He was awarded the OBE in 1990.

A foam upholstery 'Donna' - 'UP 5' easy chair and 'UP 6' ottoman, by Gaetano Pesce for B&B Italia, maker's label, stamped 'UP 2000 series design gaetano pesce B&B Italia'.
1969
$3,200-3,800

51.25in (130cm) long
QU

An elm refectory table, made by Alan Peters, the top with curved ends and hand-reeded edges.

This table was the last piece made by Alan Peters.

84in (213cm) long
$6,500-7,500
WW

A 'Sunset' mink fur child's chair, by Christophe Pillet for Cappellini, one of only nine made, sewn label 'SAGA FURS Royal and FURECO HOME', with maker's leaflet.
2007
$3,200-3,800

25.25in (64cm) wide
QU

An Italian walnut bar, after a design by Gio Ponti, the fronts mounted with lithographed views of Venice, the reverse with shelves and two drawers.

60in (152cm) wide
$2,300-2,800
SWO

A 'Sess Longue' foam seat, by Nani Prina for Sormani.
1968
$2,500-3,200

56.75in (144cm) wide
QU

A steel and leather 'Visiteur' armchair, by Jean Prouvé for Tecta, on wheels, marked 'Label Jean Prouvé'.
1948
$3,200-3,800

43in (109cm) deep
QU

A 20thC cow hide, horn, and gemstone cabochon mounted sofa, by Anthony Redmile, with silvered metal hoof feet.

The British designer Anthony Redmile was known in the 1960s and 1970s for his extravagant designs that stood out particularly through his use of unusual materials.

67.75in (172cm) wide
$6,500-7,500
BELL

A 'Petal table', by Richard Schultz for Knoll International, cast metal leg with wooden top, maker's label reading 'KNOLL ASSOCIATES INC.; 320 PARK AVENUE N.Y'.

designed 1960   *42.25in (107cm) wide*

$2,500-3,200   **QU**

A mid-20thC rosewood sideboard, by Archie Shine.

83.75in (213cm) wide

$1,300-1,500   **BELL**

ESSENTIAL REFERENCE - ETTORE SOTTSASS

Ettore Sottsass (1917-2007) was an Italian architect and designer, best known for the Postmodern furniture he produced for the Memphis group. He studied architecture in Turin and went on to become the artistic director of Poltronova in 1957, then a design consultant for Olivetti from 1958. In 1981, he co-founded the Memphis group with several other leading designers and architects. They aimed to create bright, colorful pieces in contrast to the dark colors of 1970s European furniture design. Sottsass's designs are colorful, innovative and often make use of a range of different materials.

A plastic and plate glass 'Ultrafragola' mirror, by Ettore Sottsass for Poltronova, with maker's label.

1970   *76.75in (195cm) high*

$5,000-6,500   **QU**

A Skovby of Denmark extending hardwood dining table, the top with three radiating leaves turning to activate a patent spring-loaded extension housed in the cylindrical support below, manufacturer's label.

59in (150cm) wide extended

$750-900   **HT**

A 'Suvretta' chipboard bookcase, by Ettore Sottsass for Memphis, with green and white plastic laminate.

1981   *80.25in (204cm) wide*

$5,500-6,500   **QU**

A 'Beverly' chipboard and plastic laminate sideboard, by Ettore Sottsass for Memphis, with metal badge 'Memphis Milano Ettore Sottsass 1981 Made in Italy'.

1981 100.5in (225cm) high

$5,500-7,000   **QU**

ESSENTIAL REFERENCE - HENRIK THOR-LARSEN

Henrik Thor-Larsen was born in Denmark in 1932. He has worked as a graphic and industrial designer in Denmark, Norway and Switzerland. His first major success was the design of a plastic sports car. After designing car seats for Saab, he turned his interests to chairs. His most famous design is the Ovalia Egg Chair, first produced in 1968.

An 'Ovalia' easy chair and stool, by Henrik Thor-Larsen for Torlan, Staffanstorp, Sweden, with integrated loudspeakers.

1968   *chair 52in (132cm) high*

$5,500-6,500   **QU**

A steel, ply and leather 'Costes' armchair, by Philippe Starck for Driade.

1988   *33.75in (85.5cm) high*

$550-650   **QU**

An Andrew Varah 'Umbrella Men' surrealist three-door gentleman's wardrobe, designed by Andrew Varah, each door modeled as a gentleman's overcoat and boots, the central figure with a peg leg, hanging on a clothes hanger, each with an umbrella, mixed exotic veneers comprising Brazilian rosewood coats and boots, pressure dyed tabu veneers for shirts, satinwood coat hangers oak and burr oak background, metal door furniture, stamped to metal furniture 'AV' and paper label to reverse of each cabinet.

The 'Umbrella Men' wardrobes (cupboards) were produced in about five variations between 1987 and 2003. Each one is unique.
1989   *81.5in (207cm) high*
$3,800-5,000   **WW**

A Heinz Witthoeft pinewood and black leather 'Tail 4' armchair.
1959   *25.5in (65cm) wide*
$2,500-3,200   **QU**

An orange polyester and fibreglass furniture set, by Günter Beltzig Wuppertal for Brüder Beltzig Design, comprising three 'Floris' chairs and a table, shallow chip to the end of the table top.

Only about 30 examples of these sets were produced.
1967   *chairs 42.5in (108cm) high*
$38,000-50,000   **QU**

A red 'Corona - EJ 605' easy chair with ottoman, by Poul Volther for Eric Jörgensen.
1961   *chair 38.25in (97cm) high*
$3,800-4,400   **QU**

A 'Knotted Rouge chair', by Marcel Wanders for Cappellini, no.1/99 of a limited special edition, with certificate.
1996   *28.25in (72cm) high*
$5,500-6,500   **QU**

A pair of 'GE 672' bent plywood armchairs, by Hans J. Wegner for Getama, with linen covers.

Wegner's easy chairs had been presented by Getama at the Scandinavian Furniture Fair Malmö 1967. The 'Hammock chair' is also part of the series. The interesting thing about the 'GE 672' chairs was that they were stackable. Unfortunately, their production was very elaborate and expensive, thus manufacture was discontinued rather quickly.
1967   *28.25in (71.5cm) high*
$3,200-3,800   **QU**

A '5668' nutwood sideboard, by Edward Wormley for Dunbar Furniture, with maker's badge.
c1954   *61.5in (156cm) wide*
$7,500-9,000   **QU**

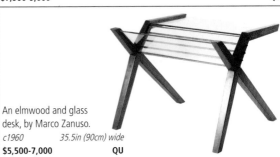

An elmwood and glass desk, by Marco Zanuso.
c1960   *35.5in (90cm) wide*
$5,500-7,000   **QU**

A handwoven wool and linen 'Orfeo' carpet, by Renata Bonfanti, signed 'Renata Bonfanti copia n. 12.'

1961 *124in (315cm) long*

$6,500-7,000 **QU**

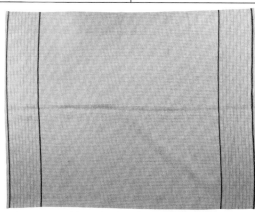

A 1950s cream and blue wool carpet, by Ingrid Dessau, marked 'ID'.

78.25in (199cm) long

$2,500-3,200 **QU**

A rare 'Tapipardo' pure new wool carpet, by Roberto Gabetti, Aimaro Isola, Luciano Re and Guido Drocco, for Paracchi or Arbo, from the 'Tapizoo' series, with maker's label.

1970 *98.5in (250cm) long*

$8,000-9,000 **QU**

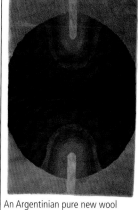

A 1960s cream, gray, blue and red wool carpet, attributed to Ulla Lagerheim.

98.5in (250cm) wide

$1,300-1,900 **QU**

A 'Le Coq' - 'Brahma' woolen tapestry, by Jean Lurçat for Atelier Tabard, framed.

1956 *39.25in (100cm) square*

$2,500-3,200 **QU**

An Argentinian pure new wool carpet, monogrammed '102 809'.

115in (283cm) wide

$1,500-1,900 **QU**

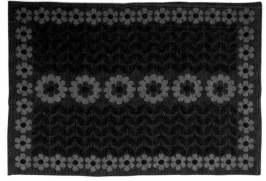

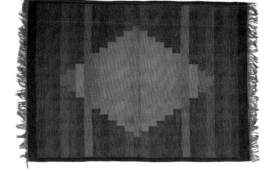

A 1950s Swedish wool on cotton carpet, marked 'BW'.

89.75in (228cm) wide

$750-900 **QU**

A 1950s Swedish wool on cotton carpet, marked 'AMB'.

102.25in (260cm) wide

$650-750 **QU**

A black cycladic pot, by Hans Coper, impressed seal mark.

c1972   *7.5in (19cm) high*

$25,000-32,000   **WW**

A 1950s Guido Gambone faience vase, marked 'Donkey, GAMBONE ITALY', one chip in the glaze.

11in (28cm) high

$3,200-3,800   **QU**

A 1950s Guido Gambone earthenware vase, marked 'Donkey, GAMBONE ITALY'.

5.75in (40cm) high

$1,900-2,500   **QU**

A stoneware bowl, by Shoji Hamada, painted tenmoku brush design to the well, the rim with resist design in wooden box.

Hamada, Bernard Leach and Yanagi flew to Santa Fe New Mexico, in 1953, to see first-hand the old handmade pots, and textiles, having been inspired by Native American pottery. At San Ildefonso they met Maria Martinez the renowned potter.

c1955   *16.5in (42cm) diam*

$9,000-10,000   **WW**

A large white raku mounted blade form, by Peter Hayes (b.1946), with textured finish, on black raku stand with copper bands, unsigned.

35.5in (90cm) high

$1,300-1,500   **WW**

A Madoura Pottery Edition Picasso platter, by Pablo Picasso (1881-1973), 'Still life, Ramie 219', impressed marks.

15.25in (39cm) wide

$11,000-13,000   **WW**

A ceramic ashtray, by Pablo Picasso, 'Oiseau a la Huppe', from an edition of 500, incised 'Edition Picasso' and with the Edition Picasso and Madoura Plein Feu pottery stamps.

c1952   *6in (15cm) diam*

$1,300-1,800   **BELL**

An earthenware dish, by Pablo Picasso for Madoura pottery, Vallauris, 'Colombe Sur Lit de Paille', from an edition of 300, painted marks on reverse 'CR', 'MADOURA' and 'D'APRES PICASSO', impressed maker's mark.

1949   *15in (38cm) wide*

$7,000-7,500   **L&T**

A Poole Pottery Studio plate, by Tony Morris, painted with a geometric sun-face motif, printed Studio mark.

10.5in (27cm) diam

$650-750   **WW**

ESSENTIAL REFERENCE - DAME LUCIE RIE

Lucie Rie (1902-95) was born in Vienna and studied at the Vienna Kunstgewerbeschule before setting up her first pottery studio in 1925. By 1938, she was forced to flee Austria and moved to Britain. She established a pottery workshop in London, first producing buttons and later a range of handcrafted holloware. From 1946 to 1958, the ceramist Hans Coper worked alongside her at the pottery. Rie's wares were austere, angular and elegant in shape, finished with a variety of different glazes. They were decorated simply, often with incised parallel lines. She received the CBE in 1981 and became a Dame in 1991.

A 20thC stoneware bottle vase, by Dame Lucie Rie, covered in a pitted and speckled buff glaze, impressed seal mark.

6in (15cm) high

$5,000-6,500   WW

A 20thC small footed stoneware bowl, by Dame Lucie Rie D.B.E., the rim highlighted with darker brown impressed seal mark.

5.5in (14cm) diam

$5,000-6,500   WW

A footed bowl, by Dame Lucie Rie, glazed to the foot in a mat blue glaze with pitting and lavender to the interior, the exterior running blue over turquoise, the rim with bronze running highlights, impressed seal mark.

An added bonus with this piece is that it comes with a letter from Dame Lucie Rie about the bowl.

1988   *9.25in (23.5cm) diam*

$25,000-32,000   WW

A 1980s stoneware bottle vase, by Dame Lucie Rie, the top rim with running bronze band impressed seal mark.

9in (23cm) high

$20,000-25,000   WW

A stoneware vase, by Dame Lucie Rie, glazed with bands of Dolomite white and muted blue with hints of rusty red, impressed seal mark.

9.75in (25cm) high

$11,000-13,000   WW

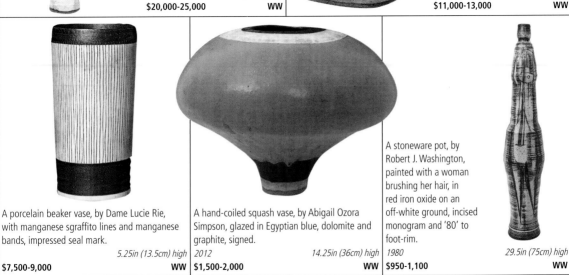

A porcelain beaker vase, by Dame Lucie Rie, with manganese sgraffito lines and manganese bands, impressed seal mark.

5.25in (13.5cm) high

$7,500-9,000   WW

A hand-coiled squash vase, by Abigail Ozora Simpson, glazed in Egyptian blue, dolomite and graphite, signed.

2012   *14.25in (36cm) high*

$1,500-2,000   WW

A stoneware pot, by Robert J. Washington, painted with a woman brushing her hair, in red iron oxide on an off-white ground, incised monogram and '80' to foot-rim.

1980   *29.5in (75cm) high*

$950-1,100   WW

MODERN DESIGN

A Barovier & Toso 'Variazione Christian Dior' bottle and stopper, designed by Ercole Barovier, clear glass with 'Scozzese' web.

c1969   *9in (23cm) high*
$6,500-7,500   **QU**

A Barovier & Toso 'Intarsio' vase, designed by Ercole Barovier.

c1961-63   *6.75in (17cm) high*
$2,500-3,200   **QU**

A pair of Venini Latimo glass birds, designed by Fulvio Bianconi, both with etched Venini mark.

hen 7.25in (18.5cm) high
$2,500-3,200   **LAW**

A Venini & C. 'Pezzato' vase, designed by Fulvio Bianconi, model no.4398, acid stamped 'venini murano ITALIA'.

1951   *9in (23cm) high*
$10,000-11,000   **QU**

A Venini & C. bottle-shaped 'Pezzato' vase, designed by Fulvio Bianconi, acid stamped 'venini murano ITALIA'.

c1950   *14.25in (36cm) high*
$9,000-10,000   **QU**

A 1950s/60s Gino Cenedese wall plate, designed by Fulvio Bianconi, with horse figures, diamond cut, signed 'Fulvio Bianconi'.

13.5in (34cm) high
$1,900-2,500   **QU**

A 1950s Gino Cenedese glass Aquarium, underwater scene with two fish.

7in (18cm) high
$500-650   **QU**

A Venini & C. 'Bambù' vase, designed by Elena Cutolo, engraved 'venini 2006 4/9 E.C.'.

2006   *15.5in (39.5cm) high*
$3,800-5,000   **QU**

A De Majo 'Murrine' vase, designed by Vittorio Ferro, carved 'de Majo. Murano. Maestro V. Ferro pezzo unico 1992-9614; C.A.'.

1992   *12.5in (31.5cm) high*
$1,000-1,250   **QU**

An A.Ve.M. 'Murrine incatenate' vase, designed by Anzolo Fuga, with blue, red, green and yellow fused murrhines, red ribbons.

c1960   *14.5in (37cm) high*

$2,500-3,200   **QU**

An A.Ve.M. vase, designed by Anzolo Fuga, with fused murrines and rings of various colors.

1960-68   *16.5in (42cm) high*

$1,900-2,500   **QU**

An A.Ve.M. 'Murrine incatenate' vase, designed by Anzolo Fuga, made by 'Incalmo' technique.

1960   *10.75in (27.5cm) high*

$2,300-2,800   **QU**

A 1980/90s Kyohei Fujita vessel, with silvered metal mounting, engraved 'Kyohei Fujita'.

6in (15cm) high

$7,500-9,000   **QU**

An Aureliano Toso 'Oriente' vase, designed by Dino Martens, model no.3121 (Nabucco).

c1953   *9.25in (23.5cm) high*

$6,500-7,500   **QU**

An A.Ve.M. 'Murrine' vase, attributed to Aldo Nason, with distributor mark 'Caliari Venini, Turin'.

c1950   *6.25in (16cm) high*

$1,300-1,500   **QU**

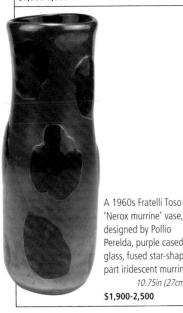

A 1960s Fratelli Toso 'Nerox murrine' vase, designed by Pollio Perelda, purple cased glass, fused star-shaped part iridescent murrines.

10.75in (27cm) high

$1,900-2,500   **QU**

A Seguso Vetri d'Arte 'Sommerso' vase, designed by Flavio Poli.

1963   *8in (20.5cm) high*

$1,900-2,500   **QU**

A Murano glass vase, possibly by Flavio Poli for Seguso.

1957   *15in (38cm) long*

$1,000-1,250   **SWO**

Judith Picks

When I'm asked 'What should I collect?', I always answer that you should buy something you love, something that will make you smile when you walk into a room.

And I find that with these Pianon birds. They have such character - such individual charm. They typify the optimism and humor that pervaded the island of Murano post-war and they are quite addictive. When you buy one, you are then tempted by the whole set. Although no work of art, it is pleasing to find this bird with his original box, which is very unusual.

A Pulcini glass bird, designed by Alessandro Pianon for Vistosi, with a spherical orange body, with darker splatter decoration and murrine glass eyes above clear crystal base, with copper wire legs, complete with original box.

Alessandro Pianon was born in Venice in 1931 and died there in 1984. He studied architecture at Venice University. In 1956 he worked at Vistosi's, designing its logo. In 1962 he opened a design studio.

c1962   *8.5in (21.5cm) high*
$4,500-5,000   **FLD**

A Vistosi Pulcini glass bird, designed by Alessandro Pianon, the blown blue glass body internally decorated with red and blue plumage, applied glass cane eyes, on copper feet, unsigned.

12.5in (32cm) high
$4,500-5,000   **WW**

A Vistosi Pulcini glass bird, designed by Alessandro Pianon, with applied glass cane eyes, on copper feet, unsigned.

7in (18cm) high
$3,800-4,400   **WW**

A Vistosi Pulcino glass bird sculpture, by Alessandro Pianon, olive green glass body with internal applied murrines, on copper wire feet.

c1965   *8.25in (21cm) high*
$7,500-9,000   **TEN**

A 20thC alexandrite and calcedonia glass, 'Cobra', by Dino Rosin.

Dino Rosin was born in Venice in 1948. At the age of twelve, he left school and began work as an apprentice at the Barovier and Toso glassworks where he remained until he joined his brothers, Loredano and Mirko, at their factory, Artvet, in 1963. Dino continued at Artvet until 1975 when he moved to Loredano's newly established studio as his assistant. There Dino collaborated with his brother for almost 20 years. In 1988, Dino Rosin was invited to Pilchuck Glass School in the state of Washington to teach solid freehand glass sculpture with Loredano and the American glass artist, William Morris. In 1992, Loredano died and Dino assumed the role of 'maestro'.

19in (48cm) high
$500-650   **SWO**

A 20thC abstract-form clear and calcedonia glass, by Dino Rosin, signed.

15.5in (39cm) high
$800-950   **SWO**

A Venini post-war veiled glass vase, by Carlo Scarpa, in deep ruby red, with a satin battuto finish, with three line acid mark.

11in (28cm) high
$1,800-2,300   **FLD**

A Vetreria Archimede Seguso 'A losanghe' vase, designed by Archimede Seguso.

1951   *8.5in (21.5cm) high*
$3,200-3,800   **QU**

An Archimede Seguso 'Disgiunzione' object, clear glass with blue and green spots and air bubbles, engraved 'Archimede Seguso'.

1994 *12.5in (13.5cm) high*

$1,900-2,500 QU

An Effetre International vase, designed by Lino Tagliapietra, with maker's plastic label.

1987 *13.75in (35cm) high*

$3,200-3,800 QU

A Fratelli Toso 'Stellato' vase, designed by Ermanno Toso, with aventurine, fused star-shaped murrines.

c1960 *9.25in (23.5cm) high*

$2,500-3,800 QU

A Tsuchida Yasuhiko vase, with 'Incalmo' rim, included gold foil, 'Battuto' surface cut, dark purple foot, engraved 'Tsuchida Yasuhiko 2001'.

2001 *14in (35.5cm) high*

$1,000-1,100 QU

A S.A.L.I.R. vase, designed by Tono Zancanaro, engraved scene with figures standing on the shore, engraved 'TONO 1956'.

1956 *15.25in (38.5cm) high*

$5,000-6,500 QU

A Fratelli Toso 'Murrine' vase, designed by Ermanno Toso, with fused flower-shaped murrines.

c1960 *11.25in (28.5cm) high*

$1,000-1,250 QU

ESSENTIAL REFERENCE - SAM HERMAN

Sam Herman was born in Mexico in 1936. He studied Fine Art at the University of Wisconsin, then moved to Britain, where he worked at Edinburgh College of Art and the Royal College of Art, London. From 1969 to 1974, he was head of the glass department at the Royal College of Art, where he taught his students to work directly with molten glass. He was significant within the Studio Glass movement, which encouraged designers to craft their work themselves. In 1969 he and Michael Harris founded the studio Glasshouse in London. In 1974 he set up Australia's first hot glass studio at the Jam Factory, Adelaide. Over his career, Herman has worked as a designer, painter, glassblower and sculptor. After a twenty-year hiatus, he returned to glassblowing in 2007. He now lives in London and Mallorca and is still working.

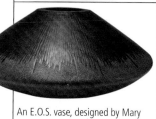

An E.O.S. vase, designed by Mary Ann 'Toots' Zynsky, with fused crushed oxides, line-cut, engraved 'TOOTS ZYNSKY 06/92 EOS MURANO'.

1992 *16.5in (42cm) wide*

$3,800-5,000 QU

A luster glass vase, by Sam Herman, etched marks to base 'SAMUEL J. HERMAN/1978/ SA1893'.

1978 *8.75in (22cm) high*

$1,500-2,000 L&T

A luster glass vase, by Sam Herman, the clear and red glass body with trailed inclusions, etched mark to base 'SAMUEL J. HERMAN / 1973'.

1973 *8.25in (21cm) high*

$1,300-1,900 L&T

A yellow plastic and brass table light, attributed to Carl Auböck.

c1958   *14.25in (36cm) high*

$1,000-1,250   QU

A 'Cactus' table light, by Giovanni Bassi for Studio Luce, chrome-plated sheet metal with neon pink Plexiglas.

1969   *21.75in (55.5cm) high*

$3,200-3,800   QU

A 'Super' plastic and fiberglas table light, by Martine Bedin for Memphis, with painted sheet metal and rubber wheels, with maker's label, in original box.

1981   *24in (61cm) long*

$750-900   QU

A 'Medusa' table light, by Olaf von Bohr for Valenti, Milan, aluminum lamellae, chrome-plated metal rings.

1968   *25.75in (65cm) high*

$2,300-2,800   QU

A 'Genesy' black polyurethane floorlamp, by Zaha Hadid for Artemide, LED and halogenous bulbs with touch dimmer switch, with maker's mark.

2009   *72.5in (184cm) high*

$6,500-7,500   QU

A table light, attributed to Angelo Lelli for Arredoluce, Monza.

c1958   *9.75in (24.5cm) high*

$3,200-3,800   QU

A 'Kalashnikov AK-47' gilded aluminum table light, by Philippe Starck for Flos, the shade made of black plastic and paper, marked 'happiness is a warm gun', with maker's label.

c2005   *37in (94cm) high*

$1,900-2,500   QU

A plastic and fiberglas 'Plan' ceiling light, by Enrico Botta for Sundown.

1968   *20.75in (53cm) wide*

$1,300-1,900   QU

A 1960s tubular metal ceiling light, by Angelo Mangiarotti for Candle.

39.25in (99.5cm) high

$3,200-3,800   QU

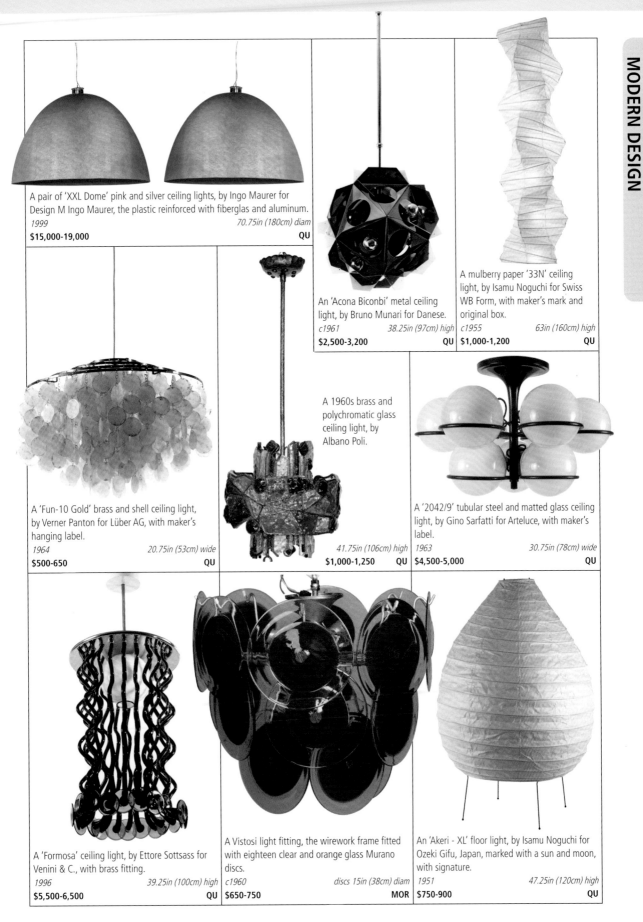

A pair of 'XXL Dome' pink and silver ceiling lights, by Ingo Maurer for Design M Ingo Maurer, the plastic reinforced with fiberglas and aluminum.
1999 70.75in (180cm) diam
$15,000-19,000 QU

An 'Acona Biconbi' metal ceiling light, by Bruno Munari for Danese.
c1961 38.25in (97cm) high
$2,500-3,200 QU

A mulberry paper '33N' ceiling light, by Isamu Noguchi for Swiss WB Form, with maker's mark and original box.
c1955 63in (160cm) high
$1,000-1,200 QU

A 1960s brass and polychromatic glass ceiling light, by Albano Poli.

A 'Fun-10 Gold' brass and shell ceiling light, by Verner Panton for Lüber AG, with maker's hanging label.
1964 20.75in (53cm) wide
$500-650 QU

1000-1,250 QU

A '2042/9' tubular steel and matted glass ceiling light, by Gino Sarfatti for Arteluce, with maker's label.
1963 30.75in (78cm) wide
$4,500-5,000 QU

A 'Formosa' ceiling light, by Ettore Sottsass for Venini & C., with brass fitting.
1996 39.25in (100cm) high
$5,500-6,500 QU

A Vistosi light fitting, the wirework frame fitted with eighteen clear and orange glass Murano discs.
c1960 discs 15in (38cm) diam
$650-750 MOR

An 'Akeri - XL' floor light, by Isamu Noguchi for Ozeki Gifu, Japan, marked with a sun and moon, with signature.
1951 47.25in (120cm) high
$750-900 QU

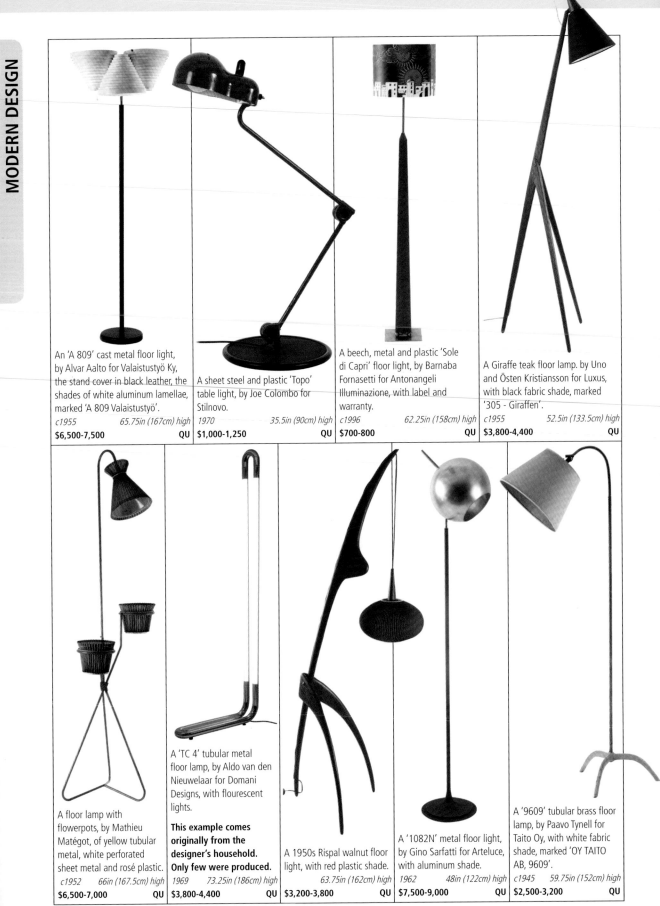

An 'A 809' cast metal floor light, by Alvar Aalto for Valaistustyö Ky, the stand cover in black leather, the shades of white aluminum lamellae, marked 'A 809 Valaistustyö'.

c1955   65.75in (167cm) high

$6,500-7,500   QU

A sheet steel and plastic 'Topo' table light, by Joe Colombo for Stilnovo.

1970   35.5in (90cm) high

$1,000-1,250   QU

A beech, metal and plastic 'Sole di Capri' floor light, by Barnaba Fornasetti for Antonangeli Illuminazione, with label and warranty.

c1996   62.25in (158cm) high

$700-800   QU

A Giraffe teak floor lamp. by Uno and Östen Kristiansson for Luxus, with black fabric shade, marked '305 - Giraffen'.

c1955   52.5in (133.5cm) high

$3,800-4,400   QU

A floor lamp with flowerpots, by Mathieu Matégot, of yellow tubular metal, white perforated sheet metal and rosé plastic.

c1952   66in (167.5cm) high

$6,500-7,000   QU

A 'TC 4' tubular metal floor lamp, by Aldo van den Nieuwelaar for Domani Designs, with flourescent lights.

This example comes originally from the designer's household. Only few were produced.

1969   73.25in (186cm) high

$3,800-4,400   QU

A 1950s Rispal walnut floor light, with red plastic shade.

63.75in (162cm) high

$3,200-3,800   QU

A '1082N' metal floor light, by Gino Sarfatti for Arteluce, with aluminum shade.

1962   48in (122cm) high

$7,500-9,000   QU

A '9609' tubular brass floor lamp, by Paavo Tynell for Taito Oy, with white fabric shade, marked 'OY TAITO AB, 9609'.

c1945   59.75in (152cm) high

$2,500-3,200   QU

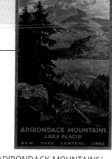

'ADIRONDACK MOUNTAINS/
LAKE PLACID, designed by Walter
L. Greene (1870-1956), printed
by Latham Litho & Ptg. Co., Long
Island City, repaired tear through
right image.

**With their route passing through
one of the Northeast's most
scenic areas, the New York
Central Line chose to let Mother
Nature be its spokesperson
by showing the scenery its
passengers could enjoy rather
than the trains that would carry
them. Walter Greene was the art
director at General Electric from
1903-1940.**

c1935   *40.25in (102cm) high*
$7,000-8,000   **SWA**

'L'ARMENIE SOVIETIQUE', designed
by Sergey Igumnov (1900-1942),
repaired tears.
1935   *35.5in (90cm) high*
$3,500-4,000   **SWA**

'ORIENT CRUISES', designed by
Andrew Johnson, minor creases,
tears in lower image.

**Andrew Johnson was a
commercial designer whose work
was marked by an attractive
modernity.**

c1933   *39.75in (101cm) high*
$4,500-5,000   **SWA**

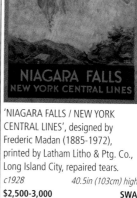

'NIAGARA FALLS / NEW YORK
CENTRAL LINES', designed by
Frederic Madan (1885-1972),
printed by Latham Litho & Ptg. Co.,
Long Island City, repaired tears.
c1928   *40.5in (103cm) high*
$2,500-3,000   **SWA**

'FIFTH AVENUE NEW YORK /
The World's Greatest Shopping
Street / TRAVEL BY TRAIN',
designed by Frederic Kimball
Mizen (1888-1965), printed by
Latham Litho & Ptg. Co., Long
Island City.
1932   *39.75in (101cm) high*
$6,500-7,000   **SWA**

'NEW YORK / THE UPPER BAY
FROM LOWER MANHATTAN',
designed by Leslie Ragan
(1897-1972), printed for
Latham Litho Co., Long Island
City.
1935   *41in (104cm) high*
$6,500-7,500   **SWA**

'NEW YORK THE UPPER BAY FROM LOWER MANHATTAN'

Judith Picks

A powerful Art Deco
image of one of the last
century's most famous
American trains. In the
1930s, technology began
to reflect the sleek, aerodynamic lines of
the Art Deco movement, and the new
20th Century Limited, designed by Henry
Dreyfuss, was the pride of the New York
Central Line, which ran from New York
to Chicago. This image has been featured
by the United States Postal Service on a
series of stamps commemorating the 1930s
and is among the top American Art Deco
posters ever designed.

'THE New 20TH CENTURY LIMITED / NEW YORK - 16
hours - CHICAGO', designed by Leslie Ragan (1897-
1972), printed by Latham Litho Co., Long Island City,
repaired tears and creases.
1939   *40.75in (103.5cm) high*
$15,000-18,000   **SWA**

THE *New* 20TH CENTURY LIMITED
NEW YORK-*16 hours*-CHICAGO
NEW YORK CENTRAL SYSTEM

'SWEDISH AMERICAN LINE /
GOTHENBURG - NEW YORK',
designed by Harry Hudson Rodmell
(1896-1984), printed by Ronald
Massey, London.

**Rodmell enrolled into the Hull
School of Art in 1912 and that
same year designed his first
magazine cover. More than just
a maritime artist, he was also a
very active commercial designer.**

c1928   *40in (101.5cm) high*
$4,000-5,000   **SWA**

'TOMORROWLAND / rocket jets/ FLY ONE YOURSELF', designed by Ken Chapman, printed for Walt Disney Productions, repaired tear at bottom right edge.

Tomorrowland first opened in California's Disneyland in 1955, then in Florida and internationally in the following decades. The attraction was Walt Disney's futuristic vision of the world - a sort of permanent World's Fair for innovation and imagination.

1967   *54in (137cm) long*
$1,500-2,000   **SWA**

'THE "SILVER WING" DE LUXE / IMPERIAL AIRWAYS', designed by Charles C. Dickson, printed by De Montfort Press, London, repaired tears in margins.

The Armstrong Whitworth Argosy entered the Imperial Airways fleet in 1926. In May 1927, Imperial launched its 'Silver Wing' service, considered the world's first luxury air service... passengers enjoyed a meal service and hot drinks plus a bar!

c1927   *40in (101.5cm) high*
$12,000-14,000   **SWA**

ESSENTIAL REFERENCE - WAR POSTER

One of the most striking American posters issued during the war, this World War I recruitment poster distills the horrors of a German invasion of America into a savage, primitive, sexually charged theme. A red-tongued and drooling gorilla, whose helmet reads 'Militarism,' is clutching a desperate maiden with her dress torn off in one paw and a bloody club, reading 'Kultur,' in the other. He is stepping over the sea into America, leaving a burned down and ravaged Europe behind him. The phallic and bloody cudgel and the beast's power over the semi-nude girl, give urgency to the enlistment call. As the beast steps onto American shores, recruits are invited both to fight militarism and to vie for the eroticized figure of raped Liberty. Popular folklore has it that this image was the influence for King Kong.

'DESTROY THIS MAD BRUTE / ENLIST', designed by H.R. Hopps (1869-1937), printed by Schmidt Lithograph Co., San Francisco, expertly repaired tear through image, restoration in upper right corner.

c1917   *42in (106.5cm) high*
$13,000-16,000   **SWA**

2 DAYS TO EUROPE / HAMBURG - AMERICAN LINE', designed by Jupp Wiertz (1881-1939), printed for Eschebach & Schaefer, Leipzig, minor creases.

1936   *32.5in (82.5cm) high*
$10,000-12,000   **SWA**

'WAKE UP, AMERICA! / CIVILIZATION CALLS EVERY MAN WOMAN AND CHILD!', designed by James Montgomery Flagg (1870-1960), printed by the Hegeman Print, New York, repaired tears.

1917   *41.5in (105.5cm) high*
$4,500-5,500   **SWA**

'WAKE UP AMERICA DAY / APRIL 19 1917', designed by James Montgomery Flagg (1870-1960), replaced and overpainted margins.

On April 6, 1917, the United States Congress declared war on Germany. Over the next two weeks, the Recruiting Committee of the Mayor's Committee on National Defense organized one of New York's largest public recruiting campaigns in history. The day chosen to 'Wake Up America' was April 19, the anniversary of the Revolutionary War battles of Lexington and Concord.

1917   *39.75in (101cm) high*
$9,000-10,000   **SWA**

'I WANT YOU FOR U.S. ARMY', designed by James Montgomery Flagg (1870-1960), printed for Leslie-Judge Co., New York, minor repaired tears.

1917   *40in (101cm) high*
$7,000-8,000   **SWA**

'HE'S WATCHING YOU', designed by Glen Grohe (1912-1956), printed by the U.S. Government Printing Office, Washington, D.C., creases and restoration in margins and image.

This is one of the most powerful American images produced during the World War II. It is a terrifying, hypnotizing vision of a German soldier with his eyes staring straight out at the viewer, rising ominously above the bold typography. This is the larger of two formats.

1942   *39.5in (100.5cm) high*
$2,000-2,500   **SWA**

Every antique illustrated in Miller's Antiques has a letter code, which identifies the dealer or auction house that sold it. The list below is a key to these codes. In the list, auction houses are shown by the letter A and dealers by the letter D.

Inclusion in this book in no way constitutes or implies a contract or a binding offer on the part of any of our contributors to supply or sell the goods illustrated, or similar items, at the prices stated.

AH Ⓐ
HARTLEY'S
www.hartleysauctions.co.uk

ALTE Ⓐ
ALTEA MAPS
www.alteagallery.com

APAR Ⓐ
ADAM PARTRIDGE
AUCTIONEERS & VALUERS
www.adampartridge.co.uk

ARTC Ⓐ
ARTCURIAL
www.artcurial.com

BE & H&L Ⓐ
BEARNES, HAMPTON & LITTLEWOOD
www.bhandl.co.uk

BELL Ⓐ
BELLMANS
www.bellmans.co.uk

BER Ⓐ
BERTOIA AUCTIONS
www.bertoiaauctions.com

BOL Ⓐ
BOLDON AUCTION GALLERIES
www.boldonauctions.co.uk

BLEA Ⓐ
BLEASDALES LTD.
www.bleasdalesltd.co.uk

BLO Ⓐ
DREWEATTS & BLOOMSBURY
www.bloomsburyauctions.com

BLNY Ⓐ
BLOOMSBURY AUCTIONS NEW YORK
ny.bloomsburyauctions.com

BRI Ⓐ
BRIGHTWELLS
www.brightwells.com

CA Ⓐ
CHISWICK AUCTIONS
www.chiswickauctions.co.uk

CAN Ⓐ
THE CANTERBURY AUCTION GALLERIES
www.thecanterburyauctiongalleries.com

CHEF Ⓐ
CHEFFINS
www.cheffins.co.uk

CHOR Ⓐ
CHORLEY'S
www.chorleys.com

CLV Ⓐ
CLEVEDON SALEROOMS
www.clevedon-salerooms.com

CM Ⓐ
CHARLES MILLER
www.charlesmillerltd.com

CSB Ⓓ
CHENU SCRIVE BERARD
Tel: 0033 472 777801

DN Ⓐ
DREWEATTS & BLOOMSBURY
www.dreweatts.com

DNW Ⓐ
DIX NOONAN WEB
www.dnw.co.uk

DRA Ⓐ
RAGO ARTS
www.ragoarts.com

DSA Ⓐ
DAVID STANLEY AUCTIONS
www.davidstanley.com

DUK Ⓐ
DUKE'S
www.dukes-auctions.com

DW Ⓐ
DOMINIC WINTER
www.dominic-winter.co.uk

ECGW Ⓐ
EWBANK'S
www.ewbankauctions.co.uk

FELL Ⓐ
FELLOWS AUCTIONEERS
www.fellows.co.uk

FIS Ⓐ
AUKTIONSHAUS DR FISCHER
www.auctions-fischer.de

FLD Ⓐ
FIELDINGS AUCTIONEERS
www.fieldingsauctioneers.co.uk

FRE Ⓐ
FREEMAN'S
www.freemansauction.com

GBA Ⓐ
GRAHAM BUDD AUCTIONS
www.grahambuddauctions.co.uk

GHOU Ⓐ
GARDINER HOULGATE
www.gardinerhoulgate.co.uk

GORL Ⓐ
GORRINGES
www.gorringes.co.uk

GRV Ⓓ
GEMMA REDMOND VINTAGE
www.gemmaredmondvintage.co.uk

GTH Ⓐ
GREENSLADE TAYLOR HUNT
www.gth.net

H&C Ⓐ
HISTORICAL & COLLECTABLE
www.historicalandcollectable.com

H&H Ⓐ
H & H AUCTION ROOMS
hhauctionrooms.co.uk

HALL Ⓐ
HALLS
hallsgb.com/fine-art

HAN Ⓐ
HANSONS AUCTIONEERS
www.hansonsauctioneers.co.uk

HANN Ⓐ
HANNAMS
www.hannamsauctioneers.com

HAY Ⓐ
INGLES & HAYDAY
www.ingleshayday.com

HICK Ⓓ
HICKMET FINE ART
www.hickmet.com

HT Ⓐ
HARTLEY'S
www.hartleysauctions.co.uk

HW Ⓐ
HOLLOWAY'S
www.hollowaysauctioneers.co.uk

JDJ Ⓐ
JAMES D. JULIA INC.
www.juliaauctions.com

JN Ⓐ
JOHN NICHOLSONS
www.johnnicholsons.com

JON Ⓐ
ROGERS JONES & CO.
www.rogersjones.co.uk

KEY Ⓐ
KEYS
www.keysauctions.co.uk

L&T Ⓐ
LYON & TURNBULL
www.lyonandturnbull.com

LAW Ⓐ
LAWRENCE'S AUCTIONEERS LTD.
www.lawrencesbletchingley.co.uk

LC Ⓐ
LAWRENCE'S AUCTIONEERS OF CREWKERNE
www.lawrences.co.uk

LOC Ⓐ
LOCKE & ENGLAND
www.leauction.co.uk

LOCK Ⓐ
LOCKDALES
www.lockdales.com

LOW Ⓐ
**LOWESTOFT PORCELAIN
AUCTIONS**
www.lowestoftchina.co.uk

LSK Ⓐ
LACY SCOTT & KNIGHT
www.lsk.co.uk

M&DM Ⓐ
M&D MOIR
www.manddmoir.co.uk

MAB Ⓐ
MATTHEW BARTON LTD.
www.matthewbartonltd.com

MAI Ⓐ
MOORE ALLEN & INNOCENT
www.mooreallen.co.uk

MART Ⓐ
MARTEL MAIDES LTD.
www.martelmaidesauctions.com

MOR Ⓐ
MORPHETS
www.morphets.co.uk

MTZ Ⓐ
METZ AUKTION
www.metz-auktion.de

NAG Ⓐ
NAGEL
www.auction.de

PBE Ⓐ
**PAUL BEIGHTON
AUCTIONEERS**
www.pbauctioneers.co.uk

PFR Ⓐ
PETER FRANCIS
www.peterfrancis.co.uk

PFW Ⓐ
P.F. WINDIBANK
www.windibank.co.uk

POOK Ⓐ
POOK & POOK
www.pookandpook.com

PHI Ⓐ
PHILLIPS
www.phillips.com

PSA Ⓐ
POTTERIES AUCTIONS
www.potteriesauctions.com

PW Ⓐ
**PETER WILSON FINE ART
AUCTIONEERS**
www.peterwilson.co.uk

QU Ⓐ
QUITTENBAUM
www.quittenbaum.de

RGA Ⓓ
**RICHARD GARDNER
ANTIQUES**
www.richardgardnerantiques.co.uk

ROS Ⓐ
ROSEBERYS
www.roseberys.co.uk

SK Ⓐ
SKINNER INC.
www.skinnerinc.com

SWA Ⓐ
SWANN GALLERIES
www.swanngalleries.com

SWO Ⓐ
SWORDERS
www.sworder.co.uk

TEAR Ⓐ
MCTEAR'S
www.mctears.co.uk

TEN Ⓐ
TENNANTS
www.tennants.co.uk

TOO Ⓐ
TREADWAY TOOMEY
treadwaygallery.com

TOV Ⓐ
TOOVEY'S
www.tooveys.com

TRI Ⓐ
TRING MARKET AUCTIONS
www.tringmarketauctions.co.uk

TS Ⓐ
TAMLYNS
www.tamlynsprofessional.co.uk

W&W Ⓐ
WALLIS & WALLIS
www.wallisandwallis.co.uk

WAD Ⓐ
WADDINGTON'S
www.waddingtons.ca

WHP Ⓐ
W & H PEACOCK
www.peacockauction.co.uk

WKA Ⓐ
**AUKTIONSHAUS IM KINSKY
GMBH**
www.imkinsky.com

WW Ⓐ
WOOLLEY & WALLIS
www.woolleyandwallis.co.uk

This is a list of auctioneers that conduct regular sales. Auction houses that would like to be included in the next edition should contact us at info@millers.uk.com

ALABAMA
Vintage Auctions
Tel: 205 429 2457

ARIZONA
Dan May & Associates
Tel: 480 941 4200

Old World Mail Auctions
www.oldworldauctions.com

ARKANSAS
Hanna-Whysel Auctioneers
Tel: 501 855 9600

Ponders Auctions
www.pondersauctions.com

CALIFORNIA
Bonhams & Butterfields
www.bonhams.com

I M Chait Gallery
www.chait.com

Cuschieri's Auctioneers & Appraisers
Tel: 650 556 1793

eBay, Inc.
www.ebay.com

H.R. Harmer
Tel: 714.389.9178

Michaan's
www.michaans.com

San Rafael Auction Gallery
www.sanrafaelauction.com

L H Selman Ltd.
www.paperweight.com

Slawinski Auction Co.
www.slawinski.com

Sotheby's
www.sothebys.com

NORTH CAROLINA
Robert S Brunk Auction Services Inc.
www.brunkauctions.com

Raynors' Historical Collectible Auctions
www.hcaauctions.com

SOUTH CAROLINA
Charlton Hall Galleries Inc.
www.charltonhallauctions.com

COLORADO
Pacific Auction
www.pacificauction.com

Pettigrew Auction Company
Tel: 719 633 7963

Priddy's Auction Galleries
Tel: 800 380 4411

Stanley & Co.
Tel: 303 355 0506

CONNECTICUT
The Great Atlantic Auction Company
Tel: 860 963 2234

Norman C Heckler & Company
www.hecklerauction.com

Lloyd Ralston Toys
www.lloydralstontoys.com

Winter Associates Inc.
www.auctionsappraisers.com

NORTH DAKOTA
Curt D Johnson Auction Co.
www.curtdjohnson.com

SOUTH DAKOTA
Fischer Auction Company
www.fischerauction.com

FLORIDA
Auctions Neapolitan
www.auctionsneapolitan.com

Burchard Galleries/Auctioneers
www.burchardgalleries.com

Arthur James Galleries
Tel: 561 278 2373

Kincaid Auction Company
www.kincaid.com

Albert Post Galleries
Tel: 561 582 4477

TreasureQuest Auction Galleries Inc.
www.tqag.com

GEORGIA
Arwood Auctions
Tel: 770 423 0110

Great Gatsby's
www.greatgatsbys.com

Red Baron's Auction Gallery
www.redbaronsantiques.com

Southland Auction Inc.
Tel: 770 818 2418

IDAHO
The Coeur d'Alene Art Auction
www.cdaartauction.com

INDIANA
AAA Historical Auction Service
Tel: 260 493 6585

Heritage Auction Galleries
www.historical.ha.com

Lawson Auction Service
lawsonauction.com

Schrader Auction
www.schraderauction.com

Stout Auctions
www.stoutauctions.com

Strawser Auctions
www.strawserauctions.com

ILLINOIS
The Chicago Wine Company
www.tcwc.com

Hack's Auction Center
www.hacksauction.com

Leslie Hindman Inc.
www.lesliehindman.com

Sotheby's
Tel: 312 475 7900

Susanin's Auction
www.susanins.com

John Toomey Gallery
www.johntoomeygallery.com

IOWA
Jackson's Auctioneers & Appraisers
www.jacksonsauction.com

Tubaugh Auctions
www.tubaughauctions.com

KANSAS
CC Auction Gallery
Tel: 785 632 6062

Spielman Auction
Tel: 316 256 6558

KENTUCKY
Hays & Associates Inc.
Tel: 502 584 4297

Steffen's Historical Militaria
Tel: 859 431 4499

LOUISIANA
Estate Auction Gallery
Tel: 504 383 7706

New Orleans Auction Galleries
www.neworleansauction.com

MAINE
James D. Julia Inc.
www.jamesdjulia.com

Thomaston Place Auction Galleries
www.thomastonauction.com

Maryland Hantman's Auctioneers & Appraisers
www.hantmans.com

Richard Opfer Auctioneering Inc.
www.opferauction.com

Sloans & Kenyon
www.sloansandkenyon.com

Theriault's
www.theriaults.com

MASSACHUSETTS
Douglas Auctioneers
www.douglasauctioneers.com

Eldred's
www.eldreds.com

Grogan & Company Auctioneers
www.groganco.com

Shute Auction Gallery
Tel: 508 588 0022

Skinner Inc.
www.skinnerinc.com

White's Auctions
www.whitesauctions.com

Willis Henry Auctions Inc.
www.willishenry.com

MICHIGAN
Frank H. Boos Gallery
Tel: 248 643 1900

DuMouchelle Art Galleries Co.
www.dumouchelles.com

MINNESOTA
Tracy Luther Auctions
Tel: 651 770 6175

Rose Auction Galleries
www.rosegalleries.com

MISSOURI
Selkirk Auctioneers
www.selkirkauctions.com

Simmons & Company Auctioneers
www.simmonsauction.com

MONTANA
Allard Auctions
www.allardauctions.com

Stan Howe & Associates
Tel: 406 443 5658 / 800 443 5658

NEW HAMPSHIRE
Paul McInnis Inc. Auction Gallery
www.paulmcinnis.com

Northeast Auctions
www.northeastauctions.com

R O Schmitt Fine Art
www.roschmittfinearts.com

NEW JERSEY
Bertoia Auctions
www.bertoiaauctions.com

Dawson & Nye
www.dawsonandnye.com

Rago Arts & Auction Center
www.ragoarts.com

NEW MEXICO
Altermann Galleries
www.altermann.com

NEW YORK
Antiquorum
www.antiquorum.com

Christie's
www.christies.com

Copake Auction Inc.
www.copakeauction.com

Samuel Cottone Auctions
Tel: 716 658 3180

Doyle New York
www.doylenewyork.com

Guernsey's Auction
www.guernseys.com

William J Jenack Auctioneers
www.jenack.com

Keno Auctions
www.kenoauctions.com

Mapes Auction Gallery
www.mapesauction.com

Phillips
www.phillips.com

Sotheby's
www.sothebys.com

Stair Galleries
www.stairgalleries.com

Swann Galleries
www.swanngalleries.com

OHIO
Belhorn Auction Services
www.belhorn.com

Cincinnati Art Galleries LLC.
www.cincinnatiartgalleries.com

The Cobbs Auctioneers LLC.
www.thecobbs.com

Cowan's Historic Americana Auctions
www.cowanauctions.com

Garth's Auction Inc.
www.garths.com

Treadway Toomey
www.treadwaygallery.com

Wolf's Auction Gallery
Tel: 216 575 9653

OKLAHOMA
Buffalo Bay Auction Co.
www.buffalobayauction.com

OREGON
O'Gallery
www.ogallerie.com

PENNSYLVANIA
Noel Barrett
www.noelbarrett.com

William Bunch Auctions
www.williambunchauctions.com

Concept Art Gallery
www.conceptgallery.com

Freeman's
www.freemansauction.com

Hunt Auctions
www.huntauctions.com

Pook & Pook
www.pookandpook.com

Sanford Alderfer Auction Co.
Tel: 215 393 3023
Email: info@alderauction.com

Charles A. Whitaker Auction Co.,
www.whitakerauction.com

RHODE ISLAND
Gustave White Auctioneers
Tel: 401 841 5780

TENNESSEE
Kimball M Sterling Inc.
www.sterlingsold.com

TEXAS
Austin Auctions
www.austinauction.com

Dallas Auction Gallery
www.dallasauctiongallery.com

Heritage Auction Galleries
www.ha.com

UTAH
America West Archives
www.americawestarchives.com

VIRGINIA
Green Valley Auctions Inc.
www.greenvalleyauctions.com

Ken Farmer Auctions & Estates
www.kenfarmer.com

Phoebus Auction Gallery
www.phoebusauction.com

WASHINGTON DC
Seattle Auction House
www.seattleauctionhouse.com

Weschler's
www.weschlers.com

WISCONSIN
Milwaukee Auction Galleries
Tel: 414 271 1105

CANADA

ALBERTA
Hall's Auction Services Ltd.
www.hallsauction.com

Hodgins Art Auctions Ltd.
www.hodginsauction.com

Lando Art Auctions
www.landoartauctions.com

BRITISH COLUMBIA
Maynards Fine Art Auction House
www.maynards.com

Waddington's
www.waddingtons.ca

Heffel Fine Art Auction House
www.heffel.com

ONTARIO
Empire Auctions
www.empireauctions.com

Ritchies
www.ritchies.com

A Touch of Class
www.atouchofclassauctions.com

Waddington's
www.waddingtons.ca

Walkers
www.walkersauctions.com

Robert Deveau Galleries
robertdeveaugalleries.com

Heffel Fine Art Auction House
www.heffel.com

Sotheby's
www.sothebys.com

QUEBEC
Empire Auctions
www.montreal.empireauctions.com

Iegor - Hôtel des Encans
www.iegor.net

Montréal Auction House
pages.videotron.com/encans

Specialists who would like to be listed in the next edition, or have a new address or telephone number, should contact us at info@millers.uk.com. Readers should contact dealers before visiting to avoid a wasted journey.

AMERICAN PAINTINGS
James R Bakker Antiques Inc.
www.bakkerart.com

Jeffrey W Cooley
www.cooleygallery.com

AMERICANA & FOLK ART
American West Indies Trading Co. Antiques & Art
www.goantiques.com/members/awind-iestrading

Augustus Decorative Arts Ltd.
www.portrait-miniatures.com

Thomas & Julia Barringer
Tel: 609 397 4474
Email: tandjb@voicenet.com

Bucks County Antique Center
Tel: 215 794 9180

Garthoeffner Gallery Antiques
www.garthoeffnergallery.com

Allan Katz Americana
www.allankatzamericana.com

Olde Hope Antiques Inc.
www.oldehope.com

Pantry & Hearth,
www.pantryandhearth.com

J B Richardson
Tel: 203 226 0358

The Rookery Bookery
therookerybookery.com

Cheryl & Paul Scott
Tel: 603 464 3617
Email: riverbendfarm@tds.net

The Stradlings
Tel: 212 534 8135

Patricia Stauble Antiques
Tel: 207 882 6341

Throckmorton Fine Art
www.throckmorton-nyc.com

Jeffrey Tillou Antiques
www.tillouantiques.com

ANTIQUITIES
Frank & Barbara Pollack
Tel: 847 433 2213
Email: barbarapollack@comcast.net

ARCHITECTURAL ANTIQUES
Garden Antiques
www.bi-gardenantiques.com

Cecilia B Williams
Tel: 301 865 0777

ARMS & MILITARIA
Faganarms
www.faganarms.com

BAROMETERS
Barometer Fair
www.barometerfair.com

BOOKS
Bauman Rare Books
www.baumanrarebooks.com

CARPETS & RUGS
Collins Gallery
www.collinsgallery.com

Karen & Ralph Disaia
www.orientalrugsltd.com

Quadrifoglio Gallery
www.quadrifogliogallery.com

CERAMICS
Charles & Barbara Adams
Tel: 508 760 3290
 Email: adams_2430@msn.com

Mark & Marjorie Allen
www.antiquedelft.com

Jill Fenichell
By appointment Tel: 212 980 9346
Email: jfenichell@yahoo.com

Mellin's Antiques
www.mellinsantiques.com

Philip Suval, Inc
Tel: 540 373 9851
Email: jphilipsuval@aol.com

COSTUME JEWELRY
Deco Jewels Inc.
Tel: 212 253 1222

Terry Rodgers & Melody
www.melodyrodgers.com

Roxanne Stuart
Tel: 215 750 8868
gemfairy@aol.com

Bonny Yankauer
bonnyy@aol.com

CLOCKS
Kirtland H. Crump
www.kirtlandcrumpclocks.com

RO Schmitt Fine Art
www.roschmittfinearts.com

DECORATIVE ARTS
Susie Burmann
Tel: 603 526 5934
rsburmann@tds.net

H L Chalfant Antiques
www.hlchalfant.com

Brian Cullity
www.briancullity.com

Gordon & Marjorie Davenport
Tel: 608 271 2348
Email: GMDaven@aol.com

Ron & Penny Dionne
Tel: 860 487 0741

Peter H Eaton Antiques
www.petereaton.com

Leah Gordon Antiques
www.leahgordon.com

Samuel Herrup Antiques
www.samuelherrup.com

High Style Deco
www.highstyledeco.com

R Jorgensen Antiques
www.rjorgensen.com

Bettina Krainin
www.bettinakraininantiques.com

William E Lohrman
Tel: 845 255 6762

Macklowe Gallery
www.macklowegallery.com

Milly McGehee
Tel: 410 653 3977
Email: millymcgehee@comcast.net

Jackson Mitchell Inc.
Tel: 302 656 0110
Email: JacMitch@aol.com

Lillian Nassau
www.lilliannassau.com

Perrault-Rago Gallery
www.ragoarts.com

Sumpter Priddy Inc.
Tel: 703 299 0800
www.sumpterpriddy.com

James L Price Antiques
Tel: 717 243 0501
Email: jlpantiques@earthlink.net

R J G Antiques
www.rjgantiques.com

John Keith Russell Antiques Inc.
www.jkrantiques.com

Israel Sack
 Tel: 212 399 6562

Lincoln & Jean Sander
Tel: 203 938 2981
Email: sanderlr@aol.com

Kathy Schoemer American Antiques
www.kathyschoemerantiques.com

Jack & Ray Van Gelder
Tel: 413 369 4660

Van Tassel/Baumann American Antiques
Tel: 610 647 3339

Anne Weston & Associates LLC
www.anne-weston.com

DOLLS
Sara Bernstein Antique Dolls & Bears
www.sarabernsteindolls.com

Theriault's
www.theriaults.com

FURNITURE
American Antiques
Tel: 207 354 6033
Email: acm@midcoast.com

Antique Associates
www.aaawt.com

Barbara Ardizone Antiques
www.barbaraardizone.com

Artemis Gallery
www.artemisantiques.com

Joanne & Jack Boardman
Tel: 815 756 359
Email: boardmanantiques@comcast.net

Boym Partners Inc.
www.boym.com

Joan R Brownstein
www.joanrbrownstein.com

Carswell Rush Berlin Inc.
www.american-antiques.net

Evergreen Antiques
www.evergreenantiques.com

Douglas Hamel Antiques
www.shakerantiques.com

Eileen Lane Antiques
www.eileenlaneantiques.com

Lost City Arts
www.lostcityarts.com

GENERAL
Alley Cat Lane Antiques
www.rubylane.com/shops/alleycatlane

Bucks County Antiques Center
Tel: 215 794 9180

Camelot Antiques
www.about-antiques.com

Manhatten Arts & Antiques Center
www.the-maac.com

Showcase Antiques Center
showcaseantiquesofcny.com

South Street Antique Markets
Tel: 215 592 0256

GLASS
Brookside Art Glass
www.wpitt.com

Holsten Galleries
www.holstengalleries.com

Antiques by Joyce Knutsen
Tel: 315 637 8238 (Summer)
Tel: 352 567 1699 (Winter)

Paul Reichwein
Tel: 717 569 7637

JEWELRY
Ark Antiques
Tel: 203 498 8572

Arthur Guy Kaplan
Tel: 410 752 2090
Email: rkaplan8350@comcast.net

LIGHTING
Chameleon Fine Lighting
www.chameleon59.com

MARINE ANTIQUES
Hyland Granby Antiques
www.hylandgranby.com

METALWARE
Wayne & Phyllis Hilt
www.hiltpewter.com

ORIENTAL
Marc Matz Antiques
www.marcmatz.com

Mimi's Antiques
www.mimisantiques.com

PAPERWEIGHTS
The Dunlop Collection
Tel: 704 871 2626 or (800) 227 1996

SILVER
Alter Silver Gallery Corp.
Tel: 212 750 1928 or 917 848 1713
Email: aftersilvergallery@mac.com

Argentum
www.argentum-theleopard.com

Chicago Silver
www.chicagosilver.com

Jonathan Trace
Tel: 914 658 7336

Imperial Half Bushel
www.imperialhalfbushel.com

TEXTILES
Pandora de Balthazar
www.pandoradebalthazar.com

Colette Donovan
Tel: 978 346 0614
Email: colettedonovan@adelphia.net

M Finkel & Daughter
www.samplings.com

Cora Ginsburg
www.coraginsburg.com

Nancy Goldsmith
Tel: 212 696 0831

Andrea Hall Levy
Tel: 646 441 1726
barangrill@aol.com

Stephen & Carol Huber
www.antiquesamplers.com

Fayne Landes Antiques
Tel: 610 658 056

Charlotte Marler
Tel: 212 367 8808
Email: char_marler@hotmail.com

Stephanie's Antiques
Tel: 212 633 6563

TRIBAL ART
Arte Primitivo
www.arteprimitivo.com

Marcy Burns American Indian Arts
www.marcyburns.com

Morning Star Gallery
www.morningstargallery.com

Myers & Duncan
Tel: 212 472 0115
Email: jmyersprimitives@aol.com

Elliott & Grace Snyder
www.elliottandgracesnyder.com

Trotta-Bono American Indian Art
www.trottabono.com

20THC DESIGN
Mix Gallery
www.mixgallery.com

Moderne Gallery
www.modernegallery.com

Modernism Gallery
www.modernism.com

R Gallery
www.r20thcentury.com

CANADIAN SPECIALISTS

CANADIANA
Antiquites Gerard Funkenberg

& Jean Drapeau
Tel: 819 842 2725

The Blue Pump
Tel: 416 944 1673
Email: john@thebluepump.com

Ingram Antiques & Collectibles
Tel: 416 484 4601

CERAMICS
Cynthia Findlay
www.cynthiafindlay.com

Pam Ferrazzutti Antiques
www.pamferrazzuttiantiques.com

FINE ART
Barbara M Mitchell
Tel: 416 699 5582
Email: fineartsbarbara@hotmail.com

FURNITURE
Croix-Crest Antiques
Tel: 506 529 4693

Faith Grant
www.faithgrantantiques.com

Lorenz Antiques Ltd.
Tel: 416 487 2066
Email: info@lorenzantiques.com

Maus Park Antiques
www.mausparkantiques.ca

Milord Antiques
Tel: 514 933 2433
Email: showroom@milordantiques.com

Richard Rumi & Co. Antiques
www.rumiantiques.com

Shand Galleries
Tel: 416 260 9056

GENERAL
Toronto Antiques Centre
www.torontoantiquesonking.com

JEWELRY
Fraleigh Jewellers
www.fraleigh.ca

Fiona Kenny Antiques
www.fionakennyantiques.com

SILVER
Richard Flensted-Holder
By appointment only Tel: 416 961 3414

Louis Wine Ltd.
www.louiswine.com

INDEX

INDEX

INDEX TO ADVERTISERS